Pepper Adams' Joy Road

Studies in Jazz

The Institute of Jazz Studies
Rutgers—The State University of New Jersey

To see a complete list of titles for the Studies in Jazz series, please visit us at https://rowman.com/Scarecrow.

Pepper Adams' Joy Road

An Annotated Discography

Gary Carner

Studies in Jazz, No. 69

The Scarecrow Press, Inc.
Lanham, Maryland • Toronto • Plymouth, UK
and
Institute of Jazz Studies
Rutgers—The State University of New Jersey
1998

SCARECROW PRESS, INC.

Published in the United States of America
by Scarecrow Press, Inc.
A wholly owned subsidary of
The Rowman & Littlefield Publishing Group, Inc.
4501 Forbes Boulevard, Suite 200
Lanham, Maryland 20706
www.rowman.com

Estover Road
Plymouth PL6 7PY
United Kingdom

British Library Cataloguing in Publication Information Available

Library of Congress Cataloging-in-Publication Data
Carner, Gary.
  Pepper Adams' Joy Road : an annotated discography / Gary Carner.
    p. cm. -- (Studies in jazz ; No. 69)
  Includes bibliographical references and index.
  ISBN 978-0-8108-8256-0 (cloth : alk. paper) -- ISBN 978-0-8108-8257-7
(electronic) 1. Adams, Pepper, 1930-1986--Discography. 2. Jazz--
Discography. I. Title.
  ML156.7.A32C37 2012
  016.7887'165092--dc23
                                                        2012016351

♾™ The paper used in this publication meets the minimum requirements of
American National Standard for Information Sciences—Permanence of
Paper for Printed Library Materials, ANSI/NISO Z39.48–1992.
Manufactured in the United States of America.

For Lewis Porter

Contents

Foreword

While correct, "Annotated Discography" by no means says all about this fascinating record of a great musician's career and life. For decades, Gary Carner has devoted himself to tracing every musical step by Pepper Adams, from the very first teenaged endeavor, captured by a recording device, professional or amateur, issued or not. And he has enhanced the carefully gathered discographical details with additional information, musical, technical and personal, about the performance circumstances, more often than not obtained from participants and observers, as well as from interviews, published and personal, with the man himself.

Quite a man, too—not only one of the outstanding practitioners of the baritone saxophone, but a brilliant, complicated guy, whom I had the distinct pleasure of knowing. If there is a subtext here, it would be the fact that Pepper was the only white musician in the "Detroit Invasion" that descended upon the New York jazz scene in the late 1950s, accepted as a "primus inter pares" by his black colleagues—and friends. Early on, you will find an amusing anecdote about Alfred Lion's first reaction to Pepper's music: the founder of Blue Note Records refused to believe that the player on the demo tape the young baritonist had submitted was not black, going so far as to calling him a liar. Pepper would of course go on to participate in many a Blue Note session—if Lion ever apologized, we'll never know.

Good discographies are certainly very useful tools, but it is highly uncommon for a discography, even an annotated one, to also qualify as a good read. But *Pepper Adams' Joy Road* most definitely is. It brings the man as well as his music to life. Read—and listen—well!

—Dan Morgenstern

Acknowledgments

A very special thanks goes to Lewis Porter, Michael Fitzgerald, and Frank Basile for reading my manuscript and making enormously helpful comments and suggestions.

Additional special thanks goes to my editor, Bennett Graff, at Scarecrow Press, for all his guidance and dedication. Thanks also to the Scarecrow art department for the groovy cover, and to Sally Craley, Rayna Andrews, and Laura Reiter.

Also, thanks to Dan Morgenstern for writing the foreword, and to Pepper Adams' colleagues who have written endorsements. Many thanks and hugs to my daughter, Erin Carner, for formatting my manuscript, and thanks to Jana Herzen at Motema Music for encouraging me to finally finish the book.

I've included below as complete a list as possible of those individuals and institutions that have helped me with my research over the last 27 years. I'm sure there are some very kind people that I've somehow omitted. For them, my apologies and sincere appreciation for all your assistance.

* * *

Chapter 1: Claudette Adams, Pepper Adams, Gary Alderman, Larry Appelbaum, Kevin Bales, Frank Basile, Rod Baum, Kenny Berger, Mark Berger, Lars Bjorn, Willie Bolar, Bess Bonnier, Clora Bryant, Don Buday, Charles Burrell, Kenny Burrell, Blasko Camberwell, Jay Cameron, R.L. Carter, Noal Cohen, Bob Cornfoot, Michael Cuscuna, Peter Danson, Evrard Deckers, Chris DeVito, Len Dobbin, Art Farmer, Tom Fewlass, Michael Fitzgerald, Tommy Flanagan, Frank Foster, Curtis Fuller, Jim Gallert, Frank Gant, Joie Gifford, Phil Gilbert, Ira Gitler, Ray Glassman, Norb Grey, Johnny Griffin, Lionel Hampton, Barry Harris, Jim Harrod, Alan Hartwell, John Hasselback, Pat Henry, Philippe Hirigoyen, Major Holley, Clayton Hulet, IAJRC Bruce Davidson Lending Library, Institute of Jazz Studies, Hugh Jackson, Charles Johnson, Sheila Jordan, Howard Kanovitz, Lee Katzman, Orrin Keepnews, Red Kelly, Maurice King, Ron Kolber, Yusef Lateef, Hugh Lawson, Pete Leinonen, Peter Leitch, Phil Levine, Debra Hall Levy, Mel Lewis, H. Lukas Lindenmaier, John Marabuto, Ron Marabuto, Bill Miner, John Miner, Dan Morgenstern, Will Moyle, Hod O'Brien, Dan Olson, Phil Pastras, Cecil Payne, Bill Perkins, Gene Perrin, Bob Pierson, Herb Pomeroy, Bob Porter, Lewis Porter, Ken Posten, John Reid, Max Roach, Sonny Rollins, Boris Rose, Jimmy Rowles, Stacy Rowles, Oliver Shearer, Michael Sparke, Alvin Stillman, Bob Sunenblick, Arthur Taylor, Joe Termini, Toots Thielemans, Fred Tompkins, Peter Susan Townsley, Rudy Tucich, Dave Usher, Claude Williamson, Bob Weinstock, Bozy White, Bob Wilber, Jurgen Wolfer, Arthur Zimmerman.

Chapter 2: Claudette Adams, Pepper Adams, Tony Argo, Bill Barron, Frank Basile, Eddie Bert, John Bunch, Kenny Burrell, Ron Carter, Teddy Charles, Joe Cinderella, Jimmy Cobb, Noal Cohen, D. Russell Connor, Michael Cuscuna, Peter Danson, Walter Davis Jr., Evrard Deckers, Larry Dickson, Len Dobbin, Mike Fitzgerald, Tommy Flanagan, Hans Fridlund, Don Friedman, John Frosk, Curtis Fuller, Johnny Griffin, Louis Hayes, Jimmy Heath, Billy Higgins, Philippe Hirigoyen, Freddie Hubbard, Dave Hunt, Institute of Jazz Studies, Laymon Jackson, Hank Jones, Dick Katz, Orrin Keepnews, Jimmy Knepper, Peter Leitch, Virgil Matheus, Hal McKusick, John Miner, Dan Morgenstern, Frank Nash, Fred Norsworthy, Ted O'Reilly, Cecil Payne, Bob Porter, Lewis Porter, Boris Rose, Charlie Rouse, Lorne Schoenberg, Oliver Shearer, Herb Snitzer, Sam Stephenson, Bob Sunenblick, Arthur Taylor, Rudy Tucich, Billy Ver Planck, Bob Weinstock, Keith White, Bob Wilber, Phil Woods, Tony Zano, Mike Zwerin.

Chapter 3: Claudette Adams, Pepper Adams, Danny Bank, Frank Basile, Marcus Belgrave, Eddie Bert, Jackie Byard, Teddy Charles, Noal Cohen, George Coleman, Bob Cranshaw, Michael Cuscuna, Peter Danson, Richard Davis, Evrard Deckers, Len Dobbin, Jerry Dodgion, Mike Fitzgerald, Otto Flueckiger, Frank Foster, Curtis Fuller, Lionel Hampton, Roland Hanna, Jimmy Heath, Philippe Hirigoyen, Andrew Homzy, Institute of Jazz Studies, Milt Jackson, Lee Jeske, Bruce Jones, Hank Jones, Clifford Jordan, George Kanzler, Gene Kee, Jimmy Knepper, Mel Lewis, Ron Ley, Andy McGhee, Charles McPherson, John Miner, Billy Mitchell, Dan Morgenstern, Jimmy Owens, Cecil Payne, Bob Porter, Lewis Porter,

Jerome Richardson, Mickey Roker, Evan Spring, Bob Sunenblick, Arthur Taylor, Clark Terry, Bill Titone, Rudy Tucich, Billy Ver Planck, Harry Weinger, Bob Weinstock, Jimmy Witherspoon, Phil Woods.

Chapter 4: Claudette Adams, Pepper Adams, David Amram, Kenny Barron, Frank Basile, Bill Berry, Eddie Bert, Cecil Bridgewater, Thierry Bruneau, Ron Carter, Teddy Charles, Bob Colmer, Bob Cornfoot, Bob Cranshaw, Michael Cuscuna, Harold Danko, Richard Davis, Alan Dawson, Evrard Deckers, Len Dobbin, Jerry Dodgion, Jon Faddis, Mike Fitzgerald, Tommy Flanagan, Frank Foster, Curtis Fuller, Earl Gardner, Steve Gilmore, Jens Jorn Gjedsted, Bob Gold, Albert Goldman, Bill Goodwin, Roland Hanna, Billy Harper, Johan Helø, Joe Henderson, Philippe Hirigoyen, Marv Holladay, Jan Horne, Freddie Hubbard, Per Husby, Institute of Jazz Studies, Shin-ichi Iwamoto, Jeremy Kahn, George Kanzler, Dick Katz, Amos Kaune, Colin Kellam, Bill Kirchner, Bruce Klauber, Jack Kleinsinger, Jimmy Knepper, Mel Lewis, Jan Lohmann, Mike Lipskin, Ole Matthiessen, Charles McPherson, John Miner, Tony Mosa, John Mosca, George Mraz, Jan Mulder, Walter Norris, Fred Norsworthy, Dick Oatts, Hod O'Brien, Ted O'Reilly, Jimmy Owens, Don Palmer, Niels-Henning Orsted Pederson, Agustin Pérez, Gene Perla, Bob Porter, Lewis Porter, Rufus Reid, Jerome Richardson, Mickey Roker, Howard Rye, Randy Sandke, Al Schackman, Rhoda Scott, Wayne Shorter, Thorbjørn Sjøgren, Gary Smulyan, Marvin Stamm, Bob Sunenblick, Lew Tabackin, Toots Thielemans, Fred Tompkins, McCoy Tyner, Marc Vasey, Cedar Walton, Bill Watrous, Bob Weinstock, Andre White, Bob Wilber, Glenn Wilson, Jimmy Witherspoon, Mike Wolff, Phil Woods, Reggie Workman, Ed Xiques.

Chapter 5: Claudette Adams, Pepper Adams, Barry Altschul, David Amram, Iris Andringa, Juul Anthonissen, Peter Anthonissen, Georges Arvanitas, Steve Bagby, Erik Bakker, Tommy Banks, Bill Barron, Kenny Barron, Frank Basile, Bess Bonnier, Ed Berger, Kenny Berger, Johs Bergh, Mark Berger, Eddie Bert, Peter Bevan, Aad Bos, Joshua Breakstone, Cecil Bridgewater, Dee Dee Bridgewater, Nick Brignola, Tom Bronsvoort, Walter Bruyninckx, Leonard Bukowski, Ronnie Burrage, Carl Burnett, Benny Carter, Tony Cennamo, Denny Christianson, George Coleman, Bob Colmer, Gerhard Conrad, Eddie Cook, Keith Copeland, Bob Cornfoot, John Craig, Søren Damving, Franco d'Andrea, Richard Davis, James L. Dean, Evrard Deckers, Rein de Graaff, Coen de Jong, Don DePalma, Freddie Deronde, Joop de Roo, Jeroen de Valk, Len Dobbin, Jackie Docherty, Paquito D'Rivera, Ray Drummond, Jon Faddis, Mark Feldman, Mike Fitzgerald, Tommy Flanagan, Ricky Ford, Frank Foster, André Francis, Don Friedman, Michael Frohne, Curtis Fuller, Everett Gates, Cliff Gorman, Noreen Grey, Roland Hanna, Per Møller Hanson, Danny Harrington, Billy Hart, Kees Hazevoet, Jimmy Heath, Dave Helland, Kevin Henriques, Willy Heremans, Michel Herr, Phil Hey, John Hicks, Philippe Hirigoyen, Paul Holmberg, Gerard Hoogeveen, Jan Horne, Tim Horner, Eddie House, Clint Houston, Per Husby, Chubby Jackson, Laird Jackson, Howard Johnson, Hank Jones, Mike Jordan, J-M Juilland, Jeremy Kahn, Gabe Katell, Dick Katz, Colin Kellam, Ken Kellett, Jack Kleinsinger, Matti Konttinen, Piet Koster, Lex Lammen, René Laanan, Pat LaBarbera, Claude Lèfevre, Peter Leitch, Cindy Ley, Ulla Lexander, Ron Ley, Patrick Linder, Colin Logan, Jaap Lüdeke, Dean Magraw, Dee Marabuto, Ron Marabuto, Francisco Martinelli, Andy McKee, Jill McManus, Daniel Meyer, Don Miller, Mark Miller, Mark Morganelli, Erik Moseholm, Will Moyle, Michael G. Nastos, Gui Nézan, Gerry Niewood, Alfie Nillson, Cisco Normand, Fred Norsworthy, Hod O'Brien, Colm O'Sullivan, Jimmy Owens, Don Palmer, Charles Papasoff, Stan Patrick, Agustin Pérez, Joel Patterson, Bill Perkins, Allen Pittman, Bob Porter, Lewis Porter, Bill Potts, Angel Rangelov, John Reid, Rufus Reid, Red Rodney, Jimmy Rowles, Michel Ruppli, Thorbjørn Sjøgren, Earl Sauls, Al Schackman, Oliver Shearer, Ib Skovgaard, Arlene Smith, Derek Smith, Carol Sloane, Marvin Stamm, Bob Sunenblick, Naoki Suzuki, Ron Sweetman, Lew Tabackin, Marcello Tonolo, Nobby Totah, Clark Terry, Miel Vanattenhoven, Marc Nam den Hoof, Carrie van der Schagt-van Sloten, Piet van Engelen, Roger Vanhaverbeke, René Vincent, Bert Vuijsje, P.J. Washburn, George Wattiau, Bob Weir, Michael Weiss, Roger Wernboe, André White, Keith White, Ray Whitehouse, Claude Williamson.

Additionally, special thanks to the following institutions:

Belgian BRT Radio, Brussels
Danish Radio, Copenhagen
Dutch Vara Radio, Hilversum
Granada TV, London
Institute of Jazz Studies, Newark, NJ
Metropole Orkest
Nederlandse Omroepprogramma Stichting NOS, Hilversum
Norsk Jazzarchiv, Oslo

Norsk Rikskringkasting, Oslo
La Phonothètique de la Radio Suisse Romande, Lausanne
Radio France, Paris
Royal Norwegian Embassy, Brussels
Swedish National Radio, Stockholm
TV-Byen, Søborg
OY Yleisradio, Helsinki

How to Use This Book

The first line of each entry is the leader(s), if known, or the name that historically has defined an ensemble. Next to the leader is the album's title, but only in the case where (1) all the tunes are done on an LP, and (2) all the tunes are issued on that session, not broken up over various dates.

Each entry's second line is an alphanumeric code, derived from the session's recording date. Lower case letters are appended to a code as a suffix when more than one session exists on a given day. Conversely, upper case letters are used to distinguish dates from each other when only the month and year, or year, are known.

Beneath the alphanumeric code is the recording date, location, and personnel. Throughout the book, two-letter United States postal codes are used to help identify the location of less well-known American cities. Specific information on instrumentation is denoted by asterisks, footnotes, symbols, or additional text that is stripped into a listing. Personnel abbreviations are as follows:

acl alto clarinet
arr arranger
as alto saxophone
b bass
bcl bass clarinet
bfl bass flute
bs baritone saxophone
btb bass trombone
btp bass trumpet
cga conga
cl clarinet
cond conductor
dm drums
e-b electric bass

engh English horn
e-p electric piano
fl flute
flh flugelhorn
frh French horn
g guitar
mc Master of Ceremonies
org organ
p piano
perc percussion
ss soprano saxophone
synth synthesizer
tb trombone
tp trumpet

ts	tenor saxophone	vln	violin
tu	tuba	voc	vocals
vib	vibraphone	vtb	valve trombone

After a session's first paragraph of data is a listing of titles, if known, and a listing of the title's original issue, with label information. Where known, if the country (or region) of origin is not the U.S., that location is abbreviated thusly:

Arg	Argentina	It	Italy
Bel	Belgium	Neth	Netherlands
Braz	Brazil	NZ	New Zealand
Can	Canada	J	Japan
Eng	England	P	Poland
Eu	Europe	R	Russia
F	France	Sp	Spain
Ger	Germany	Swe	Sweden
Gr	Greece	Swiss	Switzerland
Ire	Ireland	YU	the former Yugoslavia

All titles in boldface indicate that Pepper Adams solos on that tune. In some cases, record company matrix numbers are included to the left of a title. If a space exists to the right of a title, it's to be read as a ditto; that is, the same as the listing directly above it.

Often underneath an entry is an annotation, which commonly includes any known reissues, as well as supporting historical data. Much of the oral history commentary that makes up many of the annotations is transcribed from interviews I've conducted about Pepper Adams.

All media is included—recordings, audience tapes, film, videotape, TV and radio broadcasts, private recordings, overdubs, etc.—and, wherever known, I distinguish 78s, 45s, 16rpm, and EPs, from LPs, 45rpm LPs, and CDs. Not included, however, are any issues on 8-track and cassette tape.

Although many of Adams' recordings as a leader and sideman have been reissued, some very fine recordings remain unissued and unheard by those who grew up with CDs. It's hoped that these dates will soon be reissued, not just sought by collectors. More importantly, of course, it's hoped that this book inspires readers, even ardent fans, to listen anew to the recordings of the great Pepper Adams that are readily available.

Discographies are never done. Technology turns over every generation, necessitating a new wave of reissues, and collectors are continually discovering new things. Please send any corrections, additions, and comments to gc-pepperadamsblog.blogspot.com.

Preface

Throughout jazz's illustrious history, live and studio performances have been frozen in time on recordings, preserving for listeners the musical traditions passed down from generation to generation by jazz's great improvisers. Because of recordings' pivotal role in conveying jazz's oral tradition, it can be argued that recordings are jazz's most basic and enduring artifact. If that's indeed the case, then discography—books that list these recordings—is jazz's most fundamental reference work.

A jazz musician's discography is a musical story. It shows the people he played with, the venues he played, the progression of his art over time, the maturation of his repertoire, the compositions he wrote. It functions as a life chronology and a buying guide.

What you have in your hands is Pepper Adams' story, as told by his recordings. It's the culmination of three decades of research on Adams' recorded work—from the LP and cassette era to VHS, CDs, DVDs, and now YouTube—that began in 1984, when I worked with Adams on his memoirs during the last two years of his life.

After much of our work was done, in 1985 I moved from New York to Boston to study jazz musicology with Lewis Porter. I was already well along on the biographical aspects of Adams' life, but I needed to learn from an expert about discographical research, and to round out my knowledge of jazz history, especially the 1920 and '30s. Apart from all that Lewis Porter taught me (and it was considerable), during that time I adopted an overarching strategy to my Adams research: I would, at the very least, try to interview everyone still alive who recorded with Adams, with the aim of verifying published and anecdotal discographical information. The end result was vastly improved data, plus two things I hadn't anticipated: The first was the discovery of many unknown recordings. The other was learning fascinating new details of well-known sessions, sometimes in glorious detail, that cast entirely new light on the creative process and on the business of jazz.

While busy making sense of this, in 1987 Evrard Deckers, an independent researcher working in Belgium, asked me to review the discog-

raphy he was compiling on Pepper Adams. After a few years of corre-
spondence, and a trip to Belgium, in 1992 Deckers and I decided to collaborate on a co-authored work. It was a wonderful division of labor,
since I'd focus on my archival materials and North American research
while Deckers could mine the many resources available in Europe. This
was before the internet and Google era, so geography mattered far more
than it does now. Evrard Deckers contributed much new information,
especially regarding reissues, European radio broadcasts, and audience
recordings, before he died in his sleep at home in 1997.

In the fifteen years since his death, however, this book has become
an entirely different entity. The biggest change is the addition of transcribed interview material that took me two years to complete. It occurred to me that some of my interview material only pertained to Adams' discography, and was too nuanced to be used in an Adams
biography. If not used here, it would never be published.

Also new to the manuscript, I've identified Adams' solos, so that
listeners can focus on these recordings, as opposed to those he did as a
sideman or studio player. Moreover, much new recorded material, and a
new generation of reissues, has been released since 1997, necessitating a
great deal of additional research.

The format of the discography, too, has been completely overhauled
to better conform to current standards and make it more legible. Annotations and footnotes, for example, have been redesigned, LP titles have
been added, and subtle changes have been instituted, such as adding the
country of origin and identifying 78s, 45s, LPs, CDs, VHS, and DVDs.

Joy Road is so named not just to riff on one of Adams' great compositions. I chose it to also capture the essence of Adams' life on the road,
playing jazz with a cast of thousands, some of whom are quoted in this
book. It's also my tribute to Adams' great recorded oeuvre, his 43 magnificent compositions, and the joy he derived from playing the baritone
saxophone.

Much about Adams' personality is woven throughout the annotations, especially among younger musicians that witnessed Adams' final
illness. In a sense, I've tried, like documentary filmmaker Ken Burns, to
infuse my work with a kind of "emotional archeology." Those who are
interested in getting a still deeper understanding of Adams' life might
enjoy my companion volume, a full-length biography of Adams, tentatively entitled *In Love with Night*. I'm planning to finish it well before
2030, the centennial of Pepper Adams' birth. In the meantime, please

consult pepperadams.com, the website I maintain as the historical record of his life and work.

Gary Carner
Braselton, GA

Chapter One
The Early Years: 1947-1958

OLIVER SHEARER
470900
September 1947, unissued demo recording, United Sound Studios, Detroit: Willie Wells tp; Pepper Adams cl; Tommy Flanagan p; Oliver Shearer vib, voc; Charles Burrell b; Patt Popp voc.

a   **Shearer Madness** (Ow!)
b   Medley: Stairway to the Stars
    A Hundred Years from Today

These tracks exist on one 12-inch pressing and were never released commercially. In a conversation with the author in 1988, guitarist Kenny Burrell said that United Sound was on Second or Third Avenue near West Grand Boulevard. The owners were "the main guys that wanted to record us," he said, "when we wanted to make a record on our own in Detroit. They seemed to be sympathetic to jazz. If we wanted to go into the studio, that's where we went."

Oliver Shearer, in an interview with the author in 1988, said,

Tommy [Flanagan] had been playing with Rudy Rutherford and all these people, and Bobbie Caston. At sixteen, Tommy was playing professionally, so, whether this was [his] first record date, I couldn't answer that....It definitely was Pepper's!...He wasn't excited or nervous. I'm on there, writing on the spot. I'm humming shit that I want him to play, and he played every note! I tell him about an ending: I hummed this ending. I didn't know what the hell it was myself, and he played it. He had good facility on that clarinet, and he had a jazz feeling.

According to Adams' college roommate, Bob Cornfoot, in an interview with the author in 1987, Shearer paid for the session. "I think [Shearer] wanted to have one that he could take around with him and play as a demo," said Cornfoot.

Adams first began playing baritone saxophone in December 1947, three months after this session, when he was working for six weeks in the record department at Grinnell's, Detroit's largest music store. A used Bundy baritone had come into the instrument repair shop on trade. Adams bought it and began to get gigs right away.

CHARLES JOHNSON
500700A

c. Summer 1950, Detroit: Elliot Escoe tp; Maurice King as; Yusef Lateef ts; Pepper Adams bs; Willie Anderson p; Oliver Gill b; Charles Johnson dm.

a	PR-1	Midnight Mood	Prize 78: 705
b		Midnight Mood	Prize unissued
c		Rompin' on the Ramp	Prize unissued

According to Yusef Lateef, in remarks made to the author in 1989, this date would have been done no earlier than 1950, after Lateef left Dizzy Gillespie's band and returned to Detroit.

In an interview with the author in 1989, Charles Johnson said that Odessa Malone produced the session. "[She] had a small recording company, the Odessa Malone Recording Company," said Johnson. "The studio was near Hastings [Street]. We made it on a home recording machine, a very primitive machine. How I got ahold of Pepper, I was rehearsing a big band at the time and Pepper was rehearsing with me."

About -a and -b, Maurice King, in an interview with the author in 1989, said,

> That was my composition and my band. This band could have been named "Charles Johnson" because I wasn't letting anything go in my name at that time, but this is my band! That tenor solo was written....Willie Anderson was one of the best blues players in the city, [and] that was background that I had for him. All those riffs and things like that: Those were things that I used for blues singers and different things when they...had no music.

See also 500700B.

About -c, Charles Johnson told the author in 1989 that the acetate broke, so the group re-recorded it on 500700B.

"Bill Evans" and "Park Adams" are listed on the record label for Yusef Lateef and Pepper Adams respectively. "Bill Evans" was the stage name that Lateef used until he converted to Islam in the early 1950s, though his real surname is Huddleston. "Park Adams" was Adams' birth name, and musicians in Detroit in the 1940s and 1950s used it interchangeably with "Pepper Adams," though increasingly less so over time. Adams' nickname carried over from seventh grade in Rochester, New York, predating his family's relocation to Detroit in 1947. Ultimately, "Pepper" became his accepted name, except among his oldest of friends, such as Elvin Jones. Upon his move to New York City in January 1956, "Pepper" was the name that was commonly used.

See 500700B.

CHARLES JOHNSON
500700B
c. Summer 1950, Detroit: same as preceding c. Summer 1950, except Yusef Lateef or Louis Barnet ts; Charles Johnson or unknown dm.

a   PR-2   Rompin' on the Ramp   Prize 78: 705

About -a, Maurice King told the author in 1989 that he believes Louis Barnet played the tenor solo, not Yusef Lateef.

The group's name, as listed on the label, is the Charles Johnson Orchestra. The personnel on the label lists Johnson on drums, yet Johnson, in his 1989 interview with the author, said he didn't feel he played on this session.

See 500700A notes.

510000
Early 1951, unissued recording, Sam's Record Store, Detroit: Billy Horner tp; Bob Pierson ts; Pepper Adams bs; unknown p; unknown b; unknown dm; unknown voc.

According to Bob Pierson, in an interview with the author in 1989, this date was recorded in the back room of Sam's. Adams enlisted in the U.S. Army on 12 July 1951, so the date was done sometime beforehand.

HUGH JACKSON
520700
July 1952, Ann Arbor MI: Frank Keys tp; Larry McCrorey ts; Pepper
Adams bs; Bu Bu Turner p, voc; Ron Penney b; Hugh Jackson dm.

a   **Yardbird Suite**   Vitaphone unissued
b   **Dancing in the Dark**
c   Medley: If You Could See Me Now[1]
        Blue Champagne[2]
        Autumn in New York[3]
        Body and Soul[4]
d   **Out of Nowhere**
e   **Oh! Henry**
f   **Our Delight**
g   **Fine and Dandy**
h   **Blue Room**

[1] Rhythm section only.
[2] Adams and rhythm section.
[3] Keys and rhythm section.
[4] McCrorey and rhythm section.

These tracks exist on one 12-inch pressing. Saxophonist Frank Basile
has pointed out that "U.N. Owen," the pseudonym for Adams on the record label, is both a character from the Agatha Christie novel *And Then
There Were None* and a homophone for "unknown."

It's likely that Adams was on leave, before being shipped off to Ko-
rea, and he chose the pseudonym U.N. Owen in case this session was
commercially released. Saxophonist Bob Pierson, in an interview with
the author in 1989, said, "Probably he had joined the union...and that
was maybe off the books. If it isn't a kosher date, why, you can get in a
lot of trouble."

Hugh Jackson told the author in 1988 that Larry McCrorey was, at
that time, a student at the University of Michigan, and that the recording
was made somewhere on Liberty Street, three blocks from campus.

AUTHOR'S NOTE
Private recordings made during the period 1953-1956 at the Blue Bird
Inn, Klein's Show Bar, and probably the World Stage and West End Ho-
tel, comprise part of the collections of saxophonist Joe Brazil, impresario

Willie Bolar, and jazz fan Terry Weiss. These collections contain recordings of Pepper Adams in performance with Wardell Gray, Sonny Stitt, Miles Davis, Thad Jones, Billy Mitchell, and many of the foremost Detroit musicians of Adams' generation, such as Tommy Flanagan, Kenny Burrell, Barry Harris, Elvin Jones, Yusef Lateef, Frank Foster, Curtis Fuller, Doug Watkins, and Paul Chambers. Additionally, because Detroit in the 1950s was one of the major jazz centers in the United States, and, thus, an important destination for traveling musicians, these three collections also contain recordings that capture in performance many significant soloists of that time who were touring as singles or with ensembles. Barry Harris told the author in 1995 that Joe Brazil's collection also includes jam sessions that Brazil recorded at his house in Detroit. Many, if not all, of Brazil's tapes were recorded on Ampex quarter-track reels.

THAD JONES-PEPPER ADAMS
540400
April 1954, unissued demo recording, United Sounds Studios, Detroit:
Thad Jones tp; Pepper Adams bs; Major Holley b; Walter Smith dm.

a   **I Love You**
b   **I Love You**
c   **Old Geoff**
d   **Old Geoff**
e   **Minority Opinion**
f   **Minority Opinion**
g   **Esme**

These tracks exist on two pressings: -a, -b, -c, -d are on one LP, -e, -f, -g are on the other.

Thad Jones joined the Count Basie band in May 1954, replacing Joe Wilder. After listening to these recordings in 1989, historian Dan Morgenstern told the author that he felt this session's concept—its instrumentation and use of contrapuntal lines—was inspired by Gerry Mulligan and Chet Baker's piano-less quartet recordings of 1952.

See 470900 notes regarding United Sound.

ELVIN JONES
540600
c. June 1954, unissued demo recording, United Sound Studios, Detroit:
Pepper Adams bs; Barry Harris p; Beans Richardson b; Elvin Jones dm.

a   **Shiloh**
b   **Bitty Ditty**
c   **Elusive**
     Rhythm section only:
d   Tenderly

The tracks exist on one twelve-inch acetate. *See* 470900 about United Sound.

This group was the working house band at Detroit's Blue Bird Inn. Harris had replaced Tommy Flanagan in May 1954.

According to Ira Gitler, in a conversation with the author in 1987, Adams brought these tracks to Bob Weinstock of Prestige Records, with the hope of getting a record deal. As the author wrote, in a 1990 article for *Jazzforchung,* on the same trip to New York, Adams also played the tracks for Alfred Lion at Blue Note Records:

> Lion's reaction to Adams' playing was "very interesting," Adams told me [in 1984], something that *might* explain some of the negative reactions that critics felt toward my playing, which didn't seem to be necessarily shared by musicians, for the most part, nor by the public. Lion, Adams said, refused to believe that it was him playing: "That's not you," Lion said. "That's a black baritone player. You're lying, that's not *you!*" Another thing that Alfred said, Adams continued, is: "You know, that's a black baritone player who is a rhythm and blues player trying to learn how to play jazz." Now, that's sort of a clue to me to what I *think* confused critics, to a great extent, and made them so violently antagonistic to the way I played. My feeling is to play with a strong swing sense, a really strong rhythmic base, and also to play with a sophisticated harmonic approach. And, I think, to many critics, these were supposed to be two antithetical things. The people that played with a real strong swing are supposed to be the straightahead, basic players, and the people that play with a sophisticated harmonic approach are supposed to be the intellectual players that don't swing. So, if you get someone doing these two things at once, there's obviously something very wrong with him!

SONNY STITT
550328
28 March 1955, World Stage, Detroit: Sonny Stitt ts; Pepper Adams bs;
Kenny Burrell g; Tommy Flanagan p; Bill Burrell e-b; Hindal Butts dm.

Free Arts LP. This concert was produced and recorded by the New
Music Society to showcase its members. From the program notes, written
by drummer Rudy Tucich: "This concert is being recorded and will be
the first release on our own label, Free Arts Records. Your cooperation in
the recording will be greatly appreciated. We would also like to have you
give us your suggestion for the name of our first concert album." Two
other bands performed at the concert, one led by Yusef Lateef (with
Sonny Red, Bernard McKinney, Barry Harris, Alvin Jackson, and Elvin
Jones), the other by Ali Jackson (with Norman Pockgrandt and Mike
Lawton).

PEPPER ADAMS
550500A
c. May 1955, World Stage, Detroit: Yusef Lateef ts; Pepper Adams bs;
Tommy Flanagan or Barry Harris p; Beans Richardson or Alvin Jackson
b; Jack Thomas, Frank Gant, or Elvin Jones dm; Willie Bolar mc.

Transition unissued. Recorded sometime after 550328. According to
Adams' friend, Alvin Stillman, in a conversation with the author in 1987,
this was one of two live commercial recordings made at the World Stage.

PEPPER ADAMS
550500B
c. May 1955, unissued recording, Dave Usher's basement, Detroit:
Curtis Fuller tb; Pepper Adams bs; Tommy Flanagan or Barry Harris p;
Ernie Farrow b; Hindal Butts dm.

According to Curtis Fuller, in an interview with the author in 1989,
Usher (the former owner of Emanon and Dee Gee records) recorded the
group, though it's not known if Usher intended it for commercial release.
In April 1955 Curtis Fuller replaced Kenny Burrell in the house band at
Klein's, when Burrell left to join Oscar Peterson. Upon Burrell's departure, Adams became the group's musical director, and the above ensemble was the resident band until Adams and Flanagan's move to New

York in January 1956. Pianist Hugh Lawson served as Flanagan's sub, if Flanagan took another gig.

DAVE COLEMAN
551107
7 November 1955, Cambridge MA: Tommy Ball tp; Bud Pearson as; Pepper Adams bs; Dick Wetmore vln; Pat Petracco g; Everett Evans b; Paul Drummond dm; Dave Coleman arr.

a   Backstreet   Transition LP: TRLP-30

    -a on Transition-Blue Note (J) LP: GXF-3126, Toshiba-EMI (J) CD: TOCJ-5889.

PEPPER ADAMS-CURTIS FULLER
560420
20 April 1956, Cambridge MA: Curtis Fuller tb; John Coltrane ts; Pepper Adams bs; Roland Alexander p*; Paul Chambers b; Philly Joe Jones dm.

a   **Trane's Strain***   Transition LP: TRLP-30
b   **High Step**   Blue Note LP: BN-LA-451-H2
c   **Nixon, Dixon and Yates Blues**

    -a on Blue Note LP: BN-LA-451-H2, Transition-Blue Note (J) LP: GXF-3126, Blue Note (Ger) LP: BST-84481/2, Blue Note CD: CDP-7-84437-2, Fresh Sound (Sp) CD: FSRCD-610, Toshiba-EMI (J) CD: CJ28-5160.
    -b on Blue Note LP: BN-LA-451-H2, Blue Note (Ger) LP: BST-84481/2, Blue Note CD: CDP-7-84437-2, Fresh Sound (Sp) CD: FSRCD-610, Toshiba-EMI (J) CD: CJ28-5160.
    -c on Blue Note LP: BN-LA-451-H2, Blue Note (Ger) LP: BST-84481/2, Blue Note CD: CDP-7-84437-2, Fresh Sound (Sp) CD: FSRCD-610, Toshiba-EMI (J) CD: CJ28-5160.
    According to Curtis Fuller, in an interview with the author in 1989, Adams and Fuller had a working group (*see* 550500B) called "Bones and Bari," and Transition's original intent was to produce a co-led date as Transition LP: TRLP-8. "We did enough for two dates," Fuller told the author. Instead, only -a was originally released, and that on a sampler.
    According to discographer David Wild, in 1977 Curtis Fuller told record producer Michael Cuscuna, "The record date was to have featured

Fuller and Pepper Adams (with a tentative title of *Salt and Pepper*). It was to have used part of the Miles Davis Quintet, then performing in town." Davis' group was at Storyville from 16-30 April 1956.

In an interview with the author in 1984, Pepper Adams remembered the date:

> The first records that I was on that achieved any kind of distribution was really a sampler thing. When I first moved from Detroit to New York [in January 1956, a few] months later there was a record date in Boston for a company that was brand new at the time called Transition. There were two horn players—John Coltrane and myself—and Paul Chambers. I think it was Philly Joe, and it was supposed to be Red Garland, but he didn't show up, so there was confusion around the piano chair. It was very strange. It was an odd studio, hours late getting started. The whole thing was all very awkward, uncomfortable, but we actually did record the equivalent of an album....I think the first thing they put out was a sampler of several dates [Transition] had done, and it had one track of blues: This thing with Curtis, John, and myself as the front line.

About Alexander replacing Garland, Curtis Fuller told the author in 2006, Alexander "was a tenor player who was going to Berklee [School of Music]. He wanted to hear Trane and Pepper, and asked me [if he could] come down." In 1989 Fuller told the author, "Roland happened to be sitting there...and [producer Tom Wilson] said, 'It's going to be you then.'"

KENNY CLARKE–JAZZMEN: DETROIT
560430
30 April 1956, Van Gelder Studio, Hackensack NJ: Pepper Adams bs; Tommy Flanagan p; Kenny Burrell g; Paul Chambers b; Kenny Clarke dm.

a	69191	**Cottontail**	Savoy LP: MG-12083
b	69192	But Not for Me[1]	Vogue (F) LP: 600-143
c	69193	**Your Host**	Savoy LP: MG-12083
d	69194	**Tricrotism**	Savoy LP: SJL-1111
e	69195	**Tom's Thumb**	Savoy LP: MG-12083

[1]Duet for Burrell and Clarke.

-a on Savoy LP: SJL-1111, Savoy (Ger) LP: WL-70515, Byg (F) LP: 529-117, Vogue (F) LP: 600-143, Savoy CD: SV-0176, Savoy CD: SV-0243, Proper Box (Eng) CD: 120. Vogue (F) CD: 650-143, Fresh Sounds (Sp) CD: FSR-CD-645, Nippon-Columbia (J) CD: COCB-53953.

-b on Vogue (F) LP: 600-143, Vogue (F) CD: 650-143, Fresh Sounds (Sp) CD: FSRCD-645, Savoy CD: SV-0176, Proper Box (Eng) CD: 120.

-c on Savoy LP: SJL-1111, Savoy (Ger) LP: WL-70515, Byg (F) LP: 529-117, Vogue (F) LP: 600-143, Savoy CD: 0190, Savoy CD: SV-0176, Savoy CD: SV-0243, Proper Box (Eng) CD: 120, Vogue (F) CD: 650-143, Fresh Sounds (Sp) CD: FSR-CD-645, Nippon-Columbia (J) CD: COCB-53953.

-d on Proper Box (Eng) CD: 120, Vogue (F) LP: 600-143, Vogue (F) CD: 650-143, Vogue (F) CD: 660-512, Fresh Sounds (Sp) CD: FSRCD-645, Denon-Savoy (J) CD: SVY-17189.

-e on Savoy LP: SJL-1111, Savoy (Ger) LP: WL-70515, Byg (F) LP: 529-117, Vogue (F) LP: 600-143, Savoy CD: SV-0176, Savoy CD: SV-0243, Proper Box (Eng) CD: 120, Vogue (F) CD: 650-143, Fresh Sounds (Sp) CD: FSRCD-645, Denon-Savoy (J) CD: SVY-17304, Nippon-Columbia (J) CD: COCB-53953.

According to trumpeter Art Farmer, in an interview with the author in 1988, Savoy, at this time, typically recorded at Van Gelder on Wednesday. 30 April 1956 was a Monday, so likely an anomaly?

About the group of Detroit musicians that moved to New York in 1956, Kenny Burrell, in an interview with the author in 1988, said:

When we first came [to New York], it wasn't that easy. Tommy [Flanagan] and I stayed with my auntie up in Harlem and we weren't working that much. Finally, we started getting some gigs. Kenny Clarke was one of the few guys that helped us. We used to go down to the Café Bohemia and sit in. Tommy, Pepper, all of us would go down there to get ourselves heard. This was in '56. People like Kenny Clarke, a very benevolent man, would welcome young-sters to come up on the bandstand and play, and, therefore, it en-abled him to hear us, and other people to hear us, and, consequently, I'm sure he asked [Savoy producer] Ozzie Cadena about putting him together with these guys from Detroit, as a result. (Kenny Clarke was more or less the house drummer at Savoy, and the dates were being produced at that time by Ozzie Cadena. [Clarke] was also very active at Prestige. Kenny Clarke and Art Taylor were guys on call.) So Ozzie decided to put us—the Detroit guys that just moved to New York in the middle '50s—together with Kenny Clarke. We put our heads together and came up with some tunes.

On a 1978 Rochester, New York radio interview, conducted by Will Moyle, Pepper Adams said, "When Kenny Clarke got this date, he called me and asked me to set up a group to record."

In an interview with the author in 1984, Adams said, it's "a good album." "It was more of a collective," Adams continued, "of which I was one of the contributors. I think Tommy, and Kenny, and I each had an original tune on there, and then we worked out an arrangement between ourselves. It was on Savoy. For a small label, they had decent distribution, so it was the first time my name appeared on a record that was likely to be in more than eight stores on any given day."

Regarding Rudy Van Gelder's original studio, that was located in his home in Hackensack, Adams told the author in 1984,

> You could walk a couple of blocks and there was a bar that would serve you draft beer in big plastic containers. This was just so you didn't have to worry about returning them. Get a sandwich and a beer and eat in the yard; [Rudy] wouldn't let us in the house....He's extremely meticulous. When he's in the studio, he's very conscious about dust and fingerprints and all that. He wears black gloves in the studio at all times, and generally wears an all-black costume, and tends to look a little bit like the invader force in Army war games. He was able to consistently record jazz well at a time when it was not being done....When he started in the late '40s, and on through the early fifties, he was certainly at the top of the field, day in and day out turning out quality recordings. I guess part of that meticulousness paid off. He kept his pianos in perfect condition. Not every recording studio bothers.

See 560509.

KENNY CLARKE–JAZZMEN: DETROIT
560509
9 May 1956, Van Gelder Studio, Hackensack NJ: Same as 30 April 1956:

a	69204	**You Turned the Tables on Me**	Savoy LP: MG-12083
b	69205	**Afternoon in Paris**	
c	69206	**Apothegm**	

-a on Savoy LP: SJL-1111, Savoy (Ger) LP: WL-70515, Byg (F) LP: 529-117, Vogue (F) LP: 600-143, Proper Box (Eng) CD: 120, Vogue (F) CD: 650-143, Denon-Savoy (J) CD: SVY-17248, Denon-Savoy (J) CD: SVY-1728, Nippon Columbia (J) CD: COCB-5395.

-b on Savoy LP: SJL-1111, Savoy (Ger) LP: WL-70515, Byg (F) LP: 529-117, Vogue (F) LP: 600-143, Proper Box (Eng) CD: 120, Vogue (F) CD: 650-143, Nippon Columbia (J) CD: COCB-5395.

-c on Savoy LP: SJL-1111, Savoy (Ger) LP: WL-70515, Byg (F) LP: 529-117, Vogue (F) LP: 600-143, Savoy CD: SV-0176, Savoy CD: SV-0243, Proper Box (Eng) CD: 120, Vogue (F) CD: 650-143, Nippon Columbia (J) CD: COCB-5395.

See 560430 notes regarding Van Gelder's studio.

STAN KENTON
561103
3 November 1956, Macumba Club, San Francisco: Ed Leddy, Lee Katzman, Phil Gilbert, Dennis Grillo, Tom Slaney tp; Bob Fitzpatrick, Kent Larsen, Jim Amlotte tb; Kenny Shroyer btb; Irving Rosenthal, Joe Mariani frh; Jay McAllister tu; Lennie Niehaus as; Bill Perkins, Richie Kamuca ts; Pepper Adams bs; Stan Kenton p; Ralph Blaze g; Don Bagley b; Mel Lewis dm; Laurindo Almeida perc.*

a	Evening (Rendezvous at Sunset)	Artistry LP: AR-106
b	Stomping at the Savoy	
c	Artistry in Rhythm*	private recording
d	What's New	
e	My Old Flame	
f	**I Concentrate on You**	Artistry LP: AR-106
g	Collaboration	private recording
h	Intermission Riff	
i	**Royal Blue**	
j	Artistry in Rhythm*	
k	Stomping at the Savoy	
m	Love for Sale*	
n	Yesterdays	Artistry LP: AR-106
o	Winter in Madrid	private recording
p	El Congo Valiente*	
q	piano interlude	
r	Fuego Cubano*	
s	La Suerte de los Tontos*	

t   Evening (Rendezvous at Sunset)
u   Jump for Joe
v   My Old Flame
w   **Take the "A" Train**
x   Theme and Variations
y   La Suerte de los Tontos*
z   Young Blood
aa   Cherokee
bb   Out of Nowhere   Artistry LP: AR-106
cc   **King Fish**   private recording
dd   Under a Blanket of Blue
ee   **Swing House**

It's not clear whether -a, -b, -f, -n, -bb were taken from this session or from 561106.

Some of this material may be on Sounds of Yesteryear (Eng) CD: DSOY-814. The CD claims to include music from the 3 November concert, but three of the tunes on the CD weren't played that evening.

Originally cut on 78s, then converted to reel tape, by Wally Heider.

Adams joined the Kenton band in New York on 25 May 1956, upon bassist Oscar Pettiford's recommendation. On 24 November, after a two week engagement at the Macumba Club, Adams, Lee Katzman, and Mel Lewis resigned from Kenton to start their own band in Los Angeles. In an interview with Peter Danson in *Coda*, Adams spoke about the Kenton tour:

[Oscar Pettiford] damn near strong-armed me into that gig.…It was a situation where I wasn't at all sure I wanted to play in the Stan Kenton Band, and Stan was not at all sure he wanted me to play in his band, but Oscar Pettiford was convinced that that's what I should do, and, so, by God, that's what I wound up doing for about five months.…Actually, the band I played in was not that bad. We still had, at that time, a professional band. It was soon after that he started cutting his payroll drastically. But, at that time, there were still a number of fine players. Mel Lewis was the drummer. Unfortunately, we never had a solid bass player. We went through a whole bunch of them—briefly Red Mitchell, and that was fine—so it was very difficult to make that band swing.…We did not play much of the "progressive" type stuff. In other words, we never played any of those awful Bob Graettinger or Bill Russo arrangements. Maybe once or twice, and that was it. We would play a lot of

Bill Holman arrangements, which were always musical, and a lot of Johnny Richards' things, some of which were just beautiful, gorgeous writing. We had three or four of Gerry Mulligan's charts: Limelight, which is a joy to play, that was a beauty. So certain things were obligatory during my tenure once a night. But, generally speaking, we were playing quality music and playing it quite well.

According to Phil Gilbert (in a 1988 letter to the author) and Mel Lewis (in a 1989 interview with the author), there weren't any solo spots for baritone in Kenton's book when Adams joined the band. Historically, Kenton's arrangements featured alto and tenor saxophone, but especially alto, due to the band's long lineage of alto soloists, such as Art Pepper, Bud Shank, Lennie Niehaus, Charlie Mariano, Dave Schildkraut, and Lee Konitz. Nevertheless, as Gilbert wrote, "Bill Perkins and Lennie Niehaus offered [Adams] *their* solo spots, since they were obviously aware of his incredible talent! Kenton quickly realized he had a superior talent on hand and began to open up the charts with solos for Pepper to fill." As Lewis explained: "We saw in Pepper a 'major' [player] right there. I mean, you saw it. You knew right away. It was a matter of getting Kenton to give him more and more [solos]."

Regarding Pepper Adams' influence on the Kenton band, Lennie Niehaus told an interviewer that Adams' phrasing was different from all the horn players in the band, and, eventually, the entire band phrased like Adams. Commemorating Adams' enduring influence, Niehaus, in the late 2000s, wrote a big band chart, *Pepper*.

Pepper Adams' influence on Bill Perkins was equally profound. About Adams, Perkins told interviewer Les Tomkins in 1987, "When he came with Stan Kenton's band in 1956, he just turned me around musically and mentally, although it didn't come out in my playing till many years later—but in my mind I heard this incredible player, and, when I play baritone, I hear him."

See 561104 notes, and sessions 561104, 561106, 561107, 561108, 561109, 561110, 561111, 561117, 561118.

STAN KENTON
561104
4 November 1956, private recording, Macumba Club, San Francisco: Same as 3 November 1956, except Archie LeCoque tb replaces Bob Fitzpatrick; Laurindo Almeida perc*:

a   The Opener
b   I Remember You
c   Sophisticated Lady
d   Walking Shoes
e   Autumn Nocturne
f   **King Fish**
g   Jump for Joe
h   Winter in Madrid
i   Young Blood
j   My Old Flame
k   **Intermission Riff**
m   Stella by Starlight
n   Under a Blanket of Blue
o   **Swing House**
p   Theme and Variations
q   What's New
r   Winter in Madrid
s   Love for Sale*
t   **My Funny Valentine**
u   My Old Flame
v   **The Big Chase**
w   **I Concentrate on You**
x   Stella by Starlight
y   Cherokee
z   Artistry in Rhythm*
aa The Opener
bb **I Concentrate on You**
cc **Swing House**
dd Love for Sale*
ee Evening (Rendezvous at Sunset)
ff **The Big Chase**
gg What's New
hh Cherokee
ii Theme and Variations
jj El Congo Valiente
kk **King Fish**
mm 23° North, 82° West*
nn Stomping at the Savoy
oo Yesterdays
pp Out of Nowhere

qq La Suerte de los Tontos
rr **Royal Blue**
ss Autumn Nocturne
tt Opus in Chartreuse
uu Theme and Variations
vv **My Funny Valentine**
ww **I Concentrate on You**
xx Fearless Finlay
yy My Old Flame
zz **The Big Chase**
aaa The Peanut Vendor*

Originally cut on 78s, then converted to reel tape, by Wally Heider. In a 1984 interview with Pepper Adams, Adams told the author,

Of course, [in Kenton's] band, like most bands, there were hardly any solos in the baritone chair anyway....Gradually, they started getting used to what I was doing, so more and more solos started coming my way....They even resurrected one thing to become a feature for me, which was pretty unusual. They had done a tour with Charlie Parker, and so they had an arrangement that Bill Holman had written on My Funny Valentine for Bird to play in front of the band on tour. So they pulled this out of the inactive book and put it into the book for me to play as a feature tune. It was terrific! It had been crafted for Bird, so it's all saxophone solo, and it's about seven minutes long, so it made a great feature. I got to do that every night, and, by the time I left the band in San Francisco, I was getting more solos than anybody and I was still unknown. I think it was when we were in San Francisco that Ralph Gleason, the critic for *Down Beat,* wrote the first article about me that had appeared in any of the major publications.

See 561103 notes and sessions 561103, 561104, 561106, 561107, 561108, 561109, 561110, 561111, 561117, 561118.

STAN KENTON
561106
6 November 1956, Macumba Club, San Francisco: Same as 3 November 1956; Laurindo Almeida perc*:

a   The Opener   Artistry LP: AR-103

b	Sophisticated Lady	private recording
c	Walking Shoes	Artistry LP: AR-103
d	**King Fish**	
e	Love for Sale*	private recording
f	Autumn Nocturne	
g	**The Big Chase**	Artistry LP: AR-106
h	**Swing House**	Artistry LP: AR-103
i	Evening (Rendezvous at Sunset)	
j	**Intermission Riff**	Artistry CD: ARCD-002
k	Winter in Madrid	private recording
m	**I Concentrate on You**	
n	Stomping at the Savoy	
o	Theme and Variations	
p	What's New	Artistry LP: AR-103
q	My Old Flame	private recording
r	Opus in Chartreuse	
s	Lover Man	
t	Cherokee	
u	El Congo Valiente	Artistry LP: AR-103
v	La Suerte de los Tontos	private recording
w	Happy Birthday[1]	
x	Walking Shoes	Artistry LP: AR-103
y	Sophisticated Lady	private recording
z	Artistry in Rhythm*	
aa	**Take the "A" Train**	
bb	I Remember You	Artistry LP: AR-103
cc	Young Blood	
dd	**My Funny Valentine**	
ee	23° North, 82° West	Artistry CD: ARCD-002
ff	All the Things You Are	Artistry LP: AR-103
gg	Fearless Finlay	
hh	Theme and Variations	private recording
ii	**I Concentrate on You**	
jj	Out of Nowhere	
kk	**Royal Blue**	Artistry LP: AR-103
mm	El Congo Valiente	private recording
nn	**Swing House**	Artistry LP: AR-103
oo	La Suerte de los Tontos	private recording
pp	Yesterdays	Artistry CD: ARCD-002

[1]Piano and band vocal.

Artistry LP: AR-103 claims a 5 November 1956 recording date, but Pirie and Mueller's reference work *Artistry in Kenton* doesn't include an entry for that date. All of the tracks released by Artistry correspond to a 6 November recording date.

It's not clear whether -i, -m, -n, -jj, and -pp were taken from 6 November or from 561103.

Regarding -c and -x, it's not clear which of the two tracks is included on Artistry LP: AR-103.

Regarding -h and -nn, it's not clear which of the two tracks is included on Artistry LP: AR-103.

-a, -c, -d, -h, -j, -p, -u, -x, -bb, -cc, -dd, -ee, -ff, -gg, -kk, -nn, -pp on Artistry CD: ARCD-002.

Some of this material may be on Sounds of Yesteryear (Eng) CD: DSOY-814. *See* 561103 note.

Originally cut on 78s, then converted to reel tape, by Wally Heider.

See 561103 and 561104 notes, plus sessions 561103, 561104, 561107, 561108, 561109, 561110, 561111, 561117, 561118.

STAN KENTON
561107
7 November 1956, private recording, Macumba Club, San Francisco:
Same as 3 November 1956:

a   The Opener
b   **Royal Blue**
c   All the Things You Are
d   Jump for Joe
e   **Swing House**
f   La Suerte de los Tontos

Originally cut on 78s, then converted to reel tape, by Wally Heider.

See 561103 and 561104 notes, plus sessions 561103, 561104, 561106, 561108, 561109, 561110, 561111, 561117, 561118.

STAN KENTON
561108
8 November 1956, private recording, Macumba Club, San Francisco:
Same as 3 November 1956; Laurindo Almeida perc*:

a   The Opener

b   Sophisticated Lady
c   Walking Shoes
d   Autumn Nocturne
e   **Swing House**
f   What's New
g   Cherokee
h   El Congo Valiente
i   **I Concentrate on You**[*]
j   Evening (Rendezvous at Sunset)
k   Opus in Chartreuse
m   Yesterdays
n   Love for Sale[*]
o   The Nearness of You
p   23° North, 82° West[*]
q   Intermission Riff
r   Street of Dreams
s   La Suerte de los Tontos
t   piano interlude
u   Theme and Variations
v   Young Blood
w   Winter in Madrid
x   **Royal Blue**
y   Stella by Starlight
z   Out of Nowhere
aa   September Song
bb   Stomping at the Savoy
cc   I Remember You
dd   Under a Blanket of Blue
ee   **King Fish**
ff   Love for Sale[*]
gg   Artistry in Rhythm[*]
hh   **My Funny Valentine**
ii   **The Big Chase**
jj   My Old Flame
kk   **Take the "A" Train**
mm   Tenderly
nn   Fearless Finlay
oo   I'm Glad There is You
pp   Pennies from Heaven
qq   **The Way You Look Tonight**

Originally cut on 78s, then converted to reel tape, by Wally Heider.
See 561103 and 561104 notes, plus sessions 561103, 561104, 561106, 561107, 561109, 561110, 561111, 561117, 561118.

STAN KENTON
561109
9 November 1956, private recording, Macumba Club, San Francisco:
Same as 3 November 1956; Laurindo Almeida perc*:

a   The Opener
b   Sophisticated Lady
c   Walking Shoes
d   **Swing House**
e   Street of Dreams
f   La Suerte de los Tontos
g   **Intermission Riff**
h   23° North, 82° West*
i   Stomping at the Savoy
j   Under a Blanket of Blue
k   Young Blood
m   Theme and Variations
n   **I Concentrate on You**
o   My Old Flame
p   Love for Sale*
q   Yesterdays
r   Out of Nowhere
s   September Song
t   **The Big Chase**
u   Artistry in Rhythm*
v   Opus in Chartreuse
w   What's New
x   Winter in Madrid
y   **Royal Blue**
z   Stella by Starlight
aa Cherokee
bb Laura
cc The Peanut Vendor*
dd piano interlude
ee **I Concentrate on You**
ff The Nearness of You

gg **Take the "A" Train**
hh El Congo Valiente
ii Autumn Nocturne
jj 23° North, 82° West*
kk **My Funny Valentine**
mm **Between the Devil and the Deep Blue Sea**
nn My Old Flame
oo Laura
pp **King Fish**
qq Artistry in Rhythm*

Originally cut on 78s, then converted to reel tape, by Wally Heider.
See 561103 and 561104 notes, plus sessions 561103, 561104, 561106, 561107, 561108, 561110, 561111, 561117, 561118.

STAN KENTON
561110
10 November 1956, private recording, Macumba Club, San Francisco:
Same as 3 November 1956, except Archie LeCoque tb replaces Bob Fitzpatrick; Laurindo Almeida perc*:

a The Opener
b Sophisticated Lady
c Walking Shoes
d **Swing House**
e piano and bass interlude
f Theme and Variations
g El Congo Valiente
h Artistry in Rhythm*
i What's New
j **Royal Blue**
k 23° North, 82° West*
m Love for Sale*
n Winter in Madrid
o Young Blood
p My Old Flame
q **Take the "A" Train**
r The Opener
s Stomping at the Savoy
t Stella by Starlight

u   Cherokee
v   Theme and Variations
w   **Intermission Riff**
x   Collaboration
y   **The Big Chase**
z   La Suerte de los Tontos
aa Artistry in Rhythm*
bb Under a Blanket of Blue
cc I'm Glad There is You
dd I Remember You
ee Laura
ff Royal Blue
gg Artistry in Rhythm*
hh **My Funny Valentine**
ii Opus in Turquoise (Opus in Azure)
jj Street of Dreams
kk The Peanut Vendor*

Originally cut on 78s, then converted to reel tape, by Wally Heider.
See 561103 and 561104 notes, plus sessions 561103, 561104,
561106, 561107, 561108, 561109, 561111, 561117, 561118.

STAN KENTON
561111
11 November 1956, private recording, Macumba Club, San Francisco:
Same as 3 November 1956; Laurindo Almeida perc*:

a   Sophisticated Lady
b   Walking Shoes
c   The Opener
d   Autumn Nocturne
e   **I Concentrate on You***
f   **Swing House**
g   I Remember You
h   Street of Dreams
i   **Intermission Riff**
j   Winter in Madrid
k   Stomping at the Savoy
m   **My Funny Valentine**
n   Love for Sale*

o What's New
p My Old Flame
q Stella by Starlight
r **Take the "A" Train**
s El Congo Valiente
t Sophisticated Lady
u Walking Shoes
v **Swing House**
w Evening (Rendezvous at Sunset)
x **Intermission Riff**
y **Royal Blue**
z Artistry in Rhythm*
aa The Man I Love[1]
bb Stomping at the Savoy
cc Autumn Nocturne
dd La Suerte de los Tontos
ee Yesterdays
ff Theme and Variations
gg drum solo
hh Love for Sale*
ii Spring Is Here
jj Lover Man
kk Cherokee
mm **Take the "A" Train**
nn Out of Nowhere
oo Laura
pp 23° North, 82° West*
qq My Old Flame
rr Young Blood
ss El Congo Valiente
tt Evening (Rendezvous at Sunset)
uu **I Concentrate on You**
vv Where or When
ww Winter in Madrid
xx **King Fish**
yy **My Funny Valentine**
zz **Royal Blue**
aaa Autumn Nocturne
bbb **The Big Chase**
ccc My Old Flame

ddd Out of Nowhere
eee Under a Blanket of Blue
fff Artistry in Rhythm[*]

[1]Kenton piano solo.

Originally cut on 78s, then converted to reel tape, by Wally Heider.
See 561103 and 561104 notes, plus sessions 561103, 561104,
561106, 561107, 561108, 561109, 561110, 561117, 561118.

STAN KENTON
561117
17 November 1956, Macumba Club, San Francisco: Same as 3 November-
ber 1956; Laurindo Almeida perc*:

a	Walking Shoes	Magic CD (F): DAWE-50
b	Autumn Nocturne	
c	Artistry in Rhythm[*]	
d	Winter in Madrid	
e	My Old Flame	
f	La Suerte de los Tontos	
g	**I Concentrate on You**	
h	Theme and Variations	
i	Young Blood	
j	Collaboration	
k	Stella by Starlight	
m	Cherokee	
n	**Intermission Riff**	
o	Laura	
p	Stomping at the Savoy	
q	Out of Nowhere	
r	Opus in Chartreuse	private recording
s	El Congo Valiente	Magic CD (F): DAWE-53
t	Fuego Cubano	
u	**The Big Chase**	
v	**My Funny Valentine**	
w	The Opener	
x	I Remember You	
y	Harlem Nocturne	
z	**Between the Devil and the Deep Blue Sea**	
aa	**Swing House**	

bb Love for Sale*
cc Sophisticated Lady   private 78
dd **Royal Blue**   Magic CD (F): DAWE-53
ee Artistry in Rhythm*

-g also on Magic CD (F): DAWE-53.

-z probably on Artistry LP: AR-106.

Regarding -w, Pirie and Mueller, in their discography *Artistry in Kenton,* do not list the tune. It seems likely, however, that only performances from 17 November are included on both Magic releases.

Some of this material may be on Sounds of Yesteryear (Eng) CD: DSOY-814. *See* 561103 note.

Originally cut on 78s, then converted to reel tape, by Wally Heider.

See 561103 and 561104 notes, plus sessions 561103, 561104, 561106, 561107, 561108, 561109, 561110, 561111, 561118.

STAN KENTON
561118
18 November 1956, private recording, Macumba Club, San Francisco:
Same as 3 November 1956; Laurindo Almeida perc*:

a   The Opener
b   Autumn Nocturne
c   Artistry in Rhythm*
d   Winter in Madrid
e   My Old Flame
f   Don't Take Your Love from Me
g   **King Fish**
h   Where or When
i   **I Concentrate on You**
j   Lover Man
k   Evening (Rendezvous at Sunset)
m   All the Things You Are
n   Fearless Finlay

Originally cut on 78s, then converted to reel tape, by Wally Heider.

See 561103 and 561104 notes, plus sessions 561103, 561104, 561106, 561107, 561108, 561109, 561110, 561111, 561117.

MEL LEWIS–GOT'CHA
561119
19 November 1956, Sands Ballroom, Oakland CA: Ed Leddy tp; Jerry
Coker, Richie Kamuca ts; Pepper Adams bs; John Marabuto p; Dean
Reilly b; Mel Lewis dm.

a **In a Mellow Tone**   San Francisco LP: JR-2
b **Leave Your Worries Behind**
c **One for Pat**

All tracks on Fresh Sound (Sp) LP: FSR-B-10905, Fresh Sound (Sp)
CD: FSR-CD-073
In an interview with the author in 1988, Pat Henry, the producer of
the session, said, "Jerry Coker was playing on the date because…Bill
Perkins got attacked by some toughs up in Chinatown, next to where the
Macumba [Club] was, and he couldn't play." Coker subbed for Perkins
in the Kenton band, and was the logical choice for the recording.
According to drummer Ron Marabuto, in a 1989 interview with the
author, "When they did that record date, what was happening was [Pep-
per] and all those guys were playing with Stan Kenton's band, and this
local disk jockey, [Pat Henry], put together the date. They needed a piano player, so this guy's a friend of my dad's, so he got my dad on it."
According to John Marabuto, in an interview with the author in
1988, "I'm sure we did each [tune] twice….It was after the [Kenton] job.
Everybody was beat, especially the guys from Stan Kenton's band. The
trumpet player, Ed Leddy, was the first trumpet player with Stan Kenton.
His chops were wiped [out]. We went from, I'd say, two to four in the
morning, because the guys had to come [over] from San Francisco."
See 561120.

MEL LEWIS–GOT'CHA
561120
20 November 1956, Sands Ballroom, Oakland CA: Same as 19 November 1956:

a **A Winter's Tale**   San Francisco LP: JR-2
b **Sir Richard Face**
c **'enry 'iggins 'ead**
d **El Cerrito**

All tracks on Fresh Sound (Sp) LP: FSR-B-10905, Fresh Sound (Sp) CD: FSR-CD-073
See 561119 notes.

LENNIE NIEHAUS–ZOUNDS!
561210
10 December 1956, Contemporary Studios, Los Angeles: Frank Rosolino tb; Vince DeRosa frh; Jay McAllister tu; Lennie Niehaus as; Bill Perkins ts; Pepper Adams bs; Red Mitchell b; Mel Lewis dm.

a	**The Sermon**	Contemporary LP: C-3540
b	**With the Wind and the Rain in Your Hair**	
c	Four	
d	Blues for Susie	

All tracks on Vogue (Eng) LP: LAE-12222, Vogue (Eng) LP: LDC-150, Vogue (F) LP: JSLP-50035, King (J) LP: K2OP-6010, Original Jazz Classics CD: OJCCD-1892-2

STAN KENTON
561212
12 December 1956, Hollywood CA: Ed Leddy, Lee Katzman, Phil Gilbert, Pete Candoli, Don Paladino tp; Bob Fitzpatrick, Kent Larsen, Jim Amlotte tb; Kenny Shroyer btb; Irving Rosenthal, Erik Kessler frh; Jay McAllister tu*; Lennie Niehaus, Charlie Mariano as; Bill Perkins, Richie Kamuca ts; Pepper Adams bs; Stan Kenton p; Ralph Blaze g; Don Bagley b; Mel Lewis dm; Laurindo Almeida perc.

a	16275	Mexican Dance	Creative World LP: ST-1066
b	16276	Sophisticated Samba	Creative World LP: ST-1040
c	16277	Opus in Beige*	Capitol (Eng) LP: OU-2001
	Saxes and rhythm section only:		
d	16278	Sentimental Serenade	Creative World LP: ST-1066

-c on Capitol (Neth) LP: 5C052-80799, Emigold (Neth) LP: DAG-124, Capitol CD: 724354231025.

DAVE PELL–A PELL OF A TIME
570117a
17 January 1957, Los Angeles: Jack Sheldon tp; Bob Burgess tb; Dave Pell ts; Pepper Adams bs; Marty Paich p; Tommy Tedesco g; Tom Kelly b; Mel Lewis dm.

a	H2JB0265	**Grey Flannel**	RCA-Victor LP: LPM-1524
b	H2JB0266	Angel Eyes	
c	H2JB0267	**Them There Eyes**	

All tracks on Fresh Sound (Sp) LP: NL-45627, Blue Sounds (Sp) CD: ND-74408.
See 570123 and 570320.

STAN KENTON–VOICES IN MODERN
570117b
17 January 1957, Hollywood CA: Ed Leddy tp; Bob Fitzpatrick, Kent Larsen, Jim Amlotte, John Halliburton tb; George Roberts btb; Lennie Niehaus, Charlie Mariano as; Bill Perkins, Richie Kamuca ts; Pepper Adams bs; Stan Kenton p; Ralph Blaze g; Red Mitchell b; Mel Lewis dm; vocal choir [Modern Men]: Bob Smart, Tony Katics, Paul Salamunovich, Al Oliveri.

a	16441	All about Ronnie	Capitol LP: T-810
b	16442	Walk Softly	
	Leddy out:		
c	16443	Sunday's Child	Capitol unissued
	Brass out:		
d	16444	After You	Capitol LP: T-810

-a on Capitol 45: EAP2-810, Capitol (Eng) LP: LCT-6138, Collectors' Choice CD: CCM-354.
-b on Capitol 45: EAP3-810, Capitol (Eng) LP: LCT-6138, Collectors' Choice CD: CCM-354.
-d on Capitol 45: EAP3-810, Capitol (Eng) LP: LCT-6138, Collectors' Choice CD: CCM-354.
See 570222 and 570304.

DAVE PELL–A PELL OF A TIME
570123
23 January 1957, Los Angeles: Same as 17 January 1957:

a   H2JB0269 **Jazz Goes to Siwash**   RCA-Victor LP: LPM-1524
b   H2JB0270 Sandy Shoes
c   H2JB0271 **Love Me or Leave Me**

All tracks on Fresh Sound (Sp) LP: NL-45627, Blue Sounds (Sp) CD: ND-74408.
See also 570320.

SHORTY ROGERS–PLAYS RICHARD RODGERS
570130
30 January 1957, Los Angeles: Shorty Rogers flh; Conte Candoli, Pete Candoli, Harry Edison, Al Porcino, Maynard Ferguson tp; Milt Bernhart, Bob Burgess, Frank Rosolino tb; John Halliburton btb; Sam Rice tu; Herb Geller as; Bill Holman, Jack Montrose ts; Pepper Adams bs; Pete Jolly p; Red Mitchell b; Stan Levey dm.

a   H2JB0313 Mountain Greenery   RCA-Victor LP: LPM-1428
b   H2JB0314 On a Desert Island with Thee

All tracks on RCA (Eng) LP: RD-27018, Fresh Sound (Sp) LP: NL-45643, BMG-RCA (Sp) CD: 74321433882.
See 570201 and 570204a.

SHORTY ROGERS–PLAYS RICHARD RODGERS
570201
1 February 1957, Los Angeles: Same as 30 January 1957, except George Roberts btb replaces John Halliburton:

a   H2JB0317 **I've Got Five Dollars**   RCA-Victor LP: LPM-1428
b   H2JB0318 **I Could Write a Book**

-a on RCA (Eng) LP: RD-27051, RCA (Eng) LP: RD-27018, Fresh Sound (Sp) LP: NL-45643, BMG-RCA (Sp) CD: 74321433882.
-b on RCA (Eng) LP: RD-27018, Fresh Sound (Sp) LP: NL-45643, BMG-RCA (Sp) CD: 74321433882.

See 570130 and 570204a.

SHORTY ROGERS–PLAYS RICHARD RODGERS
570204a
4 February 1957, Los Angeles: Shorty Rogers tp, flh; Conte Candoli tp; Herb Geller as; Bill Holman ts; Pepper Adams bs; Pete Jolly p; Red Mitchell b; Stan Levey dm.

a   H2JB0315 **The Girl Friend**   RCA-Victor LP: LPM-1428
b   H2JB0316 **Like a Ship without a Sail**
c   H2JB0319 **Thou Swell**

   -a on RCA (Eng) LP: RD-27018, Fresh Sound (Sp) LP: NL-45643, BMG-RCA (Sp) CD: 74321433882.
   -b on RCA (Eng) LP: RD-27018, Fresh Sound (Sp) LP: NL-45643, BMG-RCA (Sp) CD: 74321433882.
   -c on RCA (Eng) LP: RD-27051, RCA (Eng) LP: RD-27018, Fresh Sound (Sp) LP: NL-45643, BMG-RCA (Sp) CD: 74321433882.
   See also 570201.

SHORTY ROGERS
570204b
4 February 1957, TV broadcast, Los Angeles: Shorty Rogers flh; Conte Candoli, Pete Candoli, Harry Edison, Al Porcino, Maynard Ferguson tp; Milt Bernhart, Bob Burgess, Frank Rosolino tb; George Roberts btb; Sam Rice tu; Herb Geller as; Bill Holman, Bill Perkins, Jack Montrose ts; Pepper Adams bs; Pete Jolly p; Red Mitchell b; Stan Levey dm; Kay Brown voc.*

a   Short Stop
b   Infinity Promenade
c   Wow*
d   Medley: various spirituals*
e   unknown title

   -b on Los Angeles Jazz Institute/Lighthouse CD: LAJI: 003.
   The band performed on Bobby Troup's KABC program *Stars of Jazz*. It isn't clear if both the audio and video still exist. Another Troup *Stars of Jazz* program with Shorty Rogers was recorded for TV on 2 June

1956, and later released on Calliope and Zeta (F), but Adams was not in the band. Adams was working in New York throughout the summer.

STAN KENTON–VOICES IN MODERN
570222
22 February 1957, Hollywood CA: Same as 17 January 1957, except add Jack Costanzo bongos* and Ann Richards voc†:

a   16222   Eager Beaver   Capitol LP: T-810
b   16623   Temptation*
c   16624   Softly†

    -a on Capitol 45: EAP1-810, Capitol (Eng) LP: LCT-6138, Collectors' Choice CD: CCM-354.
    -b on Capitol 45: EAP3-810, Capitol (Eng) LP: LCT-6138, Collectors' Choice CD: CCM-354.
    -c on Capitol 45: EAP1-810, Capitol (Eng) LP: LCT-6138.
    See 570117b and 570304.

QUINCY JONES–GO WEST, MAN
570301
1 March 1957, Los Angeles: Buddy Collette, Bill Perkins, Walter Benton ts; Pepper Adams bs; Carl Perkins p; Leroy Vinnegar b; Shelly Manne dm; Quincy Jones producer.

a   5465   **Bright Moon**   ABC-Paramount LP: ABC-186
b   5468   **The Oom Is Blues**
c   5471   Medley: What's New[1]
    5472   **We'll Be Together Again[2]**
    5473   Time on My Hands[3]
    5474   You Go to My Head[4]
    5475   Laura[5]

[1]Perkins and rhythm section.
[2]Adams and rhythm section.
[3]Collette and rhythm section.
[4]Rhythm section only.
[5]Benton and rhythm section.

    -a on ABC-Paramount LP: ABC-782, ABC-Paramount LP: SR-3037, HMV (Eng) LP: CLP-1157, Jasmine (Eng) LP: JASM-1048, Fresh

Sound (Sp) LP: 054-252278-1, Columbia-Nippon (J) LP: YW-8511, Columbia-Nippon (J) LP: YW-8553, Probe (J) LP: IPR-88047, ABC-Paramount (J) LP: VIM-5572, GRP-Impulse CD: GRD-115, GRP-Chessmates CD: GRD-828, CTI (Ger) CD: PDCTI-1108-2, MCA-Warner-Pioneer (J) CD: 28P2-2484.

-b on ABC-Paramount LP: ABC-782, ABC-Paramount LP: SR-3037, HMV (Eng) LP: CLP-1157, Jasmine (Eng) LP: JASM-1048, ABC-Paramount (J) LP: VIM-5572, Columbia-Nippon (J) LP: YW-8511, Columbia-Nippon (J) LP: YW-8553, Probe (J) LP: IPR-88047, GRP-Impulse CD: GRD-115, GRP-Chessmates CD: GRD-828, CTI (Ger) CD: PDCTI-1108-2, Fresh Sound (Sp) LP: 054-252278-1, MCA-Warner-Pioneer (J) CD: 28P2-2484.

-c on ABC-Paramount LP: SR-3037, HMV (Eng) LP: CLP-1157, Jasmine (Eng) LP: JASM-1048, Fresh Sound (Sp) LP: 054-252278-1, Columbia-Nippon (J) LP: YW-8511, Columbia-Nippon (J) LP: YW-8553, Probe (J) LP: IPR-88047, ABC-Paramount (J) LP: VIM-5572, GRP-Impulse CD: GRD-115, GRP-Chessmates CD: GRD-828, CTI (Ger) CD: PDCTI-1108-2, MCA-Warner-Pioneer (J) CD: 28P2-2484.

According to the ABC company log, three sessions produced by Quincy Jones were recorded on 25 February, 26 February, and 1 March. In his liner notes to the Jasmine LP reissue, Ralph J. Gleason wrote that Jones put together three different bands, each one invited to their own session. "The third date," Gleason wrote, "was for saxophones and has Buddy Collette, Bill Perkins and Pepper Adams on baritone (the most exciting soloist on that instrument since Serge Chaloff came up)." The ABC company log specifies that -c was recorded on 1 March.

STAN KENTON–VOICES IN MODERN
570304
4 March 1957, Hollywood CA: Same as 17 January 1956, except Karl DeKarske btb replaces George Roberts; add Ramon Rivera bongos:

a	16653	Lullaby of the Leaves	Capitol LP: T-810
b	16654	Dancing in the Dark	
c	16659	Sophisticated Lady	
d	16660	Orchids in the Moonlight	Capitol unissued

-a on Capitol 45: EAP2-810, Capitol (Eng) LP: LCT-6183, Collectors' Choice CD: CCM-354.

-b on Capitol 45: EAP1-810, Capitol (Eng) LP: LCT-6183, Collectors' Choice CD: CCM-354.

-c on Capitol (Eng) LP: LCT-6183, Collectors' Choice CD: CCM-354.

See also 570222.

BOB KEENE–SOLO FOR SEVEN
570311
11 March 1957, Los Angeles: Bob Burgess tb; Bob Keene cl; Pepper Adams bs; Dick Johnson p; Red Norvo vib; Ralph Peña b; Dick Wilson dm.

a	**I Won't Dance**	Andex LP: A-4001
b	There'll Never Be Another You	

All tracks on Fresh Sound (Sp) LP: FSR-641.

According to record producer Bob Sunenblick, in an interview with the author in 1987, "Pepper said that, in Japan, some Japanese guy went running up to him and wanted him to sign the record. He said, 'I paid $75 for this record!' Pepper thought it was one of the shittiest records he ever made!"

See 570321a.

LENNIE NIEHAUS–LIGHTHOUSE ALL-STARS
570312
12 March 1957, Contemporary Studio, Los Angeles: Conte Candoli tp; Frank Rosolino tb; Lennie Niehaus as; Richie Kamuca ts; Pepper Adams bs; Dick Shreve p; Howard Rumsey b; Stan Levey dm.

a	Funny Frank	Contemporary LP: C-3517
b	That's Rich	
c	If You Are There	

All tracks on Contemporary LP: C-3517, Contemporary LP: C-2515, Original Jazz Classics LP: OJC-451, Vogue (F) LP: JSLP-50036, Vogue (Eng) LP: LAE-12271, Original Jazz Classics CD: OJCCD-451-2.

DAVE PELL–A PELL OF A TIME
570320
20 March 1957, Los Angeles: Same as 17 January 1957, except Ray
Sims tb and Paul Moer p replace Bob Burgess and Marty Paich respectively:

a   H2JB0268 **Suze Blues**   RCA-Victor LP: LPM-1524
b   H2JB0272 G Tune
c   H2JB0273 Cameo

According to discographer Walter Bruyninckx, -a has the same ma-
trix number as the alternate track on 570117a.
   All tracks on Fresh Sound (Sp) LP: NL-45627, Blue Sounds (Sp)
CD: ND-74408.
See also 570123.

BOB KEENE–SOLO FOR SEVEN
570321a
21 March 1957, Los Angeles: Same as 11 March 1957, except Paul Moer
p, Red Mitchell b, Shelly Manne dm replace Dick Johnson, Ralph Peña
and Dick Wilson respectively:

a   **Can't We Be Friends**   Andex LP: A-4001
b   I Hear Music
c   **Once in Love with Amy**
d   Caravan   Fresh Sound (Sp) LP: FSR-641

   -b, -c on Fresh Sound (Sp) LP: FSR-641.
See 570311 notes.

HERBIE HARPER–JAZZ CITY PRESENTS . . .
570321b
21 March 1957, Jazz City, Los Angeles: Don Fagerquist, Clora Bryant tp;
Herbie Harper tb; Herb Geller as; Bill Perkins ts; Pepper Adams bs;
Claude Williamson p; Curtis Counce b; Mel Lewis dm.

a   **Lady Be Good**   Bethlehem LP: BCP-80

   -a on Fresh Sound (Sp) LP: 2017, Toshiba-EMI (J) CD: TOCJ-
62053.

The theme of Lady Be Good is never stated. According to historian Lewis Porter, the title is more properly Rifftide or Hackensack.

Recorded on Jazz City's last night before it closed for business.

MAYNARD FERGUSON
570406
6 and 13 April 1957, Mutual Radio broadcasts, Birdland, New York: Maynard Ferguson, Joe Burnett tp; Bob Burgess tb; Jimmy Ford, Joe Maini as; Willie Maiden ts; Pepper Adams bs; Larry Bunker dm; other musicians.

Collector Boris Rose told the author that he recorded both shows on reel tape (#358 for 6 April, and reels #140, 332, or 353 for 13 April).

Pepper Adams, after working with Ferguson occasionally during early 1957, left Los Angeles on c. 22 March with three members of Ferguson's band to play a series of gigs across the country, culminating c. 4 April in a two-week engagement in New York at Birdland. The tour east would get Adams to New York in time for his 20 April Prestige date with John Coltrane, and it nicely filled up his calendar. The agreement with Ferguson was that Adams would drive the musicians to New York and, upon arrival, Ferguson would reimburse Adams for his passengers' travel expenses. Things, however, hardly went as planned. Although Adams wouldn't identify his travel companions in a 1984 interview with the author, Adams did mention how "terrified" he was while, in each major city on the trip, all three musicians left him waiting in his car while they bought heroin. To make matters worse, according to Adams' friend Len Dobbin, upon reaching New York, Ferguson refused to pay Adams for transportation expenses, saying, "You don't have that in writing." Adams left Ferguson's band at the end of the Birdland stint, joining Chet Baker's group. Adams' four-month tour with Baker got him back to Los Angeles, where he recorded his first two dates as a leader.

PEPPER ADAMS–MODERN JAZZ SURVEY: BARITONES AND FRENCH HORNS
570420
20 April 1957, Van Gelder Studio, Hackensack NJ: John Coltrane ts; Pepper Adams, Cecil Payne bs; Mal Waldron p; Doug Watkins b; Arthur Taylor dm.

a	1208	**Dakar**	Prestige [16rpm] LP: 16-6
b	1209	**Mary's Blues**	

c 1210   **Route 4**
d 1211   **Velvet Scene**
e 1212   **Witches Pit**
f 1213   **Cat Walk**

-a on Prestige 45: 45-315, Prestige LP: PR-7280, Prestige LP: P-24104, Prestige LP: P-7313, Original Jazz Classics LP: OJC-393, Fantasy LP: F-393, Transatlantic (Eng) LP: PR-7280, Prestige (Ger) LP: 0902054, Prestige (J) LP: LPJ-70020, Victor (J) LP: SMJ-6541, Prestige CD: P-9316, Prestige CD: P-30650, Prestige CD: 16PCD-4405-2, Original Jazz Classics CD: OJCCD-393-2, Original Jazz Classics CD: OJCCD-203393, Carrère (F) CD: CA-98-927, JVC-Victor (J) CD: VICJ-2122, JVC (J) CD: 41319.

All other tracks on Prestige LP: PR-7280, Prestige LP: P-24104, Prestige LP: P-7313, Original Jazz Classics LP: OJC-393, Fantasy LP: F-393, Transatlantic (Eng) LP: PR-7280, Prestige (Ger) LP: 0902054, Prestige (J) LP: LPJ-70020, Victor (J) LP: SMJ-6541, Prestige CD: P-9316, Prestige CD: P-30650, Prestige CD: 16PCD-4405-2, Original Jazz Classics CD: OJCCD-393-2, Original Jazz Classics CD: OJCCD-203393, Carrère (F) CD: CA-98-927, JVC-Victor (J) CD: VICJ-2122, JVC (J) CD: 41319.

According to saxophonist Kenny Berger, who interviewed Adams about this recording, Pepper Adams led the date, yet he didn't choose most of the tunes, nor design the recording conceptually, as he normally would for a date of his own. Interestingly, as with most Adams dates, however, there are two Adams original compositions, Mary's Blues and Witches Pit. *See* 570712 notes for Adams' description of his first date as a leader.

Mary's Blues, written by Adams on 25 November 1956, is a different composition from the same title written by John Coltrane. (See Pepper Adams and John Coltrane at pepperadams.com for a full explanation.) Adams told saxophonist Kenny Berger, "The name came from the fact that the recording date took place on Good Friday." Since the tune had been written months beforehand, what Adams meant was that the title of Mary's Blues was retained in honor of the session taking place on Good Friday.

According to trumpeter Art Farmer, in an interview with the author in 1988, Prestige, at this time, typically recorded at Van Gelder on Friday. 20 April 1957 was a Saturday, so it's possible that the date was an anomaly, or it carried over until Saturday morning. *See* 560430 notes regarding Van Gelder's studio.

According to Prestige owner Bob Weinstock, in an interview with the author in 1988,

> Teddy Charles supervised it. I talked it over with him and I figured it would be interesting to put Cecil together with the new boy on the scene, Pepper. That was his first date on Prestige. [This LP was issued with a running speed of 16rpm, not the customary 33rpm. 16rpm] was an experiment. You had that speed on the phonographs, but it just didn't sell. People weren't interested. You could get two records instead of one. Nobody cared anyway. It was a viable thing: They used it in the studios for transcriptions and everything. It's just [that] people weren't interested.

JOHNNY MANDEL–THE JAMES DEAN STORY
570700

July or August 1957, Los Angeles: Don Fagerquist, Ray Linn tp; Milt Bernhart tb; Charlie Mariano, Herbie Steward as; Bill Holman, Richie Kamuca ts; Pepper Adams bs, bcl; Claude Williamson p; Monty Budwig b; Mel Lewis dm; Mike Pacheco bongos*; Johnny Mandel arr; GUESTS: Chet Baker tp, voc; Bud Shank as, fl.

a		Fairmount, Indiana	Pacific Jazz LP: WP-2005
b	1907	Jimmy's Theme*	
c	1908	Let Me Be Loved	
d		The Search*	
e		Lost Love[1]	
f		People	
g		The Movie Star*	
h		Rebel at Work[2]	
i		Success, and then What?	
j		Hollywood*	
k		Let Me Be Loved	Pacific Jazz (Eu) CD: 0777-7-95251-2-6

[1]Baker, Shank, and rhythm section.
[2]Baker, Holman, and rhythm section.

-a on Kimberley LP: LP-2016, Kimberley LP: LPS-11016, Vogue (Eng) LP: VA-160125, Fresh Sound (Sp) LP: 054-260898-1, Pacific Jazz (Eu) CD: 0777-7-95251-2-6, Toshiba-EMI (J) CD: TOCJ-5313.

-b on World Pacific LP: WP-641, World Pacific LP: PJ-1257, World Pacific LP: JWC-514, Kimberley LP: LP-2016, Kimberley LP: LPS-11016, Vogue (Eng) LP: VA-160125, Fresh Sound (Sp) LP: 054-260898-1, Toshiba-EMI (J) LP: PJ-0514, Toshiba-EMI (J) LP: PJ-2005, Blue Note CD: CDBN-7-80707-2, Blue Note (Eng) CD: BNZ-303, Pacific Jazz (Eu) CD: 0777-7-95251-2-6, Toshiba-EMI (J) CD: TOCJ-5313, Toshiba-EMI (J) CD: 6893.

-c on World Pacific LP: WP-641, Kimberley LP: LP-2016, Kimberley LP: LPS-11016, Vogue (Eng) LP: VA-160125, Fresh Sound (Sp) LP: 054-260898-1, Capitol CD: CDP-7-89292-2, Pacific Jazz (Eu) CD: 0777-7-95251-2-6, Toshiba-EMI (J) CD: TOCJ-5313.

-d on Kimberley LP: LP-2016, Kimberley LP: LPS-11016, Vogue (Eng) LP: VA-160125, Fresh Sound (Sp) LP: 054-260898-1, Pacific Jazz (Eu) CD: 0777-7-95251-2-6, Toshiba-EMI (J) CD: TOCJ-5313.

-e on Kimberley LP: LP-2016, Kimberley LP: LPS-11016, Vogue (Eng) LP: VA-160125, Fresh Sound (Sp) LP: 054-260898-1, Pacific Jazz (Eu) CD: 0777-7-95251-2-6, Toshiba-EMI (J) CD: TOCJ-5313.

-f on Kimberley LP: LP-2016, Kimberley LP: LPS-11016, Vogue (Eng) LP: VA-160125, Fresh Sound (Sp) LP: 054-260898-1, Pacific Jazz (Eu) CD: 0777-7-95251-2-6, Toshiba-EMI (J) CD: TOCJ-5313.

-g on Kimberley LP: LP-2016, Kimberley LP: LPS-11016, Vogue (Eng) LP: VA-160125, Fresh Sound (Sp) LP: 054-260898-1, Pacific Jazz (Eu) CD: 0777-7-95251-2-6, Toshiba-EMI (J) CD: TOCJ-5313.

-h on Kimberley LP: LP-2016, Kimberley LP: LPS-11016, Vogue (Eng) LP: VA-160125, Fresh Sound (Sp) LP: 054-260898-1, Capitol CD: CDP-7-89292-2, Pacific Jazz (Eu) CD: 0777-7-95251-2-6, Toshiba-EMI (J) CD: TOCJ-5313.

-i on Fresh Sound (Sp) LP: 054-260898-1, Pacific Jazz (Eu) CD: 0777-7-95251-2-6, Toshiba-EMI (J) CD: TOCJ-5313.

-j on Fresh Sound (Sp) LP: 054-260898-1, Pacific Jazz (Eu) CD: 0777-7-95251-2-6, Toshiba-EMI (J) CD: TOCJ-5313.

-k on Pacific Jazz (Eu) CD: 0777-7-95251-2-6, Toshiba-EMI (J) CD: TOCJ-5313.

Johnny Mandel arranged three of the arrangements, Bill Holman the others. It's believed that Mandel was the leader of this session, the music of which is adapted from Leith Stevens' original soundtrack to *The James Dean Story.*

This date was not recorded in Los Angeles on 8 November 1956, as was previously believed. Adams was in San Francisco from 1 November until at least 23 November 1956 with the Stan Kenton band, playing a long engagement at the Macumba Club. Moreover, as researcher Blasko Chamberlain pointed out in a letter to the author in 2008, "The orchestral score that is used in the film was recorded in May 1957, and, as the World Pacific album is a spin-off from this, it must have been done later." In 1957 Adams worked in Los Angeles only twice: at Peacock Lane with Chet Baker from c. 6-15 July (when he was also recording 570712 for Mode), and, again, from c. 5-14 August.

In a conversation with the author in 1989, Mel Lewis said that Pepper Adams played baritone sax and bass clarinet on this date. Adams rented the bass clarinet for the session, said Lewis, and "it sounded excellent." Other than his work in Benny Goodman's band (*see* 581115, 581117, 581118, 590417), this is the only known time that Adams appears on a recording session playing bass clarinet. For years, Mel Lewis told the author in 1988, Lewis encouraged Adams to "double" on bass clarinet, since he felt it would make Adams more marketable. Adams consistently refused to play anything other than clarinet, and he would only play clarinet for an occasional jingle or when necessary in a big band setting. Once Adams' last clarinet was stolen in the early 1970s, while on tour with the Thad Jones-Mel Lewis Orchestra, he would never play the clarinet again.

PEPPER ADAMS–PEPPER ADAMS QUINTET
570712
12 July 1957, Radio Recorders, Hollywood CA: Stu Williamson tp*; Pepper Adams bs; Carl Perkins p; Leroy Vinnegar b; Mel Lewis dm.

a	**Unforgettable***	Mode LP: MOD-112
b	**Baubles, Bangles and Beads***	
c	**Freddie Froo***	
d	**My One and Only Love**	
e	**Muezzin'***	

-a on Interlude LP: MO-502, Interlude LP: ST-1002, VSOP LP: LP-5, Teichiku-Overseas (J) LP: ULS-1867, VSOP CD: CD-5, West Wind (Ger) CD: WW-2053, Fresh Sound (Sp) CD: FSR-CD-2246, Toy's Factory (J) CD: TFCL-88914.

-b on Vintage LP: VJR-31736, Interlude LP: MO-502, Interlude LP: ST-1002, VSOP LP: LP-5, Teichiku-Overseas (J) LP: ULS-1867, VSOP CD: CD-5, West Wind (Ger) CD: WW-2053, Fresh Sound (Sp) CD: FSR-CD-2246, Toy's Factory (J) CD: TFCL-88914.

-c on Coronet EP: CX-196, Interlude LP: MO-502, Interlude LP: ST-1002, VSOP LP: LP-5, Teichiku-Overseas (J) LP: ULS-1867, VSOP CD: CD-5, West Wind (Ger) CD: WW-2053, Fresh Sound (Sp) CD: FSR-CD-2246, Toy's Factory (J) CD: TFCL-88914.

-d on Vintage LP: VJR-31736, Interlude LP: MO-502, Interlude LP: ST-1002, VSOP LP: LP-5, Teichiku-Overseas (J) LP: ULS-1867, VSOP CD: CD-5, West Wind (Ger) CD: WW-2053, Fresh Sound (Sp) CD: FSR-CD-2246, Toy's Factory (J) CD: TFCL-88914.

-e on Coronet EP: CX-196, Interlude LP: MO-502, Interlude LP: ST-1002, VSOP LP: LP-5, Teichiku-Overseas (J) LP: ULS-1867, VSOP CD: CD-5, West Wind (Ger) CD: WW-2053, Fresh Sound (Sp) CD: FSR-CD-2246, Toy's Factory (J) CD: TFCL-88914.

In a conversation with the author in 1984, Pepper Adams discussed this date:

After I left Kenton, and during the time I spent in California, I did an album for a company that was called Mode Records. This Mode album was the first one under my own name, and over which I had full artist control. Since Mode went out of business, the masters have been sold, I guess, several times. I guess that's had several different incarnations. I've always tried in my albums to present some kind of a statement with the album: To have at least a couple of originals, minimum, and try to find some uncommon standards to play, and present an overall mood and change of mood and pacing, and present something that had some intrinsic value. I was able to spend enough time on the project to write out stuff, and have a rehearsal, be able to go to the studio with as much out of the way in advance as possible, so there would be as little between ourselves and the realization of the project. I certainly wouldn't consider this one of my better albums, but at least it showed some thought had gone into its preparation.

SHORTY ROGERS–PORTRAIT OF SHORTY
570715
15 July 1957, Los Angeles: Shorty Rogers tp, flh; Al Porcino, Conrad Gozzo, Don Fagerquist, Conte Candoli, Pete Candoli tp; Frank Rosolino, Harry Betts tb; Bob Enevoldsen vtb; George Roberts btb; Herb Geller as,

ts; Bill Holman, Richie Kamuca, Jack Montrose ts; Pepper Adams bs; Lou Levy p; Monte Budwig b; Stan Levey dm.

a H2JB3148 **A Geophysical Ear**   RCA-Victor LP: LPM-1561
b H2JB3149 The Line Backer
c H2JB3150 Play! Boy
d H2JB3151 Saturnian Sleigh Ride

-a, -b on RCA-Victor LP: LPS-1561, RCA (F) LP: PL-42828, RCA (F) LP: NL-89585, RCA CD: 51561, RCA-Victor CD: 09026-63537-2, Cloud Nine CD: 61105, RCA (F) CD: 07863-51561-2, RCA-BMG (Ger) CD: 74321-21882-2, Fresh Sounds (Sp) CD: 74321-61105-2.

-c on RCA-Victor LP: LPS-1561, Playboy LP: PB-1957, Columbia (Eng) LP: 33CX-1529/1530, Columbia (F) LP: FPX-167, RCA (F) LP: PL-42828, RCA (F) LP: NL-89585, RCA CD: 51561, RCA CD: 09026-63537-2, Cloud Nine CD: 61105, RCA-BMG (Ger) CD: 74321-21882-2, Fresh Sounds (Sp) CD: 74321-61105-2.

-d on RCA-Victor LP: LPS-1561, RCA (F) LP: PL-42828, RCA (F) LP: NL-89585, RCA CD: 51561, RCA-Victor CD: 09026-63537-2, Cloud Nine CD: 61105, RCA (F) CD: 07863-51561-2, Le Chant du Monde (F) CD: 5741631/40, RCA-BMG (Ger) CD: 74321-21882-2, Fresh Sounds (Sp) CD: 74321-61105-2.

See 570811.

SHORTY ROGERS–PORTRAIT OF SHORTY
570811
11 August 1957, Los Angeles: Same as 15 July 1957:

a H2JB3152 **Martian's Lullaby**   RCA-Victor LP: LPM-1561
b H2JB3153 **Bluezies**
c H2JB3154 Grand Slam
d H2JB3155 **Red Dog Play**

-a on RCA-Victor LP: LPS-1561, RCA (Ger) LP: CL-89807, RCA (F) LP: PL-42828, RCA (F) LP: 430-277, RCA (F) LP: NL-89585, RCA CD: 51561, RCA CD: 09026-63537-2, Cloud Nine CD: 61105, RCA (F) CD: 07863-51561-2, RCA-BMG (Ger) CD: 74321-21882-2, Fresh Sounds (Sp) CD: 74321-61105-2.

-b on RCA-Victor LP: LPS-1561, RCA (F) LP: PL-42828, RCA (F) LP: NL-89585, Cloud Nine CD: 61105, RCA CD: 51561, RCA CD:

09026-63537-2, RCA (F) CD: 07863-51561-2, RCA-BMG (Ger) CD: 74321-21882-2, Fresh Sounds (Sp) CD: 74321-61105-2.

-c on RCA-Victor LP: LPS-1561, RCA (F) LP: PL-42828, RCA (F) LP: NL-89585, Cloud Nine CD: 61105, RCA CD: 51561, RCA CD: 09026-63537-2, Le Chant du Monde (F) CD: 5741631/40, RCA (F) CD: 07863-51561-2, RCA-BMG (Ger) CD: 74321-21882-2, Fresh Sounds (Sp) CD: 74321-61105-2.

-d on RCA-Victor LP: LPS-1561, RCA (Ger) LP: CL-89807, RCA (F) LP: PL-42828, RCA (F) LP: NL-89585, RCA CD: 51561, RCA CD: 09026-63537-2, Cloud Nine CD: 61105, RCA (F) CD: 07863-51561-2, RCA-BMG (Ger) CD: 74321-21882-2, Fresh Sounds (Sp) CD: 74321-61105-2.

See 570715.

PEPPER ADAMS–CRITICS' CHOICE
570813
13 or 14 August 1957, Los Angeles: Lee Katzman tp*; Pepper Adams bs; Jimmy Rowles p; Doug Watkins b; Mel Lewis dm.

a	**Minor Mishap***	World Pacific LP: PJM-407
b	**High Step***	
c	**Zec***	
d	**Alone Together***	
e	**5021***	
f	**Blackout Blues**	
g	**Blackout Blues**	World Pacific unissued

According to Pacific Jazz check stubs found in Adams' materials, a 4.5-hour session was done on 13 August and a 4-hour session was done on 14 August. It's not known what tracks were taken from either session.

-a on World Pacific 45: PJM-407-1, World Pacific 45: PJM-407-2, Vogue (Eng) LP: LAE-12134, King (J) LP: GXF-3137, Toshiba-EMI (J) LP: PJ-0407, Mighty Quinn (Ire) CD: MQP-1103, Fresh Sound (Sp) CD: FSR-CD-2246, Toshiba-EMI (J) CD: TOCJ-50225.

-b on Vogue (Eng) LP: LAE-12134, King (J) LP: GXF-3137, Toshiba-EMI (J) LP: PJ-0407, Mighty Quinn (Ire) CD: MQP-1103, Fresh Sound (Sp) CD: FSR-CD-2246, Toshiba-EMI (J) CD: TOCJ-50225.

-c on World Pacific LP: JWC-508, Vogue (Eng) LP: LAE-12154, Vogue (F) LP: LDM-30-086, King (J) LP: GXF-3137, Toshiba-EMI (J) LP: PJ-0508, Toshiba-EMI (J) LP: PJ-0407, Mighty Quinn (Ire) CD:

MQP-1103, Fresh Sound (Sp) CD: FSR-CD-2246, Toshiba-EMI (J) CD: TOCJ-50225.

-d on World Pacific 45: PJM-407-1, World Pacific 45: PJM-407-2, Vogue (Eng) LP: LAE-12134, King (J) LP: GXF-3137, Toshiba-EMI (J) LP: PJ-0407, Mighty Quinn (Ire) CD: MQP-1103, Fresh Sound (Sp) CD: FSR-CD-2246, Toshiba-EMI (J) CD: TOCJ-50225.

-e on Vogue (Eng) LP: LAE-12134, King (J) LP: GXF-3137, Toshiba-EMI (J) LP: PJ-0407, Mighty Quinn (Ire) CD: MQP-1103, Fresh Sound (Sp) CD: FSR-CD-2246, Toshiba-EMI (J) CD: TOCJ-50225.

-f on Vogue (Eng) LP: LAE-12134, King (J) LP: GXF-3137, Toshiba-EMI (J) LP: PJ-0407, Mighty Quinn (Ire) CD: MQP-1103, Fresh Sound (Sp) CD: FSR-CD-2246, Toshiba-EMI (J) CD: TOCJ-50225.

An edited version of -f, renamed Four Funky Folk, is -f with its 12-bar bass introduction deleted, and augmented with an extra chorus of piano solo taken from -g. This edited track is on World Pacific LP: JWC-512, Vogue (Eng) LP: LAE-12224, King (J) LP: PFJ-5045, Toshiba-EMI (J) LP: PJ-0512.

About his second date as a leader, Pepper Adams told the author the following in 1984:

> The projection was, at the time the album was recorded, to call the album *Peppermill*. The people at World Pacific actually spent some money to take advantage of that name. They rented an enormous peppermill from Hollywood Ranch Market and had the photograph taken by William Claxton, who was very well known for his cover photography at that time. (He was a celebrity in his own right. Later, he became the director of films. A very nice man, I never saw him since.) One of my few experiences going to a truly professional photographer's studio, with the enormous rolls of different colored paper, so that you have a no-horizon background—all this. So they go to great lengths to have my photograph taken by this eminent professional, and [have me] seated behind this enormous pepper-mill. However, before the album was issued, I won the *Down Beat* New Star Award, which is the equivalent to what they now call Talent Deserving Wider Recognition. So, they changed the album to Critics' Choice, except I'm still getting questions about why is there an album cover with me sitting behind that enormous pawn! The trumpet player was Lee Katzman, and Jimmy Rowles was the pianist. I had never met Jimmy Rowles, but I remembered him off of records and had decided that this was someone I would like to work with. I certainly made a very good blind choice there, because he was terrific! And, Douglas Watkins and Mel Lewis. Here again I

was able to incorporate some originals, some standards, and get a general blend and mix of things that I thought created a single artistic statement. So, from that point of view, I think it was successful.

According to Jimmy Rowles, in a conversation with the author in 1987, there were no rehearsals for this session.

I had a ball there. I always got a kick out of Lee. That was the first time I ever saw or met Watkins. He was very good. I enjoyed him very much. Yeah, he was a new feel, which I *really* liked! I was sure sorry to hear about his [death. Doug Watkins died in a car crash at age 27 on 5 February 1962, while driving to San Francisco from Arizona with Roland Alexander and Bill Hardman.] That was a drag! After the date, I had a little VW that was running real good, and I took him over to where he had checked in. I drove him over, and took him around a little bit, because he'd never been here, and he *really* got a wang out of that car, you know? He just thought it was great! He'd never ridden in one, and, he told me, he decided: "I'm going to get one of these!" And that's what he had when that guy, I understand a farmer, ran a stop sign and came out and broadsided him.

HUGH JACKSON
570910
c. 10 September 1957, private recording, Ann Arbor MI: Frank Keys tp*; Bernard McKinney euphonium; Pepper Adams bs; Barry Harris p; Beans Richardson b; Hugh Jackson dm.

a **High Step**
b **Wee Dot**[*]
c Medley[*]: You Go to My Head[1]
       These Are the Things I Love[2]
       Embraceable You[3]
       I Didn't Know about You[4]
d **Ray's Idea**

[1]Keys and rhythm section.
[2]McKinney and rhythm section.
[3]Rhythm section only.
[4]Adams and rhythm section.

These tracks exist on one 12-inch pressing.

McKinney changed his professional name to Kiane Zawadi in the late 1960s.

SHAFI HADI–THE RAREST ON DEBUT
570915

15 September 1957, New York: Clarence Shaw tp; Shafi Hadi ts; Pepper Adams bs; Wynton Kelly p; Henry Grimes b; Dannie Richmond dm; unknown perc.*

a	Autumn in New York	Mythic Sound (It) LP: MSLP-003
b	Autumn in New York	
c	Long Ago and Far Away	
d	Long Ago and Far Away	
e	Long Ago and Far Away	
f	Long Ago and Far Away	
g	Long Ago and Far Away	
h	We Got Blue	
i	We Got Blue	
j	Joldi	
k	Joldi	
m	**Joldi**	
n	Joldi	
o	Joldi	
p	**Joldi**	
q	**Joldi**	
r	**Joldi**	
s	untitled composition*	
t	untitled composition*	
u	Stella by Starlight	
v	Stella by Starlight	

-a, -b, -e, -f, -g, -p on Debut CD: 12DCD-4402-2, Original Jazz Classics CD: OJCCD-1821-2, Carrère (F) CD: CA-100-012, Victor (J) CD: VICJ-23053.

-h and unknown versions of Autumn in New York, Long Ago and Far Away, Stella by Starlight, and Untitled Original Composition on Essential Jazz Classics (Sp) CD: EJC-55474.

-i on Wax Time LP: 771713, Original Jazz Classics CD: OJCCD-1821-2, Essential Jazz Classics (Sp) CD: EJC-55474.

-r, -s, -t, -u, -v on Original Jazz Classics CD: OJCCD-1821-2.

In a conversation with Ben Young, broadcast on New York's WKCR-FM, Henry Grimes confirmed that Wynton Kelly was the pianist on this date.

The date was originally recorded for Charles Mingus' Debut Records, but the session was not released until 1987.

A.K. SALIM–PRETTY FOR THE PEOPLE
570917
17 September 1957, Van Gelder Studio, Hackensack NJ: Kenny Dorham tp; Buster Cooper tb; Johnny Griffin ts; Pepper Adams bs; Wynton Kelly p; Paul Chambers b; Max Roach dm; Chino Pozo cga*; A.K. Salim arr.

a	70125	**Blu-Binsky***	Savoy LP: MG-12118
b		**Blu-Binsky***	Savoy CD: 93006-2
c	70126	**R. U. 1. 2.***	Savoy LP: MG-12118
d	70127	**Pretty for the People**	
e		**Pretty for the People**	Savoy CD: 93006-2
f	70128	**Ba-Lu-Ee-Du***	Savoy LP: MG-12118
g	70129	Shirley Ray*	
h	70130	**Takin' Care of Business***	

All tracks on Savoy CD: 93006-2, Denon-Savoy (J) CD: SVY-17092, Savoy (Ger) CD: 7567-93006-2, Fresh Sound (Sp) CD: FSR-474-2.

According to trumpeter Art Farmer, in an interview with the author in 1988, Savoy, at this time, typically recorded at Van Gelder on Wednesday. 17 September 1957 was a Tuesday, so it's possible the session was an anomaly, or it carried over until Wednesday morning. *See* 560430 notes regarding Van Gelder's studio.

According to Johnny Griffin, in an interview with the author in 1988, "I knew A. K. since I was a kid, because he was formerly an alto saxophonist. He had to stop playing because he had problems with his pulmonary system: respiratory, lung, or something. When I grew up, he had stopped playing. I think he gave me an alto mouthpiece when I was a kid."

LEE MORGAN–THE COOKER
570929

29 September 1957, Van Gelder Studio, Hackensack NJ: Lee Morgan tp; Pepper Adams bs; Bobby Timmons p; Paul Chambers b; Philly Joe Jones dm.

a	105	**A Night in Tunisia**	Blue Note LP: BLP-1578
b	106	**Heavy Dipper**	
c	107	**Just One of Those Things**	
d		**Just One of Those Things**	Mosaic LP: MD4-162
e	108	**Lover Man**	Blue Note LP: BLP-1578
f	109	**New-Ma**	

-a on Blue Note 45: 45-1692, Blue Note LP: BST-81578, Blue Note LP: B1-91138, Blue Note-Classics LP: BN-1578-200, Blue Note 45: [180g vinyl Gray-Hoffman remaster LP], Mosaic LP: MQ6-162, Blue Note (F) LP: BST-81578, Blue Note (J) LP: BLP-1578, King (J) LP: GXK-8132, Blue Note CD: CDP-7-91138-2, Blue Note CD: 9084, Blue Note CD: 6431, Mosaic CD: MD4-162, Blue Note (Eu) CD: 0946-3-62643-2-5, Toshiba-EMI (J) CD: TOCJ-1578, Toshiba-EMI (J) CD: TOCJ-7072, Toshiba-EMI (J) CD: TOCJ-6431, Toshiba-EMI (J) CD: TOCJ-9084. According to producer Michael Cuscuna, in a conversation with the author in 1988, this monophonic track has a different out theme edited onto it than subsequent stereo releases. (The first stereo release was Blue Note LP: BST-81578.)

-b on Blue Note LP: BST-81578, Blue Note-Classics LP: BN-1578-200, Blue Note LP: BN-LA-224-G, Blue Note 45: [180g vinyl Gray-Hoffman remaster LP], Mosaic LP: MQ6-162, Blue Note (F) LP: BST-81578, Blue Note (J) LP: BLP-1578, King (J) LP: GXK-8132, Mosaic CD: MD4-162, Blue Note CD: 9084, Blue Note CD: 6431, Blue Note (Eu) CD: 0946-3-62643-2-5, Toshiba-EMI (J) CD: TOCJ-9084, Toshiba-EMI (J) CD: TOCJ-1578, Toshiba-EMI (J) CD: TOCJ-7072, Toshiba-EMI (J) CD: TOCJ-6431.

-c on Blue Note LP: BST-81578, Blue Note LP: BN-LA-224-G, Blue Note-Classics LP: BN-1578-200, Mosaic LP: MQ6-162, Blue Note 45: [180g vinyl Gray-Hoffman remaster LP], Blue Note (Ger) LP: BN-WG-BST-84446, Blue Note (F) LP: BST-81578, Blue Note (J) LP: CJ28-5037, Blue Note (J) LP: BLP-1578, King (J) LP: GXK-8132, Blue Note CD: 9084, Blue Note CD: 6431, Mosaic CD: MD4-162, Blue Note (Eu) CD: 0946-3-62643-2-5, Toshiba-EMI (J) CD: TOCJ-9084, Toshiba-EMI (J) CD: TOCJ-1578, Toshiba-EMI (J) CD: TOCJ-7072, Blue Note (J) CD: CDP- 7-95591-2, Toshiba-EMI (J) CD: TOCJ-6431.

-d on Mosaic LP: MQ6-162, Mosaic CD: MD4-162, Blue Note (Eu) CD: 0946-3-62643-2-5, Toshiba-EMI (J) CD: TOCJ-1601, Toshiba-EMI (J) CD: TOCJ-6431, Toshiba-EMI (J) CD: TOCJ-9084.

-e on Blue Note LP: BST-81578, Blue Note-Classics LP: BN-1578-200, Mosaic LP: MQ6-162, Blue Note 45: [180g vinyl Gray-Hoffman remaster LP], Blue Note (F) LP: BST-81578, Blue Note (J) LP: BLP-1578, King (J) LP: GXK-8132, Blue Note CD: 9084, Blue Note CD: 6431, Mosaic CD: MD4-162, Blue Note (Eu) CD: 0946-3-62643-2-5, Toshiba-EMI (J) CD: TOCJ-5828, Toshiba-EMI (J) CD: TOCJ-6431, Toshiba-EMI (J) CD: TOCJ-9084, Toshiba-EMI (J) CD: TOCJ-1578, Toshiba-EMI (J) CD: TOCJ-7072.

-f on Blue Note LP: BST-81578, Blue Note 45: [180g vinyl Gray-Hoffman remaster LP], Blue Note-Classics LP: BN-1578-200, Mosaic LP: MQ6-162, Blue Note (F) LP: BST-81578, Blue Note (J) LP: BLP-1578, King (J) LP: GXK-8132, Blue Note CD: 9084, Blue Note CD: 6431, Mosaic CD: MD4-162, Blue Note (Eu) CD: 0946-3-62643-2-5, Toshiba-EMI (J) CD: TOCJ-6431, Toshiba-EMI (J) CD: TOCJ-9084, Toshiba-EMI (J) CD: TOCJ-1578, Toshiba-EMI (J) CD: TOCJ-7072, Toshiba-EMI (J) CD: TOCJ-5828.

See 560430 notes regarding Van Gelder's studio.

HANK MOBLEY–POPPIN'
571020
20 October 1957, Van Gelder Studio, Hackensack NJ: Art Farmer tp; Hank Mobley ts; Pepper Adams bs; Sonny Clark p; Paul Chambers b; Philly Joe Jones dm.

a **Gettin' Into Something**   Blue Note (J) LP: LT-3066
b **Poppin'**
c **East of Brooklyn**
d **Tune Up**
e **Darn that Dream**

All tracks on King (J) LP: GXF-3066, King (J) LP: GXK-8163, Mosaic LP: MQ10-181, Mosaic CD: MD6-181, Toshiba-EMI (J) CD: TOCJ-1620.

At least 12 takes were done at this session. First released in Japan, the original American cover art included the catalog # Blue Note BNLP-1620.

See 560430 notes regarding Van Gelder's studio.

SONNY RED
571112
12 November 1957, Van Gelder Studio, Hackensack NJ: Sonny Red as;
Pepper Adams bs; Wynton Kelly p; Doug Watkins b; Elvin Jones dm.

a	**Watkins Products**	Regent LP: RMG-6069
b	**Red's Head**	
c	**Stop**	Savoy LP: MG-12123

-a on Savoy CD: SV-0161, Denon CD: SVY-17136, Fresh Sound
(Sp) CD: FSR-CD-491, Denon-Savoy (J) CD: COCB-53403, Columbia
(J) CD: COJY-9145.
-b on Savoy CD: SV-0161, Denon CD: SV-0161, Fresh Sound (Sp)
CD: FSR-CD-491, Denon-Savoy (J) CD: COCB-53403, Columbia (J)
CD: COJY-9145.
-c on Savoy LP: SJC-408, Savoy (Ger) LP: WL-70839, London
(Eng) LP: LTZ-C15143, Savoy CD: SV-0161, Savoy CD: SV-0178, Sa-
voy CD: SV-0183, Fresh Sound (Sp) CD: FSR-CD-491, Savoy (J) CD:
COCB-50310, Denon-Savoy (J) CD: COCY-9825.
Regent is a subsidiary of Savoy. According to Art Farmer, in an in-
terview with the author in 1988, Savoy, at this time, typically recorded at
Van Gelder on Wednesday. 12 November 1957 was a Tuesday, so it's
possible the date was an anomaly, or it carried over until Wednesday
morning. *See* 560430 notes regarding Van Gelder's studio.

PEPPER ADAMS–THE COOL SOUND OF PEPPER ADAMS
571119
19 November 1957, Van Gelder Studio, Hackensack NJ: Bernard
McKinney euphonium; Pepper Adams bs; Hank Jones p; George Duvivier b; Elvin Jones dm.

a	**Bloos, Blooze, Blues**	Regent LP: MG-6066
b	**Seein' Red**	
c	**Seein' Red**	Savoy LP: SJL-1142
d	**Like ... What Is This**	Regent LP: MG-6066
e	**Skippy**	

-a on Savoy LP: MG-12211, Savoy LP: SLJ-1142, Savoy (Ger) LP:
WL-70514, Pye (Eng) LP: NPL-28007, Savoy CD: SV-0198, Fresh
Sound (Sp) CD: FSR-CD-491, Sony-Columbia (J) CD: 53524.

-b on Savoy LP: MG-12211, Savoy LP: SLJ-1142, Savoy (Ger) LP: WL-70514, Pye (Eng) LP: NPL-28007, Savoy CD: SV-0198, Fresh Sound (Sp) CD: FSR-CD-491, Sony-Columbia (J) CD: 53524.

-c on Savoy LP: SLJ-1142, Pye (Eng) LP: NPL-28007, Savoy (Ger) LP: WL-70514.

-d on Savoy LP: MG-12211, Savoy LP: SLJ-1142, Pye (Eng) LP: NPL-28007, Savoy (Ger) LP: WL-70514, Savoy CD: SV-0198, Fresh Sound (Sp) CD: FSR-CD-491, Sony-Columbia (J) CD: 53524.

-e on Savoy LP: MG-12211, Savoy LP: SLJ-1142, Pye (Eng) LP: NPL-28007, Savoy (Ger) LP: WL-70514, Savoy CD: SV-0198, Fresh Sound (Sp) CD: FSR-CD-491, Sony-Columbia (J) CD: 53524.

According to trumpeter Art Farmer, in an interview with the author in 1988, Savoy, at this time, typically recorded at Van Gelder on Wednesday. 19 November 1957 was a Tuesday, so it's possible that the date was an anomaly, or it carried over until Wednesday morning. *See* 560430 notes regarding Van Gelder's studio.

In a conversation with the author in 1984, Pepper Adams discussed his third date as a leader:

[This is] the only time I can think of where I had my name out as a leader and, yet, really didn't function that way. It was just everybody going in the studio and play a little bit, leave the studio, and then they make an album up out of it. So, it does not add up that well. I did it partially for the "bread," and also because it was an opportunity for Bernard McKinney to make a record date on which he played some solos. He plays marvelous, and, at that time, he hadn't recorded at all. Actually, no one was interested in recording me anyway, so Savoy would do it, but they would do it on their basis, which means very little money and no studio time, so there was no opportunity to do anything else. I was able to get a terrific rhythm section, with Hank and George Duvivier and Elvin, so it's not a bad album.

During a 19 November 1985 after-hours interview, conducted in Calgary by saxophonist John Reid, Pepper Adams said,

I think we did that in under two hours at Rudy's: Get in the studio, and get out again as quick as we could. Savoy was not spending any money for studio time to do a second take on things. As a matter of fact, on that reissue there are two takes of one of the tunes, and the reason they had to do that was to make it a decent length album. Savoy was not the only company at that time; There were a number of others that were making twelve-inch albums with no more than fifteen minutes of music a side, because, if they got more than thirty minutes of music, they'd have to pay for a "triple record date." But, by keeping it that low, they'd just pay for a double date, which, in those days, was, I think, $60 a person. I think scale was then about $30 or $35 dollars for a three-hour date, the date being three hours or fifteen minutes of recorded music, whichever came first. Anyway, they were really shortchanging the purchaser on the amount of music on the recording by doing it that way, but they saved themselves a little bit of money.

McKinney changed his professional name to Kiane Zawadi in the late 1960s.

DOUG WATKINS
571206
6 December 1957, Van Gelder Studio, Hackensack NJ: Idrees Sulieman tp; Frank Rehak tb; Pepper Adams bs; Bill Evans p; Doug Watkins b; Louis Hayes dm.

a   1402   **Roots**   Prestige New Jazz LP: P-8202

-a on Original Jazz Classics LP: OJC-062, Carrère (F) LP: CA-68-399, Victor (J) LP: SMJ-6605, Original Jazz Classics CD: OJC-062-2, Victor (J) CD: VICJ-23084.

According to Prestige owner Bob Weinstock, in a conversation with the author in 1988, "I just decided to put Pepper with Bill Evans and Idrees, some real young, new players. It was supposed to be a New Star type of thing."

According to guitarist Peter Leitch, in an interview with the author done in 1987:

Pepper told me the story of that session. It was [arranger] Alonzo Levister's date. He was supposed to write the arrangements. [He] doesn't play on the record, but is credited with the arrangements. I don't really know anything about him, except that he was around in the '50s....Pepper told me about riding out to Van Gelder's with him, and the session was a total fiasco. Alonzo was drunk, and the arrangements were just not together. I got the impression that they weren't copied properly, and they spent the whole session trying to get these arrangements together, and, finally, there was about twenty minutes left and Bob Weinstock said, "Enough of this crap. Let's get a blues. Just get a medium blues." So they put together this riff that ended up being called Roots, and they played for twenty minutes on it, which filled up the whole side of the record. When they reissued it is when [Pepper and I] discussed it. He wanted some money for the reissue, which I doubt he ever got.

Compositional credit for the tune Roots was awarded to Doug Watkins, hence the date falling under his leadership.
See 560430 notes regarding Van Gelder's studio.

TOOTS THIELEMANS–MAN BITES HARMONICA
571230
30 December 1957, Reeves Sound Studio, New York: Toots Thielemans harmonica, g*; Pepper Adams bs; Kenny Drew p; Wilbur Ware b; Arthur Taylor dm.

a   **East of the Sun**   Riverside LP: RLP-12-257
b   **18th Century Ballroom**[*]
c   **Soul Station**[*]
d   **Fundamental Frequency**
e   **Strutting with Some Barbecue**
f   **Isn't It Romantic**

All tracks on Riverside LP: RS-1125, Original Jazz Classics LP: OJC-1738, Victor (J) LP: SMJ-6308, Original Jazz Classics CD: OJCCD-1738-2, Riverside CD: VICJ-60698, Carrère (F) CD: CA-99-954, JVC-Victor (J) CD: VICJ-60698, JVC-Victor (J) CD: 41779.
In an interview with the author in 1990, Thielemans mentioned that Riverside owner Orrin Keepnews suggested that Thielemans use Pepper Adams on this date because he felt that a low-pitched instrument, such as a baritone, would nicely counterbalance the timbre of a harmonica.

AUTHOR'S NOTE
Private recordings of Pepper Adams, in many different small group settings, were made by Joe Segal at various clubs that he operated in Chicago, at least as early as 1958, through Adams' last appearance in 1984. *See* 580000A, 731216, 751128, 751129, 751130, 760302, 760303, 760304, 760305, 760306, 760307, 760308, 780125, 780126, 770411, 770412, 770413, 770414, 780127, 780128, 780129, 820804, 820805,

820806, 820807, 820808, 831111, 831112, 841228, 841229, 841230, 841231.

PEPPER ADAMS
580000A

c. 1958, private recording, Jazz Showcase, Chicago: Curtis Fuller tb; Sonny Stitt ts; Pepper Adams bs; unknown p; unknown b; unknown dm.

In an interview with the author in 1989, trombonist Curtis Fuller spoke of a date that was recorded at Joe Segal's club near Rush Street. *See* Author's Note above.

Saxophonist Ron Kolber, in an interview with the author in 2005, said that he was in the audience for this show:

> Joe Segal had the Jazz Showcase in the ballroom at the Lincoln Hotel on Clark Street. Pepper came in, and he was playing, and the audience was sort of not into it or whatever. So Sonny Stitt came in, took out his horn, and walked on stage, and he says, "Well, let me straighten this whole thing out." Pepper just smiled that enigmatic smile of his. He was leaning on his baritone. He had it down on the floor, and he was leaning on the top of it. Sonny was playing *all* his licks, all the Sonny Stitt licks, and, really, he sounded great. When he got to the end of his thing, the piano player played, Pepper hooked up his baritone, and just waited, smiling. And then it came Pepper's turn, and he just *wasted* Sonny Stitt! He played so magnificently that Sonny said, *"Jesus Christ!* I'm getting out of here, man!"* It was uptempo, and Pepper played chorus after chorus, and it got hotter and hotter, and Sonny was just standing there wide-eyed. He couldn't believe what he was hearing. He took Sonny's licks and turned them backwards and forwards and sideways. It was absolutely marvelous! When I looked at the audience, everybody's mouth was open in amazement. Pepper wasted the whole place! But, the nice thing was, they embraced when it was over. The rest of the evening was just marvelous with the two of them.

GENE AMMONS
580103

3 January 1958, Van Gelder Studio, Hackensack NJ: Jerome Richardson fl; John Coltrane as; Gene Ammons, Paul Quinichette ts*; Pepper Adams bs; Mal Waldron p; Jamil Nasser b; Arthur Taylor dm.

a   1426   **Ammon Joy***   Prestige LP: PR-7201

| b | 1427 | **Groove Blues**[*] | |
| c | 1428 | **The Real McCoy**[*] | Prestige LP: PR-7132 |

Richardson, Ammons, Adams, and rhythm section:

| d | 1429 | **That's All** | |

Coltrane, Ammons, and rhythm section:

| e | 1430 | It Might as Well Be Spring | Prestige LP: PR-7201 |

Richardson, Ammons, and rhythm section:

f	1431	Cheek to Cheek	Prestige LP: PR-7132
g	1432	Jug Handle	Prestige LP: PR-7201
h	1433	Blue Hymn	Prestige LP: PR-7132

-a on Prestige LP: P-24098, Original Jazz Classics LP: OJC-723, Prestige (J) LP: SMJ-6555, Prestige CD: 16PCD-4405-2, Original Jazz Classics CD: OJCCD-723-2, Avid (Eng) CD: AMSC-1029.

-b on Prestige LP: P-24098, Original Jazz Classics LP: OJC-723, Prestige (J) LP: SMJ-6555, Original Jazz Classics CD: OJCCD-723-2, Prestige CD: 16PCD-4405-2, Avid (Eng) CD: AMSC-1029.

-c on Prestige LP: P-24098, Franklin Mint LP: FM-88, Original Jazz Classics LP: OJC-651, Prestige CD: 16PCD-4405-2, Original Jazz Classics CD: OJCCD-651-2, Prestige (Ger) CD: PRCD-11005-2.

-d on Prestige LP: P-24098, Original Jazz Classics LP: OJC-651, Original Jazz Classics CD: OJCCD-651-2.

-e on Prestige LP: P-24098, Original Jazz Classics LP: OJC-723, Prestige (J) LP: SMJ-6555, Original Jazz Classics CD: OJCCD-723-2, Prestige CD: 16PCD-4405-2, Avid (Eng) CD: AMSC-1029.

-f on Prestige LP: P-24098, Original Jazz Classics LP: OJC-651, Original Jazz Classics CD: OJCCD-651-2.

-g on Prestige LP: P-24098, Prestige LP: PR-7306, Franklin Mint LP: FM-88, Prestige (J) LP: SMJ-6555, Original Jazz Classics LP: OJC-723, Original Jazz Classics CD: OJCCD-723-2, Avid (Eng) CD: AMSC-1029, Prestige (Ger) CD: PRCD-11005-2.

-h on Prestige 45: PR-45-121, Prestige Bluesville LP: BVLP-1010, Prestige LP: P-24098, Franklin Mint LP: FM-88, Original Jazz Classics LP: OJC-651. Original Jazz Classics CD: OJCCD-651-2, Prestige (Ger) CD: PRCD-11005-2.

According to Bob Porter, Prestige 45: PR-45-121 was released in two parts to comprise both sides of a 45rpm single.

Jamil Nasser changed his name from George Joyner sometime after this recording.

According to Prestige owner Bob Weinstock, in a conversation with the author in 1988, "Gene liked [Pepper's playing] very much. We used to speak a lot." Regarding Waldron's role as staff arranger and contractor, Weinstock said, "Yeah, I'd talk with Mal and he'd round up the guys for the dates and write little arrangements."

According to Bob Porter, in his liner notes for Prestige LP: P-24098, Quinichette was added to the roster because Ammons was late for a flight and it was feared he would miss the session. Moreover, Coltrane played Ira Gitler's alto saxophone, possibly because his tenor was under repair. This might be the only recording of Coltrane on alto. "Ammons," Porter wrote, "invariably named Pepper Adams as one of his favorite musicians, always emphasizing the big sound which has been an Adams trademark."

See 560430 notes regarding Van Gelder's studio.

COZY COLE
580208
8 February 1958, Nola's Penthouse Studios, New York: Joe Wilder, Bernie Privin, Harold Johnson tp; Urbie Green, Frank Rehak, tb; Peanuts Hucko cl; John Muenzenberger as; Barney Bigard ts, cl; Pepper Adams bs; Bert Farber p; Dick Hyman org; Al Caiola g; Wendell Marshall b; Cozy Cole dm.

| a | Topsy 1 | Love 45: 5003 |
| b | Topsy 2 | Love 45: 5004 |

All tracks on Coral 45: 65584, London (Eng) 45: 45-HL-8750, London (It) 45: 45-HL-8750, Love LP: 5005, Love CD: 5005, Love CD: 504, Orchard CD: 6699-101074-61.

Chapter Two
Donald Byrd-Pepper Adams Quintet: 1958-1961

THELONIOUS MONK
580225a

25 February 1958, Reeves Sound Studios, New York: Donald Byrd tp; Johnny Griffin ts; Pepper Adams bs; Thelonious Monk p; Wilbur Ware b; Philly Joe Jones dm.

a   Coming on the Hudson   Milestone LP: M-9124
b   Coming on the Hudson   Milestone unissued

-a on Milestone LP: 68-154, Riverside LP: R-22, Riverside LP: 99-912, Riverside LP: RIV-4005/4, Victor (J) LP: VIJ-4039, Riverside CD: 15RCD-022-2, Riverside CD: VDJ-25010/24, Lone Hill (Sp) CD: LHJ-10360-2.

According to Orrin Keepnews, in his liner notes for Milestone LP: M-9124, Coming on the Hudson is "the sole reminder of an attempted album that would have had Griffin and Rollins as a unique two-tenor team, and Art Blakey as the drummer. But we never assembled that combination in the studio. Monk was to have contacted Sonny and Art; neither one appeared; and both later insisted to me quite convincingly that they had never been told. Late evening phone calls brought in Philly Joe Jones and Pepper Adams, but after this run-through of what was then a brand new composition, on which only Griffin and the leader solo, Thelonious decided not to continue."

According to Johnny Griffin, in a conversation with the author in 1988, Monk left the session abruptly, after two tracks were recorded, because he was upset with the condition of the piano. Griffin said,

> I don't think Monk was too happy about doing the date at the time. He had wanted Sonny Rollins on the date, and he wanted Art

Blakey on the date, and both of them said he never informed them about the date, so he wound up with Philly Joe Jones. Monk didn't act satisfied about anything....We ran over a couple of tunes. He wasn't satisfied with the piano, and they gave him another piano and he struck the piano and the leg came loose and hit the floor, and that was all he could bear! He took a graceful exit without saying a word! I was supposed to record the next day with a quartet, and, so, without losing that studio time...we decided we could do a date anyway, which was good for Orrin Keepnews, because he didn't want to lose the studio time he had rented for [Monk]. I think the date turned out pretty good. [*See* 580225b.] Oh yeah, those musicians are fantastic!

In a 1987 discussion with the author about Pepper Adams and Monk, guitarist Peter Leitch said,

I just know what Pepper told me. I mentioned this [session] to Pepper, and, at first, he couldn't quite remember what date it was, and then he said, "Oh, that's the session where the piano collapsed." That was the first recording of that tune, by the way. (It was later recorded by the Monk quartet with Griffin at the Five Spot. That's the only other place, I believe, that it has appeared anywhere in the Monk discography, and it's a wonderful piece of music, but it's very difficult.) It was just basically a run-through. In no way was it a final take. You can hear it too: It's real raggedy, there's no way. They managed to do that: They rehearsed it, and did that one run-through, and the piano collapsed. Monk left, and Pepper and Griffin, and possibly Donald Byrd—I'm not sure whether Donald Byrd was involved in this—went to a bar near the studio, because they didn't know what was going to happen with the date. They hung in the bar for awhile and somebody from Riverside came and got them—and they had gotten Kenny Drew—and they did a Johnny Griffin sextet record....I remember [Pepper] saying that they only did that one tune and then the piano collapsed. Monk freaked and left. He told me that he had disagreements with Monk about chord changes. He wasn't specific. I guess on probably the way things should be notated.

JOHNNY GRIFFIN–JOHNNY GRIFFIN SEXTET
580225b
25 February 1958, Reeves Sound Studios, New York: Donald Byrd tp; Johnny Griffin ts; Pepper Adams bs; Kenny Drew p; Wilbur Ware b; Philly Joe Jones dm.

a **Stix' Trix**   Riverside LP: RLP-12-264
b **What's New**
c **Johnny G. G.**
d **Catharsis**
   Griffin and rhythm section:
e Woody'n You

-a on Riverside (Ger) LP: RIV-001, Riverside (Ger) LP: RLP-264, Victor (J) LP: SMJ-6285, Original Jazz Classics CD: OJCCD-1827-2, Riverside (Ger) CD: CDRIVM-001, JVC (J) CD: 41369.

-b on Original Jazz Classics CD: OJCCD-1827-2, Riverside (Ger) LP: RLP-264, Victor (J) LP: SMJ-6285, JVC (J) CD: 41369.

-c on Milestone LP: M-47054, Riverside (Ger) LP: RLP-264, Victor (J) LP: SMJ-6285, Original Jazz Classics CD: OJCCD-1827-2, Victor (J) CD: VDJ-1547, JVC (J) CD: 41369.

-d on Milestone LP: M-47054, Riverside (Ger) LP: RLP-264, Victor (J) LP: SMJ-6285, Original Jazz Classics CD: OJCCD-1827-2, Victor (J) CD: VDJ-1547, JVC (J) CD: 41369.

-e on Riverside LP: RLP-12-284, Riverside (Ger) LP: RLP-264, Victor (J) LP: SMJ-6285, Original Jazz Classics CD: OJCCD-1827-2, JVC (J) CD: 41369.

See 580225a notes.

PEPPER ADAMS
580300
c. March 1958, private recording, Howard Kanovitz's loft, New York: Pepper Adams bs; Don Friedman p; Henry Grimes b; Elvin Jones dm.

In a discussion with the author in 1989, painter Howard Kanovitz said that he taped this band in performance at his loft at 122 Second Avenue.

According to Don Friedman, in an interview with the author in 1988, "There used to be a jam session loft scene in New York down on the Lower East Side. One of the guys was Larry Rivers, who's a well-known painter—and Howie Kanovitz. They were painters. They also played: Howie was a trombone player and Larry was a saxophone player. They had a big loft down there and I used to go down there and play, and Elvin used to go down there and play, and I'm sure that's where I first met Pepper Adams, because I know he went down there and played too."

PEPPER ADAMS-JIMMY KNEPPER – PEPPER-KNEPPER QUINTET
580325
25 March 1958, Beltone Studios, New York: Jimmy Knepper tb; Pepper Adams bs, p*; Wynton Kelly p, org†; Doug Watkins b; Elvin Jones dm.

a   58-XY-413 **Minor Catastrophe**   Metrojazz LP: E-1004
b   58-XY-414 **All Too Soon**
c   58-XY-415 **Beaubien**
d   58-XY-416 **Adams in the Apple**
e   58-XY-417 **Riverside Drive**
f   58-XY-418 **I Didn't Know about You** *†
g   58-XY-419 **Primrose Path**

-a on Jazz Workshop (F) LP: JW-003, Polydor-Metrojazz (J) LP: MM-2093, Fresh Sounds (Sp) CD: FSRCD-344, American Jazz Classics (Sp) CD: 99011, Verve (Neth) CD: 840-040-2.

-b on Jazz Workshop (F) LP: JW-003, Polydor-Metrojazz (J) LP: MM-2093, Fresh Sounds (Sp) CD: FSRCD-344, American Jazz Classics (Sp) CD: 99011.

-c on Jazz Workshop (F) LP: JW-003, Polydor-Metrojazz (J) LP: MM-2093, Fresh Sounds (Sp) CD: FSRCD-344, American Jazz Classics (Sp) CD: 99011.

-d on Jazz Workshop (F) LP: JW-003, Polydor-Metrojazz (J) LP: MM-2093, Fresh Sounds (Sp) CD: FSRCD-344, American Jazz Classics (Sp) CD: 99011.

-e on Jazz Workshop (F) LP: JW-003, Polydor-Metrojazz (J) LP: MM-2093, Fresh Sounds (Sp) CD: FSRCD-344, American Jazz Classics (Sp) CD: 99011.

-f on Jazz Workshop (F) LP: JW-003, Polydor-Metrojazz (J) LP: MM-2093, Fresh Sounds (Sp) CD: FSRCD-344, American Jazz Classics (Sp) CD: 99011.

-g on Jazz Workshop (F) LP: JW-003, Polydor-Metrojazz (J) LP: MM-2093, Fresh Sounds (Sp) CD: FSRCD-344, American Jazz Classics (Sp) CD: 99011.

Pepper Adams told his friend Bob Cornfoot that, during the time it took Wynton Kelly to leave the piano chair and sit at the organ so he could begin his organ solo on -f, Adams sat in on piano and comped with the rhythm section.

This is Adams' fourth date as a leader or co-leader, and, similar to his Savoy date with Bernard McKinney (*see* notes for 571119), it's not a date that has much of Adams' personal stamp. For one thing, Adams only contributed one original tune, Beaubien, and it's a simple blues line at that. Usually, Adams' dates as a leader have at least two of his originals, and, typically, they're ambitious pieces. Moreover, *Pepper-Knepper,* somewhat of a gimmick, was Leonard Feather's idea. In an interview with the author in 1988, Jimmy Knepper remembered the session: "Leonard Feather called me up to do a record with Pepper: *Pepper and Knepper....*I remember going over to [Pepper's] apartment in the Village. We played a couple of tunes down and showed up for the date....[Feather] was the A&R man. He had one or two tunes [of his] that he had us play." Adams, however, likely chose fellow Detroiters Doug Watkins and Elvin Jones, because, at this time, he was working with them at the Five Spot. Also, Adams probably had no issue with recording two Ellington tunes.

MANNY ALBAM–JAZZ NEW YORK
580408
8 April 1958, New York: Bernie Glow, Donald Byrd, Ernie Royal tp; Jim Dahl tb; Bob Brookmeyer vtb; Tom Mitchell btb; Gene Quill as, cl; Zoot Sims, Al Cohn ts; Pepper Adams bs; Dick Katz p; Milt Hinton b; Osie Johnson dm; Manny Albam arr.

a   Thruway   Dot LP: DLP-9004
b   **The Nether Regions**

-a on Dot LP: DLP-25879, Dot LP: SLP-29004, Fresh Sound (Sp) LP: M-39342, Aris-MCA CD: 874706, Lone Fresh Sounds (Sp) CD: FSR-631, Lone Hill (Sp) CD: LHJ-10118-2, Hill (Sp) CD: LHJ-10196, MCA-Victor (J) CD: MVCZ-58.
-b on Aris-MCA CD: 874706, Fresh Sounds (Sp) CD: FSR-631, Lone Hill (Sp) CD: LHJ-10118-2, Lone Hill (Sp) CD: LHJ-10196.

In Dom Cerulli's liner notes to the LP, Albam said the following about the band: "I used six brass and four reeds with rhythm rather than the more conventional seven brass and five reeds with rhythm. I find the smaller band a little more wieldy [sic]. I can write both small and big band things, and the band is small enough or big enough to be either."

See 580412, 580425.

MANNY ALBAM–JAZZ NEW YORK
580412
12 April 1958, New York: Same as 8 April 1958, except Nick Travis tp; Jerome Richardson ts, fl; Joe Benjamin b replace Donald Byrd, Zoot Sims and Milt Hinton respectively:

a	**They All Laughed**	Dot LP: DLP-9004
b	Fresh Flute	

All tracks on Dot LP: SLP-29004, Fresh Sound (Sp) LP: M-39342, Aris-MCA CD: 874706, Fresh Sounds (Sp) CD: FSR-631, Lone Hill (Sp) CD: LHJ-10118-2, Lone Hill (Sp) CD: LHJ-10196, MCA-Victor (J) CD: MVCZ-58.

See also 580425.

PEPPER ADAMS–10 TO 4 AT THE FIVE SPOT
580415
15 April 1958, Five Spot Café, New York: Donald Byrd tp; Pepper Adams bs; Bobby Timmons p; Doug Watkins b; Elvin Jones dm; Jon Hendricks* and Oliver Shearer voc.†

a	**'Tis**	Riverside LP: RLP-12-265
b	**The Long Two Four** (Off to the Races)	
c	**Hastings Street Bounce**	
d	**Yourna**	
e	**Stuffy** * †	Riverside unissued
	Adams and rhythm section:	
f	**You're My Thrill**	Riverside LP: RLP-12-265

All tracks on Riverside LP: RSLP-1104, Milestone LP: M-47044, Original Jazz Classics LP: OJC-031, Carrère (F) LP: CA-68-932, Original Jazz Classics CD: OJCCD-031-2, Victor (J) LP: SMJ-6129.

This is Adams' fifth date as a leader. Approximately 25 tunes in four or five sets were recorded during the course of the evening, but the LP's title derives its name from the actual time the set used on the recording began. (*See* Adams' comments to Ben Sidran below.)

In an interview with the author in 1988 Oliver Shearer said -e was recorded but never released. "Riverside let me and Jon come in there to do one song with that group," said Shearer, "and Pepper played a solo on it....Jon Hendricks had just written the lyrics to Stuffy for me, as he did writing the lyrics for Moanin' and After Hours for me, to be used in a recording for Columbia [*see* 600700]."

On a 19 April 1982 Toronto radio interview conducted by Ted O'Reilly, Pepper Adams discussed the date: "This was a time when Elvin was still not being seriously considered, certainly by a lot of critics and even some musicians. Since his playing was so different from anything else that was being played at that time—his own concept of a time feeling and that really loose kind of swing, which is what I particularly enjoyed about him—I took a lot of heat for using Elvin as a drummer for the three months that this band was together from a lot of different sources. And some of it appeared in print: that the rest of the band wasn't too bad but the drummer isn't even professional; because he didn't sound like anybody else, so they were turned off by him."

According to Pepper Adams in an interview with Peter Danson in *Coda,* "I had a lot of arguments for hiring Elvin, but Joe and Iggy Termini stood behind my judgment and we went in there and had a powerhouse band all summer. Fascinating place to work, too. It had a lot of interesting people who were regulars in there. W.H. Auden used to come in frequently. He lived just a couple of blocks away. A lot of the modern painters—Larry Rivers; Dwight McDonald, Esquire's film critic; Lionel Stander."

On a 1986 NPR radio interview conducted by Ben Sidran, Pepper Adams was asked what it's like to play a ballad feature (track -f) with a piano so horribly out of tune:

I tell you, it's excruciating! Really! Because I completely lose track of where the core of the intonation is, if indeed there is one, and, so, very quickly, instead of just competing with an out-of-tune piano, I have lost all track of intonation within myself, so I'm not even sure to what extent my intonation on my own instrument is. To use the Irish expression, "Something like that'd make your face hurt!" It's tough, and was probably made even worse by the fact that everything on that album is from the very last set. I think we did three or

four sets in there, and this was when stereo was first coming in, if
you notice by the date there, and it was Riverside's first attempt at
recording stereo on a live date. So we completed the earlier part of
the evening. I think Ray Fowler was the engineer, if I'm remembering correctly. Orrin Keepnews was there, of course, overseeing
things, and he says, "Well, I think we've got a lot of really great
music there. I think we can even start packing up now." Orrin had
Elvin and myself to the bar for a drink, and Ray Fowler comes running up and says, "One of our microphone leads has been out all
night! Nothing is on stereo!" That was part of the whole point:
Their first live stereo recording, so we quickly had to do one more
set, and that's the entire album. And Elvin Jones had a black eye.
Not from any disagreement. He had had a wisdom tooth removed a
couple of days earlier, on which the roots had gone back so far that
its removal caused a blood vessel to burst inside, giving him a rather
spectacular black eye. If you've never seen Elvin with a black eye,
you're really missing something there!

Regarding the Five Spot piano, Adams told the author in 1984, "It
was not in good shape, so it couldn't hold a tuning. It would slip in the
course of one night! [With] live recordings there, even if you tuned the
piano at the beginning of the night, by the middle of the second set it's
not in tune."

At various times during the run at the Five Spot, Tommy Flanagan,
Roland Hanna, and Don Friedman sat in for Bobby Timmons.

MANNY ALBAM–JAZZ NEW YORK
580425
25 April 1958, New York: Same as 8 April 1958 except Art Farmer tp;
Frank Socolow ts; Eddie Costa p, vib replace Donald Byrd, Zoot Sims,
Dick Katz respectively:

a   In a Mist   Dot LP: DLP-9004
b   **Dot's Right**
c   Hebe, the Cups Please!

All tracks on Dot LP: SLP-29004, Fresh Sound (Sp) LP: M-39342,
Aris-MCA CD: 874706, Fresh Sounds (Sp) CD: FSR-631, Lone Hill
(Sp) CD: LHJ-10118-2, Lone Hill (Sp) CD: LHJ-10196, MCA-Victor (J)
CD: MVCZ-58.

See also 580412.

GENE AMMONS–BLUE GENE
580502
2 May 1958, Van Gelder Studio, Hackensack NJ: Idrees Sulieman tp; Gene Ammons ts; Pepper Adams bs; Mal Waldron p; Doug Watkins b; Arthur Taylor dm; Ray Barretto cga.

a	1509	**Blue Greens and Beans**	Prestige LP: PR-7146
b	1510	**Hip Tip**	
c	1511	**Scamperin'**	
d	1512	**Blue Gene**	

-a on Prestige 45: PR-45-140, Original Jazz Classics LP: OJC-192, Esquire (Eng) LP: 32-147, Analog Productions [45rpm] LP: LAP-7146-45, Original Jazz Classics CD: OJCCD-192-2, Avid (Eng) CD: AMSC-1029. According to record producer Bob Porter, Prestige 45: PR-45-140 was released in two parts to comprise both sides of a 45rpm single.

-b on Original Jazz Classics LP: OJC-192, Esquire (Eng) LP: 32-147, Analog Productions [45rpm] LP: LAP-7146-45, Original Jazz Classics CD: OJCCD-192-2, Avid (Eng) CD: AMSC-1029.

-c on Original Jazz Classics LP: OJC-192, Esquire (Eng) LP: 32-147, Analog Productions [45rpm] LP: LAP-7146-45, Original Jazz Classics CD: OJCCD-192-2, Avid (Eng) CD: AMSC-1029.

-d on Prestige LP: PR-7306, Esquire (Eng) LP: 32-147, Original Jazz Classics LP: OJC-192, Analog Productions [45rpm] LP: LAP-7146-45, Original Jazz Classics CD: OJCCD-192-2, Avid (Eng) CD: AMSC-1029.

See 560430 notes regarding Van Gelder's studio.

BILLY VER PLANCK–THE SOUL OF JAZZ
580505
5 May 1958, Van Gelder Studio, Hackensack NJ: Joe Wilder tp; Bill Harris tb; Bobby Jaspar ts; Pepper Adams bs; Eddie Costa p; George Duvivier b; Arthur Taylor dm; Billy Ver Planck arr.

a	**You Gotta Be a Good Man**	World Wide LP: MG-20002
b	**Each Side of the River**	
c	**Where You Gonna Run To**	
d	**I Can't Believe It**	

e   What Could I Do
f   **Royal Garden Blues**

See 560430 notes regarding Van Gelder's studio.

MANNY ALBAM
580516
16 May 1958, Town Hall, New York: Bernie Glow, Ernie Royal, Nick
Travis tp; Jim Dahl, Frank Rehak tb; Tom Mitchell btb; Gene Quill as,
cl; Jerome Richardson ts, fl; Al Cohn, Pepper Adams bs; Dick Katz p;
Milt Hinton b; Osie Johnson dm; Manny Albam arr; GUESTS: Don Elliott mellophone; Paul Horn as, fl; Hal McKusick as, bcl; Georgie Auld ts;
Steve Allen p, vib:

a   **A Little Eye-Opener**   Dot LP: DLP-9003
b   My Funny Valentine
c   **Blues Over Easy**
d   Blues Over Easy   Dot LP: DLP-3188

-a and -b is performed by the band, without guests.

-c is an edited version of the original performance, performed by the band
without guests, that includes the opening chorus, six solos, the out chorus, and
an added band chorus that was played as an encore.

-d is a different edited version of the original performance that includes the
last five solos done that night (all played by the added guests), one of which is a
four-hand piano solo by Katz and Allen.

-a on Dot LP: DLP-25679, Victor (J) LP: VIM-5025, Fresh Sounds
(Sp) CD: FSR-631, Lone Hill (Sp) CD: LHJ-10118-2.

-b on Victor (J) LP: VIM-5025, Fresh Sounds (Sp) CD: FSR-631,
Lone Hill (Sp) CD: LHJ-10118-2.

-c on Fresh Sounds (Sp) CD: FSR-631, Lone Hill (Sp) CD: LHJ-
10118-2.

-d on Victor (J) LP: VIM-5025, Fresh Sounds (Sp) CD: FSR-631,
Lone Hill (Sp) CD: LHJ-10118-2.

JERRY VALENTINE—OUTSKIRTS OF TOWN
580829
29 August 1958, Van Gelder Studio, Hackensack NJ: Art Farmer, Idrees
Sulieman tp; Buster Cooper tb; Jerome Richardson as, fl; Jimmy Forrest
ts; Pepper Adams bs; Ray Bryant p; Tiny Grimes g; Wendell Marshall b;

Osie Johnson dm; Jerry Valentine arr.

a	1571	Sent for You Yesterday, Here	
		You Come Today	Prestige LP: PR-7145
b	1572	Blue Flute	
c	1573	I'm Gonna Move to the Outskirts of Town	
d	1574	**I Wanna Blow, Blow, Blow**	
e		**I Wanna Blow, Blow, Blow**	Prestige unissued
f	1575	**Jelly Jelly**	Prestige LP: PR-7145
g	1576	**Blues A-Swingin'**	

-a on Prestige LP: PR-7787, Original Jazz Classics LP: OJC-1717, Esquire (Eng) LP: 32-110, Original Jazz Classics CD: OJCCD-1717-2.

-b on Prestige 45: 132, Prestige LP: PR-7787, Original Jazz Classics LP: OJC-1717, Esquire (Eng) LP: 32-110, Original Jazz Classics CD: OJCCD-1717-2.

-c on Prestige LP: PR-7787, Original Jazz Classics LP: OJC-1717, Esquire (Eng) LP: 32-110, Original Jazz Classics CD: OJCCD-1717-2.

-d on Prestige LP: PR-7787, Original Jazz Classics LP: OJC-1717, Esquire (Eng) LP: 32-110, Original Jazz Classics CD: OJCCD-1717-2.

-e on Prestige New Jazz LP: 8293, Prestige LP: PR-7787, Original Jazz Classics LP: OJC-1717, Esquire (Eng) LP: 32-110, Original Jazz Classics CD: OJCCD-1717-2, Jazz Classics CD: OJCCD-987.

-f on Prestige LP: PR-7787, Original Jazz Classics LP: OJC-1717, Esquire (Eng) LP: 32-110, Original Jazz Classics CD: OJCCD-1717-2.

-g on Prestige LP: PR-7787, Original Jazz Classics LP: OJC-1717, Esquire (Eng) LP: 32-110, Original Jazz Classics CD: OJCCD-1717-2.

See 560430 notes regarding Van Gelder's studio.

WHITEY MITCHELL–GET THOSE ELEPHANTS OUTA HERE
581006
6 October 1958, Beltone Studios, New York: Blue Mitchell tp; Frank Rehak tb; Pepper Adams bs; André Previn p; Red Mitchell p, b; Whitey Mitchell b; Frankie Capp dm.

a	**Get Those Elephants Outa Here**[1]	Metrojazz LP: E-1012
b	**My One and Only Love**[2]	
c	In the Wee Small Hours of the Morning[3]	
d	**Moten Swing**[4]	
e	**Monster Rally**[5]	

f   **Three Cheers**[6]
g   **Blues for Brian**[7]
h   Fraternity[8]

[1]Full ensemble, with both Red Mitchell and Whitey Mitchell on b.
[2]Full ensemble, with both Red Mitchell and Whitey Mitchell on b.
[3]Rhythm section only, with Red Mitchell p, Previn out.
[4]Full ensemble, except Red Mitchell p, Previn out.
[5]Both Red Mitchell and Whitey Mitchell on b, Previn out.
[6]Red Mitchell p, Previn and Rehak out.
[7]Both Red Mitchell and Whitey Mitchell on b, add Rehak and Previn.
[8]Duo for Red Mitchell p and b, and Whitey Mitchell b.

Regarding the original matrix numbers 58-XY-1041 through 58-XY-1049 that appear in Ruppli and Novitsky's MGM label discography, historian Mike Fitzgerald has written that the tune order is unknown and a ninth track may remain unissued.

All tracks on Metrojazz LP: SE-1012, MGM LP: 665007, MGM (Eng) LP: C-803, Fresh Sound (Sp) CD: FSR-CD-444.

BENNY GOODMAN
581115
15 November 1958, Engineers Hall, New York: John Frosk, E. V. Perry, Allen Smith, Benny Ventura tp; Buster Cooper, Rex Peer, Hale Rood tb; Benny Goodman cl; Herb Geller, Jimmy Sands as; Bob Wilber, Arthur Clarke ts; Pepper Adams bs, bcl; Russ Freeman p; Turk Van Lake g; Milt Hinton b; Shelly Manne dm, Donna Musgrove voc.*

a	9535	Mission to Moscow	Chess LP: LP-1440
b	9660	Oh, Baby	
c		Oh, Baby	Limelight CD: 820-820-2
d		Autumn Nocturne	Gala (Swe) EP: FPK-703
e		**Happy Session Blues**	Columbia LP: CL-1324
f		**Happy Session Blues**	Wax Time LP: 771680
g		**Happy Session Blues**	Columbia unissued
h		**Happy Session Blues**	
i		How Deep Is the Ocean*	
j		How Long Has This Been Going On*	

-a on Chess 45: 1742, Gala (Swe) EP: FPK-703, Chess LP: LP-1440, Chess LP: LS-1440, Jazz Reactivation (Eng) LP: JR-155, Barclay (F)

LP: 84103, Chess (Neth) LP: 9283-047, Bellaphon (Ger) LP: BJS-4025, Limelight CD: 820-820-2, MCA CD: CHD-31264, Universal CD: 31264, Charly (Eng) CD: CPCD-82632.

-b on Gala (Swe) EP: FPK-703, Chess LP: LP-1440, Chess LP: LS-1440, Jazz Reactivation (Eng) LP: JR-155, Chess (Neth) LP: 9283-047, Barclay (F) LP: 84103, Bellaphon (Ger) LP: BJS-4025, Limelight CD: 820-820-2, Musicmasters CD: CIJ-60201-Y, Limelight CD: 844-318-2, MCA CD: CHD-31264, Universal CD: 31264, Nimbus (Eng) CD: NI-2714-15, Charly (Eng) CD: CPCD-82632.

-c on Musicmasters CD: CIJ-60201-Y, Music Heritage Society CD: MHS-522431-L, Essential Jazz Classics (Sp) CD: EJC-55506.

-d on Limelight CD: 820-820-2, Musicmasters CD: CIJ-60201-Y, Limelight CD: 844-318-2, Musical Heritage Society CD: MHS-522431-L, Nimbus (Eng) CD: NI-2714-15, Essential Jazz Classics (Sp) CD: EJC-55506.

-e on Columbia LP: JJ-1, Columbia LP: JS-1, Columbia LP: CS-8129, Wax Time LP: 771680, Philips (Eng) LP: BO-7511-L, Philips (Eng) LP: BBL-7318, Philips (Eng) LP: SBBL-539, Philips (Neth) LP: 840-054-BY, Sony (F) LP: SOP2-31, CBS (J) LP: SOPZ-31, Musicmasters CD: CIJ-60201-Y, Limelight CD: 844-318-2, Nimbus (Eng) CD: NI-2714-15, Sony (F) CD: 476-523-2, Essential Jazz Classics (Sp) CD: EJC-55472.

-f on Musicmasters CD: CIJ-60201-Y, Limelight CD: 820-820-2, Musical Heritage Society CD: MHS-522431-L, Essential Jazz Classics (Sp) CD: EJC-55472.

Prior to this recording date, Adams had toured with Benny Goodman's big band from 15 October-14 November. According to Pepper Adams, in an interview with the author in 1984,

I got the gig because I was recommended by André Previn, who later apologized. He said, when he thought about it later, that he thought maybe it wasn't such a good idea. I had to reassure him: "No, it was interesting." Benny is known for his crotchets, I think— well, irritable at times, and eccentric, certainly. Wardell Gray did a brief tour with Goodman in '49 or so and he had a memorable statement about it when he came home to Detroit. People asked him what it was like playing with Benny Goodman, and Wardell said, "Well, you know, it seems for years I've been hearing Benny Goodman stories, and some of them were pretty outrageous and I tended to disregard at least fifty percent of them. But now, after having spent some time touring with Benny, I'm gonna believe every one of them!" Actually, I got on with Benny very well. I remember talking to him about recording the Bartok trio. He always treated me very well, but, at the rehearsals, I saw him treat other people rather shabbily....Benny's book has always been well taken care of, so there was some good writing in the book, so it was fun to play. Rehearsals were interminable, but they were fun because there was a good quantity of good music. Not all of it, but a lot of it was very good.

In a 1989 interview with the author, Bob Wilber said that Pepper Adams borrowed Wilber's bass clarinet to play the bass clarinet parts that were part of Goodman's baritone saxophone book. *See* 58117, 58118, 590417.

BENNY GOODMAN
581117
17 November 1958, Engineers Hall, New York: Same as 15 November 1958, omit Musgrove:

a	9536	Benny Rides Again	Chess LP: LP-1440
b		Benny Rides Again	Limelight CD: 820-820-2
c	9537	The Earl	Chess LP: LP-1440
d		The King and Me	Chess unissued

-a on Chess LP: LPS-1440, Chess (F) LP: 9283-047, Chess (Neth) LP: 9283-047, Jazz Reactivation (Eng) LP: JR-155, Nimbus (Eng) CD: NI-2714-15, Barclay (F) LP: 84103, Bellaphon (Ger) LP: BJS-4025, Musicmasters CD: CIJ-60201, Limelight CD: 820-820-2, Limelight CD: 844-318-2, MCA-Chess CD: GRD-2-812, MCA CD: CHD-31264, Universal CD: 31264, Charly (Eng) CD: CPCD-82632.
-b on Musicmasters CD: CIJ-6-0201-Y, Musical Heritage Society CD: MHS-522431-L, Essential Jazz Classics (Sp) CD: EJC-55506.
-c on Chess LP: LPS-1440, Barclay (F) LP: 84103, Chess (F) LP: 9283-047, Chess (Neth) LP: 9283-047, Jazz Reactivation (Eng) LP: JR-155, Bellaphon (Ger) LP: BJS-4025, MCA CD: CHD-31264, Universal CD: 31264, Nimbus (Eng) CD: NI-2714-15, Charly (Eng) CD: CPCD-82632.
See 581115, 581118.

BENNY GOODMAN
581118
18 November 1958, Engineers Hall, New York: Same as 15 November 1958, omit Musgrove:

a	The King and Me	Columbia LP: CL-1324
b	The King and Me	Essential Jazz Classics (Sp) CD: EJC-55472
c	What a Difference a Day Makes	Columbia LP: CL-1324
d	What a Difference a Day Makes	Essential Jazz Classics (Sp) CD: EJC-55472
e	Batunga Train	Columbia LP: CL-1324
f	Batunga Train	Musicmasters LP: 20142
g	Clarinet à la King	Columbia LP: CL-1324
h	Macedonia Lullaby	
i	Macedonia Lullaby	Essential Jazz Classics (Sp) CD: EJC-55472

-a on Columbia LP: CS-1324, Columbia LP: TL-STA-354, Columbia LP: CS-8129, Columbia LP: P4M-5678, Wax Time LP: 771680, Philips (Eng) LP: BO-7511L, Philips (Eng) LP: SBBL-539, Philips (Eng) LP: BBL-7318, Philips (Neth) LP: 840-054-BY, CBS (J) LP: SOPZ-31, Essential Jazz Classics (Sp) CD: EJC-55472.

-c on Columbia LP: CS-1324, Columbia LP: CS-8129, Columbia LP: P4M-5678, Wax Time LP: 771680, Philips (Eng) LP: BO-7511L, Philips (Eng) LP: SBBL-539, Philips (Eng) LP: BBL-7318, Philips (Neth) LP: 840-054-BY, CBS (J) LP: SOPZ-31, Musicmasters CD: CIJ-60201-Y, Limelight CD: 820-820-2, Limelight CD: 844-318-2, Nimbus (Eng) CD: NI-2714-15, Essential Jazz Classics (Sp) CD: EJC-55472.

-d on Musicmasters CD: CIJ-60201-Y, Limelight CD: 820-820-2, Musical Heritage Society CD: MHS-522431-L.

-e on Columbia LP: CS-1324, Columbia LP: CS-8129, Columbia LP: P4M-5678, Wax Time LP: 771680, Philips (Eng) LP: BO-7511L, Philips (Eng) LP: SBBL-539, Philips (Eng) LP: BBL-7318, Philips (Neth) LP: 840-054-BY, CBS (J) LP: SOPZ-31, Limelight CD: 820-820-2, Essential Jazz Classics (Sp) CD.

-f on Columbia LP: CS-1324, Limelight CD: 820-820-2, Limelight CD: 844-315-2, Musicmasters CD: CIJ-60142-Z, Essential Jazz Classics (Sp) CD: EJC-55472.

-g on Columbia LP: CS-1324, Columbia LP: CS-8129, Columbia LP: CL-2483, Columbia LP: CS-9283, NARC LP: KM8P-1006, Philips (Eng) LP: BO-7511L, CBS (Eu) LP: 52368, Columbia LP: KG-31547, Wax Time LP: 771680, Philips (Eng) LP: SBBL-539, Philips (Eng) LP: BBL-7318, Parade CD: PAR-2029, Essential Jazz Classics (Sp) CD: EJC-55472.

-h on Columbia LP: CS-8129, Columbia LP: TL-STA-354, Columbia LP: P4M-5678, Wax Time LP: 771680, Philips (Eng) LP: BBL-7318, Philips (Neth) LP: 840-054-BY, CBS (J) LP: SOPZ-31, Musicmasters CD: CIJ-60142-Z, Essential Jazz Classics (Sp) CD: EJC-55472.

See 581115, 581117.

DONALD BYRD–OFF TO THE RACES
581221
21 December 1958, Van Gelder Studio, Hackensack NJ: Donald Byrd tp; Jackie McLean as; Pepper Adams bs*; Wynton Kelly p; Sam Jones b; Arthur Taylor dm.

a **Sudwest Funk***   Blue Note LP: BLP-4007
b **Lover Come Back to Me***
c **Off to the Races*** (The Long Two Four)
d **Paul's Pal***
e **Down Tempo***
f When Your Love Has Gone

-a on Blue Note LP: BST-84007, Mosaic CD: MD4-194, Blue Note (Eu) CD: 0946-3-62658-2-7, Blue Note (J) CD: TOCJ-9050, Toshiba-EMI (J) CD: TOCJ-4007, Toshiba-EMI (J) CD: TOCJ-6465, Toshiba-EMI (J) CD: TOCJ-8653.

-b on Blue Note LP: BST-84007, Mosaic CD: MD4-194, Blue Note (Eu) CD: 0946-3-62658-2-7, Toshiba-EMI (J) CD: TOCJ-5934, Blue Note (J) CD: TOCJ-9050, Toshiba-EMI (J) CD: TOCJ-4007, Toshiba-EMI (J) CD: TOCJ-6465, Toshiba-EMI (J) CD: TOCJ-8653.

-c on Blue Note LP: BST-84007, Blue Note LP: BN-B2S-5256, Mosaic CD: MD4-194, Blue Note (Eu) CD: 0946-3-62658-2-7, Blue Note (J) CD: TOCJ-9050, Toshiba-EMI (J) CD: TOCJ-4007, Toshiba-EMI (J) CD: TOCJ-6465, Toshiba-EMI (J) CD: TOCJ-8653.

-d on Blue Note LP: BST-84007, Mosaic CD: MD4-194, Blue Note (Eu) CD: 0946-3-62658-2-7, Blue Note (J) CD: TOCJ-9050, Toshiba-

EMI (J) CD: TOCJ-4007, Toshiba-EMI (J) CD: TOCJ-6465, Toshiba-EMI (J) CD: TOCJ-8653.

-e on Blue Note LP: BST-84007, Mosaic CD: MD4-194, Blue Note (Eu) CD: 0946-3-62658-2-7, Blue Note (J) CD: TOCJ-9050, Toshiba-EMI (J) CD: TOCJ-4007, Toshiba-EMI (J) CD: TOCJ-6465, Toshiba-EMI (J) CD: TOCJ-8653.

-f on Blue Note LP: BST-84007, Mosaic CD: MD4-194, Blue Note (Eu) CD: 0946-3-62658-2-7, Blue Note (J) CD: TOCJ-9050, Toshiba-EMI (J) CD: TOCJ-4007, Toshiba-EMI (J) CD: TOCJ-6465, Toshiba-EMI (J) CD: TOCJ-8653.

At least 12 takes were done at this session.

As Pepper Adams pointed out to interviewer Len Dobbin on 23 February 1986, the traveling band was customarily billed *The Donald Byrd-Pepper Adams Quintet,* but records made by the Quintet for Blue Note were solely in Byrd's name, because Byrd, not Adams, signed the Blue Note contract.

See 560430 notes regarding Van Gelder's studio.

CHET BAKER
581230
30 December 1958, Reeves Sound Studios, New York: Chet Baker tp; Herbie Mann fl; Pepper Adams bs; Bill Evans p; Kenny Burrell g*; Paul Chambers b; Connie Kay dm.

a   **Alone Together**   Riverside LP: RLP-12-299
b   **How High the Moon**
c   **If You Could See Me Now**
d   **You'd Be So Nice to Come Home To**
e   **Early Morning Mood**   Riverside LP: RLP-12-294
     Baker and rhythm section, Evans out:
f   September Song*
g   It Never Entered My Mind*

-a on Riverside LP: RSLP-1135, Original Jazz Classics LP: OJC-087, Carrère (F) LP: CA-68-950, Victor (J) LP: VIJ-4075, Original Jazz Classics CD: OJCCD-087-2, Carrère (F) CD: CA-98-950.

-b on Riverside LP: RSLP-1135, Original Jazz Classics LP: OJC-087, Carrère (F) LP: CA-68-950, Victor (J) LP: VIJ-4075, Original Jazz Classics CD: OJCCD-087-2, Carrère (F) CD: CA-98-950.

-c on Riverside LP: RSLP-1135, Original Jazz Classics LP: OJC-087, Carrère (F) LP: CA-68-950, Victor (J) LP: VIJ-4075, Original Jazz Classics CD: OJCCD-087-2, Carrère (F) CD: CA-98-950.

-d on Riverside LP: RSLP-1135, Original Jazz Classics LP: OJC-087, Carrère (F) LP: CA-68-950, Victor (J) LP: VIJ-4075, Original Jazz Classics CD: OJCCD-087-2, Carrère (F) CD: CA-98-950.

-e on Riverside LP: RSLP-1134, Original Jazz Classics LP: OJC-256, Original Jazz Classics CD: OJCCD-087-2, Carrère (F) CD: CA-98-950.

-f on Riverside LP: RSLP-1134, Original Jazz Classics LP: OJC-256, Original Jazz Classics CD: OJCCD-087-2, Carrère (F) CD: CA-98-950.

-g on Riverside LP: RSLP-1134, Original Jazz Classics LP: OJC-256, Original Jazz Classics CD: OJCCD-087-2, Carrère (F) CD: CA-98-950.

After this session, Baker and Adams play a 4-5 week gig in New York, fronting a quintet with Don Friedman and Doug Watkins. *See* 590119.

THELONIOUS MONK
590100
January-February 1959, private recordings of various rehearsals, Hall Overton's loft, New York: Donald Byrd tp; Eddie Bert tb; Robert Northern frh; Jay McAllister tu; Phil Woods as; Charlie Rouse ts; Pepper Adams bs; Thelonious Monk, Hall Overton p; Sam Jones b; Arthur Taylor dm.

Rehearsals for Monk's Town Hall concert (*see* 590228) were taped by photographer and neighbor W. Eugene Smith at Hall Overton's loft at 821 Sixth Avenue. Musicians would arrive, after their club dates, beginning at 2 am, staying often until 7 or 8 am. Besides performances by the band, these tapes also include conversations with Monk and Overton, as they collaborate on band orchestrations. As Monk biographer Robin D. G. Kelley pointed out to Sara Fishko on her WYNC radio program, "The common lore is that Hall Overton essentially took Monk's music and masterfully came up with these arrangements. Clearly, the tapes suggest that not only was Monk the master, in some ways, but Overton really did try to be true to [Monk's] conception." Seventeen tapes totaling nine hours are part of the Smith Collection at Duke University. For a description of Overton's loft, *see* 591224.

"I got a call from Jules Colomby," said Eddie Bert, in an interview in 1988 with the author:

> He was like a manager for Monk, and things like that. Monk told him who to get. We rehearsed at Hall Overton's, on Sixth Avenue, down around 28th Street. It was Hall's pad up on the second floor, I think it was, and we rehearsed for about a month for that Town Hall thing. It was a lot of work....I think that Hall Overton did an amazing job on the arrangements. He caught Monk just the way Monk was. He did a great job!...At that point, that music was very new. What [Overton] did was transcribe Monk's choruses—and the melodies, naturally—but some of [Monk's] choruses were transcribed for that [band's] instrumentation....At most of the rehearsals, Hall played the piano. I remember there was one point where Hall said, "Hey, Monk!" (Monk was in the other room. We were rehearsing.) He said, "Monk, are you ever going to play the piano parts?" So Monk said, "I'm dancing! I want to make sure the band is getting the right beat." He was in the other room dancing, because that's the way he feels the band.

Phil Woods, in an interview with the author in 1989, said, "When we got good, Monk would dance around the band. We knew we were getting close to the music when Monk would start dancing."

CHET BAKER
590119
19 January 1959, Reeves Sound Studios, New York: Same as 30 December 1958, except Burrell out and Philly Joe Jones dm replaces Kay:

a **'Tis Autumn**   Riverside LP: RLP-12-299
b **You and the Night and the Music**
   Baker and rhythm section:
c Time on My Hands

All tracks on Riverside LP: RSLP-1135, Original Jazz Classics LP: OJC-087, Carrère (F) LP: CA-68-950, Victor (J) LP: VIJ-4075, Original Jazz Classics CD: OJCCD-087-2, Carrère (F) CD: CA-98-950.
   Baker's quintet, with Adams, Don Friedman, Doug Watkins, were in the midst of a 4-5 week run in New York that began in early January.

THELONIOUS MONK
590200
February 1959, private recordings of various rehearsals, Hall Overton's loft, New York: See 590100.

URBIE GREEN
590202
2 February 1959, New York: John Frosk, Burt Collins, Marky Markowitz, John Carisi tp; Urbie Green, Billy Byers, Marshall Hawk tb; Eddie Bert btb; Hal McKusick, Rolf Kuhn as, cl; Don Lanphere ts; Pepper Adams bs; John Bunch p; Barry Galbraith g; Teddy Kotick b; Nick Stabulas dm.

a	K2PB0961	The Message	Fresh Sound (Sp) LP: NL-46033
b	K2PB0962	I'm Confessin'	
c	K2PB0963	But Not for Me	
d	K2PB0964	Goodnight My Love	
e	K2PB0965	**One O'Clock Jump**	

Originally recorded by RCA Victor, this session was first released in 1986. All tracks on Lone Hill (Sp) CD: LHJ-10309. *See* 590203.

URBIE GREEN
590203
3 February 1959, New York: Same as 2 February 1959, except Dick Hafer ts replaces Lanphere:

a	K2PB0966	I'm Through with Love	Fresh Sound (Sp) LP: NL-46033
b	K2PB0967	**Whirlaway**	
c	K2PB0968	I'm in a Dancing Mood	
d	K2PB0969	**Early Autumn**	
e	K2PB0970	When You're Smiling	

Originally recorded by RCA Victor, this session was first released in 1986. All tracks on Lone Hill (Sp) CD: LHJ-10309. *See* 590202.

CHARLES MINGUS–BLUES AND ROOTS
590204

4 February 1959, Atlantic Studios, New York: Willie Dennis, Jimmy Knepper tb; John Handy, Jackie McLean as; Booker Ervin ts; Pepper Adams bs; Mal Waldron,* Horace Parlan p; Charles Mingus b, voc; Dannie Richmond dm.

a	3346	E's Flat Ah's Flat Too*	Atlantic LP: SD-1305
b		**E's Flat Ah's Flat Too***	Rhino CD: R2-75205
c	3347	My Jelly Roll Soul	Atlantic LP: SD-1305
d		**My Jelly Roll Soul**	Rhino CD: R2-75205
e	3348	**Tensions**	Atlantic LP: SD-1305
f		Tensions	Rhino CD: R2-75205
g	3349	**Moanin'**	Atlantic LP: SD-1305
h	3350	Cryin' Blues	
i	3351	Wednesday Night Prayer Meeting	
j	4732	Wednesday Night Prayer Meeting	
			Atlantic LP: SD-5006
k	4733	Wednesday Night Prayer Meeting	

-a on Atlantic LP: KSD-1305, Wax Time LP: 771680, Atlantic (Ger) LP: ATL-50232, London (Eng) LP: LTZ-K15194, London (Eng) LP: SANK-6087, Warner Jazz (F) LP: 60039, Warner-Pioneer (J) LP: P-6999A, Warner Jazz (J) LP: 81227-8708-1, Atlantic CD: SD-1305-2, Rhino CD: R2-75205, Rhino CD: R2-72871, Warner Jazz CD: 3617, Atlantic (Eu) CD: 81227-3617-2, Atlantic (Ger) CD: 7567-81336-7, Atlantic (Ger) CD: 781-336-2, Avid (Eng) CD: AMSC-1026, London (Eng) CD: CD-1305-2, Essential Jazz Classics (Sp) CD: EJC-55474, Essential Jazz Classics (Sp) CD: EJC-R2-72871.

-c on Atlantic LP: KSD-1305, Franklin Mint LP: FM-28, Wax Time LP: 771680, London (Eng) LP: LTZ-K15194, London (Eng) LP: SANK-6087, Atlantic (Ger) LP: ATL-50232, Warner Jazz (F) LP: 60039, Warner-Pioneer (J) LP: P-6999A, Warner Jazz (J) LP: 81227-8708-1, Atlantic CD: SD-1305-2, Rhino CD: R2-75205, Rhino CD: R2-72871, Atlantic (Eu) CD: 81227-3617-2, Warner Jazz CD: 3617, Atlantic (Ger) CD: 781-336-2, Atlantic (Ger) CD: 7567-81336-7, Avid (Eng) CD: AMSC-1026, London (Eng) CD: CD-1305-2, Essential Jazz Classics (Sp) CD: EJC-55474, Essential Jazz Classics (Sp) CD: EJC-R2-72871.

-e on Atlantic LP: KSD-1305, Wax Time LP: 771680, Atlantic (Ger) LP: ATL-50232, London (Eng) LP: LTZ-K15194, London (Eng) LP:

SANK-6087, Warner Jazz (F) LP: 60039, Warner-Pioneer (J) LP: P-6999A, Warner Jazz (J) LP: 81227-8708-1, Atlantic CD: SD-1305-2, Rhino CD: R2-75205, Rhino CD: R2-72871, Warner Jazz CD: 3617, Atlantic (Eu) CD: 81227-3617-2, Atlantic (Ger) CD: 781-336-2, Atlantic (Ger) CD: 7567-81336-7, London (Eng) CD: CD-1305-2, Avid (Eng) CD: AMSC-1026, Essential Jazz Classics (Sp) CD: EJC-55474, Essential Jazz Classics (Sp) CD: EJC-R2-72871.

-g on Atlantic LP: SD2-302, Atlantic LP: KSD-1305, Wax Time LP: 771680, Atlantic (Eu) LP: K-50232, Atlantic (Ger) LP: ATL-50232, London (Eng) LP: LTZ-K15194, London (Eng) LP: SANK-6087, Warner Jazz (F) LP: 60039, Warner-Pioneer (J) LP: P-4505/6A, Warner-Pioneer (J) LP: P-6999A, Warner Jazz (J) LP: 81227-8708-1, Atlantic CD: SD-1305-2, Rhino CD: R2-75205, Rhino CD: R2-72871, Warner Jazz CD: 3617, Atlantic (Eu) CD: 81227-3617-2, Atlantic (Ger) CD: 781-336-2, Atlantic (Ger) CD: 7567-81336-7, London (Eng) CD: CD-1305-2, Avid (Eng) CD: AMSC-1026, Essential Jazz Classics (Sp) CD: EJC-55474, Essential Jazz Classics (Sp) CD: EJC-R2-72871.

-h on Atlantic LP: KSD-1305, Atlantic LP: SD3-600, Wax Time LP: 771680, Atlantic (Eu) LP: WE-313, Atlantic (Ger) LP: ATL-60143, Atlantic (Ger) LP: ATL-50232, Warner Jazz (F) LP: 60039, London (Eng) LP: LTZ-K15194, London (Eng) LP: SANK-6087, Warner-Pioneer (J) LP: P-6999A, Warner Jazz (J) LP: 81227-8708-1, Atlantic CD: SD-1305-2, Rhino CD: R2-75205, Rhino CD: R2-72871, Warner Jazz CD: 3617, Atlantic (Eu) CD: 81227-3617-2, Atlantic (Ger) CD: 781-336-2, Atlantic (Ger) CD: 7567-81336-7, London (Eng) CD: CD-1305-2, Avid (Eng) CD: AMSC-1026, Essential Jazz Classics (Sp) CD: EJC-55474, Essential Jazz Classics (Sp) CD: EJC-R2-72871.

-i on Atlantic LP: KSD-1305, Atlantic LP: SD-1555, Atlantic LP: SD2-316, Wax Time LP: 771680, Atlantic (Ger) LP: ATL-60143, Atlantic (Ger) LP: ATL-50232, Curcio-I Grandi del Jazz (It) LP: GJ-74, Atlantic (Eng) LP: K-781-907-1, London (Eng) LP: LTZ-K15194, London (Eng) LP: SANK-6087, Warner Jazz (F) LP: 60039, Warner-Pioneer (J) LP: P-6999A, Warner Jazz (J) LP: 81227-8708-1, Atlantic CD: SD-1305-2, Atlantic CD: 8122-71257-2, Rhino CD: R2-75205, Rhino CD: R2-72871, Warner Jazz CD: 3617, Atlantic (Eu) CD: 81227-3617-2, Atlantic (Ger) CD: 781-336-2, Atlantic (Ger) CD: 7567-81336-7, Atlantic (Eng) CD: K-781-907-2, London (Eng) CD: CD-1305-2, Avid (Eng) CD: AMSC-1026, Essential Jazz Classics (Sp) CD: EJC-55474, Essential Jazz Classics (Sp) CD: EJC-R2-72871.

-j and -k are edited versions of -i. Both on Rhino CD: R2-75205.

Moanin' is different from the same title written by Bobby Timmons. The introduction to Mingus' version, as first stated by Adams, has been used widely as theme music on radio programs and in film, most recently in two documentaries: Michael Moore's *Bowling for Columbine* and Christian Charles' *Jerry Seinfeld: Comedian.*

In an interview with the author in 1988, Jimmy Knepper had the following to say about Adams' part on Moanin': "He played this riff for about four minutes and then played a solo. Playing something like that over and over again for four minutes and you're really whipped!"

According to Adams, in an interview with Peter Danson in *Coda,* "When I listened to [the album], I was astonished at how good the album sounded. There was so much confusion in the studio, it was difficult to believe that it was so well organized....[Moanin'] was one of those things that was just put together in the studio with Mingus singing out, 'You play this, you play that,' which means you had to play the God damn figure like an hour and a half. By the time we got around to making the actual recording, I was damn near on my knees."

According to Adams, in an interview with Mike Bloom in *Klacto,*

We went in to do that date with a band that had not worked together before. Several of us had worked with Charles in clubs at various times, but not that exact group. There was very little in the way of written music. Most of it was making things up and fitting them together. A lot of repetition went on before we got things started. Remember that phrase on Moanin' that I had to play over and over again—that ground bass figure? It starts out with me playing that phrase at the bottom of the horn, and then I just continue as other layers of horns are added. Then, on the out chorus, it starts with everybody and then it comes down to just me, so I've got to play that damn thing over and over again, really grinding it out—which, for a single performance, OK, but in a studio with about fifteen false starts?

According to historians Lewis Porter and Michael Fitzgerald, additional alternate tracks were likely destroyed in an Atlantic warehouse fire.

JERRY VALENTINE–STASCH
590205
5 February 1959, Van Gelder Studio, Hackensack NJ: Idrees Sulieman tp; Jerome Richardson as fl; Coleman Hawkins ts; Pepper Adams bs;

Ray Bryant p; Roy Gaines g; Wendell Marshall b; Walter Bolden dm;
Jerry Valentine arr.

a	1708	Stasch	Swingville LP: SVLP-2013
b	1709	Since I Fell for You	
c	1710	Roll 'em Pete	
d	1711	Trust in Me	
e	1712	**Skrouk**	
f	1713	**My Babe**	

-e on Prestige (Ger) LP: 0902117, Solar (Eu) CD: 4569873, Prestige
(Ger) CD: PRCD-11006-2, Prestige (Ger) CD: PRCD-24124-25.
    All tracks on Prestige (Ger) LP: 0902117, Solar (Eu) CD: 4569873,
Prestige (Ger) CD: PRCD-24124-25.
    See 560430 notes regarding Van Gelder's studio.

THELONIOUS MONK
590228
28 February 1959, Town Hall, New York: Donald Byrd tp; Eddie Bert tb;
Robert Northern frh; Jay McAllister tu; Phil Woods as; Charlie Rouse ts;
Pepper Adams bs; Thelonious Monk p; Sam Jones b; Arthur Taylor dm.

Rouse and rhythm section:

a	Blue Monk	Milestone LP: M-9115
b	Straight No Chaser	Milestone CD: MCD-9199-2
c	In Walked Bud	Milestone LP: M-9115
d	'Round Midnight	Riverside unissued
e	Rhythm-a-Ning	Milestone LP: M-9115

Full band:

f	Thelonious	Riverside LP: RLP-1138
g	Friday the 13th	Riverside LP: RLP-12-300
h	Monk's Mood	
i	Off Minor	
j	Crepescule with Nellie	
k	**Little Rootie Tootie**	Milestone (J) LP: VIJ-4032
m	**Little Rootie Tootie**	Riverside LP: RLP-12-300

-a on Riverside LP: R-022, Riverside LP: RIV-4006, Riverside LP:
RLP-300, Riverside LP: RS-3313, Riverside CD: RCD-30190-25, Riverside CD: 15RCD-022-2, Milestone CD: MCD-9199-2, Riverside (Eu)

LP: 673-022-1, Carrère (F) CD: 99-913, Essential Jazz Classics (Sp) CD: EJC-55525, Victor (J) LP: VIJ-5102/23, Victor (J) CD: VJD-25010/24.

-b on Riverside LP: R-022, Riverside LP: RIV-4006, Riverside LP: RLP-300, Riverside LP: RS-3313, Riverside CD: 15RCD-022-2, Riverside (Eu) LP: 673-022-1, Carrère (F) CD: 99-913, Victor (J) LP: VIJ-5102/23, Victor (J) CD: VJD-25010/24.

-c on Riverside LP: R-022, Riverside LP: RIV-4006, Riverside LP: RLP-300, Riverside LP: RS-3313, Riverside CD: 15RCD-022-2, Riverside CD: RCD-30190-25, Milestone CD: MCD-9199-2, Riverside (Eu) LP: 673-022-1, Carrère (F) CD: 99-913, Essential Jazz Classics (Sp) CD: EJC-55525, Victor (J) LP: VIJ-5102/23, Victor (J) CD: VJD-25010/24.

-d on Riverside LP: RLP-300, Riverside LP: RS-3313, Riverside (Eu) LP: 673-022-1.

-e on Riverside LP: R-022, Riverside LP: RIV-4006, Riverside LP: VDJ-1589, Riverside LP: RLP-300, Riverside LP: RS-3313, Riverside CD: 15RCD-022-2, Milestone CD: MCD-9199-2, Giants of Jazz CD: CD-53008, Riverside CD: RCD-30190-25, Riverside (Eu) LP: 673-022-1, Carrère (F) CD: 99-913, Bella Musica (It) CD: BM-CD31-4037, Melodiya (R) LP: M60-49407-004, Essential Jazz Classics (Sp) CD: EJC-55525, Victor (J) LP: VIJ-5102/23, Victor (J) CD: VJD-25010/24.

The complete take of -f is on Riverside LP: R-022, Riverside LP: RIV-4006, Riverside LP: RLP-300, Riverside LP: RS-3313, Milestone LP: M-9115, Carrère (F) LP: 68-146, Victor (J) LP: VIJ-4032, Victor (J) LP: VIJ-5102/23, Original Jazz Classics CD: OJCCD-135-2, Riverside CD: 15CD-022-2, Riverside CD: RCD-30190-25, Riverside (Eu) LP: 673-022-1, Carrère (F) CD: 99-913, Carrère (F) CD: CA-98-914, Carrère (F) CD: CD-022-2, Essential Jazz Classics (Sp) CD: EJC-55525, Riverside (J) CD: VICJ-41723, Victor (J) CD: VJD-25010/24. An abridged version is on Riverside LP: RLP-12-300, Riverside LP: RS-1138, Riverside LP: RS-3313, Milestone LP: M-47033, Original Jazz Classics LP: OJC-135, Riverside (Eu) LP: 673-022-1, Victor (J) LP: SMJ-6183, Riverside (J) CD: VICJ-41723. According to Eddie Bert, in a 1988 interview with the author, "the one that they put out on the album that was released first was just a short version, because [Monk] didn't like his chorus. Later on they put the whole thing out."

-g on Riverside LP: RLP-12-300, Riverside LP: R-022, Riverside LP: RIV-4006, Riverside LP: RLP-9-483/4, Riverside LP: RS-1138, Riverside LP: RLP-1138, Riverside LP: RS-3313. Milestone LP: M-47033, Original Jazz Classics LP: OJC-135, Riverside (Eu) LP: 673-022-1, Victor (J) LP: SMJ-6183, Victor (J) LP: VIJ-5102/23, Original Jazz

Classics CD: OJCCD-135-2, Riverside CD: 15RCD-022-2, Riverside
CD: RCD-30190-25, Carrère (F) CD: CD-022-2, Carrère (F) CD: CA-
98-914, Carrère (F) CD: 99-913, Essential Jazz Classics (Sp) CD: EJC-
55525, Riverside (J) CD: VICJ-41723, Victor (J) CD: VJD-25010/24.

-h on Riverside LP: RLP-12-300, Riverside LP: RS-3313, Riverside
LP: RS-1138, Riverside LP: RLP-1138, Riverside LP: RS-3037, River-
side LP: RLP-3503, Riverside LP: RLP-93503, Riverside LP: R-022,
Riverside LP: RIV-4006, Milestone LP: M-47033, Original Jazz Classics
LP: OJC-135, Riverside (Eu) LP: 673-022, Victor (J) LP: VIJ-5102/23,
Victor (J) LP: SMJ-6183, Original Jazz Classics CD: OJCCD-135-2,
Riverside CD: 15CD-022-2, Riverside CD: RCD-30190-25, Riverside
(Eu) LP: 673-022-1, Carrère (F) CD: CD-022-2, Carrère (F) CD: 99-913,
Carrère (F) CD: CA-98-914, Essential Jazz Classics (Sp) CD: EJC-
55525, Riverside (J) CD: VICJ-41723, Victor (J) CD: VJD-25010/24.

-i on Riverside LP: RLP-12-300, Riverside LP: RLP-9-3503, River-
side LP: SR-7941, Riverside LP: RS-1138, Riverside LP: RLP-1138,
Riverside LP: RS-3313, Riverside LP: R-022, Riverside LP: RIV-4006,
Milestone LP: M-47033, Original Jazz Classics LP: OJC-135, Victor (J)
LP: VIJ-5102/23, Original Jazz Classics CD: OJCCD-135-2, Riverside
CD: 15RCD-022-2, Riverside CD: RCD-30190-25, Riverside (Eu) LP:
673-022-1, Carrère (F) CD: CD-022-2, Carrère (F) CD: 99-913, Carrère
(F) CD: CA-98-914, Essential Jazz Classics (Sp) CD: EJC-55525, River-
side (J) CD: VICJ-41723, Victor (J) CD: VJD-25010/24.

-j on Riverside LP: RLP-1138, Riverside LP: R-022, Riverside LP:
RIV-4006, Milestone LP: M-47033, Warner-Pioneer (J) LP: 15646-2,
Victor (J) LP: VIJ-5102/23, Riverside CD: 15CD-022-2, Riverside CD:
RCD-30190-25, Original Jazz Classics CD: OJCCD-135-2, Carrère (F)
CD: CD-022-2, Carrère (F) CD: 99-913, Carrère (F) CD: CA-98-914,
Essential Jazz Classics (Sp) CD: EJC-55525, Riverside (J) CD: VICJ-
41723, Victor (J) CD: VJD-25010/24.

-k on Riverside LP: RLP-300, Riverside LP: RS-3313, Riverside LP:
RLP-421, Riverside LP: RLP-9421, Riverside LP: R-022, Riverside LP:
RIV-4006, Riverside LP: RS-1138, Riverside LP: RLP-1138, Riverside
LP: RS-3047, Milestone LP: M-47033, Milestone LP: M-47064, Original
Jazz Classics LP: OJC-135, Franklin Mint LP: FM-27, Riverside (Eu)
LP: 673-022-1, Philips (Ger) LP: P-14701, Victor (J) LP: SMJ-6183,
Victor (J) LP: VIJ-4032, Victor (J) LP: VIJ-5102/23, Riverside CD:
RCD-30190-25, Riverside CD: 15CD-022-2, Milestone CD: MCD-
47064-2, Original Jazz Classics CD: OJCCD-135-2, Riverside (Ger) CD:
FCD-60-018, Carrère (F) CD: CD-022-2, Carrère (F) CD: 99-913, Car-

rère (F) CD: CA-98-914, Essential Jazz Classics (Sp) CD: EJC-55525, Riverside (J) CD: VICJ-41723, Victor (J) CD: VJD-25010/24. According to Orrin Keepnews, in Robert Palmer's liner notes to Milestone LP: M-47033, "The intro and the first few bars were lost" because of miscommunication between Monk and the engineers when changing reels of tape. To correct this, the band played an encore (-m) and the theme from -m was spliced onto the beginning of -k and used as -k's theme.

About Adams' solo on -k, photographer Herb Snitzer, in an interview with the author in 1989, said,

> He was swinging and the crowd was clapping. It was really electric! At the end of the concert, when they finished the last piece, somebody came out on stage and asked everybody to stick around because they were going to do Little Rootie Tootie again [track -m]; that something happened with the machine, it malfunctioned, and they have to redo it. And, so, they did it again and Pepper blew again, but, in my mind, it was *nowhere* as wonderful as the first time that he did it….I remember the sense that he was just so much more intricate. The solo just seemed so much more developed the first time around, and much more powerful. It was like the way that Coltrane would start and, then, the next thing you know, he's into six different philosophical attitudes.

-m on Milestone LP: M-47033, Milestone LP: M-47064, Milestone CD: MCD-47064-3, Original Jazz Classics CD: OJCCD-135-2, Riverside CD: 15CD-022-2, Riverside CD: RCD-30190-25, Riverside (Ger) CD: FCD-60-018, Carrère (F) CD: CD-022-2, Carrère (F) CD: CA-98-914, Riverside (J) CD: VICJ-41723.

According to photographer Herb Snitzer, in an interview with the author in 1989,

> The thing that I remember the most was that the band was really up, and Monk was up. They were all very excited about being together as a group and playing at Town Hall, because, in those days, Town Hall…was a very important gig for a musician. If a new musician came on the scene, that musician would be either at the Village Vanguard or at the Five Spot, and then the next big statement would be whether that person could fill Town Hall. And so, Town Hall was very important in terms of an aspiring musician of any kind— classical or jazz. It was filled that night and everybody was excited….It wasn't just the in-circle of jazz devotees. People were be-

ginning to realize that this guy is really good and inventive. The thing that I liked about it, because of my own personal interest in civil rights issues, is that it was an integrated band. Still, by 1959, there was a lot of resentment on the part of blacks about the advantages that white musicians had over them at that particular time and that era. There were many, many racial incidents that were occurring within the area of jazz that people don't really talk about very much....The band played really super and the crowd was very responsive.

According to historian Dan Morgenstern, in an interview with the author in 2005,

There was a wonderful moment when Monk—he didn't mean to—completely upstaged my dear, old friend, Martin Williams, who was emceeing. Martin was saying something between numbers, and Monk, sitting at the piano while Martin was talking, got up very slowly. (He was a large man. Definitely, when he moved around, people would look at him.) There was a towel in the back of the piano, so he walked around and got to the towel, and, then, very slowly, he unfolded the towel and starting mopping his head and his face, and it *completely* upstaged poor Martin. Everybody was just digging Monk and the towel! The musicians, of course, were noticing that and were all laughing.

On a 27 April 1977 Toronto radio interview that was conducted by Ted O'Reilly, Pepper Adams discussed the date:

We had three or four rehearsals. [Monk] was very pleased and very serious about the whole thing and we had a number of bookings for the band as well: college concerts, we had a whole tour set up.... The reviews were absolutely atrocious. The reviews just put the band away to such an extent that the concert tour was cancelled. We only performed one time again as a band, at the Randall's Island Jazz Festival almost two years later. It's considered now, I gather, to be one of the classic, watershed, great recordings. That seems to be the general opinion. However, the critical opinion at the time of the concert was that it was atrocious; that Monk's music should not be approached and performed in this manner.

On a 1986 NPR radio interview that was conducted by Ben Sidran, Pepper Adams discussed the date again:

When we were rehearsing for the concert, there was talk— in fact, it was supposed to be definite—that a concert tour of about three weeks had been set up for the group that was to begin something like four weeks after the concert. We're to do the Town Hall concert, have three or four weeks, add some more pieces to the repertoire, have further rehearsals—paid for—and then go on this tour of concerts, primarily colleges, I believe. That was the whole theory, and that, in fact, was part of the package that I was approached with initially, when I was asked to play in this band for Town Hall, which sounded fine. It was certainly enjoyable. The rehearsals were just great! We had a lot of fun! We go on, play the concert, and the immediate reviews that we received were so bad that all of the rest of the concerts were cancelled.

Actually, my basic memory of the situation was that it was a case of the immediate reaction being bad, that is in the New York daily press, or weekly press as in [the] *Village Voice,* which, I believe, would have been Nat Hentoff in those days. However, the *New York Times,* for Monday, 2 March '59:...There is mention of some of the titles that the ten-piece band played....Then it says, "Mr. Monk's determination to impose his musical personality on his musicians, and the surging, sweaty efforts of the musicians to wrestle with Mr. Monk's music, give the discs a raw excitement,"—he's speaking of previous Monk recordings with a smaller group—he says, "but none of this could be found in the bland, workaday performances of the large group with which Mr. Monk played Saturday evening. The arrangements smoothed out the characteristically Monkian lumps and bumps, diluted his tartness, and robbed the works of their zest. It was a pipe-and-slippers version of music that is naturally querulous. John S. Wilson."

In a 1984 interview with the author, Adams said,

It was a terrific band. It was marvelous. Thelonious had a little swell of popularity there, and so they started setting up this band [for] the concert, people got excited, and they had a tour booked of concerts and colleges, and things like that, supposed to be all set, supposed to keep us busy for about four months. Then we did the concert at Town Hall and the reviews came out, and the reviews were so horrible that everyone cancelled on the concert tour. And then about six or eight months later the record came out and pretty soon it starts being considered a classic recording, you know! Now it has a very high critical reputation. At the time, however, the critics thought it was really awful.

According to Monk's son, T.S. Monk, in the booklet for the Essential Jazz Classics reissue, "The Town Hall concert was really the kick-off for what was going to be a tour. I think it was an eight-city tour, that never occurred, because the reviews were so bad, Riverside got scared."

Eddie Bert, in an interview in 1988 with the author, said, "I really don't know the plans, because there was no itinerary given out or anything like that, but we were supposed to tour and nothing happened."

BENNY GOODMAN–SWING INTO SPRING
590410

10 April 1959, TV broadcast, CBS Studio, New York: John Frosk, Buck Clayton, Irwin Berger, Allen Smith tp; Urbie Green, Hale Rood, Buster Cooper tb; Bennie Goodman cl, voc; Gerald Sanfino, Hymie Shertzer as; Arthur Clarke, Herb Geller ts; Pepper Adams bs; Hank Jones p; Kenny Burrell g; Jack Lesberg b; Shelly Manne, Roy Burnes dm; Phil Kraus perc; vocal choir; CBS studio orchestra; Dave Garroway host; GUESTS: Andre Previn p; Lionel Hampton vib; Ella Fitzgerald*, Peggy Lee†, Donna Musgrove, The Hi-Los voc.

a	Let's Dance[1]	A&R LP: 2000
b	Swing into Spring[2]	
c	Medley[3]:	
	'S Wonderful*	
	Things Are Swingin†	
	'S Wonderful*†	
d	Concertina for Clarinet[4]	
e	Bach Goes to Town[5]	
f	Swing Low, Sweet Clarinet[6]	
g	Air Mail Special[7]	A&R LP: 2001
h	Why Don't You Do Right†[8]	
i	Like Young[9]	A&R unissued
j	Mountain Greenery*[10]	A&R LP: 2001
k	Ah! Men, Ah! Women*†[11]	A&R LP: 2000
m	I Must Have that Man*[12]	
n	Medley[13]:	
	'Sweet Georgia Brown	
	I'm Just Wild about Harry†	
	Sweet Lorraine	

The Gentleman Is a Dope[*]
When a Woman Loves a Man[†]
The Glory of Love[*][†]

o   Medley[14]:   A&R LP: 2001
Let's Dance
A String of Pearls
Goody Goody[15]
You Turned the Tables on Me[16]
One O'Clock Jump

p   Swing into Spring[*][†][17]
q   's Wonderful[18]
r   Goodbye[19]
s   Swing into Spring[20]

[1]Full Goodman band.
[2]Vocal choir only.
[3]Vocalists are accompanied by a quintet of Goodman, Hampton, Previn, Lesberg, and Burnes.
[4]Goodman and studio orchestra perform the Adagio and Andante from Weber's Concertino, Opus 26.
[5]Full Goodman band.
[6]Vocal chorus with Goodman band.
[7]Goodman, Hampton, Previn, Lesberg, and Burnes.
[8]Full Goodman band with Peggy Lee.
[9]Previn and vocal chorus.
[10]Goodman band and Fitzgerald.
[11]Goodman, Fitzgerald, Lee on vocals, with Previn p.
[12]Fitzgerald, with Goodman, Previn, Lesberg, Burnes.
[13]Goodman, Hampton, Previn, Lesberg, and Burnes. Goodman sings on first, third, and final tune.
[14]Full Goodman band.
[15]Hi-Los feature.
[16]Hi-Los feature with Musgrove.
[17]Full band, Fitzgerald, Lee, Hi-Los, and chorus.
[18]Full band, Fitzgerald, Lee, Hi-Los, and chorus.
[19]Full Goodman band.
[20]Full Goodman band.

The original reference recording of part of this live broadcast was produced by Texaco and pressed as a private, 12-inch LP by Columbia, without a record number. Much of the audio was much later released by

A&R, and the TV show was released on VHS by Nostalgia Family and on DVD by Jazz Legends.

-c on Giants of Jazz LP: COJ-1011.

BENNY GOODMAN
590417

17 April 1959, privately recorded rehearsal, New York: Taft Jordan tp, unknown tp section; Rex Peer tb, unknown tb section; Bennie Goodman cl; Herb Geller, Bob Wilber as; Buddy Tate ts; unknown ts; Pepper Adams bs, bcl; Hank Jones p; Turk Van Lake g; Scott LaFaro b; Roy Burnes dm; Donna Musgrove voc.

a   Mission to Moscow
b   Bach Goes to Town
c   Clarinet à la King
d   Clarinet à la King
e   Clarinet à la King

This was a rehearsal for Goodman's upcoming three-week tour of the U.S. and Canada. Dakota Staton and the Ahmad Jamal trio were traveling as part of the tour.

Bob Wilber told the author, in a 1989 interview, that Pepper Adams borrowed Wilber's bass clarinet to play the bass clarinet parts that were part of the Goodman baritone saxophone book.

DONALD BYRD–BYRD IN HAND
590531

31 May 1959, Van Gelder Studio, Hackensack NJ: Donald Byrd tp; Charlie Rouse ts; Pepper Adams bs; Walter Davis Jr. p; Sam Jones b; Arthur Taylor dm.

a   **Witchcraft**   Blue Note LP: BLP-4019
b   **Here Am I**
c   **Devil Whip**
d   **Bronze Dance**
e   **Clarion Calls**
f   **The Injuns**

-a on Blue Note LP: BLP-4019, Blue Note LP: BST-84019, Blue Note [45rpm] LP: LMM-4019, Toshiba-EMI (J) LP: ICJ-80093, Blue

Note CD: CDP-7243-5-42305-2-3, Mosaic CD: MD4-194, Poll Winners CD: PWR-27250, Blue Note CD: CDBN-7-84019-2, Blue Note CD: B21Y-84019, Blue Note CD: 42305, Blue Note CD: CDP-7-84019-2, Blue Note (Eng) CD: BNZ-165, Toshiba-EMI (J) CD: BNJ-71070, Toshiba-EMI (J) CD: TOCJ-4019.

-b on Blue Note 45: BN 45-1763, Blue Note LP: BLP-4019, Blue Note LP: BST-84019, Blue Note [45rpm] LP: LMM-4019, Toshiba-EMI (J) LP: ICJ-80093, Blue Note CD: CDP-7243-5-42305-2-3, Mosaic CD: MD4-194, Poll Winners CD: PWR-27250, Blue Note CD: CDBN-7-84019-2, Blue Note CD: B21Y-84019, Blue Note CD: 42305, Blue Note CD: CDP-7-84019-2, Blue Note (Eng) CD: BNZ-165, Toshiba-EMI (J) CD: BNJ-71070, Toshiba-EMI (J) CD: TOCJ-4019.

-c on Blue Note LP: BLP-4019, Blue Note LP: BST-84019, Blue Note [45rpm] LP: LMM-4019, Toshiba-EMI (J) LP: ICJ-80093, Blue Note CD: CDP-7243-5-42305-2-3, Mosaic CD: MD4-194, Poll Winners CD: PWR-27250, Blue Note CD: CDBN-7-84019-2, Blue Note CD: B21Y-84019, Blue Note CD: 42305, Blue Note CD: CDP-7-84019-2, Blue Note (Eng) CD: BNZ-165, Toshiba-EMI (J) CD: BNJ-71070, Toshiba-EMI (J) CD: TOCJ-4019.

-d on Blue Note LP: BLP-4019, Blue Note LP: BST-84019, Blue Note [45rpm] LP: LMM-4019, Toshiba-EMI (J) LP: ICJ-80093, Blue Note CD: CDP-7243-5-42305-2-3, Mosaic CD: MD4-194, Poll Winners CD: PWR-27250, Blue Note CD: CDBN-7-84019-2, Blue Note CD: B21Y-84019, Blue Note CD: 42305, Blue Note CD: CDP-7-84019-2, Blue Note (Eng) CD: BNZ-165, Toshiba-EMI (J) CD: BNJ-71070, Toshiba-EMI (J) CD: TOCJ-4019.

-e on Blue Note LP: BLP-4019, Blue Note LP: BST-84019, Blue Note [45rpm] LP: LMM-4019, Toshiba-EMI (J) LP: ICJ-80093, Blue Note CD: CDP-7243-5-42305-2-3, Mosaic CD: MD4-194, Poll Winners CD: PWR-27250, Blue Note CD: CDBN-7-84019-2, Blue Note CD: B21Y-84019, Blue Note CD: 42305, Blue Note CD: CDP-7-84019-2, Blue Note (Eng) CD: BNZ-165, Toshiba-EMI (J) CD: BNJ-71070, Toshiba-EMI (J) CD: TOCJ-4019.

-f on Blue Note LP: BLP-4019, Blue Note LP: BST-84019, Blue Note [45rpm] LP: LMM-4019, Blue Note (Neth) LP: 1A158-83391/4, Toshiba-EMI (J) LP: ICJ-80093, Blue Note CD: CDP-7243-5-42305-2-3, Mosaic CD: MD4-194, Poll Winners CD: PWR-27250, Blue Note CD: CDBN-7-84019-2, Blue Note CD: B21Y-84019, Blue Note CD: 42305, Blue Note CD: CDP-7-84019-2, Blue Note (Eng) CD: BNZ-165, Toshiba-EMI (J) CD: BNJ-71070, Toshiba-EMI (J) CD: TOCJ-4019.

At least 16 takes were done at this session.

See Adams' comment on 581221 for an explanation as to who led the working band.

See 560430 notes regarding Van Gelder's studio.

CHET BAKER–PLAYS THE BEST OF LERNER AND LOEWE 590721

21 July 1959, Reeves Sound Studios, New York: Chet Baker tp; Zoot Sims as, ts; Herbie Mann ts*, fl; Pepper Adams bs; Bob Corwin p; Earl May b; Clifford Jarvis dm.

a   The Heather on The Hill   Riverside LP: RLP-12-307
b   I've Grown Accustomed to Her Face
c   **On the Street Where You Live**
d   **Almost Like Being in Love**[*]

All tracks on Fantasy LP: 1152, Original Jazz Classics CD: 201372, Riverside CD: 1152, Jazzland CD: 9020470162, Riverside CD: 12307, Fantasy CD: RIVCD-1152, Universal (J) CD: UCCO-9295, JVC (J) CD: 41327.

CHET BAKER–PLAYS THE BEST OF LERNER AND LOEWE 590722

22 July 1959, Reeves Sound Studios, New York: Same as 21 July 1959, except Bill Evans p replaces Corwin; Mann on ts only:

a   I Could Have Danced All Night   Riverside LP: RLP-12-307
b   I Talk to the Trees
c   **Show Me**[1]
d   Thank Heaven for Little Girls[2]

[1]Baker, Adams, and rhythm section.
[2]Baker, Sims, and rhythm section.

All tracks on Fantasy LP: 1152, Original Jazz Classics CD: 201372, Riverside CD: 1152, Jazzland CD: 9020470162, Riverside CD: 12307, Fantasy CD: RIVCD-1152, Universal (J) CD: UCCO-9295, JVC (J) CD: 41327.

PHILLY JOE JONES
591117
17 November 1959, Reeves Sound Studios, New York: Blue Mitchell tp;
Julian Priester tb; Bill Barron ts; Pepper Adams bs; Dolo Coker p; Jimmy
Garrison b; Philly Joe Jones p, dm.

a   **Battery Blues**   Riverside LP: RLP-12-313
b   **Julia**
c   **I'll Never Be the Same**
     Rhythm section only; Philly Joe Jones (on overdubbed piano) re-
     places Coker:
d   Gwen

-a on Riverside LP: RSLP-1159, Milestone LP: M-47016, Original
Jazz Classics LP: OJC-484, Carrère (F) LP: CA-68-129, Riverside-
Carrère (F) LP: CA-68-964, Victor (J) LP: SMJ-6193, Milestone CD:
MCD-47016, Original Jazz Classics CD: OJCCD-484-2.
-b on Riverside LP: RSLP-1159, Original Jazz Classics LP: OJC-
484, Riverside-Carrère (F) LP: CA-68-964, Victor (J) LP: SMJ-6193,
Original Jazz Classics CD: OJCCD-484-2.
-c on Riverside LP: RSLP-1159, Original Jazz Classics LP: OJC-
484, Riverside-Carrère (F) LP: CA-68-964, Victor (J) LP: SMJ-
6193,Original Jazz Classics CD: OJCCD-484-2.
-d on Riverside LP: RSLP-1159, Original Jazz Classics LP: OJC-
484, Riverside-Carrère (F) LP: CA-68-964, Victor (J) LP: SMJ-6193,
Original Jazz Classics CD: OJCCD-484-2.

PHILLY JOE JONES
591118
18 November 1959, Reeves Sound Studios, New York: Same as 17 November, except omit Mitchell:

a   **Gone**   Riverside LP: RLP-12-313
     Priester, Barron, and rhythm section:
b   Joe's Delight
c   Joe's Debut

-a on Riverside LP: RSLP-1159, Milestone LP: M-47016, Original
Jazz Classics LP: OJC-484, Carrère (F) LP: CA-68-129, Riverside-

Carrère (F) LP: CA-68-964, Victor (J) LP: SMJ-6193, Milestone CD: MCD-47016, Original Jazz Classics CD: OJCCD-484-2.

-b on Riverside LP: RSLP-1159, Original Jazz Classics LP: OJC-484, Riverside-Carrère (F) LP: CA-68-964, Victor (J) LP: SMJ-6193, Original Jazz Classics CD: OJCCD-484-2.

-c on Riverside LP: RSLP-1159, Original Jazz Classics LP: OJC-484, Riverside-Carrère (F) LP: CA-68-964, Victor (J) LP: SMJ-6193, Original Jazz Classics CD: OJCCD-484-2.

PEPPER ADAMS
591200
c. December 1959, New York: Pepper Adams bs; Tommy Flanagan p; George Duvivier b; Dannie Richmond dm.

Possibly recorded by Stinson. According to Adams' friend Len Dobbin, Adams did this session in late 1959-early 1960 and brought the proposed album cover (with a band photograph on it) with him to the Little Vienna in Montreal, where he was playing an engagement. *See* 600513. This is Adams' sixth date as a leader.

SIXTH AVENUE LOFT JAM SESSION
591224
24 December 1959, Eugene Smith's loft, New York: Jerry Lloyd tp; Zoot Sims ts; Pepper Adams bs, p*; Mose Allison, Dave McKenna, Bob Brookmeyer p; Jim Hall g; Bill Takas, Bill Crow b; Jerry Segal dm.

a	**This Can't Be Love**[1]	Jazz Magnet CD: JAM-2002
b	**Stomping at the Savoy**[2]	
c	**Groovin' High**[3]	
d	Zoot and Drums[4]	
e	821 Blues[5]	
f	When the Sun Comes Out[6]	
g	I'll Remember April*[7]	Jazz Magnet unissued

[1]Lloyd, Sims, Adams, with rhythm section (Alison, Takas, Segal)
[2]Lloyd, Sims, Adams, with rhythm section (Alison, Takas, Segal)
[3]Lloyd, Sims, Adams, with rhythm section (Alison, Takas, Segal)
[4]Duet for Sims and Segal.
[5]Sims and rhythm section (possibly Brookmeyer on piano, Takas, Segal).
[6]Sims and rhythm section (McKenna, Takas, Segal).
[7]Sims and rhythm section (Adams on piano, Hall, either Crow or Takas).

About -g, Sam Stephenson, the curator of the W. Eugene Smith collection at Duke University, wrote to the author in 1999:

> Pepper was there Christmas Eve, 1959 for a session with Zoot Sims, Mose Allison, Jerry Segal, Bill Crow, Bill Takas, Jim Hall, and a number of unidentified others. Mose had been trying to leave for hours, but everybody kept begging him to stay because he was the only piano player. Finally, Mose leaves amidst many audible complaints. Some noodling by the musicians ensues until they finally take up I'll Remember April, first as just a duo between Zoot and Hall, then with full band. After a few minutes it becomes clear that somebody is playing piano. After they complete the tune, Zoot says, "Hey, Pep, how'd you learn to play the piano like that? You are pretty good, man." Pep says, "It's just something I like to do every now and then. I get some enjoyment out of it. It's fun." Zoot: "Well, man, you aren't bad. Let's play another one." Pepper: "The only problem is that I only know three songs on piano and we already played two of them tonight." Zoot: "Well, let's play the other one you know."

This jam session was recorded by photographer W. Eugene Smith or painter David X. Young at their loft at 821 Sixth Avenue. Other titles, yet to be catalogued, are part of Smith's archive at Duke. In the mid-'50s Young rented some of his space to Hall Overton, who then, in 1957, sublet a portion of it to Smith. Smith took 20,000 photographs of the many Monday night jam sessions.

Douglas Martin, in his *New York Times* obituary of David X. Young, wrote of Smith and Young's

> rodent infested, illegally rented loft [that] became a citadel of jazz improvisation and experimentation in the 1950s and '60s....The loft, in an industrial building at 821 Avenue of the Americas [at that time called Sixth Avenue], near 28th Street, became a gathering place for the greats of jazz....Known simply as "the Sixth Avenue Loft," it was one of maybe a half-dozen places where musicians gathered....Situated in the heart of the flower district, it was the epicenter of what became known as loft jazz....There was no lock on the loft's front door, and it was considered bad form to arrive before 11 p.m. There always seemed to be many pretty women present, and ample bourbon and marijuana. It was a spot where Salvador Dali, Norman Mailer, or Willem de Kooning might show up, entourage in tow...."The place was desolate, really awful," Young said in

Double Take. "The buildings on both sides were vacant. There were mice, rats and cockroaches all over. You had to keep cats around to fend them off. Conditions were beyond miserable. No plumbing, no heat, no toilet, no electricity, no nothing." With $300 and some instruction from his grandfather, he made the place livable. Because occupying an industrial building was illegal, he bribed a building inspector with $75 each Christmas, he said, and kept big plywood boxes over the beds to hide them.

TONY ARGO–JAZZ ARGOSY
600000
c. 1960, Van Gelder Studio, Englewood Cliffs NJ: Ernie Royal tp; Frank Rehak tb; Jim Buffington frh; Bill Barber tu; Hal McKusick as, ts, fl, piccolo, cl; Pepper Adams bs, cl; Tony Argo p, accordion; Joe Cinderella g; Bill Phillips b; Charli Persip dm.

a   'Round Midnight   Savoy LP: MG-12157
b   Gypsy in My Soul
c   Lover Man
d   **Sixpence**
e   **Walkin'**
f   Laura
g   **Half Nelson**
h   Serenade in Blue

According to the arranger of the date, Joe Cinderella, in a conversation with the author in 1988,

> I just called the guys up and they came in and sight-read what we had to do. We did the best we could. I wasn't too happy with the recording, as I think back now. A lot was lost. I'm not talking about Tony Argo's performance, I'm talking about Rudy's performance....I had things in there for piccolo and flute that you don't even hear on the date. I hate to put Rudy down. You know what my sentiments always were about Rudy Van Gelder? With a rhythm section and two horns, he was excellent. As soon as you start bringing in a small band or big band, he just didn't have it, as far as I'm concerned. That was something I was a little unhappy about, but Pepper sounded great on the thing.

In a 1988 interview with the author, Tony Argo explained his approach for the date:

> What I was trying to do with the accordion was the thing that got us together, actually, because there were some excellent jazz accordionists that were on the scene, but they really weren't playing jazz as we played it....It was more of a Benny Goodman kind of jazz, those type of clichés. It wasn't searching. It was sort of a premeditated kind of jazz, if that's possible. With the accordion, I played more like a horn. I was taking breaths in my choruses. I would try to think like a horn player, so the uniqueness of doing that was something that got us together to try to do an album. When I did that album, I was a little bit inhibited because I realized halfway through the session that I wasn't on a separate track, so certain things were coming out, like where the guitar was on the track with me. It was too loud, and I couldn't get him down, and stuff like that. The only tracks that I thought were really excellent balances were the ballads. Aside from that, I think that Pepper was the outstanding soloist on the whole album. I really think so. Oh, just exceptional! He's so forceful, no matter what the situation is, he can go right through it....
>
>   The accordion is such a love of mine, and I'm trying to get over the hump of having it accepted. One of the reasons I did it with the prominent horn players was to look at the accordion in the capacity of the horn, doing what a horn can do. What I did [that] was a mistake, I think, was that...I'm laying back, waiting for my chorus, which really didn't give me a chance to get into what the accordion can do, because you can either play the chord style or the single note style....Not to put Rudy down, but, in retrospect, the balance that was set for the ballads was ideal. It was perfect. What happened is he didn't bring up my volume when we were playing the swinging tunes. The worst part of it is that I couldn't play with the relaxation that I did on the ballads, and, once you start messing with your anatomy, and trying to play hard, it just screws the whole thing up.

OLIVER SHEARER
600100
January 1960, possibly Columbia 30th Street Studio, New York: Buck Clayton tp; Bernard McKinney euphonium; Jackie McLean as; Bill Barron ts, fl; Pepper Adams bs; Tommy Flanagan p; Kenny Burrell g; Oliver Shearer vib, perc; Doug Watkins b; Elvin Jones dm.

a   64668   This Land, Part 1   Columbia unissued

b		This Land, Part 1
c		This Land, Part 1
d		This Land, Part 1
e		This Land, Part 1
f		This Land, Part 1
g		This Land, Part 1
h		This Land, Part 1
i		This Land, Part 1
j		This Land, Part 1
k		This Land, Part 2

Clayton, McLean, Burrell out:

m	64669	**This Land, Part 2**
n		This Land, Part 2
o		**This Land, Part 2**
p		This Land, Part 2
q		This Land, Part 2
r		**This Land, Part 2**
s		Shed Some Light
t		Shed Some Light
u		Shed Some Light
v		Shed Some Light

-a through -k were issued matrix number 64668; -m through -v were issued matrix number 64669.

In a 1988 interview with the author, Oliver Shearer said,

John Hammond was discovering me like he did George Benson. He liked my voice: "If everybody had one tenth of your talent, I'd be satisfied." He wanted me to do [a] Johnny Mathis, but I surprised him, and I said, "Look, I'll do one side vocal and one side instrumental." (*See* 600700 for the vocal date.) Bill Barron played beautifully. I didn't even know Bill Barron was going to be on the date. [I] was [expecting] Benny Golson...and Benny Golson sent Bill Barron—the first time I ever saw Bill Barron. I was a little bit perturbed because John Hammond was so finicky, man. He was already mad enough that he was giving me the date to sing, and I'm bringing in all these cats. Doug [Watkins] showed up a half hour late, and Elvin had to leave at five, and it was my first date! It was pandemonium in there. Pepper sat up all night to help me write out an arrangement...on Shed Some Light. He wrote the arrangement on this thing because the shit that I had written was so fucked up.

Pepper said, "Oh, man, this is all wrong!" It was kind of spacey. This came out of a Russian traditional hymn that swung.... [Hammond] was discovering me. When you get one of those guys that are discovering you, you're supposed to just bow down. He told Kenny later on, "I'm just trying to make him some money." I just didn't have sense enough to go along with his program. I was shocked out of my wits that he would get me in Columbia. This was before any of the other guys, like Tommy or Kenny. Why me? I didn't even go out after it. Ahmad Jamal's guys got me the date with John Hammond. They just played a tape of me singing one song with them, and, bang, then all of a sudden, here I was. So instead of me going to Kenny and them and saying, "Well, let's get this date together," I said, "Well, shit, I'm going to go in there and do my instrumental"....I didn't know what I was doing. I was just getting ready [to study music.] So before I dared to tell John I wanted to do it, I took it by Miles. I let Miles hear it. Miles liked it. I took it over to Coltrane....Miles told me my song was pretty and Trane played on it. Then I had this idea of the two horns—the lower horns with euphonium and baritone—and the tenor in between, and it worked. And Jackie McLean on the slow one, it was like another Charlie Parker.

Bernard McKinney changed his professional name to Kiane Zawadi in the late 1960s.
See also 600701.

URBIE GREEN
600200
February 1960, Fine Recording, New York: Nick Travis, John Bello, Don Ferrara, Doc Severinsen tp; Urbie Green, Bobby Byrne tb; Gil Cohen btb; Hal McKusick as; Rolf Kuhn as, cl; Ed Wasserman ts, fl; Pepper Adams bs; Dave McKenna p; Barry Galbraith g; Milt Hinton b; Don Lamond dm.

a   At Last   Command LP: RS-815-SD
b   Prisoner of Love
c   Dream
d   Moonlight Serenade

All tracks on Lone Hill (Sp) CD: LHJ-10308.

According to writer Marc Myers, Command was one of the first record companies to market their recordings to audiophiles. To improve sound fidelity, and stand out among the competition, Command used 35mm film, instead of magnetic tape, for their masters.

TEDDY CHARLES
600400
Spring 1960, Bell Sound Studios, New York: Donald Byrd tp; Pepper Adams bs; Bill Evans p; Paul Chambers b; Philly Joe Jones dm; Earl Zindars timpani, perc; Teddy Charles producer.

a   Prophecy   Warwick LP: W-5003-ST
b   **Ping Pong Beer**
c   Quiet Temple

This stereo concept album featured various percussion instruments that moved from speaker to speaker. Teddy Charles ran Warwick Records.
  -a on Alomar LP: AS-110, TCB LP: 1004, Fresh Sound (Sp) LP: FSR-640, Century (J) LP: 20ED-5017, Collectables CD: COL-CD-6132, Fresh Sound (Swiss) CD: FSR-CD-210.
  -b on Warwick 45: M-663, TCB LP: 1004, Fresh Sound (Sp) LP: FSR-640, Century (J) LP: 20ED-5017, Collectables CD: COL-CD-6132, Fresh Sound (Swiss) CD: FSR-CD-210.
  -c on TCB LP: 1004, Fresh Sound (Sp) LP: FSR-640, Century (J) LP: 20ED-5017, Collectables CD: COL-CD-6132, Fresh Sound (Swiss) CD: FSR-CD-210.

TONY ZANO–THE GATHERING PLACE
600427
27 April 1960, Plaza Sound Studios, New York: Burt Collins, Jerry Tyree, Rick Kiefer, Chet Ferretti tp; Eddie Bert, Frank Rehak, Curtis Fuller tb; Mike Zwerin vtb; Bill Barber tu; Charlie Mariano, Vinnie Dean as; Dick Hafer, Frank Socolow ts; Pepper Adams bs; Tommy Flanagan p; Sal Salvador g; Paul Chambers b; Charli Persip dm; Tony Zano arr.

a   I Got Rhythm   Balmore LP: SL-381
b   They Can't Take that Away from Me
c   Ballad for Dee

TONY ZANO–THE GATHERING PLACE
600428
28 April 1960, New York: Same as 27 April 1960, except add Jean Purretta voc*, and Bill Elton tb replaces Rehak:

a	To a Certain Miss	Balmore LP: SL-381
b	Loss	
c	Gathering Place	
d	It Ain't Necessarily So*	Balmore unissued
e	What Fool Sensation*	
f	Why Must This Be Love*	

PEPPER ADAMS
600513
13 May 1960, private recording, Little Vienna, Montreal: Pepper Adams bs; Keith White p; Stan Zadak b; Billy Barwick dm.

a **Bluesology**
b **Scrapple from the Apple**
c **What's New**
d **'Tis**
e **Woody 'n You**
f **Moment's Notice**
g **Stablemates**
h **Lover Man**

According to Keith White, in a 1987 interview with the author,

I ran into Mr. [Frank] Nash. He wanted me to be the house piano player at his Little Vienna Restaurant, a small coffee house on Stanley Street, across from the YMCA. I didn't really want to, because I was too busy, but, anyway, he talked me into it. At first he wanted me to do the booking, then he wanted me to play the piano. I tried to get Mobley. I tried to get a whole bunch of people. Pepper was the only guy that was available. The reason that I thought of him, since he wasn't really a big name at the time, was from a guy by the name of Jerry Taylor, who was a [Canadian] drummer and had tipped me off about this guy that he played with once in Montreal in 1958. I was corresponding with [Jerrry] because I was living in Miami previous to this in 1958, and he was raving about this guy on baritone:

that this guy was "the greatest!" and everything. So I thought of him, you see, from [Jerry's] praise.

I got [Pepper] to come up and play for the weekend [Friday-Sunday, 6-8 May 1960], and he came up on the train. Actually, I had gotten him for Art Roberts to play with, because Art was supposed to be playing the piano, as I recall, and then Art bowed out. I can't remember why, but I know he didn't want to make the gig, so I came down to do the gig, and I didn't know what to expect. You see, I didn't know this guy at all. I walk in, and here's this guy, and he's immaculately attired. He was in a suit, with a bow tie, and all this. I couldn't believe it! For a jazz gig, especially at the Little Vienna? And I came in and I didn't have any socks on. You know, my usual attire, and he started to chastise me because he wanted to know how come I came to a job looking like this. I said, "Man, this is the Little Vienna, not the Waldorf Astoria!" I thought he was kidding at first, but he wasn't. He was quite serious. He took the job very seriously. So I thought, "Who's this guy?" Anyway, when I started to play with him, I could see that he was a "monster," a giant. The first night we sort of got to know each other a little bit. The second night—he liked to drink. I could drink a little bit in those days too, but I couldn't keep up with him. He'd have three glasses to my one, and then be ready for three more!

The first weekend went very successfully and Mr. Nash was very pleased. He was jumping up and down. "Hey, that man is very good on the horn!" he said. "We must have him again!" Anyway, I tried to get Mobley. Mobley was in jail. I tried to get Coltrane. He was going to come the next weekend or something. Then I tried to get Kenny Dorham. I even tried to get Bill Evans, because I really wasn't into playing, and he didn't want to make it either. So, I phoned Pepper again and he said, "Sure I'll come back!" He liked Montreal.

He came up on the train again. He brought his horn and two books, Dostoevsky's *Crime and Punishment* and *The Brothers Karamazov.* Then I got to know him a little better. You see, what he liked to do is, he liked to blow and he liked to fuck. There was some house of joy that was nearby. This guy wasn't that big, but he had this tremendous energy! He got this huge sound out of the baritone. He'd play these sets, and he'd come out with all this tremendous stuff, and, then, between sets, he'd run off and he'd get laid. He'd come back, "Ah, that feels better!" and he'd go and he'd blow another set! He'd be drinking in the interim, and, then, after the next set, he says, "I'm going back." I said, "Jesus Christ, man!" I had a tough time keeping up with him, with the drinking, let alone the other business! So, off he goes again, and back he comes, and that's all he did between sets the subsequent weekend, Friday, Saturday, and Sunday [13-15 May]. I didn't notice it the first week.

The tape recording was done on Friday, the second week, and that was done in stereo. I took the tape recorder down. I thought maybe Pepper might be upset about the tape recorder, but he didn't care. We experimented. We played Coltrane's Moment's Notice. He'd never played it before, and I don't think I'd ever played it. We tried stuff like that.

[At the first engagement, a week earlier,] we were in his room at the rooming house. He said he wanted to play Witchcraft, and I said, "Man, I don't know the changes." He says, "Oh, yeah, you know." I said, "What are the chord changes?" He said, "Well, I don't think of the changes too much." "Don't bullshit me, man! Don't give me that stuff!" Bird used to say that, and that's bullshit, because he knew his changes backwards and forwards. So he looked at me kind of funny. So then, finally, I said, "Look: if you want me to play the tune, you're going to have to give me the changes, and that's all there is to it." So he says, "O.K, O.K." So then I bring out this piece of paper, borrow this pen, and then he gives me the changes. And he gives me the changes like Bill Evans gives the changes: "Well, the first change, a G minor ninth with a superimposed…" and he's going on like this. "So you put in the tritone substitution…" He *really* knew his changes, and every two beats there was a different change. Very complicated. I wrote all this stuff down, and then he said, "O.K." I said, "Now you're talking." He said, "Well, you know, I don't really like to do that." "Yeah, yeah, yeah," because maybe it made it sound too intellectual or something. A lot of those guys thought that it sounded too pedantic.

When I got the paper, I sat down at the piano. I had the paper on my lap because there was no front to the piano. So we played the tune with the changes, and we struggled through it. But he liked that tune. He liked tunes that were complicated like that, that had complex changes to them, and he'd make every change. He'd be whipping through every change, so he knew exactly what he was doing. For his particular style of playing, I guess it was what suited him, because of the way he ran the notes on his changes. It was a challenge to him. If they were coming at him every two beats, then it was a challenge to him how to lay his patterns onto those changes so that it made an integrative whole. These guys play patterns, but, don't forget, they make up the patterns! Even though they play patterns, they're playing their own patterns. This is different from a regular pattern player who is playing maybe Sonny Stitt patterns or John Coltrane patterns.

What Bird used to do was he would practice in the bathroom. He used to go up into the bathroom and, what he was working out, he'd just run over these fingerings on his horn, and then he'd try them on the job. But he'd work out all that stuff beforehand. He'd think in his mind about which notes were the optimum notes for that particular run that he was doing—which would sound the best—and then he'd finger it on his horn so that, when he got to the job, he could play it, and then he'd hear what it sounded like. Bird, of course, is also a true improviser, as well as a pattern player, but so was Pepper. Pepper did both. The patterns that Pepper has are his own patterns. He's worked them out. When you hear him play, you know that it's Pepper. Even if he played alto, you'd still know that it was Pepper.

I don't know how he did it, because I never got into that with him, but I'm sure that he learned from Bird. Bird learned listening to Art Tatum that that's an approach to playing; that you work out whatever you're going to do beforehand—Bill Evans did the same thing—so, when you're stuck, you don't get hung up. At least you can play something which sounds OK that gets you through to some time when you can think of something to do. So, I think, in that way, that Pepper probably learned from Bird that that was the way to approach playing jazz.

HOWARD McGHEE–DUSTY BLUE
600613

13 June 1960, New York: Howard McGhee tp; Bennie Green tb; Roland Alexander ts, fl; Pepper Adams bs; Tommy Flanagan p; Ron Carter b; Walter Bolden dm.

a		Dusty Blue	Bethlehem LP: BCP-6055
b		Park Avenue Petite	
c		Flyin' Colours	
d		**Groovin' High**	
		McGhee and rhythm section:	
e		The Sound of Music	
f		Sleep Talk	
g		I Concentrate on You	
h	6580	With Malice Towards None	
i		Cottage for Sale	

-h on Bethlehem 45: 45-11095, Rhino CD: R2-75818, Rhino-WEA
CD: 75818, Solar (Eu) CD: 4569888, Affinity (Eng) LP: AFF-156, Af-
finity (Eng) CD: AFF-765, Parlophone (Eng) LP: PMC-1181, EMI (J)
CD: TOCJ-62033, Toshiba-EMI (J) CD: 6363.

All other tracks on Parlophone (Eng) LP: PMC-1181, Rhino CD: R2-
75818, Rhino-WEA CD: 75818, Solar (Eu) CD: 4569888, Affinity (Eng)
CD: AFF-765, EMI (J) CD: TOCJ-62033, Toshiba-EMI (J) CD: 6363.

OLIVER SHEARER
600701
1 July 1960, possibly Columbia 30th Street Studio, New York: Freddie
Hubbard tp; Urbie Green tb; Pepper Adams bs; Bobby Timmons p;
Henry Grimes b; Lex Humphries dm; Oliver Shearer voc.

a   Stuffy   Columbia unissued
b   Sleep, Baby, Sleep
c   After Hours

According to Oliver Shearer, in a 1988 interview with the author,
"We didn't finish the whole thing. We did Avery Parrish's After Hours.
Jon Hendricks wrote lyrics for me for that. Jon Hendricks wrote the lyrics for [Bobby Timmons'] Moanin' for *me* and [Hendricks's group] recorded it later themselves, because I never recorded it. John Hammond
paid Jon Hendricks to write the lyrics for Moanin' because I wanted to
do it." *See also* 580415.

See 600100 for an explanation of the derivation of this date.

WOODY HERMAN
600720
20 July 1960, audience recording, Court Theater, Chicago: Ziggy Harrell, Don Rader, Bill Chase, John Bennett, Bill Berry tp; Jimmy Guinn,
Kent McGarity, Bob Jenkins tb; Woody Herman cl, as, voc*; Gordon
Brisker, Don Lanphere, Mickey Folus ts; Pepper Adams bs; Martin Harris p; Alex Cirin b; Jimmy Campbell dm.

a   **Woodchopper's Ball**
b   Midnight Sun
c   **Montmartre Bus Ride**
d   Skylark
e   The Preacher

f   I Can't Get Started
g   Blues Groove (Country Cousins)
h   If I Were a Bell†
i   I Guess I'll Have to Change My Plans*
j   Opus de Funk
k   Off Shore
m   Medley:
         The Blues on Parade
         My Momma Done Told Me*
         Amen*
         Stars Fell on Alabama*
         Caldonia*
n   The New Golden Wedding

†Rhythm section feature.

Adams took a three-week tour with the Woody Herman band, starting on 2 July, to get him from New York to the Midwest so he could join Don-ald Byrd in Cleveland for their quintet's three-month tour, beginning on 26 July.

DONALD BYRD–LIVE AT THE HALF NOTE
601111
11 November 1960, Half Note, New York: Donald Byrd tp; Pepper Adams bs; Duke Pearson p; Laymon Jackson b; Lex Humphries dm; Ruth Mason Lion mc.

a	take 1	**Mr. Lucky**	Blue Note CD: CDBN-7-46540-2
b	take 2	**Kimyas**	Blue Note unissued
c	take 3	A Portrait of Jennie*	Blue Note unissued
d	take 4	One More for the Road	Blue Note unissued
e	take 5	**Jeannine**	Blue Note LP: BLP-4061
f	take 6	**Pure D. Funk**	
g	take 7	**My Girl Shirl**	Blue Note LP: BLP-4060
h	take 8	**Soulful Kiddy**	
i		A Portrait of Jennie*	
j		**Chant**	Blue Note CD: CDP-7-46539-2
k		**Pure D. Funk**	Blue Note unissued
m		**Mr. Lucky**	Blue Note unissued
n		**That's All**	Blue Note unissued

o	**Kimyas**	Blue Note LP: BLP-4061
p	**Cecile**	Blue Note LP: BLP-4060
q	**Pure D. Funk**	Blue Note unissued
r	When Sunny Gets Blue	Blue Note LP: BLP-4061
s	**Between the Devil and the Deep Blue Sea**	
		Blue Note CD: CDP-7-46540-2
t	**Child's Play**	Blue Note CD: CDP-7-46539-2
u	**Mr. Lucky**	Blue Note unissued
v	**Pure D. Funk**	Blue Note unissued
w	A Portrait of Jennie[*]	Blue Note unissued
x	**Pure D. Funk**	Blue Note unissued

[*]Byrd and rhythm section.

-a on Blue Note CD: CDBN-8-57187-2, Blue Note CD: CDP-7243-5-90881-2-9, Blue Note CD: B21Y-46540, Blue Note (Eng) CD: CDBNZ-15, Toshiba-EMI (J) CD: C28-5136.

-e on Blue Note LP: BST-84061, Blue Note LP: B1-80679, Blue Note LP: B1-28263, Blue Note (Eng) LP: BNSLP-2, King (J) LP: GXK-8105, Toshiba-EMI (J) LP: BN-4061, Blue Note CD: CDBN-7-46540-2, Blue Note CD: CDP-7-80679-2, Blue Note CD: B21Y-46540, Blue Note CD: 8-28263-2, Blue Note CD: CDBN-8-57187-2, Blue Note CD: CDP-7243-5-90881-2-9, Blue Note (Eng) CD: BNZ-300, Blue Note (Eng) CD: CDBNZ-15, Toshiba-EMI (J) CD: TOCJ-5779, Toshiba-EMI (J) CD: TOCJ-4061, Toshiba-EMI (J) CD: TOCJ-9506, Toshiba-EMI (J) CD: C28-5136.

-f on Blue Note LP: BST-84061, King (J) LP: GXK-8105, Toshiba-EMI (J) LP: BN-4061, Toshiba-EMI (J) LP: W-5505, Blue Note CD: CDBN-8-57187-2, Blue Note CD: CDP-7243-5-90881-2-9, Toshiba-EMI (J) CD: TOCJ-4061, Toshiba-EMI (J) CD: TOCJ-9506.

-g on Blue Note LP: BST-84060, King (J) LP: GXK-8104, Toshiba-EMI (J) LP: BNJ-71100, Toshiba-EMI (J) LP: BN-4060, Blue Note CD: CD-7-46539-2, Blue Note CD: CDBN-8-57187-2, Blue Note CD: CDP-7243-5-90881-2-9, Blue Note CD: B21Y-46539, Blue Note (Eng) CD: BNZ-14, Toshiba-EMI (J) CD: TOCJ-4060, Toshiba-EMI (J) CD: TOCJ-9505, Toshiba-EMI (J) CD: C28-5135.

-h on Blue Note LP: BST-84060, King (J) LP: GXK-8104, Toshiba-EMI (J) LP: BNJ-71100, Toshiba-EMI (J) LP: BN-4060, Blue Note CD: CD-7-46539-2, Blue Note CD: CDBN-8-57187-2, Blue Note CD: CDP-

7243-5-90881-2-9, Toshiba-EMI (J) CD: TOCJ-4060, Toshiba-EMI (J) CD: TOCJ-9505.

-i on Blue Note LP: BST-84060, King (J) LP: GXK-8104, Toshiba-EMI (J) LP: BNJ-71100, Toshiba-EMI (J) LP: BN-4060, Blue Note CD: CD-7-46539-2, Blue Note CD: CDBN-8-57187-2, Blue Note CD: CDP-7243-5-90881-2-9, Blue Note CD: B21Y-46539, Blue Note (Eng) CD: BNZ-14, Toshiba-EMI (J) CD: TOCJ-4060, Toshiba-EMI (J) CD: TOCJ-9505, Toshiba-EMI (J) CD: C28-5135.

-j on Blue Note CD: CD-7-46539-2, Blue Note CD: CDBN-8-57187-2, Blue Note CD: CDP-7243-5-90881-2-9, Blue Note CD: B21Y-46539, Blue Note (Eng) CD: BNZ-14, Toshiba-EMI (J) CD: C28-5135.

-o on Blue Note LP: BST-84061, King (J) LP: GXK-8105, Toshiba-EMI (J) LP: BN-4061, Blue Note CD: CDBN-7-46540-2, Blue Note CD: CDBN-8-57187-2, Blue Note CD: CDP-7243-5-90881-2-9, Blue Note CD: B21Y-46540, Blue Note (Eng) CD: CDBNZ-15, Toshiba-EMI (J) CD: TOCJ-4061, Toshiba-EMI (J) CD: TOCJ-9506, Toshiba-EMI (J) CD: C28-5136.

-p on Blue Note LP: BST-84060, King (J) LP: GXK-8104, Toshiba-EMI (J) LP: BNJ-71100, Toshiba-EMI (J) LP: BN-4060, Blue Note CD: CD-7-46539-2, Blue Note CD: CDBN-8-57187-2, Blue Note CD: CDP-7243-5-90881-2-9, Toshiba-EMI (J) CD: TOCJ-4060, Toshiba-EMI (J) CD: TOCJ-9505.

-r on Blue Note LP: BST-84061, King (J) LP: GXK-8105, Toshiba-EMI (J) LP: BN-4061, King (J) LP: K18P-9127, Blue Note CD: CDBN-8-57187-2, Blue Note CD: CDBN-7-46540-2, Blue Note CD: B21Y-46540, Blue Note CD: CDP-7243-5-90881-2-9, Blue Note (Eng) CD: CDBNZ-15, Toshiba-EMI (J) CD: TOCJ-4061, Toshiba-EMI (J) CD: TOCJ-9506, Toshiba-EMI (J) CD: C28-5136.

-s on Blue Note CD: CDBN-8-57187-2, Blue Note CD: CDP-7243-5-90881-2-9, Blue Note CD: B21Y-46540, Blue Note (Eng) CD: CDBNZ-15, Toshiba-EMI (J) CD: C28-5136.

-t on Blue Note CD: CDBN-8-57187-2, Blue Note CD: CDP-7243-5-90881-2-9, Blue Note CD: B21Y-46539, Blue Note (Eng) CD: BNZ-14, Toshiba-EMI (J) CD: C28-5135.

According to Laymon Jackson, in an interview with the author in 1989, the band was at the Half Note for the weekend, Friday-Sunday, and all of the material was recorded on Friday night:

We left Denver, Colorado, and then we came to Chicago, I think, and then went back to New York and we's [sic] getting ready to make a record date, this thing *Donald Byrd at the Half Note*.

[Drummer] Joe Dukes was messing up or something, and Byrd told him he wasn't going to use him. Byrd brought him back to New York and fired him! After he fired Joe Dukes, then he hired Lex Humphries. Lex used to work with Byrd and Pepper....I was real happy and excited! I was just up there with the big boys! My name was going to be on the record with Pepper and Byrd....Oh, man, [Pepper] is the master at counterpoint and harmonizing, because on that record, on My Girl Shirl, I don't know where he got that part that he played....I don't think Duke wrote that part that Pepper was playing. Just let Pepper hear it and he'll put the harmony to it!

Saxophonist Jimmy Heath told the author, in a conversation in 1988, "I used to love the way they played Mr. Lucky." *See* Adams' comment on 581221 for an explanation as to who led this working band.

PEPPER ADAMS–MOTOR CITY SCENE
601115
mid-November 1960, New York: Donald Byrd tp; Pepper Adams bs; Tommy Flanagan p; Kenny Burrell g; Paul Chambers b; Louis Hayes dm.

a **Philson**   Bethlehem LP: BCP-6029
b **Trio**
c **Libeccio**
d Bitty Ditty
   Byrd and rhythm section:
e Stardust

All tracks on Bethlehem LP: BCP-6056, Bethlehem (J) LP: 22AP-128, Bethlehem CD: 20-30182, Bethlehem CD: CDGR-167, Rhino-WEA CD: R2-75993, Bethlehem CD: 9629, Charly (Eng) CD: SNAP-039-CD, Music Club (Eng) CD: MCCD-577, Bethlehem (Ger) CD: BET-6000-2, Lone Hill (Sp) CD: LHJ-10134, EMI-Toshiba (J) CD: TOCJ-9629, JVC Victor (J) CD: VIC-J-61474, EMI-Toshiba (J) CD: TOCJ-6360.

This is Adams' seventh date as a leader. Regarding the pseudonym "Hey Lewis" that first appeared in the personnel on the original release, Louis Hayes, in an interview with the author in 1988 said, "They intentionally did that because I was with Vee Jay Records at the time." Throughout the recorded history of jazz, this riffing of a musician's name has been a common way to circumvent contractual obligations. According to Pepper Adams, in an interview with the author in 1984,

> There were a lot of distractions because the studio was so bad; a lot of breakdowns because the studio wasn't functioning. That's not an album I'm very happy with at all. Another thing that was *very* disappointing was we had Kenny Burrell on the record, so I wrote some things as if it was a frontline of three horns, voicing Kenny with the trumpet and baritone, which, acoustically, worked beautifully and had an interesting blend, and I was very happy with the way my writing turned out. As it is recorded, it doesn't make any sense at all because of the damn studio and the goddamn engineer. And also, one thing in particular: We had dynamics that were *impressive,* starting very softly, and very misterioso, and then, all of a sudden, build up to a rather stark crescendo. It was dramatic as hell in the studio! On the record it is all exactly the same level of volume because the engineer obviously noticed, "There's something wrong with these fellows. They play soft and they play loud. Here: I can fix that!" and then evened it right out. So, anyway, that's one that I'm not proud of in the least. It's frustrating, because it represents rather a lost opportunity because I think there was some music played in the studio that's not on the record.

To make matters even worse, Pepper told the author about other problems with the date:

> When Donald Byrd and I had a band together, the last gig we played, the club folded. We never got paid [and] the union demanded their money anyway. You know, it was all a terrible scene. I just barely got back to New York and I knew, once I got to New York, I was straight because I had record check money at the union. It turns out, that's a date we never got paid for, and I did most of the writing, so it's almost $1,000 I [was] supposed to have picked up, and I never got a penny. So not only do I come home broke, I go to the union to try to get money that's supposed to be there, and that's not there....Mingus was working the Five Spot. I went to the Five Spot: Either I told him the story or he heard it from somebody. Anyway, I was hired starting the next night. That was nice! It was terrific!

DONALD BYRD-PEPPER ADAMS
601213

c. 13 December 1960, private recording, Curro's, Milwaukee: Donald Byrd tp; Pepper Adams bs; Herbie Hancock p; Laymon Jackson b; Lex Humphries dm.

In a 1989 interview with the author, Laymon Jackson said that Donald Byrd had made a private recording at Curro's. "In 1984," Jackson said, "Byrd was telling me that he's going to put out an album, because when we was in Milwaukee, me and him and Herbie and Pepper [were] playing for some dancers there, and Byrd had a reel-to-reel and he was recording it." The gig at Curro's ran from 13-20 December. This was Hancock's first gig with the quintet outside of his hometown of Chicago. As Hancock explained in *Vanity Fair,* just a week or two earlier "Donald Byrd discovered me when there was a blizzard in Chicago and his regular piano player couldn't make [their gig at the Counter Joint]. The guys in the band liked my playing, so I joined them and went to New York." It was Pepper Adams' friend, Chicago-based baritone saxophonist Ron Kolber, who recommended Hancock. Duke Pearson had already expressed an interest in leaving the band, prevailing weather conditions notwithstanding.

PEPPER ADAMS-DONALD BYRD – OUT OF THIS WORLD
610100

January 1961, New York: Donald Byrd tp; Pepper Adams bs; Herbie Hancock p; Teddy Charles vib*; Laymon Jackson b; Jimmy Cobb dm.

a	61WA70	**Mr. Lucky**	Warwick LP: W-2041
b		**Mr. Lucky**	Fresh Sound (Sp) LP: FSR-669
		Byrd and rhythm section:	
c	61WA71	It's a Beautiful Evening*Warwick LP: W-2041	
		Full band:	
d		**I'm an Old Cowhand**	Fresh Sound (Sp) LP: FSR-669
e		**Curro's**	Warwick LP: W-2041
f		**Curro's**	Fresh Sound (Sp) LP: FSR-669
g		**Bird House**	Warwick LP: W-2041
h		**Bird House**	Fresh Sound (Sp) LP: FSR-669
i		**Out of This World**	Warwick LP: W-2041
j		**Out of This World**	Fresh Sound (Sp) LP: FSR-669
k		**Great God**	Warwick unissued

Adams and rhythm section:

m   **Day Dream**   Warwick LP: W-2041
n   **Day Dream**   Fresh Sound (Sp) LP: FSR-669

-a on Warwick 45: 650, Manhattan (Eng) LP: MAN-5022, Fresh Sound (Sp) LP: FSR-638, TCB (Swiss) LP: 1002, Phonogram (J) LP: RJ-7179, Starburst (Eng) CD: 1010, Fresh Sound (Sp) CD: FSR-335, Fresh Sound (Swiss) CD: CD-137, Guide Internationale du Disque (Swiss) CD: JA-CD 9023, Rockin' Chair-Tecval (Swiss) CD: CD-461, Canyon (J) CD: 20ED-5068, Century (J) CD: 20ED-5068.

-b on Royal Collection LP: RC-83144, Star Jazz LP: SJAZZ-4, Premier LP: CBR-1030, Manhattan (Eng) LP: MAN-5021, Movieplay (P) LP: 10056, Fresh Sound (Sp) LP: FSR-669, TCB (Swiss) LP: 1006, Canyon (J) CD: 20ED-5067, Century (J) CD: 20ED-5067.

-c on Cambria LP: CR-5144, Star Jazz LP: SJAZZ-4, Premier LP: CBR-1030, Manhattan (Eng) LP: MAN-5027, Movieplay (P) LP: 10056, Fresh Sound (Swiss) CD: CD-137, Fresh Sound (Sp) LP: FSR-638, TCB (Swiss) LP: 1002, Phonogram (J) LP: RJ-7179, Starburst (Eng) CD: 1010, Fresh Sound (Sp) CD: FSR-335, Rockin' Chair-Tecval (Swiss) CD: CD-461, Guide Internationale du Disque (Swiss) CD: JA-CD 9023, Canyon (J) CD: 20ED-5068, Century (J) CD: 20ED-5068.

-d on Manhattan (Eng) LP: MAN-5026, TCB (Swiss) LP: 1006, Fresh Sound (Swiss) CD: CD-137, Rockin' Chair-Tecval (Swiss) CD: CD-461, Guide Internationale du Disque (Swiss) CD: JA-CD 9023, Canyon (J) CD: 20ED-5067, Century (J) CD: 20ED-5067.

-e on Almor LP: AS-110, Cambria LP: CR-5144, Happy Bird LP: B-90173, Royal Collection LP: RC-83144, Star Jazz LP: SJAZZ-4, Premier LP: CBR-1030, Manhattan (Eng) LP: MAN-5021, Movieplay (P) LP: 10056, TCB (Swiss) LP: 1002, Fresh Sound (Sp) LP: FSR-638, Phonogram (J) LP: RJ-7179, Starburst (Eng) CD: 1010, Fresh Sound (Sp) CD: FSR-335, Canyon (J) CD: 20ED-5068, Century (J) CD: 20ED-5068. Spliced version of -e combined with -f on Fresh Sound (Swiss) CD: CD-137, Rockin' Chair-Tecval (Swiss) CD: CD-461, Guide Internationale du Disque (Swiss) CD: JA-CD 9023.

-f on Manhattan (Eng) LP: MAN-5022, Tobacco Road (Ger) LP: B-2618, TCB (Swiss) LP: 1006, Canyon (J) CD: 20ED-5067, Century (J) CD: 20ED-5067. Spliced version of -e combined with -f on Fresh Sound (Swiss) CD: CD-137, Rockin' Chair-Tecval (Swiss) CD: CD-461, Guide Internationale du Disque (Swiss) CD: JA-CD 9023.

-g on Star Jazz LP: SJAZZ-4, Premier LP: CBR-1030, Manhattan (Eng) LP: MAN-5027, Movieplay (P) LP: 10056, Fresh Sound (Sp) LP: FSR-638, TCB (Swiss) LP: 1002, Phonogram (J) LP: RJ-7179, Starburst (Eng) CD: 1010, Fresh Sound (Swiss) CD: CD-137, Fresh Sound (Sp) CD: FSR-335, Rockin' Chair-Tecval (Swiss) CD: CD-461, Guide Internationale du Disque (Swiss) CD: JA-CD 9023, Canyon (J) CD: 20ED-5068, Century (J) CD: 20ED-5068.

-h on Tobacco Road (Ger) LP: B-2619, Manhattan (Eng) LP: MAN-5026, TCB (Swiss) LP: 1006, Canyon (J) CD: 20ED-5067, Century (J) CD: 20ED-5067.

-i on Star Jazz LP: SJAZZ-4, Premier LP: CBR-1030, Manhattan (Eng) LP: MAN-5027, Movieplay (P) LP: 10056, TCB (Swiss) LP: 1002, Fresh Sound (Sp) LP: FSR-638, Phonogram (J) LP: RJ-7179, Starburst (Eng) CD: 1010, Fresh Sound (Sp) CD: FSR-335, Fresh Sound (Swiss) CD: CD-137, Rockin' Chair-Tecval (Swiss) CD: CD-461, Guide Internationale du Disque (Swiss) CD: JA-CD 9023, Canyon (J) CD: 20ED-5068, Century (J) CD: 20ED-5068.

-j on Manhattan (Eng) LP: MAN-5026, Tobacco Road (Ger) LP: B-2619, TCB (Swiss) LP: 1006, Canyon (J) CD: 20ED-5067, Century (J) CD: 20ED-5067.

-m on Manhattan (Eng) LP: MAN-5022, TCB (Swiss) LP: 1002, Fresh Sound (Sp) LP: FSR-638, Phonogram (J) LP: RJ-7179, Starburst (Eng) CD: 1010, Fresh Sound (Sp) CD: FSR-335, Canyon (J) CD: 20ED-5068, Century (J) CD: 20ED-5068. Spliced version of -g combined with -h on Fresh Sound (Swiss) CD: CD-137, Rockin' Chair-Tecval (Swiss) CD: CD-461, Guide Internationale du Disque (Swiss) CD: JA-CD 9023.

-n on Royal Collection LP: RC-83144, Star Jazz LP: SJAZZ-4, Premier LP: CBR-1030, Manhattan (Eng) LP: MAN-5021, Tobacco Road (Ger) LP: B-2618, Manhattan Movieplay (P) LP: 10056, TCB (Swiss) LP: 1006, Canyon (J) CD: 20ED-5067, Century (J) CD: 20ED-5067. Spliced version of -g combined with -h on Fresh Sound (Swiss) CD: CD-137, Rockin' Chair-Tecval (Swiss) CD: CD-461, Guide Internationale du Disque (Swiss) CD: JA-CD 9023.

This is Adams' eighth date as a leader. The band did this recording during the period 1-8 January, before the group left for Chicago to work at Bird House (10-22 January), or after they returned from Chicago, c. 24-31 January. Pepper Adams told the author in 1984,

Although the band was ours as co-leaders, Donald Byrd was the one under contract to the record company, so it became his band when

we recorded. Except, we did do one album during a brief lapse of
Donald's contract at Blue Note on a short-lived label called Warwick, and, that too has been reissued to death in various different
forms. I wasn't aware of all of them. Jimmy Cobb told me that he
had found it in a supermarket under a completely different title. Because, when they sell these things, they don't pay any royalties on
them anymore, and they pick them up cheap so they can put them
out cheap. So, they can wind up on the rack in the supermarket.
That was Herbie Hancock's first record.

Laymon Jackson told the author, in an interview in 1989, "It was just
a regular date. It just went along great. We had two rehearsals at Pepper's house."

DONALD BYRD-PEPPER ADAMS
610300
c. March 1961, TV broadcast, Indianapolis: Donald Byrd tp; Pepper Adams bs; Herbie Hancock p; Laymon Jackson b; Joe Dukes dm.

a   **I'm An Old Cowhand**

Saxophonist Larry Dickson told the author, in an interview in 1988,
that the band performed this tune on a daytime talk show, possibly the
Jim Gerard Show, while in Indianapolis for an engagement at Embers
from 6-19 March. It isn't clear if either the audio or video still exist.

DONALD BYRD - CHANT
610417
17 April 1961, Van Gelder Studio, Englewood Cliffs NJ: Donald Byrd
tp*; Pepper Adams bs; Herbie Hancock p; Doug Watkins b; Teddy Robinson dm.

a	**I'm an Old Cowhand***	Blue Note LP: LT-991
b	**You're Next***	
c	**Great God***	
d	**Chant***	
e	**Sophisticated Lady**	
f	**Cute***	Blue Note unissued
g	**That's All***	Blue Note LP: LT-991

-a on Blue Note (Eng) LP: LBR-1024, King (J) LP: GXK-8183, Mosaic CD: MD4-194.

-b on Blue Note (Eng) LP: LBR-1024, King (J) LP: GXK-8183, Mosaic CD: MD4-194.

-c on United Artists (Eng) LP: UALP-21, Blue Note (Eng) LP: LBR-1024, King (J) LP: GXK-8183, Mosaic CD: MD4-194.

-d on Blue Note (Eng) LP: LBR-1024, King (J) LP: GXK-8183, Mosaic CD: MD4-194.

-e on Blue Note (Eng) LP: LBR-1024, King (J) LP: GXK-8183, Mosaic CD: MD4-194.

-g on Blue Note (Eng) LP: LBR-1024, King (J) LP: GXK-8183, Mosaic CD: MD4-194.

At least 20 takes were done at this session. The date was first released in 1979. According to Laymon Jackson, in an interview with the author in 1989, Sophisticated Lady was a feature for Pepper Adams in their club dates during the two and a half years that Jackson toured with the band: "Pepper had an album by this bass player he used to let me listen to: the guy that played with Duke Ellington, Jimmy Blanton. He had something where Jimmy Blanton was bowing Sophisticated Lady. I think that's why he fell in love with it. Blanton really played, and he wouldn't let that record get out of his sight! Every time I'd go to his house, I'd tell him to play it." *See* Adams' comment on 581221 for an explanation as to who led this working band.

QUINCY JONES
610422
22 April 1961, radio broadcast, Birdland, New York: Clark Terry, Johnny Coles tp; Curtis Fuller, Frank Rehak, Mickey Gravine tb; Julius Watkins frh; Phil Woods as; Eric Dixon ts; Pepper Adams bs; Patti Bown p; Les Spann g, fl; other musicians; Quincy Jones cond.

a   G'won Train
b   Caravan
c   Stockholm Sweetnin'
d   The Midnight Sun Will Never Set
e   Airmail Special

An acetate of this broadcast was made by collector Boris Rose. *See also* 610429. In his 22 April 1961 *New York Times* article about Jones' twenty piece orchestra, John S. Wilson discussed the above personnel, who he said comprised "an array of soloists almost without precedent in a jazz band." According to historian Mike Fitzgerald, additional band-members might be Jimmy Maxwell, John Bello, Jimmy Nottingham, Joe Newman tp; Melba Liston, Britt Woodman tb; Paul Faulise btb; Joe Lopes as; Jerome Richardson ts; Art Davis b; Stu Martin dm.

QUINCY JONES
610429
29 April 1961, radio broadcast, Birdland, New York: Same as 22 April 1961:

a   Cherokee
b   G'won Train
c   The Midnight Sun Will Never Set
d   Caravan

See also 610422.

DONALD BYRD–THE CAT WALK
610502
2 May 1961, Van Gelder Studio, Englewood Cliffs NJ: Donald Byrd tp; Pepper Adams bs; Duke Pearson p; Laymon Jackson b; Philly Joe Jones dm.

a   **Say You're Mine**   Blue Note LP: BLP-4075
b   **Hello Bright Sunflower**
c   **Each Time I Think of You**
d   **Duke's Mixture**
e   **The Cat Walk**
f   **Cute**

All tracks on Blue Note LP: BST-84075, Blue Note [45rpm] LP: LMM-4075-45, Blue Note-EMI Pathe-Marconi (F) LP: 9991-4010504-1-5, EMI CD: 7128, Blue Note CD: 4075, EMI CD: 6562, Blue Note CD: AWMXR-0009, Blue Note (Eu) CD: 0946-3-74226-2-5, Toshiba-EMI (J) LP: BN-4075, Toshiba (J) CD: TOCJ-4075, Mosaic CD: MD4-194.

At least fifteen takes were done at this session. According to Laymon Jackson, in an interview with the author in 1989,

Byrd called up Lex and he couldn't find Lex. Lex's wife said she didn't know where he was. Lex was in one of his things then, so

Byrd said, "Call Philly Joe," and they called Philly Joe. They went by and picked up Philly Joe and we went to Englewood to Rudy's place. Philly Joe went in the restroom. I was in the restroom and Philly Joe got something out of his hat and snorted it up his nose and came back out there! That thing on Cute: That's one take.

See Adams' comment on 581221 for an explanation as to who led this working band.

DONALD BYRD-PEPPER ADAMS
610624
24 June 1961, Jorgie's, St. Louis: Donald Byrd tp; Pepper Adams bs; Herbie Hancock p; Cleveland Eaton b; Teddy Robinson dm.

a	**Jorgie's**	VGM LP: 0002
b	**6 M's**	
c	**Hush**	
d	**Amen**	
e	**Little Girl Blue**	VGM unissued
f	**I'm an Old Cowhand**	
g	**Kimyas**	
	Rhythm section only:	
h	Like Someone in Love	VGM LP: 0003
	Byrd and rhythm section:	
i	I Remember Clifford	VGM unissued

-a, -b, -c, -d, -h on Solar (Eu) CD: 4569914.

This was privately recorded during the Quintet's two-week engagement. According to Virgil Matheus, owner of VGM, some of this material has been released on LP in Europe on the Can Am label.

METROPOLITAN JAZZ OCTET
610700
c. July 1961, Universal Recording Studios, Chicago: Tom Hilliard tp; Pepper Adams as; Ron Kolber bs; other musicians.

Ron Kolber told the author in 2005 that Adams sat in on alto saxophone for this rehearsal. Kolber was a close friend of Adams, so it seems likely that Adams sat in as a favor, because the band had studio time reserved and a vacancy in their alto chair. The Donald Byrd-Pepper Adams Quintet played opposite the Metropolitan Jazz Octet sometime during c.

July 1961. Other musicians in the group might be Ed Haley tp; Ed Avis vtb; Angelo Principali p; Gerry Lofstrum b; Jim Gianas dm.

MONICA ZETTERLUND
610800
c. *August 1961, New York:* Donald Byrd tp; Pepper Adams bs; unknown p; unknown b; unknown dm; Monica Zetterlund voc.

Possibly recorded by Hanover. According to journalist Hans Fridlund, in a 1989 letter to the author, Sweden-based singer Zetterlund was an old friend of Pepper Adams' "since a never released Leonard Feather date in the U.S.A. in the early '60s. A long since defunct record company, the name of which escapes me (Hanover?), tried to push Monica overseas, with guys like Donald Byrd and Pepper in the lineup."

WILLIE WILSON
610802
2 August 1961, Bell Sound Studios, New York: Freddie Hubbard tp; Willie Wilson btb; Pepper Adams bs; Duke Pearson p; Thomas Howard b; Lex Humphries dm.

a	**Minor Mishap**	Prestige unissued
b	**Minor Mishap**	Prestige unissued
c	**Minor Mishap**	Black Lion (Ger) CD: BLCD-760122
d	**Minor Mishap**	Prestige LP: PR-7729
e	**Blues for Alvina**	Prestige unissued
f	**Blues for Alvina**	Prestige unissued
g	**Blues for Alvina**	Black Lion (Ger) CD: BLCD-760122
h	**Blues for Alvina**	Prestige LP: PR-7729
i	The Nearness of You*	Prestige unissued
j	The Nearness of You*	Prestige unissued
k	The Nearness of You*	Prestige LP: PR-7729
m	**Number Five**	Prestige unissued
n	**Number Five**	Prestige unissued
o	**Number Five**	Black Lion (Ger) CD: BLCD-760122
p	**Number Five**	Prestige unissued
q	**Number Five**	Prestige LP: PR-7729
r	**Lex**	Prestige unissued
s	**Lex**	Black Lion (Ger) CD: BLCD-760122
t	**Lex**	Prestige unissued

u	Lex	Prestige LP: PR-7729
v	Time After Time[*]	Prestige unissued
w	Time After Time[*]	Prestige LP: PR-7729
x	Apothegm	Prestige unissued
y	Apothegm	Prestige unissued
z	Apothegm	Prestige unissued
aa	Apothegm	Prestige LP: PR-7729
bb	Apothegm	Prestige unissued
cc	Apothegm	Black Lion (Ger) CD: BLCD-760122
dd	Apothegm	Prestige unissued
ee	Apothegm	Prestige unissued
ff	Apothegm	Prestige unissued
gg	Apothegm	Prestige unissued
hh	Apothegm	Prestige unissued
ii	Apothegm	Prestige unissued
jj	Apothegm	Prestige unissued
kk	Apothegm	Prestige unissued

[*]Wilson and rhythm section.

-c on Black Lion (Ger) LP: BLP-60122, Solar (Eu) CD: 4569883, Black Lion (Ger) CD: BLCD-760122, Guilde Internationale du Disque (Swiss) CD: JA-CD-2058.

-d on Fontana (Eng) LP: 883-290-JCL, Fontana (Sp) LP: JFL-136, Black Lion (Ger) LP: BLP-60122, Original Jazz Classics CD: OJCCD-1939-2, Solar (Eu) CD: 4569883, Black Lion (Ger) CD: BLCD-3701, Black Lion (Ger) CD: BLCD-760122, Guilde Internationale du Disque (Swiss) CD: JA-CD-2058, Trio-Kenwood (J) LP: PA-3081.

-g on Solar (Eu) CD: 4569883, Black Lion (Ger) CD: BLCD-3702, Black Lion (Ger) CD: BLCD-760122.

-h on Fontana (Eng) LP: 883-290-JCL, Fontana (Sp) LP: JFL-136, Black Lion (Ger) LP: BLP-60122, Original Jazz Classics CD: OJCCD-1939-2, Solar (Eu) CD: 4569883, Black Lion (Ger) CD: BLCD-760122, Guilde Internationale du Disque (Swiss) CD: JA-CD-2058, Trio-Kenwood (J) LP: PA-3081.

-k on Fontana (Eng) LP: 883-290-JCL, Fontana (Sp) LP: JFL-136, Black Lion (Ger) LP: BLP-60122, Original Jazz Classics CD: OJCCD-1939-2, Solar (Eu) CD: 4569883, Black Lion (Ger) CD: BLCD-760122, Guilde Internationale du Disque (Swiss) CD: JA-CD-2058, Trio-Kenwood (J) LP: PA-3081.

-o on Solar (Eu) CD: 4569883, Black Lion (Ger) CD: BLCD-760122.

-q on Fontana (Eng) LP: 883-290-JCL, Fontana (Sp) LP: JFL-136, Black Lion (Ger) LP: BLP-60122, Original Jazz Classics CD: OJCCD-1939-2, Solar (Eu) CD: 4569883, Black Lion (Ger) CD: BLCD-760122, Guilde Internationale du Disque (Swiss) CD: JA-CD-2058, Trio-Kenwood (J) LP: PA-3081.

-s on Solar (Eu) CD: 4569883, Black Lion (Ger) LP: BLP-60122, Black Lion (Ger) CD: BLCD-760122, Guilde Internationale du Disque (Swiss) CD: JA-CD-2058.

-u on Fontana (Eng) LP: 883-290-JCL, Fontana (Sp) LP: JFL-136, Black Lion (Ger) LP: BLP-60122, Original Jazz Classics CD: OJCCD-1939-2, Solar (Eu) CD: 4569883, Black Lion (Ger) CD: BLCD-760122, Guilde Internationale du Disque (Swiss) CD: JA-CD-2058, Trio-Kenwood (J) LP: PA-3081.

-w on Fontana (Eng) LP: 883-290-JCL, Fontana (Sp) LP: JFL-136, Black Lion (Ger) LP: BLP-60122, Original Jazz Classics CD: OJCCD-1939-2, Solar (Eu) CD: 4569883, Black Lion (Ger) CD: BLCD-760122, Guilde Internationale du Disque (Swiss) CD: JA-CD-2058, Trio-Kenwood (J) LP: PA-3081.

-aa on Original Jazz Classics CD: OJCCD-1939-2, Solar (Eu) CD: 4569883, Black Lion (Ger) CD: BLCD-760122, Guilde Internationale du Disque (Swiss) CD: JA-CD-2058.

-cc on Fontana (Eng) LP: 883-290-JCL, Fontana (Sp) LP: JFL-136, Black Lion (Ger) LP: BLP-60122, Solar (Eu) CD: 4569883, Black Lion (Ger) CD: BLCD-760122, Guilde Internationale du Disque (Swiss) CD: JA-CD-2058, Trio-Kenwood (J) LP: PA-3081.

This was originally recorded for Fred Norsworthy's Jazztime label (later renamed Jazzline), but not released. Both Pepper Adams and the producer of the date, Fred Norsworthy, told the author that this session was led by Willie Wilson. Fred Norsworthy, in an interview with the author in 1987, said,

> We were going to do the album, and Willie Wilson showed up with Duke Pearson, but no one else showed up. So there's quite harried phone calls and we called Pepper in. Originally, it was going to be Kenny Dorham, so he didn't show so we got Freddie Hubbard. The original bass player was Wilbur Ware, and it turned out that Wilbur was doing some duo work with Duke in the studio and then he split and forgot there was a record date, so we used Willie's friend, Thomas Howard, who happened to be at the date. I'd originally seen

[Willie] with the Dizzy Gillespie Big Band. I think, had he lived, he would have been probably one of the original, good players, but, as you know, he consumed a quart of paint thinner—whatever it was—and committed suicide.

DONALD BYRD–ROYAL FLUSH
610921

21 September 1961, Van Gelder Studio, Englewood Cliffs NJ: Donald Byrd tp; Pepper Adams bs*; Herbie Hancock p; Butch Warren b; Billy Higgins dm.

a	**Jorgie's***	Blue Note LP: BLP-4101
b	**Shangri-La***	
c	**Hush***	
d	**6M's***	
e	**Requiem***	
f	**Child's Play***	Blue Note unissued
g	I'm a Fool to Want You	Blue Note LP: BLP-4101

-a on Blue Note 45: BN-45-1854, Blue Note LP: BST-84101, King (J) LP: GXK-8127, Mosaic CD: MD4-194, Blue Note CD: 62632, Blue Note (Eu) CD: 0946-3-62632-2-9, Toshiba-EMI (J) CD: TOCJ-4101, Toshiba-EMI (J) CD: TOCJ-7185, Toshiba-EMI (J) CD: TOCJ-9157.

-b on Blue Note LP: BST-84101, King (J) LP: GXK-8127, Mosaic CD: MD4-194, Blue Note CD: 62632, Blue Note (Eu) CD: 0946-3-62632-2-9, Blue Note (F) CD: 4-97517-2, Toshiba-EMI (J) CD: TOCJ-4101, Toshiba-EMI (J) CD: TOCJ-7185, Toshiba-EMI (J) CD: TOCJ-9157.

-c on Blue Note 45: BN-45-1853, Blue Note LP: BST-84101, King (J) LP: GXK-8127, Mosaic CD: MD4-194, Blue Note CD: 62632, Blue Note (Eu) CD: 0946-3-62632-2-9, Toshiba-EMI (J) CD: TOCJ-4101, Toshiba-EMI (J) CD: TOCJ-7185, Toshiba-EMI (J) CD: TOCJ-9157, Blue Note (J) CD: TOCJ-66060.

-d on Blue Note 45: BN-45-1853, Blue Note LP: BST-84101, King (J) LP: GXK-8127, Mosaic CD: MD4-194, Blue Note CD: 62632, Blue Note (Eu) CD: 0946-3-62632-2-9, Toshiba-EMI (J) CD: TOCJ-4101, Toshiba-EMI (J) CD: TOCJ-7185, Toshiba-EMI (J) CD: TOCJ-9157.

-e on Blue Note LP: BST-84101, King (J) LP: GXK-8127, Mosaic CD: MD4-194, Blue Note CD: 62632, Blue Note (Eu) CD: 0946-3-62632-2-9, Toshiba-EMI (J) CD: TOCJ-4101, Toshiba-EMI (J) CD: TOCJ-7185, Toshiba-EMI (J) CD: TOCJ-9157.

-g on Blue Note LP: BST-84101, King (J) LP: GXK-8127, Mosaic CD: MD4-194, Blue Note CD: 62632, Blue Note (Eu) CD: 0946-3-62632-2-9, Toshiba-EMI (J) CD: TOCJ-4101, Toshiba-EMI (J) CD: TOCJ-7185, Toshiba-EMI (J) CD: TOCJ-9157, Blue Note (J) CD: BN TOCJ-66054.

At least 26 takes were done at this session. According to Billy Higgins, in an interview with the author in 1989, "I was living around the corner from where they were rehearsing. I think the drummer didn't show up so [Blue Note A&R man] Ike Quebec got me on the record date. There was a rehearsal at a place called the White Whale, where me and Sonny Clark was playing." According to Donald Byrd, in the original liner notes to this recording, "Pepper and Herbie and I went to rehearse one day at a place called the White Whale in New York. We found two musicians working there—Butch Warren, the bass player from Washington, D.C., and Billy Higgins, the drummer from Los Angeles who'd worked with Ornette Coleman. They both seemed to fit our requirements fine, so that's how the quintet was put together." *See* Adams' comment on 581221 for an explanation as to who led this working band.

Chapter Three
Journeyman: 1961-1965

LIONEL HAMPTON
611209

9 December 1961, Metropole Café, New York: Dave Gonsalves, Virgil Jones, Floyd Jones, Richard Williams tp; Vince Prudente, Harleem Rasheed, Lester Robinson tb; Bobby Plater, Ed Pazant as; Andy McGhee, John Neely ts; Pepper Adams bs; Kenny Lowe p; Billy Mackel g; Lionel Hampton vib; Lawrence Burgan b; Wilbert Hogan dm; Pinocchio James voc.

a	At the Metropole	Glad-Hamp LP: GHLP-3050
b	Encore	
c	After You've Gone	Glad-Hamp LP: GHLP-1005
d	They Say It's Wonderful	
e	It's All Right with Me	
f	Take My Word	
g	McGhee	

-c, -e, -g on Hindsight CD: HCD-242.
According to Pepper Adams, in an interview with the author in 1984,

I don't know how to say this without offending a lot of folks, but I don't think the emphasis in Lionel's bands has ever been on music particularly. I consider it more like a sideshow, much of the time. Although they had some capable players, and tried to play as well as possible, there just wasn't that much emphasis placed upon playing well. It was showbiz! I think everything was done about as cheaply as possible, and the payroll kept about as low as it conveniently could be kept, which explains a lot of the turnover that happened all the time. A large part of it was sub-professional; just not the quality of music one would expect a professional band to play! And then,

when you have bad quality of arrangements, no matter how good
the ensemble work sounds, it's still going to sound bad! The rehearsals for the band were wasted time because nothing ever got accomplished for us. We'd just get together as a band and sit there.

According to Adams' friend Ron Ley, in an interview with the author in 1988, Pepper Adams had described the Hampton ensemble to him
as a "rag-tag band that was a very demoralized group of musicians who
were poorly treated, underpaid—generally a rotten gig."

PONY POINDEXTER
620216
16 February 1962, possibly Columbia 30th Street Studio, New York: Pony Poindexter, Sonny Red, Eric Dolphy as; Jimmy Heath, Clifford Jordan ts; Pepper Adams bs; Gildo Mahones p; Ron Carter b; Elvin Jones
dm.

a	CO69687	B Frequency	Epic LP: LA-16035
b	CO69688	**Lanyop**	
c		**Lanyop**	CBS LP: FC-38509
d	CO69689	Catin' Latin	Epic unissued

According to discographer Walter Bruyninckx, -d has been issued
the same matrix number as -a on 620510.
-a on Epic LP: BA-17035, Epic (F) LP: EPC-65889, Epic CD: 8869-
7-11212-2-3, Koch (Ger) CD: KOC-CD-8591, Koch (Ger) CD: KOC-
CD-385912, CBS-Sony (J) CD: ECPU-10, Epic-Sony (J) CD: ESCA-
5058.
-b on Epic LP: BA-17035, Epic (F) LP: EPC-65889, Epic CD: 8869-
7-11212-2-3, Koch (Ger) CD: KOC-CD-8591, Koch (Ger) CD: KOC-
CD-385912, CBS-Sony (J) CD: ECPU-10, Epic-Sony (J) CD: ESCA-
5058.
The session's arranger, Gee Kee, in a 1988 conversation with the
author, said,

We had some problems with that date. It's the same old crap, man!
Teo Macero was A&R-ing the date, and…Jon [Hendricks, the pro-
ducer] and Pony were so uptight about kissing his ass—no better
way of putting it—that there were a few tunes where one more take,
we felt, really would have made it, and you're getting this flack:
"No, man! No, man! That's cool! That's cool!" In fact, on one of

the tunes, I made a mistake in transposition on one or two notes: "Oh, that's all right! Nobody'll hear it! Nobody'll hear it! Nobody'll hear it!" The most satisfying thing I got out of it was, maybe two years later, Pepper said, "Keys—[he always called me Keys]—I really had a chance to hear that date we did." He said, "Gee, that was a great date! If we could have done it a couple more times, I could've filled in a lot more things that I would've done, but it was such a hassle!" In fact, we *were* being hassled—clock-wise....[Teo] was the one in control. He could have said, "It's cool." They were concerned about upsetting him. That's the whole deal. [Macero's] two tunes—B Frequency and Artistry in Rhythm—they took ages with them....Jon hired me to do the charts for that date. He pulled some strings to get Pony the date, I'm pretty sure....

This is when stereo just began to be a thing. There had to be a gimmick attached to it. (Hey, you can't win!) The concept was to play up the stereo thing: You're supposed to have shit jump out of both speakers. The closest I came to where it made any sense to me was on Blue [*see* 620418], because the tempo was slow enough and the changes were slow enough where maybe you could have two saxophones doing one thing on one side, and, after that, doing something in the center, and two maybe then doing something in the right, and that sort. That's what it was. There's always some price! Part of the idea was to make a stereo gimmick out of it. That was the day of the demo tapes, you know? "Come on, you gotta hear my tape! I got airplanes flying across the room and trains running through a tunnel," and all that kind of crap, right? It was fun with Blue, because it did give me another thing to go for. Something like Blue was ideal, because the lines were long enough, and so much of it had to do with backgrounds, so you could kind of play background in two sections or more, off against one another, and still off against the lead voice.

The others—come on! But, to be fair about it, that wasn't the entire album. It was suggested, "Well, maybe you can get going on that thing." I think Blue more or less kind of took the heat off....If it wasn't for Jon and Pony getting uptight, it would have been a fun date in all respects. You got to figure it this way: They were all comrades, right? It should have been a very loose thing, but you really couldn't settle down and relax. Pony was a nervous goddamn wreck and Jon was in an Uncle Tom fucking bag. I'm very bitter about it because it was an important thing to me. I was finally getting a chance to really do a straightahead jazz session, and then you have to go through all this garbage, where the people, to my mind, who should have been most concerned with the success of the date, from the standpoint of the music, seemed to be so in fear of Teo and the clock.

BLUE MITCHELL
620307
7 March 1962, Plaza Sound Studios, New York: Blue Mitchell, Clark Terry tp; Julius Watkins frh; Jerome Richardson as, fl; Jimmy Heath ts; Pepper Adams bs; Wynton Kelly p; Sam Jones b; Albert Heath dm.

a   I Can't Get Started   Riverside LP: RLP-414
b   Hootie Blues

-a on Riverside LP: RLP-9414, Milestone LP: M-47055, Prestige LP: P-24112, Original Jazz Classics CD: OJCCD-837-2, Fantasy CD: 837, Riverside CD: VIC-60693, JVC-Victor (J) CD: 41660, JVC-Victor (J) CD: VICJ-41560.
-b on Riverside LP: RLP-9414, Original Jazz Classics CD: OJCCD-837-2.
According to Jimmy Heath, in a conversation in 1989 with the author, "I was a staff arranger, basically, for Riverside, so I was doing a lot of arrangements for a lot of groups at that time....I had already done a ten-piece band of my own, so that's why I continued almost in the same instrumentation....The sound that [Pepper] got within the section was what I wanted to hear."
See 620308.

BLUE MITCHELL
620308
8 March 1962, Plaza Sound Studios, New York: Same as 7 March 1962:

a   **Blue on Blue**   Riverside LP: RLP-414
b   A Sure Thing

-a on Riverside LP: RLP-9414, Riverside CD: VIC-60693, Fantasy CD: 837, Original Jazz Classics CD: OJCCD-837-2, JVC-Victor (J) CD: 41660, JVC-Victor (J) CD: VICJ-41560.
-b on Riverside LP: RLP-9414, Riverside CD: VIC-60693, Fantasy CD: 837, Original Jazz Classics CD: OJCCD-837-2, JVC-Victor (J) CD: 41660, JVC-Victor (J) CD: VICJ-41560.
See 620307.

RED GARLAND – RED'S GOOD GROOVE
620322
22 March 1962, Plaza Sound Studio, New York: Blue Mitchell tp; Pepper Adams bs; Red Garland p; Sam Jones b; Philly Joe Jones dm.

a	**Red's Good Groove**	Jazzland LP: JLP-87
b	**Our Love Is Here to Stay**	
c	**This Time the Dream's on Me**	
d	**Take Me in Your Arms**	
e	**Excerent**	
f	**Falling in Love with Love**	
g	Strike Up the Band	Jazzland unissued

All issued tracks on Jazzland LP: JLP-987, Jazzland LP: LPJW-025, Victor (J) LP: VIJ-5047, Original Jazz Classics CD: OJCCD-10642-5, Victor (J) CD: VICJ-23766, JVC (J) CD: 41824.

PONY POINDEXTER
620418
18 April 1962, possibly Columbia 30th Street Studio, New York: Pony Poindexter ss, as; Phil Woods, Sonny Red as; Sal Nistico, Clifford Jordan ts; Pepper Adams bs; Tommy Flanagan p; Ron Carter b; Charli Persip dm.

a	CO70070	Basin Street Blues	Epic LP: LA-16035
b	CO70071	**Mickey Mouse March**	
c	CO70072	Skylark	
d	CO70073	Blue	

All tracks on Epic LP: BA-17035, Epic (F) LP: EPC-65889, Epic CD: 8869-7-11212-2-3, Koch (Ger) CD: KOC-CD-8591, Koch (Ger) CD: KOC-CD-385912, CBS-Sony (J) CD: ECPU-10, Epic-Sony (J) CD: ESCA-5058.
See 620216 and 620510.

PONY POINDEXTER
620510
10 May 1962, possibly Columbia 30th Street Studio, New York: Pony Poindexter as, ss; Phil Woods, Gene Quill as; Dexter Gordon, Billy

Mitchell ts; Pepper Adams bs; Gildo Mahones p; Bill Yancey b; Charli Persip dm.

a	CO69689	**Catin' Latin**	Epic LP: LA-16035
b	CO75264	Pony's Express	
c	CO75265	Artistry in Rhythm	
d	CO75266	**Salt Peanuts**	
e	CO75267	Struttin' with Some Barbecue	
f		**Rudolph the Red-Nosed Reindeer**	Columbia LP: CS-8693

-f on Columbia LP: PC-36803, Harmony LP: KH-32529, Columbia CD: CK-40166.

All other tracks on Epic LP: BA-17035, Epic (F) LP: EPC-65889, Epic CD: 8869-7-11212-2-3, Koch (Ger) CD: KOC-CD-8591, Koch (Ger) CD: KOC-CD-385912, CBS/Sony (J) CD: ECPU-10, Epic/Sony (J) CD: ESCA-5058.

See 620216 and 620418.

CHARLES MINGUS
621012
12 October 1962, Town Hall, New York: Snooky Young, Ernie Royal, Ed Armour, Rolf Ericson, Lonnie Hillyer, Clark Terry, Richard Williams tp; Jimmy Cleveland, Eddie Bert, Willie Dennis, Britt Woodman, Paul Faulise tb; Quentin Jackson btb; Buddy Collette, Charles McPherson, Charlie Mariano, Eric Dolphy as; Romeo Penque oboe; Zoot Sims, George Berg ts; Pepper Adams, Jerome Richardson bs; Danny Bank contrabass cl; Toshiko Akiyoshi,* Jaki Byard p; Les Spann g; Milt Hinton b; Charles Mingus b, voc†; Dannie Richmond dm; Grady Tate perc; Warren Smith vib, perc.

a	Freedom*†	Blue Note CD: CDP-7243-8-28353-2-5
b	Clark in the Dark*†	United Artists LP: UAJ-14024
c	Osmotin'* (Monk, Bunk or Vice Versa)	Blue Note CD: CDP-7243-8-28353-2-5
d	Epitaph Part 1*	United Artists LP: UAJ-14024
e	Peggy's Blue Skylight* (Black Light)	

f   Epitaph Part 2*
g   My Search*
h   Portrait   Blue Note CD: CDP-
                                                 7243-8-28353-2-5
i   Duke's Choice (Don't Come Back)   United Artists LP: UAJ-
                                                 14024
j   Please Don't Come Back from the Moon   Blue Note CD: CDP-
                                                 7243-8-28353-2-5
k   **In a Mellow Tone**   United Artists LP: UAJ-
                                                 14024
m   Epitaph Part 1   Blue Note CD: CDP-
                                                 7243-8-28353-2-5

Forty seconds of silent footage of -a appear in Thomas Reichman's film *Mingus*.

-a on Blue Note CD: CDBN-8-28353-2, Blue Note (Eu) LP: BNS-40034.

-b on United Artists LP: UAJS-15024, United Artists LP: UA-82002, United Artists LP: UA-27002, United Artists LP: UA-67002, Solid State LP: SS-18024, Blue Note LP: 1601061, Blue Note (Eu) LP: BNS-40034, Blue Note (Eu) LP: BNS-40034, United Artists (Eng) LP: ULP-1068, United Artists (F) LP: UA-38002, United Artists (Ger) LP: 669012, Solid State (Ger) LP: 18024K, Blue Note (Neth) LP: 5C058-60106, King (J) LP: K18P-9225, Toshiba-EMI (J) LP: LBJ-60064, Blue Note CD: CDBN-8-28353-2, Blue Note CD: BN (P) 8E074-60106.

-c on Blue Note CD: CDBN-8-28353-2.

-d on United Artists LP: UAJS-15024, United Artists LP: UA-82002, United Artists LP: UA-27002, United Artists LP: UA-67002, Solid State LP: SS-18024, Blue Note (Eu) LP: BNS-40034, Blue Note (Eu) LP: BNS-40034, United Artists (Eng) LP: ULP-1068, United Artists (F) LP: UA-38002, United Artists (Ger) LP: 669012, Solid State (Ger) LP: 18024K, Blue Note (Neth) LP: 5C058-60106, King (J) LP: K18P-9225, Toshiba-EMI (J) LP: LBJ-60064, Blue Note LP: 1601061, Blue Note CD: CDBN-8-28353-2, Blue Note CD: BN (P) 8E074-60106.

-e on United Artists LP: UAJS-15024, United Artists LP: UA-82002, United Artists LP: UA-27002, United Artists LP: UA-67002, Solid State LP: SS-18024, Blue Note LP: 1601061, Blue Note (Eu) LP: BNS-40034, United Artists (Eng) LP: ULP-1068, United Artists (F) LP: UA-38002, United Artists (Ger) LP: 669012, Solid State (Ger) LP: 18024K, Blue Note (Neth) LP: 5C058-60106, King (J) LP: K18P-9225, Toshiba-EMI

(J) LP: LBJ-60064, Blue Note CD: CDBN-8-28353-2, Blue Note CD: BN (P) 8E074-60106.

-f on United Artists LP: UAJS-15024, United Artists LP: UA-82002, United Artists LP: UA-27002, United Artists LP: UA-67002, Solid State LP: SS-18024, Blue Note LP: 1601061, Blue Note (Eu) LP: BNS-40034, Blue Note (Eu) LP: BNS-40034, United Artists (Eng) LP: ULP-1068, United Artists (F) LP: UA-38002, United Artists (Ger) LP: 669012, Solid State (Ger) LP: 18024K, Blue Note (Neth) LP: 5C058-60106, King (J) LP: K18P-9225, Toshiba-EMI (J) LP: LBJ-60064, Blue Note CD: CDBN-8-28353-2, Blue Note CD: BN (P) 8E074-60106.

-g on United Artists LP: UAJS-15024, United Artists LP: UA-82002, United Artists LP: UA-27002, United Artists LP: UA-67002, Solid State LP: SS-18024, Blue Note LP: 1601061, Blue Note (Eu) LP: BNS-40034, United Artists (Eng) LP: ULP-1068, United Artists (F) LP: UA-38002, United Artists (Ger) LP: 669012, Solid State (Ger) LP: 18024K, Blue Note (Neth) LP: 5C058-60106, King (J) LP: K18P-9225, Toshiba-EMI (J) LP: LBJ-60064, Blue Note CD: CDBN-8-28353-2, Blue Note CD: BN (P) 8E074-60106.

-h on Blue Note CD: CDBN-8-28353-2.

-i on United Artists LP: UAJS-15024, United Artists LP: UA-82002, United Artists LP: UA-27002, United Artists LP: UA-67002, Solid State LP: SS-18024, Blue Note LP: 1601061, Blue Note (Eu) LP: BNS-40034, Blue Note (Eu) LP: BNS-40034, United Artists (Eng) LP: ULP-1068, United Artists (F) LP: UA-38002, United Artists (Ger) LP: 669012, Solid State (Ger) LP: 18024K, Blue Note (Neth) LP: 5C058-60106, King (J) LP: K18P-9225, Toshiba-EMI (J) LP: LBJ-60064, Blue Note CD: CDBN-8-28353-2, Blue Note CD: BN (P) 8E074-60106.

-j on Blue Note CD: CDBN-8-28353-2.

-k on United Artists LP: UAJS-15024, United Artists LP: UA-82002, United Artists LP: UA-27002, United Artists LP: UA-67002, Solid State LP: SS-18024, Blue Note LP: 1601061, Blue Note (Eu) LP: BNS-40034, Blue Note (Eu) LP: BNS-40034, United Artists (Eng) LP: ULP-1068, United Artists (F) LP: UA-38002, United Artists (Ger) LP: 669012, Solid State (Ger) LP: 18024K, Blue Note (Neth) LP: 5C058-60106, King (J) LP: K18P-9225, Toshiba-EMI (J) LP: LBJ-60064, Blue Note CD: CDBN-8-28353-2, Blue Note CD: BN (P) 8E074-60106.

Brian Priestley, in his liner notes to the Blue Note CD reissue, said, "After clearing the hall, the band stayed behind and recorded a further take of Epitaph Part 1." -m is this additional take. -m also on Blue Note CD: CDBN-8-28353-2.

As Whitney Balliett wrote about Mingus in the *New Yorker,* this concert, "with thirty all-star musicians on hand, was meant to be a summation of Mingus' work, but, as so often happened in his involuted life, it went wrong. The concert, moved forward five weeks at the behest of the company that was to record it, became an interminable four-hour rehearsal, in which copyists were still at work onstage and almost nothing was played in its entirety."

According to Pepper Adams, in an interview with the author in 1984, "I heard that record, and not only is the sound awful, [but] there were a couple of really good things that we played that night—not all of it was good, but the good things were not on the record....I actually did some of the writing, but I was paid for it, of course. Paid very well, as a matter of fact. That part was nice. I had two things that were completed, on time, were rehearsed, and performed well, and they're not on the record." -j was one of the orchestrations that Adams wrote for the concert that was performed and finally released in 1994 on Blue Note.

Adams' arrangements were not the only things not included on the original release. Of the roughly one hour of music recorded at Town Hall, only 36 minutes of music was on the original LP. According to Brian Priestley's notes for Blue Note's *Charles Mingus: Complete Town Hall Concert,* four tracks were abbreviated and five weren't included. That's because, as Gene Santoro pointed out in the *Village Voice,* "United Artists asked concert promoter [George] Wein to secretly edit the two hours or so of tapes into a record for release. Wein had no music, no outline, no clue about structure or intention. He didn't ask Mingus, who terrified him. So in a single session that ran from 2 to 6am, Wein cut the music by 50 percent, and, in the process, jumbled pieces and titles."

According to Clark Terry, in an interview with the author in 1988,

We were hired by Mingus. We were told it was a concert at Town Hall, so the dress, we assumed, or maybe we were told, was tuxedo/black tie....Prior to that, there was an awful lot of confusion, because the music, which was written for this concert, never was sufficiently rehearsed. It was just ridiculous trying to get through it. I don't know if it was because of the copying, or the late arrival of the parts, or what the heck it was, but it was catastrophic, and it was obvious, before we opened the curtain, that we were *not* going to perform a concert that night with that music. So, we walk on the stage and nobody had actually seen Mingus the last minutes before curtain time (assuming that everybody was going to, at the last minute, get presentable for the concert, whatever they were going to wear). Mingus had on dungarees, and everything, backstage. When the curtain came up, he walks out on stage with the same garb on that he wore backstage—sweatshirt, dungarees, tennis shoes, and whatnot, just like he would sit out in his backyard—and we're in Town Hall! He walks up to the mic and says, if I remember correctly (I don't know the exact words, something to this effect): "Well, I don't know what you folks out there are here for tonight, but we came to work. This is a record date," which, of course, shocked the hell out of all of us behind [the curtain.] We had no idea. None whatsoever! Then, after we found out that's what it was, well, we're there now! So, some of them took off their jackets and rolled up their sleeves: "O.K., let's get to it!" Some of us just stayed as we were. [Mingus] says, "Well, let's get things started here. Just start playing some blues," so he had Dolphy come down and do his little bit with him, with the *weep, bap, bo-bip-bap bo-bap* conversation with him, and then he calls me down and says, "You start this thing off." I said, "Well, what is it, Mingus? What's it all about?" "I don't know. Just play!" And that's why he called it Clark in the Dark, because I was in the dark! The other thing that was very vivid about this was there was this big siren in the back of the bandstand, and, for some strange reason, Ernie Royal found this and he rang this thing rather loudly. I don't know if it was on the album or not. It was really a totally fucked up afternoon! It was the most bizarre and chaotic scene I have ever witnessed!

According to Charles McPherson, in an interview with the author in 1987,

That was the one where all of the music wasn't finished yet and he had, actually, copyists copying parts on the stage while the concert was in progress! That was a fiasco!…Even though the arrangements were being written and copied on the stage, there were moments where it was great, because some of the music was real interesting, so it was a funny evening. People were laughing. I mean, a lot of people weren't "drugged," because they expect this out of Mingus. They expected some bizarre event to go down, and it always did, and that was part of the "Mingus Show": Not just the music, but who he argues with, or who he gets into a fight with, or what happens; will he break his bass? or anything. I'll put it to you this way: He was cognizant of the fact that it could be considered a show. He was aware that some people could interpret it that way, but I really think he was being himself. I don't think anything he did was out of character for him. It wasn't like, "Oh, Let me do this, even though this is against my nature." No, I think everything he did was within the realm of his personality, but I think he was well aware that some of this would be considered bizarre and, actually, interesting.

Historian Dan Morgenstern said, "I was there as well, and I recall that Joe Glaser got up on stage (a rare sight indeed) and told the audience that anyone who wanted their money back could go to the box office and get it."

Journalist George Kanzler said, "I was at that concert....I do remember Mingus telling us all to go out across the street and buy a bottle at the liquor store (causing a big line outside that little store) to bring back in while we waited for him to have charts finished by copyists backstage."

According to trombonist Jimmy Knepper, in an interview with the author in 1988,

I wasn't there. I prepared the music and then Mingus and I had a falling out. He slapped me and broke off one of my capped teeth, so that was the end of working with Mingus for about twenty years. I was copying the music for him, and he kept adding horns until he ended up with about six or seven saxophones, six trombones, six trumpets. The producer didn't expect that, and Mingus had the idea that it was going to be an open record date with an audience witnessing it. He wasn't really prepared. He didn't have a lot of music of his own to play. The day before the rehearsal—there was supposed to be a rehearsal at midnight—the afternoon before, he called me to come up to his apartment. I had done the copying before, and then the very last arrangements came in from Gene Roland, Ed Armour, and Fess Williams, Mingus' uncle. His apartment was at 130th and Fifth Avenue. I went up there and Mingus said, "I want you to write some backgrounds for solos," and I said, "No, Mingus, this is your music. You should write it," at which point he blew up and he slapped me....I went back, got all the copying done, came in, and dropped it on the floor at the rehearsal.

The day of the concert, Knepper visited his dentist, who pulled his broken cap. According to writer Gene Santoro, his dentist recommended a bridge, and, due to the fracas with Mingus, Knepper lost an octave of range. Knepper filed a civil suit against Mingus for damages.

"At that concert," said Eddie Bert to the author in 1988,

Mingus was walking around with a derby hat and hanging around with Fess Williams, [who] had the other band. I think they played at intermission or something. We get on the stage and Melba Liston is still doing some arrangements: There's a table set up and there's three or four chairs around the table in the front of the band. The house was just about sold out and Mingus goes up in the front—we all got tuxedos on—and he says, "Ladies and Gentlemen, this is not a concert. This is a recording and we don't need you, and, if you want to get your money back, you can go to the box office and get your money back!" and half the place left! We were still rehearsing, because the thing wasn't down enough. Parts were still coming in and all that. He said [to us], "Take your jackets off because we're going to be here for a while." Most of the guys took their jackets off. I don't know if you ever saw the picture of the band on the cover? Well, me and Quentin Jackson don't have our jackets off because we figured we were going to have to run, and I don't want to be scuffling with a jacket! I figured the tomatoes and all this stuff is going to come flying at us because some of the people got mad....

Mellow Tone was the last tune that was done. It was a fake tune. At that point, there was so much pressure, really, for getting the concert over. The reason that we played that was because the stagehands would've had to get paid extra because we went into overtime. As soon as the stagehands have to get paid, that means a lot of bread. We don't get paid but they get paid, so you got to close the curtain—and they were closing the curtain on us. So, if you hear that tune, they were closing the curtain! And, right at the end, there's a big thing that goes *bwaaaaaa!* That was me, because I was glad to get the hell out of there! *Bwaaaaaa*, and then I walked out! You can hear that right at the end of the record. The guy that produced the concert, I understand, got fired from the record company.

CHARLES MINGUS
621019
19 October 1962, radio broadcast, Birdland, New York: Ed Armour tp; Don Butterfield tu*; Charles McPherson as; Pepper Adams bs; Jaki Byard p; Charles Mingus b; Dannie Richmond dm.

a	My Search (I Can't Get Started)*	Session LP: 118
b	**Monk, Bunk and Vice Versa**	
c	**Please Don't Come Back from the Moon***	
d	Eat That Chicken*	Music Room Special
		LP: MRS-5046

All tracks on Music Room Special LP: MRS-5046, Rare Live Recordings (Eng) CD: RLR-88661, Jazz View (Eng) CD: COD-028.

CHARLES MINGUS
621026
26 October 1962, WADO radio broadcast, Birdland, New York: Same as 19 October 1962, delete Butterfield:

a	Eat That Chicken	Yadeon (J) CD: 501
b	**Monk, Bunk and Vice Versa** (Osmotin')	Ozone LP: 19
c	**O.P.**	
d	My Search[1] (I Can't Get Started)	

[1]Adams out.

-a on Music Room Special LP: MRS-OZO-14, Yadeon (J) CD: CD-501, Rare Live Recordings (Eng) CD: RLR-88661.
-b on Music Room Special LP: MRS-OZO-14, Yadeon (J) CD: CD-501, Rare Live Recordings (Eng) CD: RLR-88661.
-c on Music Room Special LP: MRS-OZO-14, RLR CD: 88661, Yadeon (J) CD: CD-501, Rare Live Recordings (Eng) CD: RLR-88661. An edited version of -c on i Maestri del Jazz (It) LP: MJP-1067.
-d on Yadeon (J) CD: CD-501, Rare Live Recordings (Eng) CD: RLR-88661.
This date includes the likely world premiere of O.P., Mingus' dedication to bassist Oscar Pettiford.

TEDDY CHARLES
630423
23 April 1963, New York: Jerome Richardson ts, fl; Zoot Sims ts; Pepper Adams bs; Eric Dolphy bcl; Hall Overton p; Jimmy Raney g; Teddy Charles vib; Teddy Kotick b; Osie Johnson dm.

a	Scheherazade Blue	United Artists LP: UAL-3365
b	Love for Three Oranges March	
c	**Borodin's Bossa Nova**	

All tracks on United Artists LP: UAS-6365, London (Eng) LP: LTZ-K15034, Jazz Beat (Sp) CD: 533.

TEDDY CHARLES
630506
6 May 1963, New York: Jerome Richardson ts, fl; Jimmy Giuffre ts, cl; Pepper Adams bs; Tommy Newsom bcl; Hank Jones p; Jim Hall g; Teddy Charles vib; Teddy Kotick b; Osie Johnson dm.

a **Dance Arabe**   United Artists LP: UAL-3365
b **Etude**

All tracks on United Artists LP: UAS-6365, London (Eng) LP: LTZ-K15034, Jazz Beat (Sp) CD: 533.

MARCUS BELGRAVE
630620
20 June 1963, Graystone Ballroom, Detroit: Marcus Belgrave tp; George Bohanon, Paul Riser tb; Benny Maupin ts: Pepper Adams bs; Kirk Lightsey p; Cecil McBee b; George Goldsmith dm.

a 049317   Odom's Cave   Motown unissued
b 049318   These Are the Things I Love
c 049319   Express Way
d   Elsie's Promenade

MARCUS BELGRAVE
630626
26 June 1963, Graystone Ballroom, Detroit: Same as 20 June 1963:

a 017219   Sweet and Lovely   Motown unissued
b   Oasis
c   Elaine My Dear
d   Dues Unpaid

JIMMY WITHERSPOON
630700
c. Summer 1963, CBC TV broadcast, Toronto: Dizzy Reece tp; John Gilmore ts; Pepper Adams bs; John Hicks p; Ali Jackson b; Charli Persip dm; Jimmy Witherspoon voc.

This program was entitled *Sixty Minutes with Spoon,* produced by Darrell Duke. It isn't clear if the audio or video still exist.

PEPPER ADAMS – PLAYS THE MUSIC OF CHARLIE MINGUS
630909
9 September 1963, New York: Thad Jones tp; Pepper Adams bs; Hank Jones p; Paul Chambers b; Dannie Richmond dm.

a 061204 **Strollin' Honies** (Nostalgia in Times Square) Jazz Workshop LP: JWS-219
b 061205 **Carolyn**
c 061214 Song with Orange (Orange Was the Color of Her Dress Then Blue Silk)
d 061216 **Incarnation** (Reincarnation of a Lovebird)
e 061302 **Black Light** (Peggy's Blue Skylight)
f 061304 **Fables of Faubus**

All tracks on Jazz Workshop (Eu) LP: JW-018, Victor/Tamla Motown (J) LP: SMJ-7475, Fresh Sound (Sp) CD: FSR-CD-177, Fresh Sound (Sp) CD: FSR-CD-341, Fresh Sound (Sp) CD: FSR-CD-604.
According to Motown ledgers, as many as 51 total takes were done on this and its companion session. *See* 630912.
This is Adams' ninth date as a leader.
According to Adams, in an interview with Peter Danson in *Coda*,

Thad arranged three or four of them, and I arranged three, and Mingus wrote one thing himself specifically for the date [track -d], which was marvelous. That one he finished on time, then got it in so we could look at it and record it. And, of course, with Thad and I doing the rest of the writing, everything was done. Mingus came to the date and just watched in open-mouth astonishment at the fact that a date could be done smoothly, without rancor, no screaming, no throwing things. Just professional musicians who have the music ready, and go in and play it and get a good performance. He just couldn't believe that record dates were like that.

PEPPER ADAMS – PLAYS THE MUSIC OF CHARLIE MINGUS
630912
12 September 1963, New York: Thad Jones tp; Benny Powell tb; Charles McPherson as; Zoot Sims ts; Pepper Adams bs; Hank Jones p; Bob Cranshaw b; Dannie Richmond dm.

a 061212 **Better Git It in Your Soul**   Jazz Workshop LP: JWS-219

b   061213   **Haitian Fight Song**
c   061215   Portrait

All tracks on Jazz Workshop (Eu) LP: JW-018, Victor/Tamla Motown (J) LP: SMJ-7475, Fresh Sound (Sp) CD: FSR-CD-177, Fresh Sound (Sp) CD: FSR-CD-341, Fresh Sound (Sp) CD: FSR-CD-604. *See* 630909.

PEPPER ADAMS
631203
3 December 1963, New York: Thad Jones tp; Quentin Jackson tb; Jerome Richardson ts, bcl; Jerry Dodgion as, cl; Pepper Adams bs; Roland Hanna p; George Duvivier b; Grady Tate dm.

a   065101   **Moten Swing**   Motown unissued
b   065102   **One Mint Julep**
c   065103   **Port of Rico**
d   065104   **Azurte**

This is Adams' tenth date as a leader.
According to Jerome Richardson, in an interview with the author in 1987,

I did an A&R job for a company—it was my one job as an A&R man—because they wanted something different and they had signed Pepper. They wanted me to do an updated thing on Pepper; not a complete jazz thing, they wanted me to try to do a more commercial thing with Pep. Thad wrote the charts on it. I picked all those tunes. I was trying to find something, according to what they wanted, to change his image. We talked about bringing back some of these old tunes and putting them in a different perspective for Pepper.

LIONEL HAMPTON
640707
c. 7 July 1964, WNEW TV broadcast, possibly Plugged Nickel, Chicago: Martin Banks, Jimmy Owens, Al Bryant tp; Garnett Brown, Sam Hurt tb; Ed Pazant, Bobby Plater as; Andy McGhee ts; Fred Jackson ts; Pepper Adams bs; Billy Mackel g; Lionel Hampton vib, voc; Lawrence Burgan b; Floyd Williams dm.

According to historian Otto Flueckiger, this was a 25-minute broadcast. The band played at least two different engagements in Chicago from 6-12 July. It isn't clear if the audio or video still exist.

Adams toured with Lionel Hampton's band beginning in January 1964, and stayed with the band until the end of August. Jimmy Owens and Andy McGhee quit before the band left in July for Europe, partly because it was Hampton's intention to scale down the size of the band for the upcoming tour. This was Adams' first trip to Europe. *See* 640723, 640724, 640725, and 611209 notes.

LIONEL HAMPTON
640723
23 July 1964, audience recording, Antibes Jazz Festival, Juan-les-Pins, France: Martin Banks, Benny Bailey tp; Bobby Plater as, fl; Ed Pazant ts, cl; Pepper Adams, Cecil Payne bs; Billy Mackel g; Lionel Hampton vib, voc; Lawrence Burgan b; Floyd Williams dm.

a   Sophisticated Lady

See 640707, 640724, 640725, and 611209 notes.

LIONEL HAMPTON
640724
24 July 1964, audience recording, Casino, Divonne-les-Bains, France: Same as 23 July 1964, omit Bailey:

a   Medley:
         Flying Home
         unknown title
b   Undecided
c   **Broadway**
d   unknown blues
e   Midnight Sun
f   Avalon
g   Tenderly
h   **Flying Home**
i   And the Angels Sing
j   Medley:
         unknown blues
         Hey Ba-Ba-Re-Bop

Caldonia
k Hello, Dolly
m **C Jam Blues**
n Medley:
   unknown title
   unknown title
   Hava Nagila
   On the Sunny Side of the Street

A silent film of this performance was produced by historian Otto
Flueckiger.
See 640707, 640723, 640725, and 611209 notes.

LIONEL HAMPTON
640725
25 July 1964, audience recording, Casino, Knokke, Belgium: Same as 24
July 1964.

See 640707, 640723, 640724, and 611209 notes.

OLIVER NELSON
641110
10 November 1964, Van Gelder Studio, Englewood Cliffs NJ: Thad Jones
tp; Phil Woods as; Phil Bodner ts, engh; Pepper Adams bs; Roger Kellaway p; Richard Davis b; Grady Tate dm; Oliver Nelson arr; GUEST: Ben
Webster ts.*

a	90199	Midnight Blue*	Impulse LP: A-75
b	90200	Goin' to Chicago Blues	
c	90201	Blues for "Mr. Broadway"*	
d	90202	One for Phil	Impulse LP: A-9101
e	90203	**One for Bob**	Impulse LP: A-75

-a on Impulse LP: AS-75, Impulse LP: IMP-212, MCA-Impulse LP:
MCA-29052, Jasmine (Eng) LP: JAS-21, Victor (Eng) LP: CLP-1868,
Victor (J) LP: VIM-5562, Impulse Nippon-Columbia (J) LP: YP-8502-
AI, GRD-Impulse CD: GRD-121, Impulse CD: GRP-212, Impulse CD:
IMPD-212, GRP CD: 512122, MCA-Impulse CD: MCAD-5888, Univer-
sal-Impulse CD: 19131, Universal CD: [Starbucks sampler], Impulse
(Eu) CD: IMPD-12122, MCA-Impulse (Eu) CD: 2292-54643-2, Bou-

tique (Ger) CD: 0600-75318-2147, Impulse (J) CD: UCCI-9068, Impulse (J) CD: YX-8568, MCA-Impulse (J) CD: 32XD-618, Impulse (J) CD: UCCI-9151, Impulse (J) CD: MVCJ-19131, MCA-Victor (J) CD: MVCI-23075.

-b on Impulse LP: AS-75, Impulse LP: IMP-212, MCA-Impulse LP: MCA-29052, Victor (Eng) LP: CLP-1868, Jasmine (Eng) LP: JAS-21, Victor (J) LP: VIM-5562, Impulse Nippon-Columbia (J) LP: YP-8502-AI, Impulse CD: GRP-212, Impulse CD: IMPD-212, GRP CD: 512122, MCA-Impulse CD: MCAD-5888, Universal-Impulse CD: 19131, Impulse (Eu) CD: IMPD-12122, MCA-Impulse (Eu) CD: 2292-54643-2, Impulse (J) CD: YX-8568, MCA-Impulse (J) CD: 32XD-618, MCA-Victor (J) CD: MVCI-23075, Impulse (J) CD: UCCI-9068, Impulse (J) CD: UCCI-9151, Impulse (J) CD: MVCJ-19131.

-c on Impulse LP: AS-75, Impulse LP: IMP-212, MCA-Impulse LP: MCA-29052, Jasmine (Eng) LP: JAS-21, Victor (Eng) LP: CLP-1868, Columbia (J) LP: YP-8502-AI, Victor (J) LP: VIM-5562, MCA-Impulse CD: MCAD-5888, GRD-Impulse CD: GRD-121, Verve CD: 314-543-808-2, Impulse CD: GRP-212, Impulse CD: IMPD-212, GRP CD: 512122, Universal-Impulse CD: 19131, Impulse (Eu) CD: IMPD-12122, Impulse (Eu) CD: 2292-54643-2, Impulse (J) CD: YX-8568, MCA-Impulse (J) CD: 32XD-618, MCA-Victor (J) CD: MVCI-23075, Impulse Nippon-Impulse (J) CD: UCCI-9068, Impulse (J) CD: UCCI-9151, Impulse (J) CD: MVCJ-19131.

-d on Impulse LP: AS-9101, Impulse CD: GRP-212, Impulse CD: IMPD-212, GRP CD: 512122, Universal-Impulse CD: 19131, Impulse (Eu) CD: IMPD-12122.

-e on Impulse LP: AS-75, Impulse LP: IMP-212, MCA-Impulse LP: MCA-29052, Jasmine (Eng) LP: JAS-21, Victor (Eng) LP: CLP-1868, Victor (J) LP: VIM-5562, Impulse Nippon-Columbia (J) LP: YP-8502-AI, Impulse CD: GRP-212, Impulse CD: IMPD-212, MCA-Impulse CD: MCAD-5888, GRP CD: 512122, Universal-Impulse CD: 19131, Impulse (Eu) CD: IMPD-12122, MCA-Impulse (Eu) CD: 2292-54643-2, Impulse (J) CD: YX-8568, MCA-Impulse (J) CD: 32XD-618, MCA-Victor (J) CD: MVCI-23075, Impulse (J) CD: UCCI-9068, Impulse (J) CD: UCCI-9151, Impulse (J) CD: MVCJ-19131.

On a 23 February 1986 radio interview, conducted in Montreal by Len Dobbin, Pepper Adams said the following: "It was a lot of fun. It was some hard music, but it came off very well. Among other things, it won the Grande Prix du Disque in France, so, somehow, the photograph in the interior of the album got reproduced in numerous French magazines. That was [taken] after the date was all over, and Oliver and I were in a celebratory mood."

See 641111.

OLIVER NELSON
641111
11 November 1964, Van Gelder Studio, Englewood Cliffs NJ: Same as 10 November 1964, add Danny Moore tp*; GUEST: Ben Webster ts†:

a   90204   **Blues and the Abstract Truth*** Impulse LP: A-75
b   90205   The Critic's Choice*
c   90206   Night Lights¹†   Impulse LP: A-100
d   90207   **Theme from "Mr. Broadway"** Impulse LP: A-75
e   90208   **Blues O'Mighty**

¹Adams out.

-a on Impulse LP: AS-75, Impulse LP: IMP-212, MCA-Impulse LP: MCA-29052, Impulse (Neth) LP: HAS-9101, Jasmine (Eng) LP: JAS-21, Victor (Eng) LP: CLP-1868, Victor (J) LP: VIM-5562, Impulse Nippon-Columbia (J) LP: YP-8502-AI, Impulse CD: GRP-212, Impulse CD: IMPD-212, GRP CD: 512122, Universal-Impulse CD: 19131, MCA-Impulse CD: MCAD-5888, Impulse (Eu) CD: IMPD-12122, MCA-Impulse (Eu) CD: 2292-54643-2, Impulse (J) CD: YX-8568, MCA-Impulse (J) CD: 32XD-618, MCA-Victor (J) CD: MVCI-23075, Impulse (J) CD: UCCI-9068, Impulse (J) CD: UCCI-9151, Impulse (J) CD: MVCJ-19131.

-b on Impulse LP: AS-75, Impulse LP: IMP-212, MCA-Impulse LP: MCA-29052, Affinity (Eng) LP: AFF-190, Jasmine (Eng) LP: JAS-21, Victor (Eng) LP: CLP-1868, Victor (J) LP: VIM-5562, Impulse Nippon-Columbia (J) LP: YP-8502-AI, Impulse CD: GRP-212, Impulse CD: IMPD-212, MCA-Impulse CD: MCAD-5888, GRP CD: 512122, Universal-Impulse CD: 19131, Impulse (Eu) CD: IMPD-12122, MCA-Impulse (Eu) CD: 2292-54643-2, Impulse (J) CD: YX-8568, MCA-Impulse (J) CD: 32XD-618, MCA-Victor (J) CD: MVCI-23075, Impulse (J) CD: UCCI-9068, Impulse (J) CD: UCCI-9151, Impulse (J) CD: MVCJ-19131.

-c on Impulse LP: AS-100, Impulse LP: AS-75, Impulse LP: IMP-212, MCA-Impulse LP: MCA-29052, Jasmine (Eng) LP: JAS-21, Victor (Eng) LP: CLP-1868, Victor (J) LP: VIM-5562, Impulse Nippon-Columbia (J) LP: YP-8502-AI, MCA-Impulse CD: MCAD-588, Impulse

CD: GRP-212, Impulse CD: IMPD-212, GRP CD: 512122, Universal-Impulse CD: 19131, Impulse (Eu) CD: IMPD-12122, MCA-Impulse (Eu) CD: 2292-54643-2, Impulse (J) CD: YX-8568, MCA-Impulse (J) CD: 32XD-618, MCA-Victor (J) CD: MVCI-23075, Impulse (J) CD: UCCI-9068, Impulse (J) CD: UCCI-9151, Impulse (J) CD: MVCJ-19131.

-d on Impulse CD: GRP-212, Impulse CD: IMPD-212, GRP CD: 512122, Universal-Impulse CD: 19131, Impulse (Eu) CD: IMPD-12122.

-e on Impulse LP: AS-75, Impulse LP: IMP-212, MCA-Impulse LP: MCA-29052, Jasmine (Eng) LP: JAS-21, Victor (Eng) LP: CLP-1868, Victor (J) LP: VIM-5562, Impulse Nippon-Columbia (J) LP: YP-8502-AI, MCA-Impulse CD: MCAD-5888, Impulse CD: GRP-212, Impulse CD: IMPD-212, GRP CD: 512122, Universal-Impulse CD: 19131, Impulse (Eu) CD: IMPD-12122, MCA-Impulse (Eu) CD: 2292-54643-2, Impulse (J) CD: YX-8568, MCA-Impulse (J) CD: 32XD-618, MCA-Victor (J) CD: MVCI-23075, Impulse (J) CD: UCCI-9068, Impulse (J) CD: UCCI-9151, Impulse (J) CD: MVCJ-19131.

According to Adams, in an interview with Peter Danson in *Coda,* "That one thing [in Blues and the Abstract Truth] that makes such a terrific exercise, with all the fourth sequences in it: that one was passed out on the first day and recorded on a subsequent date. So we all had a chance to look at that at home, thank God. The rest of it was pretty much passed out and performed right on the spot."

See 641110.

QUINCY JONES
641220
20 December 1964, New York: Jimmy Maxwell, Jimmy Nottingham, Nat Adderley, Freddie Hubbard, Joe Newman tp; J. J. Johnson, Curtis Fuller, Kai Winding, Melba Liston tb; Phil Woods, Jerry Dodgion as; James Moody as, fl; Benny Golson, Lucky Thompson ts; Roland Kirk ts, ss; Pepper Adams bs; Bobby Scott p; Milt Jackson vib; Bob Cranshaw b; Art Blakey dm; GUEST: Dizzy Gillespie tp.

a	34247	I Had a Ball	Limelight LP: LM-82002
b	34248	Almost	
c	34249	Addie's At it Again	

-a on Limelight LP: LS-86002, Mercury LP: SRM-2-623, Mercury (Eu) LP: 134 587-MFY, Limelight (Eu) LP: 220-012-LMY, Philips

Timeless (Eng) LP: TIME-07, Philips (Eng) LP: SON-033, Mercury (Eng) LP: SMWL-21022, Limelight (Neth) LP: LM-210-012-LML, Phonogram (J) LP: 15PJ-023, Mosaic CD: MD5-237, Mercury (Eu) CD: 846-630-2.

-b on Limelight LP: LS-86002, Limelight (Eu) LP: 220-012-LMY, Mercury (Eng) LP: SMWL-21022, Limelight (Neth) LP: LM-210-012-LML, Phonogram (J) LP: 15PJ-023, Mosaic CD: MD5-237.

-c on Limelight LP: LS-86002, Mercury (Eu) LP: 134-587-MFY, Limelight (Eu) LP: 220-012-LMY, Mercury (Eng) LP: SMWL-21022, Limelight (Neth) LP: LM-210-012-LML, Phonogram (J) LP: 15PJ-023, Mosaic CD: MD5-237, Mercury (Eu) CD: 846-630-2.

According to Phil Woods, in an interview done with the author in 1989, "I was the contractor on that date. I hired the musicians. I hired Pepper. You bet your *ass* I hired Pepper!"

According to Jerry Dodgion, in an interview with the author in 1988,

Billy Byers did the arrangements. Billy Byers was the real Quincy Jones in those days. Billy and Quincy had a great partnership going. Quincy could get the job. He was very charming. He was a great writer also, but he couldn't write fast enough! He'd get a job: Say, "Tomorrow we need an album for Dinah Washington," and he would say, "Well, I can't write that fast." Billy would say, "How many tunes do you need? I'll do some." He'd give some to Al Cohn. They all helped each other. Al Cohn ghosted for a lot of people....When you ghost, you don't get any credit. But it's O.K. You get paid!...I remember Art Blakey very conscientiously listening to the playback. He said, "I want to make sure I use enough bass drum behind Dizzy because he likes bass drum," which is true.

According to Bob Cranshaw, in an interview done with the author in 1988,

It was a lot of fun. It was another one of Quincy's ventures. What I remember about the big band part of it was that it was so many people that you usually didn't see together. I remember Art [Blakey] coming in. Usually, it would have been me and it would have been Grady [Tate], but Grady came in and played the arrangement down so that Art could hear it, because Art couldn't read. Quincy is a master. Again, much like a Duke Ellington, one of his great points is he knows people. He knows all the musicians and he kind of knows—he has an idea of abilities. Quincy usually gets what he wants, like a Duke Ellington, from just placing combinations of certain people. Art was one of the people who wasn't a reader, not that he couldn't have come in and played the arrangements down and probably heard them after a couple of times, but they paid Grady. He was right there, and, of course, Grady is an excellent reader. Grady played the arrangement and then Art got on the drums and played the shit out it! Again, having that group of people together is always nice for the musicians because we don't see each other all the time, so that's like a festival. It's like Old Home Week, where all of a sudden you see guys and play with guys that wouldn't ordinarily be in that situation. I think it was done in one day.

JIMMY HEATH
650314
14 March 1965, private recording, Madison Club, Baltimore: Jimmy Heath as, ts; Pepper Adams bs; Gus Simms p; Wilbur Little b; Bertell Knox dm.

This was a Charlie Parker Memorial Concert, produced by the Left Bank Jazz Society.

Chapter 4
Thaddeus: 1965-1977

AUTHOR'S NOTE
The Thad Jones-Pepper Adams Quintet's first known gig took place at the Clifton Tap Room in Clifton NJ on c. 20-26 March 1965. The rhythm section was comprised of Hank Jones, Ron Carter, and John Dentz. Subsequent quintet gigs, predating the establishment of the Thad Jones-Mel Lewis Orchestra (*see* 651126), were a return engagement at the Clifton Tap Room on 7-8 May, a month engagement at the Five Spot (c. 18 May-13 June, with Duke Pearson replacing Hank Jones), and a gig at Slug's (20-25 July). The Quintet would finally record their only LP in April-May 1966. *See* 660426.

JIMMY HEATH
650425
25 April 1965, private recording, Murphy Fine Arts Center at Morgan State College, Baltimore: Kenny Dorham tp; Sonny Red as; Jimmy Heath ts; Pepper Adams bs; Cedar Walton p; Reggie Workman b; Roy Brooks dm.

a **Gingerbread Boy**
b Pensativa[1]
c Medley:
  It's Magic[2]
  Sophisticated Lady[3]
d **Bluesville**
e Medley:
  Be My Love[4]
  When Sunny Gets Blue[5]
f **Project S**

g   **Green Dolphin Street**

[1]Dorham and rhythm section.
[2]Red and rhythm section.
[3]Adams and rhythm section.
[4]Dorham and rhythm section.
[5]Heath and rhythm section.

This concert was recorded by the Left Bank Jazz Society. *See* 650314.

DUKE PEARSON–HONEYBUNS
650525
25-26 May 1965, Atlantic Studios, New York: Johnny Coles tp; Garnett Brown tb; James Spaulding as; George Coleman ts; Les Spann fl; Pepper Adams bs, cl; Duke Pearson p; Bob Cranshaw b; Mickey Roker dm.

a   Honeybuns   Atlantic LP: SD-3002
b   New Girl
c   You Know I Care
d   Is That So
e   Our Love
f   Heavy Legs

It's unclear what tunes from each date were released on the LP.
All tracks on Rhino Atlantic CD: 08122-7681869, Collectables CD: COL-6754, Koch (Ger) CD: KOC-8519.

THAD JONES-MEL LEWIS
651126
26, 27 or 28 November 1965, various private recordings, A&R Studios, New York: Thad Jones flh; Snooky Young, Jimmy Nottingham, Bill Berry, Jimmy Owens tp; Bob Brookmeyer vtb; Garnett Brown, Jack Rains tb; Cliff Heather btb; Jerome Richardson as, ss, cl, fl; Jerry Dodgion as, ss, fl; Joe Farrell fl, ts, ss; Eddie Daniels ts, ss, cl; Pepper Adams bs, cl; Hank Jones p; Sam Herman g; Richard Davis b; Mel Lewis dm.

The band's first New York rehearsal, prior to opening at the Village Vanguard on 7 February 1966, was conducted by Thad Jones at A&R Studios the previous November (either Friday, Saturday, or Sunday, 26-

28 November) during Thanksgiving weekend. Pepper Adams made the
first rehearsal, and Marv Holladay took his place for some of the others
before the Vanguard opening. Holladay also took Adams' chair for some
Monday nights until Summer 1966, when Jones finally persuaded Adams
to join the band full-time. According to Marv Holladay, in an interview
with the author in 1987,

> Thad started doing a homeboy routine on him, and what all his
> mother used to do for him, and everything! He wanted Pepper be-
> cause Pepper is such a phenomenal soloist. When Thad put together
> that rehearsal band, he asked Pepper to make it. Pepper told him he
> didn't want to. Pepper was a small group player and did not like
> playing with a big band. That was his thing. He never, ever played
> with a big band he really enjoyed playing with, at least at that point.
> Since he didn't want to make it, he said, "Why don't you call
> Marv?" and so they did....The band started in the Fall of '65 and it
> started with the rehearsal band. We used to rehearse at A&R Studi-
> os, after the place had shut down—always after midnight—and [en-
> gineer] Phil [Ramone] would run a tape of all the rehearsals that
> were done, and we would get to hear back what we played and re-
> hearsed. At that time they were right above Jim and Andy's on 46th.

According to Jimmy Owens, in an interview with the author in 1987,

> That was Phil Ramone's studio, and he had an engineering
> school, so he used to use his engineering students to train them to
> learn how to record a big band. They'd come in at midnight and we
> usually rehearsed until 3 o'clock. At one of the A&R rehearsals,
> Thad came up up and said, "Listen, we have this possibility of do-
> ing this gig on Monday nights. It doesn't pay a lot of money." I
> think it was $20 a night. Most of the guys in that band were studio
> musicians who had good gigs, so, hey, they were all for it. The [oth-
> er] guys—I'm sure Garnett Brown, Peppper, myself—we weren't
> doing a lot of studio work like that. But that's when we started the
> Vanguard: Instead of rehearsing Monday nights at midnight, we
> worked Monday nights at the Vanguard. I worked with the band for
> three months and I left to go to Japan with Herbie Mann.

Trombonist John Mosca told the author in a 1988 interview, "According to Mel Lewis, Jerome [Richardson] wasn't supposed to be on the
band at all. Thad's idea was to have Phil Woods be the lead alto player,

but Jerome bugged him. Jerome heard that he was starting a band and just got in his face."

Additionally, regarding personnel, in the liner notes to *Suite for Pops* (*see* 720125, 720126, 720131) Mel Lewis told writer Arnold Jay Smith, "We would have had [trombonist] Willie Dennis and [trumpeter] Nick Travis, but they passed before we formed."

BLUE MITCHELL
651212
12 December 1965, private recording, Madison Club, Baltimore: Blue Mitchell tp; Pepper Adams bs; Duke Pearson p; Ron Carter b; John Dentz dm.

This concert was recorded by the Left Bank Jazz Society.
See 650314.

THAD JONES-PEPPER ADAMS
660121
21 January 1966, WABC radio broadcast, Half Note, New York: Thad Jones flh; Pepper Adams bs; Duke Pearson p; Reggie Workman b; Mel Lewis dm.

a   **Oleo**
b   **No Refill**
c   **Little Waltz**
d   **Excerent**

This was broadcast live on Alan Grant's program *Portraits in Jazz.* About the upcoming, first Thad Jones-Mel Lewis Orchestra public performance at the Village Vanguard (*see* 660207), Grant says, on this broadcast, "I'm going to be presenting the band on February the 7th."

PEPPER ADAMS
660128
c. 28 January 1966, WABC radio broadcast, Half Note, New York: Eddie Daniels ts; Pepper Adams bs; Bob James p; Chuck Israels b; Marty Morell dm.

a   **Little Waltz**
b   **St. Thomas**

c **Solar**
d **'Round Midnight**

This was broadcast live on Alan Grant's program *Portraits in Jazz.*

JOE ZAWINUL–MONEY IN THE POCKET
660207a
7 February 1966, Atlantic Studios, New York: Blue Mitchell tp; Joe Henderson ts; Pepper Adams bs; Joe Zawinul p; Sam Jones b; Louis Hayes dm.

a 11272   **If**   Atlantic LP: SD-3004
   Solo piano:
b 11273   My One and Only Love
   Full ensemble:
c 11274   **Midnight Mood**
d 11275   Some More of Dat
   Rhythm section only:
e 11276   Sharon's Waltz
f 11277   Del Sasser
   Full ensemble:
g 11279   **Riverbed**

-b on Atlantic LP: SD-1694, Atlantic (F) LP: W-50319, Atlantic (It) LP: ATL-09006, Atlantic CD: 71675, Atlantic CD: 81712-4, Rhino-Atlantic (Eu) CD: 8122-71675-2, Warner Brothers-Atlantic Masters (Eng) CD: 8122-79822-0.
   -g on Atlantic LP: SD-5060, Atlantic (It) LP: ATL-09006, Atlantic CD: 71675, Rhino-Atlantic (Eu) CD: 8122-71675-2, Warner Brothers-Atlantic Masters (Eng) CD: 8122-79822-0.
   All other tracks on Atlantic (It) LP: ATL-09006, Atlantic CD: 71675, Rhino-Atlantic (Eu) CD: 8122-71675-2, Warner Brothers-Atlantic Masters (Eng) CD: 8122-79822-0.
   Zawinul's composition Money in the Pocket, the eighth tune on this LP, was recorded by Blue Mitchell, Clifford Jordan, Joe Zawinul, Bob Cranshaw, and Roy McCurdy on a different session the same day.
   In Cannonball Adderley's liner notes to the original release, he wrote, "Pepper's solo on Riverbed is outstanding. His handling of the difficult bridge is a lesson for all saxophone players."

THAD JONES-MEL LEWIS
660207b
7 February 1966, WABC radio broadcast, Village Vanguard, New York:
Thad Jones flh; Snooky Young, Jimmy Nottingham, Bill Berry, Jimmy Owens tp; Bob Brookmeyer vtb; Garnett Brown, Jack Rains tb; Cliff Heather btb; Jerome Richardson as, ss, cl, fl; Jerry Dodgion as, ss, fl; Joe Farrell fl, ts, ss; Eddie Daniels ts, ss, cl; Pepper Adams, Marv Holladay bs, cl; Hank Jones p; Sam Herman g; Richard Davis b; Mel Lewis dm; Alan Grant mc.

a Big Dipper   BMG (NZ) CD: 74321-51939-2
b Polka Dots and Moonbeams[1]
c **Once Around**
d All My Yesterdays
e Mornin' Reverend
f Low Down
g Lover Man
h Mean What You Say
i Don't Ever Leave Me
j Willow Weep for Me
k The Little Pixie

[1]Piano, bass, and drums only, with an improvised ending by reed section.

This is the band's first public performance. All tracks were taped for broadcast on Alan Grant's radio show *Portraits in Jazz,* and this BMG release is an Alan Grant production. Grant often promoted the musicians he liked by broadcasting them in performance on his show, as well as using the show as a platform for advertising upcoming events. (*See also* 660128.) On his 21 January 1966 program (*see* 660121), Grant took a moment to promote this historic Jones-Lewis gig.

It's not clear if both Adams and Holladay played on opening night. According to saxophonist Frank Basile, "all the section playing throughout the whole recording sounds like Pepper," and, moreover, there's no disputing Adams soloing on Once Around. Nevertheless, the band played at least three sets, and Holladay had been subbing for Adams at the band's rehearsals. Additionally, the cover to the CD booklet is a concert program, in the form of a drawing, and it lists as the band personnel both Adams and Holladay.

The band did not play the following Monday night, due to it being Valentine's Day (a potentially poor night to draw an audience). On the band's second Monday night Village Vanguard gig (21 February), Doc Holladay subbed for Adams, who was on tour with Teddy Charles until early March. Adams had left from New York with Charles' band on 16 February for a twenty-hour drive to Stout State College in Menomonie WI. From there, the group played a string of one-nighters through c. 5 March.

In an interview with the author in 2011, Teddy Charles remembered the tour: "We probably left early in the morning and drove all the way to the gig, then got some sleep after the show. That's what we used to do in those days. We all piled into my car. The tour of concerts was arranged by a woman in New York that booked a lot of classical concerts."

According to Doc Holladay, in an interview with the author in 1987, Holladay was Pepper Adams' sub on Monday nights until the summer of 1966 (*see also* 651126):

Mel [Lewis] got [Vanguard owner] Max [Gordon] talked into letting us come down. Max said, "O.K., look, you cats can come down Monday night, just one night. I'll put out a $2.50 cover charge as they come in the door, and whatever we can pull in the door you guys can have." The only money he was going to make was on the bar. So he figured, "Well, we'll try it and see." The first night we had a pretty good crowd by 11 o'clock! Not bad. Probably 2/3, 3/4 of the house. A lot of them were friends, musicians that knew us. So, after that first night, the next Monday night we went down there. Man, it was raining, and I rode down with Jerome [Richardson]. Jerome and I grabbed a cab because we were both living on that side of town. We went down to the gig, and we pulled up in front of this joint, and there was a line around the corner in the rain! The second night! We had to work our way through the crowd and find our way downstairs to get in the joint, and this was before the band was going to play.... Word of mouth got out and that place was packed from that night forward!...

It was interesting, because, as we were working our way through the crowd, we ran into musician after musician after musician: Joe Wilder and Milt Hinton, people like that. Old cats that have been established in the business. They were standing out there, waiting to get in! It was an amazing experience! It blew me away! But we got ourselves downstairs and the band started playing.... And, of course, it was interesting how quick Max decided he was going to pay us all $20 a man, instead of letting us have the door. It took him no time at all!

In 1988 Jerry Dodgion spoke with the author about the band:

> In the very beginning there wasn't very much of a book. I mean, we had six tunes, I think. By the third set we were playing a lot of the things from the first set, but they always sounded different anyway, because Thad didn't want them to sound exactly the same. In the middle of somebody's solo he'd have the whole ensemble lay out, and maybe you'd just find yourself playing with the bass; or maybe with nobody, just playing alone for a while, and then he would add the bass. He would do all this conducting and orchestrating, some-times spontaneously, like that. While you were playing a solo he might have the saxophones, all of them together, play one note, or just playing with the bass, or maybe he would add the drums. And then he would give the brass an accented chord on a cue, every once in a while. He's composing and conducting at the same time. It was really a wonderful experience, because you were a small group and you were a big band. In the band you never knew what was going to happen, so you can imagine how interesting it was for the audience!

THAD JONES-MEL LEWIS
660318
18 March 1966, radio broadcast, Hunter College, New York: Thad Jones flh; Snooky Young, Jimmy Nottingham, Bill Berry, Jimmy Owens tp; Bob Brookmeyer vtb; Garnett Brown, Jack Rains tb; Cliff Heather btb; Jerome Richardson as, ss, cl, fl; Jerry Dodgion as, ss, fl; Joe Farrell ts, ss, fl; Eddie Daniels ts, ss, cl; Pepper Adams bs, cl; Hank Jones p; Sam Herman g; Richard Davis b; Mel Lewis dm.

a   Back Bone
b   **The Little Pixie**
c   Big Dipper
d   The Second Race
e   Once Around
f   Willow Weep for Me
g   Blues and the Abstract Truth
h   Hoedown
i   unknown title

Because the band's book of arrangements was small and still evolving, they played tunes from their repertoire, as well as others by Oliver Nelson and Johnny Richards.

JIMMY WITHERSPOON–BLUES FOR EASY LIVERS
660400

c. *Spring 1966, New York:* Pepper Adams bs; Roger Kellaway p; Richard Davis b; Mel Lewis dm; Jimmy Witherspoon voc.

a **Lotus Blossom** (Marijuana)   Prestige LP: PR-7475
b **Gee Baby, Ain't I Good to You**
c **Embraceable You**
d **Blues in the Night**
e **Trouble in Mind**
f I Got it Bad (And that Ain't Good)

-e on Victor (J) LP: VIP-5007, Prestige CD: PRCD-11008-2, Prestige CD: PRCD-11008-2, Original Blues Classics CD: OBCCD-585-2.

All tracks on Victor (J) LP: VIP-5007, Prestige CD: PRCD-11008-2, Original Blues Classics CD: OBCCD-585-2.

According to trombonist Bill Watrous, who participated in this recording project, but on a different session, "Roger Kellaway wrote the music for that. They were sketch charts," he told the author in an interview in 1989. "Roger sort of laid out the plan that everyone was to follow. Basically, they were all things that 'Spoon' did, so all Roger did was simply organize everything and assign solos to various people."

PEPPER ADAMS
660403

3 April 1966, private recording, Crystal Ballroom, Baltimore: Morris Goldberg as, cl; Carlos Ward ts; Pepper Adams bs; Dollar Brand p; Donald Moore b; Mel Lewis dm.

This concert was recorded by the Left Bank Jazz Society.
See 650314.

THAD JONES-PEPPER ADAMS – MEAN WHAT YOU SAY 660426

26 April, 4 May, 9 May 1966, Plaza Sound Studios, New York: Thad Jones flh; Pepper Adams bs; Duke Pearson p; Ron Carter b; Mel Lewis dm.

a **Mean What You Say**   Milestone LP: MLP-1001
b **H and T Blues**
c **Wives and Lovers**
d **Bossa Nova Ova**
e **No Refill**
f **Little Waltz**
g **Chant**
h **Yes, Sir, That's My Baby**

It's not clear what titles were recorded on what date.

All tracks on Milestone LP: MSP-9001, Original Jazz Classics LP: OJC-464, Original Jazz Classics CD: OJCCD-464-2.

This is Adams' eleventh date as a leader.

According to Adams, in a 1983 interview with Peter Danson in *Coda,* "I think [engineer] Elvin Campbell got a little too much echo on it. I think, later on, he worked out a better way to record my sound. But musically, I think that was a marvelous set. Thad and I played together so much that the phrasing and everything just seemed to fall naturally into place."

Orrin Keepnews was upset with the satirical rendition of Yes, Sir, That's My Baby, that, according to Adams, "horrified the company" (see Arnold Jay Smith's 1977 interview in *Down Beat),* but not pianist Dick Katz (in an interview with the author in 1988):

> The very first album for Milestone Records, [for] which I was involved with Orrin Keepnews, was called *Mean What You Say,* which is the name of a famous Thad composition. A wonderful record. It was my first date as an assistant producer for Milestone, but it was really a fascinating experience because there were about six producers on this. Pepper got in the act. He insisted on one thing. Mel Lewis got in the act. He insisted on things going his way. Orrin was supposed to be in charge, [but] Duke Pearson was a bandleader. So there were all these chiefs and no Indians. So I was getting my feet wet doing that, and Orrin and I hadn't established that some-

body had to really call the shots, so anything I had to say had to go through Orrin. We had some friendly arguments about what was supposed to happen. It was a kind of a tempestuous date, you could say, but I thought the music was great! There's one Thad solo on there, one of the greatest I ever heard him play. They did a tongue-in-cheek version of Yes, Sir, That's My Baby. After they did the tongue-in-cheek first chorus and got serious, what Thad played on that is historic, in my opinion. I remember being in the booth feeling incredibly envious that I wished I was playing instead of Duke Pearson, even though he was doing a great job. It was a beautiful date! It really was!

Jerry Dodgion told the author, in an interview in 1998,

Pepper was *really* upset. The quintet album that he and Thad made: When we got to Japan [in 1968], the album was available there, but it was not called the *Thad Jones-Pepper Adams Quintet.* It was called the *Thad Jones-Mel Lewis Quintet.* He was really pissed off about that! I can understand. He made a really good record, OK? and then it gets to Japan and they've taken his name off because they think that they can sell some more records because it says *Thad Jones-Mel Lewis.*

THAD JONES-PEPPER ADAMS – MEAN WHAT YOU SAY
660504a
4 May 1966, Plaza Sound Studios, New York: See 660426.

THAD JONES-MEL LEWIS – PRESENTING THAD JONES-MEL LEWIS AND THE JAZZ ORCHESTRA
660504b
4 May 1966, A&R Studios, New York: Thad Jones flh; Danny Stiles, Bill Berry, Jimmy Nottingham, Richard Williams tp; Bob Brookmeyer vtb; Jack Rains, Tom McIntosh tb; Cliff Heather btb; Jerome Richardson as, ss, cl, bcl, fl; Jerry Dodgion as, cl, fl; Joe Farrell ts, cl, fl; Eddie Daniels ts, cl, bcl; Pepper Adams bs; Hank Jones p; Sam Herman g; Richard Davis b; Mel Lewis dm.

a	ABC Blues	Solid State LP: SS-18003
b	Kids Are Pretty People	Mosaic LP: MQ7-151
c	The Waltz You "Swang" for Me	Solid State unissued

-a on United Artists LP: UAL-17003, Capitol Record Club LP: SMAS-90890, Mosaic LP: MQ7-151, United Artists (Eng) LP: SULP-1169, United Artists (Ger) LP: 669 148, King (J) LP: GP-3022, Columbia (J) LP: YS773US, Mosaic CD: MD5-151.

-b on Mosaic LP: MQ7-151, Mosaic CD: MD5-151.

At least 11 takes were done at this session.

According to Jerry Dodgion, in an interview with the author in 1988 about Thad Jones,

> [Thad] liked the guitar for the Basie-type rhythm section sound, but he didn't want it all the time. So, a lot of times he'd have Sam [Herman] lay out, or ask him to play the shaker, so he wouldn't have a guitar line. Also, Sam was a copyist. He copied the arrangements. Sam wanted to play in the band. Thad said, "O.K." I think that's the way it was. I don't think he really wanted guitar, but, with Sam there, it was O.K. When Sam left, there was never any reason to replace him.

THAD JONES-MEL LEWIS – PRESENTING THAD JONES-MEL LEWIS AND THE JAZZ ORCHESTRA
660505
5 May 1966, New York: Same as 4 May 1966, except Herman g, shaker*:

a **Once Around**   Solid State LP: SS-18003
b Don't Ever Leave Me*

-a on United Artists LP: UA-17003, Capitol Record Club LP: SMAS-90890, Mosaic LP: MQ7-151, United Artists (Eng) LP: ULP-1169, United Artists (Ger) LP: 669-148, King (J) LP: GP-3022, Columbia (J) LP: YS773US, Mosaic CD: MD5-151.

-b on Solid State LP: SS-94, United Artists LP: UA-17003, Voices of Vista LP: 88, Capitol Record Club LP: SMAS-90890, Mosaic LP: MQ7-151, United Artists (Eng) LP: ULP-1169, United Artists (Ger) LP: 669 148, King (J) LP: GP-3022, Columbia (J) LP: YS773US, Mosaic CD: MD5-151.

At least 12 takes were done at this session.

See 660504b, 660506.

THAD JONES-MEL LEWIS – PRESENTING THAD JONES-MEL LEWIS AND THE JAZZ ORCHESTRA
660506
6 May 1966, New York: Same as 5 May 1966:

a		Willow Weep for Me	Solid State LP: SS-18003
b		**Balanced Scales = Justice**	
c		**Three and One**	
d	14972	Mean What You Say	
e		The Waltz You "Swang" for Me	Solid State unissued

-a on United Artists LP: UAL-17003, Smithsonian LP: RD-108-S25-17618, Voices of Vista LP: 88, Capitol Record Club LP: SMAS-90890, Mosaic LP: MQ7-151, United Artists (Eng) LP: ULP-1169, United Artists (Ger) LP: 669-148, King (J) LP: GP-3022, Columbia (J) LP: YS773US, Mosaic CD: MD5-151, Smithsonian CD: SMRJ-0014CD.
   -b on United Artists LP: UAL-17003, Capitol Record Club LP: SMAS-90890, Mosaic LP: MQ7-151, United Artists (Eng) LP: ULP-1169, United Artists (Ger) LP: 669-148, King (J) LP: GP-3022, Columbia (J) LP: YS773US, Mosaic CD: MD5-151.
   -c on United Artists LP: UAL-17003, Capitol Record Club LP: SMAS-90890, Voices of Vista LP: 88, Mosaic LP: MQ7-151, United Artists (Eng) LP: ULP-1169, United Artists (Ger) LP: 669-148, King (J) LP: GP-3022, Columbia (J) LP: YS773US, Mosaic CD: MD5-151.
   -d on United Artists LP: UAL-17003, Capitol Record Club LP: SMAS-90890, Blue Note LP: BNLA-392-H2, Blue Note (Eng) LP: BND-4004, United Artists (Eng) LP: ULP-1169, United Artists (Ger) LP: 669-148, Blue Note (Ger) LP: BST-84497/8, King (J) LP: GP-3022, Columbia (J) LP: YS773US, Mosaic LP: MQ7-151, Mosaic CD: MD5-151.
   At least 13 takes were done at this session.
   See 660504b, 660505.

THAD JONES-PEPPER ADAMS – MEAN WHAT YOU SAY
660509
9 May 1966, Plaza Sound Studios, New York: See 660426.

HERBIE MANN–OUR MANN FLUTE
660526

26 May 1966, Atlantic Studios, New York: Marky Markowitz, Joe Newman tp; Quentin Jackson tb; Herbie Mann fl; King Curtis ts, bs; Pepper Adams bs; Jimmy Wisner p; Charlie Macey, Al Gorgoni g; Joe Macko e-b; Bernard Purdie dm; Warren Smith perc.

a	10325	Philly Dog	Atlantic LP: SD-1464
b	10326	Scratch	
c	10327	Good Lovin'	
d	10328	Monday, Monday	

-a on Atlantic LP: SD-1544, Atlantic LP: SD-1559, Atlantic LP: SD-5074, Atlantic LP: SD-2-300, Collectables CD: COL-6830, Rhino CD: R2-71634, Atlantic (Ger) CD: 781-369-2.

-b on Atlantic LP: SD-5070, Atlantic LP: SD2-300, Collectables CD: COL-6830.

-c, -d on Collectables CD: COL-6830.

STANLEY TURRENTINE–ROUGH AND TUMBLE
660701

1 July 1966, Van Gelder Studio, Englewood Cliffs NJ: Blue Mitchell tp; James Spaulding as; Stanley Turrentine ts; Pepper Adams bs; McCoy Tyner p; Grant Green g; Bob Cranshaw b, e-b*; Mickey Roker dm.

a	1752	What Could I Do Without You	Blue Note LP: BLP-4240
b	1753	Feeling Good	
c	1754	Shake	
d	1755	Walk on By	
e	1756	And Satisfy	
f	1757	**Baptismal***	

-a on Blue Note 45: 45-1933, Blue Note LP: BST-84240, Blue Note CD: 7243-5-24552-2-5, Blue Note-EMI (J) CD: TOCJ-8714.

-b on Blue Note 45: 45-1933, Blue Note LP: BST-84240, Cema LP: S21-57590, Blue Note CD: 7243-5-24552-2-5, Blue Note CD: CDBN-7-93201-2, Blue Note-EMI (J) CD: TOCJ-8714.

-c on Blue Note LP: BST-84240, Blue Note CD: 7243-5-24552-2-5, Blue Note-EMI (J) CD: TOCJ-8714.

-d on Blue Note 45: 45-1929, Blue Note LP: L-4240, Blue Note LP: BST-84240, Cema LP: S21-57590, Blue Note CD: CDBN-7-99105-2, Blue Note CD: 8-57749-2, Blue Note CD: 7243-5-24552-2-5, Blue Note-EMI (J) CD: TOCJ-8714.

-e on Blue Note 45: 45-1929, Blue Note LP: L-4240, Blue Note LP: B1-57745, Blue Note LP: BST-84240, Blue Note CD: 8-57745-2, Blue Note CD: 7243-5-24552-2-5, Blue Note-EMI (J) CD: TOCJ-8714.

-f on Blue Note LP: BST-84240, Blue Note CD: 7243-5-24552-2-5, Blue Note-EMI (J) CD: TOCJ-8714.

At least 23 takes were done at this session.

THAD JONES-MEL LEWIS
660702

2 July 1966, radio broadcast, Newport Jazz Festival, Newport RI: Thad Jones flh; Snooky Young, Bill Berry, Jimmy Nottingham, Richard Williams tp; Bob Brookmeyer vtb; Jack Rains, Tom McIntosh tb; Cliff Heather btb; Jerome Richardson as, ss, cl, bcl, fl; Jerry Dodgion as, cl, fl; Eddie Daniels ts, cl, bcl; Joe Farrell ts, cl, fl; Pepper Adams bs, cl; Hank Jones p; Sam Herman g, shaker†; Richard Davis b; Mel Lewis dm; Joe Williams voc.*

a　The Second Race
b　Willow Weep for Me
c　**The Little Pixie**†
d　Big Dipper
e　**Come Sunday***
f　Jump for Joy*
g　Roll 'em Pete*

HERBIE HANCOCK
660719

19 July 1966, Van Gelder Studio, Englewood Cliffs NJ: Melvin Lastie cornet; Julian Priester tb; Stanley Turrentine ts; Pepper Adams bs; Herbie Hancock p; Eric Gale, Billy Butler g; Bob Cranshaw b; Bernard Purdie dm.

a　1770　unknown ballad　　　　Blue Note unissued
b　1771　unknown blues
c　1772　Soul Villa
d　1773　unknown blues No. 2

e 1774 Don't Even Go There   Blue Note CD: CDBN 4-95569-2

f 1775 You Know What To Do   Blue Note unissued

-e on Blue Note CD: 5-21484-2, Blue Note CD: B2BN-7243-4-95569-2-8, EMI (Bel) CD: 5032252.
At least 26 takes were done at this session.

STANLEY TURRENTINE–THE SPOILER
660922
22 September 1966, Van Gelder Studio, Englewood Cliffs NJ: Blue Mitchell tp; Julian Priester tb; James Spaulding as, fl; Stanley Turrentine ts; Pepper Adams bs; McCoy Tyner p; Bob Cranshaw b, e-b*; Mickey Roker dm; Joseph Rivera perc.†

a 1788 **La Fiesta**†   Blue Note LP: BLP-4256
b 1789 Sunny*†
c 1790 The Magilla†
d 1791 Maybe September
e 1792 When the Sun Comes Out
f 1793 Lonesome Lover   Blue Note CD: CDP-7-93201-2
g 1794 You're Gonna Hear from Me   Blue Note LP: BLP-4256

-a on Blue Note LP: BST-84256, Blue Note LP: 74224, Blue Note CD: 4-97156-2, Blue Note CD: CDP-7-93201-2, Blue Note CD: 0946-3-74224-2, Blue Note CD: CDP-7243-8-53359-2-1.
-b on Blue Note LP: BST-84256, Blue Note LP: 74224, Blue Note CD: 4-97156-2, Blue Note CD: CDP-7-93201-2, Blue Note CD: 0946-3-74224-2, Blue Note CD: CDP-7243-8-53359-2-1.
-c on Blue Note LP: BST-84256, Blue Note LP: 74224, Blue Note CD: CDP-7-93201-2, Blue Note CD: 0946-3-74224-2, Blue Note CD: CDP-7243-8-53359-2-1.
-d Blue Note LP: BST-84256, Blue Note LP: 74224, Blue Note CD: CDP-7-93201-2, Blue Note CD: 0946-3-74224-2, Blue Note CD: CDP-7243-8-53359-2-1.
-e Blue Note LP: BST-84256, Blue Note LP: 74224, Blue Note CD: CDP-7-93201-2, Blue Note CD: 0946-3-74224-2, Blue Note CD: CDP-7243-8-53359-2-1.
-f on Blue Note CD: 4-97156-2, Blue Note CD: 0946-3-74224-2, Blue Note CD: CDP-7243-8-53359-2-1.

-g on Blue Note LP: BST-84256, Blue Note LP: 74224, Blue Note CD: CDP-7-93201-2, Blue Note CD: 0946-3-74224-2, Blue Note CD: CDP-7243-8-53359-2-1.
At least 32 takes were done at this session.

THAD JONES-MEL LEWIS – PRESENTING JOE WILLIAMS AND THAD JONES-MEL LEWIS ORCHESTRA
660930
30 September 1966, A&R Studios, New York: Thad Jones cornet, flh; Snooky Young, Jimmy Nottingham, Bill Berry, Richard Williams tp; Bob Brookmeyer vtb; Garnett Brown, Tom McIntosh tb; Cliff Heather btb; Jerome Richardson ss, as; Jerry Dodgion as; Eddie Daniels, Joe Farrell ts; Pepper Adams bs; Roland Hanna p; Sam Herman g; Richard Davis b; Mel Lewis dm; Joe Williams voc.

a 455	Woman's Got Soul		Solid State LP: SS-18008
b 457	Get Out of My Life		
c	Nobody Knows the Way I Feel this Morning		
d	Gee, Baby, Ain't I Good to You		
e	How Sweet It Is (To Be Loved By You)		
f	Keep Your Hand on Your Heart		
g	Evil Man Blues		
h 14978	**Come Sunday**		
i	Smack Dab in the Middle		
j	It Don't Mean a Thing (If It Ain't Got that Swing)		
k	Hallelujah I Love Her So		
m	Night Time Is the Right Time (To Be With the One You Love)		

-a on Solid State LP: SS-18008, Solid State LP: SM-17008, United Artists LP: UAL-17008, Blue Note LP: B1-54360, Blue Note LP: BN-LA392-H2, Blue Note (Eng) LP: BND-4004, Blue Note (Ger) LP: BST-84497/8, King (J) LP: LAX-3161, Blue Note CD: 8-54360-2, Blue Note CD: CDBN-8-30454-2, Blue Note CD: 7243-8-30454-2-6, LRC (Ger) CD: CDC-9008.
-b on Solid State LP: SS-18008, Solid State LP: SM-17008, United Artists LP: UAL-17008, Blue Note LP: BN-LA392-H2, Blue Note (Eng) LP: BND-4004, Blue Note (Ger) LP: BST-84497/8, King (J) LP: LAX-3161, Blue Note CD: CDBN-8-30454-2, Blue Note CD: 7243-8-30454-2-6.

-c on Solid State LP: SS-18008, Solid State LP: SM-17008, United Artists LP: UAL-17008, King (J) LP: LAX-3161, Blue Note CD: CDBN-8-30454-2, Blue Note CD: 7243-8-30454-2-6, LRC (Ger) CD: CDC-9005.

-d on Solid State LP: SS-18008, Solid State LP: SM-17008, United Artists LP: UAL-17008, King (J) LP: LAX-3161, Blue Note CD: CDBN-8-30454-2, Blue Note CD: 7243-8-30454-2-6.

-e on Solid State LP: SS-18008, Solid State LP: SM-17008, United Artists LP: UAL-17008, King (J) LP: LAX-3161, Blue Note CD: CDBN-4-94888-2, Blue Note CD: 7243-8-30454-2-6, LRC (Ger) CD: CDC-9005.

-f on Solid State LP: SS-18008, Solid State LP: SM-17008, United Artists LP: UAL-17008, King (J) LP: LAX-3161, Blue Note CD: CDBN-8-30454-2, Blue Note CD: 7243-8-30454-2-6.

-g on Solid State LP: SS-18008, Solid State LP: SM-17008, United Artists LP: UAL-17008, King (J) LP: LAX-3161, Blue Note CD: 7243-8-30454-2-6, LRC (Ger) CD: CDC-9005, LRC (Ger) CD: CDC-9047.

-h on Solid State LP: SS-18008, Solid State LP: SM-17008, United Artists LP: UAL-17008, Blue Note LP: B1-54360, Blue Note LP: BN-LA392-2-H2, Blue Note (Eng) LP: BND-4004, Blue Note (Ger) LP: BST-84497/8, King (J) LP: LAX-3161, Blue Note CD: 8-54360-2, Blue Note CD: 8-55221-2, Blue Note CD: 7243-8-30454-2-6, LRC (Ger) CD: CDC-9008.

-i on Solid State LP: SS-18008, Solid State LP: SM-17008, Solid State LP: SS-94, United Artists LP: UAL-17008, King (J) LP: LAX-3161, Blue Note CD: CDBN-5-21153-2, Blue Note CD: 7243-8-30454-2-6.

-j on Solid State LP: SS-18008, Solid State LP: SM-17008, United Artists LP: UAL-17008, King (J) LP: LAX-3161, Blue Note CD: CDBN-8-21146-2, Blue Note CD: 7243-8-30454-2-6.

-k on Solid State LP: SS-18008, Solid State LP: SM-17008, United Artists LP: UAL-17008, King (J) LP: LAX-3161, Blue Note CD: 7243-8-30454-2-6, LRC (Ger) CD: CDC-9047.

-m on Solid State LP: SS-18008, Solid State LP: SM-17008, United Artists LP: UAL-17008, King (J) LP: LAX-3161, Blue Note CD: 7243-8-30454-2-6, Blue Note CD: CDBN-8-30454-2.

According to Eddie Daniels, in an interview with the author in 1988,

That was one of those dates that we did after the Vanguard on a Monday night—or early the next morning....It could have been even in the afternoon, or the evening of the next day, but, because you worked 'til three in the morning at the Vanguard, by the time you got up, you were ready to go to your gig....Joe Williams was very warm. It was all very relaxed and wonderful. Everybody had a little cameo solo in it—little spots—but they ended up being classic spots, because the record was so good that just a few bars made a difference and people noticed it. Joe sounded great with the band.... Thad would start writing the charts right after the Vanguard, with copyists copying over his shoulder. He liked to work under pressure.

BLUE MITCHELL–BOSS HORN
661117
17 November 1966, Van Gelder Studio, Englewood Cliffs NJ: Blue Mitchell tp; Julian Priester tb; Jerry Dodgion as; Junior Cook ts; Pepper Adams bs; Cedar Walton, Chick Corea* p; Gene Taylor b; Mickey Roker dm.

a	1788	O Mama Enit	Blue Note LP: BLP-4257
b	1789	Rigor Mortez	
c	1790	I Should Care	
d	1791	Millie	
e	1792	**Straight Up and Down***	
f	1793	Tones for Joan's Bones*	

All tracks on Blue Note LP: BST-84257, Mosaic LP: MQ6-178, Blue Note CD: 9562, Blue Note CD: 63813, Mosaic CD: MD4-178, Blue Note CD: CDBN-7-89282-2, Blue Note (Neth) CD: 7243-5-63814-2-1, Blue Note (Neth) CD: 5638142, Blue Note-EMI (J) CD: TOCJ-9562.
At least 42 takes were done at this session.

PEPPER ADAMS
661211
11 December 1966, private recording, Famous Ballroom, Baltimore: Frank Foster ts; Pepper Adams bs; Bobby Timmons p; Cecil McBee b; Freddie Waits dm.

This was recorded by the Left Bank Jazz Society. *See* 650314.

DAVID AMRAM
670000A
1967, film soundtrack, New York: Pepper Adams bs; other musicians.

This was for a documentary film, *We Are Young,* produced for Montreal's Expo '67. According to David Amram, in an interview with the author in 1988, "We did one for Expo '67 in Montreal (and Pepper also played on that one) that was showing the life of all across Canada, but I managed to sneak some jazz into that as well."

According to Jeffrey Stanton, in his 1977 piece about Experimental Multi-Screen Cinema:

> Francis Thompson and Alexander Hammid, who previously won an Academy Award for the 1964-1965 World's Fair three-screen movie *To Be Alive,* made a more ambitious film for the C.P.R. Cominco [Pavilion]. The subject this time was about young people, teenagers who faced life, and they used six screens to present their subject. In a sense, they were successful in drawing a convincing performance from several hundred amateur actors....Word got around that *We Are Young* was an important movie to see.

JOE HENDERSON BIG BAND
670000B
c. 1967, various private recordings, Upsurge Studios, New York: Lew Soloff, Bob McCoy, Charlie Camilleri, Mike Lawrence tp; Jimmy Knepper, Julian Priester, Curtis Fuller tb; Kiane Zawadi euphonium; Bobby Porcelli as, fl; Pete Yellin as, ss; Joe Henderson ts; Pepper Adams bs; Chick Corea, Bob Dorough, Ronnie Mathews p; Ron Carter, Junie Booth b; Joe Chambers, Roy Haynes dm.

According to Bill Kirchner's liner notes to Verve's *Joe Henderson Big Band,* Henderson taped rehearsals of his big band.

LEE MORGAN
670113
13 January 1967, Van Gelder Studio, Englewood Cliffs NJ: Lee Morgan tp; James Spaulding as, fl; Wayne Shorter ts; Pepper Adams bs; Herbie Hancock p; Ron Carter b; Mickey Roker dm.

a	1816	**Blue Gardenia**	Blue Note CDP: 7243-8-23213-2-3
b		**Blue Gardenia**	
c	1817	God Bless the Child	
d	1818	Somewhere	
e	1819	If I Were a Carpenter	
f	1820	A Lot of Livin' to Do	
g	1821	This Is the Life	

-c on Blue Note CD: CDBN-4-97154-2, Toshiba-EMI (J) CD: TOCJ-6184.
All tracks on Toshiba-EMI (J) CD: TOCJ-6184.
At least 46 takes were done at this session.
The recording was first released in 1998.

LOU DONALDSON–LUSH LIFE
670120
20 January 1967, Van Gelder Studio, Englewood Cliffs NJ: Freddie Hubbard tp; Garnett Brown tb; Lou Donaldson as; Jerry Dodgion as, fl; Wayne Shorter ts; Pepper Adams bs; McCoy Tyner p; Ron Carter b; Al Harewood dm.

a	1822	Sweet and Lovely	Blue Note (J) LP: GXF-3068
b	1823	You've Changed	
c	1824	Sweet Slumber	
d	1825	It Might as Well Be Spring	
e	1826	What Will I Tell My Heart	
f	1827	The Good Life	
g	1828	Stardust	

-c on Blue Note LP: BST-84254, King (J) LP: GXF-3068, King (J) LP: GXK-8164, Blue Note CD: CDP-7-84254-2, Blue Note CD: B21Y-84254, Blue Note CD: CDBN-8-27298-2, Blue Note (Eu) CD: 0946-3-74214-2-0, Blue Note (Eng) CD: CDBNZ-124, Liberty (J) CD: CD-4413.
-g on Blue Note LP: BST-84254, King (J) LP: GXF-3068, King (J) LP: GXK-8164, Blue Note CD: CDP-7-84254-2, Blue Note CD: B21Y-84254, Blue Note CD: CDBN (J) TOCJ-5858, Blue Note (Eu) CD: 0946-3-74214-2-0, Blue Note (Eng) CD: CDBNZ-124, Liberty (J) CD: CD-4413, Liberty (J) LP: K22P-6131/32.

All other tracks on Blue Note LP: BST-84254, King (J) LP: GXF-3068, King (J) LP: GXK-8164, Blue Note CD: CDP-7-84254-2, Blue Note CD: B21Y-84254, Blue Note (Eu) CD: 0946-3-74214-2-0, Blue Note (Eng) CD: CDBNZ-124, Liberty (J) CD: CD-4413.

At least 15 takes were done at this session. This date was first released in 1980.

THAD JONES-MEL LEWIS
670124

24 January 1967, A&R Studios, New York: Thad Jones flh; Snooky Young, Marvin Stamm, Jimmy Nottingham, Richard Williams tp; Bob Brookmeyer vtb; Tom McIntosh, Garnett Brown tb; Cliff Heather btb; Phil Woods as, cl; Jerry Dodgion as, fl; Joe Farrell ts, cl, fl; Eddie Daniels ts, cl; Pepper Adams bs, cl; Roland Hanna p; Sam Herman g, shaker*; Richard Davis b; Mel Lewis dm.

a	Theme from "Hawaii"*	Solid State 45: SD-2506
b	**Sophisticated Lady**	
c	Willow Tree	Mosaic CD: MD5-151

All tracks on Mosaic LP: MQ7-151, Mosaic CD: MD5-151.

At least 11 takes were done on this session.

According to Mel Lewis, in an interview done with the author in 1988,

Hawaii was up for an Academy Award [as Best Film] and United Artists owned the picture. And, if they would have won the Academy Award—and this tune was also up for an Academy Award—they wanted to be prepared for a possible Academy Award hit. If it did, they wanted as many records out on it as possible, and they thought it would be a good idea (to give us a break) if we would do a big band recording, because there wouldn't be any other big band recordings on this tune. There'd be studio orchestras, or the original, so they thought it might be a good cover, and we might get a good crack that way. So they gave us a single session....Thad did this arrangement on Hawaii and Garnett Brown wrote Sophisticated Lady. They put it out just when the Academy Awards came out, with the hopes that it would hit. The picture did not win, and neither did the score.

Solid State was, at the time, also owned by United Artists, and Lewis said this was the only recording ever done by the band solely for 45 rpm.

According to Phil Woods, in an interview with the author in 1989, "I used to sub for Jerome Richardson on Thad Jones-Mel Lewis' band on Monday nights."

THAD JONES–MEL LEWIS
670126
26 January 1967, TV broadcast, KYW Studios, Philadelphia: Thad Jones flh; Snooky Young, Roger DeLilio, Marvin Stamm, Richard Williams tp; Bob Brookmeyer or Garnett Brown, Jack Rains, Tom McIntosh tb; Cliff Heather btb; Jerome Richardson, Jerry Dodgion as, ss, fl; Eddie Daniels ts, ss, cl, Joe Farrell ts, ss; Pepper Adams bs, cl; Roland Hanna p; Sam Herman g; Bill Crow b; Mel Lewis dm; Joe Williams*, Mike Douglas voc.†

a Hallelujah I Love Her So*
b Nobody Knows the Way I Feel This Morning*
c **Once Around**
d **Three and One**
e Smack Dab in the Middle*†

The band appeared on the *Mike Douglas Show* during a week that featured various big bands.

BOBBY HACKETT–CREOLE COOKIN'
670130
30 January 1967, A&R Studios, New York: Bobby Hackett cornet; Jimmy Maxwell, Rusty Dedrick tp; Lou McGarity tb; Bob Brookmeyer vtb; Jerry Dodgion as; Bob Wilber ss, cl; Zoot Sims ts; Pepper Adams bs; Dave McKenna p; Wayne Wright g; Buddy Jones b; Morey Feld dm.

a	102020	Lazy Mood	Verve LP: V-8698
b	102021	Fidgety Feet	Verve unissued
c	102022	Basin Street Blues	
d	102023	Royal Garden Blues	Verve LP: V-8698

-a on Verve LP: V6-8698, Verve LP: 1574, Lone Hill (Sp) CD: LHJ-10377, Polydor (J) CD: POJJ-1574.

-d on Verve LP: V6-8698, Verve LP: 1574, Lone Hill (Sp) CD: LHJ-10377, Polydor (J) CD: POJJ-1574.

According to the date's arranger, Bob Wilber, in an interview with the author in 1989,

> It was a challenge because Bobby [Hackett] told me about the date. He says, "Yeah, man, we gotta do all these songs." I said, "Not again! Not these!" He said, "Yeah." I said, "Bobby, you mind if I don't do them traditionally? I want to do something different." So on every one of the songs I tried to do something different than the usual thing....[Pepper] was always in my mind, when I had an assignment that required a baritone player, because he was an old friend and he was super-competent—could read anything.

See 670313, 670330, 670502.

JIMMY RUSHING–EVERYDAY I HAVE THE BLUES
670210
10 February 1967, Capitol Studios, New York: Clark Terry tp, unknown tp section; unknown tb section; Oliver Nelson as; Bob Ashton ts; unknown ts; Pepper Adams bs; Shirley Scott org†; Hank Jones p√, org*; Kenny Burrell gΔ; George Duvivier b; Grady Tate dm; Jimmy Rushing voc; GUEST: Dicky Wells tb.

a   Baby Don't Tell on Me*   Bluesway LP: BLS-6005
b   Berkeley Campus Blues*
c   Blues in the Dark*
d   Every Day I Have the Blues√
e   Evil Blues†Δ
f   Keep the Faith, Baby√
g   I Left My Baby√
h   You Can't Run Around*
i   Undecided Blues*

-a on Il Jazz (It) 45: SMDJ-063, Bluesway LP: BL-3005, Affinity (Eng) LP: CDX-13, Charly (Eng) LP: CDX-13, HMV (Eng) LP: CSD-3632, Bluesway (J) LP: SR-448, Impulse (Eu) CD: 547-967-2.

-b on Bluesway LP: BLS-657, Bluesway LP: BL-3005, Affinity (Eng) LP: CDX-13, Charly (Eng) LP: CDX-13, HMV (Eng) LP: CSD-3632, Bluesway (J) LP: SR-448, Impulse (Eu) CD: 547-967-2.

-c on Bluesway LP: BLS-657, Bluesway LP: BL-3005, Affinity (Eng) LP: CDX-13, Charly (Eng) LP: CDX-13, HMV (Eng) LP: CSD-3632, Bluesway (J) LP: SR-448, Impulse (Eu) CD: 547-967-2.

-d on Bluesway LP: BLS-657, Bluesway LP: BL-3005, Affinity (Eng) LP: CDX-13, Charly (Eng) LP: CDX-13, HMV (Eng) LP: CSD-3632, Bluesway (J) LP: SR-448, Impulse (Eu) CD: 547-967-2.

-e on Bluesway LP: BL-3005, Affinity (Eng) LP: CDX-13, Charly (Eng) LP: CDX-13, HMV (Eng) LP: CSD-3632, Bluesway (J) LP: SR-448, Impulse (Eu) CD: 547-967-2.

-f on Bluesway LP: BL-3005, Affinity (Eng) LP: CDX-13, Charly (Eng) LP: CDX-13, HMV (Eng) LP: CSD-3632, Bluesway (J) LP: SR-448, Impulse (Eu) CD: 547-967-2.

-g on on Il Jazz (It) 45: SMDJ-063, Bluesway LP: BLS-657, Bluesway LP: BL-3005, Affinity (Eng) LP: CDX-13, Charly (Eng) LP: CDX-13, HMV (Eng) LP: CSD-3632, Bluesway (J) LP: SR-448, Impulse (Eu) CD: 547-967-2.

-h on Bluesway LP: BLS-657, Bluesway LP: BL-3005, Affinity (Eng) LP: CDX-13, Charly (Eng) LP: CDX-13, HMV (Eng) LP: CSD-3632, Bluesway (J) LP: SR-448, Impulse (Eu) CD: 547-967-2.

-i on Il Jazz (It) 45: SMDJ-063, Bluesway LP: BLS-657, Bluesway LP: BL-3005, Affinity (Eng) LP: CDX-13, Charly (Eng) LP: CDX-13, HMV (Eng) LP: CSD-3632, Bluesway (J) LP: SR-448, Impulse (Eu) CD: 547-967-2.

According to Pepper Adams' appointment book, this was an Oliver Nelson date done at 151 West 46 Street from 8-11pm.

STANLEY TURRENTINE
670217
17 February 1967, Van Gelder Studio, Englewood Cliffs NJ: Donald Byrd tp; Julian Priester tb; Jerry Dodgion as, fl; Joe Farrell ts, fl; Stanley Turrentine ts; Pepper Adams bs, cl; Kenny Barron p; Bucky Pizzarelli g; Ron Carter b; Mickey Roker dm.

a	1839	She's a Carioca	Blue Note LP: BN-LA-394-H2
b	1840	Samba do Aviao	
c	1841	Manha de Carnaval	Blue Note LP: LT-993
d	1842	What Now My Love	
e	1843	Night Song	Blue Note LP: BN-LA-394-H2
f	1844	Here's that Rainy Day	Blue Note LP: LT-993
g	1845	Blues for Del	

-a on Blue Note (Eng) LP: BND-4006, Blue Note (Ger) LP: BST-84506, Blue Note CD: 8-35283-2, Blue Note-Capitol (Eu) CD: 0946-3-85193-2-4.

-b on Blue Note (Eng) LP: BND-4006, Blue Note (Ger) LP: BST-84506, Blue Note CD: 8-35283-2, Blue Note-Capitol (Eu) CD: 0946-3-85193-2-4.

-c on Blue Note (Eng) LP: LBR-1026, United Artists (Eng) LP: LBR-1026, King (J) LP: GXK-8189, Blue Note-Capitol (Eu) CD: 0946-3-85193-2-4, Blue Note (J) CD: CJ-28-5170.

-d on Blue Note (Eng) LP: LBR-1026, United Artists (Eng) LP: LBR-1026, King (J) LP: GXK-8189, Blue Note-Capitol (Eu) CD: 0946-3-85193-2-4.

-e on Blue Note (Eng) LP: BND-4006, Blue Note (Ger) LP: BST-84506, Blue Note-Capitol (Eu) CD: 0946-3-85193-2-4.

-f on Blue Note (Eng) LP: LBR-1026, United Artists (Eng) LP: LBR-1026, King (J) LP: GXK-8189, Blue Note-Capitol (Eu) CD: 0946-3-85193-2-4.

-g on Blue Note (Eng) LP: LBR-1026, United Artists (Eng) LP: LBR-1026, King (J) LP: GXK-8189, Blue Note-Capitol (Eu) CD: 0946-3-85193-2-4.

At least 41 takes were done at this session. Some of this material was first released in 1979.

BOBBY HACKETT–CREOLE COOKIN'
670313
13 March 1967, A&R Studios, New York: Bobby Hackett cornet; Jimmy Maxwell, Rusty Dedrick tp; Cutty Cutshall tb; Bob Brookmeyer vtb; Jerry Dodgion as; Bob Wilber as, cl; Zoot Sims ts; Pepper Adams bs; Dave McKenna p; Wayne Wright g; Buddy Jones b; Morey Feld dm.

a	102308	Tin Roof Blues	Verve LP: V-8698
b	102309	Muskrat Ramble	
c	102310	New Orleans	
d	102311	When the Saints Go Marching In	Verve LP: V-8698
e	102312	Basin Street Blues	Verve unissued

-a on Verve LP: V6-8698, Verve LP: 1574, Verve (Eu) CD: 845-153-1, Verve (Eu) CD: 845-153-2, Lone Hill (Sp) CD: LHJ-10377, Polydor (J) CD: POJJ-1574.

-b on Verve LP: V6-8698, Verve LP: 1574, Lone Hill (Sp) CD: LHJ-10377, Polydor (J) CD: POJJ-1574.

-c on Verve LP: V6-8698, Verve LP: 1574, Verve (Eu) CD: 845-153-1, Lone Hill (Sp) CD: LHJ-10377, Polydor (J) CD: POJJ-1574.

-d on Verve LP: V6-8698, Verve LP: 1574, Lone Hill (Sp) CD: LHJ-10377, Polydor (J) CD: POJJ-1574.

See 670130, 670330, 670502.

BOBBY HACKETT–CREOLE COOKIN'
670330
30 March 1967, A&R Studios, New York: Same as 13 March 1967, except James Morreale tp replaces Maxwell:

a	102505	High Society	Verve unissued
b	102506	Do You Know What It Means to Miss New Orleans	
c	102507	Original Dixieland One-Step	

See 670130, 670313, 670502.

BARRY HARRIS–LUMINESCENCE
670420
20 April 1967, New York: Slide Hampton tb; Junior Cook ts; Pepper Adams bs; Barry Harris p; Bob Cranshaw b; Lenny McBrowne dm.

a	**Luminescence**	Prestige LP: PRLP-7498
b	Like This	
c	**Nicaragua**	
d	**Dance of the Infidels**	
e	**Webb City**	
f	My Ideal	
g	**Even Steven**	

All tracks on Prestige (J) LP: SHJ-7469, Original Jazz Classic CD: OJCCD-924-2.

THAD JONES–MEL LEWIS
670427
27 April 1967, Village Vanguard, New York: Thad Jones cornet; Snooky Young, Bill Berry, Jimmy Nottingham, Richard Williams, Marvin Stamm tp; Bob Brookmeyer vtb; Tom McIntosh, Garnett Brown tb; Cliff

Heather btb; Jerome Richardson as, ss, cl, fl; Jerry Dodgion as, fl; Eddie
Daniels ts, cl; Joe Farrell ts, fl; Pepper Adams bs, cl; Roland Hanna p;
Sam Herman g, shaker; Richard Davis b; Mel Lewis dm.

Solid State unissued. According to the Bill Kirchner's notes in the
discography of *The Complete Solid State Thad Jones-Mel Lewis Orchestra*, the band recorded on 27-28 April 1967, but all tracks from 27 April
were rejected. *See* 670428.

**THAD JONES-MEL LEWIS – LIVE AT THE VILLAGE
VANGUARD**
670428
28 April 1967, Village Vanguard, New York: Same as 27 April 1967:

a	974	**The Little Pixie**	Solid State LP: SS-18016
b		A–That's Freedom	
c		The Second Race	Solid State unissued
d		Willow Tree	Solid State LP: SS-18016
e		Quietude	Solid State unissued
f		Bächafillen	Solid State LP: SS-18016
g		Lover Man	Solid State unissued
h		Mornin' Reverend	
i		Samba con Getchu	Solid State LP: SS-18016
j		Willow Tree	Solid State unissued
k		Don't Git Sassy	Solid State LP: SS-18016

-a on Solid State LP: USS-7008, Solid State LP: USS-7008, Blue
Note LP: BN-LA392-H2, Mosaic LP: MQ7-151, Blue Note (Eng) LP:
BND-4004, Blue Note (Ger) LP: BST-84497/8, King (J) LP: GP-3023,
Blue Note CD: 60438, Mosaic CD: MD5-151, LRC (Ger) CD: CDC-
9013, LRC (Ger) CD: CDC-9022, Delta Distribution (Ger) CD: CDC-
55605.
     -b on Solid State LP: USS-7008, Solid State LP: SD-2517, Solid
State LP: USS-7008, Mosaic LP: MQ7-151, King (J) LP: GP-3023, Blue
Note CD: 60438, Mosaic CD: MD5-151, LRC (Ger) CD: CDC-9013,
LRC (Ger) CD: CDC-9022, Delta Distribution (Ger) CD: 55605.
     -c on Mosaic LP: MQ7-151, Mosaic CD: MD5-151, Blue Note CD:
60438, LRC (Ger) CD: CDC-9013, LRC (Ger) CD: CDC-9022, Delta
Distribution (Ger) CD: 55605.

-d on Solid State LP: USS-7008, King (J) LP: GP-3023, Mosaic LP: MQ7-151, Mosaic CD: MD5-151, Blue Note CD: 60438, LRC (Ger) CD: CDC-9022, Delta Distribution (Ger) CD: 55605.

-e on Mosaic LP: MQ7-151, Mosaic CD: MD5-151, Blue Note CD: 60438, LRC (Ger) CD: CDC-9013, LRC (Ger) CD: CDC-9022, Delta Distribution (Ger) CD: 55605.

-f Solid State LP: USS-7008, Mosaic LP: MQ7-151, King (J) LP: GP-3023, Blue Note CD: 60438, Mosaic CD: MD5-151, LRC (Ger) CD: CDC-9013, LRC (Ger) CD: CDC-9022, Delta Distribution (Ger) CD: 55605.

-g on Mosaic LP: MQ7-151, Blue Note CD: 60438, Mosaic CD: MD5-151.

-h on Mosaic LP: MQ7-151, Blue Note CD: 60438, Mosaic CD: MD5-151.

-i on Solid State LP: USS-7008, Mosaic LP: MQ7-151, King (J) LP: GP-3023, Blue Note CD: 60438, Mosaic CD: MD5-151.

-j on Solid State LP: USS-7008, Mosaic LP: MQ7-151, King (J) LP: GP-3023, Blue Note CD: 60438, Mosaic CD: MD5-151.

-k on Solid State LP: USS-7008, Solid State LP: SD-2517, Franklin Mint LP: FM-96, Mosaic LP: MQ7-151, King (J) LP: GP-3023, Blue Note CD: 60438, Mosaic CD: MD5-151, LRC (Ger) CD: CDC-9013, LRC (Ger) CD: CDC-9022, Delta Distribution (Ger) CD: 55605. Abridged version on LRC (Ger) CD: CDC-9021.

See 670427.

Author Bill Kirchner points out, in his discography of *The Complete Solid State Thad Jones-Mel Lewis Orchestra,* that the LRC reissue of -f "has an additional trombone chorus that was edited out of the actual master," and the LRC reissue of -b "has a full piano intro and extra trombone chorus that were edited out of the actual master."

BOBBY HACKETT–CREOLE COOKIN'
670502
2 May 1967, A&R Studios, New York: Bobby Hackett cornet; James Morreale, Rusty Dedrick tp; Cutty Cutshall tb; Bob Brookmeyer vtb; Jerry Dodgion as; Bob Wilber ss, cl; Zoot Sims, Joe Farrell ts; Pepper Adams bs; Dave McKenna p; Wayne Wright g; Buddy Jones b; Morey Feld dm.

| a | 102730 | High Society | Verve LP: V-8698 |
| b | 102731 | Original Dixieland One Step | |

c   102732   Do You Know What It Means to Miss New Orleans
d   102733   Basin Street Blues
e   102734   Fidgety Feet

All tracks on Verve LP: V6-8698, Verve LP: 1574, Lone Hill (Sp) CD: LHJ-10377, Polydor (J) CD: POJJ-1574.
See 670130, 670313, 670330.

MAYNARD FERGUSON–RIDIN' HIGH
670503
3 and 5 May 1967, Bell Sound Studios, New York: Maynard Ferguson tp, flh; Natalie Pavone, Charles Camilleri, Dick Hurwitz, Lew Soloff tp; Jimmy Cleveland, Slide Hampton tb; Jack Jeffers btb, tu; Dick Spencer as, ss; Frank Vicari, Lew Tabackin ts; Pepper Adams bs; Danny Bank bass sax, piccolo; Mike Abene p; Joe Beck g; Donald Payne e-b; Donald McDonald dm; Johnny Pacheco perc.

a   13221   **The Rise and Fall of Seven**   Enterprise LP: SD13-101
b   13222   Light Green
c   13223   **Kundalini Woman**
d   13224   Sonny
e   13325   Meet a Cheetah
f   13326   Molecules
g   13327   Wack-Wack
h   13328   Satan Speaks
i   13329   Alfie

It's not clear what tunes were recorded on either date.
Matrix numbers 13225-13324 were not used by Atlantic (Enterprise).
All tracks on Atlantic (Eng) LP: 2464-008, Wounded Bird CD: WOU-3101, Rhino-Warner Brothers CD: 6034-9797-5638.
Lew Tabackin told the author, in a 1988 interview,

We did this terrible recording with Maynard Ferguson. It was just awful. Tommy MacIntosh wrote some charts. He wrote one ballad. It wasn't that it was his fault. It was the whole production—and some of the writing was sad. McIntosh wrote this thing and there was a one-bar baritone solo on a ballad. I'm sitting next to [Pepper] and he played more notes in that one bar than most of us would play in at least a half a chorus. That was his joke. I mean, "Man, you give me a one-bar solo. Is that all you can do?" But he [thought], "I'll show you!" and he played a chorus' worth of notes in the one bar! It was really funny. McIntosh probably expected that would happen. He was around him enough to know that's probably what would happen. I thought that was really funny and a fantastic little moment. I was cracking up. I knew what he was feeling, I think. Like, "Fuck you, man! You give me a bar. It's gonna be a *real* bar!"

THE RASCALS
670525
25 May 1967, New York: Overdubs: Joe Newman tp; Joe Farrell ts; Pepper Adams bs.

a   Bit of Heaven   CBS LP: S-66292

Original band tracks recorded probably in New York c. 1967: Felix Cavaliere p, org, bass marimba, voc; Link Chamberlain g; Chuck Rainey e-b; Dino Danelli dm; Ralph MacDonald perc; vocal choir: Bruce Buono, Buddy Buono.
   -a on Columbia LP: G-30462, CBS (Eng) LP: S-64407, CBS (It) LP: S-66292, CBS (Neth) LP: S-66292, Sundazed CD: SC-6131, Sony (J) CD: SR-6451, Sony (J) CD: SICP-1697-8.

STANLEY TURRENTINE
670609
9 June 1967, Van Gelder Studio, Englewood Cliffs NJ: Blue Mitchell, Tommy Turrentine tp; Julian Priester tb; Jerry Dodgion as, fl; Stanley Turrentine ts; Al Gibbons ts, bcl; Pepper Adams bs, cl; McCoy Tyner p; Walter Booker b; Mickey Roker dm.

a	1904	With This Ring	Blue Note-Capitol (Eu)
			CD: 0946-3-85193-2-4
b	1905	Silver Tears	
c	1906	A Bluish Bag	
d	1907	Come Back to Me	
e	1908	The Days of Wine and Roses	
f	1909	Message to Michael	Blue Note unissued

At least 45 takes were done at this session.

CHARLIE BIDDLE
670620
20 June 1967, CBC radio broadcast, U.S. Pavilion at Expo '67, Montreal: Pepper Adams bs; Sadik Hakim p; Nelson Symonds g; Charlie Biddle b; Clayton Johnston dm.

a   **Cotton Tail**
b   **Lady Luck**
c   **Sophisticated Lady**
d   **Straight, No Chaser**
e   **Witchcraft**

This performance took place during Adams' six-day gig with Biddle in Montreal.

LOU RAWLS
670819
19 August 1967, Rheingold Festival, Central Park, New York: Pepper Adams bs; Lou Rawls voc; other musicians.

SONNY AND CHER
670906
6 September 1967, Atlantic Studios, New York: Pepper Adams bs; Sonny Bono, Cher voc; other musicians.

Listed in Adams' date book, this 10-1pm session for Atco may have been an overdub.

DONALD BYRD–THE CREEPER
670929
29 September 1967, Van Gelder Studio, Englewood Cliffs NJ: Donald Byrd tp; Sonny Red as; Pepper Adams bs; Chick Corea p, perc; Miroslav Vitous b; Mickey Roker dm.

a   1957   **The Creeper**   Blue Note unissued
b   1958   **Chico San**

Matrix number for -a is the same one assigned for its alternate on 671005.

DIZZY GILLESPIE
671001
1 October 1967, Village Vanguard, New York: Dizzy Gillespie tp; Garnett Brown tb*; Pepper Adams bs; Ray Nance violin†; Chick Corea p; Richard Davis b; Elvin Jones√, Mel Lewis dm.

a **Birk's Works**†√   Solid State LP: SS-18034
b **Lullaby of the Leaves***†√ Solid State LP: SS-18027
c **Blues for Max**†
d **Lover Come Back to Me**†
e **Sweet Georgia Brown***   Solid State LP: SS-18028
f **On the Trail***
g **Tour de Force***

-a on Blue Note (Neth) LP: 5C038-60107, Blue Note (Eng) LP: BNS-40035, Blue Note BN (Sp) LP: BNS-40035, Blue Note CD: CDBN-7-80507-2, LRC (Ger) CD: CDC-9011, LRC (Ger) CD: CDC-9022, Delta Distribution (Ger) CD: 55605.

-b on King (J) LP: LAX -3154, Solid State (J) LP: USS-7002, Solid State (J) LP: K23P-6713, Blue Note CD: CDBN-7-80507-2, LRC (Ger) CD: CDC-9011, LRC (Ger) CD: CDC-9022, Delta Distribution (Ger) CD: 55605, Blue Note CD: CDBN (J) TOCJ-5633. Abridged version of -b on LRC (Ger) CD: CDC-9021.

-c on Solid State LP: SS-18034, Blue Note (Neth) LP: 5C038-60107, Blue Note (Eng) LP: BNS-40035, King (J) LP: LAX-3156, King (J) LP: LAX-3154, Solid State (J) LP: USS-7002, Solid State (J) LP: K23P-6713, Blue Note CD: CDBN-7-80507-2, LRC (Ger) CD: CDC-9011, LRC (Ger) CD: CDC-9021, LRC (Ger) CD: CDC-9022, Delta Distribution (Ger) CD: 55605.

-d on King (J) LP: LAX -3154 , Solid State (J) LP: USS-7002, Solid State (J) LP: K23P-6713, Blue Note CD: CDBN-7-80507-2, LRC (Ger) CD: CDC-9011, LRC (Ger) CD: CDC-9022, Delta Distribution (Ger) CD: 55605.

-e on Solid State LP: SM-17028-A, Solid State LP: USS-7009, King (J) LP: LAX-3144, Blue Note CD: CDBN-7-80507-2, LRC (Ger) CD: CDC-9012.

-f on Solid State LP: SM-17028-A, Solid State LP: USS-7009, King (J) LP: LAX-3144, Blue Note CD: CDBN-7-80507-2, LRC (Ger) CD: CDC-9012.

-g on Solid State LP: SS-18034, Solid State LP: USS-7009, Solid State LP: SM-17028-A, United Artists LP: UALP-19, Blue Note (Neth) LP: 5C038-60107, Blue Note (Eng) LP: BNS-40035, Blue Note (Sp) LP: BNS-40035, King (J) LP: LAX-3156, King (J) LP: LAX-3144, Blue Note CD: CDBN-7-80507-2, LRC (Ger) CD: CDC-9011, LRC (Ger) CD: CDC-9022, Delta Distribution (Ger) CD: 55605.

DONALD BYRD–THE CREEPER
671005
5 October 1967, Van Gelder Studio, Englewood Cliffs NJ: Donald Byrd tp; Sonny Red as; Pepper Adams bs; Chick Corea p, perc; Miroslav Vitous b; Mickey Roker dm.

a	1957	The Creeper	Blue Note LP: LT-1096
b	1959	**Blues Well Done**	
c	1960	**Early Sunday Morning**	
d	1961	I Will Wait for You[1]	
e	1962	**Chico San**	
f	1963	**Samba Yantra**	
g	1964	**Blues Medium Rare**	

[1]Byrd and rhythm section.

Matrix number for -a is the same as its alternate on 670929.
All tracks on Mosaic CD: MD4-194.
At least 25 takes were done at this session.
First issued in 1981. *See* 670929.

BLUE MITCHELL–HEADS UP
671117
17 November 1967, Van Gelder Studio, Englewood Cliffs NJ: Blue Mitchell, Burt Collins tp; Julian Priester tb; Jerry Dodgion as, fl; Junior Cook ts; Pepper Adams bs; McCoy Tyner p; Gene Taylor b; Al Foster dm.

a	1988	Len Sirrah	Blue Note LP: BST-84272
b	1989	Togetherness	
c		Togetherness	Mosaic CD: MD4-178
d	1990	Heads Up! Feet Down!	Blue Note LP: BST-84272
e	1991	Good Humor Man	

f		Good Humor Man	Mosaic CD: MD4-178
g	1992	The Folks Who	Blue Note LP: BST-84272
		Live on the Hill	
h	1993	The People in Nassau	

-e on Blue Note LP: B1-89907, Mosaic LP: MQ6-178, Blue Note CD: 7-89907-2, Mosaic CD: MD4-178.

All other tracks on Mosaic LP: MQ6-178, Mosaic CD: MD4-178.

At least 34 takes were done at this session.

HANK CRAWFORD–DOUBLE CROSS
671120

20 November 1967, Atlantic Studios, New York: Joe Newman, Melvin Lastie tp; Tony Studd tb; Hank Crawford as; David Newman ts; Pepper Adams bs; Jack McDuff p*; Carl Lynch g; Jimmy Tyrell e-b; Bruno Carr dm.

a	13508	I Can't Stand It	Atlantic LP: SD-1503
b	13509	Glue Fingers	
c	13510	In the Heat of the Night*	
d	13511	Double Cross	
e	13512	Jimmy Mack	
f	13513	The Second Time Around	
g	13514	Mud Island Blues	

-a on Collectables CD: COL-6825.
-b on Atlantic LP: 2510, Collectables CD: COL-6825.
-c on Atlantic LP: SD2-315, Collectables CD: COL-6825.
-d on Atlantic LP: SD2-315, Collectables CD: COL-6825.
-e on Collectables CD: COL-6825.
-f on Collectables CD: COL-6825.
-g on Collectables CD: COL-6825.

THE COWSILLS
671212

12 December 1967, New York: Overdub: Pepper Adams bs; other musicians.

a	104151	The Impossible Years	MGM 45: K-14011

Original recording, made on 29 October 1968: Bob Cowsill, John Cowsill voc.
-a on Razor and Tie CD: RE-2037.

DUKE PEARSON–INTRODUCING DUKE PEARSON'S BIG BAND
671215
15 December 1967, Van Gelder Studio, Englewood Cliffs NJ: Burt Collins, Randy Brecker, Joe Shepley, Marvin Stamm tp; Garnett Brown, Julian Priester, Kenny Rupp tb; Benny Powell btb; Jerry Dodgion as, fl, pic; Al Gibbons as, bcl, fl; Frank Foster, Lew Tabackin ts; Pepper Adams bs, cl; Duke Pearson p; Bob Cranshaw b; Mickey Roker dm.

a	2000	Ready When You Are C. B.	Blue Note LP: BST-84276
b	2001	Ground Hog	
c	2002	Mississippi Dip	
d	2003	A Taste of Honey	
e	2004	Bedouin	
f	2005	New Time Shuffle	
g	2006	**Straight Up and Down**	
h	2007	New Girl	
i	2008	Time After Time	

-a on Blue Note (Eu) CD: CDP-7243-4-94508-2, Toshiba-EMI (J) CD: TOCJ-4276, Toshiba-EMI (J) CD: TOCJ-8694.

-b on Blue Note LP: B1-54360, Blue Note CD: 8-54360-2, Blue Note (Eu) CD: CDP-7243-4-94508-2, Toshiba-EMI (J) CD: TOCJ-4276, Toshiba-EMI (J) CD: TOCJ-8694.

-c on Blue Note CD: CDBN (Eu) 5-23444-2, Blue Note (Eu) CD: CDP-7243-4-94508-2, Toshiba-EMI (J) CD: TOCJ-4276, Toshiba-EMI (J) CD: TOCJ-8694.

-d on Blue Note (Eu) CD: CDP-7243-4-94508-2, Toshiba-EMI (J) CD: TOCJ-4276, Toshiba-EMI (J) CD: TOCJ-8694.

-e on Blue Note (Eu) CD: CDP-7243-4-94508-2, Toshiba-EMI (J) CD: TOCJ-4276, Toshiba-EMI (J) CD: TOCJ-8694.

-f on Blue Note CD: CDBN-4-97155-2, Blue Note (Eu) CD: CDP-7243-4-94508-2, Toshiba-EMI (J) CD: TOCJ-4276, Toshiba-EMI (J) CD: TOCJ-8694.

-g on Blue Note (Eu) CD: CDP-7243-4-94508-2, Toshiba-EMI (J) CD: TOCJ-4276, Toshiba-EMI (J) CD: TOCJ-8694.

-h on Smithsonian LP: RD-108-S25-17618, Blue Note (Eu) CD: CDP-7243-4-94508-2, Toshiba-EMI (J) CD: TOCJ-4276, Toshiba-EMI (J) CD: TOCJ-8694.

-i on Blue Note (Eu) CD: CDP-7243-4-94508-2, Toshiba-EMI (J) CD: TOCJ-4276, Toshiba-EMI (J) CD: TOCJ-8694.

At least 54 takes were done at this session.

According to Mickey Roker, in a conversation with the author in 1991, the band rehearsed every Saturday in New York at Len Oliver's (59th Street and Broadway).

According to Bob Cranshaw, in an interview done with the author in 1988,

> Pepper and Duke Pearson went back a long time together. He was one of the mainstays of Duke Pearson's band....We didn't do a lot, no. Now and then the band played for Nancy Wilson or a couple of singers. It was kind of like a rehearsal band....
>
> Duke used to have a lot of ladies. He was a lady's man, so he would write these arrangements for these ladies so he could get to them, and the band would be his cover. We just enjoyed playing with each other, but we didn't really work a lot. Duke was usually busy at that time, because he was A&R at Blue Note. I was doing a lot of TV shows, so I could have only been involved with limited parts of whatever it was. Duke was really "out." With ladies, he really, as I say, had a "Jones." He always had two and three ladies. He'd get married and settle down for a minute.
>
> We got to the place where Mickey Roker and I became a package, because the difference in the band was that Duke never really played. He would be there, but he would be sitting out in the audience, listening to his music. I mean this guy just enjoyed hearing his stuff played. A lot of the stuff, when he was there, we just got to the place where he never played, so it made Mickey and I stronger. This was the difference, kind of, in the sound of the band, in that Duke wrote a little different. He had some very unique people in the band. Mickey was a small group drummer playing with a big band. He incorporated his small group thing. So Mickey played the big band thing much different than other drummers would approach it, because Mickey wasn't a big band drummer, but he learned to handle it. When guys would take solos, there was no Duke. Duke was out in the audience, and bullshitting, playing around, but we got used to it, because this is the way he was. Duke would bring in the band, and have a lot of ensemble playing coming from the backgrounds of

the band, but we didn't get it from Duke. Duke wasn't a strong piano player: He got to the place where he didn't play all the time. He
was involved more in executive work, and writing rather than playing....So he used us; we just experimented. We played his arrangements and helped him with his ladies, giving him cover, and that
was it. We all knew. It wasn't like we didn't know, but it wasn't a
big deal....He'd come in and would hit a couple of chords and so
forth. He had another role, and we all knew what his role was, and
that was it.

DAVID AMRAM
680100
c. January 1968, film soundtrack, New York: Pepper Adams bs; other
musicians; symphony orchestra.

This soundtrack for the documentary *U.S.* was produced for San Antonio's Hemisfair and shown at the Confluence Theater in the United
States Pavilion.
    According to David Amram, in an interview with the author in 1988,

That was a film that I wrote the music for in 1968 for the San Antonio Hemisfair, and Pepper had some great solos in that. On one
place, there was one scene that was supposed to show something
about life in Texas, so I always managed to sneak some improvising
music into whatever the situation was. So I said, "Well, Pepper, this
is supposed to be a scene celebrating life in Texas, so, in the middle
of this kind of big band arrangement I made, Pepper was playing
this fantastic solo and interpolated part of The Yellow Rose of
Texas in a different key than the tune was in—kind of snuck it in
sideways in the middle—and we almost had to stop recording because everybody almost fell out laughing! But it was such a good
take that we used it anyway. We had a whole symphony orchestra.
    It was done on three screens by Francis Thompson, who is a
documentary filmmaker. It was the opening of the San Antonio
Hemisfair. It was called *U.S.* It was kind of a documentary of the
United States, and W.H. Auden wrote the script. It was real heavy,
because it also showed some of the social problems of the '60s at
the same time, and a lot of the ghetto areas in Houston, Texas. The
Vietnam War was putting such a strain on the whole country. When
Lady Bird Johnson and some of the people from the Texas hierar-
chy came down and saw the film, they were horrified, except it got

such a big hand at the end, they let it slide. It was a beautiful, beautiful film.

JIMMY SMITH–STAY LOOSE
680110
10 January 1968, A&R Studios, New York: Snooky Young, Ernie Royal, Joe Newman tp; Garnett Brown, Jimmy Cleveland tb; Alan Raph btb; Jerome Richardson as; Joe Farrell, Hubert Laws ts; Pepper Adams bs; Jimmy Smith org, voc; Carl Lynch g; James Tyrell e-b; Grady Tate dm; Johnny Pacheco perc; vocal choir*: Carline Ray, Eileen Gilbert, Melba Moore.

a	104243	Stay Loose*	Verve LP: V6-8745
b	104244	If You Ain't Got It	
c	104245	I'm Gonna Move to the Outskirts of Town	
d	104246	Is You Is or Is You Ain't My Baby	

-a on Verve LP: V-8745, Verve LP: 2V6S-8814, Verve LP: B000467602, Verve (Eng) LP: SVLP-9128, Verve (Neth) LP: V6-8745, Verve (F) LP: 2610011, Verve (Ger) LP: 2622-006, Verve CD: 467602.
-b on Verve LP: V-8745, Verve LP: 2V6S-8814, Verve LP: B000467602, Verve (Eng) LP: SVLP-9128, Verve (Neth) LP: V6-8745, Verve (F) LP: 2610011, Verve CD: 467602.
-c on Verve LP: V-8745, Verve LP: B000467602, Verve (Eng) LP: SVLP-9128, Verve (Neth) LP: V6-8745, Verve (F) LP: 2632001, Verve CD: 467602.
-d on Verve LP: V-8745, Verve LP: B000467602, Verve (Eng) LP: SVLP-9128, Verve (Neth) LP: V6-8745, Verve (F) LP: V6-652, Verve (F) LP: 2632001, Verve CD: 467602.

ERROLL GARNER
680205a
5 February 1968, New York: Overdubs: Bernie Glow tp; Marvin Stamm tp, flh; Jimmy Cleveland, Wayne Andre tb; Don Butterfield tu; Jerome Richardson ts, fl, pic; Pepper Adams bs.

a	104361	A Lot of Livin' to Do	MGM LP: E-4520
b	104363	They've Got an Awful Lot of Coffee in Brazil	
c	104364	Cheek to Cheek	
d	104368	I Got Rhythm	

e   104497   Watermelon Man

Rhythm section tracks recorded in New York on 19 March 1968:
Erroll Garner p; Ike Isaacs b; Jimmie Smith dm; José Mangual cga.
-a on MGM LP: SE-4520, Pye (Eng) LP: NSPL-28123, MPS (Ger)
LP: 15252, MGM (Ger) LP: 68-056, MGM (Ger) LP: CRM-714, MPS
(Ger) LP: 21-297-14-4, MGM (Neth) LP: 5C064D-99438, Polydor (F)
LP: 2393-008, Telarc CD: CD-83378.
-b on MGM 45: K-13988, MGM LP: SE-4520, Pye (Eng) LP:
NSPL-28123, MPS (Ger) LP: 15252, MGM (Ger) LP: 68-056, MGM
(Ger) LP: CRM-714, MPS (Ger) LP: 21-297-14-4, MGM (Neth) LP:
5C064D-99438, Polydor (F) LP: 2393-008, Telarc CD: CD-83378.
-c on MGM 45: K-14043, MGM LP: SE-4520, Pye (Eng) LP: NSPL-
28123, MPS (Ger) LP: 15252, MGM (Ger) LP: 68-056, MGM (Ger) LP:
CRM-714, MPS (Ger) LP: 21-297-14-4, MGM (Neth) LP: 5C064D-
99438, Polydor (F) LP: 2393-008, Telarc CD: CD-83378.
-d on MGM LP: SE-4520, Pye (Eng) LP: NSPL-28123, Bull Dog
(Eng) LP: BDL-4004, MGM (Ger) LP: 68-056, MPS (Ger) LP: 68-126,
MGM (Ger) LP: CRM-714, MPS (Ger) LP: 15252, MPS (Ger) LP: 21-
297-14-4, MGM (Neth) LP: 5C064D-99438, MGM (Neth) LP: 5C064D-
99397, Polydor (F) LP: 2393-008, Polydor (F) LP: 2445-030, Telarc CD:
CD-83378.
-e on MGM 45: K-13916, MGM LP: SE-4520, Pye (Eng) LP: NSPL-
28123, MGM (Ger) LP: 68-056, MGM (Ger) LP: CRM-714, MPS (Ger)
LP: 15252, MPS (Ger) LP: 21-297-14-4, MGM (Neth) LP: 5C064D-
99438, Polydor (F) LP: 2393-008, Telarc CD: CD-83378.

GEORGE BENSON–GIBLET GRAVY
680205b
5 February 1968, A&R Studios or Capitol Recording Studios, New York:
Snooky Young, Ernie Royal tp; Jimmy Owens tp, flh; Alan Raph btb;
Pepper Adams bs; Herbie Hancock p; George Benson, Eric Gale g; Bob
Cranshaw b; Billy Cobham dm; vocal choir*: Eileen Gilbert, Andrew
Love, Albertine Robinson.

a   104355   Giblet Gravy   Verve LP: V6-8749
b   104356   Walk on By*
c   104357   Sunny

-a on Verve LP: V-8749, Verve LP: V3HB-8845, Verve LP: 314-543-754-2, Polydor (J) LP: 23MJ-3392, Universal CD: UCCV-9425, Polygram CD: 543754, Verve (Ger) CD: 823450-2.

-b on Verve LP: V-8749, Verve LP: V3HB-8845, Verve LP: 314-543-754-2, Polydor (J) LP: 23MJ-3392, Universal CD: UCCV-9425, Polygram CD: 543754, Verve (Ger) CD: 823450-2.

-c on Verve LP: V-8749, Verve LP: V3HB-8845, Verve LP: 314-543-754-2, Polydor (J) LP: 23MJ-3392, Polydor (J) Universal CD: UCCV-9425, Polygram CD: 543754.

See 680206, 680207.

GEORGE BENSON–GIBLET GRAVY
680206
6 February 1968, A&R Studios or Capitol Recording Studios, New York:
Same as 5 February 1968, Ron Carter replaces Cranshaw, Gale and vocal choir out:

a   104377   Sack o' Woe   Verve LP: V6-8749

-a on Verve LP: V-8749, Verve LP: V3HB-8845, Verve LP: 314-543-754-2, Polydor (J) LP: 23MJ-3392, Universal CD: UCCV-9425, Polygram CD: 543754, Verve (Ger) CD: 823450-2.
See 680205, 680207.

GEORGE BENSON–GIBLET GRAVY
680207
7 February 1968, A&R Studios or Capitol Recording Studios, New York:
Same as 5 February 1968, Ron Carter replaces Cranshaw, Carl Lynch* replaces Gale, and vocal choir out:

a   104378   Groovin'   Verve LP: V6-8749
b   104379   Along Came Mary*
c   104380   Sunny   Verve unissued

-a on Verve LP: V-8749, Verve LP: V3HB-8845, Verve LP: 314-543-754-2, Polydor (J) LP: 23MJ-3392, Polygram CD: 543754, Universal CD: UCCV-9425, Verve (Ger) CD: 823450-2.

-b on Verve LP: V-8749, Verve LP: V3HB-8845, Verve LP: 314-543-754-2, Polydor (J) LP: 23MJ-3392, Polygram CD: 543754, Universal CD: UCCV-9425.

See 680205, 680206.

HOUSTON PERSON–BLUE ODYSSEY
680312
12 March 1968, Impact Studio, New York: Curtis Fuller tb; Houston Person ts; Pepper Adams bs; Cedar Walton p; Bob Cranshaw b; Frankie Jones dm.

a   Blue Odyssey   Prestige LP: PR-7566
b   **Holy Land**
c   I Love You, Yes I Do
d   **Funky London**
e   Please Send Me Someone to Love
f   Starr Burstt

All tracks on Prestige LP: PR-7779, Original Jazz Classics CD: OJCCD-1045-2.

QUINCY JONES
680327
27 March 1968, film soundtrack, A&R Studios, New York: Pepper Adams bs; possibly Shirley Horn voc; other musicians.

According to Pepper Adams' 1968 appointment book, this date was done from 7-10pm. This is possibly for Jones' soundtrack to *For Love of Ivy*, since Jones was back at A&R on 13 April to record material for the film. It could also have been for Jones' soundtrack to *A Dandy in Aspic*. Unfortunately, according to historian Mike Fitzgerald, there are no entries in ABC's ledger for 27 March 1968.

THAD JONES-MEL LEWIS
680422
22 April 1968, TV broadcast, KQED Studios, San Francisco: Thad Jones flh; Snooky Young, Danny Moore, Richard Williams, Randy Brecker tp; Bob Brookmeyer vtb; Jimmy Knepper, Garnett Brown tb; Benny Powell btb; Jerome Richardson as, ss, cl, fl; Jerry Dodgion as, cl, fl; Seldon Powell ts; Eddie Daniels ts, cl, fl; Pepper Adams bs; cl; Roland Hanna p; Sam Herman g, shaker; Richard Davis b; Mel Lewis dm.

a   Just Blues   Koch CD: KOC-CD-8563

b   St. Louis Blues
c   Kids Are Pretty People
d   Don't Git Sassy

This thirty minute episode of *Jazz Casual,* produced and hosted by Ralph J. Gleason, is also available on Idem DVD: 1014.

JOE WILLIAMS AND THAD JONES-MEL LEWIS – SOMETHING OLD, NEW AND BLUE
680423

23-27 April 1968, Los Angeles: Same as 22 April 1968; Roland Hanna orgt; add possibly Terry Gibbs vib√, possibly Kenny Burrell g, Joe Williams voc, string section.*

a   5218   Young Man on the Way Up*   Solid State LP: SS-18015
b   5219   Hurry on Down
c   5220   When I Take My Sugar to Tea
d   5221   Honeysuckle Rose†
e   5222   Did I Really Live*
f   5223   Loneliness, Sorrow and Grief*
g   5224   Imagination†
h   5225   One More for My Baby
i   5226   Everyone Wants to Be Loved (By Someone)†
j   5227   Everybody Loves My Baby√
k   5228   If I Were a Bell
m   5229   Hallelujah I Love Her So   King (J) LP: GHX-3506
n   5230   Nobody Knows the Way I Feel This Morning
o   5231   How Sweet It Is (To Be Loved by You)
p   5232   Evil Man Blues

   -a on LRC (Ger) CD: CDC-9005, LRC (Ger) CD: CDC-9021, King (J) LP: GHX-3506.
   All other tracks on King (J) LP: GHX-3506, LRC (Ger) CD: CDC-9005.
   The band had a week-long engagement (22-27 April) at Marty's on the Hill in Hollywood. Discographies have cited the recording dates of this session as 22-27 April, but the band was in San Francisco on 22 April to record a TV broadcast (*see* 680422), then it had to fly to Los Angeles in time for their opening at Marty's. There wouldn't have been time to record again in Los Angeles on the same day. It's not clear what tunes

were recorded on what day, which days (among the five listed above) they recorded on, or whether the string session was added at a later date.

BARRY HARRIS–BULL'S EYE
680604
4 June 1968, New York: Kenny Dorham tp; Charles McPherson ts; Pepper Adams bs; Barry Harris p; Paul Chambers b; Billy Higgins dm.

a **Bull's Eye**   Prestige LP: PRLP-7600
b **Off Monk**
c **Barengo**
d **Oh So Basal**
   Rhythm section only:
e Clockwise
f Off Minor

All tracks on Victor (J) LP: SMJ-6276, Original Jazz Classics CD: OJCCD-1082-2.

According to Charles McPherson, in an interview with the author in 1987,

> I remember I played tenor rather than alto on that date. [It was] Barry's idea. I guess he just wanted a certain sound. He had written these three horn arrangements and he wanted the tenor as opposed to alto. I'm an alto player, so every record I do is alto. So it would've just been more of a novelty, in that respect, and so he wanted me to play the tenor and I did. I can remember the date being a great date! I mean, it was a fun record date with no problems. We just went in there and maybe had a little rehearsal on the [day of the] date. I remember having a rehearsal before the date also, but I don't think Pepper was there....Yeah, I can remember Barry showing me one of his tunes that he was going to use on the date at some place. It wasn't at the record date though. It might have been at my house, his house, or something. The music was real interesting. I thought it was recorded well also. But the band was great. I mean Paul, and Billy Higgins, and Barry! And then the horns: Kenny Dorham, I thought, played great on the record, and Pepper played great, and I'm the youngster there.

THAD JONES-MEL LEWIS – THE BIG BAND SOUND OF THAD JONES-MEL LEWIS FEATURING MISS RUTH BROWN
680618
18 June 1968, Plaza Sound Studios, New York: Thad Jones flh; Snooky Young, Richard Williams, Bill Berry, Jimmy Nottingham, Danny Moore tp; Garnett Brown, Jimmy Cleveland, Jimmy Knepper tb; Cliff Heather btb; Jerome Richardson as, ss; Jerry Dodgion as; Eddie Daniels, Seldon Powell ts; Pepper Adams bs; Roland Hanna p; Richard Davis b; Mel Lewis dm; Ruth Brown voc.

a   Yes, Sir, That's My Baby   Solid State LP: SS-18041
b   2597   Be Anything (But Be Mine)

-a on King (J) LP: GP-3173, Capitol-Blue Note CD: 7-81200-2, Blue Note CD: BN (Sp) 8-56842-2, Koch (Ger) CD: KOC-51414.
-b on Blue Note LP: BN-LA392-H2, King (J) LP: GP-3173, Blue Note (Eng) LP: BND-4004, Blue Note (Ger) LP: BST-84497/8, Capitol-Blue Note CD: 7-81200-2, LRC (Ger) CD: CDC-9008, LRC (Ger) CD: CDC-9021, Koch (Ger) CD: KOC-51414.
See 680702.

ROLAND KIRK–LEFT AND RIGHT
680619
19 June 1968, Regent Sound Studios, New York: Richard Williams tp; Dick Griffin, Benny Powell tb; Daniel Jones bassoon; Roland Kirk as, ts, ss, fl, thumb piano, celeste; Pepper Adams bs; Ron Burton p; Alice Coltrane harp; Vernon Martin b; Jimmy Hopps dm; Sonny Brown, Warren Smith perc.

a   14717   **Expansions**   Atlantic LP: SD-1518

-a on Rhino-Atlantic LP [180 gram]: SD-1518, Atlantic (Eng) LP: ATL-588178, Atlantic (Ger) LP: ATL-40235, Atlantic (Sp) LP: WEA-40235, Collectables CD: COL-634032, 32 Jazz CD: 32060.
According to historian Lewis Porter, in a conversation with the author in 1985, Kirk plays a straight soprano and alto saxophone, though Kirk referred to them as the manzello and stritch respectively.
Various discographies list the recording date of this portion of Kirk's project as taking place on 18 June 1968, but Adams' appointment book lists a three-hour Roland Kirk session for Atlantic taking place on

Wednesday, 19 June, with an itemization of how much he was paid for the session.

THAD JONES-MEL LEWIS – THE BIG BAND SOUND OF THAD JONES-MEL LEWIS FEATURING MISS RUTH BROWN
680702
2 July 1968, Plaza Sound Studios, New York: Same as 18 June 1968:

a		**Trouble in Mind**	Solid State LP:
			SS-18041
b		Sonny Boy	
c		Bye Bye Blackbird	
d		I'm Gonna Move to the Outskirts	
		of Town	
e		Black Coffee	
f	2596	You Won't Let Me Go	
g	2595	Fine Brown Frame	

-f on Blue Note LP: BN-LA392-H2, Blue Note (Eng) LP: BND-4004, Blue Note (Ger) LP: BST-84497/8, King (J) LP: GP-3173, Capitol-Blue Note CD: CDP-7-81200-2, Koch (Ger) CD: KOC-51414.
-g on Blue Note LP: BN-LA392-H2, Blue Note (Eng) LP: BND-4004, Blue Note (Ger) LP: BST-84497/8, King (J) LP: GP-3173, Capitol-Blue Note CD: CDP-7-81200-2, Koch (Ger) CD: KOC-51414, Denon (J) CD: DC-8517.
All other tracks on Solid State LP: SS-18041, King (J) LP: GP-3173, Capitol-Blue Note CD: CDP-7-81200-2, Koch (Ger) CD: KOC-51414.
See 680618.

681003
c. 3 October 1968, Eastern Sound Studio, Toronto: Pepper Adams bs; other musicians.
As discussed in a radio interview on 4 October 1968 with Ted O'-Reilly, Adams had a recording session planned at Eastern Sound Studio during his engagement at George's Spaghetti House.

ARETHA FRANKLIN
681016
16 October 1968, New York: Overdubs: Bernie Glow, Joe Newman, Ernie Royal, Snooky Young, Richard Williams, tp; Jimmy Cleveland, Ur-

bie Green, Tom Mitchell, Benny Powell tb; George Dorsey, Frank Wess as; King Curtis, Seldon Powell ts; David Newman ts, fl; Pepper Adams bs.

a	14329	You Send Me	Atlantic LP: SD-8186
b	14330	See Saw	
c	14335	Tracks of My Tears	Atlantic LP: SD-8212
d	14336	I Take What I Want	Atlantic LP: SD-8186
e	14337	I Can't See Myself Leaving You	

Original tracks to -a and -b recorded in New York on 16 April 1968: Aretha Franklin p, voc; Spooner Oldham org; Jimmy Johnson g; Jack Jennings vib; Jerry Jemmott or Tommy Cogbill e-b; Roger Hawkins dm; Louis Goicdecha, Manuel Gonzales perc.

Original tracks to -c, -d, -e recorded in New York on 18 April 1968: Aretha Franklin p, voc; Spooner Oldham org; Jimmy Johnson g; Jack Jennings vib; Jerry Jemmott or Tommy Cogbill e-b; Roger Hawkins dm; Louis Goicdecha, Manuel Gonzales perc.

-a on Atlantic 45: 45-2518, Atlantic LP: SD-2518, Atlantic LP: SD-8227, Atlantic (F) LP: 0920044, Atlantic (F) LP: 60030, Atlantic CD: 8227-2, Atlantic CD: R2-71273, Rhino CD: R2-72576.

-b on Atlantic 45: 45-2574, Atlantic (Eng) 45: 584206, Atlantic LP: SD-8224, Atlantic LP: SD-8227, Atlantic LP: SD-2574, Atlantic LP: SD-18204, Atlantic LP: OS-13063, Atlantic (F) LP: 60030, Atlantic (F) LP: 0920044, Atlantic CD: 8227-2, Atlantic CD: R2-71273.

-c on Atlantic 45: 45-2603, Atlantic LP: SD-2603, Atlantic (F) LP: 60030, Rhino CD: R2-71523, Rhino CD: R2-71063.

-d on Atlantic (F) LP: 60030, Atlantic (F) LP: 0920044, Rhino CD: R2-71273, Rhino CD: R2-71063.

-e on Atlantic 45: 45-2619, Atlantic LP: SD-2619, Atlantic (F) LP: 0920044, Rhino CD: R2-71273, Rhino CD: R2-71063.

See 681017, 681105, 681120.

ARETHA FRANKLIN
681017
17 October 1968, New York: Overdubs: Ernie Royal, Snooky Young or Bernie Glow, Richard Williams, Joe Newman tp; Jimmy Cleveland, Urbie Green or Tom Mitchell, Benny Powell tb; George Dorsey, Frank Wess as; King Curtis, Seldon Powell ts; David Newman ts, fl; Pepper Adams bs.

a   14331   Today I Sing the Blues   Atlantic LP: SD-8212
b   14332   The House that Jack Built   Atlantic LP: SD-8227
c   14333   I Say A Little Prayer for You   Atlantic LP: SD-8186
d   14334   Night Time Is the Right Time
e   14894   I Say a Little Prayer for You   Atlantic unissued

Original tracks recorded in New York on 17 April 1968: Aretha
Franklin p, voc; Spooner Oldham org; Jimmy Johnson g; Jack Jennings
vib; Jerry Jemmott or Tommy Cogbill e-b; Roger Hawkins dm; Louis
Goicdecha, Manuel Gonzales perc.
    -a on Atlantic LP: 7-81230-1, Atlantic CD: 7-81230-2, Rhino CD:
R2-71523, Rhino CD: R2-72942, Rhino CD: RHM2-7737, Rhino CD:
R2-71063.
    -b on Atlantic 45; 45-2546, Atlantic 45: OS-13059, Atlantic (Eng)
45: 45-2464007, Atlantic LP: SD-2546, Atlantic LP: OS-13059, Atlantic
CD: 8227-2, Rhino CD: R2-71063.
    -c on Atlantic (Eng) 45: 584206, Atlantic LP: SD-8224, Atlantic LP:
SD-8227, Atlantic LP: SD-8295, Atlantic LP: SD-8305, Atlantic (F) LP:
0920044, Atlantic CD: 8227-2, Atlantic CD: R2-71273, Rhino CD: R2-
71063.
    -d on Atlantic (F) LP: 60030, Atlantic (F) LP: 0920044, Rhino CD:
R2-71273, Rhino CD: R2-72942, Rhino CD: R2-71063.
    -e on Atlantic 45: 45-2546, Atlantic (Eng) LP: 2464007.
    See 681016, 681105, 681120.

THAD JONES-MEL LEWIS – MONDAY NIGHT
681021
21 October 1968, Village Vanguard, New York: Thad Jones flh; Snooky
Young, Jimmy Nottingham, Richard Williams, Danny Moore tp; Jimmy
Cleveland, Garnett Brown, Jimmy Knepper tb; Cliff Heather btb; Jerome
Richardson as, ss, fl; Jerry Dodgion as, fl; Seldon Powell, Eddie Daniels
ts, cl; Pepper Adams bs, cl; Roland Hanna p; Richard Davis b; Mel
Lewis dm.

a   2983   Mornin' Reverend   Solid State LP: SS-18048
b   Kids Are Pretty People
c   St. Louis Blues
d   The Waltz You "Swang" for Me
e   Say It Softly
f   The Second Race

According to Pepper Adams' 1968 appointment book, this date was recorded on Monday night, 21 October, not on Thursday, 17 October, as listed in various discographies. Adams was paid his customary $20 for the gig, plus an additional amount from United Artists for the recording.

-a on Blue Note LP: BN-LA392-H2, Blue Note (Eng) LP: BND-4004, United Artists (Eng) LP: UAS-29016, Sunset (Eng) LP: GLS-50249, Blue Note (Ger) LP: BST-84497/8, King (J) LP: GP-3024.

All other tracks on United Artists (Eng) LP: UAS-29016, King (J) LP: GP-3024, Mosaic LP: MQ7-151, Mosaic CD: MD5-151.

ARETHA FRANKLIN
681105
5 November 1968, New York: Overdubs: Ernie Royal, Snooky Young or Bernie Glow, Richard Williams, Joe Newman tp; Jimmy Cleveland, Urbie Green or Tom Mitchell, Benny Powell tb; Frank Wess, George Dorsey as; King Curtis, Seldon Powell ts; David Newman ts, fl; Pepper Adams bs.

a	15333	So Long	Atlantic LP: SD-8212
b	15334	Talk to Me	Rhino CD: R2-272188
c	15335	I'll Never Be Free	Atlantic LP: SD-8212
d	15336	Pitiful	
e	15337	Ramblin'	
f	15338	Gentle on My Mind	
g	15339	Bring It on Home to Me	Atlantic LP: SD-8212
h	15340	I Can't Turn You Loose	Atlantic unissued

Original tracks to -a, -b, -c recorded in New York on 23 September 1968: Junior Mance p; Kenny Burrell g; Ron Carter b; Grady Tate dm; Aretha Franklin voc.

Original tracks to -d, -e recorded in New York on 24 September 1968: Junior Mance p; Kenny Burrell g; Ron Carter b; Bruno Carr dm; Aretha Franklin voc.

Original tracks to -f recorded in New York on 24 September 1968: Aretha Franklin p, voc; Joe Zawinul e-p; Kenny Burrell g; Jack Jennings vib; Ron Carter b; Bruno Carr dm; vocal choir: Evelyne Greene, Wyline Ivey.

Original tracks to -g and -h recorded in New York on 25 September 1968: Joe Zawinul e-p; Kenny Burrell g; Ron Carter b; Bruno Carr dm; Aretha Franklin voc.

-a on Rhino CD: R2-71523.

-b on Rhino CD: R2-272188.

-c on Rhino CD: R2-71523.

-d on Atlantic LP: 7-81230-1, Atlantic (F) LP: 921075, Atlantic (F) LP: 60030, Atlantic CD: 81230-2, Rhino CD: R2-71523, Rhino CD: R2-71063.

-e on Atlantic LP: 7-81230-1, Atlantic CD: 7-81230-2, Rhino CD: R2-71452, Rhino CD: R2-72942, Rhino CD: R2-71523.

-f on Atlantic 45: 45-2619, Atlantic (F) LP: 60030, Rhino CD: R2-71523.

-g on Atlantic LP: 7-81230-1, Atlantic CD: 81230-2, Rhino CD: R2-71523.

See 681016, 681117, 681120.

ARETHA FRANKLIN
681120

20 November 1968, New York: Overdubs: Bernie Glow, Ernie Royal, Snooky Young, Richard Williams, Joe Newman tp; Jimmy Cleveland, Urbie Green, Tom Mitchell, Benny Powell tb; Frank Wess, George Dorsey as; King Curtis, Seldon Powell ts; David Newman ts, fl; Pepper Adams bs.

a	15341	Crazy He Calls Me	Atlantic LP: SD-8212
b	15342	Elusive Butterfly	
c	15343	If You Gotta Make a Fool of Somebody	
d	15344	River's Invitation	

Original tracks to -a and -b recorded in New York on 26 September 1968: Joe Zawinul e-p; Jack Jennings vib; Ron Carter b; Bruno Carr dm; Louis Golcdecha, Manuel Gonzales perc; Aretha Franklin voc; vocal choir: Evelyne Greene, Wyline Ivey.

Original tracks to -c and -d recorded in New York on 27 September 1968: Joe Zawinul e-p; Kenny Burrell g; Ron Carter b; Bruno Carr dm; Louis Golcdecha, Manuel Gonzales perc; Aretha Franklin voc.

-a on Atlantic LP: 7-81230-1, Atlantic CD: 7-81230-2, Rhino CD: R2-71523, Rhino CD: R2-71784, Rhino CD: R2-72576.

-b on Rhino CD: R2-71523.

-c on Rhino CD: R2-71523.

-d on Rhino CD: R2-71523, Rhino CD: R2-71063, Rhino CD: R2-72942, Rhino CD: RHM2-7737, Rhino CD: R2-71063.

See 681016, 681117, 681105.

DUKE PEARSON–NOW HEAR THIS
681202
2 December 1968, Van Gelder Studio, Englewood Cliffs NJ: Burt Collins, Jim Bossy, Randy Brecker, Joe Shepley, Marvin Stamm tp; Garnett Brown, Jimmy Cleveland, Kenny Rupp tb; Benny Powell btb; Jerry Dodgion as, fl, piccolo; Al Gibbons as, bcl, fl; Frank Foster, Lew Tabackin ts; Pepper Adams bs; Duke Pearson p; Bob Cranshaw b; Mickey Roker dm; Andy Bey voc.*

a	3056	The Days of Wine and Roses	Blue Note unissued
b	3057	Here's that Rainy Day	
c	3058	Minor League	
d	3059	I'm Tired of Cryin' Over You*	

See 681203.

DUKE PEARSON–NOW HEAR THIS
681203
3 December 1968, Van Gelder Studio, Englewood Cliffs NJ: Same as 2 December 1968; Andy Bey voc*:

a	3056	The Days of Wine and Roses	Blue Note LP: BST-84308
b	3057	Here's that Rainy Day	
c	3058	Minor League	
d	3059	I'm Tired of Cryin' Over You*	
e	3060	Disapproachment	
f	3061	**Make it Good**	
g	3062	Amanda	
h	3063	Dad Digs Mom (And Mom Digs Dad)	
i	3064	Tones for Joan's Bones	

-a on Blue Note (Ger) LP: BST-84308K, Blue Note (Eu) CD: CDP-7243-4-94508-2, Toshiba-EMI (J) CD: TOCJ-4276.

-b on Blue Note (Ger) LP: BST-84308K, Blue Note (Eu) CD: CDP-7243-4-94508-2, Toshiba-EMI (J) CD: TOCJ-4276.

-c on Sunset (Eng) LP: SLS-50249, Blue Note (Ger) LP: BST-84308K, Blue Note (Eu) CD: CDP-7243-4-94508-2, Toshiba-EMI (J) CD: TOCJ-4276.

-d on Blue Note (Ger) LP: BST-84308K, Blue Note (Eu) CD: CDP-7243-4-94508-2, Toshiba-EMI (J) CD: TOCJ-4276.

-e on Blue Note (Ger) LP: BST-84308K, Blue Note (Eu) CD: CDP-7243-4-94508-2, Toshiba-EMI (J) CD: TOCJ-4276.

-f on Blue Note (Ger) LP: BST-84308K, Blue Note (Eu) CD: CDP-7243-4-94508-2, Toshiba-EMI (J) CD: TOCJ-4276.

-g on Blue Note (Ger) LP: BST-84308K.

-h on Blue Note (Ger) LP: BST-84308K.

-i on Blue Note (Ger) LP: BST-84308K, Blue Note (Eu) CD: CDP-7243-4-94508-2, Toshiba-EMI (J) CD: TOCJ-4276.

-a, -b, -c, -d are alternates to all titles on 681202, yet assigned identical matrix numbers.

At least 62 takes were done at this session.

About Make it Good, Lew Tabackin told the author in 1988,

> I remember doing one of the dates we did with Duke Pearson, the second date. [Pepper and I] had one piece we were both featured on, and we played one take and they said, "O.K. it's fine." I wasn't particularly happy, and [Pepper] wasn't particularly happy, but they were happy. (Meanwhile, all the other cats would get up there and do it three times.) "I want to do this again! I want to do this again!" [Pepper] got bugged. He said, "Man, everybody's getting two, three shots at it. We only get one."

See 681202.

PEPPER ADAMS–ENCOUNTER
681211
11-12 December 1968, Nola Sound Studios, New York: Zoot Sims ts; Pepper Adams bs; Tommy Flanagan p; Ron Carter b; Elvin Jones dm.

a	**In and Out**	Prestige LP: PR-7677
b	**Star-Crossed Lovers**	
c	**Cindy's Tune**	
d	**Serenity**	
e	**Elusive**	
f	**Punjab**	
g	**Verdandi (Mean Streets)**	
h	**Verdandi (Mean Streets)**	Prestige unissued
	Adams, Flanagan, and Carter:	

i   **I've Just Seen Her**   Prestige LP: PR-7677
    Rhythm section only:
j   unknown title   Prestige unissued

This is Adams' twelfth date as a leader. It's not clear what tunes were released from either session.

All tracks on Prestige (F) LP: PR-7677, Bellaphon (Ger) LP: BJS-40151, Victor (J) LP: SMJ-7544, Art Union (J) LP: ART-27, Original Jazz Classics CD: OJCCD-892-2.

According to Prestige owner Bob Weinstock, in a conversation with the author in 1988, this date "was bought by Don Schlitten (who worked for me) from Fred Norsworthy." Norsworthy had produced the date independently, but Weinstock wasn't involved in the project. By the time it was sold to Prestige, Weinstock had sold the company and he was transitioning out as owner.

According to Pepper Adams, as told to interviewer Albert Goldman on 19 June 1975,

> the date was an awful lot of fun. It was made for an independent producer, a rather impressed little English cat, Fred Norsworthy, and his idea was to sell it to a major company. So we did it independently. We figured, with Zoot Sims, Elvin Jones, Ron Carter... He couldn't get any company to listen to the tape, and finally wound up selling it to Prestige, which meant giving it away. He lost money on the deal, it doesn't get any distribution, it doesn't get heard, very difficult to even get complimentary copies out of the people.

In an interview with the author in 1984, Pepper Adams said,

> I'm really happy with that album. I like the way that one turned out, and I think it was a good mix of originals. A couple of Joe Henderson tunes I really like on there—I think that came out extremely well. [Fred Norsworthy] couldn't get any one of these companies to listen to it. Not to buy it, but even to listen to it! And so, finally, he sold it to Prestige, just to get some money back so the project wouldn't be a total loss. He may have been naive using me. If he had let me off the date, and had Zoot Sims with Tommy Flanagan, Ron Carter, and Elvin Jones, they might have listened to it. They might even have bought it! But [it was] having my name on it—since it was universally known that I was always written about bad-

ly in the magazines at that time—that kept them from even wasting their time in the office listening. But Fred Norsworthy is no fool. He's been in the record business for many years, on many sides of it, and so he thought he had a viable thing, and he knew he had a damn good record. What discouraged him was that no one would even listen.

According to Fred Norsworthy, in an interview with the author in 1987,

How it all started was I called Pepper up and said, "Gee, I'd like to produce an album for you," but I said, "I don't have anybody to put it out with." Fine, so we met a couple of times and I said, "You pick the musicians." I said, "Whatever you want to do, the tunes, everything." Fine. So a week later he calls me back and says, "O.K., book the studio, here's what I got: Zoot, Tommy Flanagan, Elvin Jones, and Ron Carter." At that time, of course, they weren't the super-big names they are now....

For the date, Zoot flew in from Boston....Olga [Gust] was the lady at the time I was going with. She was the lady that put the money up for the date. We went in and did the date. It went pretty smooth, as a matter of fact. We did it in two days. We did half the album one day, and half the album the other. There was some other takes on it. We did two takes of Verdandi, and, if I remember, there was a couple of other tunes. In fact, Tommy Flanagan cut a trio thing, but it just ended up: After the final soloist, it just ended up and that was it. But, basically, it went pretty smoothly. The whole album took like a total of six and a half hours to do. They just went right in and did it....It was exactly the way he wanted to do it!...

I approached Dick Bock, at the time with Pacific Jazz, and he primarily then was into the pop jazz, like Les McCann, Monty Alexander, the Jazz Crusaders, and the Pepper Adams date didn't fit the format for the label. I had approached Blue Note, but that didn't fit their format either. Then, finally, after about a year, my friend, Don Schlitten who [had photographed the session, and] at the time was with Prestige, said, "Hey! Wait a minute. I think we can use it," so Don negotiated the deal and it came out on Prestige. Still in the catalog!

Tommy Flanagan told the author in 1988 that he wrote Verdandi (-g, -h) as a drum feature for Elvin Jones, when they toured Sweden in the late 1950s with J.J. Johnson's group. Flanagan renamed the tune by 1989, when he recorded it on his own date for Timeless. Flanagan also mentioned that Adams used to call -b "Cross-Eyed Lovers."

690130
30 January 1969, New York: Overdubs: Pepper Adams bs; other musicians.

According to Pepper Adams' 1969 appointment book, this was an Atlantic overdub done from 11-2pm.

690221
21 February 1969, probably Atlantic Studios, New York: Ernie Royal tp; Pepper Adams bs; other musicians.

According to Pepper Adams' 1969 appointment book, two dates were done for Atlantic: 10-1:30pm and 2-6pm. Ernie Royal is the contractor for these sessions.

690228
28 February 1969 , probably Atlantic Studios, New York: Pepper Adams bs; other musicians.

According to Pepper Adams' 1969 appointment book, this Atlantic date was done from 10:30-3:30pm.

HANK CRAWFORD
690321
21 March 1969, New York: Overdubs: Bernie Glow, Ernie Royal, Joe Newman, Snooky Young tp; Jimmy Cleveland, Benny Powell tb; Frank Wess as; Seldon Powell ts; Pepper Adams bs.

a	16300	Groovin'*	Atlantic LP: SD-1523
b	16302	Ain't No Way*	
c	16303	I Can't See Myself Leaving You†	
d	16304	Since You've Been Gone†	
e	16305	Going Down Slow†	
f	16306	Lady Soul√∆	
g	16308	Baby, I Love You√	
h	16309	Soul Serenade√	

i   16310   Going Down Slow√

Original tracks recorded at Atlantic Recording Studio, New York, on
12-13 February: Hank Crawford as, pΔ; David Newman ts, fl; Paul Griffin p, e-p, org; Eric Gale g; Ron Carter,* Jerry Jemmott,† Chuck Rainey√
e-b; Bernard Purdie dm. String section, conducted by Gene Orloff, added
at a subsequent session. Never Let Me Go (16301) and Take a Look
(16307) were recorded without horn overdubs.
    -a on Atlantic 45: 45-2688, Rhino CD: R2-71554, Rhino CD: R2-
71673, Collectables CD: COL-1126, Collectables CD: COL-6244, Atlan-
tic-Rhino-Warner (Eu) CD: 8122-79939-3.
    -b on Atlantic 45: 45-2688, Atlantic LP: SD-1557, Collectables CD:
COL-6244, Collectables CD: COL-1126, Collectables CD: COL-6244.
    -c on Collectables CD: COL-1126, Collectables CD: COL-6244.
    -d on Collectables CD: COL-1126, Collectables CD: COL-6244.
    -e on Collectables CD: COL-1126, Collectables CD: COL-6244.
    -f on Collectables CD: COL-1126, Collectables CD: COL-6244.
    -g on Collectables CD: COL-1126, Collectables CD: COL-6244.
    -h on Collectables CD: COL-1126, Collectables CD: COL-6244.
    -i on Collectables CD: COL-1126, Collectables CD: COL-6244.

THE NICE
690501
1 May 1969, New York: Overdubs: Joe Newman tp; unknown tb; unknown ts; Pepper Adams bs.

a   For Example   Immediate (Eng) LP: IMSP-026

Original track recorded at Trident Studios, London, c. 1969: Keith
Emerson p, org; Lee Jackson e-b, voc; Brian Davison dm, perc.
    -a on Immediate (Eng) LP: IMSP-026, Immediate (Eng) LP:
IMOCS-102, Immediate (Eng) LP: Z-12-52002, Castle Music CD:
CMETD-055.
    Keith Emerson writes about this session in his autobiography:

The Nice were hoping to complete their third album in the States.
Apart from using live performances, they were looking forward to
working with the great jazz players of New York, especially to
complete a piece called For Example, that I'd worked on in Copenhagen, and subsequently laid down a backing track in London's

Trident Studios. I'd brought our eight-track pre-recorded tape with us in the hope that New York's sound engineers could squeeze in my first arrangement for trumpet, trombone, tenor sax, and baritone sax. Clutching manuscripts, I nervously entered the studio to be introduced to the line-up. Pepper Adams on baritone sax! The same Pepper Adams who had played on my all-time favourite album, *Thelonious Monk at Town Hall.* I couldn't believe it! Dissolving instantly into one of those blubbering fans that only so recently had started to invade my life, I passed out my handwritten scores. The trumpet player (I forget his name) was hopelessly drunk and a source of embarrassment to the rest. I excused his condition, even though Pepper discreetly told me that I need not pay him. But I was in too much awe having legends working for me. Remembering the other fallen heroes such as Bird, I could only feel compassion for the trumpet player's sad condition.

ARIF MARDIN
690513
13 May 1969, New York: Overdubs: Ernie Royal, Al Porcino, Herb Pomeroy, Joe Newman tp; Jimmy Cleveland, Benny Powell, Garnett Brown tb; Frank Wess, Charlie Mariano as; King Curtis, Seldon Powell ts; Pepper Adams bs.

| a | 17014 | Listen Here | Atlantic LP: SD-8222 |
| b | 17021 | Midnight Walk | |

Original tracks recorded in Muscle Shoals AL in late April 1968: Jimmy Johnson g; Eddie Hinton g, harmonica; Barry Beckett org, p, e-p; David Hood e-b; Roger Hawkins dm, perc.

THAD JONES-MEL LEWIS
690528
28 May 1969, A&R Studios, New York: Thad Jones flh; Snooky Young, Jimmy Nottingham, Danny Moore, Richard Williams tp; Eddie Bert, Benny Powell, Jimmy Knepper tb; Cliff Heather btb; Jerome Richardson, Jerry Dodgion as, ss, cl; Joe Farrell, Eddie Daniels ts, cl; Pepper Adams bs, cl; Roland Hanna p; Barry Galbraith, Sam Jones g; Richard Davis b, e-b; Mel Lewis dm.

| a | Central Park North | Solid State unissued |
| b | Tow Away Zone | |

According to Adams' appointment book, Adams attended this date but missed the next two Thad Jones-Mel Lewis recording sessions (17-18 June), because of his previous commitment to teach (15-29 June) at the Wilmington Music School Jazz Camp.

DAVID AMRAM
690630
30 June 1969, film soundtrack, New York: Pepper Adams bs; other musicians.

a	Anatolia	Warner Brothers LP: WS-1824
b	Love Is Never Out of Style	
c	Mountain Snow	
d	Sunny Days	
e	Blue Tomorrow	
f	The Zephyr March of the Nicotine Fiends	
g	Old Country Soul	
h	Other Dreams	
i	Childhood Dreams	
j	Definitely Blue	
k	Ancestral Dreams	
m	Kazoo Story	
n	Anatolia	

-b on Warner Brothers (Eng) LP: K-26122.
This is the soundtrack to *The Arrangement,* directed by Elia Kazan. A DVD of the film is available on Warner Home Video.
According to David Amram, in an interview with the author in 1988, "I was able to record the soundtrack in New York City, and Pepper played on that and played beautifully."

690702
2 July 1969, New York: Overdubs: Pepper Adams bs; other musicians.

According to Pepper Adams' 1969 appointment book, this Atlantic date was done from 2-5pm.

THAD JONES-MEL LEWIS
690825

c. 25 August 1969, BBC radio broadcast, Ronnie Scott's, London: Thad Jones flh; Snooky Young, Al Porcino, Danny Moore, Richard Williams tp; Eddie Bert, Ashley Fennell, Jimmy Knepper tb; Cliff Heather btb; Jerome Richardson, Jerry Dodgion as, ss, cl; Eddie Daniels ts, cl; Joe Henderson ts; Pepper Adams bs, cl; Roland Hanna p; Richard Davis b; Mel Lewis dm.

This performance was taped during their one-week engagement 25-30 August, though it's not known if the audio still exists. This was the orchestra's first of many trips to Europe.

THAD JONES-MEL LEWIS
690901
1 September 1969, BBC radio broadcast, Opposite Lock, Birmingham: Same as c. 25 August 1969:

It's not known if the audio still exists.

THAD JONES-MEL LEWIS
690902
2 September 1969, SR radio broadcast, Konserthuset, Stockholm: Same as c. 25 August 1969:

a   Low Down
b   Backbone
c   Kids Are Pretty People
d   The Jive Samba[1]
e   Willow Tree
f   Two Ways On
g   Don't Git Sassy
h   Willow Weep for Me
i   The Second Race
j   After Paris
k   Central Park North
m   **Once Around**

[1]Various musicians play percussion instruments.

THAD JONES-MEL LEWIS
690903
3 September 1969, DR TV broadcast, TV-Byen, Søborg, Denmark: Same
as c. 25 August 1969:

a   Central Park North*   Kay Jazz (Eng) VHS: KJ-092
b   **Come Sunday**
c   The Groove Merchant
d   **Once Around**
e   The Second Race   Kay Jazz (Eng) unissued
f   Willow Weep for Me
g   The Jive Samba*
h   Tow Away Zone

*Various musicians play percussion instruments.

THAD JONES-MEL LEWIS
690905
*5 September 1969, SDT TV broadcast, Beethoven Saal's Stuttgarter
Liederhalle, Stuttgart:* Same as c. 25 August 1969:

a   The Second Race
b   The Groove Merchant
c   **Once Around**
d   Willow Weep for Me
e   Don't Git Sassy
f   Willow Tree
g   Tow Away Zone
h   The Jive Samba[1]

[1]Various musicians play percussion instruments.

It's not clear if the video still exists.

THAD JONES-MEL LEWIS
690907
7 September 1969, WDR radio broadcast, Sartory-Festsaal, Cologne:
Same as c. 25 August 1969:

a   Don't Git Sassy

b   Kids Are Pretty People
c   **The Little Pixie**
d   Central Park North

Portions of this date were broadcast on the German television program *Jazzorama-Die Jazz Scene Köln*. The show also featured the Kenny Clarke-Francy Boland Big Band and the Kurt Edelhagen Orchestra, in a Battle of the Big Bands format. It's not clear if the video still exists. *See* notes on 690909, 690911, 690912.

THAD JONES-MEL LEWIS
690908
8 September 1969, ORTF TV broadcast, Maison de l'ORTF, Paris: Same as c. 25 August 1969:

a   Low Down   Royal Jazz (Ger) CD: RJD-511
b   Don't Ever Leave Me
c   Mean What You Say
d   Willow Tree
e   **Once Around**
f   Don't Git Sassy
g   Willow Weep for Me   Royal Jazz (Ger) unissued
h   Tow Away Zone
i   unknown title
j   Backbone
k   The Groove Merchant
m   **The Little Pixie**

All issued tracks on Jeal (F) CD: RJD-511.

THAD JONES-MEL LEWIS
690909
9 September 1969, NRU-NOS TV broadcast, De Doelen Concert Hall, Rotterdam: Same as c. 25 August 1969:

a   **Three and One**
b   Don't Ever Leave Me
c   A–That's Freedom
d   The Groove Merchant
e   Backbone

f   Willow Weep for Me
g   Lover Man
h   The Jive Samba[1]

[1]Various musicians play percussion instruments.

Part of the Battle of the Big Bands tour that also included the Kenny Clarke-Francy Boland Big Band and the Kurt Edelhagen Orchestra. *See* notes on 690907, 670911, 690912.

THAD JONES-MEL LEWIS
690911
11 September 1969, DRS-2 radio broadcast, Stadtcasino, Basel: Same as c. 25 August 1969:

a   The Second Race   TCB Music (Swiss) CD: TCB-02042
b   Don't Ever Leave Me
c   The Waltz You "Swang" for Me
d   A–That's Freedom
e   **Come Sunday**
f   Don't Git Sassy
g   Bible Story[1]
h   The Groove Merchant
i   Central Park North   TCB Music (Swiss) unissued

[1]Piano solo.

Part of the Battle of the Big Bands tour that also included the Kenny Clarke-Francy Boland Big Band and the Kurt Edelhagen Orchestra. See notes on 690907, 690909, 690912.
    -h on LRC (Ger) CD: CDC-9021, LRC (Ger) CD: CDC-29004.
    All other issued tracks on LRC (Ger) CD: CDC-29004.

THAD JONES-MEL LEWIS
690912
12 September 1969, HR radio broadcast, Jahrhunderthalle, Frankfurt: Same as c. 25 August 1969:

Part of the Battle of the Big Bands tour. *See* notes on 690907, 690909, 690911. It's not known if the audio still exists.

ELVIN JONES – POLY-CURRENTS
690926a
26 September 1969, Van Gelder Studio, Englewood Cliffs NJ: George
Coleman ts; Joe Farrell ts√, engh, fl, bfl; Fred Tompkins fl*; Pepper Adams bs; Wilbur Little b; Elvin Jones dm; Candido Camero cga.†

a	5210	**Mr. Jones**†√	Blue Note LP: BN-LA-110-F
b	5211	Yes*[1]	
c	5212	Agappe Love†[2]	
d	5213	**Agenda**†[3]	
e	5214	Whew!√[4]	
f		One's Native Place†	Blue Note unissued
g		unknown title	Blue Note unissued

[1]Farrell on bfl, Tompkins, Little, and Jones only.
[2]Farrell on fl.
[3]Farrell on engh.
[4]Coleman and rhythm section.

-a on Blue Note LP: 784-331-1, Blue Note (F) LP: BST-84331, Blue
Note (Ger) LP: BST-84438, Toshiba-EMI (J) LP: BNJ-71095, Blue Note
CD: CDP-7-84331-2, Blue Note CD: CDBN-7-84331-2, Blue Note CD:
B21Y-84331, Mosaic CD: MD8-195.
    All issued tracks on Blue Note LP: 784-331-1, Blue Note (F) LP:
BST-84331, Toshiba-EMI (J) LP: BNJ-71095, Blue Note CD: CDP-7-
84331-2, Blue Note CD: B21Y-84331, Blue Note CD: CDBN-7-84331-
2. Mosaic CD: MD8-195.
    At least 14 takes were done at this session.

690926b
26 September 1969, A&R Studios, New York: Pepper Adams bs; other
musicians.

    According to Pepper Adams' appointment book, Adams had a ses-
sion for CBS from 7-10pm.

PEPPER ADAMS
690928
28 September 1969, private recording, Famous Ballroom, Baltimore:

Richard Williams tp; Pepper Adams bs; Duke Pearson p; Richard Davis b; Mel Lewis dm.

a   **Billie's Bounce**
b   **How Deep Is the Ocean**
c   **What Is This Thing Called Love**
d   **Stella by Starlight**

Recorded by the Left Bank Jazz Society, this was originally billed as the Thad Jones-Pepper Adams Quintet, but Richard Williams subbed for Jones.
See 650314.

FRED TOMPKINS–COMPOSITIONS OF FRED TOMPKINS 691000

c. October 1969, New York: Richard Jones frh; Al Gibbons as; Joe Farrell ts; Pepper Adams bs; Wilbur Little b; Elvin Jones dm; Fred Tompkins arr.

a   Compound   Festival LP: 9001
b   Shh!

All tracks on FKT CD: [no catalog number].
See 700500A.

Regarding Compound, in a letter to the author, written in 2002, Tompkins wrote that Adams' solo is written, and that Tompkins reversed Farrell and Jones' solos on the CD reissue.

Regarding Adams, Tompkins wrote in the same letter:

He was a very bright person and had a slightly dry, satirical sense of humor. He was great sight-reader too. I know that because, at the Compound session, he played this long, written out solo at the end quite well, but I was pretty sure he hadn't practiced it much. (These were busy session players who didn't have a lot of free time.) At one point, I apologized for not putting in breath marks, so Pepper just looked up at me and said, "Don't worry, Fred. I won't forget to breathe."

GEORGE GRUNTZ
691010
10 October 1969, film soundtrack, New York: Pepper Adams bs; other musicians.

According to Pepper Adams' 1969 appointment book, this was an industrial film date.

MOSE ALLISON–HELLO THERE UNIVERSE
691016
16 October 1969, New York: Richard Williams, Jimmy Nottingham tp; Jerome Richardson as, fl; Joe Henderson ts; Pepper Adams,* Seldon Powell† bs; Mose Allison p, org, voc; Bob Cranshaw b; Joe Cocuzzo dm.

a	17915	I'm Smashed*	Atlantic LP: SD-1550
b	17916	Monsters of the Id*	
c	17917	Wild Man on the Loose†	

All tracks on Collectables CD: COL-6534.

MOSE ALLISON–HELLO THERE UNIVERSE
691021
21 October 1969, New York: Same as 16 October 1969, except Joe Farrell ts replaces Henderson, Powell out:

| a | 17962 | **Hymn to Everything** | Atlantic LP: SD-1550 |
| b | 17963 | **Somebody's Gotta Move** | |

All tracks on Collectables CD: COL-6534.

691031
31 October 1969, New York: Overdubs: Pepper Adams bs; other musicians.

According to Pepper Adams' 1969 appointment book, this was a 4.5 hour date for Atlantic.

691103
3 and 10 November 1969, New York: Ernie Royal tp; Pepper Adams bs; other musicians.

According to Pepper Adams' 1969 appointment book, 3 November was a 3.5 hour session. Both dates were possibly RCA overdubs, for which Ernie Royal functioned as the likely contractor.

691203
3 December 1969, Van Gelder Studio, Englewood Cliffs NJ: Pepper Adams bs; other musicians.

According to Pepper Adams' 1969 appointment book, this session, possibly an overdub, was done for CTI from 2-5pm.

THAD JONES-MEL LEWIS AND JAZZ WAVE, LTD.
691206
6 December 1969, DR radio broadcast, Tivoli Gardens, Copenhagen: Thad Jones flh; Snooky Young, Al Porcino, Danny Moore, Marvin Stamm tp; Benny Powell, Julian Priester, Jimmy Knepper tb; Bob Burgess btb; Jerome Richardson as, ss, fl; Jerry Dodgion as, cl, fl; Eddie Daniels ts, cl, fl; Joe Henderson ts; Pepper Adams bs, cl; Roland Hanna p; Richard Davis b; Mel Lewis dm; GUESTS: Freddie Hubbard tp; Jeremy Steig fl; Jimmy McGriff org; Kenny Burrell g; Ron Carter b; Louis Hayes dm.

It's not known if audio still exists.
According to Jimmy Knepper, in an interview with the author in 1988, "We were on a tour with Freddie Hubbard, Kenny Burrell, Jimmy McGriff, Jeremy Steig. There were all these small bands, and they all did their bit. And then the Thad Jones band: We played about one tune, and that was all we had to do in these concerts. Then, they brought everybody out for the last tune, and whoever was out in front played the solos on one of Thad's tunes, and that was the end of the concert." *See* 691207, 691208, 691210, 691211, 691212, 691213, 691214.
Regarding Joe Henderson, Jerry Dodgion told the author, in a 1988 interview, "When we were playing on the concerts, sometimes he'd walk away from the microphone because he saw that it was being recorded. We all signed the same contract and it said they were recording. He and Mel used to argue about that all the time."

THAD JONES-MEL LEWIS AND JAZZ WAVE, LTD.
691207
7 December 1969, HR radio broadcast, Kongresshalle, Frankfurt: Same

as 6 December 1969; Freddie Hubbard tp√; Jimmy McGriff org*; Kenny Burrell g†; Ron Carter bΔ:

a   Don't Git Sassy   Blue Note LP: BST-89905
b   Lil' Darlin'*[1]
c   Greensleeves†[2]
    Hubbard, Hanna, Carter, Hayes:
d   Without a Song√Δ   Blue Note unissued
e   Hubtones√Δ
f   Space Track√Δ   Blue Note CD: 50999-236957-26

[1]McGriff and orchestra.
[2]Burrell, Davis, and Lewis.

-a on Blue Note-Capitol CD: 7-89287-2, Koch CD: KOC-CD-8563. *See* 691206, 691208, 691210, 691211, 691212, 691213, 691214.

THAD JONES-MEL LEWIS AND JAZZ WAVE, LTD.
691208
8 December 1969, RAI radio broadcast, Cisterna Theatre, Milan: Same as 6 December 1969:

Solid State unissued. *See* 691206, 691207, 691210, 691211, 691212, 691213, 691214.

RICHARD DAVIS–MUSES FOR RICHARD DAVIS
691209
9 December 1969, Villingen, Germany: Freddie Hubbard tp; Jimmy Knepper tb; Jerry Dodgion as; Eddie Daniels ts; Pepper Adams bs; Roland Hanna p; Richard Davis b; Louis Hayes dm.

a   Milktrain[1]   MPS (Ger) LP: 15266-ST
b   A Child Is Born[2]
c   Softly As in a Morning Sunrise[3]
d   **What Is It[4]**
e   Muses for Richard Davis[5]
f   **Toe Nail Moon[6]**

[1]Hubbard out.
[2]Duet for Hanna and Davis.

[3]Rhythm section only.
[4]Knepper, Adams, and rhythm section.
[5]Duet for Hubbard and Davis.
[6]Hubbard out.

All tracks on Pausa LP: PR-7022, MPS (Ger) LP: 2120-725, Teichiku (J) LP: ULX-14-P.
According to Eddie Daniels, in an interview with the author in 1988,

> Joe Henderson was in the [Thad Jones-Mel Lewis] band at that time and Joe couldn't do it, so I ended up doing the *Muses* albums....It was just all very impromptu. It was supposed to be a paid jam session, which ended up being released as an album. I did [another] one with Freddie Hubbard called the *Hub of Hubbard* on the same day. Sonny Lester produced those, and it was done for a millionaire who had a studio in the Black Forest somewhere. We took a long bus ride and meandered for hours.

According to Jimmy Knepper, in an interview with the author in 1988, "They had this date and they took some of us....We rode a bus for hours and hours through the snows of Switzerland to get to the Black Forest, and we realized there wasn't any material for this date. So [each of us] turned out a tune and made some semi-arrangements. We didn't have any time to polish it or anything. They split us up into different little bands."

Jerry Dodgion told the author, in a 1988 interview, "Evidently, in advance, before the tour left, they had arranged for Richard Davis to record and Freddie [Hubbard] to do one too. It was supposed to be Joe Henderson, and Joe balked at the contract that we had all signed. Joe was trying to get out of it."

THAD JONES-MEL LEWIS AND JAZZ WAVE, LTD.
691210
10 December 1969, SDR radio broadcast, Donauhalle, Ulm, Germany:
Same as 6 December 1969; Freddie Hubbard tp*; Jeremy Steig fl√; Jimmy McGriff orgΔ; Kenny Burrell g†:

a	The Groove Merchant	Blue Note unissued
b	Willow Weep for MeΔ	
c	Lil' Darlin'Δ	
d	See RiderΔ	

e   Peoplet[1]   Blue Note LP: BST-89905
f   Evol Deklaw Ni (Love Walked In)† Blue Note unissued
g   Avenue C†
    Steig, Carter, and Hayes:
h   Reza√   Blue Note LP: BST-89905
i   Nardis√   Blue Note unissued
    Hubbard, Burrell, Carter, Hayes:
j   Body and Soul*†   Blue Note LP: BST-89905
    Add orchestra, delete quartet:
k   St. Louis Blues   Blue Note unissued
m   Fingers
n   Once Around*†√∆[2]   Blue Note LP: BST-89905

[1]Burrell plays unaccompanied solo.
[2]Hubbard, Steig, McGriff, Burrell, and orchestra.

-e on Blue Note CD: 50999-236957-26.
See 691206, 691207, 691208, 691211, 691212, 691213, 691214.

THAD JONES-MEL LEWIS AND JAZZ WAVE, LTD.
691211
11 December 1969, ORTF radio broadcast, Salle Pleyel, Paris: Same as
6 December 1969:

Solid State unissued. *See* 691206, 691207, 691208, 691210, 691212,
691213, 691214.

THAD JONES-MEL LEWIS AND JAZZ WAVE, LTD.
691212
12 December 1969, BBC radio broadcast, Free Trade Hall, Manchester:
Same as 6 December 1969:

Solid State unissued. *See* 691206, 691207, 691208, 691210, 691211,
691213, 691214.

THAD JONES-MEL LEWIS AND JAZZ WAVE, LTD.
691213
13 December 1969, BBC radio broadcast, Royal Festival Hall, London:
Same as 6 December 1969:

Hubbard, Hanna, Carter, Hayes:
a   Without a Song   Blue Note CD: 50999-236957-26
b   Hub Tones

See 691206, 691207, 691208, 691210, 691211, 691212, 691214.

THAD JONES-MEL LEWIS AND JAZZ WAVE, LTD.
691214
14 December 1969, BBC radio broadcast, Colston Hall, Bristol, England: Same as 6 December 1969:

Hubbard, Hanna, Carter, Hayes:
a   The Things We Did Last Summer   Blue Note CD: 50999-
                                              236957-26
b   A Night in Tunisia
c   Blues by Five

See 691206, 691207, 691208, 691210, 691211, 691212, 691213.

PEPPER ADAMS
691216
c. 16 December 1969, DR radio broadcast, Montmartre Jazzhus, Copenhagen: Toots Thielemans harmonica, g; Pepper Adams bs; Kenny Drew p; Niels-Henning Ørsted Pedersen b; Ole Streenberg dm.

PEPPER ADAMS
691217
c. 17 December 1969, DR radio broadcast, Montmartre Jazzhus, Copenhagen: Same as c. 16 December 1969, Thielemans out:

a   How Deep Is the Ocean

PEPPER ADAMS
700128
28 January 1970, SR radio broadcast, Stampen, Stockholm: Pepper Adams bs; unknown p; probably Red Mitchell b; unknown dm.

Broadcast for the program *Happy Jazz*, during Adams' two-week tour of Sweden. Five months later (*see* 700506), Adams returned to Stampen to perform with Claes Crona p; Red Mitchell b; Jon Christensen dm. It's possible that the same trio was the house rhythm section on Pepper's January gig.

BILL BERRY AND THE NEW YORK BAND
700200
c. February 1970, private recording, Roosevelt Grill, New York: Bill Berry tp; Britt Woodman tb; Carmen Leggio as; Pepper Adams bs; Dave Frishberg p; Bob Daugherty b; Sol Gubin dm; other musicians.

a   **My Ideal**

Additional bandmembers might be Danny Stiles, Bob Hamilton, Al Derisi tp; Bill Watrous tb; George Dorsey as; Al Cohn ts. This band was formed in New York in early 1970, after Berry left the Thad Jones-Mel Lewis Orchestra, and lasted, under Berry's leadership, only until August 1970, when Berry moved to California to remain a member of the relocating *Merv Griffin Show* big band. Upon resettling in Los Angeles, Berry reformulated his big band. By early 1971, Al Cohn reconstituted the original band in New York.

According to historian Mike Fitzgerald, the group began as the Bill Berry-Willis Conover Jazz Band, then morphed into the New York Band. Since radio announcer Conover was broadcasting his show, *Jazz Hour*, on the Voice of America each week (albeit from Washington, D.C.), and was also broadcasting live performances (*see* 710110, 710112, 710710, 840626), it's likely that broadcasts of this incarnation of the band were made.

According to an interview in 1989 with the author, Bill Berry said, "We used to play Sunday afternoons at the Roosevelt Hotel, when my band first started in 1970. I don't know if Pep was playing with the band or sitting in, but I know I have this tape."

CARMEN McCRAE
700300A
c. March 1970, New York: Overdubs: Joe Newman tp; Garnett Brown tb; George Dorsey as; King Curtis as, ts; Pepper Adams bs.

a	18714	Breakfast in Bed	Atlantic LP: SD-1568
b	18717	I Want You	
c	18718	I Love the Life I Live	
d	18720	More Today than Yesterday	

Original tracks recorded at Criteria Studios, Miami, on 16 February 1970: Mike Utley e-p, org; Charlie Freeman g; Jim Dickinson g, keyboards; Tom McClure b; Sammy Creason dm, perc; Carmen McRae voc. French horns, string section, and vocal choir added at another time.

-a on Atlantic CD: AMCY-1079, Collectables CD: COL-6713, Collectables CD: COL-0412.

-b on Atlantic 45-2736, Atlantic CD: AMCY-1079, Collectables CD: COL-6713, Collectables CD: COL-0412.

-c on Atlantic 45-2807, Atlantic CD: AMCY-1079, Collectables CD: COL-6713, Collectables CD: COL-0412.

-d on Atlantic CD: AMCY-1079, Collectables CD: COL-6713, Collectables CD: COL-0412.

BROOK BENTON
700300B
c. March 1970, New York: Overdubs: Joe Newman tp; Benny Powell tb; George Dorsey as; King Curtis as, ts; Pepper Adams bs.

a	18725	Don't It Make You Want to Go Home	Cotillion LP: SD-9028
b	18726	Aspen, Colorado	
c	18727	Willie and Laura Mae Jones	
d	18728	Old Man Willie	Cotillion unissued
e	18729	It's All in the Game	Cotillion LP: SD-9028
f	18730	Don't Think Twice, It's All Right	
g	18731	Are You Sincere	
h	18732	For Lee Ann	
i	18733	Born Under a Bad Sign	
j	18734	Whoever Finds This, I Love You	
k	18735	Before You See a Big Man Cry	Cotillion unissued
m	18736	Let Me Fix It	Cotillion LP: SD-9028

Original tracks recorded in Miami on 3 and 5 March 1970: Mike Utley e-p, org; Charlie Freeman, Stu Scharf g; Jim Dickinson g, keyboards; Tom McClure b; Sammy Creason dm, perc; Brook Benton voc. String section and vocal choir added, probably at a later date.

-a on Cotillion 45-44078, Atlantic (Eng) LP: 2400024, DBK Works CD: CD-506.

-m on Cotillion 45-44093, Atlantic (Eng) LP: 2400024, DBK Works CD: CD-506.

All other issued tracks on Atlantic (Eng) LP: 2400024, DBK Works CD: CD-506.

QUINCY JONES–GULA MATARI
700325
25-26 March 1970, Van Gelder Studio, Englewood Cliffs NJ: Snooky Young, Ernie Royal, Marvin Stamm, Freddie Hubbard, Danny Moore tp, flh; Wayne Andre, Al Grey, Benny Powell tb; Tony Studd btb; Hubert Laws fl; Jerome Richardson ss, as; Pepper Adams bs; Danny Bank bs, bass sax; Herbie Hancock, Bob James, Bobby Scott p, e-p; Milt Jackson vib; Toots Thielemans harmonica, g, whistling; Eric Gale g; Ray Brown b; Major Holley* b, voc; Grady Tate dm; Jimmy Johnson, Warren Smith perc; Quincy Jones arr.

a   Bridge over Troubled Water   A&M LP: SP-3030
b   Walkin'
c   Hummin'*

It's not known what tunes were recorded on what dates.
-a on A&M 45-1184-S, A&M (Eng) LP: AMLS-992, Music for Pleasure (Eng) LP: MFP-50441, A&M (Neth) LP: 88669-XAT, A&M (J) LP: AML-333, King (J) LP: SP-3030, A&M CD: 75021-0820-2, A&M (Ger) CD: 397-074-2, IMS CD: 3930302, A&M (Eu) CD: 393-030-2.
-b on A&M LP: SP6-3021, A&M (Eng) LP: AMLS-992, A&M (Neth) LP: 88669-XAT, A&M (J) LP: AML-333, King (J) LP: SP-3030, A&M CD: 75021-0820-2, IMS CD: 3930302, A&M (Eu) CD: 393-030-2.
-c on A&M (Eng) LP: AMLS-992, A&M (Neth) LP: 88669-XAT, A&M (J) LP: AML-333, King (J) LP: SP-3030, Verve CD: 314-535-271-2, A&M CD: 75021-0820-2, IMS CD: 3930302, A&M (Eu) CD: 393-030-2.
String section and vocal choir added at a later time. It's unclear to what degree this personnel is, or is not, collective, especially regarding the pianists.
See 700512.

FRED TOMPKINS–COMPOSITIONS OF FRED TOMPKINS
700500A
c. May 1970, New York: Cecil Bridgewater, Richard Williams tp; Jerome

Richardson ts; Pepper Adams bs; Ron Carter b; Billy Cobham dm; Fred Tompkins arr.

a   Two Sentiments   Festival LP: 9001

-a on FKT CD: [no catalog number]. *See* 691000.

According to Cecil Bridgewater, in an interview with the author in 1989, "Richard [Williams], I think, called me to come in and do that. Something tells me it was more like a demo date or something, originally, for the flute player, trying to get a record date."

RAY BRYANT
700500B
c. May 1970, New York: Overdubs: Joe Newman tp; Garnett Brown tb; George Dorsey as; King Curtis ts; Pepper Adams bs.

a   18949   Let It Be   Atlantic LP: SD-1564

Original tracks recorded in New York on 14 April 1970: Ray Bryant p; Chuck Rainey e-b; Jimmy Johnson dm.

-a on Atlantic 45: 45-5102, Atlantic LP: 5102, Collectables CD: COL-7922.

QUINCY JONES–GULA MATARI
700512
12 May 1970, Van Gelder Studio, Englewood Cliffs NJ: Same as 25 March 1970; Richard Davis, Ron Carter b replace Brown and Holley; Don Elliott bass marimba replaces Jackson:

a   Gula Matari   A&M LP: SP-3030

-a on A&M (Eng) LP: AMLS-992, Music for Pleasure (Eng) LP: MFP-50441, A&M (Neth) LP: 88-669-XAT, A&M (J) LP: AML-333, King (J) LP: SP-3030, A&M CD: 6550, A&M CD: 396-958-2, A&M CD: 0820-2, IMS CD: 3930302, A&M (Eu) CD: 393-030-2. Edited version on A&M LP: SP-3705, A&M (Can) LP: SP-93705, A&M (Can) LP: SP-3720, A&M-Odeon (Braz) LP: SP-3717, A&M-Odeon (Braz) LP: SA-MX-2187, A&M (Eng) LP: AMLH-63705, A&M (Eu) LP: CS-3705, A&M (J) LP: GXH-2001/2. String section and vocal choir added at a later time.

See 700325.

DONALD BYRD–ELECTRIC BYRD
700515
15 May 1970, Van Gelder Studio, Englewood Cliffs NJ: Donald Byrd tp; Billy Campbell tb; Jerry Dodgion ss, as, fl; Hermeto Pascoal fl*; Frank Foster ts, acl; Lew Tabackin ts, fl; Pepper Adams bs, cl; Duke Pearson e-p; Wally Richardson g; Ron Carter b; Mickey Roker dm; Airto Moreira perc.

a	6341	The Dude	Blue Note LP: BST-84349
b	6342	Xibaba*	
c	6343	Essence	
d	6344	Estavanico	

-a on Blue Note LP: B1-89606, Blue Note LP: B1-36195, Blue Note CD: 7-89606-2, Blue Note CD: CDBN-8-36195-2.

-b on Blue Note LP: B1-36195, Blue Note CD: CDBN-8-36195-2. Edited version on Blue Note (Eng) LP: 7243-5-24415-1-8, EMI (F) CD: 7243-5-24415-2-5.

-c, -d on Blue Note LP: B1-36195, Blue Note CD: CDBN-8-36195-2. Edited version on Blue Note (Eng) LP: 7243-5-24415-1-8, EMI (F) CD: 7243-5-24415-2-5.

At least eight takes were done at this session.

Ron Carter told the author, in an interview in 1989, that this session was recorded when Brazilian music was very popular, thus the choice, in part, of some of the material and some of the musicians.

THAD JONES-MEL LEWIS – CONSUMMATION
700525
25 May 1970, New York: Thad Jones flh; Snooky Young, Danny Moore, Al Porcino, Marvin Stamm tp; Eddie Bert, Benny Powell, Jimmy Knepper tb; Cliff Heather btb; Jerome Richardson as, ss, fl; Jerry Dodgion as, cl, fl; Joe Farrell, Billy Harper ts, fl; Eddie Daniels ts, cl, fl; Pepper Adams bs; Roland Hanna p, e-p; David Spinozza g*; Richard Davis b, e-b; Mel Lewis dm.

a	5857	A Child Is Born	Blue Note LP: BST-84346
b	5858	Us*	
c	5859	Ahunk Ahunk*	

-a on Blue Note LP: BN-LA-392-2, Franklin Mint LP: FM-36, Mosaic LP: MQ7-151, Blue Note (Eng) LP: BND-4004, Blue Note (Ger) LP: BST-844887/8, Blue Note (Neth) LP: 1A158-83401/4, King (J) LP: SR-3057, King (J) LP: GXF-3037, Solid State (J) LP: SR-3110, Mosaic CD: MD5-151, Blue Note (Eu) CD: 7243-5-38226-20, LRC (Ger) CD: CDC-9004. Edited version of -a on Blue Note (Eng) LP: UALP-19.

-b on Mosaic LP: MQ7-151, King (J) LP: SR-3057, King (J) LP: GXF-3037, Solid State (J) LP: SR-3110, Mosaic CD: MD5-151, Blue Note (Eu) CD: 7243-5-38226-20. Edited version on Blue Note 45: BN-45-1962.

-c on Mosaic LP: MQ7-151, King (J) LP: SR-3057, King (J) LP: GXF-3037, Solid State (J) LP: SR-3110, Blue Note CD: 4-97155-2, Mosaic CD: MD5-151, Blue Note (Eu) CD: 7243-5-38226-20, LRC (Ger) CD: CDC-9004. Edited version on Blue Note 45: BN-45-1962.

At least 26 takes were done at this session.

Billy Harper assumed Joe Farrell's chair in the working band, but, on this recording, Thad Jones used Farrell and Harper together to augment the reed section from five to six members. According to saxophonist Frank Basile, Thad Jones may have added the extra man to cover the flute part in the baritone book on -a.

PEPPER ADAMS
700605
5 June 1970, SR radio broadcast, Stampen, Stockholm: Pepper Adams bs; Claes Crona p; Red Mitchell b; Jon Christensen dm.

a   **Three and One**
b   **Sophisticated Lady**
c   **Mr. Wonderful**
d   **Jitterbug Waltz**

Broadcast on the program *Happy Jazz,* during Adams' two-week engagement at the club.

THAD JONES-PEPPER ADAMS
700628
28 June 1970, private recording, Famous Ballroom, Baltimore: Thad Jones tp; Pepper Adams bs; Roland Hanna p; Sam Jones b; Mel Lewis dm.

Recorded by the Left Bank Jazz Society. *See* 650314.

DON BYAS COME HOME
700703
3-4 July 1970, film soundtrack, Village Vanguard, New York: Lew Soloff, unknown tp; unknown tp; probably Marvin Stamm tp; Benny Powell, probably Jimmy Knepper, Joe Ciavardone tb; Cliff Heather btb; Jerome Richardson as, ss, fl; Jerry Dodgion as, cl, fl; Billy Harper ts, fl; Eddie Daniels ts, cl, fl; Pepper Adams bs; Roland Hanna p; possibly Reggie Johnson b; Mel Lewis dm; Thad Jones cond; GUESTS: Don Byas ts; Wilbur Ware b; Jo Jones dm.

a   Lover Man
b   Intimacy of the Blues
    Byas, Hanna, Ware, Jo Jones:
c   unknown ballad

This VARAS TV documentary, directed by Nick van den Boezem, depicts expatriate Don Byas' only return to the U.S. since his departure in 1947. Byas is filmed performing with the Thad Jones-Mel Lewis Orchestra and at the Newport Jazz Festival with Dizzy Gillespie's rhythm section. It's unclear on which day these Thad Jones-Mel Lewis tracks were recorded.

EDDIE PHYFE
710000
c. 1971, NBC TV broadcast, Washington, D.C.: Al Cohn ts; Pepper Adams bs; Eddie Phyfe dm; other musicians.

A performance by Phyfe's big band was broadcast in Washington, D.C., but it's unclear if audio or video still exist.

DAVID AMRAM
710110
10 January 1971, Voice of America radio broadcast, Philharmonic Hall, New York: David Amram frh, fl, p, perc; Jerry Dodgion as; Pepper Adams bs; Herb Bushler e-b; Al Harewood dm; American Symphony Orchestra; Kazuyoshi Akiyama cond.

a   Triple Concerto for Woodwinds, Brass, Jazz Quintet, and Orchestra:

Allegro Robusto
Andante Espressivo
Rondo alla Turca: Allegro

This world premiere performance took place at Philharmonic Hall (later renamed Avery Fisher Hall).

Pepper Adams told the author, in an interview conducted in 1984, "*Triple Concerto* refers to three units—a jazz quintet, and a woodwind quintet, and a brass quintet—[plus] the orchestra. I was one of the members of the jazz quintet, but it was just David and I that had improvised solos to play."

David Amram explained his basic approach in the liner notes for the recording (*see* 731105): "Instead of writing a piece for my jazz quintet with the orchestra as a giant back-up band, I felt the need in our musical literature for a composition where ten men from the orchestra, divided into woodwind and brass quintets, could be soloists along with the jazz quintet....I also felt that the musical materials played by ninety men in the orchestra (including six percussionists) should be based on...blues, gospel, jazz, Middle Eastern, and European classical music."

As David Amram told the author, in an interview in 1988,

Leopold Stokowski had the orchestra and I was commissioned to write this piece, and I thought, "Well, I'm going to do something with Pepper," because Pepper had come to my [Shakespeare] opera [Twelfth Night], when it was done in New York in 1969, and, as I said in my book [*Vibrations*], he was able to hear jazz influences in [it], even though no one noticed that except musicians. No critics had still picked up on that. There was a lot of that, and the search of trying to find the beautiful notes and beautiful harmonies, which always concerns people in jazz—especially like Pepper, who's always looking for new ways to make something beautiful and have every note be a winner. Just as Charlie Parker and the old jazz masters never would have a "bum note," that's the way I always tried to compose. So, Pepper was always one of the people who would encourage me to continue to do that. In the Triple Concerto, when I was writing it, Pepper said, "The only thing I can think of is just to show you the scale that Barry Harris gave me the idea of a long, long time ago." I wrote it down, but I never figured a way to use that scale in the Triple Concerto. It was just a kind of a diminished scale that you use to run against a dominant chord. It wasn't any big thing, but I thought about it, and finally used it in the Ode to Lord

Buckley, my saxophone concerto. I put a little note in the score saying, "Pepper Adams taught me this scale in 1970."

Pepper came out to hang out with me for a weekend, and he
said, "I don't know what I can do to tell you, Dave, how to write a
piece," and I said, "Well, we'll just talk." So he showed me this
scale. This was 1970 out in Long Island. We went out to this little
place at the beach and hung out. Mostly, we just played. He said,
"What is it you really want?" and I said, "I'm not really sure," so
we just spent the whole weekend jamming and talking. We were in
a conversation and I said, "Pepper, you just gave me a fantastic idea
on how to write the second movement." He said, "Well, what did I
say?" I said, "Well, when you were talking about Arnold Schoenberg, you made me realize that, when I'm writing out the twelve bar
blues, somewhere in the middle voices that no one's going to hear,
I'm going to write out a twelve tone row, but, what I'm going to do
is use a different note for each of the twelve bars and put it in the
violas and the English horns and the second French horn parts (so it
was going to be buried), so no one is ever going to know it's there
except you and me!" He said, "What?" I said, "That'll force me to
do something different." But, because of talking to Pepper, I got the
idea of trying to reharmonize a twelve bar blues in a different way
than I had ever done before. Listening to it, you'd never notice that.
He was just talking about Arnold Schoenberg and Anton Webern
and sounds and Stravinsky and Bartok and Picasso and Charlie
Parker. Also, we were watching a baseball game at the same time,
and talking about the Detroit Tigers! And cooking and admiring
some of the women on the beach. Out of all that, I suddenly got an
idea. Since I had never written twelve tone music, I said I was going
to write my first and last tone row. It was really interesting, because
Pepper was the kind of person that could present so many different
pictures and ideas, that he would make you think....

When we first started rehearsing, I had written all these things
out. We went through it and Pepper said, "I don't know if this is going to be possible to do, Dave. I think I'm going to take it home and
practice it." So he came back and said, "Naw, this is going to be all
right."

Just before the Japanese conductor Akiyama came to conduct
the symphony, he came by my apartment the day before and we
went over the score. I showed the place: I said, "This is where Mr.
Adams will solo and he's great! All the rest of it's written out regu-
larly, but he'll be soloing, and there's a few little places where I'll
solo." Akiyama was a jazz fan too. He said, "I know. He's marvel-

ous!" He said, "I'll just be listening." I watched Akiyama's face the first time we were going through it, and, everytime Pepper took a solo, he loved it. (Pepper spoke a little Japanese, from being in the Service, so he used to speak to the conductor, once in a while, and really crack him up.) In fact, [Akiyama] loved it so much, when he did it with the Toronto Symphony for the Canadian premiere...at Massey Hall...he got our whole jazz group to come up and play with the symphony, which...was unheard of, especially since we weren't an internationally known group, except maybe among musicians and a few jazz fans.

When we recorded it with the Rochester Philharmonic in 1973, I was able to get the whole group to come up there and do it. So, thank God, Pepper's solos—not only the written parts that he played, but the parts that he improvised—are documented, because what he did in his playing in the piece was to bring the baritone saxophone into the symphonic literature. *Down Beat* gave it five stars and a lot of critics, since it's been done, consider it to be one of the best pieces using a jazz group and an symphony orchestra, where both elements—the symphonic element and the jazz element—both have a place....If it hadn't been for Pepper, I never would have written a baritone saxophone part.

DAVID AMRAM
710112
12 January 1971, Voice of America radio broadcast, Philharmonic Hall, New York: David Amram frh, fl, p, perc; Jerry Dodgion as; Pepper Adams bs; Herb Bushler e-b; Al Harewood dm; American Symphony Orchestra; Kazuyoshi Akiyama cond.

a   Triple Concerto for Woodwinds, Brass, Jazz Quintet, and Orchestra:
     Allegro Robusto
     Andante Espressivo
     Rondo alla Turca: Allegro

See 710110.

DAVID AMRAM–NO MORE WALLS
710701
1 July 1971, New York: David Amram frh, fl, p, g, perc; Jerry Dodgion as; Pepper Adams bs; Sam Brown g; Jack Elliot* g, voc; George Mrgdichian oud√; Herb Bushler b, e-b, Lyle Atkinson b, perc; Al Harewood

dm; Candido Camero, Arthur Edgehill, L. J. Calderon perc†; Ali Hafid perc, dumbeg, voc; Midhat Serbagi violaΔ; Lynn Sheffield, Irena Nicolai voc.

a   **São Paulo**[1]   Flying Fish LP: GRO-752
b   **Waltz from "After the Fall"**
c   Going North[*2]
d   **Wind from the Indies†[3]**
e   **Pull My Daisy[4]**
f   **Brazilian Memories**
g   **Tompkins Square Park Consciousness Expander√Δ[5]**

[1]Sheffield and Nicolai voc.
[2]Dodgion, Adams out.
[3]Percussion quartet (Camero, Edgehill, Calderon, Hafid) on this track.
[4]Sheffield voc.
[5]Hafid voc.

-b on RCA LP: APL2-1984, RCA LP: VCS-7089-2, Flying Fish CD: 18964-0752-2.

-e on Premier CD: 1046, RCA LP: VCS-7089-2, Flying Fish CD: 18964-0752-2.

All other tracks on RCA LP: VCS-7089-2, Flying Fish CD: 18964-0752-2.

DIZZY GILLESPIE AND THE NEW YORK BAND
710710
10 July 1971, Voice of America radio broadcast, Town Hall, New York:
Burt Collins, Bob Hamilton, Bob Milliken, Danny Stiles or Joe Ferrante tp; Joe Ciavardone, Bill Watrous, Tom Malone or Quentin Jackson or Jim Morris tb; Carmen Leggio, George Dorsey as; Al Cohn ts; Ernie Wilkins or George Pemberton ts; Pepper Adams bs; Dave Frishberg p; Malcolm Cecil b; Ronnie Zito dm; Willis Conover mc; GUESTS: Dizzy Gillespie, Clark Terry tp; Ruby Braff, Jimmy McPartland cornet, Dicky Wells tb; Joe Muranyi cl; Marian McPartland, Jaki Byard p.

Collector Boris Rose told the author that he recorded this performance from a radio broadcast. Most of Rose's tapes from this period were recorded on reel tape. This concert occurred four days after Louis

Armstrong's death, and, because of that, the show became a celebration of Armstrong. *See* 700200.

HANK CRAWFORD
710900
c. September 1971, Van Gelder Studio, Englewood Cliffs NJ: Overdubs: Snooky Young, Al DeRisi tp; Wayne Andre tb; Hank Crawford as; Grover Washington Jr. ts; Pepper Adams bs.

a   Ham   Kudu LP: KU-06

   Original track recorded at Van Gelder Studio, Englewood Cliffs NJ, in August 1971: Richard Tee p, org; Phil Kraus vib; Eric Gale g; Ron Carter b; Idris Muhammad dm; Airto Moreira perc.
   -a on Kudu (Eng) LP: KUL-4, CTI (Ger) LP: KU-06, King (J) CD: KICJ-8362.

PEPPER ADAMS
710910
10 September 1971, audience recording, Half Note, New York: Pepper Adams bs; Richard Wyands p; Major Holley b; Maurice McKinley dm.

a   **Cherokee**
b   **'Tis**
c   **Stella by Starlight**
d   **Time on My Hands**
e   **'Tis**

THAD JONES-MEL LEWIS
710913
13 September 1971, audience recording, Village Vanguard, New York: Thad Jones flh; Marvin Stamm, Danny Moore, Al Porcino, Cecil Bridgewater tp; Eddie Bert, Jimmy Knepper, Benny Powell tb; Cliff Heather btb; Jerry Dodgion as, cl, fl; Ed Xiques as, ss, fl; Billy Harper ss, ts, fl; Eddie Daniels ts, cl, fl; Pepper Adams bs; Roland Hanna p; Gene Perla b; Mel Lewis dm; Dee Dee Bridgewater voc.*

a   A–That's Freedom
b   It Only Happens Every Time
c   Mean What You Say

d   Willow Tree
e   Us
f   The Best Things in Life Are Free*
g   Here's that Rainy Day*
h   Bye Bye Blackbird*
i   Central Park North
j   Come on Over My Love*
k   Mornin' Reverend
m   A Child Is Born
n   River's Invitation*
o   Kansas City*
p   Fingers

Cecil Bridgewater had taken Al Porcino's place in the band, so Porcino was subbing for another member of the trumpet section. At that time, Dee Dee Bridgewater was Cecil Bridgewater's wife.

Xiques' first gigs with the band, beginning mid-July 1971, was as a baritone sub for Pepper Adams, during the time after Adams' mother had died. According to Ed Xiques, in an interview with the author in 1988, Jerry Dodgion had recommended him for the gig and "they kept asking me back," said Xiques:

Pepper, I guess, was out of town for about a month. When I was doing the baritone thing for Pepper, the alto chair had been open and they kept trying out different guys. Jerome [Richardson] had left to go out to the West Coast, so they were trying out different alto players....I told Jerry, "If you need any other subs, let me know, so he went and asked Thad, and I just moved right over. When Pepper came back, I moved over to the alto chair, and they kept asking me back, and, after about a month, Thad said I had the gig, which was great!

JOHNNY HAMMOND SMITH
711100
c. November 1971, Van Gelder Studio, Englewood Cliffs NJ: Overdubs: Snooky Young, Al DeRisi tp, flh; Wayne Andre tb; Grover Washington Jr. as*; Harold Vick ts†; Pepper Adams bs.

a   Peace Train*†   Kudu LP: KU-04
b   I Don't Know How to Love Him

c   Wild Horses[*][†]

Original tracks recorded at Van Gelder Studio, Englewood Cliffs NJ, on c. November 1971: Johnny Hammond org; Bob Mann, George Benson, Melvin Sparks, Eric Gale g; Ron Carter b; Billy Cobham dm; Airto Moreira perc. Violin section added at a later date.

All tracks on King (J) LP: KICJ-8368, Columbia-Sony CD: 94380, King (J) CD: 2226.

711207
7 December 1971, New York: Pepper Adams bs; other musicians.

This date for CBS, possibly an overdub, was probably contracted by Garry Sherman, an arranger of various popular music artists.

711215
15 December 1971, New York: Pepper Adams bs; other musicians.

This date for CBS, possibly an overdub, was probably contracted by Larry Fallon, an arranger of various popular music artists.

ELVIN JONES–MERRY GO ROUND
711216
16 December 1971, Van Gelder Studio, Englewood Cliffs NJ: Joe Farrell ss, ts, fl, piccolo; Dave Liebman, Steve Grossman ss, ts; Pepper Adams bs; Chick Corea p, e-p, Jan Hammer p, e-p, glockenspiel; Yoshiaki Masuo g[*]; Gene Perla b, e-b[†]; Elvin Jones dm; Don Alias cga, perc.

a	9071	'Round Town[*][†][1]	Blue Note LP: BST-84414
b	9072	Brite Piece[2]	
c	9073	Lungs[3]	
d	9074	A Time for Love[*4]	
e	9075	Tergiversation[5]	
f	9076	La Fiesta[6]	
g	9077	The Children's Merry-Go-Round March[7]	

[1]Liebman, Grossman, Farrell ts; Hammer e-p; Masuo g; Perla e-b; Jones dm; Alias cga.
[2]Farrell, Liebman ss, Grossman ts; Hammer p; Perla b; Jones dm; Alias perc.

[3]Hammer p; Perla b; Jones dm, Alais perc.

[4]Farrell fl; Corea p; Masuo g; Perla b; Jones dm.

[5]Corea, Hammer e-p; Perla b; Jones dm; Alias cga.

[6]Farrell ss; Liebman ss, ts; Grossman ts; Corea p; Perla e-b; Jones dm; Alias cga.

[7]Liebman, Grossman ss; Farrell pic; Adams bs; Hammer glockenspiel; Perla b; Jones dm.

-a on Blue Note LP: B1-35636, Blue Note CD: 8-35636-2, Indies Japan-Zoom (J) CD: TOCJ-8678.

All other tracks on Mosaic CD: MD8-195, Toshiba (J) CD: TOCJ-8678.

THAD JONES-MEL LEWIS – SUITE FOR POPS
720125

25 January 1972, New York: Thad Jones cornet, flh, perc; Snooky Young tp, flh; Jon Faddis tp, perc; Cecil Bridgewater, Virgil Jones, Marvin Stamm tp; Eddie Bert, Jimmy Knepper, Quentin Jackson tb; Jack Jeffers btb, tu; Jimmy Buffington, Ray Alonge frh; Jerry Dodgion ss, as, fl; Ed Xiques as, fl, bcl; Billy Harper ts, fl; Eddie Daniels ts, fl, cl; Pepper Adams bs, cl; Roland Hanna e-p; Richard Davis b; Mel Lewis dm, perc.

a   Meetin' Place   A&M-Horizon LP: SP-701

-a on A&M-Horizon (F) LP: 985023, A&M (Neth) LP: 701, Horizon-King (J) LP: GP-3501, Horizon-Canyon (J) CD: D23Y-3821, Horizon (J) CD: POCM-5047.

Thad Jones' *Suite for Pops,* of which this is the first movement, was commissioned by Jazz Interactions (under the direction of Joe Newman) to honor Louis Armstrong after Armstrong's death on 6 July 1971. Its world premiere took place at Alice Tully Hall in New York in later 1971, though it's unclear if a tape of the performance still exists. *See* 720126, 720131, 720901, 750722.

THAD JONES-MEL LEWIS – SUITE FOR POPS
720126

26 January 1972, New York: Same as 25 January 1972:

a   The Summary   A&M-Horizon LP: SP-701
b   The Farewell   A&M-Horizon unissued
c   61st and Richard

d   Come on Over My Love

All tracks on A&M-Horizon (F) LP: 985023, A&M (Neth) LP: 701, Horizon-King (J) LP: GP-3501, Horizon-Canyon (J) CD: D23Y-3821, Horizon (J) CD: POCM-5047.
See 720125, 720131, 720901, 750722.

THAD JONES-MEL LEWIS – SUITE FOR POPS
720131
31 January 1972, New York: Same as 25 January 1972; add Dee Dee Bridgewater voc†:

a   Toledo by Candlelight   A&M-Horizon LP: SP-701
b   The Great One†
c   Come on Over My Love   A&M-Horizon unissued
d   Imagine

All issued tracks on A&M-Horizon (F) LP: 985023, A&M (Neth) LP: 701, Horizon-King (J) LP: GP-3501, Horizon-Canyon (J) CD: D23Y-3821, Horizon (J) CD: POCM-5047.
See 720125, 720126, 720901, 750722.

AUTHOR'S NOTE
On 8-9 February 1972 at A&R Studios in New York, Thad Jones conducted his arrangements for the recording of *Portuguese Soul* (Verve LP: V6-8832), featuring organist Jimmy Smith, accompanied by members of the current Thad Jones-Mel Lewis Orchestra, though Grady Tate played drums, instead of Mel Lewis, and percussionist Leonard Gibbs was added. It's likely that Pepper Adams, however, was not on these recordings, since there's no mention of the session in his 1972 appointment book, and saxophonist Frank Basile has noted that Thad Jones' baritone parts were written for a Low "A" instrument, which Adams did not play. It's possible that Ed Xiques moved over to play the baritone chair. About this date, bassist George Mraz told the author, in an interview in 1988,

It was [basically Thad's] band plus French horns. I think this is maybe not the first time I played with the band, but I know they called me to do a rehearsal, because Richard [Davis] couldn't make it. So I did the rehearsal and the music, and everything was finished, and the next day they called me at ten o'clock in the morning—Mel called me—to come to the studio. I said, "What are you doing, man? It's ten o'clock in the morning! I'm sleeping." Leave me alone! He said, "Well, Thad said to call you, so I'm calling you." "So, what's happening? Richard is not there or what?" He said, "No, Richard is here but Thad wants you to come here." So, I said, "O.K." They sent Richard home. They said he had another record date. From then on I just stayed. I went with the band to London. We played two weeks at Ronnie Scott's and [then the band] went on to Russia. I couldn't go, because I didn't have an American passport, so Richard went to Russia. It was his last gig with the band.

According to Cecil Bridgewater, in an interview with the author in 1989, "I think we did the rehearsals at Carroll's Studio. I remember there was one section where we were playing this thing through and Thad [Jones] stopped everything. He said, "Wait a minute. Wait a minute. Third trombone: That note you have there is"—I don't know what note it was—"a D-flat instead of a D-natural" or something. I was amazed! I'm trying to figure out how did he *hear* that? With all of the stuff that was going on, how could he hear that? But, he was that way."

UNIVERSAL JONES
720211
11 February 1972, New York: Thad Jones tp; Jerry Dodgion as; Pepper Adams bs; Leon Pendarvis e-p, org, b; Eugene McDaniels g, voc; Bob Woos g, b; Maurice McKinley dm; Sister Charlotte voc.

a   We All Know a Lot of Things   MGM-Verve LP: MV-5084
        (But It Don't Ever Show)
b   Takin' Care of Business
c   Feeling that Glow
d   Tuesday Morning
e   Good Love Man
f   Hello to the Wind
g   River
h   Sidewalk Man

720216
16 February 1972, New York: Pepper Adams bs; other musicians.

Pepper Adams' appointment book for 1972 lists an unspecified MGM recording date. This might be a follow-up session to 720211.

THAD JONES-MEL LEWIS
720325

c. 25 March 1972, BBC TV broadcast, Ronnie Scott's, London: Thad Jones flh, cornet; Jon Faddis, Steve Furtado, Jim Bossy, Cecil Bridgewater tp; Jimmy Knepper, Billy Campbell, Quentin Jackson tb; Cliff Heather btb; Jerry Dodgion ss, as, fl; Ed Xiques as, fl, bcl; Billy Harper ts, fl; Ron Bridgewater ts, cl, fl; Pepper Adams bs, cl; Roland Hanna p; George Mraz b; Mel Lewis dm; Dee Dee Bridgewater voc.

This program took place during the Orchestra's engagement from 20-30 March. It's unclear if audio or video still exist.

According to Cecil Bridgewater, in an interview with the author in 1989,

> We were doing the show and they wanted Thad to do a sixty-second and a thirty-second theme of their theme song. So Thad looked at me, "Come on, come on, come on, come on! Come on, we're going in here!" and I said, "Going where?" So he took me into the control booth and they played the theme song. It was written for guitar, bass, and drums. It was a rock trio. They played it through and he listened to it, and he said, "O.K., play it once more," and they played it a second time. He said, "O.K.," and he was ready to go to start writing this arrangement. Now, I had a puzzled look on my face, because I'm just beginning at that point to figure out what the melody is. He's heard the melody, the harmony, and what he was going to write on it, so he looked at me and said, "All right, let's play it once more," so they played it a third time.
>
> He and I went to this room and he started laying out the parts. He laid out the first trumpet part, second trumpet part, third trumpet part, fourth trumpet part, and he started writing out the [other] parts. I'm looking at him. I'm saying [to myself], "You can't write an arrangement like this! You got to sit down and write a score, and then copy from the score." You know, everything. But he had started writing out the actual parts. Then he said, "O.K., we'll take measures three and four and write them down here at seven and eight," or whatever it was, and so I copied that, but I then copied myself a little score. Then he said, "Right here we're going to use..." and   he sang every note in the chord, from top to bottom. I

could hear his kind of voicing, but he sang every note, and when we played it, it was what it was supposed to be!...

Just long enough to write down the notes; it was, maybe, at the most, twenty minutes, a half hour, and that was mainly just *me* re-copying stuff and putting it down. He already knew what he wanted to do, how it was going to sound. It sounded great! I think it was an hour program featuring the band. I'm assuming that we must have played several of the compositions that we'd been playing at [Ronnie Scott's]. I don't know whatever happened to that show. I never saw it, but I remember they were using several different cameras for camera angles, and all of that kind of stuff. They may have also done interviews with Thad and Mel.

Regarding the transition from Richard Davis to George Mraz, and about other subs, Cecil Bridgewater told the author the following, in a 1989 interview:

Richard had a loose kind of feeling that seemed to fit well;...a very adventurous kind of way of playing which worked well with the rhythm section of Roland [Hanna] and Mel, because Roland could go either way. Mel was somewhat traditional in his approach, so I guess Richard kind of added a wildness or looseness to it that made the rhythm section exciting to me. When George came in, he kind of emulated some of what Richard had done, but, of course, he had his own way of doing things too. I think George was maybe a little more—I don't want to say—"precise," in that he played the right notes and everything, because Richard did that too. But I think he was a little more conservative. Maybe that's the other word to use. But he came in and played the music extremely well! It was no loss in musicianship at all, just a little difference in the feeling. There were other bass players that would come in from time to time too. Ron Carter would come in and sub sometimes....Hank [Jones] would come in sometimes and sub for Roland, when Roland couldn't do it. We did a few concerts with him, and it was nice to have him in the band there. I think Tommy Flanagan came and played in the band. Herbie Hancock played some. Kenny Barron.... Miles [Davis] came by several times. Thelonious [Monk] came by, just to hear the band, and hang out at a time when he wasn't doing much of that at all!

AUTHOR'S NOTE

According to Jimmy Knepper, in an interview with the author in 1988, saxophonist Jerry Dodgion made private recordings of the Thad Jones-Mel Lewis Orchestra's U.S. State Department tour of the Soviet Union during the period 2 April-2 May 1972, while in Leningrad (October Hall), Kiev (Sports Palace), Moscow (Rossiya and Estrady Concert Halls), Rostov-on-Don (Sports Palace), Yaroslavl, and Tbilisi (Philharmonic Concert Hall). Unfortunately, these tapes were likely destroyed by fire at Evon Dodgion's residence some years later, said Jerry Dodgion in 2005. Saxophonist Billy Harper filmed the band throughout the tour, and it's possible that other bandmembers also taped some of the performances. Film footage, either produced by the U.S. or Russian governments, or done privately, may also exist. For the tour, the personnel was Thad Jones flh, cornet; Jon Faddis, Steve Furtado, Jim Bossy, Cecil Bridgewater tp; Jimmy Knepper, Billy Campbell, Quentin Jackson tb; Cliff Heather btb; Jerry Dodgion ss, as, fl; Ed Xiques as, fl, bcl; Billy Harper ts, fl; Ron Bridgewater ts, cl, fl; Pepper Adams bs; Roland Hanna p; Richard Davis b; Mel Lewis dm; Dee Dee Bridgewater, Mel Dancy voc. Though he had left the band, bassist Richard Davis replaced George Mraz, who, as a Czech citizen, couldn't obtain a visa. Vocalist Mel Dancy, who sang with the band prior to Dee Dee Bridgewater, was added as a second vocalist. Saxophonist Ron Bridgewater (Cecil Bridgewater's brother) took Eddie Daniels' place in the band, beginning with this trip.

THAD JONES-MEL LEWIS
720512
12-13 May 1972, private recordings, Jazz Showcase, Chicago: Thad Jones flh, cornet; Jon Faddis, Steve Furtado, Jim Bossy, Cecil Bridgewater tp; Jimmy Knepper, Billy Campbell, Quentin Jackson tb; Cliff Heather btb; Jerry Dodgion ss, as, fl; Ed Xiques as, fl, bcl; Billy Harper ts, fl; Ron Bridgewater ts, cl, fl; Pepper Adams bs, cl; Roland Hanna p; George Mraz b; Mel Lewis dm.

See Author's Note above 580000A entry.

GROVER WASHINGTON JR.
720601
1 June 1972, Van Gelder Studio, Englewood Cliffs NJ: Overdubs: John Frosk, Marky Markowitz, Ernie Royal, Marvin Stamm, Snooky Young, Alan Rubin tp, flh; Wayne Andre, Paul Faulise, Tony Studd tb; Ray

Alonge, Donald Corrado, Fred Klein, Brooks Tillotson frh; Grover Washington Jr. as, ts; George Marge fl, recorder, as, oboe, engh; Pepper Adams bs; Arthur Clarke fl, bs.

a	No Tears, In the End	Kudu LP: KU-07
b	All the King's Horses	
c	Where Is the Love	
d	Lean on Me	
e	Body and Soul	
f	Lover Man	
g	Love Song 1700	

Original band tracks recorded at Van Gelder Studio, Englewood Cliffs NJ, in May 1972: Bob James e-p, harpsichord; Richard Tee org; Eric Gale, Gene Bertoncini, Cornell Dupree, David Spinozza g; Ron Carter, Gordon Edwards e-b; Billy Cobham, Bernard Purdie dm; Airto Moreira perc; Ralph MacDonald cga. String section added at another date.

-a on Motown LP: M5-186-V1, Kudu (Eng) LP: KU-07, Motown (Eng) LP: TMSP-6011, Motown (Eng) LP: CSTMS-5056, Motown-Bellaphon (Ger) LP: 230-15-044, Kudu-CTI (Ger) LP: KU-07, Motown (Ger) LP: WL-72-099, Kudu (J) LP: SR-3332, Kudu (J) LP: 3040, Kudu (J) LP: LAX-3253, Motown (J) LP: VIP-4134, Motown CD: 635-186, Motown CD: 37463-5186-2, Motown CD: MCD-0830-MD, Motown CD: 012-157-617-2, Hip-O CD: B0006073-2, Motown CD: 31453-0620-2, Verve CD: B-001186502, Verve (Eu) CD: 0602517822894, Motown (Ger) CD: ZD-72-494. Edited version on Kudu 45: KU-909.

-b on Motown LP: M5-186-V1, Kudu (Eng) LP: KU-07, Motown (Eng) LP: CSTMS-5056, Motown-Bellaphon (Ger) LP: 230-15-044, Kudu-CTI (Ger) LP: KU-07, Motown (Ger) LP: WL-72-099, Kudu (J) LP: SR-3332, Kudu (J) LP: 3040, Kudu (J) LP: LAX-3253, Motown (J) LP: VIP-4134, Motown CD: 635-186, Motown CD: 37463-5186-2, Motown CD: MCD-0830-MD, Motown CD: 31453-0620-2, Verve CD: B-001186502, Verve (Eu) CD: 0602517822894, Motown (Ger) CD: ZD-72-494.

-c on Motown LP: M5-186-V1, Motown LP: M9-961-AZ, Kudu (Eng) LP: KU-07, Motown (Eng) LP: TMSP-6015, Motown (Eng) LP: CSTMS-5056, Motown-Bellaphon (Ger) LP: 230-15-044, Kudu-CTI (Ger) LP: KU-07, Motown (Ger) CD: ZL-72-168, Motown (Ger) LP: WL-72-099, Kudu (J) LP: SR-3332, Kudu (J) LP: 3040, Kudu (J) LP:

LAX-3253, Motown (J) LP: VIP-4134, Motown CD: 635-186, Motown CD: 37463-5186-2, Motown CD: MCD-0830-MD, Hip-O CD: B0006073-2, Motown CD: 31453-0620-2, Verve CD: B-001186502, Verve CD: B-001394302, Verve (Eu) CD: 0602517822894, Motown (Ger) CD: ZD-72-494. Edited versions on Kudu 45: KU-912.

-d on Motown LP: M5-186-V1, Motown LP: MD-940-AZ, Motown LP: 5307-ML, Kudu (Eng) LP: KU-07, Motown (Eng) LP: STMS-5099, Motown (Eng) LP: TMSP-6011, Motown-Bellaphon (Ger) LP: 230-15-044, Motown (Ger) CD: WL-72-125, Motown (Eng) LP: CSTMS-5056, Kudu-CTI (Ger) LP: KU-07, Motown (Ger) LP: WL-72-099, Kudu (J) LP: SR-3332, Kudu (J) LP: 3040, Kudu (J) LP: LAX-3253, Motown (J) LP: VIP-4134, Motown CD: 635-186, Motown CD: 37463-5186-2, Motown CD: MCD-0830-MD, Motown CD: 31453-0620-2, Verve CD: B-001394302, Verve CD: B-001186502, Verve (Eu) CD: 0602517822894, Motown (Ger) CD: ZD-72-494.

-e on Kudu 45: KU-909, Motown LP: M5-186-V1, Kudu (Eng) LP: KU-07, Motown (Eng) LP: CSTMS-5056, Kudu-CTI (Ger) LP: KU-07, Motown (Ger) LP: WL-72-099, Motown-Bellaphon (Ger) LP: 230-15-044, Kudu (J) LP: SR-3332, Kudu (J) LP: 3040, Kudu (J) LP: LAX-3253, Motown (J) LP: VIP-4134, CTI (J) LP: GSW-3011/2, Motown CD: 635-186, Motown CD: 37463-5186-2, Motown CD: 31453-0620-2, Verve CD: B-001186502, Motown CD: MCD-0830-MD, Verve (Eu) CD: 0602517822894, Motown (Ger) CD: ZD-72-494.

-f on Motown LP: M5-186-V1, Kudu (Eng) LP: KU-07, Motown (Eng) LP: CSTMS-5056, Kudu-CTI (Ger) LP: KU-07, Motown (Ger) LP: WL-72-099, Motown-Bellaphon (Ger) LP: 230-15-044, Metronome (Ger) LP: DALP-2/1929, Kudu (J) LP: SR-3332, Kudu (J) LP: 3040, Kudu (J) LP: LAX-3253, Motown (J) LP: VIP-4134, Motown CD: 635-186, Motown CD: 37463-5186-2, Verve CD: B-001186502, Motown CD: MCD-0830-MD, Motown CD: 31453-0620-2, Verve (Eu) CD: 0602517822894, Motown (Ger) CD: ZD-72-494.

-g on Motown LP: M5-186-V1, Kudu (Eng) LP: KU-07, Motown (Eng) LP: CSTMS-5056, Kudu-CTI (Ger) LP: KU-07, Motown (Ger) LP: WL-72-099, Motown-Bellaphon (Ger) LP: 230-15-044, Kudu (J) LP: SR-3332, Kudu (J) LP: 3040, Kudu (J) LP: LAX-3253, Motown (J) LP: VIP-4134, Motown CD: 635-186, Verve CD: B-001186502, Motown CD: MCD-0830-MD, Motown CD: 31453-0620-2, Verve (Eu) CD: 0602517822894, Motown (Ger) CD: ZD-72-494.

THAD JONES
720618
18 June 1972, NPR radio broadcast, Asbury Park NJ: Thad Jones cornet; Billy Campbell tb; Jerry Dodgion as; Pepper Adams bs; Roland Hanna p; Richard Davis b; Mel Lewis dm.

a   **Straight, No Chaser**

BOB WILBER
720619
19 June 1972, New York: Bob Wilber ss; Hal McKusick as; Sam Parkins ts; Pepper Adams bs; Dill Jones p; Larry Ridley b; Cliff Leemans dm.

10 unknown titles   Music Minus One unissued

These are Wilbur band arrangements, designed to accompany a practicing soloist. On 26-27 June 1972, a different band led by Wilber, with the same instrumentation as above, recorded the following titles (on Music Minus One LP: MMO-4085) that were likely run through on 19 June: The Days of Wine and Roses, Moon Mist, Acapulco Princess, Two Moods for Piano and Winds, The Mighty Hudson, Early Morning Blues.

MUNDELL LOWE
720706
6 July 1972, film soundtrack, A&R Studios, New York: Pepper Adams bs; other musicians.

Soundtrack to *Everything You Always Wanted to Know About Sex But Were Afraid to Ask,* directed by Woody Allen: Woody Allen Collection 1: MGM DVD. A big band can be heard in the vignette *What's My Perversion* and elsewhere.

DAVID AMRAM–SUBWAY NIGHTS
720711
11 July 1972, New York: Marky Markowitz, Thad Jones, Joe Wilder, Wilmer Wise tp; Bill Watrous tb; Jim Buffington, Earl Chapin, Tony Miranda, Brooks Tillotson frhʌ; Don Butterfield tu; David Amram fl, p, voc; Joe Henderson ts; Bobby Jones ts, cl√; Pepper Adams bs; Jane Cochran, Henry Shuman oboe; William Arrowsmith engh; Marvin Feinsmith bassoon; Sam Brown, Joe Beck g; Herb Bushler b◊, e-b; Al

Harewood dm; Chorus*: Eileen Gilbert, Hilda Harris, Randy Peyton, Carlene Ray voc; McDougal Street Composers Chorus.†

a   The Professor and the Panhandler√∆   RCA LP: LSP-4820
b   Neon Casbah†◊
c   Ballad for Red Allen√[1]
d   Mean Dean*

[1]Adams out. Wilder, Cochran, Shuman, Arrowsmith, Feinsmith here only.

ELVIN JONES–MR. JONES
720712
12 July 1972, Van Gelder Studio, Englewood Cliffs NJ: Dave Liebman ss*, ts; Steve Grossman ts; Pepper Adams bs; Jan Hammer p; Gene Perla b; Elvin Jones dm; Frank Ippolito perc; Carlos Valdes cga.

a   9995   New Breed[1]   Blue Note LP: BN-110-F
b   9996   What's Up—That's It*

[1]Liebman, Grossman ts; Perla b; Jones dm; all others out.

All tracks on Blue Note LP: 784-331-1, Blue Note (F) LP: BST-84331, Blue Note (Ger) LP: BST-84438, Toshiba-EMI (J) LP: BNJ-71095, Blue Note CD: CDP-7-84331-2, Blue Note CD: CDBN-7-84331-2, Blue Note CD: B21Y-84331, Mosaic CD: MD8-195.

Explaining why the title track, Mr. Jones (*see* 690926a), was reissued after only having been released three years earlier, Gene Perla, in an interview with the author in 1989, said the following:

George Butler was the producer of this album. We're out at Rudy's and he scheduled three days of recording for us. I think it was three hours, with a one-hour "over," each day. Elvin gave me the job, prior to the recording, of being the Musical Director-Conductor-Arranger for the album. We did rehearsals at my loft in New York. I wrote one complete side: Three tunes that were supposed to segue from one to another. You will also notice that, if you listen to the record, the two tunes (that are on one side) by me segue, one into the other. In any case, there were supposed to be three tunes to cover one side [of the LP] that were like a suite. I kind of wrote a suite. We rehearsed the thing, like I say, and then we went into the studio and did some other recording. The next thing that I knew was that, at the end of the second day's session [*see* 720713], George Butler said, "That's it. We've got enough material. I'm canceling tomorrow." So, I absolutely freaked, because I didn't have the opportunity to get the third tune done [Sweet Mama]. I really got mad, and said, "This isn't right. We had rehearsals for this. The music was sketched out. I had been hired as the arranger on here. I was considering that we had three days and I was pacing myself to do three days." One thing led to another, and, being the publisher of several of the tunes—mine and Liebman's, I believe—I withheld the publishing on one of the tunes. That caused a lack of material for the album. That's why the one tune was substituted.

According to Adams' 1972 appointment book, Adams was paid for the following day's work, even though the session was cancelled.

THAD JONES-MEL LEWIS – SUITE FOR POPS
720901
1 September 1972, New York: Thad Jones cornet, flh; Jon Faddis, Steve Furtado, Jim Bossy, Lew Soloff tp; Jimmy Knepper, Billy Campbell, Quentin Jackson tb; Cliff Heather btb; Jimmy Buffington frh*; Jerry Dodgion ss, fl; Ed Xiques as, fl, bcl; Frank Foster ts, cl; Ron Bridgewater ts, fl; Pepper Adams bs, cl; Roland Hanna e-p; George Mraz b; Mel Lewis dm.

a   Only for Now*   A&M-Horizon LP: SP-701
b   A Good Time Was Had by All

All tracks on A&M-Horizon (F) LP: 985023, A&M (Neth) LP: 701, Horizon-King (J) LP: GP-3501, Horizon-Canyon (J) CD: D23Y-3821, Horizon (J) CD: POCM-5047. *See* 720125, 720126, 720131, 750722.

PEPPER ADAMS
720924
24-25 September 1972, CKUA radio broadcasts, Room at the Top, Edmonton, Canada: Pepper Adams bs; Tommy Banks p; Bob Cairns e-b; Tom Doran dm.

Both concerts were produced by the Edmonton Jazz Society, who maintain a library of their performances.

FRIEDRICH GULDA–MUSICIAN OF OUR TIME VOL. 1
721016

c. 16 October 1972, Villingen, Germany: Benny Bailey, Ack van Rooyen, Dusko Goykovich, Palle Mikkelborg tp; Ray Premru btp; Jiggs Whigham, Bobby Lamb tb; Rolf Schneebiegl frh; Alfie Reece tu; Fatty George cl; Phil Woods cl, as; Herb Geller as; Hans Salomon ts; Ferdinand Povel ts, fl; Pepper Adams bs; Fritz Pauer, Friedrich Gulda† p; Pierre Cavalli g; Ron Carter b; Tony Inzalaco dm, perc.

a   Piano Concerto Number One   MPS (Ger) LP: 88-034-2
b   Variations for Two Pianos and Band†
c   Piano Concerto Number Two   MPS (Ger) LP: 88-050-2
d   Fantasy for Four Soloists and Band

-a and BASF (Ger) LP: 4921-119-3, MPS (Ger) LP: 15384, MPS (Ger) CD: 06024-982-8945.
-b on BASF (Ger) LP: 4921-119-3, MPS (Ger) LP: 15384, MPS (Ger) CD: 06024-982-8945.
-c on MPS (Ger) LP: 15384, MPS (Ger) CD: 06024-982-8945.
-d on MPS (Ger) LP: 15384, MPS (Ger) CD: 06024-982-8945.

It's likely that additional material was recorded with Gulda during Adams' stay in Germany, because, according to Jan Lohmann, an *Orkester Journalen* review of Adams' gig in Stockholm on 7 November 1972 mentioned that Adams was in Germany to record four albums with Gulda.

According to Phil Woods, in an interview with the author in 1989, "I was still living in Europe at that point. I think Gulda arranged for the musicians he wanted, hired the ones he wanted that were available in Europe, and I believe he flew Pepper over especially for the date."

DANISH RADIO BIG BAND
721025

25 October 1972, Radiohuset, DR radio, Copenhagen: Palle Bolvig, Benny Rosenfeld, Finn Otto Hansen, Perry Knudsen, Allan Botschinsky tp, flh; Torolf Mølgaard, Per Espersen, Erling Kroner, Axel Windfeld, Ole Kurt Jensen tb; Bent Nielsen, Per Carsten, Jesper Thilo, Uffe Karskov, Flemming Madsen reeds; Ole Kock Hansen p; Ole Molin g; Mads Vinding b; Bjarne Rostvold dm; Ray Pitts cond; GUEST: Pepper Adams bs.

a   **Straight, No Chaser**
b   **Straight, No Chaser**
c   **Time on My Hands**
d   **Time on My Hands**
e   **Sea Treasure**
f   **Faces**
g   **Here's that Rainy Day**

PEPPER ADAMS
721105
5 November 1972, audience recording, Studentbyen Jazz Club, Oslo:
Pepper Adams bs; Roy Hellvin p; Sture Janson b; probably Ole Jacob
Hanson dm.

According to pianist Per Husby, a few days later in Trondheim,
Husby (with bassist Bjørn Alterhaug and drummer Kjell Johansen)
played his first gig with Adams. In a taped narration, sent to the author in
1987, Husby said,

> Pepper Adams was actually the first American soloist that I ever
> played with, which was a good man to start with because Pepper
> [had an] extremely friendly way of handling people....I think he
> sensed we were pretty green, as we say, because he was putting his
> baritone together—it was this old baritone that he had, which was
> green somewhere on the horn—and I said, "Oh, that's a very old
> baritone." He looked at me. He hadn't put the top end on, so I said,
> "Oh, it's not complete yet!" and I'm not quite sure if he thought that
> I was even greener...and that I didn't know anything, so I thought
> the horn was supposed to be there like that, with a big hole at the
> top. But he was very friendly. We were playing some blues number
> on the concert, and I remember quoting C Jam Blues. All the time,
> when we were playing solos, he would go down on the first row and
> sit listening to us. He came up and whispered in my ear, "Yeah, C
> Jam Blues, yeah!" again, something that I thought was very encour-
> aging, just doing that, even if I knew it was a silly quote.

PEPPER ADAMS
721106
*6 November 1972, SR radio broadcast, Restaurant Guldhatten, Stock-
holm:* Jan Allan tp; Pepper Adams bs; Steffan Abeleen p; Palle Daniels-
son b; Alex Riel dm.

a **Mean What You Say**
b **In a Sentimental Mood**[1]
c **Witchcraft**
d **'Tis**
e **On the Trail**
f **I Can't Get Started**
g **Nancy With the Laughing Face**[2]
h **'Tis**

[1]Adams and rhythm section.
[2]Allan and rhythm section.

NORWEGIAN RADIO BIG BAND
721108
c. 8 November 1972, NRK radio broadcast, Oslo: Thorlief Østereng,
Atle Hammer, Bernt Steen, Finn Eriksen, Christian Beck tp; Tore Nilsen,
Frode Thingnaes, Lyder Vengbo, Øivind Westby tb; Helge Hurum as, fl;
Erik Andressen as; Harald Bergersen, Knut Riisnaes ss, ts, fl; Johan Ber-
gli bs; Roy Hellvin p; Arild Andersen b; Svein Christiansen dm;
GUEST: Pepper Adams bs.

a **No Name**
b **Ballad for Hank**
c **A Secret**

According to Johan Helø, in a letter to the author written in 1986,
these tunes were recorded in the studio, then applause was later added to
simulate a live audience.

721206
6 December 1972, Van Gelder Studio, Englewood Cliffs NJ: Overdubs:
Pepper Adams bs; other musicians.

This CTI date was listed in Adams' 1972 appointment book.

DAVID AMRAM
730118a
18 January 1973, private recording, Academy of Music, Philadelphia:
David Amram fl; Jerry Dodgion as; Pepper Adams bs; Herb Bushler e-b;
Al Harewood dm; Philadelphia Orchestra; William Smith cond.

a Triple Concerto for Woodwinds, Brass, Jazz Quintet, and Orchestra:
   Allegro Robusto
   Andante Espressivo
   Rondo alla Turca: Allegro

See 710111, 730118b, 730122.

PEPPER ADAMS
730118b
18 January 1973, audience recording, Skewer's, Philadelphia: Larry McKenna as; Andy Kahn p; Leonard Chase b; Bruce Klauber dm; GUESTS: Glenn Dodson tb*; Pepper Adams bs.

a **Now's the Time***
b **God Bless the Child**
c **Scrapple from the Apple**

According to Bruce Klauber, in a conversation with the author in 1989, Pepper Adams and Glenn Dodson sat in after both performed David Amram's *Triple Concerto* at the Academy of Music (*see* 730118a).

DAVID AMRAM
730122
22 January 1973, private recording, Academy of Music, Philadelphia: David Amram frh, fl, p, perc; Jerry Dodgion as; Pepper Adams bs; Herb Bushler e-b; Al Harewood dm; Philadelphia Orchestra; William Smith cond.

a Triple Concerto for Woodwinds, Brass, Jazz Quintet, and Orchestra:
   Rondo alla Turca: Allegro

See 730118a.

JON LUCIEN
730202
2 February 1973, New York: Overdubs: Burt Collins, Joe Shepley, Lloyd Mitchell, Marvin Stamm tp; Garnett Brown, Bill Watrous, Wayne Andre, Paul Faulise tb; Dave Tofani cl; Morty Lewis ts; Pepper Adams bs.

a Kuenda   RCA LP: APL1-0161

b   Would You Believe in Me
c   Lady Love
d   Luella
e   Shana
f   Satan
g   Rashida
h   War Song
i   Esperanza
j   Love Everlasting
k   Zenzile
m   Lady Love

Original tracks probably recorded in New York in 1972: Dave Grusin e-p; Eric Harrigan Jr. dm; Frank Malabé cga; Jon Lucien voc. Other woodwinds, background vocals, and strings added at a later date.

All titles on RCA Victor VP: AYL1-3820, RCA LP: APL1-0470, RCA (J) LP: BVJP-2815, Big Break (Eng) CD: CDBBR-B0032, BMG (J) CD: BVCP-7408, Sony (J) CD: BVCP-40139.

An edited version of -c on RCA 45: RCA-0050, Big Break (Eng) CD: CDBBR-B0032.

ERIC GALE
730205
5 February 1973, Van Gelder Studio, Englewood Cliffs NJ: Overdubs: John Frosk, Jon Faddis, Victor Paz, Randy Brecker, Marvin Stamm tp; Alan Raph, Garnett Brown tb; Tony Studd tb, baritone horn; Jerry Dodgion as, ts; Joe Farrell ts; fl; Hubert Laws piccolo; George Marge afl, bfl; Pepper Adams bs.

a   Killing Me Softly With His Song   Kudu LP: KU-11
b   Cleopatra
c   Dindi
d   White Moth
e   Tonsue Corte
f   Forecast

Original tracks recorded at Van Gelder Studio, Englewood Cliffs NJ, in January 1973: Bob James e-p; Eric Gale g; Gordon Edwards, Bill Salter e-b; Rick Marotta, Idris Muhammad dm; Ralph MacDonald, Arthur Jenkins perc. String section added at another time.

-a on Kudu 45: KU-913, CTI (F) LP: CTI-9033, CTI (Ger) LP: KU-11, CTI (Ger) LP: RVG-99-771, King (J) LP: LAX-3252, King (J) LP: SR-3346, Kudu (J) CD: KICJ-2216, Kudu (J) CD: KICJ-8361.

-b on Kudu 45: KU-913, CTI (F) LP: CTI-9033, CTI (Ger) LP: KU-11, CTI (Ger) LP: RVG-99-771, King (J) LP: LAX-3252, King (J) LP: SR-3346, Kudu (J) CD: KICJ-2216, Kudu (J) CD: KICJ-8361.

All other tracks on CTI (F) LP: CTI-9033, CTI (Ger) LP: KU-11, CTI (Ger) LP: RVG-99-771, King (J) LP: LAX-3252, King (J) LP: SR-3346, Kudu (J) CD: KICJ-2216, Kudu (J) CD: KICJ-8361.

730206
6 February 1973, Van Gelder Studio, Englewood Cliffs NJ: Overdubs: Pepper Adams bs; other musicians.

According to Adams' 1973 appointment book, the contractor of this CTI date is Bob James.

DAKOTA STATON–I WANT A COUNTRY MAN
730220
20 February 1973, Bell Sound Studios, New York: Overdubs: Burt Collins, Marvin Stamm, Cecil Bridgewater, Lew Soloff tp; Eddie Bert, Garnett Brown, Bill Watrous tb; Jerry Dodgion ss; Joe Farrell as; Frank Wess ts; Pepper Adams bs.

a	Country Man	Groove Merchant LP: GM-521
b	I Love You More Than You'll Ever Know	
c	Girl Talk	
d	Heartbreak	
e	Cherokee	Groove Merchant unissued

Original tracks recorded probably in New York c. February 1973: unknown p; Sam Jones b; possibly Grady Tate dm; Dakota Staton voc.

-a on Europa Jazz (It) LP: EJ-1033, Curcio-I Grandi del Jazz (It) LP: GJ-41, LRC (Ger) CD: CDC-9017, LRC (Ger) CD: CDC-9021, Denon (J) CD: CD-8517.

-b on Europa Jazz (It) LP: EJ-1033, Curcio-I Grandi del Jazz (It) LP: GJ-41, LRC (Ger) CD: CDC-9008, LRC (Ger) CD: CDC-9017.

-c on Europa Jazz (It) LP: EJ-1033, Curcio-I Grandi del Jazz (It) LP: GJ-41, LRC (Ger) CD: CDC-9017.

-d on Europa Jazz (It) LP: EJ-1033. Curcio-I Grandi del Jazz (It) LP: GJ-41, LRC (Ger) CD: CDC-9017.

According to Cecil Bridgewater, in an interview with the author in 1989, "It was Dakota's date. Manny [Albam] did the arrangements. I was hired, along with several other members of the [Thad Jones-Mel Lewis] band, to do that. I think they had already laid down the rhythm tracks and everything, and just brought the horns in to overdub. It might have been her own rhythm section. I'm not sure."

See 730226.

DAKOTA STATON–I WANT A COUNTRY MAN
730226

26 February 1973, Bell Sound Studios, New York: Overdubs: Burt Collins, Marvin Stamm, Cecil Bridgewater, Joe Newman tp; Eddie Bert, Garnett Brown, Bill Watrous tb; Jerry Dodgion ss; Joe Farrell as; Eddie Daniels ts; Pepper Adams bs.

a   Cry Me a River   Groove Merchant LP: GM-521
b   It's the Talk of the Town
c   Make It Easy on Yourself
d   How Did He Look

Original tracks recorded probably in New York c. February 1973: unknown p; Sam Jones b; possibly Grady Tate dm; Dakota Staton voc.

-a on Europa Jazz (It) LP: EJ-1033, Curcio-I Grandi del Jazz (It) LP: GJ-41, Laserlight CD: 15-779, LRC (Ger) CD: CDC-9017, Denon (J) CD: CD-8517.

-b on Groove Merchant LP: GM-4405, Europa Jazz (It) LP: EJ-1033, Curcio-I Grandi del Jazz (It) LP: GJ-41, Laserlight CD: 15-779, LRC (Ger) CD: CDC-9017.

-c on Europa Jazz (It) LP: EJ-1033, Curcio-I Grandi del Jazz (It) LP: GJ-41, LRC (Ger) CD: CDC-9017.

-d on Europa Jazz (It) LP: EJ-1033, Curcio-I Grandi del Jazz (It) LP: GJ-41, LRC (Ger) CD: CDC-9017.

See 730220.

THAD JONES-MEL LEWIS
730407

7 April 1973, audience recording, Clarenceville High School, Livonia MI: Thad Jones flh; Cecil Bridgewater tp, unknown tp section; unknown tb section; Jerry Dodgion ss, as, fl; unknown as, ss; Ron Bridgewater ts, cl, fl; unknown ts; Pepper Adams bs; Roland Hanna p; George Mraz b; Mel Lewis dm; Dee Dee Bridgewater voc.*

a   Don't Git Sassy
b   Willow Tree
c   **Once Around**
d   A Child Is Born
e   Fingers
f   Suite for Pops:
       Meetin' Place
       The Summary
       The Farewell
g   See See Rider*
h   **How Insensitive*[1]**
i   Bye, Bye Blackbird*
j   Tow Away Zone
k   Central Park North

[1]During Adams' solo, various members of the band play percussion instruments.

According to Adams' friend Bob Cornfoot, in an interview with the author in 1987, Clarenceville High School was located on Seven Mile and Middle Belt, and the concerts were started as a

> cultural community program in the high school auditorium, which is a nice auditorium....They were having trouble getting the thing off the ground, and they had this local gal named Midge Ellis, who was a big fan of the big band thing, and she lived in the area, so she leapt into the breach. When they said they didn't know who to book, she started booking bands on the basis that sometimes bands come into town to play a one-nighter for some industrial [gig] or a party....On a lot of those, she used to pick them up, if they were available, on an adjacent night. You could pick them up for scale and not have to pay any of the transportation, because that was already taken care of by the other gig. So, a lot of times you can pick these guys up on an off-night for comparatively little money, and a lot of them were happy to get the extra day's work, as long as they were already out on the road....They had Basie, Buddy Rich,

Woody Herman—the usual. But Don Ellis came in, and they usually had Thad, almost once a year.

DUKE PEARSON
730422
22 April 1973, private recording, Famous Ballroom, Baltimore: Lloyd Mitchell, Lowell Hershey, Joe Shepley, Virgil Jones tp; Kenny Rupp, Billy Campbell, Jerry Chamberland tb; Dave Taylor btb; Jerry Dodgion, Richie Cole as; Frank Foster, Frank Perowski ts; Pepper Adams bs; Duke Pearson p; Bob Cranshaw b; Harold White dm.

Recorded by the Left Bank Jazz Society. *See* 650314.

DAVID AMRAM
730504
4 May 1973, Westinghouse TV broadcast, Horn and Hardart Automat, New York: David Amram fl, frh; Pepper Adams bs; Charlie Chin g; Gene Perla b; Elvin Jones dm.

Broadcast by Channel 11 in New York, it's unclear if audio or video still exist. According to David Amram, in an interview with the author in 1988,

We did once a Jazz at Horn and Hardart's....It was right in the window of 57th Street, right down from Carnegie Hall. People said, "Well, jazz is dead." This was the 1970s. I was sitting in the window of Horn and Hardart's. A lot of the musicians, who were going to their concerts at Carnegie Hall in their white ties and tails, would see our little group playing right in the window, and they couldn't believe it, because some of them didn't know I played too. They saw Pepper wailing away. Some of them worked with me as a conductor, but they didn't know that I had been playing all my life. At that time the world was so far apart. So, they would stand there, laughing, making signals, saying, "I'll be back." They all came back and they all loved Pepper! All the symphony players, especially. They said, "Boy, I never heard anything like that in my life! The way that guy continues playing for fifteen minutes, without ever repeating himself. It's just phenomenal!" We'd have three-day weekends. Jack Tofoya was the one who thought up the idea. By the third weekend, they would have the orders from people who were regular Horn and Hardart patrons, then the people who were just out there scuffling (who would come and drink a cup of water, with ketchup in it, to make their soup), and some people who were jazz fans, a lot of younger people who liked rock'n'roll that had never heard jazz before, tourists who wanted to get something to eat, and a lot of people who were around the Carnegie Hall area (who were classical musicians who were coming in and sometimes hearing jazz for the first time and really flipping out and enjoying it!). We also had people dance at the very end. Pepper liked that too.

One night Pepper played Lover Man, and then someone asked us to do Horn and Hardart Succotash Blues, which was kind of a Middle Eastern blues I [sung]....Then, someone asked us to play another one that we used to play, that was a Middle Eastern piece that was called Tompkins Square Park Consciousness Expander, which Pepper played on the recording *No More Walls* [*see* 710701]. So we played those three tunes and Pepper gave me a funny look. I said, "Man, that was a great set!" He said, "Yeah, Dave, we're going to have to rename this the Dave Amram-Pepper Adams D-minor Orchestra." I said, "What do you mean?" and he said, "You were so carried away, you forgot that we were playing a two hour set and every tune was in D-minor!" He played so many different things that I didn't even think about what key we were in. I was having such a good time, plus people would request tunes. He said, "Long before we did our first and last D-minor set, I found all different variations."

He reminded me: Back in 1955, when we were playing I Got Rhythm, he used the chord changes to Crazeology, which almost went through the whole cycle of fifths, so that, while you were playing, basically, in B-flat for the first sixteen bars, you were hitting a whole bunch of other keys on the way. Pepper found out more ways to play substitutions and various harmonies. Then he said, about that time, "You are the only person I knew who would appreciate this": of playing sometimes as far away from the original key and running through everything, so that sometimes people would look at him and say, "Man, I think that guy's lost it! He's completely crazy!" Actually, what Pepper was doing was to play substitutions in another key, but he had a way of doing it to make it sound right, so that it never sounded like what they call "shucking and jiving," which would be just wiggling your fingers and playing the most bizarre, unmusical, illogical things, and saying that was modern music.

Pepper always had a way of making it, almost like Bach, where every note would be a gem. Like Charlie Parker and like all master musicians, always have it be beautiful and logical, even though it was spontaneous. We played several weekends there and we would get there early and play until the man came out with the mop, because Pepper and a lot of us at that time, and all through our lives, I guess, thank God, had an approach to music that you got there and played until you had to stop. We would get there early, supposedly to decide what we were going to play, and then we would just hang out and have great philosophical conversations and eat some of Horn and Hardart's great fifteen cent dishes, and hang out with all the different people and enjoy ourselves. It was just like an enormous party.

We got paid a minimal amount of money, but we had so much fun because it was also a chance to play with Elvin. Every time Al Harewood was busy, Elvin would come and play, because he loved Pepper so much, and Elvin, by that time, had already become internationally recognized, but, because we were such old friends, anytime we could play together was a joy and a treat. One night Channel 11 came down and televised it. In fact, it was picked up nationally. They had one great shot where Elvin was playing this fantastic drum solo and Pepper and I and Charlie Chin were standing there listening to him, and, just in the middle of the solo, an old man with a gray hat on, came creeping across in front of the band, right in front of the shot, with a cup of coffee and a bun, oblivious to all the music, to sit down at this table. Pepper cracked up! It was a news program. They said, "Jazz comes to Horn and Hardart's." The wonderful thing was it showed how you can get an audience of people, at a time when, supposedly, there was nobody interested in jazz, to come and enjoy it tremendously.

BOB DOROUGH
730620
20 June 1973, TV soundtrack, New York: Unknown brass section; unknown ts; Pepper Adams bs; Bob Dorough p; Al Schackman g; Russ Savakas e-b; Grady Tate dm, voc; other musicians.

a   Naughty Number Nine   Rhino CD: R2-72455

This three-minute soundtrack was recorded for an episode of the ABC television animated children's program *Schoolhouse Rock.*
-a on Rhino CD: 72610.

STANLEY TURRENTINE
730621
c. 21 June 1973, Van Gelder Studio, Englewood Cliffs NJ: Overdubs:
John Frosk, Randy Brecker tp, flh; Alan Raph btb; Jerry Dodgion as; Joe
Farrell ts; Pepper Adams bs.

a	Too Blue	CTI LP: 6030
b	Don't Mess with Mr. "T"	
c	Don't Mess with Mr. "T"	CTI (EU) CD: 512-7922
d	I Could Never Repay Your Love	

Original tracks recorded at Van Gelder Studio, Englewood Cliffs NJ,
on 7 June 1973: Stanley Turrentine ts; Harold Mabern e-p (out on -a);
Richard Tee org; Bob James p; Eric Gale g; Ron Carter b; Idris Muhammad dm; Rubens Bassini perc. Strings recorded at another session.

Adams' 1973 appointment cites two CTI sessions done on 21 June.

-a on CTI LP: 8011, CTI LP: CTSQ-6030, CTI (Eng) LP: CTL-19,
CTI (J) LP: GP-3102, King (J) LP: SR-3349, CTI (J) LP: 6030, CTI (J)
LP: LAX-3282, Sony CD: 90600, Masterworks CD: 88697-88843-2,
CTI (Eu) CD: 5127922, Epic-Legacy (Eu) CD: EPC-460841-2, Epic-
Legacy (Eu) CD: ZK-44173.

-b on CTI LP: 8011, CTI LP: 6048-S1, CTI LP: CTSQ-6030, CTI
(Eng) LP: CTL-19, CTI (J) LP: GP-3003, CTI (J) LP: GP-3102, King (J)
LP: SR-3349, CTI (J) LP: 6030, CTI (J) LP: LAX-3282, CTI (J) LP: K-
18-P-6286/7, Sony CD: 90600, CBS CD: ZK-45218, CBS CD: ZK-
44147, Masterworks CD: 88697-88843-2, Epic-Legacy (Eng) CD:
5022872, Epic-Legacy (Eu) CD: EPC-460841-2, Epic-Legacy (Eu) CD:
ZK-44173, Epic-Legacy (Eu) CD: ZK-45478, Epic-Legacy (Eu) CD:
E2K-86364, Epic-Legacy (Eu) CD: EK-93654, Epic-Legacy (Eu) CD:
5127922, Sony (F) CD: SMM-516042-2.

-c on Sony CD: 90600, Epic-Legacy (Eu) CD: 5127922.

-d on CTI LP: 8011, CTI LP: CTSQ-6030, CTI (Eng) LP: CTL-19,
CTI (J) LP: GP-3102, King (J) LP: SR-3349, CTI (J) LP: 6030, CTI (J)
LP: LAX-3282, Epic-Legacy (Eu) CD: EPC-460841-2, Epic-Legacy
(Eu) CD: ZK-44173, Sony CD: 90600, Masterworks CD: 88697-88843-
2, Epic-Legacy (Eu) CD: 5127922.

730710
10 and 12 July 1973, New York: Pepper Adams bs; other musicians.
These dates for Buddah were contracted by Emile Charlap.

THAD JONES-PEPPER ADAMS
730722
22 July 1973, private recording, Baltimore: Thad Jones flh; Pepper Adams bs; Roland Hanna p; George Mraz b; Mel Lewis dm.

This was recorded by the Left Bank Jazz Society. *See* 650314.

ELVIN JONES–AT THIS POINT IN TIME
730724
24 July 1973, New York: Frank Foster ss†, ts√; Steve Grossman ss, ts; Pepper Adams bs; Jan Hammer p, e-p*, synth; Cornell Dupree g; Gene Perla b; Elvin Jones dm; Warren Smith timpani; Candido Camero cga; Richie "Pablo" Landrum, Omar Clay perc.

a   13431   The Prime Element*†   Blue Note LP: BN-LA506-H2
b   13432   **Whims of Bal√**

All tracks on Blue Note CD: BN-4-93385-2, Mosaic CD: MD8-195.

ELVIN JONES–AT THIS POINT IN TIME
730725
25 July 1973, New York: Same personnel as 24 July 1973, Hammer e-p*, Gene Perla b, e-b†:

a   Pauke Tanz[1]   Blue Note CD: CDBN-4-93385-2
b   The Unknighted Nations*†[2]
c   Don't Cry*†[3]

[1]Steve Grossman ts, Hammer synth.
[2]Steve Grossman ss.
[3]Steve Grossman ss, Hammer p.

All tracks on Blue Note CD: BN-4-93385-2, Mosaic CD: MD8-195.

ELVIN JONES–AT THIS POINT IN TIME
730726
26 July 1973, New York: Same personnel as 24 July 1973, Steve Grossman ts√, Jan Hammer synth*:
a   13429   At This Point in Time   Blue Note LP: LA-506-H2

b   13430   **Currents/Pollen**[*]√

All tracks on Blue Note CD: BN-4-93385-2, Mosaic CD: MD8-195.
Edited version of -b on Blue Note (Eng) LP: 7243-5-24418-1-5, Blue
Note (F) CD: 7243-5-24418-1-5, Blue Note (F) CD: 7243-5-24418-2-2.

THAD JONES-MEL LEWIS
730814
14 August 1973, SR radio broadcast, Gröna Lund, Stockholm: Thad
Jones flh; Jon Faddis, Steve Furtado, Jim Bossy, Cecil Bridgewater tp;
Jimmy Knepper, Billy Campbell, Steve Turre tb; Cliff Heather btb; Jerry
Dodgion ss, as, fl; Ed Xiques as, bcl, fl; Billy Harper ts, fl; Ron Bridge-
water ts, cl, fl; Pepper Adams bs; Roland Hanna p; George Mraz b; Mel
Lewis dm; Dee Dee Bridgewater voc.*

a   Quietude
b   Backbone
c   Central Park North
d   **How Insensitive**^{*1}
e   Dee Dee's Blues*
f   Tiptoe
g   It Only Happens Every Time
h   The Best Things in Life Are Free*
i   A Child Is Born

[1]During Adams' solo, several members of the band play percussion instruments.

THAD JONES-MEL LEWIS
730815
15 August 1973, YLE radio broadcast, Finlandia House, Helsinki: Same
personnel as 14 August 1973, Dee Dee Bridgewater voc*:
a   A–That's Freedom
b   Willow Tree
c   Tiptoe
d   Mean What You Say
e   **Us**
f   Quiet Nights*
g   River's Invitation*

h Backbone
i Willow Weep for Me
j Central Park North
k A Child Is Born
m Fingers
n By the Time I Get to Phoenix*
o See See Rider*
p **Once Around**

PEPPER ADAMS
730816
c. 16 August 1973, DR radio broadcast, Danish Radio Studio, Copenhagen: Pepper Adams bs; Kenny Drew p; Mads Vinding b; Ed Thigpen dm.

a **Mean What You Say**
b **Civilization and Its Discontents**

THAD JONES-MEL LEWIS
730818
18 August 1973, BRT TV broadcast, Jazz Middelheim, Antwerp: Same personnel as 14 August 1973, Dee Dee Bridgewater voc*:

a Don't Git Sassy
b Don't Ever Leave Me
c Us[1]
d Willow Weep for Me
e 61st and Richard
f A Child Is Born
g Fingers
h Get Out of My Life Woman*
i Here's that Rainy Day*
j Trying Times
k Tow Away Zone
m Central Park North

[1]Jones and others play percussion.

It's unclear if video still exists.

THAD JONES-MEL LEWIS
730819
19 August 1973, ORTF radio broadcast, Open Air Theatre, Chateau-vallon, France: Same personnel as 14 August 1973, Dee Dee Bridge-water voc*:

a   A–That's Freedom
b   Suite for Pops:
       Meetin' Place
       The Summary
       The Farewell
c   See See Rider*
d   Bye Bye Blackbird*
e   The Intimacy of the Blues
f   The Best Things in Life Are Free*
g   **How Insensitive**[*1]
h   **Once Around**
i   Fingers

[1]During Adams' solo, various members of the band play percussion instruments.

THAD JONES-MEL LEWIS
730824
24 August 1973, RAI radio broadcast, Jazz Umbria, Perugia, Italy: Same personnel as 14 August 1973, Dee Dee Bridgewater voc*:

a   **Once Around**
b   Tiptoe
c   unknown blues
d   A Child Is Born
e   Central Park North
f   Bye Bye Blackbird*
g   **How Insensitive**[*1]
h   Little B's Poem*
i   Every Day I Have the Blues*
j   Fingers

[1]Various bandmembers play percussion instruments during Adams' solo.

THAD JONES-MEL LEWIS
730825
25 August 1973, NOS TV broadcast, Singer Concertzaal, International NOS Jazz Festival, Laren, Netherlands: Same personnel as 14 August 1973, Dee Dee Bridgewater voc*:

a   Samba con Getchu
b   Quietude
c   Suite for Pops:
        Meetin' Place
        The Summary
        The Farewell
d   Little B's Poem*
e   **How Insensitive***1
f   Every Day I Have the Blues*
g   Willow Weep for Me
h   A Child Is Born
i   Fingers

1Various bandmembers play percussion instruments during Adams' solo.

It's unclear if video still exists.

PEPPER ADAMS–EPHEMERA
730909
9-10 September 1973, EMI Studios, London: Pepper Adams bs; Roland Hanna p; George Mraz b; Mel Lewis dm.

a   **Ephemera**   Spotlite (Eng) LP: PA-6
b   **Bouncing with Bud**
c   **Civilization and Its Discontents**
d   **Jitterbug Waltz**
e   **Quiet Lady**
f   **Patrice**
g   **Hellure (How Are You're)**

All tracks on Zim LP: ZLS-2000, Toshiba (J) LP: ITJ-80045.
This is Adams' thirteenth date as a leader.
In 1984 Pepper Adams told the author that he had waited five years to record a date under his own name, and then, he said,

the opportunity to record was only in England and very much on the cheap. A tiny studio and a tiny piano. It was very poorly recorded, but it was done so cheaply. But this was the only person that would take a chance on putting my name on a record. We did it in two days, which was fortunate because nothing got accomplished at all the first day. For one thing, the piano was ridiculous and badly out of tune, and that was only partially fixed by the second day. But, also, the engineer had never seen an acoustic bass. Not just recorded one; he had never seen one! This, of course, is the mod England of the later '60s: "Gee, what is that thing?" And then he didn't know what fingerboard noise was, and he was hearing these sounds that he couldn't identify, and it was driving him up the wall. He would stop takes and not be able to describe what it was he had heard. It was hilarious, really!

I think, at first, these engineers just looked at it as just a kind of a throwaway gig. But, after a while, they started to get involved in what they were doing, and really paying attention, and trying to do as good a job as they could, which is not the attitude they had when they went in. I think maybe some of the dedication they saw in the studio kind of rubbed off on them and they got interested and excited in the project, which is the only thing that saved us. If they'd have maintained that same attitude toward a second day, we would not have had a record. Everything was from the second day, and, musically, I think it's fine. I'm very happy with it. The recorded sound is still laughable, but it is certainly a hell of a lot better than the way things started out.

Regarding the piano on the date, Mel Lewis said the following in a 1989 interview with the author: "It was some kind of a homemade piano. You could turn it in different directions. Weird. Very strange looking!" Roland Hanna told the author the same year, the piano "was like an animal! It kept walking away from me!"

Mark Gardner, who wrote the liner notes for the LP, was in the studio the first day to listen to the band. Approximately a week later Gardner wrote in a London newspaper that the first ninety minutes of time was spent getting a "satisfactory recording balance...but in the last two hours some fine music was made."

According to Adams' friend Mike Jordan, in a 1989 interview with the author, Adams was never paid for this date.

THAD JONES-MEL LEWIS AND MANUEL DE SICA
730913

13-14 September 1973, London: Same personnel as 14 August 1973, Manuel DeSica*, Dee Dee Bridgewater voc†:

a First Jazz Suite: PAUSA LP: PR-7012
     Brasserie
     Father
     Sing*
     Ballade
     For Life†

It's unclear what tunes are taken from which date.

All tracks on Produttori Associati (It) LP: PAZ-63, Teldec (Ger) LP: 622663.

George Mraz told the author, in an interview in 1988, "We rehearsed in some disco in Perugia, and, then, a few weeks later, we recorded in London."

According to Cecil Bridgewater, in an interview with the author in 1989, "Manuel, as far as I could tell, was not a writer of [our] kind of music. It wasn't something that we should've been doing, I don't think. I don't know what all the circumstances were at the time. I don't know if Thad and Mel thought that other things were going to come out of that, or what the deal was, but I remember doing it. Everybody wasn't that pleased about the whole deal."

Ed Xiques told the author in 1988 that Adams, at the first rehearsal in Italy, said, "Why are we playing this shit?" and that Thad and Mel glared at him disapprovingly. Jerry Dodgion, when reminded of the exchange, told the author in 1988, "Well, you see, they didn't tell him!" "Thad really saved that date," said Xiques. According to Xiques, as told to the author in 1988,

This guy, Vittorio DeSica's son, was real nervous and he had written these charts. We recorded most of the album in London, and it was a hassle, as I recall. I remember Thad and Mel and some business agent: I was sitting in front of them on the bus and they were going through all kinds of changes and business stuff about that record. They weren't going to get paid, and this and that; Some bullshit was going down. We ended up doing another track. Thad finally said, "OK, we'll do a track. We're gonna be in Perugia and we'll record it." [*See* 740729.] We needed another tune. But Thad made that record sound pretty good.

THAD JONES-MEL LEWIS
730915
15 September 1973, BBC-1 TV broadcast, London: Same personnel as 14 August 1973.

It's unclear if audio or video still exist.

STANLEY TURRENTINE
730920
c. 20 September 1973, Van Gelder Studio, Englewood Cliffs NJ: Blue Mitchell tp; Curtis Fuller tb; Stanley Turrentine ts; Pepper Adams bs; George Benson g; possibly Tony Mathews g; other musicians.

CTI unissued. Adams' 1973 appointment book cites a CTI date on 20 September, the last date Turrentine did for the label before he switched to Fantasy Records.

According to Curtis Fuller, in an interview with the author in 1989,

Creed Taylor came out and said, "What do you got all these bebop guys on here for?" That was his statement, and that blew my mind!...Pepper [played] a beautiful solo on a G-minor thing, and I played what I thought was a good solo—for *me*—and they edited that right out of the date, because it wasn't what they were trying to achieve....They had a guitar player from Ray Charles' band [along with Benson], who was supposed to be a good soul player...but he was just supposed to play the rhythm guitar thing. But Creed couldn't use the jazz players. He said, "It's not a bebop session," and he got mad at the people. A few of the arrangements, about three or four, as far as I could tell, were by Don Sebesky, who I played in Maynard Ferguson with....They edited me and Pepper right off of it. It's as if we weren't even there! There were some pretty good arrangements, because Pepper and I had some moving parts together. It wasn't coming off conceptually with everyone involved, or something we had to go over, and this is what bugged Creed, because he thought it was overarranged and everything. He just wanted it to be a funk date, rather than having a whole bunch of bebop people playing....Pepper played some interesting stuff on that date!

DAVID AMRAM
731031
31 October-3 November 1973, private recordings, Eastman Theatre, Rochester NY: David Amram frh, fl, p; Jerry Dodgion as; Pepper Adams bs; Herb Bushler e-b; Al Harewood dm; Rochester Philharmonic Orchestra; David Zinman cond.

a   Triple Concerto for Woodwinds, Jazz Quintet, and Orchestra:
     Allegro Robusto
     Andante Espressivo
     Rondo alla Turca: Allegro

The Rochester Philharmonic was able to refine the piece by playing it in perfomance over four days for their season ticket subscribers. *See* 710111.

DAVID AMRAM–TRIPLE CONCERTO
731105
5 November 1973, Civic Music Association, Rochester NY: David Amram frh, fl, p; Jerry Dodgion as; Pepper Adams bs; Herb Bushler e-b; Al Harewood dm; Rochester Philharmonic Orchestra; David Zinman cond.

a   Triple Concerto For Woodwinds,   Flying Fish LP: GRO-751
     Jazz Quintet, and Orchestra:
     Allegro Robusto
     Andante Espressivo
     Rondo alla Turca: Allegro

-a on RCA LP: ARL-1-0459, Flying Fish CD: 18964-0751-2.
See 710111.

PEPPER ADAMS
731126
26 November 1973, TV North broadcast, Captain's Cabin, Edmonton, Canada: Woody Shaw tp; Julian Priester tb; Pepper Adams bs; George McFetridge p; Clint Houston b; Clifford Barbaro dm.

a **Straight, No Chaser**
b Love for the Only One You Can't Have
c Rejects Revisited
d Papo's Tune
e **Quiet Lady**
f The Goat and the Archer
g **Civilization and Its Discontents**
h **Oleo**

According to Adams' 1973 appointment book, gigs in Edmonton from 24-26 November for the Edmonton Jazz Society culminated with this TV appearance, later broadcast by the CBC.

THAD JONES-MEL LEWIS
731209
9 December 1973, private recording, Famous Ballroom, Baltimore: Thad Jones flh; Jon Faddis, Steve Furtado, Jim Bossy, Charles Sullivan tp; Jimmy Knepper, Billy Campbell, Quentin Jackson tb; Cliff Heather btb; Jerry Dodgion ss, as, fl; Ed Xiques ss, as, cl; Frank Foster ts, ss, cl; Ron Bridgewater ts, cl; Pepper Adams bs; Hank Jones p; George Mraz b; Mel Lewis dm; Dee Dee Bridgewater voc.

Recorded by the Left Bank Jazz Society. *See* 650314.

THAD JONES-MEL LEWIS
731217
17 December 1973, private recording, Jazz Showcase, Chicago: Same as 9 December 1973.

This was originally scheduled for 16 December, but was rescheduled due to bad weather. *See* Author's Note above 580000A.

DON PALMER
740000
c. 1974, private recording, Don Palmer's apartment, New York: Richie Kamuca ss; Don Palmer as; Lee Konitz ts; Pepper Adams bs.

In a 1989 interview with the author, Don Palmer said this was "music for four saxophones—soprano, alto, tenor, and baritone—played in his living room. There may have been a classical piece or two in there," he said, "but most of the stuff was music that I had gotten my hands on, written by George Handy, and a few things that Phil Woods had written. They were originally written for the New York Saxophone Quartet....I just used to have people over to play it. Pepper played it a number of times."

740104
4 January 1974, New York: Pepper Adams bs; other musicians.

In Adams' 1974 appointment book, he cites a date for Capricorn Records.

THAD JONES-MEL LEWIS – POTPOURI
740218
18 February 1974, Sigma Sound Studios, Philadelphia: Thad Jones flh; Jon Faddis, Steve Furtado, Jim Bossy, Cecil Bridgewater tp; Jimmy Knepper, Billy Campbell, Quentin Jackson tb; Cliff Heather btb; Jerry Dodgion ss, as, fl; Ed Xiques ss, as, cl, fl; Billy Harper ts, fl; Ron Bridgewater ts, cl; Pepper Adams bs; Roland Hanna p, e-p; Buddy Lucas* harmonica, jaw harp; George Mraz b; Mel Lewis dm.

a Blues In a Minute   Philadelphia International LP: PIR-X-598
b All My Yesterdays
c **Quiet Lady**
d Don't You Worry 'Bout a Thing
e For the Love of Money*
f Yours and Mine
g Ambiance
h Living for the City*

-b on Philadelphia International 45: ZS8-3556, Philadelphia International LP: KZ-3315, Philadelphia International (Eng) LP: PIR-80411, Philadelphia International (Neth) LP: BL-33152, Columbia (A) CD: 471478-2, CBS Sony (J) CD: ECPN-48-PH.
-d on Philadelphia International 45: ZS8-3556, Philadelphia International LP: KZ-33152, Philadelphia International (Eng) LP: PIR-80411, Philadelphia International (Neth) LP: BL-33152, Columbia (A) CD: 471478-2, CBS Sony (J) CD: ECPN-48-PH.

All other tracks on Philadelphia International LP: KZ-33152, Philadelphia International (Eng) LP: PIR-80411, Philadelphia International (Neth) LP: BL-33152, Columbia (Ger) CD: 471478-2, CBS Sony (J) CD: ECPN-48-PH.

Regarding the belief among bandmembers that Thad Jones was commissioned on this date to arrange music (-d, -e, -h) that he wouldn't have otherwise done on his own, Jon Faddis, in a 1988 conversation with the author, remarked, "That might be true, but the arrangements are so outstanding! That might be...where he did the job but he didn't really enjoy doing it because of a certain authority put on him: "You have to do this, you have to do that!" I don't remember him being so upset. I don't remember playing that music so much after we did the record either."

According to Ed Xiques, in a conversation with the author in 1988, "Alban Berg is a favorite composer of mine—Pepper's too. We were sitting around in the booth there. I don't know if it was a lunch break, or something happened, or Thad was rewriting something, but we obviously had plenty of time to kill. So I asked Pepper if he felt like hearing the Lyric Suite, the string quartet. We put it on and listened to it on the big speakers. Pepper and I dug it!"

According to Jimmy Knepper, in an interview with the author in 1988, "We stayed overnight and did it in two days. A few days later they brought me down and I overdubbed some of the trombone parts."

It's not clear what tunes were released from this date or 20 February. *See* 740220.

ESTHER PHILLIPS
740219
19 February 1974, Van Gelder Studio, Englewood Cliffs NJ: Overdubs: Jon Faddis, Marvin Stamm tp; Jerry Dodgion, Pee Wee Ellis as; Pepper Adams bs.

a	RVG98774	I've Only Known a Stranger	Kudu LP: KU-14
b		I Got It Bad (And that Ain't Good)	
c		Too Many Roads	
d		You Could Have Had Me, Baby	
e		Justified	
f		Black-Eyed Blues	
g		Tangle in Your Lifeline	Sony-CTI (Eu) CD: 5127972

Original tracks recorded at Van Gelder Studio, Englewood Cliffs NJ, on 25 July 1973: Tim Hinkley p; Charlie Brown g; Boz Burrell e-b, Ron Carter b (-b only); Ian Wallace dm; Arthur Jenkins perc (-e, -f only); Esther Phillips voc. Vocal choir and strings added at subsequent sessions.

-a on Kudu LP: 919, Kudu (Neth) LP: KU-14, Kudu (J) LP: LAX-3260, Sony (Eu) CD: 5127972.

-b on Kudu LP: 919, Kudu (Neth) LP: KU-14, Kudu (J) LP: LAX-3260, CBS CD: ZK-45483, Sony (Eu) CD: 5127972000.

-c on Kudu 45: KU-917, Kudu (Neth) LP: KU-14, Kudu LP: 919, Kudu (J) LP: LAX-3260, Sony-CTI (Eu) CD: 5127972.

-d on Kudu LP: 919, Kudu (Neth) LP: KU-14, Kudu (J) LP: LAX-3260, Sony (Eu) CD: 5127972.

-e on Kudu 45: KU-917, CTI LP: 6036, Kudu (Neth) LP: KU-14, Kudu LP: 919, Kudu (J) LP: LAX-3260, Sony (Eu) CD: 5127972.

-f on CTI LP: 6036, Kudu LP: 919, Kudu (Neth) LP: KU-14, Kudu (J) LP: LAX-3260, CBS CD: ZK-45483, Sony (Eu) CD: 5127972.

THAD JONES-MEL LEWIS – POTPOURI
740220
20 February 1974, Sigma Sound Studios, Philadelphia: Same as 18 February 1974.

Philadelphia International LP: PIR X-598. It's unclear what tunes were released from this date or 18 February.

All tracks on Philadelphia International LP: KZ-33152, Philadelphia International (Eng) LP: PIR-80411, Philadelphia International (Neth) LP: BL-33152, Columbia (Ger) CD: COL-471478-2, CBS Sony (J) CD: ECPN-48-PH.

See 740218.

THAD JONES-MEL LEWIS
740226a
26 February 1974, TV broadcast, Tokyo: Thad Jones flh; Jon Faddis, Steve Furtado, Jim Bossy, Cecil Bridgewater tp; Jimmy Knepper, Billy Campbell, Quentin Jackson tb; Cliff Heather btb; Jerry Dodgion ss, as, fl; Ed Xiques ss, as, cl, fl; Billy Harper ts, fl; Ron Bridgewater ts, cl; Pepper Adams bs; Roland Hanna p; George Mraz b; Mel Lewis dm; Dee Dee Bridgewater voc.*

a   Us[1]

b   Bye Bye Blackbird*
c   Pensive Miss
d   By the Time I Get to Phoenix*
e   Tiptoe

[1]Most of the band plays various percussion instruments.

THAD JONES-MEL LEWIS
740226b
26 February 1974, FM-Tokyo radio broadcast, Yubin-Chokin Hall, To-kyo: Same as 26 February 1974; Dee Dee Bridgewater voc*:

a   Mean What You Say
b   Don't Ever Leave Me
c   **The Little Pixie**
d   Pensive Miss
e   A–That's Freedom
f   St. Louis Blues
g   Yours and Mine
h   Bye Bye Blackbird*
i   Get Out of My Life Woman*
j   Fingers

THAD JONES-MEL LEWIS
740305
5 March 1974, private film, Hibaya Park, Tokyo: Same as 26 February 1974; Dee Dee Bridgewater voc*:

a   Intimacy of the Blues
b   improvised blues*
c   **Once Around**

This film was made by bandmember Billy Harper.

THAD JONES-MEL LEWIS
740306
6 March 1974, private film, Nagoya, Japan: Same as 26 February 1974:

a   **Once Around**
b   Only for Now

c   Central Park North[1]

[1]Jones and some bandmembers play various percussion instruments.

This film was made by bandmember Billy Harper.

This date was possibly the final one in which Pepper Adams played clarinet before his last clarinet was stolen. According to Ed Xiques, in an interview with the author in 1988, Adams "left the clarinet on the bus. It was a clarinet that Eddie Daniels had given him too, or he had bought it from Eddie. A good Buffet clarinet. He felt really bad about it."

THAD JONES-MEL LEWIS
740312
12 March 1974, Yubin-Chokin Hall, Tokyo: Same as 26 February 1974; Dee Dee Bridgewater out:

a   **Mean What You Say**   Nippon-Columbia (J) LP: YX-7557
b   **The Little Pixie**

According to Mel Lewis, there are additional recorded titles from this concert. *See* 740313.

All tracks on Nippon-Columbia Denon (J) LP: YP-7046-N, Denon (J) LP: YX-7557-ND, Columbia-Nippon (J) CD: COCB-53510, Columbia-Nippon (J) CD: COCY-80752.

About this live recording, Cecil Bridgewater said the following in an interview with the author in 1989:

> That was a problem. We didn't know we were recording. But I did! I finally knew about it. What happened was we were leaving for the concert hall in Tokyo and Dee Dee, as usual, was a little late. She was always a little late doing things, so she and I and the promoter ended up riding in the last car that was going over. The rest of the band had left. The promoter was telling me, "The reason that we have to go over early for the soundcheck and everything is because we are recording," and I said, "O.K." When I got to the hall I went immediately to Thad and Mel's dressing room and talked to them about this. Mel was shocked. I was talking to Mel because Thad, when I mentioned it, went over in a corner and didn't want anything to do with it. He didn't want to discuss it. He left the business end of the stuff up to Mel (to discuss at least). I don't know whether he left it up to him to take care of otherwise. We had a discussion. I

said, "Mel, I understand we're recording tonight." He was a little shocked. He said, "Well, uh, uh, uh, what do you mean?" I said, "Well, I rode over with the promoter and he told me we're recording." I said, "Are we being compensated for it?" "Well, uh, uh, well, only if it's released." I said, "Oh, man, come on. Any time you record somebody, you're supposed to at least let them know and pay them for it." Evon—she ended becoming Evon Dodgion—Evon Taylor was there in the room and she was shocked, because she thought that evidently they had gotten some money for it or something. She was saying, "Well, Mel, you can't record anybody without paying them! What kind of way is that to do business?" So then Mel was only more angry about it. Anyway, we went ahead and did the concert, and they did the recording.

When we went back a couple of years later, the recording had come out. We were doing Frank Foster's record. [*See* 751113, 751117a.] I was talking to Mel at the recording session. I said, "Mel, O.K., what about being paid for that recording?" and Mel, again, "Well, uh, uh, uh, well, we're..." and started stammering and stuff. I said, "Mel, listen: Where's the money for that recording?" He said, "Well, you know, we decided that, if the album was released internationally, then you would get paid." I said, "No, Mel, you told me, specifically, if it was *released,* we would get paid!" He said, "Well, you know, you guys are always complaining about things! We had to use that money to pay off the rest of the trip." I said, "Oh, Mel, come on!" So then I told him, I said, "Well, listen: I don't ever want to be recorded without being paid for it!" But what I found out after that—we had that confrontation at the studio getting ready to do Frank's thing, or on a break, I think it was—was that a couple of days before that, he and Pepper had the same argument and Pepper was ready to fight him. That's what I was told. He had broken a bottle or something. He was very upset at the time. I had never seen that side of Pepper!

According to Mel Lewis, in an interview with the author in 1988,

The guy that brought us over, Takawa Isizuka, is the first one to take a real chance on us. He set up this tour, and near the end, because of the fact of where the tour ended, and then where we had to go on coming back to the States, he made a deal with Nippon-Columbia (which was owned by Denon back then, but the label was Nippon-Columbia, if you have a copy of the original record). We needed to fill out the week to make our payroll, otherwise we

would've had no work that week at all and we would've been on the
road. We had to finish the tour out and then get to the States, and
then continue our way back to New York. We had a tour in the
States of a couple of weeks to work our way back on a bus. We
were going to continue in L.A. or San Francisco and so on, but we
had a whole week open, so we needed a couple of gigs to finish out
the week's work, otherwise we would have been in trouble to pay
the guys.

Nippon-Columbia bought two concerts, with the stipulation that
they would be recorded, and, of course, we stipulated that the record
would only be available in Japan and nowhere else. It turned out
they only used four tracks from the concerts. It would be a live performance, so we figured we're just going in and doing the concert.
There was no soundcheck for [the band]. They had to come in and
do it....That's a case where, on Mean What You Say, we do the
small group thing in front. Pepper never played on that before that.
That's a one-take performance that was never done like that before
or after....

The beauty of this band was that we never did anything the way
it was supposed to be. We changed it at the moment. That particular
version starts out with the rhythm section, and, the next thing you
know, Pepper's playing, long before we get to the melody at all. He
and Thad played the line from the original recording, from the small
group version [*see* 660426], and then Pepper blew before the band
went into the arrangement itself. So, we stuck the small group version in front of the big band version, at the spur of the moment.
Denon just happened to choose that particular track for their album.

See 740313.

THAD JONES-MEL LEWIS
740313
13 March 1974, Toshi Center Hall, Tokyo: Same as 12 March 1974:

a   **Once Around**   Denon (J) LP: YX-7557
b   Back Bone

All tracks on Nippon-Columbia Denon (J) LP: YP-7046-N, Denon
(J) LP: YX-7557-ND, Columbia-Nippon (J) CD: COCB-53510, Colum-
bia-Nippon (J) CD: COCY-80752.
See 740312.

THAD JONES-MEL LEWIS
740328
28-31 March 1974, private recordings, Jazz Showcase, Chicago: Thad
Jones flh; Jon Faddis, Steve Furtado, Jim Bossy, Cecil Bridgewater tp;
Jimmy Knepper, Billy Campbell, Quentin Jackson tb; Cliff Heather btb;
Jerry Dodgion ss, as, fl; Ed Xiques ss, as, cl, fl; Billy Harper ts, fl; Ron
Bridgewater ts, cl; Pepper Adams bs; Roland Hanna p; George Mraz b;
Mel Lewis dm.

See Author's Note above 580000A.

THAD JONES-MEL LEWIS
740406
6 April 1974, audience recording, Pampa Lanes, Warren MI: Same as 28
March 1974, except Lew Soloff tp for Bossy, Benny Powell tb for
Campbell, Billy Mitchell ts for Harper, Stanley Cowell p for Hanna, Per-
cy Brice dm for Lewis; Thad Jones perc*:

a   **Come Sunday**
b   **Fingers**
c   Suite for Pops:
        Meetin' Place
        The Summary
        The Farewell
d   **Tow Away Zone**
e   Samba con Getchu*
f   I Love You[1]
g   Say It Softly
h   Quietude
i   Don't Ever Leave Me
j   A–That's Freedom
k   Kids Are Pretty People
m   Don't Git Sassy

[1]Feature for Jones and rhythm section.

This is the only known time that Mel Lewis missed a Thad Jones-
Mel Lewis Orchestra gig outside New York. This gig follows a long
stretch of work for the band, beginning with running back and forth from
New York to Philadelphia for a gig and recording 16-20 February. Then,

starting on 21 February, a six-week tour to Miami, San Francisco, Tokyo and Nagoya ensued, then back home through San Francisco, Los Angeles, San Jose, Denver, and Chicago, returning Monday night to the Village Vanguard on 1 April. It could be that, after this long stretch, Lewis (and Roland Hanna too) needed a week off, possibly for personal issues, before resuming with the band on 8 April.

This is also Adams' only known solos on Fingers and Tow Away Zone. It could be due to Lewis and Roland Hanna's absence, because simpler tunes were chosen for this gig, probably to assist the new rhythm section, and so that Adams still had features to perform for his hometown Detroit friends and fans.

ARIF MARDIN
740501
1 May 1974, New York: Overdubs: Marvin Stamm, Mel Davis tp; Tony Studd tb; Frank Wess, David Newman as; Seldon Powell ts; Pepper Adams bs; Arif Mardin e-p, arr; David Spinozza g; Ron Carter b; Grady Tate dm; Ursula Dudziak voc.

a   27698   A Sunday Afternoon Feeling   Atlantic LP: SD-1661
b   28433   Journey   Atlantic unissued

Original tracks recorded in New York on 17 October 1973 and 22 February 1974: Randy Brecker tp; Joe Farrell ts; Milcho Leviev p; Ken Bichel e-p, synth; Alex Blake e-b; Billy Cobham dm; Michal Urbaniak vln.
-a on Atlantic (I) LP: K-50089, Wounded Bird CD: WOU-661.

DAVID AMRAM
740506
6 May 1974, private recording, New York University's Loeb Student Center, New York: David Amram frh, fl; Jerry Dodgion as; Pepper Adams bs; Herb Bushler -e-b, voc; Al Harewood dm; Leonard Maltin mc.

Impresario Jack Kleinsinger would morph his concert series into *Highlights in Jazz. See* 781215.

THAD JONES-MEL LEWIS
740508
8-10 May 1974, New York: Thad Jones flh; Jon Faddis, Steve Furtado,

Jim Bossy, Cecil Bridgewater tp; Jimmy Knepper, Billy Campbell, Quentin Jackson tb; Cliff Heather btb; Jerry Dodgion ss, as, fl; Ed Xiques ss, as, cl, fl; Billy Harper ts, fl; Ron Bridgewater ts, cl; Pepper Adams bs; Roland Hanna p; George Mraz b; Mel Lewis dm.

A&M-Horizon unissued.

ESTHER PHILLIPS
740516
16 May 1974, Van Gelder Studio, Englewood Cliffs NJ: Overdubs: Marvin Stamm, Jon Faddis, John Gatchell tp, flh; Urbie Green tb; Hubert Laws fl; Jerry Dodgion as; Michael Brecker ts; Pepper Adams bs, Pee Wee Ellis chimes.

a	RVG98778	Such a Night	CTI LP: 63036
b		Doing Our Thing*	
c		Mr. Bojangles	CTI unissued
d	RVG98779	Disposable Society	CTI LP: 63036

-a, -b, and -c originally recorded at Van Gelder Studio, Englewood Cliffs NJ, on 1 May 1974: Richard Wyands p; Richard Tee p; Charlie Brown g; Gordon Edwards*, Gary King e-b; Bernard Purdie dm; Ralph MacDonald perc; Esther Phillips voc. Vocal choir and strings added on subsequent sessions.
-d originally recorded at Van Gelder Studio, Englewood Cliffs NJ, on 3 May 1974: Richard Wyands p; Bob James e-p; Richie Resnicoff g; Gary King e-b; Steve Gadd dm, perc; Esther Phillips voc.
-a on Kudu LP: KU-18.
-b on Kudu LP: KU-18.
-c on CBS CD: ZK-45483.
-d on Kudu LP: KU-18, CBS CD: ZK-45483.

PEPPER ADAMS-ZOOT SIMS
740524
c. 24 or 25 May 1974, audience recording, Three Sisters, West Paterson NJ: Zoot Sims ts; Pepper Adams bs; possibly Jimmy Rowles p; unknown b; unknown dm.

Jerry MacDonald, owner of Choice Records, had this tape in his collection at the time of his death.

TEO MACERO
740529

29 May 1974, CBS Studio, New York: Don Palmer ss; Phil Woods, Lee Konitz, Teo Macero as; Al Cohn, George Young ts; Pepper Adams bs; Benny Aronov e-p; Joe Beck g; Michael Moore b; Jimmy Madison dm; Teddi King voc.*

a	**Sax Fifth Avenue**	Teo CD: SAX-003
b	Edward	Teo unissued
c	Love Song	Teo CD: SAX-003
d	**Comp**	
e	Sensuous Holiday	
f	Hello Person*	
g	Lucy Skelton	
h	Girl from Sad County*	
i	**Jeannie**	

In a 1989 interview with the author, Don Palmer said about this session:

> It was done in the studio, where they had an audience. It was Teo's compositions....There were a lot of rehearsals for that Teo Macero date, and I remember it was fun to be there because I was, more or less, the kid in the band, at that point, and all these guys would tell stories of when they did this or that or the other thing....When [Teo] was mixing these pieces—I don't know if I mentioned something, or what got him to say this, but—he said, "I sure like a lot of baritone on the bottom!" He had the baritone very prominent in the mix. Teo says in that [*Down Beat* review] somewhere that it was Ellington's gig at the Rainbow Room, where he went in there with, I think, maybe a sax section and the rhythm section—a small band anyway, an eight or nine piece band—that inspired Teo to put together this band.

Arnold Jay Smith wrote in *Down Beat* that Don Palmer also played tenor sax at the concert and that Stan Getz played tenor as a special guest. This date was first released in 2002.

740613
13 June 1974, Van Gelder Studio, Englewood Cliffs NJ: Overdubs: Pepper Adams bs; other musicians.

Adams' appointment book cites a CTI session from 2-5pm.

THAD JONES-MEL LEWIS
740627
27 June 1974, TROS-NOS radio broadcast, De Oranjerie, Roermond, Netherlands: Thad Jones flh; Jon Faddis, Steve Furtado, Jim Bossy, Cecil Bridgewater tp; Jimmy Knepper, Billy Campbell, Quentin Jackson tb; Dave Taylor btb; Jerry Dodgion ss, as, fl; Ed Xiques ss, as, cl, fl; Billy Harper ts, fl; Ron Bridgewater ts, cl; Pepper Adams bs; Walter Norris p; George Mraz b; Mel Lewis dm.

a   The Second Race
b   Willow Weep for Me
c   Tiptoe
d   Central Park North
e   **Once Around**

THAD JONES-MEL LEWIS
740629
29 June 1974, AVRO TV broadcast, Theater Het Spant, Bussum, Netherlands: Same as 27 June 1974:

a   Blues in a Minute
b   **Once Around**
c   A Child Is Born
d   The Intimacy of the Blues
e   It Only Happens Every Time
f   Tiptoe

It's unclear if video still exists.

THAD JONES-MEL LEWIS
740630
30 June 1974, NRK TV broadcast, Kongsberg Jazz Festival, Kongsberg, Norway: Same as 27 June 1974:

a   Central Park North
b   Willow Weep for Me
c   Only for Now
d   Don't Git Sassy

It's unclear if video still exists.

THAD JONES-MEL LEWIS
740701
1 July 1974, audience recording, Club 7, Oslo: Same as 27 June 1974.

THAD JONES-MEL LEWIS
740705
5 July 1974, RTSR TV broadcast, Congress Hall, Montreux: Same as 27 June 1974; add Dee Dee Bridgewater voc*:

a   Tiptoe
b   It Only Happens Every Time
c   Suite for Pops:
            Meetin' Place
            Only for Now
            The Farewell
d   Pensive Miss
e   Blues in a Minute
f   I Love You
g   **Once Around**
h   Every Day I Have the Blues*
i   Here's that Rainy Day*
j   River's Invitation*
k   **How Insensitive***[1]
m   Fingers
n   The Intimacy of the Blues

[1]Various bandmembers play percussion instruments during Adams' solo.

-a, -b, -d on Blu Jazz (Ger) CD: BJO-32-CD.
It's unclear if video still exists.

THAD JONES-MEL LEWIS
740712
12 July 1974, audience recording, Montmartre Jazzhus, Copenhagen:
Same as 27 June 1974; add Dee Dee Bridgewater voc*:

a   Bächafillen
b   Three in One
c   How Insensitive*[1]
d   Come on Over My Love*
e   Once Around
f   Ambiance
g   Living for the City
h   All My Yesterdays
i   Here's that Rainy Day*
j   Every Day I Have the Blues*
k   Backbone
m   St. Louis Blues
n   A Child Is Born
o   Fingers
p   Quiet Nights*
q   Get Out of My Life Woman*
r   The Groove Merchant

[1]Various bandmembers play percussion instruments during Adams' solo.

THAD JONES-MEL LEWIS
740713
13 July 1974, SR radio broadcast, Folkets Park, Åhus Jazz Festival,
Åhus, Sweden: Same as 27 June 1974; add Dee Dee Bridgewater voc*:

a   The Second Race
b   Willow Weep for Me
c   **The Little Pixie**
d   Central Park North
e   Bye Bye Blackbird*
f   Get Out of My Life Woman*
g   unknown title
h   Living for the City
i   Ambiance
j   Blues in a Minute

k   **Quiet Lady**

THAD JONES-MEL LEWIS
740718
18 July 1974, BR radio broadcast, Domicile, Munich: Same as 27 June 1974; add Dee Dee Bridgewater voc*:

a   A Child Is Born
b   Here's that Rainy Day*
c   Bye Bye Blackbird*
d   Fingers
e   unknown title
f   Ambiance
g   Kansas City*
h   Didn't Ya*
i   St. Louis Blues

This was recorded during the band's engagement from 15-23 July.

OLAF STILETTI
740719
c. 19 July 1974, Munich: Overdubs: Cecil Bridgewater, Jim Bossy tp; Billy Campbell tb; Ed Xiques reeds; Pepper Adams bs.

a   Funky Entertainer   Warner Brothers LP: WB-56-073Y
b   Golden Age of Rock'n Roll
c   (I Can't Get No) Satisfaction
d   Nights in White Satin
e   It's Only Rock'n Roll
f   White Room
g   Living for the City
h   Papa Was a Rolling Stone
i   Jim Dandy
j   With a Little Help from My Friends

Original tracks recorded at Union Studio, Munich c. 1974: Olaf Stiletti ss, ts, fl; Gottfried Böttger, Thor Baldurson keyboards; Karl Allaut g; Lothar Meid b; Keith Forsey dm.

THAD JONES
740728
28 July 1974, RAI radio broadcast, Umbria Jazz Festival, Todi, Italy:
Thad Jones cornet; Jerry Dodgion as, fl; Pepper Adams bs; Roland Hanna p; George Mraz b; Mel Lewis dm.

a   **Straight, No Chaser**
b   **Alone Together**
c   **Autumn Leaves**
d   **What Is This Thing Called Love**

-b on soundtrack to the film *Jazz in Piazza,* directed by Pino Adriano. *See 740729.*

THAD JONES-MEL LEWIS
740729
29 July 1974, RAI radio broadcast, Umbria Jazz Festival, Perugia, Italy:
Same as 27 June 1974; add Dee Dee Bridgewater voc*:

a   **Once Around**
b   Tiptoe
c   Ambiance
d   Blues in a Minute
e   By The Time I Get to Phoenix*
f   Every Day I Have the Blues*
g   Fingers
h   **The Little Pixie**

-h on Pausa LP: PR-7012, Teldec (Ger) LP: 6-22663, Produttori Associati (It) LP: PA-63, and on the soundtrack to the film *Jazz in Piazza,* directed by Pino Adriano. *See 740728.*

BENNY CARTER
741023
23 October 1974, film soundtrack, A&R Studios, New York: Thad Jones flh; Jon Faddis, Steve Furtado, Jim Bossy, Cecil Bridgewater tp; Jimmy Knepper, Billy Campbell, Quentin Jackson tb; Dave Taylor btb; Jerry Dodgion ss, as, fl; Ed Xiques ss, as, cl, fl; Billy Harper ts, fl; Ron Bridgewater ts, cl; Pepper Adams bs; Walter Norris p; George Mraz b; Mel Lewis dm; unknown voc; Benny Carter cond.

Soundtrack to the animated children's film *People People People,* directed by John and Faith Hubley, with music arranged and conducted by Benny Carter.

According to Ed Xiques, in an interview with the author in 1988, "I was so thrilled to do that. He used Thad's band to do this Bicentennial film. It was beautiful! It seemed to go very smoothly, as I recall, and Benny is such a gentleman and a wonderful musician. It was just a pleasure. I felt great being part of it....We didn't rehearse, as I recall. We just went in, we had the charts, and we played it."

THAD JONES-MEL LEWIS
741108
8-9 November 1974, PBS TV broadcast, Rochester NY: Thad Jones flh; Jon Faddis, Steve Furtado, Jim Bossy, Cecil Bridgewater tp; Jimmy Knepper, Billy Campbell, Quentin Jackson tb; Dave Taylor btb; Jerry Dodgion ss, as, fl; Ed Xiques ss, as, cl, fl; Billy Harper ts, fl; Ron Bridgewater ts, cl; Pepper Adams bs; Walter Norris p; George Mraz b; Mel Lewis dm.

According to John Faddis, in an interview with the author in 1988, the band played on the top floor of a hotel for the program *Live from the Top.* It's unclear if audio or video still exists.

THAD JONES-MEL LEWIS
741127
27-30 November 1974, private recordings, Jazz Showcase, Chicago: Same as 8 November 1974.

See Author's Note above 580000A.

THAD JONES-MEL LEWIS
750126
26 January 1975, audience recording, Music Hall Ballroom, Cincinnati: Same as 8 November 1974.

THAD JONES-MEL LEWIS
750130
30 January 1975, TV broadcast, Los Angeles: Same as 8 November 1974.

It's unclear if audio or video still exist.

PEPPER ADAMS
750209
9 February 1975, private recording, Bach Dynamite and Dancing Society, Half Moon Bay CA: Pepper Adams bs; John Marabuto p; George Mraz b; Ron Marabuto dm.

a　**Mean What You Say**
b　**Quiet Lady**
c　**Civilization and Its Discontents**
d　**Three Little Words**
e　**Sophisticated Lady**
f　**Ephemera**
g　**'Tis**

PEPPER ADAMS
750420
20 April 1975, audience recording, St. James Infirmary, New York: Tommy Turrentine, Lonnie Hillyer tp†; Pepper Adams bs; Hod O'Brien p; unknown p*; Cameron Brown b; Jimmy Lovelace, Zahir Batin dm.

Adams and rhythm section:
a　**High Step**
b　**Civilization and Its Discontents**
c　**'Tis**
d　**Moment's Notice**
e　**Sophisticated Lady**
f　**On Green Dolphin Street†**
g　**What Is This Thing Called Love†**
h　**'Tis †**
i　**Parisian Thoroughfare*†**

According to David Amram, in an interview with the author in 1988, St. James Infirmary "was about the size of five or six phone booths. It was the tiniest place. I think it held sixty people when it was packed. That was just before Seventh Avenue started getting all the jazz places."

PEPPER ADAMS
750517
17 May 1975, private recording, Gulliver's, West Paterson NJ: Pepper
Adams bs; Tommy Flanagan p; George Mraz b; Al Harewood dm.

a   **Afternoon in Paris**
b   **How Am I to Know**
c   **Cherokee**
d   **Ephemera**
e   **A Child Is Born**
f   **Half Nelson**
g   **Falling in Love with Love**
h   unknown title[1]
i   **What Is This Thing Called Love**
j   **I Let a Song Go Out of My Heart**

[1]Rhythm section only.

DIZZY GILLESPIE
750703
3 July 1975, private recording, Buddy's Place, New York: Jon Faddis tp;
Dizzy Gillespie tp, perc; unknown tp section; Melba Liston tb; unknown
tb section; Billy Mitchell as; Buddy Pierson as, fl; Jimmy Heath ts, fl;
Turk Mauro ts; Pepper Adams bs; Mike Longo p; Milt Jackson vib*; Ben
Brown e-b; Mickey Roker dm; Azzedin Weston perc.

a   **Una Mas**
b   Whisper Not
c   Lover Come Back to Me
d   Things to Come*
     Jackson and rhythm section:
e   Poor Butterfly*
f   Speedball*
     Full orchestra:
g   Manteca*

Recorded during Gillespie's two-week engagement from 25 June-9
July.

THAD JONES-MEL LEWIS – SUITE FOR POPS
750722

22 July 1975, A&R Studios, New York: Thad Jones flh, cornet; Jon Faddis, Lew Soloff, Steve Furtado, Jim Bossy, Cecil Bridgewater tp; Billy Campbell, Janice Robinson, Earl McIntyre tb; Dave Taylor btb; Peter Gordon, Earl Chapin, Julius Watkins, Jim Buffington, Ray Alonge frh; Don Butterfield tuba; Jerry Dodgion, Ed Xiques as, fl; Lou Marini cl, ts, fl; Gregory Herbert ts, fl; Pepper Adams bs; Roland Hanna e-p; Steve Gilmore b; Jerry Jemmott e-b△; David Spinozza g√; Mel Lewis, Herb Lovelle dm, perc◊; Leonard Gibbs cga†.

a	The Farewell†	A&M-Horizon LP: SP-701
b	Greetings and Salutations	A&M-Horizon unissued
c	**Forever Lasting**√△◊[1]	
d	Love to One Is One to Love◊[2]	

[1]Buffington and Butterfield out.

-a on A&M-Horizon (F) LP: 985023, A&M (Neth) LP: 701, Horizon-King (J) LP: GP-3501, Horizon-Canyon (J) CD: D23Y-3821, Horizon (J) CD: POCM-5047.

Parts of -b, -c, -d have been spliced onto the released version of their respective titles. For other takes of these tunes, that are also part of the released versions on A&M-Horizon LP: SP-707, see 751216 and 760108 for -b, 760108 for -c, and 751217b for -d. The released versions of -b, -c, -d are on A&M-Horizon LP: SP-707, A&M-Horizon (Eng/Neth) LP: AMJL-707, Canyon (J) LP: D32Y-3822, Canyon (J) LP: D22Y-3911, Horizon (YU) LP: 4374, A&M-Horizon CD: CD-0810.

According to Ed Xiques regarding -a (The Farewell), "the one thing that's a shame," he told the author, in an interview in 1988, "is that [Quentin] Butter [Jackson] is replaced by Janice [Robinson]....The one thing that was a letdown was that she played those plunger solos and he wasn't there....She wasn't really into it. It might have been Butter that told me this, but she sort of fluffed it off, when he tried to show her the secrets of how to do that....We had done the record [in 1972], and something was screwed up, and we had to go back in and do it over again, and he couldn't be there, for some reason, to do some tracks over again."

Steve Gilmore told the author, in an interview in 1989, that he played with the band for approximately ten months. "I think the guy who recommended me," Gilmore said, "was Jerry Dodgion....Jerry and I are old friends." Gilmore and George Mraz shared bass duties through 1975 until Bob Bowman joined the band in 1976.

PEPPER ADAMS–JULIAN/TWELFTH AND PINGREE
750813
13 August 1975, Domicile, Munich: Pepper Adams bs; Walter Norris p; George Mraz b; Makaya Ntshoko dm.

a	**Jirge**	Enja (Ger) LP: 2060
b	**Julian**	
c	**Spacemaker**	
d	**Ad Astra**	
e	**Three and One**	
f	**'Tis**	
g	**Marmaduke**	Enja unissued
h	**Time on My Hands**	
i	**Time on My Hands**	Enja (Ger) CD: 9115-2
j	**Lady Luck**[1]	
k	**Twelfth and Pingree**	Enja (Ger) LP: 2074
m	**A Child Is Born**	
n	**Well, You Needn't**	
o	**Bossa Nouveau**	

[1]Duo for Adams and Mraz.

Recorded during Adams' two-week engagement, c. 25 July–13 August, these are Adams' fourteenth and fifteenth dates as a leader.

-b, -c, -e, and -g were broadcast on radio; -h and other tunes were broadcast on television. It's unclear if video still exists.

-a, -b, -c, -d, -e, -f on Inner City LP: IC-3014, Victor (J) LP: SMJ-6126.

-k, -m, -n, -o on Enja (Ger) CD: ENJ-9079-2, Victor (J) LP: SMJ-6160, Tokuma (J) CD: TKCD-32195.

On a 27 April 1977 Toronto radio interview, conducted by Ted O'Reilly, Pepper Adams explained how this date came about:

> [It was] the result of a mix-up....Thad and Mel's band was scheduled to go to Europe in June sometime, I believe, so Walter and George went to Munich about three weeks early to play a couple of weeks of duo at Club Domicile, and then they would have a week

off, and, with a couple of concerts in there, meet Thad and Mel's band. So everything was fine until Thad and Mel's band changed their itinerary and did not go until sometime in the middle of July, which left George and Walter in Munich with no gigs, waiting for the band to arrive. The owner of Domicile, Ernst Knauff, figured he could not really afford to have the duo in the club again so soon, since they had just done two full weeks there, so they got on the phone and called me in New York and suggested this would be a way to bail them out as well. If I would come over, they would add a drummer and we'd do a couple of weeks with the quartet, and this would bring them up to the time where the band would actually arrive and bail them out. It was great with me. It worked fine! Actually, it was about three weeks that we did with the quartet, and, with only about three or four days remaining, the representatives of Enja came in and suggested recording live in the club one album, which eventually became two albums....We had started the gig with Billy Brooks playing drums. He could not make about the last four days of the gig, and this is when Enja decided they wanted to record, and it was their suggestion that we use Makaya, which worked reasonably well.

According to Walter Norris, in an interview with the author in 1988,

The producers, Matthias Wincklemann and Horst Weber, were committed to other projects, so, when the pianist-composer Gerhard Francesconi suggested that they record Pepper, their answer was, "No." So, Francesconi, who had been listening to most of our evenings at the Domicile, proposed that Enja record live at the club, and he, Francesconi, would finance the recorded effort. Just like that! This guy is really something! But the owner of the Domicile, Ernst Knauff, objected to our having a recording made in his club, because groups want to repeat so many of the titles, that most of the audience become bored and soon leave. Well, we recorded everything with one take for each title. One take, except there was a title without piano [-h]....On this they used the second take, but the first take was good enough. So the whole night just went really great musically! Everyone involved, including the audience, was happy....One must admire the pioneering spirit of Gerhard Francesconi. He was fantastic for that! He just felt that it should be recorded, and he wanted it recorded, even if he had to pay the money, which he did, and I think he got his money back....

Pepper was a very intense performer and he always gave more than the 100% that most players wish for. He really thought of improvisation as an art, and it's never to be fitted in a category. I think a lot of people think of improvisation as a sport. I think so: As a way of kicking the ball or something. In other words, they're not thinking of it so much as art. I mean, Charlie Parker was really the first one to come along and think of it as an art. I say "art" because Pepper was so well read and Pepper was an intellectual by nature. It was just in his bones. At the same time, Pepper had a real down-to-earth attitude of making the damn music *work;* make it turn out right. This could be like a very skilled, working class attitude of, "Let's put this thing together and do the damn thing right!" He had a really good combination of these two elements, that are kind of extreme from each other, where he wanted the notes to be *really* well-chosen, really good, artistically valid. This showed up, of course, in his compositions, just like his playing.

George Mraz told the author, in an interview in 1988,

It was fun. There was a lot of reading, but we just went through it that afternoon—all of Pepper's tunes. There was a lot of interesting bass parts. I liked it. It kind of reminded me of Thad's lines for bass: good register, interesting rhythmically, also melodically. It made sense, but it was a little different than most people's writing. I don't know whether it had anything to do with harmony that much. It was just the way he heard it, more the lines themselves, because the harmonies were basic, although sometimes he threw in some unusual, indescribable turns.

THAD JONES-MEL LEWIS
750826
26 August 1975, YLE radio broadcast, Hotel Hesperia, Helsinki: Thad Jones flh; Jon Faddis, Lew Soloff, Jim Bossy, Cecil Bridgewater tp; Billy Campbell, Janice Robinson, Sam Burtis tb; Earl McIntyre btb; Jerry Dodgion, Ed Xiques ss, as, fl; Frank Foster ts; Gregory Herbert ts, fl; Pepper Adams bs; Walter Norris p; George Mraz b; Mel Lewis dm.

a   Mean What You Say
b   Pensive Miss
c   Tiptoe
d   All My Yesterdays

e   61st and Richard
f   **Once Around**
g   **The Little Pixie**
h   Lover Man
i   Central Park North
j   **Little Rascal on a Rock**
k   A Child Is Born
m   Fingers
n   Greetings and Salutations

THAD JONES-MEL LEWIS
750829
29 August 1975, SR radio broadcast, Estrad Concert Hall, Södertälje, Sweden: Same as 26 August 1975:

a   Mean What You Say
b   **Once Around**
c   Yours and Mine
d   A–That's Freedom
e   **The Little Pixie**

THAD JONES-MEL LEWIS
750830
30 August 1975, DR radio broadcast, Værkstedet, Holbæk, Denmark: Same as 26 August 1975:

a   **Once Around**
b   Willow Tree
c   Mornin' Reverend
d   Kids Are Pretty People
e   Bächafillen
f   The Second Race
g   Samba con Getchu
h   The Waltz You "Swang" for Me

THAD JONES-MEL LEWIS
750831
31 August 1975, audience recording, Montmartre Jazzhus, Copenhagen: Same as 26 August 1975:

a   Big Dipper
b   Mornin' Reverend
c   It Only Happens Every Time
d   unknown title

THAD JONES-MEL LEWIS
750902
2 September 1975, DR TV broadcast, Graabroedre Torv, Copenhagen:
Same as 26 August 1975:

a   Mean What You Say
b   A—That's Freedom
c   Don't Git Sassy

It's unclear if video still exists.

THAD JONES-MEL LEWIS
750909
9 September 1975, BR radio broadcast, Domicile, Munich: Same as 26
August 1975:

a   Suite for Pops:
         Meetin' Place
         The Summary
         The Farewell
b   Big Dipper
c   Blues in a Minute
d   All My Yesterdays
e   Us[1]

[1]Most of the band plays various percussion instruments.

This was broadcast during the band's engagement on 5-9 September.

THAD JONES-MEL LEWIS
750915
mid-September 1975, BR radio broadcast, Domicile, Munich: Same as
26 August 1975:

a   Big Dipper

b   Backbone
c   A–That's Freedom

THAD JONES-MEL LEWIS
750926
26 September 1975, CTVSC TV broadcast, Los Angeles: Thad Jones cornet, flh; Jon Faddis tp; Waymon Reed tp, flh; Jim Bossy, Cecil Bridgewater tp; Bob Brookmeyer vtb; Billy Campbell, Janice Robinson tb; Earl McIntyre btb; Jerry Dodgion, Ed Xiques ss, as, fl; Ron Bridgewater, Billy Harper ts; Pepper Adams bs; Walter Norris p, e-p; George Mraz b; Mel Lewis dm; Juanita Fleming voc.*

a   **The Little Pixie**   Kay Jazz (Eng) unissued
b   Central Park North[1]
c   Suite for Pops: Kay Jazz (Eng) VHS: KJ-092
        Meetin' Place
        Only for Now
        The Farewell
d   Here's that Rainy Day*   Kay Jazz (Eng) unissued
e   Fingers
f   A Child Is Born

[1]Most of the band plays various percussion instruments.

According to Cecil Bridgewater, in an interview with the author in 1989,

> Ron [Bridgewater] and Billy Harper got fired about the same time. Part of the deal was they weren't smiling enough or something. That's what was said. I don't think Thad was too unhappy with the way they were playing. I don't think that was it. The story went that Billy didn't want to play on a song or something, and he'd look at my brother and see if he wanted to play on it at that time. It was something backwards like that. I think they wanted Gregory Herbert to come into the band, for his experience and so forth and so on. Ron had taken off to do some things with McCoy Tyner, and Gregory came in and filled in for him. Ron and I had been rooming together, so Gregory and I ended up rooming together. We were down in Miami. We did something down there, then went on to St. Louis, I believe. Ron had taken that time off, and then they decided they wanted to keep Gregory, I think, in the band, so they finally let Ron

go. I can't remember exactly how they told him, but he wasn't all that displeased about it. It was a drag to be fired, but he said, "O.K.," because he had another gig. It wasn't that bad.

I remember [Billy's firing.] What happened was it was a Monday night at the Vanguard, and Thad, I guess, devised a plan by which [band manager] Sherman Darby was going to fire Billy, and then he was supposed to tell Billy to go talk with Thad, and then Thad was going to hire him back, but he was going to explain some things to him, because they weren't happy with the fact that Billy didn't seem to be enjoying being in the band. He wasn't smiling and happy, and so forth and so on, but that was pretty much just Billy's way. Ever since I've known him, he's been that way. The thing that happened was Thad and Billy had the conversation *before* Sherman fired him, and Sherman didn't know that, so Sherman told Billy he was fired, and Mel was standing there. Billy said, "Mel, did you hear what he said?" and Mel said, "Well, uh, yeah, yeah, um—." He said, "Well, am I fired?" He said, "Well, yeah, but why don't you go talk to Thad." He said, "No! Does Sherman have the right to fire me?" and Mel said, "Well, yes," and he said, "Well, then I'm fired!" and he said, "Well, no, why don't you talk to Thad about it!" etc, etc. He said, "No, if Sherman says I'm fired, then I'm fired!" and that was where Billy left it. He said, "Fine, thank you," because Thad and Billy had already had their conversation, for whatever it was worth. I don't know what their conversation consisted of. I think Billy may have been ready to go out of the band anyway. He had some other projects he was working on, with his own group, and he and I were working with Max [Roach] at the time, so it didn't throw him off too badly. He just felt, "Well, O.K., you thought you were going to pull one on me? I got you."

THAD JONES-MEL LEWIS
750928
28 September 1975, private recording, Famous Ballroom, Baltimore:
Thad Jones flh; Jim Bossy, Waymon Reed, Steve Furtado, Cecil Bridgewater tp; Billy Campbell, Alex Kofman, Janice Robinson tb; Earl McIntyre btb; Jerry Dodgion ss, as, fl; Ed Xiques ss, as, cl; Gregory Herbert ts, ss, cl, fl; Frank Foster ts, ss, cl; Pepper Adams bs; Walter Norris p; George Mraz b; Mel Lewis dm.

Recorded by the Left Bank Jazz Society. *See* 650314.

THAD JONES-MEL LEWIS
751026
26 October 1975, FM-Tokyo radio broadcast, Tokyo: Thad Jones flh; Al Porcino, Waymon Reed, Sinclair Acey, Cecil Bridgewater tp; Billy Campbell, Janice Robinson, John Mosca tb; Earl McIntyre btb; Jerry Dodgion as, ss, fl; Ed Xiques as, fl; Frank Foster ts; Gregory Herbert ts, fl; Pepper Adams bs; Walter Norris p; George Mraz b; Mel Lewis dm.

According to the Thad Jones-Mel Lewis Orchestra 1975 Japan Tour itinerary, as prepared by All Art Promotion, the band had a live studio appearance from 3-4pm, listed as "Denon Live Concert." It's unclear if this was intended for commercial release, or if audio still exists. (*See also* 751102.) This appearance was the first performance of the band's four-week tour of Japan. Vocalist Juanita Fleming joined the band in California for the Japanese tour.

According to John Mosca, in an interview with the author in 1988, "I think I was replacing Alex Kofman," said Mosca. Kofman was

a Russian immigrant, and he couldn't get a visa to go to Japan.... When I started playing on the band, I was playing third trombone, and I thought my part was the most important part in the band. And I'm sure everybody else felt that way about his part. That was something that I've heard Clark Terry say about Duke Ellington too. He'd ask everybody, "Do you like your part? How do you feel about your part?" Even inside guys too. [Thad Jones and Duke Ellington] are two guys operating on the same level compositionally. They would write for guys in the band. There *are* certain things that were written for Pepper, obviously. Some of these things with complex changes, you could tell they were right down the middle of the plate for Pepper. They were just perfect for him. But Thad, being a big band veteran himself, knew that guys come and go, so things were adaptable.

THAD JONES-MEL LEWIS
751101
1 November 1975, audience recording, Hitot-Subashi University, Tokyo: Same as 26 October 1975:

a   Us[1]
b   Kids Are Pretty People
c   The Groove Merchant

d   Willow Tree
e   Don't Git Sassy

[1]Most of the band plays various percussion instruments.

THAD JONES-MEL LEWIS
751102
2 November 1975, FM-Tokyo radio broadcast, Tokyo: Same as 26 October 1975:

According to the Thad Jones-Mel Lewis Orchestra 1975 Japan Tour itinerary, as prepared by All Art Promotion, the band had a second FM-Tokyo live studio appearance from 3-4pm. As before (*see* 751026), it was promoted by Denon, though it's unclear whether this was intended for commercial release, or if the audio still exists.

THAD JONES-MEL LEWIS
751105
5 November 1975, audience recording, Gunma Kenminkaikan Hall, Maebashi, Japan: Same as 26 October 1975:

a   Quietude
b   The Waltz You "Swang" for Me
c   Bächafillen
d   The Groove Merchant
e   **Little Rascal on a Rock**
f   Giant Steps
g   Greetings and Salutations

THAD JONES-MEL LEWIS
751106
6 November 1975, audience recording, Festival Hall, Osaka: Same as 26 October 1975:

a   **Once Around**
b   **Quiet Lady**
c   Willow Weep for Me
d   Central Park North
e   Suite for Pops:
         Meetin' Place

The Summary
The Farewell
f   Tow Away Zone

THAD JONES-MEL LEWIS
751107
7 November 1975, audience recording, Ishibashi Bunka Hall, Karume, Japan: Same as 26 October 1975:

a   **Once Around**
b   Fingers
c   Big Dipper
d   Willow Weep for Me
e   Samba con Getchu
f   Ambiance
g   Second Race
h   Blues in a Minute
i   Only for Now

THAD JONES-MEL LEWIS
751108
8 November 1975, audience recording, Ken Bunka Center, Kagoshima, Japan: Same as 26 October 1975:

a   Mean What You Say
b   It Only Happens Every Time
c   Tiptoe
d   **Thank You**
e   Giant Steps
f   Suite for Pops:
     Meetin' Place
     The Summary
     The Farewell
g   Fingers
h   Intimacy of the Blues

THAD JONES-MEL LEWIS
751110
10 November 1975, audience recording, Kenmin Kaikan, Toyama, Japan: Same as 26 October 1975:

a   **Three and One**
b   Mean What You Say
c   A Child Is Born
d   Central Park North
e   **Us**[1]
f   Yours and Mine
g   Say It Softly
h   Ambiance

[1]Most of the band plays various percussion instruments.

THAD JONES-MEL LEWIS
751111
11 November 1975, audience recording, Sangyo Kaigan, Kyoto: Same as 26 October 1975:

a   The Second Race
b   It Only Happens Every Time
c   St. Louis Blues
d   Willow Tree
e   Don't Git Sassy
f   **Once Around**
g   **Little Rascal on a Rock**
h   Backbone
i   Fingers

THAD JONES-MEL LEWIS
751112
12 November 1975, audience recording, Shi Kokaido, Nagoya, Japan: Same as 26 October 1975, add Juanita Fleming voc*:

a   The Groove Merchant
b   Kids Are Pretty People
c   The Waltz You "Swang" for Me
d   **Thank You**
e   **The Little Pixie**
f   Giant Steps
g   **Little Rascal on a Rock**
h   Bächafillen
i   Bye Bye Blackbird*

j   Until Its Time for Me to Go*
k   Bird of Beauty*
m   Don't Git Sassy
n   Fingers

FRANK FOSTER–GIANT STEPS
751113
13 November 1975, Mouri Studio, Tokyo: Thad Jones flh*; Al Porcino, Waymon Reed, Sinclair Acey, Cecil Bridgewater tp; Billy Campbell, Janice Robinson, John Mosca tb; Earl McIntyre btb; Jerry Dodgion, Ed Xiques as, fl; Frank Foster ts, cl; Gregory Herbert ts, fl; Pepper Adams bs; Walter Norris p; George Mraz b; Mel Lewis dm.

a   Cecilia Is Love*   Nippon-Columbia Denon (J) LP: YQ-7522-AX
b   Japan Suite*:
        Shitsu-Mon (The Question)
        Tan-Kyu (The Search)
c   Giant Steps   Nippon-Columbia Denon (J) unissued

-a on Nippon-Columbia Denon (J) LP: YX-7576.
-b on Nippon-Columbia Denon (J) LP: YX-7576.
According to Frank Foster, in an interview with the author in 1989,

They wanted an album under my leadership—under my name—with my compositions and arrangements, and they wanted a big band, so we had the best one going at the time! They just had me take over that band for that one session. I had done three of these—Giant Steps, Now that She's Away, Cecilia Is Love [*see* 751117a]. The Japanese Suite I wrote while traveling through Japan, using the bullet [train], and the Japanese countryside, and the colorful scenes in the cities as inspiration: Speeding past Mount Fuji writing music! I thought it came out very good, because the band was of such quality that it couldn't have come out but so bad! I was very happy with the fact that I was able to finish these two tunes on a trip, because usually I can't finish nothing on a trip!

Cecil Bridgewater told the author, in an interview in 1989,

We were getting ready to do that *Giant Steps* album and Frank was working on the Japanese Suite that we did on there. He was sitting on the train, every day writing. He was writing like somebody else would write a letter. Frank is sitting there writing out the score, and he'd hand the score to Ed Xiques, who was doing the copying. When we got to where we were going, and we'd go play the concert, Frank would be up half the night writing, get on the train the next day, write some more, hand the scores to Ed, and Ed would copy them. He was writing without piano, without benefit of his horn or anything else. Thad did that a lot too, so, I think probably traveling with Basie year-round, they didn't have time to sit down near a rehearsal studio, or at their homes with a piano, and work out things. They got to the point where they could hear it in their heads and write it....I remember [on] the date that we did, Frank Foster's *Giant Steps* album, [Pepper] had a case of beer sitting there. He finished it off as we were doing the date, but it didn't seem to impair his abilities.

According to Ed Xiques, in an interview in 1988, Thad conducted the band for Frank Foster to enable Foster to play in the reed section. About Thad Jones, Xiques said, "It seemed like he was almost getting in the way, like sabotaging it, in a sense....Maybe Thad was jealous because he wasn't doing an album there? I don't know what was going on, but I remember talking to Jerry [Dodgion] about it. It was kind of subtle, more of an attitude. Maybe he could have been more helpful."

FRANK FOSTER – GIANT STEPS
751117a
17 November 1975, Mouri Studio, Tokyo: Same as 13 November 1975, Thad Jones flh*:

a   Giant Steps   Nippon-Columbia Denon (J) LP: YQ-7522
b   Now That She's Away*
c   Now That She's Away*   Nippon-Columbia Denon (J) unissued

All tracks on Nippon-Columbia Denon (J) LP: YX-7576.
See 751113.

THAD JONES-MEL LEWIS
751117b
17 November 1975, NHK radio broadcast, Yubin Chokin Hall, Tokyo: Same as 26 October 1975:

a   The Second Race

b Only for Now
c Don't Git Sassy
d 61st and Richard
e A Child Is Born
f Fingers
g Greetings and Salutations
h It Only Happens Every Time
i A-Hunk A-Hunk
j **Once Around**

THAD JONES-MEL LEWIS
751118
18 November 1975, audience recording, Shimin Kaikan, Sendai, Japan:
Same as 26 October 1975, add Juanita Fleming voc*:

a All My Yesterdays
b The Groove Merchant
c Willow Tree
d Samba con Getchu
e Cecilia Is Love
f **Thank You**
g Giant Steps
h Blues in G*
i Fingers
j Tow Away Zone
k **Us**[1]

[1]Most of the band plays various percussion instruments.

THAD JONES-MEL LEWIS
751119
19 November 1975, audience recording, Noguchi Hideyo Kinenkan, Tokyo: Same as 26 October 1975, add Juanita Fleming voc*:

a Blues in a Minute
b Yours and Mine
c **Quiet Lady**
d Willow Weep for Me
e Bächafillen
f Suite for Pops:

      Meetin' Place
      The Summary
      The Farewell
g   Until Its Time for Me to Go*
h   Medley*:
      Stormy Monday Blues
      Every Day I Have the Blues
      Kansas City
i   Tow Away Zone
j   Tow Away Zone

THAD JONES-MEL LEWIS
751120
20 November 1975, audience recording, Shi Kokaido, Niigata, Japan:
Same as 26 October 1975, add Juanita Fleming voc*:

a   A–That's Freedom
b   **Thank You**
c   St. Louis Blues
d   It Only Happens Every Time
e   Central Park North
f   Cecilia Is Love
g   Now that She's Away
h   Giant Steps
i   Bye Bye Blackbird*
j   Fingers
k   Greetings and Salutations

THAD JONES-MEL LEWIS
751122
22 November 1975, audience recording, Great American Music Hall,
San Francisco: Same as 26 October 1975:

a   Greetings and Salutations
b   Intimacy of the Blues
c   Evol Deklaw Ni (Love Walked In)
d   **Once Around**
e   A–That's Freedom
f   **Thank You**
g   Tiptoe

h   Samba con Getchu

PEPPER ADAMS
751123a
23 November 1975, audience recording, Bach Dynamite and Dancing Society, Half Moon Bay CA: Cecil Bridgewater tp; Jerry Dodgion as; Frank Foster ts, ss; Pepper Adams bs; John Marabuto p; George Mraz b; Ron Marabuto dm.

a   **Mean What You Say**[1]
b   Softly As in a Morning Sunrise[2]
c   **Donna Lee**[3]
d   **The Days of Wine and Roses**[4]
e   **What Is This Thing Called Love**[5]
f   **I Can't Get Started**[6]
g   **Oleo**[7]

[1]Full ensemble.
[2]Bridgewater, Dodgion and rhythm section.
[3]Full ensemble.
[4]Foster, Adams, and rhythm section.
[5]Full ensemble.
[6]Full ensemble.
[7]Foster, Adams, and rhythm section.

According to Cecil Bridgewater, in an interview with the author in 1989, "Thad was supposed to do that and, at the last minute, bowed out and put me in there."

THAD JONES-MEL LEWIS
751123b
23 November 1975, audience recording, Great American Music Hall, San Francisco: Same as 26 October 1975:

a   Big Dipper
b   Willow Weep for Me
c   Mean What You Say
d   It Only Happens Every Time
e   Cecilia Is Love
f   **Once Around**
g   Central Park North

h   **Thank You**
i   61st and Richard
j   The Second Race
k   A Child Is Born
m   Tow Away Zone
n   Greetings and Salutations
o   Only for Now
p   **Little Rascal on a Rock**
q   Giant Steps
r   Intimacy of the Blues

J.F.K. HIGH SCHOOL JAZZ BAND
751124a
24 November 1975, audience recording, John F. Kennedy High School, Richmond CA: J.F.K. High School Jazz Band; GUEST: Pepper Adams bs.

a   **Didi's Waltz**
b   **Didi's Waltz**

This was a high school clinic and a rehearsal for the school's concert later that evening. *See* 751124b.

PEPPER ADAMS
751124b
24 November 1975, audience recording, John F. Kennedy High School, Richmond CA: Pepper Adams bs; John Marabuto p; George Mraz b; Ron Marabuto dm; GUEST: Peter Apfelbaum ts.*

a   **Hellure**
b   **E-7/A7 Vamp**
c   **Wrap Your Troubles in Dreams**
d   **In a Sentimental Mood**
e   **Lester Leaps In***

See 751124a.

THAD JONES-MEL LEWIS
751127
27 November 1975, audience recording, La Bastille, Houston: Same as 26 October 1975; GUEST: Arnett Cobb ts*:

a The Second Race[*1]
b Blue and Sentimental[*2]
Cobb out:
c Backbone
d **Thank You**
e Cecilia Is Love
f Fingers

[1]Feature for Cobb and orchestra.
[2]Jones, Cobb, and rhythm section.

THAD JONES-MEL LEWIS
751128
28-30 November 1975, private recordings, Jazz Showcase, Chicago:
Same as 26 October 1975.

See Author's Note above 580000A.

THAD JONES-MEL LEWIS
751207
7 December 1975, audience recording, Clarenceville High School, Livonia MI: Same as 26 October 1975, except Ralph LaLama ts for Herbert, Steve Gilmore b for Mraz:

a **Once Around**
b Willow Weep for Me
c Tiptoe
d **Thank You**
e Giant Steps
f The Second Race
g Yours and Mine
h Central Park North[1]
i A Child Is Born
j Greetings and Salutations

[1]Jones and some bandmembers play various percussion instruments.

PEPPER ADAMS
751212
12 December 1975, audience recording, Three Sisters, West Paterson

NJ: Pepper Adams bs; Mike Melillo p; Steve Gilmore b; Bill Goodwin dm.

a   **Just Friends**
b   **Have You Called Her Today**
c   **Sweet Sue**
d   **Witchcraft**
e   **Well, You Needn't**
f   **Julian**
g   **Perdido**
h   **Alone Together**
i   **Bossa Nouveau**
j   **D-flat blues**

According to Steve Gilmore, in an interview with the author in 1989, "Pepper brought in an entire [book] of music for those dates and it was very hard music! They were just tunes that we would blow on, but they were *very* difficult tunes! They were his tunes. The changes were hard. It was fun. As I recall, I took the music home that night—some of the lead-sheets—and took them to the piano and looked at them for a minute. It was a little more successful the second night."

According to Bill Goodwin, in an interview with the author in 1989, the gig

> was like going fifteen rounds with a heavyweight champ. [There are] certain saxophone players who—I don't want to say they kick your ass, but it's a very physical experience. It's not unusual, I think, in the real greats, the real heavyweights, the guys who play real strong and real committed like Pepper did. I never played with Coltrane, for example, but I used to hear him play a lot, and I used to wonder what it would feel like, and I remember that weekend playing with Pepper: I said, "I bet you it must feel something like this to play with Coltrane," because it was so strong, and he played so fast, and so many notes, and he swung so hard. This is being in the presence of a master—not just a master, but somebody who played as if there was no tomorrow; at all times! The really best guys have that....He's one of the strongest guys I ever played with, and I've played with a lot of good guys. I'd put him in the very highest category, with Phil [Woods]. As far as playing the saxophone, he's just the master of the saxophone, the master of bebop, equally in a category with Phil, and Zoot [Sims], and guys I think of

who are super-strong players. Joe Farrell is another. Lew Tabackin is one. These guys, they don't take any prisoners! I really like that. Freddie Hubbard plays that way....Yeah, I couldn't pick up my arms at the end of the night, both nights. He had me playing as hard, and pushing as hard, as I could. I don't see how you could help it! He brings it out....It makes you feel like you're a real jazz musician and you're playing the real stuff.

See 751213.

PEPPER ADAMS
751213
13 December 1975, audience recording, Three Sisters, West Paterson NJ: Same as 12 December 1975:

a **Solar**
b **A Child Is Born**
c **'Tis**
d **Falling in Love with Love**
e **Stars Fell on Alabama**

See 751212.

THAD JONES-MEL LEWIS – NEW LIFE
751216
16 December 1975, A&R Studios, New York: Thad Jones flh; Al Porcino, Waymon Reed, Sinclair Acey, Cecil Bridgewater tp, flh; Billy Campbell, Janice Robinson, John Mosca tb; Earl McIntyre btb; Ray Alonge, Jimmy Buffington, Peter Gordon, Julius Watkins frh; Jerry Dodgion, Ed Xiques as, fl; Frank Foster ts; Gregory Herbert ts, fl; Pepper Adams bs; Roland Hanna e-p; Barry Finnerty e-g; George Mraz b; Mel Lewis dm.

a   Greetings and Salutations   A&M-Horizon unissued

Part of -a has been spliced onto the released version of this title. For other takes of this tune that are also part of the released version on A&M-Horizon SP-707, see 750722, 760108.
The released version of -a is on A&M-Horizon LP: SP-707, A&M-Horizon (Eng/Neth) LP: AMJL-707, Horizon (YU) LP: LP-4374, Can-

yon (J) LP: D32Y-3822, Canyon (J) LP: D22Y-3911, A&M-Horizon
CD: CD-0810.

THAD JONES-MEL LEWIS – NEW LIFE
751217a
17 December 1975, A&R Studios, New York: Same as 16 December
1975; omit Alonge, Buffington, Gordon, Watkins, Finnerty; Roland
Hanna celeste*:

a   **Thank You**   A&M-Horizon LP: SP-707
b   Love and Harmony*   A&M-Horizon unissued
c   Love and Harmony*

-a on Franklin Mint LP: FM-96, A&M-Horizon (Eng/Neth) LP:
AMJL-707, Canyon (J) LP: D32Y-3822, Canyon (J) LP: D22Y-3911,
Horizon (YU) LP: LP-4374, A&M-Horizon CD: CD-0810.

Parts of -b and -c have been spliced together to form the released
version on A&M-Horizon LP: SP-707. This track on A&M-Horizon
(Eng/Neth) LP: AMJL-707, Canyon (J) LP: D32Y-3822, Canyon (J) LP:
D22Y-3911, Horizon (YU) LP: LP-4374, A&M-Horizon CD: CD-0810.

Regarding Pepper Adams' solo style, Jerry Dodgion, in an interview
with the author in 1988, said that Adams "would do some amazing stuff!
He would start a solo with sometimes a very humorous introduction or
startling beginning, certainly different than what came before!" About
Adams' solo on Jerry Dodgion's composition Thank You (-a), Dodgion
said, "Oh, it's wonderful, yeah! When we were recording, I said, 'This is
the take! I know this is going to be the take because that's the solo, no
matter what the rest of the band does!' And that was the only full take!"
Dodgion added that Adams had told him, "'Since that's sort of [Dodg-
ion's] fond tribute [to Ellington and Strayhorn], I thought to take a little
bit of a Paul Gonsalves approach wouldn't be out of line.' I said, 'Whatever you did, it's wonderful.' So he was thinking that maybe it was his
way of doing a tribute to Paul Gonsalves actually."

Regarding -a, Pepper Adams told Robert Ronzello in a 1982 interview, "I think Jerry Dodgion had that kind of a strong contrast in mind
when he put my solo in at that point of the tune....It's not often that I
hear a recorded solo and think, 'Well, that's about as good as I can do on
that tune.' In terms of Thank You, perhaps I could have played a better
solo, but maybe it would have been difficult to find one that would be

more striking to sit at that particular point in relationship to the arrangement that surrounded it."

About Pepper Adams' solo on Thank You, saxophonist Glenn Wilson told the author in 1987, Adams "told me that his horn was all fucked up. It was leaking like crazy. He said these notes didn't work, but he was going to come blasting in on them anyway."

Regarding Cecil Bridgewater's composition, Love and Understanding (-b, -c), Bridgewater told the author in 1989, Thad

> was always encouraging me to write for the band...so, when he came up with this date, he said, "Listen: I want you to write something for the band. What I'm going to try to do this time is, instead of having it like a blowing date, I want it to be more arranged. I want more of the stuff written out, so it's not just solo, solo, solo." So I said, "O.K., let me work on something." I came up with [Love and Harmony]. Matter of fact, we were in Japan, I think, when I finished it and we first rehearsed it....I had been so enamored with Thad's writing before I ever got in his band, hearing the records and so forth. When I got in the band, I would sometimes ask him questions and he would never really answer the question with a direct answer, which was probably better, because, if he told me exactly what to do, then I would have done that, and that would have been it. He would make you use your imagination; to use your own abilities and come up with your way of doing it. But a lot of times I'd hear something that the band was doing and I'd go get the parts out, take them home, study them, and bring them back the next Monday night or whenever, and put them back in the book. That was a way for me to learn.

THAD JONES-MEL LEWIS – NEW LIFE
751217b

17 December 1975, A&R Studios, New York: Same as 16 December 1975; Lou Marini ts, cl replaces Foster; Peter Gordon frh replaces Watkins; Steve Gilmore b replaces Mraz; add Herb Lovelle dm:

a Love to One Is One to Love   A&M-Horizon unissued
b Love to One Is One to Love

Parts of -a and -b have been spliced onto the released version on A&M-Horizon LP: SP-707. *See* 750722 for the other take of this tune that is also used in the released versions on A&M-Horizon LP: SP-707.

The released version is also on A&M-Horizon (Eng/Neth) LP: AMJL-707, Canyon (J) LP: D32Y-3822, Canyon (J) LP: D22Y-3911, Horizon (YU) LP: LP-4374, A&M-Horizon CD: CD-0810.

THAD JONES-MEL LEWIS – NEW LIFE
760108

8 January 1976, A&R Studios, New York: Thad Jones flh*; Al Porcino tp; Waymon Reed tp, flh; Sinclair Acey, Cecil Bridgewater tp; Billy Campbell, Janice Robinson, John Mosca tb; Earl McIntyre btb; Peter Gordon, Jimmy Buffington, Ray Alonge, Julius Watkins frh; Jerry Dodgion, Ed Xiques as, ss, fl; Lou Marini cl; Gregory Herbert ts, fl; Frank Foster ts; Pepper Adams bs; Roland Hanna e-p; George Mraz b; Mel Lewis dm.

a	Greetings and Salutations	A&M-Horizon unissued
b	Greetings and Salutations	
c	**Forever Lasting***	
d	**Forever Lasting***	

Parts of -a and -b, and parts of -c and -d, have been spliced onto the released versions of their respective titles. *See* 750722 and 751216 for other takes of these tunes that are also used in the released versions on A&M-Horizon LP: SP-707. The released versions are also on A&M-Horizon (Eng/Neth) LP: AMJL-707, Canyon (J) LP: D32Y-3822, Canyon (J) LP: D22Y-3911, Horizon (YU) LP: LP-4374, A&M-Horizon CD: CD-0810.

THAD JONES-MEL LEWIS – NEW LIFE
760110

10 January 1976, A&R Studios, New York: Thad Jones flh; Al Porcino, Waymon Reed, Sinclair Acey, Cecil Bridgewater tp; Billy Campbell, Janice Robinson, John Mosca tb; Earl McIntyre btb; Don Butterfield tuba*; Jerry Dodgion ss, fl; Ed Xiques as, ss, fl; Gregory Herbert ts, fl; Frank Foster ts, cl; Pepper Adams bs; Walter Norris p; George Mraz b; Mel Lewis dm.

a	**Little Rascal on a Rock***	A&M-Horizon LP: SP-707
b	Cherry Juice	

-a on A&M-Horizon (Eng-Neth) LP: AMJL-707, TRB (Yugo) LP: LP-4374, Canyon (J) LP: D32Y-3822, Canyon (J) LP: D22Y-3911, A&M-Horizon CD: CD-0810.

-b on Smithsonian LP: RD-108-S25-17618, A&M-Horizon (Eng-Neth) LP: AMJL-707, Horizon (YU) LP: LP-4374, Canyon (J) LP: D32Y-3822, Canyon (J) LP: D22Y-3911, A&M-Horizon CD: CD-0810, Smithsonian CD: SMRJ-0014-CD.

Regarding Pepper Adams' solo on -a, Jerry Dodgion, in an interview with the author in 1988 said, "That's a great example of how he could play on difficult chord changes. He's playing melody. It doesn't sound like he's just running chords. He's making music with the challenge."

According to Ed Xiques, in an interview with the author in 1988,

> The band hardly ever rehearsed. A lot of times Thad wouldn't have the music ready, and he would write for a recording date: Sometimes it wouldn't be ready until *then*. But occasionally, like Cherry Juice, for instance, I remember one time he brought that down to the club. In fact, Pepper wasn't there. I was playing baritone that night. A hard saxophone soli. The tempo that we originally played it at was like a medium tempo, but, then, before long, Thad was counting that thing off at a blazing tempo. Those intervals in the saxophone soli—the lead part isn't that hard, but all the other parts are a bitch! You've got wide leaps in there, and the thing is moving along like crazy!

THAD JONES-MEL LEWIS
760113
13 January 1976, BR radio broadcast, Domicile, Munich: Thad Jones flh; Al Porcino, Waymon Reed, Sinclair Acey, Cecil Bridgewater tp; Billy Campbell, Janice Robinson, John Mosca tb; Earl McIntyre btb; Jerry Dodgion ss, as, fl; Ed Xiques ss, fl; Gregory Herbert as, ts, fl; Sal Nistico ts; Pepper Adams bs; Walter Norris p; Steve Gilmore b; Mel Lewis dm.

a   Evol Deklaw Ni (Love Walked In)
b   The Waltz You "Swang" for Me
c   Ahunk, Ahunk
d   Backbone
e   Willow Weep for Me
f   Bächafillen

In a 1988 author interview John Mosca said, "we went over in '76 to open the new Domicile for three weeks. (There was an old Domicile, that was a small, little joint that the band used to squeeze in to.) That gig was noteworthy because we had Sal Nistico sit in with the band for a week, and then Bobby Jones played for two weeks, or vice versa."

THAD JONES-MEL LEWIS
760125
25 January 1976, WDR radio broadcast, Cologne: Same as 13 January 1976, Jiggs Whigham tb replaces Campbell:

a   Quietude
b   Tiptoe
c   **Once Around**
d   **Thank You**
e   Fingers
f   St. Louis Blues
g   Love and Harmony
h   Don't Git Sassy
i   Mean What You Say
j   The Second Race

According to John Mosca, in an interview with the author in 1988,

> I remember doing a double hit-and-run to make that job: The gig at the Domicile ended late, like three in the morning; We got on the bus and drove to Cologne and did a radio broadcast [then returned to Munich]. Jiggs Whigham subbed on trombone for Billy Campbell, who had a tooth pulled in Munich. Billy liked to drink too, and, of course, the dentist also gave him some pills to take, so he was gone. He couldn't play.

THAD JONES-MEL LEWIS
760302
c. 2-8 March 1976, private recordings, Jazz Showcase, Chicago: Thad Jones flh; Al Porcino, Waymon Reed, Sinclair Acey, Cecil Bridgewater tp; Billy Campbell, Janice Robinson, John Mosca tb; Earl McIntyre btb; Jerry Dodgion ss, as, fl; Ed Xiques ss, fl; Gregory Herbert as, ts, fl; Frank Foster ts; Pepper Adams bs; Mike Wolff p; Steve Gilmore b; Mel Lewis dm.

According to Mike Wolff, in a conversation with the author, the band played a one-week engagement. *See* Author's Note above 580000A entry.

THAD JONES-MEL LEWIS
760320
late March 1976, HR radio broadcast, Frankfurt: Thad Jones flh; Al Porcino, Waymon Reed, Sinclair Acey, Cecil Bridgewater tp; Jiggs Whigham, Janice Robinson, John Mosca tb; Earl McIntyre btb; Jerry Dodgion ss, as, fl; Ed Xiques ss, fl; Gregory Herbert as, ts, fl; Sal Nistico ts; Pepper Adams bs; Walter Norris p; Steve Gilmore b; Mel Lewis dm.

It's unclear if audio still exists.

LALO SCHIFRIN
760400
c. April 1976, Van Gelder Studio, Englewood Cliffs NJ: Overdubs: Jon Faddis tp; Billy Campbell, Wayne Andre, Barry Rogers tb; Dave Taylor btb; Joe Farrell as, fl; Jerry Dodgion, George Marge, Hubert Laws fl*; Pepper Adams bs.

a   Black Widow   CTI LP: 5000
b   Medley:
        Theme from "Moonglow"
        Theme from "Picnic"
        Theme from "Jaws"*
c   Turning Point
d   Flamingo
e   Quiet Village
f   Baia
g   Dragonfly
h   Frenesi   CTI (J) LP: GXP-6003

-a, -b, and -c originally recorded in New York on 29 March 1976: Lalo Schifrin p; Clark Spangler keyboards; Eric Gale (-a, -e only), Jerry Friedman, John Tropea g; Anthony Jackson e-b; Andy Newmark dm. All other tracks originally recorded in New York on 30 March 1976: Personnel same as 29 March 1976, except add Don Alias, Carter Collins, Sue Evans, Carlos Martin perc. For both sessions, string section and vocal choir added at another time.

-a on CTI (Ger) LP: 63-001, CTI (J) LP: GXP-6003, CTI (J) LP: GP-3071, CTI (J) LP: LAX-3173, Legacy CD: ZK-65128, Sony (F) CD: 5048372, Epic-Legacy (Sp) CD: CD-5060292, CTI (J) CD: KICJ-8329.

-b (Jaws only) on CTI LP: OJ-29, CTI LP: OJL-2, CTI (Sp) LP: CTSP-005, CTI (F) LP: 42579.

-b (entire medley) on CTI (Ger) LP: 63-001, CTI (J) LP: GP-3071, CTI (J) LP: LAX-3173, CTI (J) LP: GXP-6003, Legacy CD: ZK-65128, Sony (F) CD: 5048372, Epic-Legacy (Sp) CD: CD-5060292, CTI (J) CD: KICJ-8329.

-c on CTI LP: OJ-29, CTI (Ger) LP: 63-001, CTI (J) LP: GP-3071, CTI (J) LP: LAX-3173, CTI (J) LP: GXP-6003, Legacy CD: ZK-65128, Sony (F) CD: 5048372, Epic-Legacy (Sp) CD: CD-5060292, CTI (J) CD: KICJ-8329.

-d on CTI (J) LP: GXP-6003, CTI (Ger) LP: 63-001, CTI (J) LP: GP-3071, CTI (J) LP: LAX-3173, Legacy CD: ZK-65128, Sony (F) CD: 5048372, Epic-Legacy (Sp) CD: CD-5060292, CTI (J) CD: KICJ-8329.

-e on CTI (Ger) LP: 63-001, CTI (J) LP: GP-3071, CTI (J) LP: LAX-3173, CTI (J) LP: GXP-6003, Legacy CD: ZK-65128, Epic-Legacy (Sp) CD: CD-5060292, Sony (F) CD: 5048372, CTI (J) CD: KICJ-8329.

-f on CTI LP: OJL-2, CTI LP: OJ-29, CTI (F) LP: 42579, CTI (Ger) LP: 63-001, CTI (J) LP: GP-3071, CTI (J) LP: LAX-3173, CTI (J) LP: GXP-6003, Legacy CD: ZK-65128, Epic-Legacy (Sp) CD: CD-5060292, Sony (F) CD: 5048372, CTI (J) CD: KICJ-8329.

-g on CTI LP: OJL-2, CTI (Ger) LP: 63-001, CTI (J) LP: GP-3071, CTI (J) LP: LAX-3173, CTI (J) LP: GXP-6003, Legacy CD: ZK-65128, Epic-Legacy (Sp) CD: CD-5060292, Sony (F) CD: 5048372, CTI (J) CD: KICJ-8329.

-h on CTI (J) LP: GXP-6003, Legacy CD: ZK-65128, Epic-Legacy (Sp) CD: CD-5060292.

THAD JONES-MEL LEWIS
760505
5-9 May 1976, private recordings, Jazz Showcase, Chicago: Thad Jones flh; Al Porcino, Waymon Reed, Sinclair Acey, Cecil Bridgewater tp; Billy Campbell, Janice Robinson, John Mosca tb; Earl McIntyre btb; Jerry Dodgion ss, as, fl; Ed Xiques ss, fl; Gregory Herbert as, ts, fl; Frank Foster ts; Pepper Adams bs; Mike Wolff p; Bob Bowman b; Mel Lewis dm.

See Author's Note above 580000A entry.

RHODA SCOTT – RHODA SCOTT IN NEW YORK WITH THE THAD JONES-MEL LEWIS ORCHESTRA
760602

2-3 June 1976, Media Sound Studio, New York: Thad Jones flh; Al Porcino, Lynn Nicholson, Earl Gardner, Cecil Bridgewater tp; Billy Campbell, John Mosca, Clifford Adams tb; Earl McIntyre btb; Jerry Dodgion ss, as, fl; Ed Xiques as, fl; Gregory Herbert ts, cl, fl; Larry Schneider ts, cl; Pepper Adams bs; Rhoda Scott org; Harold Danko e-p*; Bob Bowman b; Mel Lewis dm.

a	Mach II*	Barclay (F) LP: 90068
b	Tanikka*	
c	Rhoda Map*	
d	R & R*	
e	Charlotte's Waltz*	
f	Walkin' About*	
g	Take a Ladder	
h	La Solitude*	Universal-EmArcy (F) CD: 981120-6
i	Quand Je Monte Chez Toi*	

It's unclear what tunes are from what date.

-a, -b, -c, -d, -e, -f, -g on King (J) LP: GP-3084.

All tracks on EmArcy CD: 813590-2, Universal-EmArcy (F) CD: 9811206.

Regarding the collaboration, Rhoda Scott told writer Marc Myers, "When Mel Lewis came to Paris, he visited the Bilboquet Club, where I was playing. He sat in and loved the experience so much that he said we should make a record together and that Thad would do the arrangements. I brushed it off. I said, 'No way, I'm not going back to New York to do it.' But my husband [and manager, Raoul Saint-Yves] thought it was a terrific idea and we rolled forward."

According to an email Rhoda Scott sent to historian Lewis Porter in 2011, "The first seven tunes were…on the first release because the people at Barclay didn't want to include the two French tunes. Thad and Mel were disappointed about that. It was Thad who had asked me for some French tunes to include.…Thad did the arrangements just prior to the recording date, and the parts were arriving progressively; As we recorded, the copyist would arrive with the next tune."

Earl Gardner told the author in 2006 that he joined the trumpet section in May 1976, by which time Sinclair Acey had left the band and Lynn Nicholson, Harold Danko, and Bob Bowman had also joined.

Regarding the vacancy in the piano chair, Harold Danko told the author in a 1989 interview, "Walter [Norris] had already left. They were trying some different guys. [Allan Zavod may have tried out.] I think the last guy to do it before me was Mike Wolff. Mike did it for a time, but it was a transitional thing." Danko joined the band just prior to this recording. "I remember we had some gigs and the Rhoda Scott record, and I made a lot of money that [first full] week," said Danko, "so I thought, 'Wow! This is great!'" Danko stayed almost two years with the band: "It was great," said Danko. "I really enjoyed just about every minute."

THAD JONES-MEL LEWIS
760618
18 June 1976, NOS radio broadcast, De Doelen Concert Hall, International NOS Jazz Festival, Rotterdam: Thad Jones flh, perc; Al Porcino, Lynn Nicholson, Earl Gardner, Frank Gordon tp; Billy Campbell, John Mosca, Clifford Adams tb; Earl McIntyre btb; Jerry Dodgion ss, as, fl; Ed Xiques ss, fl; Gregory Herbert ts, cl, fl; Larry Schneider ts, cl; Pepper Adams bs; Harold Danko p; Bob Bowman b; Mel Lewis dm.

a   Second Race
b   Kids Are Pretty People
c   The Groove Merchant
d   **Thank You**
e   **Little Rascal on a Rock**
f   Mean What You Say
g   **Once Around**
h   **My Centennial**[1]

[1]Jones and some bandmembers play various percussion instruments.

Beginning with the band's Summer 1976 European tour, Frank Gordon took Cecil Bridgwater's chair in the band.

PEPPER ADAMS
760620
20 June 1976, NOS radio broadcast, De Doelen Concert Hall, Interna-

tional NOS Jazz Festival, Rotterdam: Pepper Adams bs*; Walter Norris p; Red Mitchell b.

a   A Child Is Born
b   **Twelfth and Pingree***
c   **Cottontail/Oleo***
d   **Julian***
e   Drifting
f   **Ebb and Flow***
g   **'Tis** *

THAD JONES-MEL LEWIS
760708
8 July 1976, TV broadcast, Domicile, Munich: Same as 18 June 1976:

a   **Once Around**   ZDF-Musikkanal (Ger) VHS
b   Quand Je Monte Chez Toi
c   Kids Are Pretty People
d   Love and Harmony*
e   Cherry Juice
f   **My Centennial**[1]

[1]Thad Jones and some bandmembers play various percussion instruments.

Recorded during the band's engagement 22 June-8 July. According to John Mosca, in an interview with the author in 1988, the band played three weeks at the Domicile, toured for eight weeks, and then returned to the Domicile for another three weeks near the end of the tour. *See* 760909.

THAD JONES-MEL LEWIS
760710
10 July 1976, RTSR radio broadcast, Casino, Montreux: Same as 18 June 1976:

a   Mornin' Reverend
b   Willow Weep for Me
c   ABC Blues
d   **Thank You**
e   **Little Rascal on a Rock**

f   Love and Harmony
g   Greetings and Salutations
h   Giant Steps

THAD JONES-MEL LEWIS
760714
14 July 1976, audience recording, HNITA Jazz Club, Heist-op-den-Berg, Belgium: Same as 18 June 1976:

a   Quietude
b   Pensive Miss
c   Tiptoe
d   Kids Are Pretty People
e   Mornin' Reverend
f   Blues in a Minute
g   **Thank You**
h   Mach II
i   The Groove Merchant
j   Yours and Mine
k   **Once Around**
m   Walkin' About
n   La Solitude
o   Take a Ladder
p   Fingers

Regarding the HNITA Club, according to John Mosca, in an interview with the author in 1988, "it was not a jazz club, in the sense that we mean in New York. It's a club: They get together, and they had records there. It wasn't a bar per se. It was a big room over the police station, and that's where these guys would get together. It was the space they could get."

About the band's performance there, Mosca said, "Pepper's right in the middle of Once Around, which is a fast, minor solo for him. He's burning away, really tearing it up, and a police car comes with a siren on, and he goes right into I Don't Want to Set the World on Fire. I swear, right in the middle of this solo, and it broke everybody up. It was very funny!"

See 750714.

THAD JONES-MEL LEWIS
760715
15 July 1976, audience recording, HNITA Jazz Club, Heist-op-den-Berg,
Belgium: Same as 18 June 1976:

a   Evol Deklaw Ni (Love Walked In)
b   Ceora
c   **The Little Pixie**
d   A–That's Freedom
e   Lover Man
f   **Three and One**
g   Greetings and Salutations
h   **Thank You**
i   The Groove Merchant
j   Love and Harmony
k   Take a Ladder
m   Walkin' About
n   A Child Is Born
o   **My Centennial**[1]
p   The Intimacy of the Blues

[1]Jones and some bandmembers play various percussion instruments.

See 760714.

THAD JONES-MEL LEWIS
760716
16 July 1976, radio broadcast, North Sea Jazz Festival, The Hague:
Same as 18 June 1976.

It's unclear if audio still exists.

THAD JONES-MEL LEWIS
760719
19 July 1976, RAI radio broadcast, Teatro Romano, Verona, Italy: Same
as 18 June 1976:

a   **Once Around**
b   Walkin' About
c   Love and Harmony

d   The Second Race
e   **Thank You**

THAD JONES-MEL LEWIS
760722
22 July 1976, RF radio broadcast. Antibes Jazz Festival, Juan-les-Pins, France: Same as 18 June 1976:

a   **Three and One**
b   **My Centennial**[1]

[1]Thad Jones and some bandmembers play various percussion instruments.

THAD JONES-MEL LEWIS
760724
24 July 1976, TVE TV broadcast, Sitges, Spain: Same as 18 June 1976: GUEST: Tete Montoliu p*:

a   Mach II
b   The Groove Merchant
c   Kids Are Pretty People
    Danko out:
d   A Child Is Born*

Broadcast on the program *Jazz Vivo,* though it's not known if the video still exists. According to John Mosca, in an interview with the author in 1988,

> This was a "famous" ride. We drove from Sitges, which is basically Barcelona, back to Munich with one bus driver. Thirty hours! I flew. Every once in a while you do this. You save your money up, and, once in a while, you fly. Me, Earl McIntyre, and Earl Gardner flew. We had an extra day and a half on the beach, and we still beat the band back. Horrible ride!

THAD JONES-MEL LEWIS
760726
late July 1976, SWF radio broadcast, Domicile, Munich: Same as 18 June 1976:

a   Cherry Juice
b   Mach II
c   Come on Over My Love
d   Walkin' About
e   **My Centennial**[1]
f   **The Little Pixie**
g   A–That's Freedom
h   Mornin' Reverend
i   Central Park North
j   It Only Happens Every Time
k   Oregon Grinder
m   Take a Ladder

[1]Jones and some bandmembers play various percussion instruments.

This was broadcast during the band's engagement 26 July-2 August.

THAD JONES-MEL LEWIS
760806
6 August 1976, Polish Radio, Jazz Jantar, Sopot, Poland: Same as 18
June 1976:

a   Fingers   Poljazz (P) LP: Z-SXL-637
b   **Thank You**
c   Take a Ladder
d   Greetings and Salutations
e   A Child Is Born   Fresh Sound (Sp) CD: FSR-69320-2
f   The Intimacy of the Blues

-a, -b, -c, -d on Poljazz (P) LP: Z-SX-637.
All tracks on Fresh Sound (Sp) CD: FSR-69320-2, Jazz View (Ger)
CD: COD-017, Gambit (Sp) CD: 69320.
According to Ed Xiques, in an interview with the author in 1988,

They were recording, and a bunch of us were concerned about it,
because we weren't getting any money for it. We started playing the
concert and Larry Schneider deliberately played off-mic on the solos because nobody had said anything that we were going to do a
record or anything. There was some resentment about that. Thad
and Mel may not have even known about it....There's nothing you

can do about it. They have you over there. It might even have been
in the contract. Sometimes they write that in, that they have the
right to record you. They issue records all the time that jazz artists
never get paid for.

In producer Bo Johnson's liner notes, he wrote, "This record was
made courtesy of Thad Jones and Mel Lewis, who allowed Poljazz to
bring out the recording so that the Orchestra's music would be available
to the Polish record audience....In connection with the 1978 European
tour with [the] Thad Jones-Mel Lewis Orchestra, it was decided...that
even the rest of the European audience should have the chance of sharing
this record."

Regarding what it was like touring in an Eastern European country,
and about the possibility of Polish police informants spying on the band,
Harold Danko, in an interview with the author in 1989, said, "Oh yeah,
there was kind of an entourage in Poland that was jazz-society-type people, that seemed to be really interested in the music, and then there were
some other people that were *there* on the tour. I never delved into who or
what they might be, but I thought possibly they're *watching.* "

THAD JONES-MEL LEWIS
760818
18 August 1976, audience recording, Norrköping, Sweden: Same as 18
June 1976:

a   Big Dipper
b   All My Yesterdays
c   But a Feeling
d   unknown ballad
e   **Three and One**
f   Don't Git Sassy
g   Willow Weep for Me
h   **Little Rascal on a Rock**
i   Don't You Worry 'Bout a Thing
j   **Thank You**
k   **My Centennial**[1]
m   The Intimacy of the Blues

[1]Jones and some bandmembers play various percussion instruments.

THAD JONES
760905
5 September 1976, audience recording, Har-Monika, Munich: Thad
Jones flh, cornet; Pepper Adams bs; Harold Danko p; Bob Bowman b;
Mel Lewis dm.

a **Straight, No Chaser**
b **Sophisticated Lady**
c **unknown rhythm changes**
d **A–That's Freedom**
e **Chelsea Bridge**
f **In a Mellow Tone**
g **Buzzy**
h **I Can't Get Started**

THAD JONES-MEL LEWIS – LIVE IN MUNICH
760909
9 September 1976, Domicile, Munich: Same as 18 June 1976:

a Mach II   A&M-Horizon LP: SP-724
b A–That's Freedom
c Mornin' Reverend
d **Come Sunday**
e Central Park North

Recorded during the band's engagement 5-9 September.
All tracks on Victor-Phonogram (J) LP: HOJ-2010.
Jerry Dodgion told the author, in an interview in 1988,

That's the record that won the Grammy, and it's one of our worst
records. We were nominated several times. There [were] a couple of
them that were nominated that were very good, and, everytime, we
kept getting beat by Duke Ellington or…But the time we really got
pissed off is when Miles Davis won in that category for *Bitches
Brew*. They called it a "big band." Thad and Mel were really pissed
off. They said, "Well, that's Columbia Records pulling their weight
again. That's all it is. They can do whatever they wanted to." But it
wasn't fair. It wasn't a big band. It was a lot of people, and a lot of
them not playing at the same time either.

Ed Xiques told the author, in an interview in 1988,

That club is great to play in. That was fun! I remember Central Park
North being real long. I thought the solos were too long. Someone
told me that Mel [Lewis] thought that was actually the best record
the band had made ensemble-wise. He may be right. We were playing in there every night, and the band really felt good!

THAD JONES–MEL LEWIS
760913
13 September 1976, BR radio broadcast, Passau, Germany: **Same as 18
June 1976:**

a   Blues in a Minute
b   Tiptoe
c   Oregon Grinder
d   **Two as One**
e   **Once Around**
f   The Groove Merchant

THAD JONES–MEL LEWIS
760915
15 September 1976, SDR radio broadcast, Musikpodium, Stuttgart:
Same as 18 June 1976:

a   Walkin' About
b   The Jive Samba[1]
c   Tiptoe
d   It Only Happens Every Time
e   Yours and Mine
f   **Three and One**
g   Mornin' Reverend
h   Mach II
i   **Two as One**
j   Oregon Grinder
k   Willow Weep for Me
m   Cherry Juice
n   A–That's Freedom
o   Blues in a Minute
p   Evol Deklaw Ni (Love Walked In)

q **Thank You**

[1]Various musicians play percussion instruments.

Regarding Gregory Herbert, Harold Danko told the author in 1989,

Gregory just could ignite the band. I remember once, in, I think it was, Stuttgart, where Thad was in a *horrible* mood, because Thad would stop drinking, now and then, and then it was horrible when Thad stopped drinking, because he'd get really grumpy. *Oh,* yeah, we'd just pray for him to start: "Start drinking again, Thad, please! Just drink and make it easy on us." But he had stopped drinking and he was just horribly grumpy, and I remember Gregory kind of had this look in his eye. We played a blues. I think it was Number 4 (The Second Race, or whatever), and Gregory just was determined, was looking at Thad, pointing the bell of the horn at Thad, and playing the most drenchingly blues-influenced kind of lines and just downhome kind of thing until Thad finally broke out with a big smile. Gregory would do that kind of thing. He had great passion in his playing.

THAD JONES–MEL LEWIS
760916
16 September 1976, SDR TV broadcast, Waldshut, Germany: Same as 18 June 1976:

a Samba con Getchu
b Ambiance
c Cherry Juice
d **My Centennial**[1]
e Walkin' About

[1]Jones and some bandmembers play various percussion instruments.

It's unclear if video still exists.

THAD JONES-MEL LEWIS
760919
19 September 1976, HR radio broadcast, Frankfurt: Same as 18 June 1976:

a   Mach II
b   **Thank You**
c   Walkin' About
d   **Two as One**
e   Fingers

According to John Mosca, in an interview with the author in 1988,

> Bob Bowman got married three weeks before he went out [on this tour]. I think, when we got back [to New York], he packed up his shit and went back to Kansas. He drove back home. He was really in rough shape. He was a young guy, really idealistic, and had just gotten married. Thad and Mel both could carry on pretty good on the road, along with everybody else. I think, in the course of the tour, a girlfriend changed hands inside the band.

THAD JONES-PEPPER ADAMS
760923
23 September 1976, DR radio broadcast, Montmartre Jazzhus, Copen-hagen: Thad Jones cornet; Pepper Adams bs; Kenny Drew p; Hugo Rasmussen b; Svend-Erik Nørregaard dm.

a   **Sophisticated Lady**
b   **Gone with the Wind**
c   **Fly Me to the Moon**
d   **What Is This Thing Called Love**
e   **Now's the Time**
f   **'Tis**
g   **How Long Has This Been Going On**

THAD JONES-PEPPER ADAMS
760924
24 September 1976, DR radio broadcast, Montmartre Jazzhus, Copen-hagen: Same as 23 September 1976.

It's unclear if audio still exists.

THAD JONES-MEL LEWIS
761100A
November 1976, radio broadcast, Agora Ballroom, Cleveland: Thad

Jones flh; Earl Gardner, Jeff Davis tp; Waymon Reed tp, flh; Frank Gordon tp; Billy Campbell, Clifford Adams, John Mosca tb; Earl McIntyre btb; Lawrence Feldman as, ss, bcl, fl; Ed Xiques ss, as, fl; Gregory Herbert, Larry Schneider ts, cl, fl; Pepper Adams bs; Harold Danko p; Rufus Reid b; Mel Lewis dm.

a **Little Rascal on a Rock**
b Bächafillen
c Cecilia Is Love
d **The Little Pixie**
e Take a Ladder

THAD JONES-MEL LEWIS
761100B
November 1976, radio broadcast, Academy of Music, Philadelphia: Same as November 1976 Cleveland broadcast, except Lynn Nicholson tp for Davis, and Jerry Dodgion as, ss for Feldman:

a The Second Race
b Willow Weep for Me
c Take a Ladder
d Ambiance
e **My Centennial**[1]

[1]Jones and some bandmembers play various percussion instruments.

PEPPER ADAMS
770216
16 February 1977, audience recording, Torengebouw, Heist-op-den-Berg, Belgium: Pepper Adams bs; Tony Bauwens p; Roger Vanhaverbeke b; Freddy Rottier dm.

a **Just Friends**
b **Autumn Leaves**
c **Lover Man**
d **Stomping at the Savoy**
e **Have You Met Miss Jones**
f **A Child Is Born**
g **Stella by Starlight**
h **Mean What You Say**

i **Julian**
j **'Tis**

Recorded by the HNITA Jazz Club. *See* 750714 note.

PEPPER ADAMS
770218
18 February 1977, BRT radio broadcast, Germana Jazzklub, Lauwe, Belgium: Same as 16 February 1977.

It's unclear if audio still exists.

PEPPER ADAMS
770221
21 February 1977, audience recording, New Dixieland, Knokke, Belgium: Same as 16 February 1977.

PEPPER ADAMS
770222
22 February 1977, audience recording, Restaurant La Redoute, s'Gravenwezel, Belgium: Same as 16 February 1977; GUESTS: Eddy House as*; Johnny Kay p†:

a **P/A...Pepper Adams**
b **A Child Is Born**
c **What Is This Thing Called Love**
d **On the Sunny Side of the Street*†**
e **Misty*†**
f **Scrapple from the Apple*†**

This was the first public performance of the Tony Bauwens' composition P/A...Pepper Adams, and, at this concert, it was still unnamed.

PEPPER ADAMS
770224
24 February 1977, audience recording, Queen of the South, Genk, Belgium: Same as 16 February 1977.

PEPPER ADAMS
770228
28 February 1977, BRT radio broadcast, Witte Hoed at the Royal Ander-lecht Sporting Club Bar, Anderlecht, Belgium: Same as 16 February 1977:

a   **Mean What You Say**
b   **A Child Is Born**
c   **Ephemera**
d   **P/A...Pepper Adams**

THAD JONES-MEL LEWIS
770411
11-14 April 1977, private recordings, Jazz Showcase, Chicago: Thad Jones flh; Earl Gardner, Lynn Nicholson tp; Waymon Reed tp, flh; Frank Gordon tp; Billy Campbell, John Mosca, Clifford Adams tb; Earl McIntyre btb; Jerry Dodgion ss, as, fl; Ed Xiques as, ss; Gregory Herbert, Larry Schneider ts, cl, fl; Pepper Adams bs; Harold Danko p; Rufus Reid b; Mel Lewis dm.

See Author's Note above 580000A entry.

THAD JONES-MEL LEWIS
770430
c. 30 April 1977, audience recording, West Virginia University, Morgantown WV: Same as 11 April 1977:

a   Mach II
b   Kids Are Pretty People
c   Tiptoe
d   Ambiance
e   **The Little Pixie**
f   Big Dipper
g   **Thank You**
h   Oregon Grinder
i   Body and Soul

THAD JONES
770501
c. 1 May 1977, audience recording, Kilcawley Center at Youngstown

State University, Youngstown OH: Thad Jones cornet; Lawrence Feldman as; Gregory Herbert ts; Pepper Adams bs; Harold Danko e-p; Rufus
Reid b; Mel Lewis dm; Youngstown State University Jazz Band.

a   **Straight, No Chaser**[1]
b   **Sophisticated Lady**[2]
c   Mood Indigo[3]
d   **In a Mellow Tone**
e   Second Race[4]

[1]Jones, Herbert, Adams, and rhythm section.
[2]Adams and rhythm section.
[3]Jones and rhythm section.
[4]Feldman and University Jazz Band.

According to saxophonist Glenn Wilson, as told to Jim Newsom,
"We brought Thad Jones and Pepper Adams in because Harold Danko, a
great piano player who was playing with Thad at that time, was a gradu-
ate of Youngstown. I was Pepper's roadie, taking him to dinner and running him around town."

JOHN SPIDER MARTIN–ABSOLUTELY
770600

c. June 1977, Trackmaster Audio, Buffalo: Jimmy Owens, Billy Skinner
tp, flh; John Spider Martin ts; Pepper Adams bs; Dave Loeb p, e-p, cl;
Russeau Taylor g; Joe Locke vib; Oscar Alston*, Steve Davis e-b; Billy
Hart dm; Riccardo Felice perc.

a   Never Can Say Goodbye   Improv LP: 7118
b   You Are So Beautiful
c   That's Nice
d   Uh-Ah*

After Martin and Adams had discussed whether a certain take was
acceptable, they learned from the engineer that the take had been erased.
Adams said that this was the most unprofessional thing he had ever seen
in his thirty years of recording.

THAD JONES-MEL LEWIS
770701
1 July 1977, radio broadcast, Carnegie Hall, New York: Thad Jones flh, perc; Earl Gardner, Larry Moses, Jeff Davis, Frank Gordon tp; Billy Campbell, John Mosca, Clifford Adams tb; Earl McIntyre btb; Jerry Dodgion, Ed Xiques ss, as, cl, fl; Richard Perry, Dick Oatts ts, cl, fl; Pepper Adams bs; Harold Danko p; Rufus Reid b; Mel Lewis dm; GUESTS: Dizzy Gillespie tp*; Hank Jones p†; Elvin Jones dm√.

a   The Second Race
b   Don't Git Sassy
    Thad Jones, Hank Jones, Rufus Reid, Elvin Jones:
c   Straight, No Chaser†√
d   Sweet Georgia Brown†√
    Full orchestra, except Hank Jones and Elvin Jones replace Danko and Lewis respectively:
e   A Child Is Born*†√
f   **My Centennial***†√[1]

[1]Thad Jones and some bandmembers play various percussion instruments.

According to Dick Oatts, in a conversation with the author in 2005, both he and Richard Perry joined the band in June prior to the upcoming European tour.

THAD JONES-MEL LEWIS
770709
9 July 1977, RAI radio broadcast, Teatro Sportivo, Casale Monferrato: Thad Jones flh, perc; Earl Gardner, Larry Moses, Jeff Davis, Frank Gordon tp; Billy Campbell, John Mosca, Clifford Adams tb; Earl McIntyre btb; Jerry Dodgion, Ed Xiques ss, as, cl, fl; Richard Perry, Dick Oatts ts, cl, fl; Pepper Adams bs; Harold Danko p; Rufus Reid b; Mel Lewis dm; Aura Rully voc.*

a   Take a Ladder
b   Kids Are Pretty People
c   The Groove Merchant
d   **Thank You**
e   The Second Race
f   Mach II

g   Willow Weep for Me
h   61st and Richard
i   Here's that Rainy Day*
j   Don't Git Sassy

THAD JONES-MEL LEWIS
770711
11 July 1977, RF radio broadcast, Les Jardin des Arènes de Cimiez, La Grande Parade du Jazz, Nice: Same as 9 July 1977; omit Rully, GUEST: Kai Winding tb:

a   **The Little Pixie**
b   A Child Is Born
c   The Second Race
d   Big Dipper
e   **Thank You**
f   Mach II

NEW YORK JAZZ REPERTORY COMPANY
770712a
12 July 1977, audience recording of rehearsal, Les Jardin des Arènes de Cimiez, La Grande Parade du Jazz, Nice: Jon Faddis, Jimmy Maxwell, Joe Newman tp; Clark Terry tp, voc*; John Mosca, Kai Winding tb; Earl McIntyre btb; Eddie Barefield cl, as; Benny Carter as; Arnett Cobb, Buddy Tate ts; Pepper Adams bs; Dick Hyman p; Bucky Pizzarelli g; George Duvivier b; Alan Dawson dm.

a   Every Tub
b   Every Tub
c   Moten Swing
d   Doggin' Around
e   Doggin' Around
f   Doggin' Around
g   Blue and Sentimental
h   Rock-a-Bye Basie
i   Miss Thing
j   Miss Thing
k   Harvard Blues*

See 770712b.

NEW YORK JAZZ REPERTORY COMPANY
770712b
12 July 1977, RF radio broadcast, Les Jardin des Arènes de Cimiez, La Grande Parade du Jazz, Nice: Same as 12 July 1977 rehearsal, Clark Terry voc*; GUEST: Count Basie p†:

Hyman out:
a   Every Tub†
b   Moten Swing†
c   Doggin' Around†
Add Hyman, Basie out:
d   Blue and Sentimental
e   Rock-a-Bye Basie
f   Miss Thing
g   Harvard Blues*
h   **Broadway**
i   One O'Clock Jump

In a conversation with the author, conducted in 1988, Alan Dawson said, "I didn't work with the repertory band per se. I did play on one set with the repertory band when they were doing some of the old Basie stuff. You know, the way they set that up in Nice is that, if you go there as a freelancer, you work with a whole lot of different people."

THAD JONES-MEL LEWIS
770713
13 July 1977, RF TV broadcast, Les Jardin des Arènes de Cimiez, La Grande Parade du Jazz, Nice: Same as 9 July 1977, omit Rully:

a   Don't Git Sassy
b   Walkin' About
c   I Love You
d   Evol Deklaw Ni (Love Walked In)
e   It Only Happens Every Time
f   61st and Richard
g   Ambiance

It's unclear if video still exists.

THAD JONES-MEL LEWIS
770714
14 July 1977, RF radio broadcast, Les Jardin des Arènes de Cimiez, La Grande Parade du Jazz, Nice: Same as 9 July 1977; Aura Rully voc*; GUEST: Eddie Daniels ts†:

a	The Groove Merchant	Blu Jazz (Ger) CD: BJO-32-CD
b	Medley*:	Blu Jazz (Ger) unissued
	Flying Home	
	Route 66	
c	A Child Is Born	
d	And I Love You So	Blu Jazz (Ger) CD: BJO-32-CD
e	Take a Ladder†	Blu Jazz (Ger) unissued
f	Mach II	
g	The Second Race	Blu Jazz (Ger) CD: BJO-32-CD

THAD JONES-MEL LEWIS
770715
15 July 1977, RF TV broadcast, Les Jardin des Arènes de Cimiez, La Grande Parade du Jazz, Nice: Same as 9 July 1977; Aura Rully voc*:

a	Evol Deklaw Ni (Love Walked In)	Blu Jazz (Ger) unissued
b	It Only Happens Every Time	
c	61st and Richard	
d	Here's that Rainy Day*	
e	Route 66*	
f	**My Centennial**[1]	
g	Low Down	Blu Jazz (Ger) CD: BJO-32-CD
h	Yours and Mine	
i	**Three and One**	

[1]Thad Jones and some bandmembers play various percussion instruments.

It's unclear if video still exists.

NEW YORK JAZZ REPERTORY COMPANY
770717a
17 July 1977, FR3 TV broadcast, Les Jardin des Arènes de Cimiez, La Grande Parade du Jazz, Nice: Jon Faddis, Jimmy Maxwell, Joe New-

man; John Mosca, Billy Campbell tb; Earl McIntyre btb; Bob Wilber as, ss; Eddie Daniels ts, cl; Zoot Sims, Billy Mitchell ts; Pepper Adams bs; Dick Hyman p arr; Raymond Fol p*; George Duvivier b; Bobby Rosengarden, Sam Woodyard dm.†

a **East St. Louis Toodle-Oo**[1]
b Double Check Stomp[2]
c Jungle Nights in Harlem[3]
d Doctor E.K.E.*†
e Harlem Airshaft
f Blue Goose
g **Jumpin' Punkins**
h Chelsea Bridge
i **Main Stem**

[1]Faddis, Campbell, Mitchell, and Sims out.
[2]Newman, McIntyre, Mitchell, and Adams out.
[3]Sims and Mitchell out.

It's unclear if video still exists.

THAD JONES
770717b
17 July 1977, audience recording, Les Jardin des Arènes de Cimiez, La Grande Parade du Jazz, Nice: Thad Jones flh, cornet; Tony Scott, Billy Mitchell ts*; Pepper Adams bs; Harold Danko p; Rufus Reid b; Mel Lewis dm.

a **Mean What You Say**
b **Oleo***

THAD JONES-MEL LEWIS
770717c
17 July 1977, audience recording, Les Jardin des Arènes de Cimiez, La Grande Parade du Jazz, Nice: Same as 9 July 1977; Aura Rully voc*:

a Mach II
b **Two as One**
c Suite for Pops:
        Meetin' Place

The Summary
The Farewell
d   Here's that Rainy Day[*]
e   **Billie's Bounce**
f   Fingers

THAD JONES-MEL LEWIS
770720
20 July 1977, audience recording, Milan: Same as 9 July 1977, omit Rully:

a   Evol Deklaw Ni (Love Walked In)
b   The Second Race
c   **Thank You**
d   Take a Ladder
e   Here's that Rainy Day
f   **Little Rascal on a Rock**
g   Willow Weep for Me
h   **My Centennial**[1]

[1]Thad Jones and some bandmembers play various percussion instruments.

THAD JONES-MEL LEWIS
770727
27 July 1977, audience recording, Club 7, Oslo: Same as 9 July 1977; Aura Rully voc*:

a   Rhoda Map
b   And I Love You So[1]
c   The Big Dipper
d   **Two as One**
e   Here's that Rainy Day[*]
f   Airmail Special[2]
g   61st and Richard
h   **Three and One**
i   Yours and Mine
j   Backbone
k   Tiptoe
m   A Child Is Born[3]
n   Route 66[*]

o   Fingers
p   Say It Softly
q   The Groove Merchant
r   I Can't Get Started[4]

[1]Jones and some bandmembers play various percussion instruments.
[2]Jones and rhythm section.
[3]Jones and rhythm section.
[4]Jones and rhythm section.

THAD JONES-MEL LEWIS
770800A
c. early August 1977, audience recording, Scandinavia: Same as 9 July 1977, omit Rully:

a   Low Down   Editoriale Pantheon (It) CD: JCD-11
b   Yours and Mine
c   The Oregon Grinder
d   **Three and One**
e   And I Love You So
f   Tiptoe
g   The Second Race
h   The Groove Merchant

The band's August tour schedule: 29 July-6 August (Copenhagen), 7 August (Gavle, Sweden), 8 August (Stockholm), 9 August (Lund, Sweden), 10 August (Aarhus, Denmark), 11 August (Copenhagen), 12-13 August (Stockholm), 14 August (Jonkoping, Sweden), 15 August (Goteborg, Sweden), 16 August (Oslo), 17 August (Boras, Sweden), 18 August (Vasteras, Sweden), 19 August (travel), 20-21 August (Helsinki), 22 August (Uppsala, Sweden), 23 August (Vaxjo, Sweden).

THAD JONES-MEL LEWIS
770800B
c. early August 1977, private videotape, possibly Tivoli Gardens, Copenhagen: Same as 9 July 1977, omit Rully:

a   Once Around
b   The Little Pixie
c   **My Centennial**[1]

[1]Thad Jones and some bandmembers play various percussion instruments.

Saxophonist Gary Smulyan wrote to the author in 2004: "I saw a video when I was in Sweden of an outdoor concert with Thad and Mel in Copenhagen (Dexter Gordon walks across the screen!) where Pepper plays his ass off on My Centennial." A few years earlier, Smulyan had also told the author of outdoor footage taken of the Thad Jones-Mel Lewis Orchestra in Copenhagen, near the Strøget. It's not clear if all three tracks are from this same concert.

THAD JONES-MEL LEWIS
770808
8 August 1977, audience recording, Restaurant Atlantic, Stockholm: Same as 9 July 1977, omit Rully:

a   Ambiance
b   Oregon Grinder
c   **My Centennial**[1]

[1]Thad Jones and some bandmembers play various percussion instruments.

THAD JONES-MEL LEWIS
770811
11 August 1977, audience recording, Montmartre Jazzhus, Copenhagen: Same as 9 July 1977, omit Rully.

THAD JONES-MEL LEWIS
770816
16 August 1977, radio broadcast or audience recording, Club 7, Oslo: Same as 9 July 1977, omit Rully.

It's unclear if audio still exists.

THAD JONES-MEL LEWIS
770820a
20 August 1977, audience recording, Hotel Hesperia, Helsinki: Same as 9 July 1977, omit Rully, Clifford Adams voc*:

a   Take a Ladder
b   Ambiance

c   The Groove Merchant
d   Samba con Getchu
e   **Little Rascal on a Rock**
f   Willow Weep for Me
g   Oregon Grinder
h   Body and Soul
i   **My Centennial**[1]
j   Route 66*
k   It Only Happens Every Time
m   Mach II
n   **Two as One**
o   Walkin' About

[1]Jones and some bandmembers play various percussion instruments.

MONICA ZETTERLUND–IT ONLY HAPPENS EVERY TIME 770820b

20-21 August 1977, Sound Track Recording Studios, Helsinki: Thad Jones flh, perc; Earl Gardner, Larry Moses, Jeff Davis, Frank Gordon tp, flh; John Mosca, Billy Campbell, Clifford Adams tb; Earl McIntyre btb; Jerry Dodgion, Ed Xiques as, ss, cl, fl; Richard Perry, Dick Oatts ts, cl, fl; Pepper Adams bs; Harold Danko p; Rufus Reid b; Mel Lewis dm; Monica Zetterlund voc.

a   It Only Happens Every Time[1]   EMI Svenska (Swe) LP:
                                            7C-O62-35454
b   He Was Too Good to Me
c   The Groove Merchant
d   Love to One Is One to Love
e   The Second Time Around

[1]Jones and some bandmembers play various percussion instruments.

All tracks on Inner City LP: IC-1082, Trio-Kenwood (J) LP: PAP-9165, EMI (Neth) CD: 7243-4-75205-2-5.
It's not known what material was taken from either session.
In a 1987 interview with the author, Rufus Reid said,

That was interesting. That's when I really began to really see how fantastic Thad was, in terms of his writing skills, because he didn't have all the music completed on schedule, but, on route, on the bus, he wrote two arrangements. I sat and watched him for maybe three, four, five hundred miles. We did those [long rides]. Most big bands do those, but, I tell ya, without a *piano*—and then, when we got a chance to get to the studio, he had already done three things, and we rehearsed those things, so, while we were already playing and recording those things, the new things he was writing were being copied, and the counterpoint and the music that was coming out was awesome to me. He was doing that in his head! He always waited until the last minute.

According to Harold Danko, in an interview with the author in 1989,

Thad wrote some gorgeous charts. Yeah, he loved to leave it right until the very end, and then he'd just get nuts, and, over a couple of days, he'd come up with everything he needed to do—or almost everything, anyway....[Pepper] knew Monica. He was very close with some other people there—Hans Fridlund and his wife, Annika—and they were close with Monica. They were old friends, so it just seemed like Pepper was involved in the workings on a personal level.

In a letter to the author about the Zetterlund recording, dated 28 July 1989, journalist Hans Fridlund wrote:

[Pepper] was *very* instrumental to get [this date] together, since Thad, as usual, messed up the whole working schedule....Thad, of course, hadn't even begun to write these charts. So work was slow in the studio, and a finishing-off session was arranged in the Stockholm Radio House on the band's return to Sweden (*see* 770823). Bosse Broberg helped with copyists; Thad writing desperately in an adjoining studio to finish in time to get on the bus for the next booked gig, in Southern Sweden; and Pepper coming up with the idea of just he and Monica and the rhythm section to record a few "fillers" for the album. Producer Gunnar Lindqvist, formerly the recently deceased Lars Gullin's producer and staunchest supporter, had Pepper and Monica do two Gullin tunes, Silhouette (with "long notes" from the horns as a backup—hardly a real chart) and Happy Again, an out-and-out quartet number, with the singing added later on. The lyrics weren't even written at the time.

According to Ed Xiques, in an interview with the author in 1988,

I stayed up all night copying music for this date, as [Thad] was writing it. For two or three days I was copying music. I was up all night the day of the recording. They were in the studio and I'm still copying. [Thad] would finally finish the chart, I would finish copying it, he would hand me the pages. He was sitting at a piano and I was at a table, and, as he finished a page, he would hand it to me and I would finish the parts. Then I would come in and rehearse the chart while he was still writing....It was a big scene because Thad wasn't prepared. Thad had known about it way in front, but kept putting it off. He worked that way. He would work under pressure.

About the Zetterlund date, according to John Mosca, in an interview with the author in 1988, Pepper Adams

was a great ensemble player as well. He had "big ears." When we were doing the Monica Zetterlund date, they had us set up kind of weird in the studio. The saxes were across the way, and the brass was over here, and right after, maybe the first time through something, [Pepper] came right over to me and said, "What do you want to do here, because I'm playing with the trombones." He already knew his place in the chart, which is one of those things that, when you're playing in a big band ensemble, you really need to know who you're doubling with, and he already had checked out that he was with the trombones in this spot and he wanted to know how we were going to phrase. I guess I was playing lead, and he was asking me what we were going to do.

THAD JONES-MEL LEWIS
770821
21 August 1977, audience recording, Hotel Hesperia, Helsinki: Same as 9 July 1977:

a   Rhoda Map
b   **Thank You**
c   **The Little Pixie**
d   Yours and Mine
e   **Centennial**[1]

[1]Jones and some bandmembers play various percussion instruments.

MONICA ZETTERLUND–IT ONLY HAPPENS EVERY TIME
770823
23 August 1977, Swedish Radio, Stockholm: Same as 20 August 1977:

a   Long Daddy Green   EMI Svenska (Swe) LP: 7C-O62-35454
    Zetturlund, Adams, and rhythm section:
b   **Happy Again**
c   **Silhouette**[1]

[1]The tune is augmented by occasional big band chords. See Hans Fridlund's comments on 770820a.

All tracks on Inner City LP: IC-1082, Trio-Kenwood (J) LP: PAP-9165, EMI-Svenska (Swe) CD: 7243-4-75205-2-5.

This was Adams' last performance with the Thad Jones-Mel Lewis Orchestra.

See 770820a.

Chapter 5
International Soloist: 1977-1986

PEPPER ADAMS
770918
18 September 1977, Bach Dancing and Dynamite Society, Half Moon Bay CA: Pepper Adams bs; John Marabuto p; Bob Maize b; Ron Marabuto dm.

a **Dewey Square**   Just Jazz CD: JJCD-1004
b **Body and Soul**
c **Bossa Nouveau**
d **How Long Has This Been Going On**
e **Blues Out**

All tracks on Culture Press CD: 2003.
Bennet Blaustein produced a videotape of this concert (with an interview with Adams afterwards) but, according to producer Pat Britt, the remaining copy is damaged and undecipherable.
According to a letter to the author from Joel Patterson, dated 10 June 1988,

This show was coming up and they needed a third hand. We spent that afternoon setting up two cameras and taping all the wires to the floor of a bar that was right on the water. There were a few descending decks out the back, and the sand and shore, and the setting sun. Blondie—Bennet had a blonde buddy; wish I could remember his name—would run the tape machine, mounted on the bar, Bennet would do close-ups and solos, and I would keep an overall group shot to cut back to. The combo was four players and, when they were cooking, the ceiling tiles rocked....After the show, Pepper sat down in the bright lights of the empty hall (no stage) and talked for ten minutes to a guy from a radio station? a musicological stringer?

and this was recorded; Pepper very open, and laughing easily as he chatted with this historian, who asked him about touring or his roots or something.

DAVID AMRAM–HAVANA/NEW YORK
771001

c. 1 October 1977, Variety Sound Studios, New York: Thad Jones tp, flh; David Amram frh, fl, p, g, perc; Jerry Dodgion as; Billy Mitchell ts; Pepper Adams, George Barrow bs; Eddie Gomez b; Candido Camero cga; Ray Mantilla cga, perc; Johnny Rodriguez Jr., Los Papines, Nicky Marrero perc; Alfredo De La Fe perc, violin; vocal choir*: Bonnie Koloc, Rahni Kugel, Illana Morillo, Patti Smyth.

a   **Havana/New York**   Flying Fish LP: FF-057
b   **Para los Papines***

All tracks on Flying Fish CD: 18964-0057-2.

PEPPER ADAMS
771010

10 October 1977, RF radio broadcast, Jazz Pulsations, Nancy, France: Pepper Adams bs; Georges Arvanitas p; Jacky Samson b; Charles Saudrais dm.

a   **Just Friends**
b   **Ephemera**
c   **I Can't Get Started**
d   **Oleo**

VLADIMIR COSMA
771019

19 October 1977 film soundtrack, Paris: Tony Russo, Pierre Dutour, Michel Barrot tp; unknown tp; Jacques Bolognési, Christian Guizien, Hamid Belocine tb; Mark Steckar btb; Raymond Guiot fl; Al Newman, Alain Hato as; Tony Coe ts, cl; Jean-Louis Chautemps ts; Pepper Adams bs; Maurice Vander p, e-p; Michel Gaudry b; Sam Woodyard dm.

a   **Les Sax Brothers**[1]   Déesse (F) LP: DDLX-157
b   **Jalousie-Blues**

c **Nous Irons Tous au Paradis**
d Le Souvenir de L'eléphant[2]
e Parker par Coeur
f All My Evening Birds   Largo (F) CD: 0015163

[1]Brass out.
[2]String section added, possibly at a later date.

Soundtrack to the film *Nous Irons Tous au Paradis (We Will All Go to Heaven),* directed by Yves Robert.

PEPPER ADAMS
771028
28 October 1977, audience recording, Aix-en-Provence, France: Pepper Adams bs; Georges Arvanitas p; Jacky Samson b; Charles Saudrais dm.

It's unclear if the audio still exists.

PEPPER ADAMS–LIVE IN EUROPE
771104
4 November 1977, Alhambra, Bordeaux: Pepper Adams bs; Georges Arvanitas p; Jacky Samson b; Charles Saudrais dm.

a **Bossa Nouveau**   Impro (F) LP: 02
b **Ephemera**
c **Min and Maj Blues**
d **Body and Soul**
e **Dear Old Stockholm**   Futura-Impro (F) CD: 10415

All tracks on Impro (F) CD: CD-151952, EPM Musique (F) CD: 151952, Futura-Impro (F) CD: 10415, Buda (F) CD: 329849-1519522.

PEPPER ADAMS
771212
12 December 1977, audience recording, Allary, Providence RI: Pepper Adams bs; Paul Schmelling p; Bob Peterutti b; Artie Cabral dm.

a **Just Friends**
b **Quiet Lady**

c **The Song Is You**
d **In a Sentimental Mood**
e **'Tis**
f **Mean What You Say**
g **Body and Soul**
h **Bossa Nouveau**
i **I've Just Seen Her**
j **'Tis**

According to saxophonist Danny Harrington, in an interview with the author in 1989, "Allary, on North Main Street...[was] running a name jazz policy for a while, where they'd bring in some of the better players from New York to play a night or two with a local rhythm section." *See* 771214.

PEPPER ADAMS
771214
14 December 1977, audience recording, Allary, Providence RI: Same as 12 December 1977:

a **Oleo**
b **How Long Has This Been Going On**
c **Bossa Nouveau**
d **A Child Is Born**
e **'Tis**
f **Three Little Words**
g **Scrapple from the Apple**
h **Ephemera**
i **Lover**
j **Julian**
k **'Tis**

See 771212b.

NICK BRIGNOLA–BARITONE MADNESS
771222
22 December 1977, Blue Rock Studio, New York: Ted Curson* tp, flh; Nick Brignola as†, bs; Pepper Adams bs; Derek Smith p; Dave Holland b; Roy Haynes dm.

a	**Billie's Bounce***	Beehive LP: BH-7000
b	**Marmaduke***	
c	**Marmaduke***	Beehive unissued
d	**Donna Lee**	Beehive LP: BH-7000

Brignola and rhythm section:

| e | Body and Soul | |

Rhythm section only:

| f | Alone Together | |

Full ensemble:

| g | **Stablemates**† | Beehive LP: BH-01 |

All issued tracks except -g on Paddle Wheel (J) LP: GP-3183.

In an interview with the author in 1989, upon hearing that Adams wasn't happy with this project, Nick Brignola agreed:

Neither was I. That was a big farce. Initially, the intent of doing the album was [with] all good intentions. It was this new label called Beehive out of Chicago. Jim [Neumann, its owner,] liked my playing. I didn't even know this guy. So here I couldn't get recorded at all, and now, all of a sudden, this guy's flying in from Chicago and wants to do an album with me.

I just thought it would be fun to do something with the two baritones. So we got together. They said it was going to be my album—initially—and who would I want on the album? So I started to name cats that I thought were compatible (but I learned my lesson). I had worked a lot with Dave Holland. He lived near us, so I wanted Dave on there. They wanted Ted Curson to be on the album because I had been with his band. I didn't really want Ted. Nothing against Ted, but I just wanted to make it two baritones. But this was their first album, and they were trying to make a big stew out of it. Next thing I know, Roy Haynes is on the drums, and Derek Smith....I just assumed everybody knew what they were doing, and then it didn't work out.

The other problem was it was initially going to be my album, then, the day of the date, they told me it was not going to be my album: It was going to be an all-star album, because of all the guys that were around, and all that. So I completely let go of the record date. I had no control over it, and, it was a question of, "Well, what do you want to play?" And then they went over to Derek Smith and said, "And what would you like to play?" There's a trio piece

on there. It was supposed to be a baritone album. That would never
be on there. No offense to Derek, but it was just not the right way to
do an album like that. I did Body and Soul, and they decided to do
Donna Lee fast, and Pepper decided to do Marmaduke, and we got
through it, and that was it. It was a fun album and that was the end
of it, and then a month later I got a call saying that they had
changed their mind: They are going to make me the leader. Man,
was I pissed! And then, to top it off, Pepper was *really* bugged because they used a picture on the cover [in which] Pepper's more
prominent in the picture. He took offense to that, figuring that it
looked like it was going to be his album.

Reflecting back on the experience, Brignola admitted to the author, in the
same interview, how naive he was: "I didn't know anything about it:
That was my first big, major recording, in a sense. I just didn't know that
those were decisions I could have made....After that, they wanted Pepper
and I to do another one, and, at that point, he just didn't want to hear
about that company."

On a 19 November 1985 after-hours interview that was conducted in
Calgary by saxophonist John Reid, Pepper Adams said,

Any time I find myself playing, I try to play as well as I can, although, in that situation, it was extremely difficult with the rhythm
section as it was: Just not together, and the studio was physically set
up so it would have made it difficult for them to play together, but I
don't think they were even trying too hard. And, with the rhythm
section all spread out like that, then the only real hope you've got of
hearing everybody is through the earphones, but the engineer didn't
know how to set up the earphones so that you could hear everybody.
I was standing right by the piano, and [I] could hear the bass, sort
of, and [I] had to stand on tiptoe to see Roy Haynes over his drums!
He was like about twenty yards away! I put on the earphones, and
all that's in the earphones is the piano. I figure, well, this isn't going
to help at all. I mean, he's right here! That's not what I need, so I
took the damn things off and I tried to listen to Dave Holland's bass
as much as possible...If anybody was going to have anything to do
with the time, he might.

In an interview with Pepper Adams, conducted in Malmo in March
1985 by Alfie Nilsson, Adams said:

This is why I never recorded for Beehive again: If you remember, it was Nick Brignola's album and I was just a sideman. They have my picture on the cover, my name on the cover, my name on the spine, doing everything they can to make it look like my album. I wasn't even paid as a soloist on that. I went to the date thinking that it was a rock'n'roll overdub or something. In this case, I think the fellow was an amateur, but just saw a way to get some value out of having me on the record...but I took considerable offense and I let him know about it.

According to Fred Norsworthy, in an interview with the author in 1987, Norsworthy produced the recording and Neumann paid for the date. About Pepper Adams' displeasure with it, Norsworthy said,

> It turned out better than expected, in a way. I know he was a little unhappy. I think part of it was he and Jim didn't get along, And, unfortunately, Jim was rather adamant about Nick staying only on baritone, and, for some reason, Nick switched over to alto on Stablemates and that freaked Jim out, because he's very set in his ways, I guess. So, as a result, that's the reason for the trio side with Derek, Dave, and Roy Haynes. I did it as a filler, because I knew, without him putting Stablemates out at all on the album, then I had to fill the album out....
>
> At the time we did the album, Nick, unfortunately, was virtually unknown outside a hardcore bunch of people, and Jim wanted to start his Beehive Records. The original date for that, which I'd set up, was going to be Zoot Sims and Chet Baker and Nick. What happened was Chet Baker, of course, couldn't be found anywhere, so that went down the tubes. And Zoot just signed with Norman Granz, and, since Norman took exceptionally good care financially of his players, they're in no way going to record advertisement for anybody. Zoot had done the *Encounter* album [*see* 681211], and, of course, he'd love to do it, but his obligation was to Norman. So, I said, "Gee, brain wave! I'll get Pepper and do a baritone [thing]." We got Ted Curson on trumpet, since Ted and Nick had worked together for almost seventeen years. That's how it all came about, and, believe it or not, we finished the album off in approximately five and a half hours.

Regarding alternate tracks, Norsworthy continued,

There are some, but they weren't complete. For example, the first tune of the date was a Charlie Parker title [Marmaduke], and Pepper and Nick hastily ran over, kind of, the bridge, and everything like that, and, then, wham, they went in and hit it. The reason they did the tunes was to keep it very simple, because, unfortunately, there was no preparation. Pepper wasn't exactly too fond of Derek Smith. I think it basically was Derek's first all-star date that he'd ever done—I mean, outside the Famous Door sessions. I think Derek at the beginning was very over-awed. I think he was totally blown away by the caliber....Roy and I go back many years. I've known Roy since the days of Charlie Parker, and Dave Holland, I felt, was a very underrated bass player. Ron Carter, of course, at the time was under the CTI contract, so I thought Dave Holland would make a good alternate choice.

According to saxophonist Mark Berger, in an interview with the author in 1987, Pepper Adams was also unhappy with the mix on the recording. Adams told Berger that "it was mixed pretty much in Nick's favor. It made it sound like Nick had a sound that put Pepper's to shame ...like Nick was just blowing him away." Berger said that this tactic was used by Beehive on Brignola's subsequent release with Cecil Payne and Ronnie Cuber, in which Cuber's sound was doctored to favor Brignola.

In an interview with the author in 1988, drummer Andre White said that, when Pepper Adams visited Montreal for a concert at the Museum of Fine Arts (*see* 781105), "he was going on about this recording session he had done with Roy Haynes. He was *very* dragged with Roy Haynes! He was not happy!" It's probable that the recording had recently been released.

CHARLES MINGUS–SOMETHING LIKE A BIRD
780118
18 January 1978, Atlantic Studios, New York: Jack Walrath, Randy Brecker, Mike Davis tp; Slide Hampton, Jimmy Knepper tb; Ken Hitchcock ss, as; Lee Konitz, Charles McPherson, Akira Ohmori as; George Coleman as, ts; Dan Block, Michael Brecker, Ricky Ford ts; Pepper Adams, Ronnie Cuber, Craig Purpura bs; Bob Neloms p; Kenny Werner e-p; Ted Dunbar, Jack Wilkins, Larry Coryell, Danny Toan g; Eddie Gomez, George Mraz b; Joe Chambers, Dannie Richmond dm; Ray Mantilla perc.

a   36884   **Something Like a Bird**   Atlantic LP: SD-8805

-a on Atlantic (Eu) LP: 50764, Atlantic (Gr) LP: 50764, Warner-Pioneer (J) LP: P-10938A, Collectables CD: COL-6840.

According to George Coleman, in an interview with the author in 1989, "That was like a whole bunch of all-stars playing big band charts. I think Jack Walrath did most of the orchestration, but all of that was written by Mingus."

Regarding -a, in an interview with Mike Bloom in *Klacto*, Adams said, "It's the tune I think I referred to once as "All the Choruses on the Changes to Idaho that Your Family Will Ever Need.""

According to Pepper Adams, in an interview with Peter Danson in *Coda*,

> Where Ronnie and I trade choruses in eights and sevens, I begin my solo with a quote from Baby It's Cold Outside. So almost two years later, I am playing the record and I heard that, and I said, "My God, that's dumb. Why did I do that?" Then I remember we had about three feet of snow outside on that date.
>
> There was less chaos than normal with Charles' dates. In this case, the music had been ready in advance, and it had been rehearsed prior to that. He was in good spirits.

Ricky Ford told the author, in an interview in 1989 about Adams, "I don't think he had ever gotten a chance to record with Gerry Mulligan up to that point, and, subsequently, Gerry Mulligan couldn't make it and they hired Ronnie Cuber [instead. Adams] intimated that he always wanted to get a piece of Mulligan!...Pepper sounded very good on that date. He and Ronnie Cuber—I mean they really played up a storm! It was one of the standouts on the date, among so many other standouts. Pepper was one of the outstanding soloists of the twentieth century on the baritone."

See 780119, 780123.

CHARLES MINGUS–ME MYSELF AN EYE
780119
19 January 1978, Atlantic Studios, New York: Same as 18 January 1978, omit Konitz, McPherson, Werner; add Joe Chambers dm and Sammy Figueroa perc:

a   36249   Three Worlds of Drums   Atlantic LP: SD-8803

-a on Atlantic (Eu) LP: 50571, Atlantic (Eng) LP: 50571, Atlantic (F) LP: WEA-341, Warner-Pioneer (J) LP: P-10638A, Collectables CD: COL-6840.
See 780118, 780123.

CHARLES MINGUS
780123
23 January 1978, Atlantic Studios, New York: Same as 18 January 1978; Keith O'Quinn tb replaces Hampton; add John Tank ts; omit Hitchcock, Konitz, McPherson, Ohmori, Coleman, Werner, Mraz, Mantilla:

a	36250	Devil Woman	Atlantic LP: SD-8803
b		Devil Woman	Atlantic unissued
c	36251	Wednesday Night Prayer Meeting	Atlantic LP: SD-8803
d	36252	Carolyn "Keki" Mingus	
e	36885	Farewell Farwell[1]	Atlantic LP: SD-8805

[1]Michael Brecker, Randy Brecker, Dannie Richmond out.

-a on Atlantic (Eu) LP: 50571, Atlantic (Eng) LP: 50571, Atlantic (F) LP: WEA-341, Warner-Pioneer (J) LP: P-10638-A, Collectables CD: COL-6840.
-c on Atlantic (Eu) LP: 50571, Atlantic (Eng) LP: K-781-907-1, Atlantic (F) LP: WEA-341, Warner-Pioneer (J) LP: P-10638-A, Atlantic (Eng) CD: 781-907-2, Collectables CD: COL-6840.
-d on Atlantic (Eu) LP: 50571, Atlantic (Eng) LP: 50571, Atlantic (F) LP: WEA-341, Warner-Pioneer (J) LP: P-10638-A, Collectables CD: COL-6840.
-e on Atlantic (Eu) LP: 50764, Warner-Pioneer (J) LP: P-10938-A, Collectables CD: COL-6840.
This session had been scheduled for 20 January 1978, but a snow storm postponed it for three days.
According to Pepper Adams, in an interview with Peter Danson in *Coda*, "there was a blues thing [Devil Woman] on which I made a private joke for Charles. I started a solo with a quote from Lips Page's tune We Got Fish for Supper, but played in the wrong key, and persisted in

the wrong key for quite a while. And I was watching Charles out of the corner of my eye, while I was doing this, and he was just cracking up. It was something we'd used as a private, inside joke."

See 780118, 780119.

CHET BAKER
780125

25-29 January 1978, private recordings, Jazz Showcase, Chicago: Chet Baker tp; Pepper Adams bs; Willie Pickens p; Steve Rodby b; Wilbur Campbell dm.

See Author's Note above 580000A entry.

DAVID AMRAM
780130

30 January 1978, WTTW TV broadcast, Chicago: David Amram frh, fl, perc; Jerry Dodgion as; Pepper Adams bs; Alfredo De La Fe violin; Brian Torff e-b; Al Harewood dm; Ray Mantilla, Nicky Morrero perc; 42 members of the Chicago Symphony Orchestra; GUESTS: Dizzy Gillespie tp, perc, voc; Jethro Burns mandolin; Bonnie Kolac, Floyd Westerman, Steve Goodman voc.

a   **Pull My Daisy**[1]
b   En Memoria de Chano Pozo
c   Summer Nights and Winter Rain[2]
d   Crab Grass[3]
e   unknown title[4]
f   unknown blues[5]
g   **Rondo alla Turca: Allegro**

[1]Amram and Koloc voc.
[2]Goodman voc.
[3]Burns on this track only; Gillespie perc, Amram voc.
[4]Westerman voc.
[5]Amram, Gillespie, Goodman voc.

According to David Amram, this PBS special, *David Amram and Friends,* was, apart from the symphonic piece that concluded the show, a tribute to percussionist Chano Pozo, and it was recorded for the program

Sound Stage. According to Amram, in an interview with the author in 1988, Pepper Adams played

all the Latin and jazz pieces, and then, at the end, he was dressed up in tails, like we all were, for the finale, when we recorded, with members of the Chicago Symphony, the last movement of [Amram's] *Triple Concerto.* We had a rehearsal with the symphony members. I think 42 members of the symphony came in. We had just a forty minute run-through, but they were such "scarifyingly" brilliant symphonic players that they were able to read it once or twice and then it sounded as good as I ever heard it played in my life....

Since Pepper and Jerry and Al Harewood had played it before so many times, when they went out to eat supper, they came back a little late because they already knew their part inside out. They were tired, because we had been recording all the other stuff. I said, "Look: Just come back just so we can at least go through it once, so the orchestra can at least hear what your part sounds like, because I want to do a little work on some of the parts." The bass player, Brian Torff, came, and he hadn't played the piece before, so he got there early so he could be sure to get his part. And I knew what it sounded like, and I was doing a lot of the soloing on Pakistani flute anyway, and conducting it, so I wasn't worried about them there.

They showed up about 25 minutes after the musicians had gone through it the first time to get used to the different tempos. There was a lot of complex stuff with the Middle Eastern writing and all that. They came strolling back in, smiling and laughing and looking happy. Some of the people in the symphony, not knowing them, and not really knowing the piece and what it was going to sound like, were kind of shocked to see some of the people strolling in, because, in the symphony world, everything starts exactly on the second and stops exactly on the second. Then, when they heard everybody play, then they suddenly changed, because they could hear what fantastic players Jerry and Pepper and Al were. Plus, knowing the piece as they did, they really put it right in the pocket.

Just before we made the first take, we had some time, and I thought it would just be nice to, in the interest of the brotherhood and sisterhood of all musicians, introduce the members of our group. Jazz teaches us to be together, and realize [that] every living musician is almost like part of your family, in the true sense, because that's the way jazz players are, and the way symphony players used to be, and still are when they're able to have the right conditions. But sometimes, in the symphony world, players lose that feeling because it's so competitive, and becomes so impersonal, and, very often, the conductors spoil the whole atmosphere and take away that good musicianly fraternal feeling. So, I thought it would be nice just to bring everyone together and introduce the members of our group. So I introduced Al Harewood, and said what a magnificent blessing it had been for me to play with him all those years; how it inspired me to write certain parts of the piece. And Brian Torff: What a great young bass player he was, coming in and playing for the first time. How nice it was to have him be part of this program too. And Jerry Dodgion, who had been a musician's musician. They all stood up and took a little bow. The symphony kind of applauded politely, and then I said, "Finally, then, there's the man here who, when I wrote the piece, the only part that wasn't composed and written out, where there's any improvisation, aside from a few little parts of my own, were for this man, who's inspired generations of musicians to look at the baritone saxophone and music in a whole different way: Pepper Adams." Pepper stood up, and they were about to applaud, and he turned around and he said, "Ladies and Gentlemen. It's nice to play with an orchestra of note." At the same time, he had a cigarette and a beer bottle in his hand when he stood up, but he looked so professorial, at the same time, with his glasses and his crew cut and his tails. When he stood up, with his cigarette and his beer bottle, looking like a crazed bank president, and then he said that, the orchestra first looked at him, with the beer bottle and the cigarette, in sort of a state of semi-shock. There was a silence, and then all 42 members of the Chicago Symphony cracked up laughing!

See 780131.

DAVID AMRAM
780131
31 January 1978, WTTW TV broadcast, Chicago: Same as 30 January 1978.

It's unclear what material from this date or 780130 comprised the television broadcast. It's likely that some, if not all, of the material performed on 780130 was performed here.

PEPPER ADAMS
780318
18 March 1978, private recording, Gulliver's, West Paterson NJ: Pepper
Adams bs; Tommy Flanagan p; Frank Tusa b; Ron Marabuto dm;
GUEST: Bill Evans ts.*

a   **Half Nelson**
b   **Time on My Hands**
c   **Three Little Words**
d   **Chelsea Bridge**
e   **'Tis**
f   **Apothegm**
     Rhythm section only:
g   A Blue Time
     Full ensemble:
h   **Body and Soul**
i   **Sweet Georgia Brown**
j   **'Tis**
k   **I've Just Seen Her**
m   **What Is This Thing Called Love***
n   **I Love You***

EASTMAN JAZZ ENSEMBLE
780327
27 March 1978, audience recording, Eastman Theater, Rochester NY:
Eastman Jazz Ensemble; GUEST: Pepper Adams bs.

a   **Salt and Pepper**
b   **unknown title**
c   **Blues Antigua**
d   **Motion Suspended**
     Adams and rhythm section:
e   **Body and Soul**

Adams dedicated -e to Everett Gates, a professor at Eastman, and an
early mentor to Adams who was in the audience. Regarding Adams' performance of Body and Soul, Gates, in an interview with the author in
1988, said, "That completely floored me!" In 1942, when Pepper Adams
was eleven years old, Adams started visiting Gates on a regular basis at

Gates' home in Rochester, New York. They used to listen to music and discuss jazz and music theory. "He came to the house," Gates continued, "and one day he said,

> "Do you know Body and Soul?" I said, "Sure." "Well," he said, "could you write it out for me?" I said, "Sure." At that time he was going to get a saxophone. So I wrote it out in D-flat, which of course was the key we always used, rather than any other when we're playing. When we were improvising, it was always D-flat. And, so I wrote it out with the chords. He said, "There's a record by Coleman Hawkins." I said, "Yes, he made that a couple of years ago." He said, "Well, he's all over the place." I said, "Yes, it's very complicated and he gets up even to the high harmonics on the saxophone, like high G, so you have to be pretty advanced to control those." So he said, "I wonder: Could you write me out a little improvisation that's simple? Something simple I can play?" I said, "Sure. You can play this either on tenor, or you can play it on a clarinet." So he got so he could play that, [and] this is what [he began his solo with] when he played at the Eastman Theater with the Eastman Jazz Ensemble. (He played this just with a rhythm section, and the other things he had played with a big band.) And, unbelievably, he played that, and then, of course, he went into his own [thing]. Well, of course, I was just overcome with what he had done there!

PEPPER ADAMS
780430
30 April 1978, KGO TV broadcast, San Francisco: Pepper Adams bs; Larry Vuckovich p; Bob Maize b; Clarence Becton dm.

According to Adams' 1978 appointment book, Adams was paid for an appearance on ABC-TV. KGO is an ABC affiliate. Judging from the amount Adams was paid, it's likely that he only played one tune with the house rhythm section on Sonny Buxton's show, *AM Weekend.* It's unclear if audio or video still exist. *See* 781112.

PEPPER ADAMS–REFLECTORY
780614
14 June 1978, CI Recording, New York: Pepper Adams bs; George Mraz b; Roland Hanna p; Billy Hart dm.

a	**Reflectory**	Muse LP: MR-5182
b	**Sophisticated Lady**	
c	**Etude Diabolique**	
d	**Claudette's Way**	
e	**I Carry Your Heart**	
f	**That's All**	

-c on Franklin Mint LP: FM-72, Muse CD: CDMR-5182, Camden-BMG (Neth) CD: 74321-610882.

All tracks on Franklin Mint LP: FM-72, Muse-WEA (F) LP: MR-5182, Muse CD: CDMR-5182, Camden-BMG (Neth) CD: 74321-610882.

This is Adams' sixteenth date as a leader.

According to Adams, in an interview with Peter Danson in *Coda*, "I think Elvin Campbell has captured my sound the best, particularly on the *Reflectory* and *The Master* albums (*see* 800311). He used two microphones—one close, and one high and fairly distant—and put them on separate tracks and then remixed." Adams told the author in 1984 that he was most proud of both these recordings.

According to Billy Hart, in an interview with the author in 1988,

Of all the record dates I've ever done—I've never really counted them, but I'm sure it's around 200 record dates—Pepper is the only one that I ever worked with that seemed to know exactly how long every tune would be. I mean, he was so clear and so explicit: He would know the tempo, he would know how many choruses, and he would know how long each tune would take. Consequently...his were easy, and they were quick, because he was so thorough! He left nothing to guess. But he didn't stifle, he didn't impede your creativity in any way! It enhanced it by being so clear!

First of all, he'd have [all the parts] written very clearly. Then he would describe, in his very clear way, exactly what it was: "This is eight bars with a four bar tag, and I want this with brushes, but then this is that, and this should be Latin here, and it should build here, and I think this is going to take about five minutes and roughly forty seconds."

Another thing, he was like they say J.J. [Johnson] is: You're never worried about *his* solo any way. He was always going to take a great solo. I mean, solo after solo after solo. (Now, I'm trying to think of whose other record date we were on, because the other guy didn't like his solo, so we did take after take, but every solo that Pepper took was a masterpiece! It might have been Peter Leitch, I don't really remember [*see* 841117].) So on Pepper's own dates, if *we* got it right, that was it! He didn't have to take his solo over!

If the ending had a thing to it, he really showed you what it was. You never had to think, "Boy, I see this, but how am I going to play it?" He told you exactly what it was. It's one thing to think it out. I think out all my arrangements. But he knew how to articulate what it was. He knew the jazz language, like Hank Jones knows the jazz language—three or four generations of it. He can quote very articulately from the '30s to the '80s. Pepper didn't [always] have to say it. He would play it. He would play something and you could tell that it might have been a '30s or '40s type thing, "classic style," whether it was Fats Waller, Ben Webster.

I only know that I was affected to play a certain way by the way he played—unmistakably. Man, there's been a lot of great baritone saxophone players, and I've enjoyed and loved everyone I heard, from Cecil Payne to Ronnie Cuber, Mulligan, Carney. Serge [Chaloff] was bad and Leo [Parker]'s from my hometown, but there was something about the first time I heard Pepper to the last time. It stuck right in me immediately, like that was it! The same thing like the first time I heard Coltrane: That was it for me!

THE WIZ
780621a
21 June 1978, film soundtrack, A&R Studios, New York: Collective personnel: Bernie Glow, Jon Faddis, Ernie Royal, Marvin Stamm, Randy Brecker, Lew Soloff, Burt Collins, Chuck Findley, Joe Wilder, Clark Terry, Tom Bahler, Randy Brecker, Daniel Cahn tp; Eddie Bert, Wayne Andre, Urbie Green, Sonny Russo, George Flynn tb; Ray Alonge frh; Don Butterfield, Howard Johnson tuba; Hubert Laws fl; Johnny Mince cl; Jerome Richardson, Phil Bodner, Michael Brecker, Seldon Powell, Frank Wess, Walt Levinsky, John Campo, Ray Beckstein, Danny Bank reeds; Pepper Adams bs; Dick Hyman, Derek Smith, Bob James, Dave Grusin, Quincy Jones, Kenny Ascher, Thom Brodwell keyboards; Toots Thielemans harmonica; Eric Gale g; Carmen Mastren banjo; Ron Carter, Milt Hinton, John Beal b; Anthony Jackson e-b; Mel Lewis, Steve Gadd, Steve Little, Grady Tate, Harvey Mason dm; Paulinho DaCosta, Dave Friedman, Bill Lavorgna perc.

a   Overture   MCA LP: 11649
b   The Feeling that We Have
c   Can I Go On
d   Glinda's Theme
e   He's the Wizard
f   Medley:
        Soon As I Get Home
        Home
g   You Can't Win
h   Ease on Down the Road
i   What Would I Do If I Could Feel
j   Slide Some Oil to Me
k   Ease on Down the Road
m   (I'm a) Mean Ole Lion
n   Ease on Down the Road
o   Poppy Girls
p   Be a Lion
q   End of the Yellow Brick Road
r   Emerald City Sequence
s   So You Wanted to See the Wizard
t   Is This What Feeling Gets
u   Don't Nobody Bring Me No Bad News
v   A Brand New Day
w   Believe in Yourself
x   The Good Witch Glenda
y   Believe in Yourself
z   Home

Soundtrack to the film version of *The Wiz*, directed by Sidney Lu-
met. A separate recording was made of the Broadway stage production.
    -e on MCA LP: MCA-2-14000, Universal CD: B-0010577-02, MCA
CD: 11649.
    -g on Epic 45: 28-50658, MCA LP: MCA-2-14000, Sony-Epic CD:
E5K-926600, Universal CD: B-0010577-02, MCA CD: 11649.
    -h on Atlantic-WEA (It) 45: W-10640, MCA (Sp) 45: 6832168,
MCA LP: MCA-2-14000, Sony-Epic CD: E5K-926600, Universal CD:
B-0010577-02, MCA CD: 11649.
    -j on MCA LP: MCA-2-14000, Universal CD: B-0010577-02, MCA
CD: 11649.

-m on MCA LP: MCA-2-14000, Universal CD: B-0010577-02, MCA CD: 11649.

-r on MCA LP: MCA-2-14000, Universal CD: B-0010577-02, MCA CD: 11649.

-v on MCA LP: MCA-2-14000, Universal CD: B-0010577-02, MCA CD: 11649.

-z on MCA LP: MCA-2-14000, Universal CD: B-0010577-02, MCA CD: 11649.

All tracks on MCA CD: 11649, MCA LP: MCA-2-14000, Universal CD: B-0010577-02, MCA CD: 11649.

It's unclear on what tunes Adams performs.

This was likely done on several dates, possibly, in Adams' case, as overdubs, with vocals and vocal choirs, and strings added at subsequent sessions. *See* 780624.

WALTER BISHOP JR–CUBICLE
780621b
21 June 1978, CI Recording, New York: Randy Brecker tp, flh; Curtis Fuller tb; Rene McLean ss, as, ts; Pepper Adams bs; Walter Bishop Jr. p, e-p; Joe Caro g; Bob Cranshaw, Mark Egan e-b†; Billy Hart dm; Ray Mantilla perc; Carmen Lundy voc.*

a	Valley Land*†	Muse LP: MR-5151
b	**My Little Suede Shoes**	
c	Those Who Chant	
d	**Summertime†**	
e	**Now, Now that You've Left Me**	
f	**Cubicle**	

MICKEY TUCKER–MISTER MYSTERIOUS
780623
23 June 1978, Van Gelder Studio, Englewood Cliffs NJ: Cecil Bridgewater tp; Frank Foster ss, ts, fl; Pepper Adams bs; Mickey Tucker p; Cecil McBee b; Eddie Gladden dm; Ray Mantilla cga*; Azzedin Weston cga, perc.†

a	Plagio†	Muse LP: MR-5174
b	A Prayer	
c	**Mister Mysterious**	

d   **Taurus Lullaby**[*][†]
     Piano solo:
e   Cecilitis
     Full band:
f   **Basic Elements**

THE WIZ
780624
24 June 1978, film soundtack, New York: Same as 780621a.

DON FRIEDMAN–HOT KNEPPER AND PEPPER
780626
26 June 1978, Downtown Sound Studio, New York: Jimmy Knepper tb;
Pepper Adams bs; Don Friedman p; George Mraz b; Billy Hart dm.

a   **Audobon**   Progressive LP: P-7036
b   **Audobon**   Progressive CD: PCD-7036
c   **Audobon**   Progressive unissued
d   **Audobon**
e   **I'm Getting Sentimental Over You** Progressive LP: P-7036
f   **I'm Getting Sentimental Over You** Progressive CD: PCD-7036
g   **Hellure**   Progressive LP: P-7036
h   **Groovin' High**
i   Medley:
          Alfie[1]
          Laura[2]
          Prelude to a Kiss[3]
          I Got It Bad (And that Ain't Good)
j   **Beautiful Love**   Progressive CD: PCD-7036
k   **Beautiful Love**
m   **Beautiful Love**   Teichiku (J) LP: KUX-102-G

[1]Piano solo.
[2]Knepper and rhythm section.
[3]Rhythm section only.

-a on Progressive CD: PCD-7036, Teichiku (J) LP: KUX-102-G.
-b on Progressive CD: PCD-7036.
-e on Progressive CD: PCD-7036, Teichiku (J) LP: KUX-102-G,

-f on Progressive CD: PCD-7036.

-g on Progressive CD: PCD-7036, Teichiku (J) LP: KUX-102-G.

-h on Progressive CD: PCD-7036, Teichiku (J) LP: KUX-102-G.

-i on Progressive CD: PCD-7036, Teichiku (J) LP: KUX-102-G.

-j on Progressive CD: PCD-7036.

-k on Progressive CD: PCD-7036.

-m on Teichiku (J) LP: KUX-102-G.

Don Friedman told the author in 1987,

It was a strange date because I think originally [producer Gus Stati-ris] asked me some time before we actually did this date if I would do a date with Pepper and Jimmy Knepper. Sure, I wanted to! And then the thing got postponed or cancelled, and I just kind of put it out of my mind. I didn't think we were going to do it anymore, and then, one night, I got a call from him and he asked me to come into the studio the next day and do the date with Pepper and Jimmy Knepper. That's the way he operated. So, we had no time to re-hearse. Nothing. Then, we went there and we played.

In a way, it was my date, but, in a way, it was everybody's date, because everybody was making suggestions because of the fact that we didn't rehearse before. I know Pepper wanted to play Audobon, and then we decided to do a ballad medley and everybody picked a tune....The album came off very well, and, considering that, as I say, we had no rehearsals....It was a blowing session, except that, what we did is, we went over the tunes once at least before we actu-ally did a take. We said, "Let's end this way," and that kind of stuff. After the date [Pepper, George, and I] went to a bar which is now called 55 Bar. At that time it was just a neighborhood bar, and we just hung out there. I remember that Pepper and George got into a drinking thing. They really got out....They got so wasted, it was unbelievable! I left them there, finally.

LIONEL HAMPTON–50th ANNIVERSARY CONCERT
780630
30 June 1978, Carnegie Hall, Newport-New York Jazz Festival, New York: Jimmy Maxwell, Doc Cheatham, Cat Anderson tp; Joe Newman tp, flh; Eddie Bert, John Gordon, Benny Powell tb; Earle Warren as, cl, fl; Bob Wilber cl; Charles McPherson as; Arnett Cobb, Paul Moen ts; Pepper Adams bs; Ray Bryant p; Billy Mackel g; Lionel Hampton p, vib,

dm, voc; Chubby Jackson b; Panama Francis dm; GUEST: Teddy Wilson p.*

a	On the Sunny Side of the Street	Sutra LP: SU2-1006
b	Hamp's the Champ	
c	unknown blues	Pair CD: P-1235
d	Nearness of You	
e	Stomping at the Savoy	Sutra LP: SU2-1006
f	**Flying Home**	
g	Hamp's Boogie Woogie	
h	I'm Confessin' (That I Love You)	
i	Misty	

Hampton, Wilson, Jackson, and Francis:

j   Tea for Two*
k   Avalon*
m   More than You Know*
n   Runnin' Wild*
o   Flying Home*

Hampton, Bryant, Jackson, and Francis:

p   Carnegie Hall Blues

-a on Sutra LP: 1198, Timeless (Neth) LP: SJP-142, Cashbox (Arg) LP: CB-10050, Philips-Phonogram (J) LP: 25PJ-004, Philips-Phonogram (J) LP: 20PJ-0027, Pair CD: P-1235, Half Note CD: 4201-2, Sutra CD: SU-2008, Unidisc (Can) CD: B-70-P-8, Timeless-Bellaphon (Ger) CD: SJPCD-142, Philips (J) CD: EJD-3049, Philips-Phonogram (J) CD: 32JD-10059.

-b on on Sutra LP: 1198, Timeless (Neth) LP: SJP-142, Cashbox (Arg) LP: CB-10050, Philips-Phonogram (J) LP: 20PJ-0027, Philips-Phonogram (J) LP: 25PJ-004, Pair CD: P-1235, Half Note CD: 4201-2, Sutra CD: SU-2008, Unidisc (Can) CD: B-70-P-8, Timeless-Bellaphon (Ger) CD: SJPCD-142, Philips (J) CD: EJD-3049, Philips-Phonogram (J) CD: 32JD-10059.

-c on Sutra CD: SU-2008, Unidisc (Can) CD: B-70-P-8.

-d on Sutra CD: SU-2008, Unidisc (Can) CD: B-70-P-8.

-e on Sutra LP: 1198, Timeless (Neth) LP: SJP-142, Cashbox (Arg) LP: CB-10050, Philips-Phonogram (J) LP: 25PJ-004, Philips-Phonogram (J) LP: 20PJ-0027, Pair CD: P-1235, Half Note CD: 4201-2, Sutra CD: SU-2008, Unidisc (Can) CD: B-70-P-8, Timeless-Bellaphon (Ger) CD:

SJPCD-142, Philips (J) CD: EJD-3049, Philips-Phonogram (J) CD: 32JD-10059.

-f on on Sutra LP: 1198, Timeless (Neth) LP: SJP-142, Cashbox (Arg) LP: CB-10050, Philips-Phonogram (J) LP: 25PJ-004, Philips-Phonogram (J) LP: 20PJ-0027, Pair CD: P-1235, Half Note CD: 4201-2, Sutra CD: SU-2008, Unidisc (Can) CD: B-70-P-8, Timeless-Bellaphon (Ger) CD: SJPCD-142, Philips (J) CD: EJD-3049, Philips-Phonogram (J) CD: 32JD-10059.

-g on Sutra LP: 1198, Timeless (Neth) LP: SJP-142, Cashbox (Arg) LP: CB-10050, Pair CD: P-1235, Half Note CD: 4201-2, Sutra CD: SU-2008, Unidisc (Can) CD: B-70-P-8.

-h on Sutra LP: 1198, Timeless (Neth) LP: SJP-142, Cashbox (Arg) LP: CB-10050, Pair CD: P-1235, Half Note CD: 4201-2, Sutra CD: SU-2008, Unidisc (Can) CD: B-70-P-8.

-i on Sutra LP: 1198, Timeless (Neth) LP: SJP-142, Cashbox (Arg) LP: CB-10050, Pair CD: P-1235, Half Note CD: 4201-2, Sutra CD: SU-2008, Unidisc (Can) CD: B-70-P-8.

-j on Sutra LP: 1198, Timeless (Neth) LP: SJP-142, Cashbox (Arg) LP: CB-10050, Pair CD: P-1235, Half Note CD: 4201-2, Sutra CD: SU-2008, Unidisc (Can) CD: B-70-P-8.

-k on Sutra LP: 1198, Timeless (Neth) LP: SJP-142, Cashbox (Arg) LP: CB-10050, Pair CD: P-1235, Half Note CD: 4201-2, Sutra CD: SU-2008, Unidisc (Can) CD: B-70-P-8.

-m on Timeless (Neth) LP: SJP-142, Cashbox (Arg) LP: CB-10050, Pair CD: P-1235, Half Note CD: 4201-2, Sutra CD: SU-2008, Unidisc (Can) CD: B-70-P-8.

-n on Timeless (Neth) LP: SJP-142, Cashbox (Arg) LP: CB-10050, Pair CD: P-1235, Half Note CD: 4201-2, Sutra CD: SU-2008, Unidisc (Can) CD: B-70-P-8.

-o on Timeless (Neth) LP: SJP-142, Cashbox (Arg) LP: CB-10050, Philips-Phonogram (J) LP: 25PJ-004, Philips-Phonogram (J) LP: 20PJ-0027, Pair CD: P-1235, Timeless-Bellaphon (Ger) CD: SJPCD-142, Philips-Phonogram (J) CD: 32JD-10059, Sutra CD: SU-2008, Unidisc (Can) CD: B-70-P-8.

-p on Timeless (Neth) LP: SJP-142, Cashbox (Arg) LP: CB-10050, Philips-Phonogram (J) LP: 25PJ-004, Philips-Phonogram (J) LP: 20PJ-0027, Pair CD: P-1235, Timeless-Bellaphon (Ger) CD: SJPCD-142, Philips-Phonogram (J) CD: 32JD-10059, Philips (J) CD: EJD-3049, Sutra CD: SU-2008, Unidisc (Can) CD: B-70-P-8.

Hampton's band played Carnegie Hall on 30 June, then played the Newport Jazz Festival in Saratoga NY on 1-2 July, before leaving from New York for their European tour on c. 4 July.

According to Chubby Jackson, in an interview with the author in 1989,

> Lionel is an enigma in a lot of ways. It was an all-star pick-up band. We had possibly three days of rehearsals in a rehearsal hall and then right square into Carnegie Hall to do a concert. We had rehearsed a number of songs, and, when we had an afternoon soundcheck, he had picked out all the tunes we were going to play and in the order [there]of. Now, Lionel is notorious for this: We get on a bandstand and he starts to noodle at the vibraphone, and it has nothing to do with the song that was coming up next on our list. Our ears and our professionalism would take us into the [tune] and off we'd go, and it went on and on like that. Playing bass is difficult, because you're holding an instrument in you're hands, which sort of makes it difficult, for one, to lean over and, all of a sudden, find "Number 78," now that you know he's going to play it. So there were three, four, five times I didn't have the opportunity [to know what chart we were playing], because we were recording, [so I had] to just fake my way through with my ear, praying down deep that I finish when they do....You never knew who was going to get what when! That's what I meant about Lionel being an enigma on the bandstand. That album at Carnegie Hall survived, and it came out and it was swinging! I guess it can be attributed to the professional abilities of all the guys in there that, under pressure, really did it! That's where it's at. But, by the same token, the same musicians that we're discussing also would be extremely strained and pissed, and saying, "What did he do that for?" and "Why was *this?*"

LIONEL HAMPTON
780707
7 July 1978, RF radio broadcast, Les Jardins des Arènes de Cimiez, La Grande Parade du Jazz, Nice: Jimmy Maxwell, Doc Cheatham, Cat Anderson tp; Joe Newman tp, flh; Eddie Bert, John Gordon, Benny Powell tb; Earle Warren as, cl, fl; Bob Wilber cl; Charles McPherson as; Arnett Cobb, Paul Moen ts; Pepper Adams bs; Ray Bryant p; Billy Mackel g; Lionel Hampton vib, p*, voc†; Chubby Jackson b; Panama Francis dm.

a   unknown blues
b   The Nearness of You
c   Hamp's Boogie Woogie
d   Hey Ba-Ba-Re-Bop†
e   **Flying Home**
f   Flying Home*
g   unknown blues
h   In the Mood

About the Hampton band's European tour, Chubby Jackson, in an interview with the author in 1989 said, "It all started in Nice with that George Wein situation over there, and we spent maybe ten days in Nice. That was a very wild thing because it was a get-together of all of our peers, everybody we ever knew in this business."

LIONEL HAMPTON
780709
9 July 1978, RF radio broadcast, Les Jardins des Arènes de Cimiez, La Grande Parade du Jazz. Nice: Same as 7 July 1978:

a   Ain't Misbehavin'
b   Medley:
        Moment's Notice
        unknown blues
c   unknown blues
d   **Flying Home**
e   Love for Sale
f   Hamp's the Champ

LIONEL HAMPTON
780710
10 July 1978, RF radio broadcast, Les Jardins des Arènes de Cimiez, La Grande Parade du Jazz, Nice: Same as 7 July 1978; Hampton voc*, GUEST: Dizzy Gillespie tp†:

a   Airmail Special
b   Ain't Misbehavin'
c   Moment's Notice
d   On the Sunny Side of the Street*

e   St. Louis Blues
f   unknown blues
g   I Can't Get Started†
h   Love For Sale
i   Hamp's Boogie Woogie
j   Hey Ba-Ba-Re-Bop*
k   **Flying Home**
m   In the Mood

LIONEL HAMPTON
780711
11 July 1978, RF radio broadcast, Les Jardins des Arènes de Cimiez, La Grande Parade du Jazz, Nice: Same as 7 July 1978, Hampton voc*:

a   Airmail Special
b   Ain't Misbehavin'
c   Moment's Notice
d   Stomping at the Savoy
e   unknown title
f   The Nearness of You
g   Love for Sale
h   Hamp's Boogie Woogie
i   Hey Ba-Ba-Re-Bop*
j   **Flying Home**
k   In the Mood
m   In the Mood
n   unknown blues

NEW YORK JAZZ REPERTORY COMPANY
780712
12 July 1978, RF TV broadcast, Les Jardins des Arènes de Cimiez, La Grande Parade du Jazz, Nice: Jimmy Maxwell, Harry Edison, Cat Anderson tp; Joe Newman tp, voc*; Dicky Wells, John Gordon, Benny Powell tb; Earle Warren, Bob Wilber as, cl; Paul Bascomb, Paul Moen ts; Pepper Adams bs; Dick Hyman p; Bucky Pizzarelli g; Chubby Jackson b; Bobby Rosengarden dm; Helen Humes voc.†

a   Jumping at the Woodside
b   One O'Clock Jump

c   Rock-a-Bye Basie
d   Harvard Blues*
e   Lester Leaps In
f   Where Shall I Go†
g   If I Could Be with You One Hour†
h   I Want a Little Boy†
i   Goin' to Kansas City†
j   Moten Swing
k   Doggin' Around
m   Li'l Darlin'
n   Broadway

About this tribute to Count Basie, Chubby Jackson, in an interview with the author in 1989, said the following:

Quite a bit of hostility came out of that, because Jo Jones was sitting there doing nothing! A lot of the guys in the band—Earle Warren and Joe Newman, and some of those guys that had been with the Basie band—for the life of them couldn't figure out why Papa Jo wasn't on drums. As I do recall, we played some place down in Southern France and Jo was, strangely, working in some club. It was a little, pretty town. We had dinner together and he was pissed! I could see why.

LIONEL HAMPTON
780713a
13 July 1978, RF TV broadcast, Les Jardins des Arènes de Cimiez as part of La Grande Parade du Jazz, Nice: Same as 7 July 1978, Hampton voc*, GUEST: Helen Humes voc†:

a   Moment's Notice
b   Cherokee
c   Little Brown Jug
d   Memories of You
e   Stomping at the Savoy
f   Love for Sale
g   Medley:
         Hamp's Boogie Woogie
         Hey Ba-Ba-Re-Bop*†
h   Hamp's Boogie Woogie

LIONEL HAMPTON
780713b
13 July 1978, RF radio broadcast, Les Jardins des Arènes de Cimiez as part of La Grande Parade du Jazz, Nice: Same as 7 July 1978, Hampton voc*, GUEST: Helen Humes voc†:

a   Airmail Special
b   Ain't Misbehavin'
c   Moment's Notice
d   Cherokee
e   unknown blues
    Hampton and rhythm section:
f   Memories of You
    Full band:
g   unknown blues
h   unknown blues
i   Stomping at the Savoy
j   Love for Sale
k   Hey Ba-Ba-Re-Bop*†
    Hampton and rhythm section:
m   Medley:
        Hamp's Boogie Woogie
        Hey Ba-Ba-Re-Bop†
    Full band:
n   Medley:
        Hamp's Boogie Woogie
        Hey Ba-Ba-Re-Bop†
o   **Flying Home**
p   In the Mood

LIONEL HAMPTON
780714
14 July 1978, AVRO TV broadcast, Prins Willem Alexander Zaal at the Concertgebouw, Northsea Jazz Festival, The Hague: Same as 7 July 1978, Hampon voc*, GUEST: Helen Humes voc†:

a   Airmail Special
b   Moment's Notice
c   Love for Sale

d   In the Mood
e   On the Sunny Side of the Street*
f   Medley:
        Hamp's Boogie Woogie
        Hey Ba-Ba-Re-Bop*†

LIONEL HAMPTON
780716
16 July 1978, RF TV broadcast, Les Jardins des Arènes de Cimiez, La Grande Parade du Jazz, Nice: Same as 7 July 1978, Hampton voc†, GUEST: Stephane Grappelli vln*:

a   Airmail Special
b   Ain't Misbehavin'
c   Moment's Notice
d   Begin the Beguine
e   The Hucklebuck
f   unknown blues
    Grappelli, Hampton, and rhythm section:
g   Avalon*
h   Lady Be Good*
    Full band:
i   On the Sunny Side of the Street†
j   Stomping at the Savoy
k   The Nearness of You
m   Medley:
        Hamp's Boogie Woogie
        Hey Ba-Ba-Re-Bop†
n   **Flying Home**
o   In the Mood
p   The Hucklebuck
q   Take the "A" Train
r   C Jam Blues

DIZZY GILLESPIE
780717
17 July 1978, RF radio broadcast, Cour du Chateau de L'Empéri Festival de Jazz, Salon-de-Provence, France: Jimmy Maxwell, Doc Cheatham, Cat Anderson, Joe Newman tp; Kai Winding, Curtis Fuller, John

Gordon, Benny Powell tb; Earle Warren as, cl; Charles McPherson as;
Arnett Cobb, Paul Moen ts; Pepper Adams bs; Ray Bryant p; Rodney
Jones g; Ben Brown e-b; Mickey Roker dm.

a   'Round Midnight
b   Manteca

According to writer Charles Delauney, the first half of the concert was
comprised of big band charts featuring Gillespie as soloist. The second
half featured Gillespie and the rhythm section, with selected soloists
from the band, such as Kai Winding and Pepper Adams.

LIONEL HAMPTON
780718
18 July 1978, RAI radio broadcast, Umbria Jazz Festival, Perugia, Italy:
Same as 7 July 1978, GUEST: Helen Humes voc, Dizzy Gillespie tp.*

a   Airmail Special
b   Ain't Misbehavin'
c   Little Brown Jug
d   **Flying Home**
e   I Can't Get Started*

LIONEL HAMPTON
780721
21 July 1978, audience recording, Middlesbrough, England: Same as 7
July 1978:

a   Airmail Special
b   Ain't Misbehavin'
c   Moment's Notice
d   Stomping at the Savoy
e   unknown title
f   Love for Sale
g   unknown title
h   **Flying Home**
i   unknown title

PEPPER ADAMS-KAI WINDING
780804
4 August 1978, audience recording, HNITA Jazz Club, Heist-op-den-Berg, Belgium: Kai Winding tb; Greg Badolato ts; Pepper Adams bs; Nico Bunick p; Koos Serierse b; Clifford Jarvis dm.

a   **Sonnymoon for Two**
b   **Groovin' High**
c   Lover Man[1]
d   **The Theme**
e   **Reflectory**
f   **On Green Dolphin Street**
g   **I Carry Your Heart**[2]
h   **Buzzy**
i   **All the Things You Are**
j   Stella by Starlight[3]
k   **The Theme**

[1]Winding and rhythm section.
[2]Adams and rhythm section.
[3]Badolato and rhythm section.

STURE NORDIN
780815
mid-August 1978, SR TV broadcast, Mariahissen, Stockholm: Clark Terry tp, flh; Nisse Sandström ts; Calle Lundborg ts, fl; Pepper Adams bs; Lars Sjösten p; Sture Nordin b; Egil Johansen dm.

a African Igloo	Kay Jazz (Eng) unissued
b **Straight, No Chaser**[1]	
c God Bless the Child[2]	Kay Jazz (Eng) VHS: KJ-085
d **Day Dream**[3]	
e **It's from Lester Actually**	Kay Jazz (Eng) unissued
f Balladen om Olika Segeis Ytor	

[1]Terry, Adams, and rhythm section.
[2]Terry and rhythm section.
[3]Adams and rhythm section.

-c, -d on Impro-Jazz (Sp) DVD: IJ-524.

According to Clark Terry, in an interview with the author in 1988, Rolf Ericson was also on the date, though he doesn't appear on the above titles.

PEPPER ADAMS-KAI WINDING
780817
c. 17 August 1978, BRT TV broadcast, Jazz Middelheim, Antwerp: Kai Winding tb; unknown ts; Pepper Adams bs; unknown p; Koos Serierse b; Clifford Jarvis dm.

A short portion of TV footage, with a Winding solo, is posted on YouTube, but it's unclear how much additional footage exists.

PEPPER ADAMS-BENNY BAILEY
780825
25 August 1978, radio broadcast, Jazzdagar Festival, Stockholm: Benny Bailey tp; Pepper Adams bs; Lars Sjösten p; Sture Nordin b; Egil Johansen dm.

It's unclear if the audio still exists.

GUGGE HEDRENIUS
780827
27 August 1978, private recording, Balpalais, Stockholm: Benny Bailey, Bosse Broberg, Gustavo Bergalli tp; Lasse Olofsson tb; Sven Larsson btb; Wåge Finér, Christer Boustedt as; Jesper Thilo ts; Chris Holmström bs; Gugge Hedrenius p; Sture Åkerberg b; Pétur Östlund dm; Claes Janson voc*; GUEST: Pepper Adams bs.

a **Stoney Lonesome**
b **I Almost Lost My Mind***
c **In a Mellow Tone**
d Medley:
      Did She Ever Cry
      Soul Shoutin'
e Until the Real Thing Comes Along*
f **Sherri**
g Stoney Lonesome

CURTIS FULLER–FOUR ON THE OUTSIDE
780918
18 September 1978, CI Recording Studio, New York: Curtis Fuller tb; Pepper Adams bs; James Williams p; Dennis Irwin b; John Yarling dm.

a	**Four on the Outside**	Timeless (Neth) LP: SJP-124
b	**Suite-Kathy**	
c	**Hello Young Lovers**	
d	**Little Dreams**	
e	**Ballad for Gabe-Wells**	
f	**Corrida del Torro**	

All tracks on Imagem (Braz) LP: IMS-8006, Timeless (J) LP: SJP-124, Victor (J) LP: RJL-2620, Phonogram (J) LP: RJ-6052, Timeless/Bellaphon (Ger) CD: SJP-124, Phantom (J) CD: ABCJ-126.

About Adams' contribution, Curtis Fuller, in an interview with the author in 1989 said,

> To me, he made the date....I didn't want to write anything deep or hard or nothing like that. It was just to complement—something easy—the two instruments, and he loved it! It wasn't [like] Zec...or Milestones, or none of this stuff, or whatever. But it was just melodic writing and he was so lyrical. He just loved doing it....You know the easy, little lines that Chet and Mulligan used to play together? I thought, this is something easier. Sometimes a horn player, or actors, or something, get ahead of the public, you know? It's like talking down to them. We hit them with Zec and stuff; nobody wants to hear that! I figure we'd play a little more lyrical, and Pepper fit like a glove. He understood where I was coming from. It was very melodic. Oh, he loved it! You could tell by the way he played. But he could still be Pepper. I knew he was going to fly through it, and triple up, and double up that thing, and put chords in there that weren't even there! He could hear all the inner chords and workings, you know?

DAVID AMRAM–AT HOME/AROUND THE WORLD
781017
17 October 1978, Variety Sound, New York: Wilmer Wise tp; David Amram frh, fl, p, perc; Jerry Dodgion as; George Barrow ts; Pepper Adams bs; Rambling Jack Elliot g, voc; Victor Venegas b, e-b; Steve Berrios

dm, perc; Ray Mantilla, Nicky Marrero, Johnny Rodriquez Jr., Candido Camero perc; Odetta voc; vocal choir: Angela Bofill, Libby McLaren, Ilana Morrillo, Patti Smyth.

a **Traveling Blues**   Flying Fish LP: FF-094
b Birds of Montparnasse[1]
c Splendor in the Grass[2]
d **Home on the Range**[3]
e Pescau
f Kwahare[4]

[1]Dodgion, Amram, Venegas, Berrios, all percussion only.
[2]Dodgion, Amram, Venegas, Berrios only.
[3]Elliot and Odetta here only.
[4]Vocal choir here only.

All tracks on Flying Fish CD: 18964-0094-2.

PEPPER ADAMS
781105
5 November 1978, private recording, Musée des Beaux-Arts, Montreal:
Pepper Adams bs; Maury Kaye e-p; Paul Dyne b; Andre White dm.

a **Dylan's Delight**
b **A Child Is Born**
c **Mean What You Say**
d **I Carry Your Heart**
e **Bossa Nouveau**
f **In Love with Night**
g **Three Little Words**
h **Claudette's Way**
i **Oleo**

-f, -g, -h, -i privately videotaped by pianist Keith White. According to Andre White, in an interview with the author in 1988,

At the time I played with [Pepper Adams], I wasn't ready to play with him. I was 19 [years old]. (It was my Fender Rhodes, actually, for Maury! He had a hell of a time with those tunes, too. He was scuffling on those tunes.)

We had one rehearsal....It was, I think, the day before [the gig]. I had just come home from school. I had to go pick Pepper up at the corner of some street, and then we went to my basement up in [the] Roxborough [area of Montreal]. I was living with my father at the time.

I was very nervous, because, of course, I had never worked with anyone big-time and I didn't know what to expect. I didn't know whether he was going to play standards or he was just going to give us written parts. So we got into the rehearsal and I had my drums set up. Paul Dyne was there. Paul was trying to calm me down a little bit. We just sat down and Pepper announced that there was no drum parts, so I heaved a sigh of relief! He called out that, for [one] tune, there was a break on bar 30. "O.K., I have to remember to count thirty bars." The other tunes, he'd tell me to play straightahead or walk through this or whatever. Very, very simple directions. He knew that I was nervous, he knew that I was green.

My father was, basically, the impresario of the concert, and he thought that I should play drums because he didn't think there was anyone else in Montreal that could play drums. I still shouldn't have been on the concert, but, as a matter of fact, there weren't any real jazz drummers at that time that could've done the date. There was a lack of a good rhythm section at that point. There were no drummers in town!...

We went through four or five tunes. It didn't take long. It was like 45 minutes to rehearse. It was obvious that he had gone through this *hundreds* of times: coming up, playing with a rhythm section never seen before that probably weren't up to his musical standards at all. But he was used to it. He had done this a million times, just like Sonny Stitt and Milt Jackson and all of the other guys that used to tour as singles, and he knew what to expect, and hoped for the best, and that was about it. That was all he could do....Paul Dyne was probably the most competent member there. He took to the tunes right away and seemed to have no trouble reading the bass parts. That was cool. That was what Pepper was worried the most about: whether the bass player would be on. The rest would follow.

I hadn't had much experience. [Pepper] had worked with Maury maybe ten, fifteen years before. I'm not sure if it was in Montreal....I was glad to be there. It was fun and Pepper was very professional. It was cool. Nothing fell apart. It sounded O.K. It just doesn't groove like it could, because it's hard to groove when you're nineteen!...I should add, though, that [Pepper] played incredibly at the concert! Despite the rhythm section, it's very good blowing for Pepper. Also, at that concert, he had just gotten a new horn. It was almost brand new, as far as I knew, and he was really happy with that. Then I heard something like it went back, because it screwed up, and he had gotten another one. He was going through a period where he was trying to decide on one or the other.

PEPPER ADAMS
781112
12 November 1978, KGO TV broadcast, San Francisco: Pepper Adams bs; Larry Vuckovich p; Bob Maize b; Clarence Becton dm.

a **Body and Soul**
b **unknown title**

Adams appeared on Sonny Buxton's show, *AM Weekend,* with its house rhythm section. It's unclear if audio or video still exist. *See* 780430.

RIVERSIDE CITY COLLEGE JAZZ BAND
781116
16 November 1978, audience recording, Riverside CA: Riverside City College Jazz Band; GUEST: Pepper Adams bs.

a **It Only Happens Every Time**
b **A Good Time Was Had by All**
c **A Child Is Born**
d **Scrapple from the Apple**
e **Big Dipper**

BILL PERKINS–CONFLUENCE
781120
20 November 1978, Sage and Sound Studio, Hollywood CA: Bill Perkins ts†, bs√, fl◊; Gordon Goodwin ss*, ts; Pepper Adams bs; Lou Levy p; Bob Magnusson b; Carl Burnett dm.

a **Confluence**† [Don't Be a Stiff]   Interplay LP: IP-7721
b La Costa*√◊
c **Indoor Sports**†
   Goodwin out:

d **Civilization and Its Discontents**◊
e **Dylan's Delight**√
Adams out, add Goodwin:
f In Love with Night√

All tracks on Flyright (Eng) LP: FLY-214, Storyville (Ger) CD: STCD-4166, Interplay (J) CD: ABCJ-536, 3D (J) CD: MTCJ-2511.

Regarding Adams' role on the date, Bill Perkins said the following, in an interview with the author in 1988: "We communicated for eight or nine months and talked about it. That's what you have to do when you come in cold. It's *really* hard to do things that way. We had one rehearsal and we did the album, so we talked about the tunes and everything."

Bill Perkins told interviewer Les Tomkins in 1987,

I did an album with the late Pepper Adams...and that was a fulfill-ment of a long-time dream of mine....But, quite frankly, I was not prepared for playing in those days—I wish I could do them over now. I hadn't been playing jazz for years, and I wasn't really ready to play with Pepper. It was a lifetime opportunity, you know, and I did the best I could.

BISHOP NORMAN WILLIAMS–ONE FOR BIRD
781121
21 November 1978, Bear West Studios, San Francisco: Warren Gale tp; Allen Pittman flh*; Bishop Norman Williams as, fl; Marvin Williams ts†; Pepper Adams bs; Paul Arslanian p; Curtis Ohlsen b, e-b◊; Larry Hancock dm; Babatunde Lea dm, perc√.

a **About Time**†   Theresa LP: TR-105
b **Tahia's Outlook**
c **Allegra***√◊
d **The Doc Speaks**
e **Koko**
f Beth*

According to Allen Pittman, in a conversation with the author in 2005, all titles were recorded on this date. On 22 November, however, synthesizer overdubs were done by Mark Isham for -f, and conga over-dubs were done by Babatunde Lea.

In Michael Zipkin's liner notes, he quotes Bishop Norman Williams about Adams: "I always thought he was the best baritone player, but I had never seen him play until he worked at Christo's....The record company called to ask if I'd like to use Pepper on the date. I'd been thinking just the same thing."

DICK SALZMAN
781128
28 November 1978, Hyatt Regency Hotel, San Francisco: Si Perkoff p; Dick Salzman vib; Bob Maize b; Tony Johnson dm; GUEST: Pepper Adams bs.

a   **Undecided**
b   **Mean to Me**
c   **Little Suede Shoes**
d   **Sophisticated Lady**
e   **The Song Is You**
f   **Love Walked In**
g   **Scrapple from the Apple**
h   **How Deep Is the Ocean**
i   **Au Privave**

HIGHLIGHTS IN JAZZ
781215
15 December 1978, private recording, New York University's Loeb Student Center, New York: Joe Wilder, Marky Markowitz tp; Al Cohn ts; Zoot Sims ts, voc; Pepper Adams bs; Barry Harris p; Jimmy Raney g; Milt Hinton b, voc; Leroy Williams, Mousey Alexander dm; Flo Handy-Cohn voc.

a   What Is This Thing Called Love[1]
b   Groovin' High[2]
c   How about You[3]
d   Just Friends[4]
e   **In a Mellow Tone**[5]
f   Medley:
        Body and Soul[6]
        My Ideal[7]
        That's All[8]

g   I'm Beginning to See the Light[9]
h   I'm in Love with You, Honey[10]
i   America the Beautiful[11]
j   Zootcase (Exactly Like You) [12]
k   Morning Fun[13]
m   Wee Dot[14]
n   Perdido[15]

[1]Cohn, Raney, Williams out.
[2]Cohn, Raney, Williams out.
[3]Raney, Hinton, Alexander only.
[4]Raney, Hinton, Alexander only.
[5]Wilder, Adams, Harris, Hinton, Williams only.
[6]Rhythm section only.
[7]Wilder and rhythm section.
[8]Adams and rhythm section.
[9]Cohn, Harris, Hinton, Alexander only.
[10]Cohn, Harris, Hinton, Alexander only.
[11]Cohn, Harris, Hinton, Alexander only.
[12]Cohn, Sims, Harris, Hinton, Alexander only.
[13]Cohn, Sims, Harris, Hinton, Alexander only.
[14]Handy-Cohn out.
[15]Handy-Cohn out.

According to Jack Kleinsinger, in an interview with the author in 1994, Pepper Adams typically performed either an obscure tune or one he composed that he hadn't yet recorded. Adams enjoyed these all-star jams, Kleinsinger pointed out, "because he was treated as a star among stars. He could be on a show with Red Rodney, Jimmy Heath, Billy Taylor, and he was just as important as they were. He got his features, a chance at the microphone, a chance to call some tunes, and everything else." The format of these concerts was based on Jazz at the Philharmonic, in that it was a leaderless collective that played unrehearsed tunes. "There was a structure," Kleinsinger told the author:

I knew what was going on, in terms of giving them an outline when they got to the hall: medium tempo opener, uptempo here, ballad here, piano feature here. The order of the program was dictated by me, but not the tunes. Within the parameters, they were free to play anything they wanted. But that insured that everybody got a chance to play, and nobody felt like a sideman. As I always say, on these shows there's no sidemen and no leader. That's the only way it's going to work....This was an audience [for whom] Pepper had become like a friend. They liked him, and they knew him and came to see him. It was over 700 people each time out. NYU was 727 seats. It was intimate, but it wasn't like playing in a club....I had one rhythm section guy for everybody on the show—[those who were working, or had recently worked, with each soloist]—so everybody had their little anchor there.

We used to have a saxophone patron. A fellow by the name of Fred Shotwell was the President of American Family Publishers, and he would fund one concert a year, with the proviso that it was a saxophone featured concert. So we had "Saxophone Inspirations," "Saxophone Supreme," "Saxophone Splendor," and then he pulled the funds and we stopped doing them. For a while we had a lot of fun with them, and Pepper was on two of them.

This was a hobby. I did it at the instigation of a couple of musician friends—Bucky Pizzarelli and Zoot Sims—who said, "Hey, get it out of your system. Get a club or rent a theater or something like that." I rented the Theater de Lys, which is now Lucille Lortel Theater, on Christopher Street. We did two shows and it was off and running. That was 21 years ago!

PEPPER ADAMS
790120
20 January 1979, audience recording, St. Louis Club, Rome: Pepper Adams bs; Franco d'Andrea p; Giovanni Tommaso b; Bruno Biriaco dm.

a **Dylan's Delight**
b **Body and Soul**

It's unclear if the audio still exists.

PEPPER ADAMS
790122
22 January 1979, audience recording, Brussels Jazz Club, Brussels: Pepper Adams bs; Georges Arvanitas p; Jacky Samson b; Charles Saudrais dm.

a **How Deep Is the Ocean**
b Con Alma[1]

c   **Mean What You Say**
d   **Gone with the Wind**
e   **A Child Is Born**
f   **In a Sentimental Mood**
g   **Honeysuckle Rose**

[1]Rhythm section only.

PEPPER ADAMS
790204
4 February 1979, audience recording, Brussels Loft, Brussels: Richard Rousselet tp; Steve Houben fl; Pepper Adams bs; Michel Herr p; Freddie Deronde b; Félix Simtaine dm.

It's unclear if the audio still exists.

HELEN MERRILL
790210
c. 10 February, c. 17 February, c. 24 February 1979, private recording of various rehearsals, New York: Pepper Adams bs; Dick Katz p; Joe Puma g; Rufus Reid b; Mel Lewis dm; Helen Merrill voc.

These were rehearsals for 790306. According to Dick Katz, in an interview with the author in 1988, "we had several rehearsals at Helen's apartment. Mel Lewis came with his brushes. [Pepper] was very helpful in fixing the arrangements. I was writing away." All the rehearsals, Katz said, were recorded.

HELEN MERRILL–CHASIN' THE BIRD/GERSHWIN
790306
6 and 9 March 1979, RCA Studios, New York: Pepper Adams bs; Dick Katz p; Joe Puma g*; Rufus Reid b; Mel Lewis dm; Helen Merrill voc.

a   **Embraceable You/Quasimodo**[*]   Inner City LP: IC-1080
b   It Ain't Necessarily So[1]
c   **Summertime**
d   I Can't Be Bothered Now[2]
e   **I Got Rhythm/Chasin' the Bird**[*]
f   **I Loves You, Porgy**[*]

g　**Someone to Watch over Me**
h　**My One and Only**　　　　　　　　Trio (J) LP: PAP-9160
i　**But Not for Me**[3]　　　　　　　　Inner City unissued

[1]Reid, Lewis, Merrill only.
[2]Katz and Merrill duet.
[3]Pepper, Katz, and Merrill only.

-c on Trio (J) LP: PAP-9160, Universal-Mercury CD: 3035, Gitanes (F) CD: CD-PY-899, Absurd (J) CD: 286, Tokuma (J) CD: TKCD-70049, Absurd (J) CD: 286, EmArcy-Mercury (J) CD: E-5588502.

All issued tracks on Gitanes (F) CD: CD-PY-899, Tokuma (J) CD: TKCD-70049, Absurd (J) CD: 286, EmArcy-Mercury (J) CD: E-5588502.

According to Dick Katz, in an interview with the author in 1987, -i was recorded "after everyone else went home. We couldn't find a way to end it, so it would take some editing to find a way to gracefully end it. Parts of it are beautiful."

According to Rufus Reid, in an interview with the author in 1988,

It was done, I think, independently and Inner City probably picked it up. I believe Dick Katz [produced it]. He was one of the arrangers on it for sure. He had done some of the other arranging for her prior to that on a couple of Milestone records....Pepper always played great, so it was always nice. It was really different between his sound on the baritone and, say, Helen Merrill's airy, haunting kind of vocal sound. It was really an interesting contrast.

According to Dick Katz, in an interview with the author in 1987, another tune might also remain unissued. At the recording session, "piano strings were breaking and the guy had to call the tuner in the middle of the thing. The whole [control] board went out at one point....The idea of Helen Merrill and Pepper Adams: Some people said, "You people are crazy! With her silky, smoky, smooth voice, you're going to put her with this gargantuan, raspy sound?" I think it worked out beautifully."
See 790210.

PEPPER ADAMS
790318
18 March 1979, audience recording, Voss Jazz Festival, Voss, Norway:

Atle Hammer tp*; Pepper Adams bs; Per Husby p; Bjørn Alterhaug b; Espen Rud dm.

a   **Unforgettable**[*]
b   **Bossa Nouveau**[*]
c   **In Love with Night**[*]
d   **Conjuration**
e   **'Tis**
f   **Claudette's Way**
g   **Civilization and Its Discontents**
h   **My Shining Hour**
i   **unknown blues**
j   **'Tis**

In a taped narration sent to the author in 1987, Per Husby said,

Pepper wasn't really an expensive guy to hire. He used to say, "If I can go home with $1,000 per week in my pocket, I'm happy." Finish piano player Esko Linnavalli once said to me, when we talked about Pepper, "You know, Pepper doesn't know anything about money. He's one of the few people that we can still hire...." What he really meant was that Pepper was one of the few who were still in it for the music....

[On] that tour, we started in Stavanger. Pepper came in, jet-lagged and all, and was not in a very good mood. So we had to assure him, "O.K., let's just have a short rehearsal, tunes that we know for tonight, and then we'll have a rehearsal tomorrow for the tour." So that's just what we did. I don't know if he even [put together] his horn. He just said, "Do you know this tune, do you know this tune?" and so on.

I remember he said, "Do you know Embraceable You?" and I hadn't played that for a while, but I thought the bass player had played it, so I said, "Oh, yes," and the bass player said, "Oh, yes," and we didn't think more about it, because we went out for dinner, and we all slept a little after that, and we went right on the gig. Pepper called, [for] the second tune, Embraceable You. It turned out that the bass player had thought that I knew the tune, and I had thought the bass player knew the tune, so we didn't know it well enough to play it, and I remember Pepper was *very* angry about that, saying something to the effect, "You said you knew it!" and he was sort of mumbling and swearing to himself. He hated any kind of conceit; people that tried to lay on him something that they weren't or couldn't [do]. I think he was very much after honesty, and people that were straight. I think the thing that he never forgot was that I promised him this salary. I think I promised him a little bit more, maybe $1,200 a week, or whatever. I said, "I don't think it is very much, but we haven't got everything set just now, so, if there's any extra money when we do the books at the end, I'll send you some extra money after you come home again." That actually happened. I sent him about $1,000 about a month after the tour had ended, and I don't think Pepper ever forgot that. Apparently, he had heard this from so many people (people saying that maybe we can get you some more, and it never materialized), and suddenly he got $1,000 just out of the blue from Norway....He also did this thing—I think that was at Voss, or Oslo—one other thing that he said that he had picked up from Thad Jones: He came over to us, looking *very* stern. He said, "Men: I'll have to see you! There's a meeting in my room in five minutes!" This was just after the first set one night.

Then he just disappeared. We were all a bit scared. "What the hell is this?" So we hurried up to his room, and there he was, sitting with a whole bottle of bourbon, glasses for the whole band, with a big smile. "Sit down, have a drink." That was the whole point of it. Apparently, that was some code language that Thad and he had used for many years that, when he wanted to have a drink with the band, or to celebrate, or be nice to the band, and wanted to get rid of all the [hanger-ons] or get out of there, he would always do this—call a band conference and everybody in the band would know that it was just an excuse for having a drink and saying, "This is good!"

PEPPER ADAMS
790320
20 March 1979, audience recording, Club 7, Oslo: Same as 18 March 1979:

a **Reflectory**
b **Just Friends**
c **Dylan's Delight**
d **Mean What You Say**
e **In Love with Night**

BILLY MITCHELL
790601

1 June 1979, audience recording, Jazz Olympics, Radisson-Muehlebach Hotel, Kansas City: Red Rodney tp; Charles McPherson as; Billy Mitchell ts; Pepper Adams bs; Barry Harris p; Ray Drummond b; Leroy Williams dm.

a **Anthropology**
b **On Green Dolphin Street**
c Embraceable You[1]
d **Blue'n Boogie**

[1]Rhythm section only.

BARRY ALTSCHUL–BEBOP
790624

c. 24 June 1979, Studio Ramses, Paris: Jean-Pierre Debarbat ts; Pepper Adams bs; Siegfried Kessler p; Jacques Vidal b; Barry Altschul dm.

a **Woody'n You**   Musica (F) LP: MUS-3014
b **Neuftemps**
c **You Can't Name Your Own Tune**
d **Valse Celtique**
   Adams and rhythm section:
e **Julian**[1]

All tracks on Musica (F) LP: MD-200, Sun (F) LP: SEB 11-006. According to Adams, in an interview with Peter Danson in *Coda,*

> I was basically disturbed about the cover, the way it's similar to the Nick Brignola *Baritone Madness* album [*see* 771222], that the company attempted to make it look as if I am a co-leader, when I was merely a sideman and had no input into the musical sides of things. Or else, had I been a co-leader, it would have been different dates in both instances. Since I was hired as a sideman, paid as a sideman, had no quality control over the album, I think I am correct in being somewhat hacked at the people who were responsible for both those dates.

In an interview with the author in 1989, Barry Altschul said,

I was in town, Pepper was in town....We both decided that it should just be a group thing, and [then] they put our names on the cover.... It was the record company that hired everybody....I knew the company people and I was in town. I called [Gérard Terrones], and he said, "Are you doing anything?" and I said, "No." He said, "Do you want to come and do this date with Pepper Adams?" and I said, "O.K." The record company got all the personnel, except for the tenor player. Pepper brought him in....I think everyone did it for the bread at that time. No rehearsals.

JEAN-PIERRE DEBARBAT
790625
c. 25 June 1979, audience recording, Paris: Jean-Pierre Debarbat ts; Pepper Adams bs; other musicians.

This group was a tentet and the tape was in Adams' collection at the time of his death.

PEPPER ADAMS
790822
22 August 1979, audience recording, Pizza Express, London: Digby Fairweather tp; Pepper Adams bs; Brian Dee, Brian Lemon p; Jimmy Gourley g; Len Skeat b; probably Tony Mann dm.

a   **Take the "A" Train**
b   **Chelsea Bridge**[1]
c   **It Don't Mean a Thing (If It Ain't Got that Swing)**
d   **Cotton Tail**

[1]Adams with guitar, bass, and drums.

PEPPER ADAMS
790824
24 August 1979, audience recording, Pizza Express, London: Pepper Adams bs; Roger Kellaway p; Jimmy Gourley g*; Harvey Weston b; Tony Mann dm.

a   **Star Eyes***
b   **Ray's Idea***
c   **Valse Celtique**

d **Bye Bye Blackbird**
e **Civilization and Its Discontents**
f **Oleo**
g **'Tis**

PEPPER ADAMS
790825
25 August 1979, audience recording, Pizza Express, London: Same as 24 August 1979, Kellaway out:

a **Embraceable You**
b **Urban Dreams**
c **Autumn Leaves**
d **'Tis**

PEPPER ADAMS
790907
7 September 1979, audience recording, Jazz Forum, New York: Pepper Adams bs; Bob Neloms p; Wayne Dockery b; John Yarling dm.

a **unknown title**
b **In Love with Night**
c **Blue Champagne**
d **'Tis**
e **Claudette's Way**
f **Pent-Up House**
g **I Carry Your Heart**

According to club owner Mark Morganelli, in an interview in 1988 with the author,

it was literally the third month of the Jazz Forum, and that would become a traditional date for Pepper. He would be the first weekend in September for the next four years, in addition to other times that I booked him. In fact, the piano player I was just talking to said, "You booked him three or four times at Cooper Square alone." I had the club from '79 there through the end of '80. Then I moved to Broadway and Bleeker: 648 Broadway at Bleeker....I had kind of a beat-up grand [piano], and, for Pepper, I would actually hire the rhythm section for him. In fact, that wound up continuing through all the gigs I booked him for. He trusted my musical judgment....I remember I would always offer him a beer, but he would always bring his own. He'd come in with a six-pack of Molson and he'd put that in my refrigerator. He was a nice guy and he knew I was running a shoestring operation....

He was just always very cool, and played his ass off! He was one of the most-known entities that I had in the beginning, and people came there—real jazz fans—and you could hear a pin drop while he was playing. He'd play these uptempo tunes, that were just burning, and he'd challenge the rhythm section to stay up with him. Then he'd play these ballads, that were just gorgeous, and put in, like, forty subs[titution chords] on these ballads; just tear the ballad apart and make it a whole new composition....It was a gig that was really looked forward to by my regular customers. People would ask me, "When are you going to have Pepper back?" He was *really* revered by all of the Jazz Forum regulars. It was a mix of people. People definitely came to check him out: Clifford Jordan, other tenor players....He would always perform a lot of original tunes that he wrote...and he always played Thad's music in his sets. Pepper's music, Thad's music, and then standards was basically his repertoire....He had a phenomenal harmonic vocabulary, as vast as any keyboard player that played there, and his conception of swing was just great.

BILL POTTS
791011
11 October 1979, private recording, Frankie Condon's, Rockville MD: Vaughn Nark, Bob Pomarleau, Kenny Smukal, Don Junker, Joe Bovello, Ron Norris tp; John Hager, Rick Lillard, Gary Hall, Howard Lamb tb; unknown btb; Ron Diehl, Tim McWright as; Jack Wolfe, Barry Weinstein ts; Art Monroe p; Paul Langosch e-b; Paul Wingo g; Chuck Redd dm; GUEST: Pepper Adams bs.*

a   Theme
b   Tin Roof Blues
c   Ballad for Trumpet
d   555 Feet High
e   Mahogany Hall
f   Momsville
g   **C Jam Blues***

h　**My Man's Gone Now**[*]
i　**Melancholy Baby**[*]
j　**Stella by Starlight**[*]
k　Summertime
m　**Bess, You Is My Woman Now**[*]
n　**Happy Blues**[*]
o　Battle Hymn of the Republic
p　**Shhhhhhh!**[*]
q　**Big Swing Face**[*]

PEPPER ADAMS
791029
29 October 1979, WWUH radio broadcast, 880 Club, Hartford CT: Pepper Adams bs; Harold Danko p; Ray Drummond b; Ron Marabuto dm.

It's unclear if audio still exists.

TEO MACERO–IMPRESSIONS OF CHARLES MINGUS
791227a
27 December 1979, 30th Street Studios, New York: Teo Macero reeds, p; Bill Evans, Dave Liebman, Alex Foster, John Stubblefield, Dick Oatts reeds; Pepper Adams bs; Biff Hannon keyboards; Bob DeVos, Jamie Glaser g; Ron Davis b; Tom Brechtlein dm; Kitt Moran voc.*

a　Oops Mr. Mingus ("Theme from "The Body Human")　　　Palo
　　　　　　　　　　　　　　　　　　　　　Alto LP: PA-8046-N
b　Blues for Duke[*]

All tracks on Teo CD: TMP-5, TEO CD: 12, Orchard CD: 4392.
See 791227b.

TEO MACERO–IMPRESSIONS OF CHARLES MINGUS
791227b
27 December 1979, 30th Street Studios, New York: John Frosk, Ted Curson, Mel Davis, Lew Soloff tp; Eddie Bert, Britt Woodman tb; Don Butterfield tu; Lee Konitz, Anthony Braxton as; John Stubblefield, Al Cohn ts; Pepper Adams bs; Mike Nock, Biff Hannon p; Larry Coryell g; Will Lee e-b; Alan Swartzberger dm.

a **Glory Be! Let the Sun Shine In**   Palo Alto LP: PA-8046-N
b Goodbye "Mr. Good Bass"
c **Two Bits and a Piece**
d Chill

All tracks on Teo CD: TMP-5, TEO CD: 12, Orchard CD: 4392.

Regarding the lack of a rehearsal, in an interview with the author in 1988, Eddie Bert said, "Teo wrote the music and we did what he wrote. Generally, with those dates, you do them right on the date."

See 791227a.

PEPPER ADAMS
800210
10 February 1980, Downtown Athletic Club, Albany NY: Pepper Adams bs; Lee Shaw p; Mike Wicks b; Stan Shaw dm.

a **It Could Happen to You**   Jazz on Jazz CD: 244554
b **Scrapple from the Apple**
c **In a Sentimental Mood**
d **Big Foot**   Jazz on Jazz unissued
e **Alone Together**   Jazz on Jazz CD: 244554
f **Secret Love**
g **unknown blues**   Jazz on Jazz unissued
h **Wrap Your Troubles in Dreams**   Jazz on Jazz CD: 244554
i **Lovers of their Time**   Jazz on Jazz unissued
j **Falling in Love with Love**
k **My Funny Valentine**
m **Star Eyes**
n **Blues in the Closet**

PEPPER ADAMS–THE MASTER
800311
11 March 1980, New York: Pepper Adams bs; Tommy Flanagan p; George Mraz b; Leroy Williams dm.

a **Enchilada Baby**   Muse LP: MR-5213
b **Enchilada Baby**   Muse unissued
c **Enchilada Baby**
d **Chelsea Bridge**   Muse LP: MR-5213

e	**Bossallegro**	
f	**Bossallegro**	Muse unissued
g	**Rue Serpente**	Muse LP: MR-5213
h	**Rue Serpente**	Muse unissued
i	**Lovers of Their Time**	Muse LP: MR-5213
j	**Lovers of Their Time**	Muse unissued
k	**My Shining Hour**	Muse LP: MR-5213

-i on Muse-Libra (Gr) CD: 7-277.

All issued tracks on Muse-Impulse CD: MCD-5213, Muse CD: 5213, Landmark CD: 5213, Camden-BMG CD: 74321-610882.

This is Adams' seventeenth date as a leader.

In a conversation with the author in 1988, drummer Billy Hart said that Pepper Adams had invited him to play on this session, but he couldn't make the date because of a previous commitment.

According to Adams, in an interview with Peter Danson in *Coda,* "I think Elvin Campbell has captured my sound the best, particularly on the *Reflectory* and *The Master* albums. He used two microphones—one close, and one high and fairly distant—and put them on separate tracks and then remixed."

Regarding Chelsea Bridge, Adams continued:

It's such a beautiful, gorgeous tune, and the recording was almost an accident. I intended the tempo to be much faster than that, and also we didn't intend the take to be that long. It's quite a long take. I think eight or nine minutes. And it kind of unbalanced the programming which we had worked out. So it was all kind of a mistake. I think Leroy Williams, who had not worked with me that much before, kind of misheard the count-off, and so the tempo started much differently than I had anticipated, and, therefore, the length got out of hand. So I was ready to go for another take immediately, and [producer] Mitch Farber said listen before you do it, and, once we had listened, we said, "No, we're not going to touch that one again. Leave it alone."

PEPPER ADAMS
800610

c. 10 June 1980, audience recording, Salt Peanuts, New York: Bob Brookmeyer vtb*; Pepper Adams bs; Jill McManus p; Chip Jackson b; Ron Marabuto dm.

a   **Half Nelson**[*]
b   **Flanagram**[*]
c   **Chelsea Bridge**[*]
d   **Sweet Georgia Brown**[*]
e   **Reflectory**
f   **Solar**
g   **Joy Road**
h   **Scratch**
i   **Claudette's Way**
j   **What Happened Will Always Exist**
k   **Splurge**
m   **Jean Marie**
n   **Zec**
o   **In Love with Night**
p   **How Long Has This Been Going On**

According to McManus, the band's engagement lasted from 10-14 June. At this gig Adams was still experimenting with a new Dukoff D-5 mouthpiece and a plastic Bari reed that he bought at Art Schell's in Midtown Manhattan on 6 June. Adams' original Berg Larson mouthpiece, after 32 years of use, had finally given out at a concert in Detroit on 5 June, and, in the thirty minutes or so he had between his return from Detroit and catching a train to Washington for his 6-7 June gig at One Step Down, Adams settled on this set-up for the time being.

PEPPER ADAMS
800710
10 July 1980, RAI TV broadcast, Pérgine, Italy: Pepper Adams bs; Franco d'Andrea p; Dodo Goya b; Bruno Biriaco dm.

a   **Bossa Nouveau**
b   **Now in Our Lives**
c   **Claudette's Way**
d   **Conjuration**

It's unclear if the video portion still exists. Adams began writing his composition Trentino at this date. Pérgine is a town very close to Trento, Italy.

PEPPER ADAMS
800807
7 August 1980, audience recording, Bull's Head, London: Pepper Adams
bs; John Woodhead p; Graham Gallery b; Tony Richards dm.

a   **Scratch**
b   **Straight, No Chaser**
c   **Lovers of Their Time**
d   **Gone with the Wind**
e   **Trentino**
f   **Conjuration**
g   **A Child Is Born**

PEPPER ADAMS
800818
*18 August 1980, CBC radio broadcast, Shoctor Theatre, Edmonton,
Canada:* Sam Noto tp; P.J. Perry as, ts; Lew Tabackin ts; Pepper Adams
bs; Mike Nock p; Michael Moore b; Bill Goodwin dm.

a   **Split Kick**
b   **Blue**
c   **Just Friends**
d   **Groovin' High**

Sponsored by the Edmonton Jazz Society, who maintain a library of
their broadcasts.
Lew Tabackin told the author in 1988 that

Oscar Peterson was supposed to be headliner opening night and, [due to
the flu], he cancelled, so Marc Vasey, who was the producer of the festival, called us all and tried to organize as many of us to come out early
and fill in for Oscar. I had to leave that same day from Los Angeles, and
I got there about ten minutes after the concert had started, which was fine. We kind of formed little ensembles. Also, at that time, Pepper
played an original, untitled piece. He played something he had just written. It was a ballad. I said, "Pepper, that sounds like some big city shit to
me." He said, "Well, that would be a good title, but I don't think the record company would go for it." So he called it Urban Dreams instead.
[*See* Earl Sauls' comments on 801101.] During the festival we played
jam sessions together....I remember Pepper and I just playing a duet,

without rhythm section, in the lounge. They almost had to physically eject us. He was more loaded than I was, but we were both feeling no pain!...

[Paraphrasing] was his thing, but he knew everything he played. A lot of times you play things that come to your head, [but] you don't know what you're playing. In fact, one day we were playing a jam session. He played a quote from Springtime for Hitler, and I didn't know it, and he kept playing it and playing it, waiting for a response, and nobody responded. Finally, out of sheer frustration, he had to tell everybody what it was!

TOMMY BANKS
800819
19 August 1980, CBC radio broadcast, Shoctor Theatre, Edmonton, Canada: Bob Tildesley tp; Bob Stroup tb; P. J. Perry as; Tommy Banks p; other musicians; GUESTS: Sam Noto tp, Pepper Adams bs.

This was produced by the Edmonton Jazz Society, who maintains a library of their broadcasts.

HELEN MERRILL
800919
19 September 1980, private recording of rehearsal, New York: Pepper Adams bs; Dick Katz p; Rufus Reid b; Mel Lewis dm; Helen Merrill voc.*

a **Rue Serpente**
b **Claudette's Way**
c **I Got Rhythm/Chasin' the Bird***
d **What Is This Thing Called Love***
e **Embraceable You/Quasimodo***

According to Dick Katz, in a conversation with the author in 2006, this was a noontime rehearsal for the group's upcoming New York engagement on 7-12 October at Fat Tuesday's.

TEO MACERO
801003
3 October 1980, New York: Pepper Adams bs; other musicians.

In Adams' appointment book he lists a Teo Macero date from 2-5pm, for which Adams was paid. Adams worked from 30 September-4 October with Macero's group at Michael's Pub, and rehersals had taken place on 24 and 29 September. It's likely that Macero brought the same group into the studio to record that was working that week.

PEPPER ADAMS
801017
17 October 1980, audience recording, Baker's Keyboard Lounge, Detroit: Pepper Adams bs; Gary Schunk p; Ken Kellett b; Pistol Allen dm; GUEST: Marv Holiday bs.*

a　**Scratch**
b　**Mean What You Say**
c　**A Child Is Born**
d　**Zec**
e　**'Tis**
f　**Tricotism**
g　**Stolen Moments**[1]
h　**Bossa Nouveau**
i　**Take the "A" Train***
j　**Satin Doll***
k　**'Tis***

[1]Rhythm section only.

Adams' gig at Baker's was 14-21 October.

PEPPER ADAMS
801101
1 November 1980, Far and Away, Cliffside Park NJ: Pepper Adams bs; Noreen Grey p; Earl Sauls b; Clarence Becton dm.

a　**Falling in Love with Love**
b　**Ephemera**
c　**How Long Has This Been Going On**
d　**What Is This Thing Called Love**
e　**Three and One**
f　**A Child Is Born**

g   **Mean What You Say**
h   **Urban Dreams**
i   **Reflectory**
j   **Happy Birthday**
k   **I Carry Your Heart**
m   **Claudette's Way**
n   **'Tis**
o   **Conjuration**
p   **I'll Remember April**

Regarding the title of -h, Adams said, in his introduction to the tune, "We'd like now to play an original ballad. We played it last night and called it Untitled Ballad. I think we might have something better for it tonight: tentatively titled Urban Dreams." *See* Lew Tabackin's comments on 800818.

Regarding Adams, Earl Sauls told the author, in a conversation in 1995,

> This was the first time we played with him. Generally, we opened with [Mean What You Say], but a lot of times he'd play the fastest tune he could think of, and, after the tune was over, he'd say, "We got that out of the way. Now we can relax and really play!" We did How Am I to Know. He used to like to play that. We didn't know it. He would say, "You've heard it, right? Come on, you can do it." After You've Gone: He always played that really fast. I don't know if he did this with other people, but, when he played with us, he would call tunes that sometimes he wasn't even sure he knew, or he'd say he wasn't sure he knew. You know, "Well, I don't know if I know this one or not, but let's try it." There's some pretty—not off-the-wall—but tunes that you wouldn't particularly call off right off the bat. Far and Away was a small place. There was no pressure. He probably never felt any pressure anyway, but there was no pressure there to do anything.
>
> His tunes are real interesting. They're very challenging to play, actually—harmonically. He would play some of Noreen's tunes, though, sometimes, and, a couple of times, he asked her about certain harmonic things, like, "Well, how would you play over this particular voicing?" or things like that, that I thought was really interesting! Some of her harmonies were a little different....

I don't know what Pepper made. I'm sure he didn't make very much money either, but it was bad for us. We used to give the drummer $50 and split whatever was left. Maybe it was $125 for the trio....I never made good money with Pepper. We didn't care about the money. We would've played for free!

Regarding the tempo Adams chose for his ballads, Sauls said, "He played them a little faster because he said that, no matter where they started, the rhythm section would always slow down, no matter who he was playing with, even with Tommy [Flanagan] and those guys." Sauls also said that Adams generally would play a cadenza at their conclusion.

PEPPER ADAMS
801123
23 November 1980, audience recording, Foyer pour Jeunes, Angers, France: Pepper Adams bs; Dominique Lofficial p; Charles Arnault b; Jean-Yves Colson dm.

a   **Conjuration**
b   **A Child Is Born**
c   **Ornithology**
d   **It Got It Bad (And that Ain't Good)**
e   **On Green Dolphin Street**
f   **There Will Never Be Another You**
g   **Sonnymoon for Two**
h   **Ephemera**
i   **Well, You Needn't**
j   **Urban Dreams**
k   **Oleo**

PEPPER ADAMS
810105
5 January 1981, audience recording, Palsson's, New York: Pepper Adams bs; Jill McManus p; Chip Jackson b; Ron Marabuto dm.

a   **Bossallegro**
b   **There Is No Greater Love**
c   **Wait Till You See Her**

McManus' gig was 5-7 January.

DIZZY GILLESPIE
810212

12-13 February 1981, private videotape of rehearsals, New York: Dizzy Gillespie tp, voc, jaw harp; Jon Faddis, Victor Paz, Marvin Stamm, Joe Wilder tp; Curtis Fuller, Slide Hampton or Janice Robinson, Melba Liston, Benny Powell tb; Paquito D'Rivera, Frank Wess as; Jimmy Heath, Frank Foster ts; Pepper Adams bs; Roland Hanna p; George Davis g; George Duvivier, Paul West b; Grady Tate dm; Candido Camero perc; Jon Hendricks voc; GUESTS: Gerry Mulligan bs; John Lewis p; Milt Jackson vib; Max Roach dm.

These were rehearsals for the PBS television broadcast *Dizzy Gillespie's Dream Band* (*see* 810216). According to Jon Faddis, some of the rehearsals were videotaped.

West was hired to play a few small group numbers. Duvivier played with the orchestra. *See* 810216 for specific tracks.

According to Curtis Fuller, in an interview with the author in 1989,

> Diz, when he got his Dream Band, you could see who's in it. Pepper was the guy *in* the band but, somehow, the people doing the show wanted Gerry Mulligan to be the featured soloist. What did [Dizzy] and Mulligan have in common? What did Mulligan do for Dizzy? He may have put him down a couple of times....Max [Roach] said to Mulligan], "What the fuck do you got to do with this?" [Mulligan] told the band, at one point, "Nice reading job. Now let's play the arrangement," and Slide Hampton took offense to that. Slide got pissed off, so he left. Dizzy had to send for Janice Robinson.

According to Cecil Bridgewater, in an interview with the author in 1989,

> When Dizzy put the Dream Band together, Pepper was his choice for the baritone chair....I talked with Max a little bit about it. He said that Gerry was strutting around a bit; he wanted the band to play some of *his* arrangements. Of course, Dizzy was such a diplomat and such a warm person that Dizzy didn't say anything. But Max felt that it was an insult to Dizzy to play [Mulligan's] arrangements for Dizzy's Dream Band. This is Dizzy's project. That

whole thing. So Max was incensed by it, and he jumped all over Gerry about it, cussed him, and so forth.

According to Jon Faddis, in an interview with the author in 1989,

Pepper was there, and one of the things that Max [Roach] was upset about was that he felt, "Every time they do a jazz show, somebody brings in Gerry Mulligan or something like that." He said, "We've got all these great saxophone players sitting here: We've got Pepper Adams and Frank Wess, Frank Foster and Paquito, Jimmy Heath. Why aren't they getting a shot?" Then Max took it *out!* He started cussing and all of that stuff, and Gerry said, "Well, I don't have to sit here and take this crap!" and he started to walk off. Dizzy tried to tell Max to chill out. And, it's really funny: When you see the show, Max and Gerry are hugging! There was so much going on. At the concert, to me, the most upsetting thing was the sound. If you hear the tape or watch the video, you can see that the sound is not really that together. In the middle of the concert, Dizzy would go up to the microphone, the microphone would be off, that kind of stuff.

See 820216.

DIZZY GILLESPIE
810216
16 Februry 1981, PBS TV broadcast, Avery Fisher Hall, New York: Same as 12 February 1981:

a	Manteca	Fox-Lorber DVD: FLV-5134
b	A Night in Tunisia	
c	Groovin' High[1]	
d	Tin Tin Deo[*2]	
e	Salt Peanuts[*†3]	
f	**Con Alma**	Fox Lorber unissued
g	The Drum also Waltzes (Mr. High Hat)[4]	
h	'Round Midnight[5]	
i	Hot House[*6]	Sony VHS: 113086-V
j	Lover Man	Fox-Lorber unissued
k	Things to Come	

[1]Mulligan featured with big band.

[2]Gillespie, Mulligan, Lewis, Jackson, West, and Roach featured as sextet separately and with the big band.

[3]Gillespie, Mulligan, Lewis, Jackson, West, and Roach featured as sextet separately and with the big band.

[4]Roach solo drum feature.

[5]Duet for Mulligan and Lewis.

[6]Gillespie, Mulligan, Lewis, Jackson, West, and Roach only.

-c on Sony VHS: 113086-V.

This TV broadcast, *Dizzy Gillespie's Dream Band*, was produced by Gary Keys and directed by Stanley Dorfman.

According to Paquito D'Rivera, Marvin Stamm, and Jon Faddis, two complete concerts were performed on the same day, some of which was televised by PBS. It's not clear what titles were taken from what set.

In an interview with the author in 1988, "I just arrived in this country," said D'Rivera:

> That was one of my first important dates. I was very honored to be called to that date. My God, there were so many monsters in that band, all those people there! I remember that, in the whole show, Pepper didn't have one solo to play. I don't know why. You say whatever you want to say. And then I felt sorry for that, because that man was my idol, you see. He was one of the people I admired for so many years. In Cuba, they love that man, the musicians there. Yeah, everybody knows Pepper Adams. That's the baritone, there: Pepper; no other one at all! Just Pepper Adams! Suddenly, I found myself sitting in that marvelous saxophone section—Frank Wess, Frank Foster, Jimmy Heath—and Pepper was there, but they didn't give a solo to Pepper. And then I said, "Hey, Pepper. You want to play my solo on Con Alma?" because I don't feel comfortable with that tune, which is true. I didn't know the harmony very well, and I didn't want to go on. I said, "You play that because I have two more solos to play," and Pepper played the solo there....
>
> We played two shows in there. It was the same program exactly. I took my solo in the afternoon concert on Salt Peanuts, at the ending, and, in the middle of the show, as rehearsed, I played Groovin' High. In the second show, the producer of the show came to me and said, "Gerry [told] me that he wants to play the solo on Groovin' High." I said, "Yes, he plays the solo after me. I play my solo and then he plays the baritone solo. It's written there." I knew what he was talking about. He said, "No, no." "I know: He wants to

play the whole thing, right?" He said, "Yeah, exactly." He came to me, and knew I just arrived and wouldn't know what to say. But Gerry played during the whole night!

Curtis Fuller, in an interview with the author in 1989, spoke about Con Alma:

Very few players can play that song. It's not an everyday song. It's like Countdown or Giant Steps. You know, you're playing E to A-flat, and stuff like that, where you don't have the common tones between the chords where you can fly through it and play this chord against that chord. No, no, no, no! Then it becomes a spelling bee, and you got to spell it or you can't play it. [Pepper] excelled at that.

According to Marvin Stamm, in an interview with the author in 2002, "The sound on the stage was so bad that, some of the times, you couldn't even hear Dizzy's solos."

Regarding the feeling among the reed players, Jimmy Heath said, in a 1989 interview with the author, "We felt slighted. I felt slighted: I got sixteen bars on the whole thing—on Manteca."

Regarding Mulligan, according to Roland Hanna, in an interview with the author in 1988,

When they hired Gerry Mulligan, they gave Gerry Mulligan two feature spots and paid him an enormous sum of money to do the gig, but they didn't pay Max [Roach] for any feature and they didn't give him an enormous sum of money. I think Max was just angry at him anyway and was going to pop him. Pepper was in the band. Why should Gerry Mulligan be a featured soloist anytime Pepper's on the scene? They had Dizzy wired for sound, and Dizzy got shocked a couple of times and told them to take all that shit off, and it turned out that...the band sounded horrible, because it was really poorly put together, and especially Gerry Mulligan's part. It sounded really bad because nobody wanted to play with Gerry Mulligan. I remember that gig very well. A lot of guys quit. Slide Hampton had written something for the band and he didn't even play. He just quit altogether.

It's a hell of a thing to have a guy sell stuff and you never got paid for video. I mean, I got paid for doing the date, but not paid for video. What kind of crap is that?...Gerry Mulligan and Max Roach got into it and almost stopped the whole show, because Max was going to pop him. Can you imagine these two sixty-year-old guys up there popping each other?

See 810212.

PEPPER ADAMS
810308
8 March 1981, audience recording, Jazz Forum, New York: Mark Morganelli tp; Pepper Adams bs; Ronnie Matthews p; Ray Drummond b; Kenny Washington dm.

a   **Four**
b   **Out of Nowhere**

See 790907.

PEPPER ADAMS
810315
15 March 1981, private recording, Baltimore: Pepper Adams bs; unknown p; unknown b; unknown dm.

Recorded by the Left Bank Jazz Society. *See* 650314.

PEPPER ADAMS
810320
20 March 1981, audience recording, Defemio's, Yonkers NY: Pepper Adams bs; Stanley Cowell p; Nobby Totah b; Al Defemio dm.

a   **Perdido**
b   **Urban Dreams**
c   **Four**
d   **Quiet Lady**
e   **Claudette's Way**

PEPPER ADAMS
810321
21 March 1981, audience recording, Defemio's, Yonkers NY: Same as 20 March 1981:

a   **It's You or No One**
b   **Chelsea Bridge**
c   **Conjuration**
d   **Star Eyes**

PEPPER ADAMS
810425
25 April 1981, audience recording, De Spieghel, Groningen, Netherlands: Pepper Adams bs; Rein de Graaff p; Henk Haverhoek b; Eric Ineke dm.

a   **Conjuration**
b   **Bossa Nouveau**
c   **Sophisticated Lady**
d   **Au Privave**
e   **Well, You Needn't**

SKYMASTERS BIG BAND
810427
27 April 1981, AVRO radio broadcast, Nick Vollebregt's Jazz Café, Laren, Netherlands: Jan Oosthof, Ack van Rooyen, Geert Sprik, Rob Bruinen, Wim Kat tp; Bart van Lier, Rudy Bosch, Pier van den Dolder tb; Eric van Lier btb; Piet Noordijk, Henny Kluvers as; Ferdinand Povel, Ruud Brink ts; Max Boeree bs; Henk Meutgeert p; Peter Tiehuis g; Koos Serierse b; Cees Kranenburg dm; Tony Nolte cond; GUEST: Pepper Adams bs.

a   **Dylan's Delight***
b   **Ephemera**
c   **Two As One***
d   **The Preacher**
e   **Au Privave***

*Adams and rhythm section.

PEPPER ADAMS
810428
28 April 1981, WDR radio broadcast, Club Subway, Cologne: Same as 25 April 1981:

It's unclear if audio still exists.

PEPPER ADAMS
810429
29 April 1981, KRO radio broadcast, KRO Studio, Hilversum, Netherlands: Same as 25 April 1981:

a   **Conjuration**
b   **Claudette's Way**
c   **Bossallegro**
d   **A Child Is Born**
e   **Three and One**

PEPPER ADAMS
810500
May 1981, audience recordings at various locations, Norway: Pepper Adams bs; Per Husby p; Arild Andersen b; Espen Rud dm.

a   **Milestones**
b   **A Child Is Born**
c   **It's You or No One**
d   **'Tis**
e   **I Let a Song Go Out of My Heart**
f   **Bossa Nouveau**
g   **How Long Has This Been Going On**
h   **Three and One**
i   **'Tis**
j   **Min and Maj Blues**

Recorded at possibly Oslo (Club Valken and Blue Note Jazzclub), Tønsberg (Handverkeren), Fredrikstad (Club Thelonious), and Lillehammer (at another Blue Note Jazzclub location), during Adams' month-long, 28 one-nighter Norwegian tour with Husby's rhythm section. Trumpeter Kenny Wheeler made three or four of the gigs.

According to Per Husby, in a taped narration, sent to the author in 1987,

I think I was the one to bring them together, because I asked Pepper, "How do you like Kenny Wheeler?" and Pepper said, "Oh, I really like his playing." I said to Pepper, "Well, have you ever played together?" and Pepper said, "No, but I'd like to." I said, "It sounds to me that it would be an interesting combination." Then I asked Kenny, and Kenny said the same thing about Pepper: that he liked Pepper very much but he never had the chance to play with him. So I got the gig together and got them together....

Arild [Andersen] had come in, instead of Bjørn Alterhaug, who had done the first tour. Bjørn is a very good, accomplished, straight bass player. Ben Webster used to love playing with him, and I know Pepper loved to play with him. Arild is slightly more modern, so it took Arild a little while to get used to playing more of that bebop stuff again. Pepper came over to me, after the first gig, and said, "Well, you know, I think I would have preferred Bjørn, but he'll come along," and I could see that he sort of took Arild under his wing, tried to get to know him, tried to be nice to him, and so on, which made Arild feel very good. After some gigs, Arild was right there with him.

It was also on one of these gigs that Pepper told me his philosophy about encores. I think he had this from Thad Jones. He said, *"Never, ever* play a fast encore! You should always play an encore that's sort of medium tempo, so that, after you've finished that, they will never want to hear another one!" So he always played Three and One or something like that.

PEPPER ADAMS
810630
30 June 1981, audience recording, Jazz Unite, Paris: Charles Davis ts*; Pepper Adams bs; Gene Adler p; Wilbur Little b; Philly Joe Jones dm.

a **Ephemera**
b **Bossallegro**
c **A Child Is Born**
d **Invitation***
e **Killer Joe***

This was recorded on the last night of the engagement (c. 25-30 June).

Vibist Oliver Shearer was in the audience, and, in an interview with the author, done in 1988, said,

This was a new, prominent jazz club in Paris, and Philly Joe had played there for a week....They...[hired] Pepper as...soloist and he's playing with the band. Charles Davis was also playing, and what have you. They went to the rehearsal, and things like that, and they didn't have too much of a rehearsal, but what disturbed Pepper that much is that Philly was taking liberties and increasing the tempos at will. It was the first time I've ever seen Pepper when he was really upset enough to apologize to the audience....I was ready to knock somebody in the mouth!...Pepper was *furious* because it seems like, everything that he wanted to play, Philly was playing a big-time "I'm the leader here," and treated him like a sideman almost. [Pepper] was a Guest Soloist, and he was paid as a Guest Soloist: Pepper was being featured with the Philly Joe group, so then he turned around and he stomped off a tempo and it goes all kinds of ways! We weren't taught like that to play. He did [the apology] on his last set on the microphone....He just said something to the effect, "I want to apologize to the audience that things weren't into the vein of what it was supposed to be," or what was rehearsed, or something like that. He didn't purposely try to "down" anybody, but he let everybody know that, if you're keeping score, don't hold me responsible!...Pepper kind of went straight to the bar and got drunk....We both got on Charles Davis, because Charles was supposed to be the Musical Director....We were in the back and we were talking about it, and Charles Davis was trying to defend Philly Joe in that he's been doing that for quite some time: He does that for his own arrangements and stuff like that. When he thinks his thing is lagging or sagging, then he ups the tempo. He'll break in on somebody with some kind of funny break or something to change it.

PEPPER ADAMS
810706
6 July 1981, RAI TV broadcast, Trento, Italy: Pepper Adams bs; Franco d'Andrea p; Dodo Goya b; Bruno Biriaco dm.

It's unclear if audio or video still exist.

PEPPER ADAMS
810709
9 July 1981, RAI radio broadcast, Parco Marsiglia, San Remo, Italy: Pepper Adams bs*; Franco d'Andrea p; Dodo Goya b; Gianni Cazzola dm.

a   **Conjuration**[*]
b   **What Is This Thing Called Love**[*]
c   Ortwein 15
d   **A Child Is Born**[*]
e   **Bossallegro**[*]

PEPPER ADAMS
810810
10 August 1981, Granada TV broadcast, The Flags, Liverpool: Pepper
Adams bs; John Horler p; Jim Richardson b; Trevor Tomkins dm.

a   **Dylan's Delight**
b   **A Child Is Born**
c   **Bossa Nouveau**
d   **Three and One**
e   **'Tis**

Broadcasted on the program *Music from The Flags.*

PEPPER ADAMS–URBAN DREAMS
810930
30 September 1981, Van Gelder Studio, Englewood Cliffs NJ: Pepper
Adams bs; Jimmy Rowles p; George Mraz b; Billy Hart dm.

a	**Dexter Rides Again**	Palo Alto LP: PAJ-8009
b	**Urban Dreams**	Palo Alto unissued
c	**Urban Dreams**	
d	**Urban Dreams**	Palo Alto LP: PAJ-8009
e	**Three Little Words**	Palo Alto unissued
f	**Three Little Words**	
g	**Three Little Words**	
h	**Three Little Words**	Palo Alto LP: PAJ-8009
i	**Time on My Hands**	Palo Alto unissued
j	**Time on My Hands**	Palo Alto LP: PAJ-8009
k	**Pent-Up House**	Palo Alto unissued
m	**Pent-Up House**	Palo Alto LP: PAJ-8009
n	**Trentino**	Palo Alto unissued
o	**Trentino**	Palo Alto LP: PAJ-8009

All issued tracks on Quicksilver LP: QS-4006, Quicksilver CD: QSCD-4006.

This is Adams' eighteenth date as a leader.

According to Adams, in an interview with Peter Danson in *Coda,*

> I am not as fond of it as I am of the Muse dates [*see* 780614, 800311]. I think, for one thing, they did not like original material. So I had to talk my ass off to get [Herb Wong] to do two of my tunes. They were dictating really clichéd, hackneyed tunes, and I had to talk them out of that. So the choice of material is not mine. Well, I'll take responsibility for it, because we finally arrived at a decision where I could at least live with the material that was chosen. That date itself is quite good.

Record producer Mark Feldman told the author, in an interview in 1988,

> I remember [Pepper Adams] telling me about the *Urban Dreams* thing. He didn't like some of the tunes on there. He didn't choose them. I think he told Bob [Sunenblick] at the time that, the way Rudy recorded Jimmy Rowles, Jimmy could have mailed his piano part in from California. That's not Rudy's fault. That's the producer's fault.

Adams and Feldman were alluding to the producer, Bob Porter, deliberately under-recording Rowles, so he was far less present than others on the date.

According to Jimmy Rowles, in a conversation with the author in 1987, there were no rehearsals for this session:

> I don't like to go out and sit in, and I don't like to sit around in the day and practice, just to keep up, so that, if I ever get a chance to do a record date, I've been practicing for four years and now I got the date and I'm ready! I'm not that hungry, so I was apprehensive about playing this date with Pepper, because he's blowing all the time and I'm not, and I'm not ready to record, really, so I felt a little bit "underneath" that way, and I was not really satisfied with what I did. I've played jobs where I haven't practiced for a long time, and I'll say to myself, after the first tune, "What the hell am I doing here? I should have turned this one down! I'm not ready." Oh, I got

a kick out of what [Pepper] did with that fast one we played, Three Little Words. Isn't that the one where we slowed down and we played half time? I told him, in front, that I wasn't ready to play any real fast tempos and, if you got one, leave me out of the choruses! I was trying to save myself. That's all. I enjoyed it. I enjoyed playing with Mraz and Billy Hart.

Record producer Bob Sunenblick told the author in 1988,

Bob Porter told me that, on the *Urban Dreams* recording, he had a very difficult time talking Pepper into doing a lot of the songs that Pepper did. I remember that one called Dexter Rides Again. Pepper didn't want to record that one. There's two or three other ones that Pepper didn't want to record. He found Pepper to be very complicated, uncompromising—but uncompromising in a negative fashion—to do recordings. The thing is, if you go back in history, the best records were made when the artist did not have complete artistic control. For instance, the Coleman Hawkins' Body and Soul, which is a masterpiece. Hawkins didn't want that issued. He thought it was horrible.

Bob Porter told the author that, since the band came very prepared, the date was knocked out in two or three hours. Alternate tracks might have been destroyed.

PEPPER ADAMS
811010
10 October 1981, audience recording, Far and Away, Cliffside Park NJ:
Pepper Adams bs; Noreen Grey p; Earl Sauls b; Ron Marabuto dm.

a **In a Mellow Tone**
b **Confirmation**
c **'Tis**

See 801101.

PEPPER ADAMS
811117
c. 17 November 1981, audience recording, Bechet's, New York: Pepper

Adams bs; Jill McManus p; Cecil McBee or Ratzo Harris b; Ron Marabuto dm.

According to McManus, this band's engagement lasted from 17-21 November.

LUIS OSCAR–TU Y ELLA
811200
c. *December 1981, West New York NJ:* Paquito D'Rivera as; Pepper Adams bs; Luis Oscar voc; other musicians.

a   Tu y Ella   Kim LP: K-715
b   Para Que
c   Que Tienes Tu para Mi
d   Primavera de Hoy
e   Ya No Quiero Pensar
f   Usted Senora

According to Paquito D'Rivera, in an interview with the author in 1988, D'Rivera invited Pepper Adams to the session as a sub for baritone saxophonist Mario Rivera.

DAVID AMRAM – LATIN-JAZZ CELEBRATION
811216
16-18 December 1981 and 29 January 1982, Hit Factory and Variety Sound Studio, New York: Joe Wilder tp; Jimmy Knepper tb; David Amram frh, fl, p, g, perc; Jerry Dodgion ss, as; Paquito D'Rivera as, fl, perc; George Barrow, David Newman ts; Pepper Adams bs; Victor Venegas e-b; Steve Berrios dm, perc; Machito claves; Machito Jr., Duduca Fonseca perc; Candido Camero cga, perc; Myra Casales cga.

a   En Memoria de Chano Pozo   Elektra-Musician LP: 60195-1
b   New York Charanga
c   Andes Breeze[1]
d   **Take the "A" Train**
e   Blue Bomba
f   Brazilian Memories
g   **Celebration**
h   Song of the Rain Forest

[1]All horns out.

It's unclear what material was used from either session. Only -d was recorded at Variety Sound.

All tracks Elektra-Musician (F) LP: WE-351, Elektra-Musician (Eng) LP: E-0195, Elektra-Musician (Ger) LP: 96-0195-1, Wounded Bird CD: WOU-195.

HIGHLIGHTS IN JAZZ
820107
7 January 1982, private recording, New York University's Loeb Student Center, New York: Bob Wilber as, ss; Sonny Fortune as*; Scott Hamilton ts; Pepper Adams bs; Tommy Flanagan p; Chris Flory g; Phil Flanigan b; Connie Kay dm; Pug Horton voc.

a   Honeysuckle Rose*
b   Summertime
c   Polka Dot Stomp
d   Medley:
        unknown Lester Young tune
        unknown Ike Quebec tune
e   **Chelsea Bridge**
f   Medley*:
        Dewey Square
        unknown title
g   **Sophisticated Lady**
h   **Chalumeau**
i   Things Ain't What They Used to Be
j   unknown title
k   unknown title*

Regarding -h, *see* 860702.
See 781215.

PEPPER ADAMS
820109
9 January 1982, audience recording, Jazz Forum, New York: Pepper Adams bs; Ronnie Mathews p; Ray Drummond b; Al Foster dm.

a   **Ephemera**
b   Gene Marie*
c   **Hi-Fly**
d   **Three and One**
e   **'Tis**
f   John Charles*
g   **Doctor Deep**
h   **Bossallegro**
i   **Old Ballad**
j   **'Tis**

*Rhythm section only.

Adams' gig was 8-9 January 1982. *See* 790907.

PEPPER ADAMS
820207
7 February 1982, private recording, Ron and Cindy Ley's house, Albany NY: J.R. Monterose ss*; Pepper Adams bs; Walter Donnaruma p; Otto Gardner b; Eddie Robinson dm.

a   **Doctor Deep**
b   **Conjuration**
c   **A Child Is Born**
d   **Bossallegro**
e   **I Carry Your Heart**
f   **'Tis**
g   **Star Eyes***

Pepper Adams mentioned to the audience that Doctor Deep was written about six weeks prior to this gig.

According to Adams' friend Cindy Ley, in a conversation with the author in 1988,

This happened in our house particularly, and in other places: I've always known when Pepper was playing his heart out, because he knew that there were people in the audience he was playing for and they were listening. There was a love being exchanged, in that I always felt that, when he did that. In a sense you could almost say, "He's playing that for me," and I'm listening because it's him, and there was something there. That communication goes back and forth, between the musician and the listener.

PEPPER ADAMS-AL JARREAU
820223
23 February 1982, audience recording of rehearsal, Shrine Auditorium, Los Angeles: Pepper Adams bs; Milcho Leviev p; Bob Magnusson b; Alex Acuna dm; Al Jarreau voc.*

a **My Shining Hour**
b **Blue Rondo à la Turk***
c **Blue Rondo à la Turk**[1]
d **My Shining Hour**
e **Blue Rondo à la Turk***
f **My Shining Hour**
g **Blue Rondo à la Turk***

[1]Piano solo.

In his 1984 interview with the author, Adams said,

It was Al Jarreau's backup people. Milcho Leviev was the piano player. He was terrific! At the rehearsal he played his version of Take Five in 4/4 time and in major. He had me on the floor! It's one of the funniest two minute renditions I ever heard!...It was all first class treatment, all the way. It was terrific: Met by a limousine at the airport, first-class accommodations in L.A. There's traditionally a party for nominees. That was great fun, and, like, the whole thing, it was all first class.

And, of course, I was told, "You have two minutes with the rhythm section, then you do a tune with Al Jarreau." My first night in California I had a rehearsal, first with the rhythm section, which was just for a very short time. How long can you rehearse for two minutes? I had never met Al Jarreau, so I was kind of wondering how was this going to go, like what sort of person is this going to turn out to be. As he turned out, he was terrific. Really nice cat. His primary concern at the rehearsal was to see that, while he was getting his exposure for singing this tune that he was doing (which was Blue Rondo à la Turk), that also I would be featured in it as well, so that I would get equal representation, which was certainly very nice of him. My Shining Hour was written as a ballad. I played it very up-tempo, and it had been on the album that had received that year's nomination, so it was appropriate from that point of view. But, the basic idea of doing something real uptempo is that, if it had not been something real uptempo, I would have had just a chance to play the melody and that would have been it! This way, there was some actual jazz improvisation taking place.

See 820224.

PEPPER ADAMS-AL JARREAU
820224
24 February 1982, NBC TV broadcast, Shrine Auditorium, Los Angeles: Same as 23 February 1982, Al Jarreau voc.*

a **My Shining Hour**
b **Blue Rondo à la Turk**[*]

This was the annual National Association of Recording Arts and Sciences *Grammy Awards* television show.

According to Dick Katz, in a conversation with the author in 1987, "We had a near mutiny in the New York Chapter because the National didn't want [Pepper] to play. They didn't think it was commercial enough, and we threatened to boycott the whole thing. We had enough of a protest to make sure he got on."

Regarding his performance, Adams, in an interview with Peter Danson in *Coda,* said, "Hey, how about that? My three minutes in the big time." *See* 820223.

PEPPER ADAMS
820302
c. 2 March 1982, audience recording, Bull's Head, London: Pepper Adams bs; Tony Lee p; Spike Heatley b; Martin Drew dm.

a **Falling in Love with Love**
b **Isn't It Romantic**
c **Dewey Square**
d **How Long Has This Been Going On**
e **'Tis**
f **Wrap Your Troubles in Dreams**

g   **I Got It Bad (And that Ain't Good)**
h   **Well, You Needn't**
i   **Witchcraft**
j   **'Tis**

Recorded during Adams' one-week tour with Tony Lee (c. 2-7 March). After this gig Adams traveled to Stockport, England to perform at Warren Buckley. While there Adams likely visited with mouthpiece maker Geoff Lawton in nearby Macclesfield. Adams chose one of Lawton's mouthpieces to replace his fragile Dukoff, and Adams stuck with this set-up for the rest of his life.

PEPPER ADAMS
820317
17 March 1982, RF TV broadcast, Maison de la Radio, Paris: Eric Le Lann tp, flh; Pepper Adams bs; Georges Arvanitas p; Jacky Samson b; Charles Saudrais dm.

a   **Conjuration**

-a was videotaped and used as a television advertisement for the group's engagement on 15-20 March at the Petit Opportun.

PEPPER ADAMS
820318
18 March 1982, RF radio broadcast, Maison de la Radio, Paris: Same as 17 March 1982:

a   **Conjuration**
b   **Binary**
c   **Doctor Deep**
d   **Dexter Rides Again**
e   **Lovers of Their Time**[1]
f   **Bossa Nouveau**
g   **Reflectory**

[1]Adams and rhythm section.

PEPPER ADAMS
820401
*1 April 1982, TROS radio broadcast, Nick Vollebregt's Jazz Café, Laren,
Netherlands:* Pepper Adams bs; Tony Bauwens p; Roger Vanhaverbecke
b; Freddy Rottier dm.

a   **Scratch**
b   **Have You Met Miss Jones**
c   **I Carry Your Heart**
d   **Joy Road**
e   **Doctor Deep**
f   **Falling in Love with Love**

PEPPER ADAMS
820406
6 April 1982, audience recording, Hasty Pudding Club, Cambridge MA:
Bob Merrill tp; Bob Mover, Jeff Zelnick as†; Pepper Adams bs; Joe
Cohn g; Ed Felson b; Jeff Williams, Jerry Adams dm.

a   **'Tis**[1]
b   **Pent-Up House**
c   **In Love with Night**[2]
d   **It's You or No One**
e   **Trentino**[3]
f   **Binary**
g   **Doctor Deep**[4]
h   **A Night in Tunisia**
i   **Mr. Lucky**
j   **'Tis**
     Full band:
k   **Oleo***†

[1]Prior to the concert, Adams plays the theme of this tune only, by himself,
as a soundcheck.
[2]Adams and rhythm section.
[3]Adams and rhythm section.
[4]Adams and rhythm section.

Due to a mishap on slippery steps in Brussels in late March, Adams' saxophone was damaged and he's forced to play his original instrument for the first time since it was replaced in December 1980.

PEPPER ADAMS
820514
14 May 1982, audience recording, Defemio's, Yonkers NY: Pepper Adams bs; Hal Galper p; Reggie Johnson b; Al Defemio dm.

a   **Minority**
b   **Blue Champagne**
c   **Half Nelson**

PEPPER ADAMS
820717
17 July 1982, audience recording, Far and Away, Cliffside Park NJ: Pepper Adams bs; Noreen Grey p; Earl Sauls b; Ron Marabuto dm.

a   **What Is This Thing Called Love**
b   **Shuffle**
c   **The Days of Wine and Roses**
d   **Waltz**
e   **Falling in Love with Love**
f   **'Tis**

See 801101.

PEPPER ADAMS
820804
4 August 1982, private recording, Blackstone Hotel, Chicago: Paul Serrano tp; Pepper Adams bs; Willie Pickens p; Eddie de Haas b; Wilbur Campbell dm.

a   If I Were A Bell[1]
b   **Doctor Deep**
c   **Joy Road**
d   **Dig**
e   **Stomping at the Savoy**
f   **What Is This Thing Called Love**

g   **Yesterdays**

[1]Rhythm section only.

See Author's Note above 580000A entry.

PEPPER ADAMS
820805
5-8 August 1982, private recordings, Blackstone Hotel, Chicago: Same
as 4 August 1982:

See Author's Note above 580000A entry.

HANK JONES
820814
*14 August 1982, NOS radio broadcast, De Meervaart, International Jazz
Festival, Amsterdam:* Pepper Adams, Nick Brignola bs; Hank Jones p;
George Mraz b; Mel Lewis dm.

a   **Nick Who's Blues**
b   **Valse Celtique**
c   **Urban Dreams**[1]
     Rhythm section:
d   Mr. Walker
e   On Green Dolphin Street
f   Sophisticated Lady[2]
     Add Adams:
g   **Reflectory**
h   **Sonnymoon for Two**
i   **Oleo**

[1]Adams and rhythm section.
[2]Brignola and rhythm section.

NOBBY TOTAH
820822
22 August 1982, audience recording, Levitt Pavillion, Westport CT: Pepper Adams bs; Hod O'Brien p; Nobby Totah b; Ray Mosca dm; Stephanie Nakasian voc.*

a **Between the Devil and the Deep Blue Sea**
b **Get Happy**
c One More for My Baby[1]
d **Urban Dreams**
e Bohemia after Dark[2]
f **Take the "A" Train**
g Medley:
      Something to Live For[3][*]
      Day Dream
      Lush Life[4]
      Chelsea Bridge
h **'Tis**

[1]Rhythm section feature.
[2]Rhythm section feature.
[3]Rhythm section feature, with vocals.
[4]Rhythm section feature.

In an interview with Nobby Totah in 1988, Totah told the author that he had played this venue with his trio in 1980-1981:

> They called me up for the following year, and I said "I'd be glad to do it, but I would like to recommend that you have Pepper Adams here." They didn't know who Pepper Adams was. I said, "He's a very important voice in jazz, and it would be a treat for your listeners to have him here, but it would cost more to bring Pepper here for a quartet instead of just a trio." I'll tell you frankly, I really wanted Pepper there also, because that's Gerry Mulligan territory. [Mulligan at the time lived in nearby Darien CT.] Everybody knows Gerry and I think Gerry is a great musician, but, when it comes to baritone, Pepper has always been my man! They said they'd think about it, and they called me back and said, "All right, we'll increase your budget so you can bring Pepper Adams." It's funny the way it happened. The day they told me, "O.K., go ahead," I had to go out of town, and I was at LaGuardia [Airport], and who should I run into but Pepper!

PEPPER ADAMS
820904
4 September 1982, WEMU radio broadcast, Hart Plaza, Mon-

treux/Detroit Kool Jazz Festival, Detroit: Pepper Adams bs; Gary
Schunk p; Ken Kellett b; Tony Pia dm.

a   **Scratch**
b   **Joy Road**
c   **Doctor Deep**
d   Vitamin E[1]
e   **Now in Our Lives**
f   **Bossa Nouveau**
g   **A Child Is Born**
h   **'Tis**

[1]Rhythm section only.

A private videotape of -a, -b, -c, -e, -f was made by the drummer's
brother.

According to Ken Kellett, in an interview with the author in 1987,
the rehearsal for this concert was done at a small recital hall at the Detroit Institute of Art. "That's where Pepper uttered the famous line, 'No
rehearsal should last as long as the gig,'" said Kellett.

According to saxophonist Mark Berger, in an interview with the author in 1987, "It was really good to see Pepper get that kind of exposure
to a national festival like that. It was in downtown Detroit. Pepper clever-
ly quoted the Stroh's [beer] theme, like he's done in other situations.
Something like that really got the crowd yelling."

PEPPER ADAMS
820905
*5 September 1982, audience recording, Baker's Keyboard Lounge, De-
troit:* Same as 4 September 1982:

a   **Julian**
b   The Break Through[1]
c   **Day Dream**
d   **'Tis**
e   **Reflectory**

[1]Rhythm section only.

PEPPER ADAMS-ROLAND HANNA
820906a
6 September 1982, WEMU radio broadcast, Veterans Memorial Hall, Montreux/Detroit Kool Jazz Festival, Detroit: Johnny Trudell tp; Pepper Adams bs; Roland Hanna p; Marian Haden b; J.C. Heard dm.

a **Just Friends**
b **In a Mellow Tone/Rosewood**
c **A Child Is Born**[1]
d **Scrapple from the Apple**
e **Oleo**

[1]Adams and Hanna duet.

DETROIT JAMS III
820906b
6 September 1982, WEMU radio broadcast, Veterans Memorial Hall, Montreux/Detroit Kool Jazz Festival, Detroit: Marcus Belgrave, Johnny Trudell tp; unknown ss; unknown as; unknown ts; Pepper Adams bs; Roland Hanna p; unknown p; unknown vib; Marian Haden b; unknown b; J.C. Heard dm.

a **C Jam Blues**[1]
b **Well, You Needn't**[2]

[1]Unknown as and ts here only. Both pianists play, though not simultaneously. Hanna, Haden, and Heard support a series of solos.
[2]Unknown ss here only. Unknown p and unknown b solo while Hanna and Haden respectively support them in the rhythm section.

PEPPER ADAMS
820906c
6 September 1982, audience recording, Baker's Keyboard Lounge, Detroit: Same as 4 September 1982:

a **I've Just Seen Her**
b **Joy Road**
c We'll Be Together Again[*]
d **Come Back to Me**
e **Tricotism**

f **How Long Has This Been Going On**
g Stolen Moments*
h **Bossa Nouveau**

*Rhythm section only.

PEPPER ADAMS
820907
7 September 1982, audience recording, Baker's Keyboard Lounge, Detroit: Same as 4 September 1982:

a **Dylan's Delight**
b **Urban Dreams**
c **Bossa Nouveau**
d **'Tis**

PEPPER ADAMS
821014
14 October 1982, audience recording, Café La Voute, Montreal: Pepper Adams bs; Stan Patrick p; Freddie McHugh b; Cisco Normand dm; Arlene Smith voc.*

a **Scratch**
b **Chelsea Bridge**
c **Three and One**
d **Falling in Love with Love***
e **How Long Has This Been Going On***
f **'Tis**
g **What Is There to Say***

Stan Patrick told the author in 1987 that the club, formerly a bank, had a jazz policy for the preceding summer months, but that they had just expanded the size of the club in time for Pepper Adams' engagement by opening up, for the first time, the vault area and putting the bandstand within it. "It was weird, but, yet, it had a certain ambiance to it," said Patrick. "I wasn't ready for this at all," Patrick explained, "because I had open heart surgery *again* the year before, and I was trying to get it back. I was unconscious for five weeks." Adams had called Patrick in advance of the gig, even though they hadn't seen each other since 1958: "Man,

I'm sure glad we are going to work together," Adams said to Patrick. "I remembered you from all these years. How are you doing? How's your playing?"

> The guys had told him before...but you don't turn down a gig from someone that great....This is the beautiful thing about Pepper: Pepper knew how to put you at ease! And, he could make you play things that you never thought you could play. The first night [14 October], everything just popped! I was amazed....[On the second night, however,] I wasn't feeling well that night at all. For some strange reason, none of us could just get into anything. The third night, everything fell into place again. He would encourage me. If I played a halfway decent little thing there, he'd say, "Yeah! O.K., Stan! Keep it up! You're gonna get it, man! Yeah, all right!"...He never screamed at us at all for messing up his music. I've worked with a lot of guys, and they don't give you a break. Very demanding: You make Mistake One, they say, "Lay out!" and I've had a lot of lay-outs called at me, but Pepper had a way of making you *want* to play. A gentle, kind manner; underneath it, there was a lot of strength. If you felt weak in the song, you could lay back on him, because you knew he would give it to you. His time was just beautiful. I think that's one of the other reasons why he and Freddie [McHugh] got along well, because Freddie was the man for time.

According to Arlene Smith, in an interview with the author in 1988, "We had a club going in Montreal, [for] which I was doing some managing and some booking....It was in the vault of an old bank. We dug all through tunnels, etc, and had, as our first guest, Pepper Adams."

About the club, saxophonist Charles Papasoff told the author, in an interview in 1987, "The club was actually in the vault, and then there was a little restaurant outside the vault, which was also part of the club. So wherever you were seated, Pepper was playing right in your face!"

Trumpeter Denny Christianson told the author in 1987,

> What struck me, when I saw him, was, what is a giant like this doing in a small, little place with fifty people listening to him? He should be center stage, down at a featured concert. That was always my frustration. This place was so small, you could only get about four people in the room where the band was playing, and everybody else had to be outside the vault. You could hear it, but you couldn't

see it! It was a very bizarre place and it didn't last long. There's
Pepper back in this hole, playing away, and there's some semblance
of an audience scattered around pillars and posts. Bizarre!

See 821015.

PEPPER ADAMS
821015
15 October 1982, audience recording, Café La Voute, Montreal: Same
as 14 October 1982, Arlene Smith voc*:

a   **Claudette's Way**
b   **Bossa Nouveau**
c   **A Child Is Born**
d   **There Will Never Be Another You***

See 821014.

PEPPER ADAMS
821112
*c. 12 November 1982, audience recording, Far and Away, Cliffside Park
NJ:* Lee Katzman tp*; Pepper Adams bs; Noreen Grey p; Earl Sauls b;
Ron Marabuto dm.

a   **Valse Celtique***
b   **Reflectory***
c   **Zec***
d   **My Shining Hour**
e   **Alone Together**
f   **'Tis**

This is their second and third set. *See* 801101.

ANGEL RANGELOV
821114
14 November 1982, audience recording, Satch's, Boston: Steve Lombar-
di, Mike Morris, Tony Gorruso tp; Andy Gravish, Dave Jensen tp, flh;
Jeff Rinear, Fuji Fujimoto, Herb Hubel, Matt Havilland tb; Mark Pinto,
Mike Rubino as, fl; Billy Pierce, Scott Robinson ts, ss; Brian Williams

bs, bcl; Makoto Ozone p; Leon Quintero g; Marshall Wood b; Klaus Suonsaari dm; Marcel Feunmayer cga, perc; Mark Ledford voc; Angel Rangelov arr; GUEST: Pepper Adams bs.

According to Angel Rangelov, in an interview with the author in 1996, Adams drove up to Boston and did the gig for $75. He stayed at the home of local disk jockey Tony Cennamo.

METROPOLE ORCHESTRA
821210a
10 December 1982, NOS radio broadcast, Hilversum, Netherlands: Jan Oosthof, Fons Diercks, Jan Hollander, Jan Vleeschouwer tp; Rudy Bosch, Chris Waldhober, probably Jan Elsink, Fred Volmer tb; Leen Oosterman frh; Piet Noordijk as, cl; Albert Beltman as, cl; Joop Mastenbroek ts, cl; Tinus Bruin or Dick Vennik ts; Wiebe Schuumans bs; Dick Schallies p; Rob Langereis b; Evert Overweg dm; harp; Rob Meijn perc; probably Eddie Koopman perc; 27 strings = 8, 7, 5, 4, 3; Rob Pronk cond; GUEST: Pepper Adams bs.

a **Urban Dreams**
b **Linger Awhile**
c **I'm All Smiles**
d **Witchcraft**
e **Gone with the Wind**

PEPPER ADAMS
821210b
10 December 1982, NOS radio broadcast, Nick Vollebregt's Jazz Café, Laren, Netherlands: Rob McConnell vtb; Piet Noordijk as*; Pepper Adams bs; Rein de Graaff p; Koos Serierse b; Eric Ineke dm.

a **Scrapple from the Apple***
b **Reflectory**
c **My Little Suede Shoes***
d **Ornithology***
e **No Refill**

PEPPER ADAMS
830115
15 January 1983, audience recording, Struggles, Edgewater NJ: Pepper
Adams bs; Peter Leitch g; Mike Richmond b.

a **Chelsea Bridge**
b **Three and One**
c **'Tis**
d **Fifty-Up**
e **Pent-Up House**
f **Reflectory**

According to Peter Leitch, in an interview with the author in 1987,

I moved [to New York] at the end of '82....I guess I wrote to him
and told him where I was going to be in New York, because, shortly
after I arrived here, there was a message from Pepper on my an-
swering machine with a gig for me....The last thing I expected
when I moved to New York was a call from Pepper Adams to go
and do a gig. It was probably the first gig I did in New York....
We worked two nights there with Mike Richmond, just the three of
us....He had learned one of my tunes, a tune called Fifty-Up, which
is a blues; one of the tunes I had sent him. We did it on the gig, I
guess, because he just liked the line. It was great! He knew exactly
what he wanted to hear. He didn't want to hear the *Fake Book*
changes on Chelsea Bridge, for example. He wanted to hear the correct stuff, which is great. We did some of his tunes and some standards.

PEPPER ADAMS
830219
*19 February 1983, audience recording, One Step Down, Washington
D.C.:* Pepper Adams bs; Reuben Brown p; Rufus Reid b; Steve Bagby
dm.

It's unclear if the audio still exists.
According to Steve Bagby, in an interview with the author in 1993,
"Rufus was cuing me on a lot of the tunes, because he knew a lot of the
tunes."

PEPPER ADAMS
830220
20 February 1983, audience recording, Penn Harris Ballroom, Camp Hill PA: Same as 19 February 1983:

a **Just Friends**
b **Quiet Lady**
c **Trentino**
d **Lovers of Their Time**
e **'Tis**
f **Green Dolphin Street**
g **Reflectory**
h **Now in Our Lives**
i **'Tis**
j **Conjuration**
k **Doctor Deep**
m **'Tis**

Recorded by the Central Pennsylvania Friends of Jazz.
According to Steve Bagby, in an interview with the author in 1993,

We had a great time. It was swinging. I just remember the sound in the ballroom. It was like playing at a concert hall. I could hear my drum come off the audience and I could hear his horn coming back. You got to hear yourself come back, so the sound settled and then the time took off....I liked playing with him because he swings, number one. For a drummer, he plays with you. It's like playing with another drummer. He would do funny quotes. I like that once in a while. Also, I could hear him play some of the altered scales. He was obviously up on modern harmony.

PEPPER ADAMS
830304
4 or 5 March 1983, audience recording, Defemio's, Yonkers NY: Pepper Adams bs; Stanley Cowell p; Jamil Nasser b; Al Defemio dm.

a **Body and Soul**
b **Caravan**
c **Blue Monk**

PEPPER ADAMS
830306
6 March 1983, audience recording, Holiday Inn, Hartford CT: Pepper
Adams bs; Don DePalma p; Nat Reeves b; Mike Duquette dm.

a **Conjuration**
b **Quiet Lady**
c **There Will Never Be Another You**
d **Now in Our Lives**
e **Valse Celtique**
f **Scratch**
g **What Is This Thing Called Love**
h **A Child Is Born**
i **Bossa Nouveau**
j **Rue Serpente**
k **'Tis**

Recorded by the Hartford Jazz Society.

HIGHLIGHTS IN JAZZ
830317
*17 March 1983, private recording, New York University's Loeb Student
Center, New York:* Red Rodney tp; Jimmy Heath ts; Pepper Adams,
Howard Johnson bs; Billy Taylor p; Victor Gaskin b; Keith Copeland
dm.

a Confirmation
b **Now in Our Lives**[1]
c Billie's Bounce

[1]Adams and rhythm section.

See 781215.

BILL BERRY BIG BAND
830325
*c. 25 March 1983, private videotape, Orange Coast College, OCC Jazz
Festival, Costa Mesa CA:* Bill Berry, Gene Goe, Blue Mitchell, Cat Anderson, Jack Sheldon tp; Britt Woodman, Jimmy Cleveland, Benny Pow-

ell, Tricky Lofton tb; Marshal Royal, Lanny Morgan as; Don Menza, Richie Kamuca ts; Jack Nimitz bs; Dave Frishberg p; Monte Budwig b; Frank Capp dm; GUESTS: Ted Curson tp; Pepper Adams bs.

It's unclear if the audio and video still exist.

PEPPER ADAMS
830326
26 March 1983, Orange Coast College, OCC Jazz Festival, Costa Mesa CA: Ted Curson tp; Pepper Adams bs; Victor Feldman p; Bob Magnusson b; Carl Burnett dm.

a	**Valse Celtique**	Interplay CD: IPCD-8608-2
b	Summertime[1]	
c	Last Resort[2]	
d	**Now in Our Lives[3]**	
e	**Oleo**	
f	**Doctor Deep**	Interplay-King (J) CD: ABCJ-556

[1]Curson and rhythm section.
[2]Rhythm section only.
[3]Adams and rhythm section.

All tracks on Interplay-King (J) CD: ABCJ-556, 3D (J) CD: MTCJ-2511.

According to producer Fred Norsworthy, in an interview with the author in 1987, "When he was working with the Victor Feldman thing, Victor found a flaw in Pepper's arrangements and they got into a kind of snit." Adams and Norsworthy discussed it again a few years later: "He kind of just smiled that little smile of his," Norsworthy said, [implying] "that Victor was right."

ORANGE COAST COLLEGE JAZZ BAND
830327
27 March 1983, private recording, Orange Coast College, OCC Jazz Festival, Costa Mesa CA: Orange Coast College Jazz Band; GUESTS: Ted Curson tp; Ted Marienthal ts; Pepper Adams bs; Brian Bromberg p.

It's unclear if the audio still exists.

PEPPER ADAMS
830328
28 March 1983, NPR radio broadcast, Four Queens Hotel, Las Vegas:
Pepper Adams bs; Bob Corwin p; Bob Badgely b; Dick Berk dm.

a **Conjuration**
b **What Is This Thing Called Love**
c **Now in Our Lives**
d **Dexter Rides Again**
e **A Child Is Born**
f **Trentino**
g **'Tis**

Saxophonist Bob Pierson recommended Adams: "I was responsible
for that," said Pierson in an interview with the author in 1988. "I talked
to Alan Grant about getting him."

ELVIN JONES
830414
14 April 1983, audience recording, Village Vanguard, New York: Pat
LaBarbera ss, ts; Pepper Adams bs; Jean-Paul Bourelly g; Andy McKee
b; Elvin Jones dm.

a **Lovers of Their Time**[1]
b **Doll of the Bride**
c **Harmonique**
d **My One and Only Love**
e **Island Birdie**

[1]Adams and rhythm section.

Andy McKee told the author in 2004 that Elvin Jones had invited
him to a rehearsal in New York, which McKee gladly attended since it
was his first chance to play with Jones. At the end of the rehearsal, much
to McKee's shock, Elvin Jones said, "That was fine. You're hired. The
gig starts tonight." McKee went home and sat for a while motionless in a
chair before getting dressed for the gig. There was never any mention by
Jones of this being any kind of a tryout, he said, and to play a six-night

run at the Vanguard with Elvin Jones, particularly this suddenly, was
rather overwhelming.

PEPPER ADAMS
830416
16 April 1983, audience recording, Far and Away, Cliffside Park NJ:
Pepper Adams bs; Noreen Grey p; Earl Sauls b; Al Harewood dm.

a   **My Shining Hour**
b   **Times Have Changed**
c   **Reflectory**
d   **No Refill**
e   **Bossallegro**
f   **What Might Have Been**
g   **Oleo**
h   **The Days Of Wine And Roses**
i   **Waltz**
j   **'Tis**
k   **My Secret Love**
m   **Rue Serpente**
n   **That's All**

See 801101.

ELVIN JONES
830417
17 April 1983, audience recording, Village Vanguard, New York: Same
as 14 April 1983, add Greg Kogan p:

a   **You're a Weaver of Dreams**
b   **E.J.'s Blues**
c   **Now in Our Lives**[1]
d   **Doll of the Bride**

[1]Adams and rhythm section, Kogan out.

See 830414.

HANK JONES
830604
4 June 1983, SR radio broadcast, Stockholm Jazz and Blues Festival,
Stockholm: Chet Baker tp, voc; Pepper Adams bs; Hank Jones p; Red
Mitchell b; Shelly Manne dm.

	Baker and rhythm section:	
a	Night Bird	Philology (It) unissued
b	Four	Philology (It) LP: W52-2
c	My Ideal	
d	But Not for Me	Philology (It) unissued
e	Chet's Blues	Philology (It) LP: W52-2
	Adams and rhythm section:	
f	**Doctor Deep**	Philology (It) unissued
g	**Consummation**	

PEPPER ADAMS
830611
11 June 1983, audience recording, Opus 40, High Woods NY: Howard
Johnson* as, bs; Pepper Adams bs; Walter Donnaruma p; Teddy Kotick
b; Eddie Robinson dm.

a   **unknown waltz**
b   **Now's the Time**[*]

Pepper Adams' performance was curtailed because, prior to the concert, he was hit in the chest with a car door that was swung open by Teddy Kotick. Because Adams was in considerable pain, Howard Johnson
was called in to substitute for Adams, although Adams did play a few
tunes.

In a 1988 conversation about Pepper Adams, record producer and
physician Mark Feldman told the author,

> I met Pepper for the first time at a concert at Opus 40. Opus 40 is
> near Kingston. It's in High Woods, which is between Saugerties and
> Woodstock. It's a beautiful site. This guy, who used to teach art at
> Bard College, took this natural quarry and built this huge sculpture.
> Walter knew the people involved in Opus 40 and that's how I think
> Pepper got the gig. In any event, one thing about this concert is that
> Pepper was in pretty bad shape. He hit himself against a car door

and he cracked a rib. He was not the same old ferocious Pepper. I was introduced to Pepper by Walter at intermission....Pepper was very happy to be there, because it's a beautiful place and the backdrop is one of the Catskill Mountains. He was just overjoyed. He was very much impressed with it, but he was in agony. Pepper was playing in Albany that weekend and they came down and played.... He told me at intermission he was having trouble breathing. He took a very slow, deep breath and he said, "Oh, it hurts me so terribly to take a deep breath." I said, 'It sounds like you fractured a rib."

According to Howard Johnson, in a conversation with the author in 1989,

The last time I played with him was up in Woodstock, where I was living at the time and where I still live sometimes. He had a job at this place called Opus 40. I went over just to hang out, but, just in case, I took my baritone, and Pepper said, "Hey, come and play with me, because I've got a pain in my side and I don't know what it is. I don't feel very comfortable playing." I had a good time. He still played great, but he just didn't play as much as he might have played. He was as great as ever. I said, "Well, you don't sound like there's anything wrong with you to me!" The next time I saw him, I said, "Did you go to the doctor?" He said, "Yeah, the doctor said I had a broken rib." I don't remember if he said how he broke it, but he said that he went to this doctor, who didn't know anything about him as a musician, and he said, "Well, just let it heal. There's no need in putting a splint on it or anything. Just don't do any deep breathing or lift anything heavy." When he told me that, he was laughing, and his rib wasn't right, and he was laughing and laughing, and—*"Ew, ew, ew!"*—he hurt his rib laughing!

ELVIN JONES
830621
21 June 1983, audience recording, Village Vanguard, New York: Frank Foster ts; Pepper Adams bs; Kenny Kirkland p; Richard Davis b; Elvin Jones dm.

a   **George and Me**
b   **Valse Celtique**

Pepper Adams was suffering with a cracked rib, due to an accident in High Woods, New York (*see* 830611).

ELVIN JONES
830622
22 June 1983, audience recording, Village Vanguard, New York: Same as 21 June 1983:

a   **Conjuration**
b   **Simone**
c   **Some Other Blues**
d   **Dobbin'**
e   The House that Love Built[1]
f   **Claudette's Way**

[1]Foster and rhythm section.

Pepper Adams finished writing Dobbin' on 21 June 1983, a few hours prior to opening a four-night stint with Elvin Jones' group at the Village Vanguard (*see* 830621). If the band did not play the tune on opening night, this is possibly its world premiere.

Pepper Adams was suffering with a cracked rib, due to an accident in High Woods, New York (*see* 830611).

ELVIN JONES
830624
24 June 1983, audience recording, Village Vanguard, New York: Same as 21 June 1983:

a   Black Nile
b   The House that Love Built[1]
c   **Valse Celtique**

[1]Foster and rhythm section.

Stafford James played the first two sets of the evening, but was replaced for the third set by Richard Davis.

Pepper Adams was suffering with a cracked rib, due to an accident in High Woods, New York (*see* 830611).

PEPPER ADAMS
830625
25 June 1983, WEMU radio broadcast, Frog Island Park, Ypsilanti MI:
Pepper Adams bs; Gary Schunk p; Ken Kellett b; Tony Pia dm.

a   **Scratch**
b   **Dobbin'**
c   **Doctor Deep**
d   **Three and One**
e   Out on Grand River[1]
f   **Now in Our Lives**
g   **Bossallegro**

[1]Rhythm section only.

Pepper Adams was suffering with a cracked rib, due to an accident in High Woods, New York (*see* 830611).

ELVIN JONES
830626
26 June 1983, audience recording, Village Vanguard, New York: Same as 21 June 1983, except Stafford James* or Richard Davis b:

a   **Mean What You Say***
b   **Black Nile***
c   **Conjuration**
d   **In a Sentimental Mood**
e   **Claudette's Way**

James played the first set, Davis played the second set.
Pepper Adams was suffering with a cracked rib, due to an accident in High Woods, New York (*see* 830611).

PEPPER ADAMS
830704
4 July 1983, audience recording, Astrolabe, Ottawa Jazz Festival, Ottawa: Pepper Adams bs; John Hicks p; Dennis Irwin b; Lorne Ellen dm.

a   **Mean What You Say**

b   **Quiet Lady**
c   **What Is This Thing Called Love**
d   **Dobbin'**
e   **Conjuration**
f   **Bossallegro**
g   **Now in Our Lives**
h   **Oleo**

At the beginning of the concert, Irwin broke a string. Killing time while Irwin repaired his bass, Adams entertained the audience with an account of his experience with Canadian immigration officials on his way to the gig.

Pepper Adams was suffering with a cracked rib, due to an accident in High Woods, New York (*see* 830611). Regarding Adams' condition in Ottawa, Hicks said, "his playing was great, but he was in a little pain," Hicks said. "I remember talking about that on the plane coming up, when we flew up from New York. You never would have known anything was wrong with him."

PEPPER ADAMS–LIVE AT FAT TUESDAY'S
830819

19 August 1983, Fat Tuesday's, New York: Kenny Wheeler tp, flh; Pepper Adams bs; Hank Jones p; Clint Houston b; Louis Hayes dm.

a	**Conjuration**	Uptown LP: UP-27-16
b	**Alone Together**	Reservoir CD: RSR-CD-113
c	**Diabolique II**	Uptown unissued
d	**Now in Our Lives**[1]	
e	Recordame[2]	
f	Oleo[3]	
g	**Doctor Deep**	Uptown LP: UP-27-16
h	**Dobbin'**	
i	**'Tis**	
j	**Everybody's Song But My Own**	Uptown unissued
k	**Quittin' Time**	Reservoir CD: RSR-CD-113
m	**Valse Celtique**	Uptown unissued
n	Old Ballad	
o	Yours Is My Heart Alone[4]	
p	Budo[5]	

q   **A Child Is Born**
r   **Dylan's Delight**

[1]Adams and rhythm section.
[2]Rhythm section only.
[3]Rhythm section only.
[4]Rhythm section only.
[5]Rhythm section only.

-a, -g, -h, -i on Reservoir CD: RSR-CD-113.
This is Adams' nineteenth date as a leader.
In a conversation with the author in 1988, drummer Billy Hart said that Pepper Adams had invited him to play on this session, but he couldn't make the date because of a previous commitment.
According to Clint Houston, in an interview with the author in 1988, rehearsals took place probably at Don Sickler's studio on 28th Street:

> It was really just a week of work. We had rehearsed those tunes, and [had] gotten them together, and the company just came down. It was, like, not really recording. They just had the microphones there, and somebody was way in the back in a booth that we never saw.... It went beautifully. Everybody was relaxed. There wasn't any heavy pressure. We all knew the tunes. I loved [Pepper's tunes]. Some of them were really difficult. It's the way he writes. He has harmonic movement in some of those tunes that are very surprising and don't go where you normally think a tune is going to go.

Regarding the final product, Houston said, "It took a while to get used to the sound of the recording. It's just a strange sound. There wasn't much we could do about it. That was all out of our hands."
Pepper Adams told the author, in a 1984 interview,

> They wanted a standard on the album. It's funny. They named several standards as possibilities. They were adamant about at least one. So, Alone Together, we agreed on that, and then they said—this is the two doctors—"That's fine. We'll have an arrangement written for you." I said, "That won't be necessary. I'll write one my damn self." I think I wrote a good one! Shit! I've recorded that before. But, anyway, this time I was able to write an arrangement to make it a little bit different. I think it came out good.

Uptown owner Mark Feldman told the author, in an interview in 1988, that Pepper Adams "felt that this was a very special situation, because he liked playing with Kenny Wheeler, who was different, and he was very happy about the rhythm section, so he enjoyed it."

About Pepper Adams, Hank Jones told the author, in a 1988 interview,

> Baritone was the instrument, the medium that he used to express his ideas, which were *endless;* absolutely endless and varied. I worked with him at Fat Tuesday's on a job, and I never ceased to be amazed at the flow of ideas—continuous flow. Every chorus was better than the last one. Now, that's genius! And absolutely flawless execution! What else can you say? You see, there are lots of ways to play the instrument. You can play an instrument with what we'd like to describe as "safe." That is, you don't take any chances. You don't go out on a limb. You play everything absolutely safe. Of course, you can get by like that. But Pepper didn't play it safe. He got out on a limb. He took chances and always made it work: harmonically, melodically, everything, in every possible way. I've never heard anybody that played like that on saxophone before. The man was just a total genius!...
>
> The word *genius* carries with it many implications and connotations. When you say, "The man is a genius," that means that he's capable of doing things that nobody else is capable of doing, or at least relatively few people. Charlie Parker had that same thing. Charlie Parker had an endless flow of ideas, which he could execute flawlessly at any tempo, with a tone that was impeccable....I was just always amazed: I used to get the impression that there was nothing that [Pepper] couldn't do. I got that same impression from Charlie Parker. There are probably things that he couldn't do, but, if there were, I don't think anybody ever invented them!...I never felt I was up to his standards, to tell you the truth. I was reaching to play along with him. Pepper would extend your thinking, your abilities. That was part of the greatness of Pepper. He would make you *play.* He would make you think more creatively because he was thinking and playing creatively.

Uptown owner Bob Sunenblick told the author in 1988,

> Personally, I found Pepper to be very difficult when I did the recordings, because you had no control over what he was going to

play. Like, for instance, that recording at Fat Tuesday's, I did want some kind of tune that other people could hang their hat on. The only tune I could get Pepper to agree with was Alone Together, which he had already recorded on World Pacific. I couldn't talk Pepper into anything! Basically, I was willing to accept Pepper's choices. He said that he played beautifully with Kenny Wheeler, so I accepted it, and it looked like a tremendous rhythm section, so I went along with this. Of all the people that I recorded, the only person that really gave me this problem was Pepper Adams, and I especially loved to record a lot of marginal, fringe type musicians.... When you wanted to make a record, and you had some idea of making some kind of—not commercial viability, but something that—for instance, you pick up the record, you see some familiar tune, and you want to hear it. Like, you want to hear Pepper play 'Round Midnight. Pepper played 'Round Midnight with Peter Leitch [*see* 841117]. I wanted, at that time, to get a feature of Pepper Adams doing it, but he wouldn't do it. He would only do it in the context of the Peter Leitch [date]. The only way to really record Pepper, it seems, and get him to play what you wanted him to play, was to not do him as a leader; do it under somebody else's name. But you wouldn't get a solo feature, so I found that kind of difficult....

I personally didn't like the sound....I tried to get Malcolm Addey to do the recording. Malcolm Addey is a recording engineer that has some portable equipment. Malcolm Addey was recording Ron Carter and Jim Hall at another club called the Village West. He got ahold of this other guy named Jim Anderson, who's done some NPR recordings. I like Jim. He was a good guy. I felt his sound wasn't really the way I like it. [Feldman] was dinking around with the cymbals of Louis Hayes. Besides that, I don't think the sound would have been good, because I think I am very faithful to Rudy Van Gelder, and I like his sound. I like his piano sound, so I didn't like Jim Anderson's piano sound. I don't like that bright kind of piano. Malcom Addey, in particular, records very bright piano, and Jim Anderson did the same thing. It was done two-track. The recording was mixed right on the date. It's almost impossible to do one of these multi-track. You don't get any separation anyway, and, so, if you have to go in the studio and mix this down, you're getting a new cost for nothing.

PEPPER ADAMS–LIVE AT FAT TUESDAY'S
830820
20 August 1983, Fat Tuesday's, New York: Same as 19 August 1983:

a	**Convection**	Uptown unissued
b	**Conjuration**	
c	**Alone Together**	
d	**Diabolique II**	
e	**Now in Our Lives**[1]	
f	Au Privave[2]	
g	Recordame[3]	
h	**Doctor Deep**	
i	**'Tis**	
j	**Everybody's Song But My Own**	
k	**Quittin' Time**	
m	**Dylan's Delight**	Reservoir CD: RSR-CD-113
n	Old Ballad	Uptown LP: UP-27-16
o	'Round Midnight[4]	Uptown unissued
p	Oleo[5]	
q	**Claudette's Way**	Reservoir CD: RSR-CD-113
r	**Diabolique II**	Uptown LP: UP-27-16
s	**'Tis**	Uptown unissued
t	**Conjuration**	
u	**Alone Together**	
v	**Diabolique II**	
w	**Doctor Deep**	
x	Moanin'[6]	
y	Yours Is My Heart Alone[7]	
z	**Dobbin'**	
aa	**Valse Celtique**	

[1]Adams and rhythm section.
[2]Rhythm section only.
[3]Rhythm section only.
[4]Rhythm section only.
[5]Rhythm section only.
[6]Rhythm section only.
[7]Rhythm section only.

-n, -r on Reservoir CD: RSR-CD-113.

This is Adams' nineteenth date as a leader.
See 830819.

BARRY HARRIS
830826a
26 August 1983, film soundtrack, Entermedia Theater, New York: Pepper
Adams bs; Barry Harris p.

a   **Donna Lee**   Kay Jazz (Eng) VHS: KJ-048

This appears in the documentary *Passing It On,* directed by David
Chan and Ken Freundlich.
-a on Rhapsody VHS: [no number], Rhapsody DVD: [no number].

BARRY HARRIS
830826b
26 August 1983, Entermedia Theater, New York: Red Rodney tp;
Clifford Jordan ts; Pepper Adams bs; Barry Harris p; Art Davis b; Leroy
Williams dm; tap dancer: probably Jimmy Slyde.*

a   Medley†:   Kay Jazz (Eng) VHS: KJ-048
      Epistrophy
      Ruby My Dear
b   **Luminescence**   private recording
c   **Lover Man**
d   **Lover Come Back to Me**
e   Easy to Love*†
f   **Valse Celtique**
g   **The Theme**

†Rhythm section only.
-a on Rhapsody VHS: [no number], Rhapsody DVD: [no number].
About the PBS television broadcast of this film, Red Rodney, in an
interview with the author in 1988, said,

> I remember that Entermedia Theater thing. In fact, I saw [Mark]
> Morganelli yesterday and he mentioned it, and I screamed at him. I
> said, "Man, you had no right to do that without telling us that it was
> going to happen, because we should be paid for that." He was the
> producer. Of course, he swears he didn't allow it, but I somehow

don't believe him. Maybe I'm being unfair; I just don't believe he didn't know. I was upset that he televised us, or had someone else do it—which he told me about yesterday. He gave the name of the person. He said, "If you call him, you can get a tape," and I said, "No, if I call him, I'll ask for a lot more than the tape, not that I would get it." I said, "Pepper sure could have used some money before he died," and that would have been very nice, if they'd have paid *something,* instead of just doing it secretively, and then we find out later that it's a TV show. It's a tape. It's been shown on television and everything....

I do remember Pepper and I backstage. In fact, he gave me a piece of music [Valse Celtique] that we played onstage. It was very difficult, and I was put out with Pepper for doing it: "Man, we don't have any time to rehearse this damn thing," but we did it....I would have said, "No, absolutely no," if it hadn't been Pepper. I know it was very difficult, I had no music stand there, I had to hold it out with my hand—it was ridiculous! We never played it before. He didn't insist. He just wanted to do it and brought it. Pepper wasn't the type to insist.

In an interview with the author in 1988, producer Mark Morganelli said,

I have reviews of the concert and people were just amazed. It was one of the best productions that's ever been done. I mean, I did it myself. I lost a lot of money. The set was from *Taking My Turn,* which was an Off-Broadway musical, (that was running with Cissy Houston, Margaret Whiting, Tiger Haynes) about aging. We did it right on the stage of *Taking My Turn.* It had 300 lights aimed at the stage, and it was an 1,100 seat theater, and I had a good sound system in place, and my Steinway there....It was Barry's group that I set up—I booked it for him—opening for Art Blakey and the Jazz Messengers, two nights.

BARRY HARRIS
830827
27 August 1983, audience recording, Entermedia Theater, New York: Same as 26 August 1983:

It's likely that most, if not all, of the tunes done on 830826b were done here.

DANNY D'IMPERIO
830930a
30 September 1983, audience recording, Eddie Condon's, New York:
John Marshall tp*; Pepper Adams bs; Pat Rebillot p; Reggie Johnson b;
Danny D'Imperio dm.

a **Star Eyes***
b **Minority***
c **Lover Come Back to Me***
d **Just You, Just Me**
e **Blues for Philly Joe***
f **Have You Met Miss Jones**
g **Scrapple from the Apple**
h **Body and Soul**
i **My Ideal***
j **Hellure**

PEPPER ADAMS
830930b
*30 September 1983, audience recording, Far and Away, Cliffside Park
NJ:* Pepper Adams bs*; Noreen Grey p; Earl Sauls b; Curtis Boyd dm.

a **That's All***
b **Star Eyes***
c I Loves You, Porgy
d **Three Little Words***

This was their second set of the night. *See* 801101.

PEPPER ADAMS
831001
1 October 1983, audience recording, Far and Away, Cliffside Park NJ:
Same as 30 September 1983; Pepper Adams bs*:

a **Dobbin'***
b **Time on My Hands***
c What's New
d **Times Have Changed***
e **Everybody's Song But My Own***

f   **Solitary Blues**[*]
g   Everything Happens to Me
h   **Three and One**[*]
i   **Witchcraft**[*]
j   **Valse Celtique**[*]
k   **What Might Have Been**[*]
m   **The Way You Look Tonight**[*]

See 801101.

PEPPER ADAMS
831014
14 October 1983, audience recording, Defemio's, Yonkers NY: Pepper
Adams bs; Hal Galper p; Reggie Johnson b; Al Defemio dm.

a   **Alone Together**
b   **Dobbin'**
c   **Isn't It Romantic**
d   **Chelsea Bridge**

PEPPER ADAMS
831015
15 October 1983, audience recording, Defemio's, Yonkers NY: Same as
14 October 1983:

a   **Lovers of Their Time**
b   **Falling in Love with Love**
c   **Chelsea Bridge**

RAY ALEXANDER–CLOUD PATTERNS
831023
23 October 1983, Eddie Condon's, New York: Pepper Adams bs*; Albert
Dailey p; Ray Alexander vib; Harvie Swartz b; Ray Mosca dm.

a   Cloud Patterns   Nerus LP: NR-4477
b   I Can't Get Started
c   **Softly As in a Morning Sunrise**[*]
d   My Foolish Heart
e   **Green Dolphin Street**[*]

f   Reflections[1]
g   Ray's Blues
h   **I Remember You***   Nerus unissued
i   **In a Sentimental Mood***[2]
j   **Thou Swell***
k   **Moment's Notice***[3]
m   **Mean to Me***
n   **unknown title***
o   **Just Friends***
p   **Bernie's Tune***
q   **Witchcraft***[4]
r   Ray's Blues

[1]Alexander solo feature.
[2]Adams and rhythm section.
[3]Adams and rhythm section.
[4]Adams and rhythm section.

All issued tracks on Nerus CD: NR-4477.

HIGHLIGHTS IN JAZZ
831110
10 November 1983, private recording, New York University's Loeb Student Center, New York: Jerry Dodgion as; Zoot Sims, Jimmy Heath ts; Pepper Adams bs; Walter Norris p; Tony Purrone g; George Mraz b; Walter Bolden dm.

a   Autumn Leaves
b   Sweet Georgia Brown
c   **Diabolique II**[1]
d   **Old Ballad**[2]
e   Billie's Bounce[3]
f   Perdido

[1]Dodgion, Adams, and rhythm section.
[2]Adams and rhythm section.
[3]Purrone solo feature.

See 781215.

PEPPER ADAMS
831111
11-12 November 1983, private recordings, Blackstone Hotel, Chicago:
Pepper Adams bs; Willie Pickens p; Eddie de Haas b; Wilbur Campbell
dm.

See Author's Note above 580000A entry.

PEPPER ADAMS
831119
19 November 1983, audience recording, Sealy's, Bloomfield NJ: Pepper
Adams bs*; Noreen Grey p; Earl Sauls b; Curtis Boyd dm.

a   **Falling in Love with Love***
b   **Wrap Your Troubles in Dreams***
c   What's New
d   **Bye Bye Blackbird***

According to Earl Sauls, in a 1995 interview with the author,

We had this gig at this place that started having jazz. It was a disco.
A very strange place. As soon as we finished playing, on went the
disco lights and music. Pepper was looking around: "What's going
on?" The piano was really sad. There was a new sound system that
was really bad. There was hardly anybody there.

See 801101.

PEPPER ADAMS
831120
20 November 1983, audience recording, Chambers, Albany NY: Pepper
Adams bs*; Tony Zano p; Teddy Kotick b Joe Hunt dm.

a   **Ephemera***
b   **A Child Is Born***
c   **Maj and Min Blues***
d   I Should Care
e   **'Tis***
f   **Now in Our Lives***

g It's You or No One
h **Dobbin'***
i **'Tis***

PEPPER ADAMS
831201
1 December 1983, TV-3 broadcast, Palau de la Música, Barcelona Jazz Festival, Barcelona: Pepper Adams bs*; Tete Montoliu p; Marc Johnson b; Victor Lewis dm.

a There Is No Greater Love
b Old Folks
c **Hellure***
d **It's You or No One***
e **A Child Is Born***

JORGE ANDERS–NEW YORK ALL STARS BIG BAND AND QUARTET
831206
6 December 1983, Blank Tape Studio, New York: Jon Faddis, Lew Soloff, Alan Rubin, Dick Sudhalter tp; Bob Alexander, George Masso, Jimmy Knepper tb; Gerry Niewood as; Jorge Anders* ts, cl; Frank Wess, Phil Bodner ts; Pepper Adams bs; John Bunch p; George Duvivier b; Mel Lewis dm.

a Como al Comienzo   RCA Victor (Arg) LP: TLP-60153
b El Duke
c Boogie Blues
d Despues de un Largo Viaje*
e Poor Butterfly*

According to Gerry Niewood, in an interview with the author in 1990, "It was a big band. Jorge had written some stuff. I had never actually played for him before but he called me to play lead alto. It was very nice music and a very nice rhythm section. It was a lot of fun to do."

According to Jorge Anders, in an interview with the author in 1990, Adams chose not to accept any solos because he was having problems with his saxophone and it needed repair.

BENNY CARTER
840626
26 June 1984, Voice of America radio broadcast, Carnegie Hall, Kool Jazz Festival, New York: Snooky Young, Jon Faddis, Lew Soloff, Harry Edison tp; Benny Powell, Birch Johnson, Paul Faulise, Dave Bargeron tb; Benny Carter, Marshal Royal, Bob Wilber as; Seldon Powell, Frank Wess ts; Pepper Adams bs; Derek Smith p; Bucky Pizzarelli g; George Duvivier, Milt Hinton bt; Oliver Jackson, Candido Camero cga* GUESTS: Dizzy Gillespie, Doc Cheatham tp; J.J. Johnson tb; Mickey Roker dm.

a   Symphony in Riffs*
b   Easy Money*
c   Blue Star*
d   Sleep*
    Cheatham, Carter, Smith, Pizzarelli, Hinton, Jackson:
e   Blues in My Heart†
f   When Lights Are Low†
    Carter, Royal, Wilber, Powell, Wess, Adams, Smith, Pizzarelli, Hinton, Jackson:
g   **Doozy**†
    Gillespie, J.J. Johnson, Carter, Smith, Pizzarelli, Duvivier, Roker:
h   A Night in Tunisia
i   The Courtship
    Full band:
j   Coalition*

According to Derek Smith, in an interview with the author in 1989, "Benny Carter came to do a ["Salute to Benny Carter"] for the Kool Jazz Festival...and Pepper was playing baritone. Even then he was coming in on some crutches. I remember we were rehearsing in Carroll's Studio and then we did the concert."

This was Adams' first gig in over six months since the Jorge Anders recording (*see* 831206). He had been recuperating since c. 15 December 1983 from a freakish accident with his car, in which its handbrake disengaged after he had momentarily parked it uphill at the sidewalk and had walked down his driveway to close his garage door. Adams' car rolled downhill, pinning him for some time between the front bumper and the garage door, crushing one of his legs. The injury necessitated near 24-

hour immobilization and bed rest for many months, and, as a conse-
quence, Adams had to cancel all work during that period.

Historian Ed Berger told the author in 2002 that Adams was not
someone who asked for help. At this concert, Adams was still incapaci-
tated, and he was still wearing a cast on his leg. Backstage at Carnegie
Hall, Adams sat in a wheelchair in his tuxedo and asked no one for assistance, said Berger. Berger, however, volunteered to help, and he wheeled
Adams into the Green Room, being especially careful not to strike ob-
jects with Adams' protruding leg cast. "It was during the soundcheck and
the actual concert," wrote Berger, in a 2006 email to the author. "I don't
remember specifically what he said, but he cracked me up with his one-
liners during these short journeys on and off stage. I remember thinking
how pleasant he was during what must have been for him an awkward
and physically uncomfortable situation."

BESS BONNIER
840713a
13 July 1984, NPR radio broacast, Kresge Court, Institute of Arts, De-
troit: Pepper Adams bs; Bess Bonnier p; Dan Jordan b; Tom Brown dm;
Carol Sloane voc.*

a   Blue 20[1]
b   **Time on My Hands**[2]
c   **Joy Road**[3]
d   **Bernie's Tune**[*]
e   The More I See You[*4]
f   I Love You Madly[*]
g   **I'm Just a Lucky So and So**[*]
h   **Cotton Tail**[*]
i   My Funny Valentine[*]

[1]Rhythm section only.
[2]Adams and rhythm section.
[3]Adams and rhythm section.
[4]Duet for piano and vocal.

-c on Noteworks LP: BB-102.
According to Carol Sloane, in an interview with the author in 1989,

I don't remember how I got that job. I don't even know how that
happened. Bess didn't...know who I was. As a matter of fact, we all
had dinner the night before the concert so we could at least meet!
She didn't really hear me sing (unless somebody got her a tape of
my singing) not until the day we rehearsed. It could very well have
been Pepper's idea.

According to Bess Bonnier, in an interview with the author in 1988,
two almost identical sets were played that evening (*see* 840713b):

First, we went to a dinner at the St. Regis Hotel with all the people
that were going to be involved in the concert. Now, the rhythm section—Tom Brown and Dan Jordan—saw no earthly reason to have
a dinner with drinks to discuss a rehearsal. Plus, the fact that everybody was paying their own tab, albeit these guys had good jobs and
wouldn't think a thing of it, if it were with their wives and they
went out to dinner. For some reason the perception was this wasn't
acceptable, so they came along grudgingly. Then there was Pepper
and Carol. Now, Carol and Pepper drank a good deal. Nothing got
done at this dinner, and Carol was not going to like me right away.
She changed her mind the next day, but I was a "chick," and, "How
did I play?" She was going to be competitive with me for Pepper's
attention. Well, I didn't need to be. I'm recognizing all this stuff.
    The next day, that all changed. Once I sat down and played for
her, she was fine. Greg Bloomfield, the guy who was running Jazz
at the Institute, put that together. The next day we had the rehearsal
and Pepper was excellent at describing his tunes and what he wanted for himself. I mean, excellent! I mean, clear as a bell! It's the
way he made the chord changes clear to me. Our minds are similar,
so that he communicated to me readily—and quietly. He conducted
his part of the rehearsal. It was exemplary. It was just excellent! Just
good style.

BESS BONNIER
840713b
*13 July 1984, NPR radio broacast, Kresge Court, Institute of Arts, De-
troit:* Same as 13 July 1984 [first show]; Pepper Adams bs*:

a   Blue 20[1]
b   **Time on My Hands**[2]
c   **Joy Road**[3]

d   **Bernie's Tune**[*]
e   The More I See You^{*4}
f   I Love You Madly[*]
g   **I'm Just a Lucky So and So**[*]
h   **Cotton Tail**[*]
i   Medley[*]:
       Never Never Land⁵
       When My Ship Comes In
j   **Stomping at the Savoy**[*]

[1]Rhythm section only.
[2]Adams and rhythm section.
[3]Adams and rhythm section.
[4]Duet for piano and vocal.
[5]Vocal a cappella.

-e on Noteworks LP: BB-102.
See 840713a.
Bob Cornfoot told the author, in a 1987 interview,

It was the second set, and they came out and they were going to do
Joy Road, or one of the other uptempo things where he was playing
with the group. Pep just said, "I'll stomp this one off," and the foot
with the cast on it went *boom-boom*. It sounded like it was going
right through the [stage floor], and everybody cringed, because they
thought of the pain that must have been shooting through that bone.

PEPPER ADAMS
840929
*29 September 1984, audience recording, Far and Away, Cliffside Park
NJ:* Pepper Adams bs*; Noreen Grey p; Earl Sauls b; Al Harewood dm.

a   **Quiet Lady**[*]
b   **Three and One**[*]
c   Too Late Now
d   **Have You Met Miss Jones**[*]
e   **That's All**[*]
f   **What Might Have Been**[*]
g   There Is No Greater Love
h   **Witchcraft**[*]

See 801101.

NOREEN GREY
841010
10 October 1984, audience recording, University of Bridgeport's Bern-
hart Center Recital Hall, Bridgeport CT: Same as 29 September 1984,
add John Marshall tp:

a   **Solitary Blues**
b   **In Room 301**
c   **What Might Have Been**
d   **One from Cattoni**
e   **Woman Is a Sometime Thing**
f   Medley:
        My Man's Gone Now[1]
        I Loves You, Porgy
        There's a Boat That's Leaving Soon for
            New York
g   **Rhythm-a-Ning**

[1]Solo piano.

PEPPER ADAMS
841015
15 October 1984, audience recording, Singapore International Jazz Fes-
tival, Singapore: Pepper Adams bs; Jeremy Kahn p; Ed Howard b; Tim
Horner dm.

a   **Conjuration**
b   **Reflectory**
c   **What Is This Thing Called Love**
d   **A Child Is Born**
e   **Dobbin'**
f   **Chelsea Bridge**
g   **Valse Celtique**
h   **Ephemera**
i   **Body and Soul**
j   **Bossa Nouveau**
k   **Doctor Deep**

m **Three and One**
n **'Tis**

According to Jeremy Kahn, in an interview with the author in 1990,

There were groups from all over the world. We were the only group
from the States. There was a band from Belgium, a band from
France, a band from Indonesia, a band from New Zealand. A friend
of mine is Tim Horner, a drummer. I played with him a lot up in
Boston. He had an old girlfriend he went to Berklee with whose father was in the import-export business, so [Tim] had a connection to
the powers that be in Singapore and found out about this festival
and decided that this would be a good way maybe to play with Pepper Adams, because he had always wanted to. So he approached
Pepper, and was able to back it up and say, "Hey, listen, I got this
gig. I might be able to put a tour together," because he had connec-
tions in Japan as well....So Tim asked Pepper if he would be into
this, and how much would he want for it, and Pepper told him, and
he said, "Well, let's go ahead and do it."

   Oh, [Pepper] was the ultimate tourist. He was loaded with cameras. He had traveled quite a bit, although I was surprised he had
never been to that part of the world before. It's funny. He cracked
me up. I'll never forget the line he said. Somebody had asked him if
he had ever been to the Far East before, and he said, "Well, yeah,
but I didn't really like it, because, the last time I was here, people
were shooting at me."

   So this wasn't Pepper's group. Tim, Ed, and I played a lot together, so we were a unit. [Tim] approached Pepper and Pepper said
O.K., so none of us were of Pepper's choosing, which became sort
of evident in varying degrees. It was subtle. I don't think he really
dug Tim or Ed or me probably all that much musically. I never
played with him again [however, *see* 851004], although we played
Body and Soul there, and he must have liked my solo, because he
turned around and said, "Oh, you really *can* play that tune, can't
you?" or something to that effect, which gratified me to no end.

   You can imagine, because I was a big fan. There's an approach
that he has to playing the diminished scale which seems to be one of
the foundations of his playing....He could find the damnest places
to put them in, and seemed to have just an untapped reservoir of different licks or figures that he could play at blinding speed with un-
canny accuracy. You hear Coltrane play a lot of diminished licks.

Sonny Stitt, definitely, and anybody that's coming out of that era, I would say, but that's sort of [Pepper's] trademark. It's not really a pianistic thing as much as it is a horn thing: I think if you dove into it, you could say, "Hey, there's one," "Hey, there's one," but his is more of a flagwaving diminished lick, which is not to say that other aspects of his playing were not fully developed as well, but that was sort of his trademark, to me anyway.

So we did this gig. We rehearsed. [They] came over to my house.…It was [Sunday, 7 October,] the day that [the Cubs] blew the pennant to the Padres, so…about an hour later, they all came over and we rehearsed. About half of the stuff was original tunes of Pepper's, and things like A Child Is Born, Body and Soul.

Well, let's see. It takes a long time to get there. We flew from [New York] to San Francisco, to either Tokyo or Hong Kong (I can't remember which), and then to Singapore. Sticking in a few layovers in each place, I think it was about 36 hours. Every time I looked over, Pepper had two more little bottles of airline booze. Something different: Jack Daniels and then vodka and then scotch. This is right after he had a real grisly accident. His car slipped out of gear while he was opening his garage door, I think. This might have been one of the first things he did. They had sent all this publicity stuff about him, [in which] he was looking probably twenty years younger, and we're wheeling this "old man" in a wheel chair. I think they were a little bit surprised, although he managed to get about with a cane. He was reading some book and he came to a passage that he thought was pretty funny and he passed the book to me and he just said, "Read these couple of paragraphs. I thought you might find them amusing." I read them and laughed dutifully. Yeah, I was totally star-struck. I had played gigs with some people up to that point, but I don't think anyone of his magnitude, where I was really going to be under the microscope.…

So, we had some girl showing us around. She was sort of our liaison. Pepper was very much a good tourist. He wanted to go all over the place, as much as his gammy [legs] would permit him.

I remember the soundcheck and rehearsal at this place. He obviously had dealt with unsympathetic, not intelligent sound system people. He sort of laid his cards out on the table: He said, "Find a level and leave it there. If I start playing louder, don't push it down, and if I start playing soft, don't push it up, because, then, what's the point of having dynamics at all?" Then, we were backstage and they brought us a bunch of sodas, and he just sort of looked at those and said, "What's this?" Either Tim or Ed produced a bottle of cognac, which Pepper basically polished off.

We did our part. We did the concert. It went O.K. He yelled at us about something. He thought that we had brought the tempo way down on a Child Is Born, I think. It had come down, but, I don't know. He was maybe a little sloshed or something, and we were just basically following him, which maybe you're not supposed to do. Maybe you just put it there and let him refer to it. I'm not sure how he felt about it. I thought it went pretty well.

He got really pissed off when they didn't have cash for him, which I guess was part of his agreement. Maybe he sort of had a chip on his shoulder. He went out and did the gig in a semi-grudging way. Tim had already been in Japan and supposedly was on good terms with some promoter, and they didn't think Pepper was a big enough name to build a tour to promote in Japan, so that's how that fell by the wayside. I guess he was just [for] a rarified audience and didn't have star power....We were supposed to play in Jakarta or something, and I'm not sure what happened with that.

According to Tim Horner, in an interview with the author in 1990,

They originally booked us at that festival for two concerts. About a week before we went there they called and said we were now going to have one. What happened was I had a friend in Singapore that I knew from Berklee, and she really loved Pepper's music, so she wanted to have him over, and she wrote me a letter. [I responded:] "Yes, I know him, and, yes, I can put it together." So I put together the group, and I said, "While we're going that far, let me try to get something else together." There was this promoter in Japan that I worked for: His name is Takao Ishizuka and he owns a company there called All Arts Promotion. He had promoted Thad and Mel's big band. He had brought them over for a tour, and he had promoted Hank Jones, and Blakey at times, Art Farmer, Helen Merrill, all kinds of people. I had the fortune to do about seven tours with him with Helen Merrill and Chris Connor, Ernestine Anderson, George Mraz, Norman Simmons, a lot of different people, so, in knowing him from those tours—he was a very sweet man to me—I called him up: "Hey, I got a band together with Pepper Adams. We're going to be in Singapore. Put together two weeks for us." He loved Pepper, but had never worked with him past the one time with Thad and Mel. So he said, "That's great! Wonderful! Let's do this," and he worked on it.

About two or three weeks before we were supposed to split, he called me up and he said, "No tour. I can't sell any tickets." He had set up several things and had no early ticket sales and he just became very antsy that he was going to lose a lot of money, even though I really had all our flights and everything to Singapore paid for. All he had to do was bring us over from Singapore, which was a lot easier than bringing us from the States. He just cancelled the whole two weeks. It was a shock. I was actually in the stage of waiting for the contract to show up, and it wasn't showing, and Pepper was, like, "What's going on?" and I said, "Pepper, I'm doing my best." I didn't really know Pepper too well, so I was getting really hot under the collar: "What am I doing here?" Oh, man, I was very nervous! We had already gotten a deposit on the Singapore thing, and a contract.

So the two weeks in Japan folded. The people from Jakarta called, and said that now they had no money, but wanted us to come over for free, and they were going to put us up and pay for our airfare and food. I just spoke for everybody at that point. I said, "No! That's not going to happen with Pepper Adams. He's not going to do that. You either come up with "x" amount of dollars and call me tomorrow or forget it." Then, after that, the people from Singapore called and said, "Were looking forward to the concert." I said, "I have a contract here for two!" and they said, "Oh no, there's a new contract in the mail. There's only one." We literally got cut down from making a lot of bread and doing a three week tour to—I believe Jeremy, myself, and Ed Howard, we all made $500; Pepper made a grand—for a one-nighter. It was crazy! We literally went half way around the world for a one-nighter!

It was a long flight. We had three stops, one in San Francisco. The timing was very strange, because Pepper at that point was very sick. We were there on October 13th. The concert was on the 15th. It was awful, man. They put together the most ridiculous menu of events for us to deal with. We got there after the 36 hours—like two in the morning, when we checked into our hotel room—and they had a press conference with all this Singapore press at 7 o'clock in the morning! We were, like, "Come on!" They would not budge an inch. They insisted, and here was Pepper, man. He was on crutches, his leg was crushed, it wasn't healing, and he had cancer and he didn't know it!

He was "juicing" heavily on the plane. They flipped out when we showed up because he had sent over a press picture of him from Thad and Mel, and he had hair—black hair—and he was in shape, and he looked really good, and here we came out, and they greeted us at the airport, and he's in a wheelchair with his leg up, and he's juiced like crazy, and he just looked like he was a hundred years old. They looked at him like, "This is not the guy we hired! Who is this?"

It was pretty bizarre, although, I must say, for the condition he was in, he played his ass off! He really was on fire! I don't know if he was real comfortable playing with us, although I think we played very well for him. He was a real particular person in his sidemen, in people he wanted to play with. Some of the cats that I heard him play with him I never considered to be really great players. But, just to put it in perspective, I think he was the kind of guy that enjoyed his company, as much as the quality of people that he played with. I think in some cases it could be a situation where he might really be with somebody [and] he enjoyed their company. I think he liked us, and I think he enjoyed what we did, and I think he respected our professionalism. He just didn't really know us, and just had met us basically for this gig. Being that we only played the one gig, and it was *very* tiring, and he was not in great shape, he was not a real happy person.

Regarding the sound system at the concert and collecting the band's fee, Horner said,

It kind of threw me, because he had so much experience. Most people that I've met—the professionals in this business that have played so many concerts—they get past that so easily. They've done so much, and have run into so many bad engineers, you just get to the point where you say, "Well, man, I'll just play. I don't care. You guys just do what you've got to do! I'm gonna play!" He wasn't like that. He was very irritated, but they had also not paid us! They were supposed to pay us before we played. He got to the point where, on the break, he refused to go back out until they came up with the money! They rounded the money up! He made his commitment to the gig, which I thought was pretty amazing in the condition he was in at the time. A guy like Pepper could have easily said, "Tim, forget Singapore. Have a nice life. I'm not going over there for

$1,000," [but] he did it. He did it, man! He held up to his commitment in a real trooper sense. It was amazing!

DENNY CHRISTIANSON
841023a

23 October 1984, CBC Radio Studios, Montreal: Denny Christianson, Roger Walls, Laflèche Doré, Ron DiLauro, Jocelyn Lapointe tp, flh; Patrice DuFour, André Verreault, Muhammad Abdul Al-Khabyyr tb; Bob Ellis btb; Joe Christie Jr. as, ss, bs, fl, pic; Pat Vetter as, cl, bs, fl; Richard Beaudet ts, cl, bs, fl; Jean Lebrun ts, ss, fl, pic; Jean Frechette bs; Kenny Alexander p; Richard Ring g; Vic Angelillo b; Cisco Normand dm; Paul Picard perc; GUEST: Pepper Adams bs.

a   **Autumn Leaves**
b   **Ephemera**
c   **A Pair of Threes**
d   **Sophisticated Lady**

According to Denny Christianson, in an interview with the author in 1987,

The first time I brought him up, in October of 1984, I wanted to put on a show that would draw well. I loved Pepper. I had tunes that were well-suited to feature baritone. A lot of the material in my book has baritone solos, as well as a couple of Alf Clausen tunes featuring bari and flugel together. That, plus Len Dobbin was a close friend of Pepper's, and, when I mentioned to Len that I was going to bring somebody in, he said "Well, why don't you bring Pepper?" I said, "Yeah, that's natural. That's a good idea." So I called him up. He said, "Sure," and I went and got all the work papers from the government and all that shit. The purpose was to come up and do a night with my band at the Blue Note, and then I talked CBC Radio into recording us the following night.

The first night we went into the Blue Note and played in front of a live audience—a good crowd and they got a hell of a show—and everybody felt real good about it, and then the next night we went into the studio and did a half hour of big band and a half hour of the small group....

After we did this together, that's when we got to know each other. We had him over for dinner. When he came up for that, I didn't know it, but he was coming off of a one-year recuperation from a broken leg....I had seen him in town in Montreal, a year or two before, with a small group thing at Winston's Café [an alternate name for La Voute; see 821014, 821015] and he was healthy, robust, and all of that, so I go out to pick him up at the airport and he's coming out with a cane, and barely dragging this huge instrument, and looked thin and pale and weak. Right away I was a little concerned. He could hardly walk. It turned out that his leg had never healed properly and he still had a crack in his leg. So, that slowed him down, and, I'm telling you, the first rehearsal we had for this October of '84 gig—I brought the band together on a Sunday afternoon, brought him over, and we rehearsed, and he was rusty. He wasn't playing well at the first rehearsal, and the guys in the band were saying, "Wow! What happened to Pepper Adams?" Next night, we get up on stage in front of a live audience and *whaaap!* He was just pacing himself! He knew he could do it. And then, the following evening, everybody's cooled out. We had a great night the night before.

Going into the CBC's Radio Studios to do this radio show, the call is for six o'clock, so I told everybody to be there at 5:30, and, for once, they were all there early. They were set up and ready to go. Six o'clock comes: CBC doesn't have any mics out, there's nothing ready. We're all waiting to go! Pepper's sitting on a stool. The whole band's fucking ready. I'm following the producer now: "What's going on?" He said, "Just wait, just wait, just wait!" Finally, an hour later, I said, "Hey, look! Do you realize what's going on? This is one of the greatest artists in the world and you're having..." Anyway, the recording engineer was getting his ass chewed out. They had found out that he had just erased a one-hour radio show for somebody else, so they're out reaming his ass. Meantime, they're making Pepper Adams wait.

Finally, at 8:15, they start—yeah!—I'm all over them: "I can't believe you bring in a world class artist and you're making him sit and wait. I don't care what your problem is..." There was nobody else in the studio. Just us. This was recorded for later replay. This is all of it. No extra cuts.

What was interesting is that, finally, at 8:15 they're ready, right? Well, I had a few subs in the band for these four cuts, and I wouldn't put them out on a record or anything, but, for what it was, it was just, *bang, bang, bang,* and it sounded terrific, and an hour and fifteen minutes later we were done. Then we did the small group thing and that was all one take stuff. In fact, it pissed us off, because we started one take and went ten minutes, and it was great! Everybody was cooking, and we said, "Did you get it?" "No." "Are you ready now?" Oh, fuck! We had to go do it again!

DENNY CHRISTIANSON
841023b
23 October 1984, CBC Radio Studios, Montreal: Denny Christianson tp; Pepper Adams bs; Kenny Alexander p; Vic Angelillo b; Cisco Normand dm.

a   **Reflectory**
b   **Binary**
c   **Claudette's Way**

See 841023a notes.

PEPPER ADAMS
841115
15 November 1984, audience recording, University of Hartford's Berkman Auditorium, West Hartford CT: Walter Fogg, Steve Wheeler tp; John Hasselback tb; Eric Matthews, Charley Socci as; Pepper Adams bs; Lisa Housholder p; unknown g; Roger Hart, Nat Reeves b; Victor Riley dm.

a   **Au Privave**
b   **Half Nelson/Ladybird**
c   **Groovin' High**

This was a lecture/demonstration, conducted by Pepper Adams, for students at the Hartt School of Music.

PETER LEITCH–EXHILIRATION
841117
17 November 1984, Van Gelder Studio, Englewood Cliffs NJ: Pepper Adams bs; John Hicks p; Peter Leitch g; Ray Drummond b; Billy Hart dm.

a   **Exhilaration**   Uptown LP: UP-27-24

b	Exhiliration	Reservoir CD: RSR-CD-118
c	'Round Midnight	Uptown LP: UP-27-24
d	'Round Midnight	Reservoir CD: RSR-CD-103
e	'Round Midnight	Uptown unissued
f	Trinkle Tinkle	Uptown LP: UP-27-24
g	Trinkle Tinkle	Uptown unissued
h	Trinkle Tinkle	
i	Trinkle Tinkle	
j	Trinkle Tinkle	
k	Trinkle Tinkle	
m	Trinkle Tinkle	
n	Played Twice	Uptown LP: UP-27-24
o	Played Twice	Uptown unissued
p	Played Twice	
q	Played Twice	
r	Played Twice	
s	Played Twice	
t	Slugs, in the Far East	Uptown LP: UP-27-24
u	Slugs, in the Far East	Uptown unissued
v	Slugs, in the Far East	
w	How Deep Is the Ocean	Uptown LP: UP-27-24
x	How Deep Is the Ocean	Uptown unissued
y	How Deep Is the Ocean	

All issued tracks on Reservoir CD: RSR-CD-118.
According to Peter Leitch, in an interview with the author in 1987,

Pepper and I got together a few times at his house, just the two of us, to rehearse the music....He had a very bad leg at that point....When I first went to rehearse with Pepper for *Exhilaration,* I had written the baritone parts for my tunes, and I had transposed the chord changes for an E-flat instrument. Pepper said, "Well, I would prefer to read chord changes in concert." But that's unusual. Usually, a person who plays a transposing instrument, in my experience, would want to see the chord changes transposed to their key. He could certainly deal with them in his key, but it was just a preference that he preferred to see them in concert.

Originally, I was going to produce that record myself. I had discussed it with Pepper, and I was thinking of doing an album of all Monk material. Pepper was up for it, and we discussed it. Gene Per-

la was going to be involved. We were going to use his studio and I
was going to produce it myself, and, I guess, try to peddle it to a
company. Then Uptown became involved...and we ended up doing
the date for Uptown. It was decided not to do an album of Monk
tunes, although we did three of them....We had one rehearsal before
the date.

Pepper was just extremely helpful, because I put a lot of pressure on myself, most of it unnecessary, but, because it was my first
date here in the States, and I was working with a pretty heavy
rhythm section, and it was my first time at Van Gelder's. Pepper
was just extremely helpful in dealing with all of it, just his manner
in the studio, his experience, basically. If he sensed at all that something was bothering me at the date, or if he sensed that I wasn't in
control, he took control in a very subtle way, just in terms of dealing
with Rudy, and dealing with the producers—very much of a calm-
ing influence.

About Pepper Adams, Uptown owner Mark Feldman told the author,
in an interview in 1988,

He had played a few gigs before that, but that was like his first coming out after his leg injury. He looked like hell. I even remember
mentioning to Bob [Sunenblick]: I said, "He looks very sick," and
Bob said, "Well, you know, he's been so depressed for so long. It
could be that. He just hasn't been getting out. But, as bad as he
looked, he played extremely well. I think some of his best playing
on record is on that Peter Leitch record....That was a great record. I
thought that was one of our better records. What I liked about it was
here's a guy making his first record for an American label, and, yet,
he surrounded himself with good players and sort of made sure that
it was a sound that they were getting; that it wasn't only you were
listening to Peter Leitch, but you were listening to all of these guys,
and he highlighted everything. He highlighted all the players, he
made sure that Pepper was equally featured, he made sure that the
material was right.

He wanted to do, originally, all Monk tunes, and I told him,
"Look, everybody knows Thelonious Monk. You should have some
of your own stuff." He does Monk very well. He plays all the tunes,
and not the common Monk tunes. I thought it was nice that there
were three Monk tunes on the record. It was the first time we ever
had anybody do 'Round Midnight. Played Twice and Trinkle Tinkle

are not the most commonly recorded Monk tunes, and Peter did an arrangement of a Monk solo, which was a unison thing between Pepper and Peter playing the melody. I thought it was a very good record: Very well conceived, very well executed, and Peter wanted those players. He wasn't going to do it any other way. Peter was sort of miffed by that fact that [Josh] Breakstone did that record with Pepper [*see* 860219]. Peter felt it was his idea—guitar and baritone, especially guitar and Pepper Adams.

Uptown owner and oncologist Bob Sunenblick told the author, in an interview in 1988,

When we did the Peter Leitch recording, Pepper had been in his house, it seems like, for at least a year. He really hadn't done much, had been in a wheelchair, rarely answered the phone. In fact, I don't think he ever answered the phone. Apparently, he was in such a lot of pain with the broken leg, that he never answered the phone. Poor healing. But, if he had a crush injury, this would have explained it, although you wouldn't expect it to last a year. When I saw him at the Peter Leitch recording, he was walking with a cane. He really looked bad. He looked like somebody who was depressed and had cancer. It's easy to say that maybe this was a pre-cancerous state, but it couldn't have been, because he ended up getting this cancer that, if you don't treat it, you die in three to four weeks: that's small cell cancer of the lung.

In an interview in 1989 with the author, Ray Drummond said,

It went fine. There were no hitches. As I remember, Billy Hart was late for the date. He didn't show up until about a quarter to one for a twelve o'clock start, and Peter, who chain smokes incessantly on dates, was really nervous. It was his first American date and all that. We had done the rehearsal already at Sickler's, so we had some idea of the music. I think we had the rehearsal several days before, if memory serves me right. We were just waiting for Billy, and then Billy showed up, had to get all set up, and then we began to record, and we got the tunes knocked out pretty quickly—all of them....At that time Peter was really into multiple takes, and it kind of wore us down a little bit on some of the material, because we just took too many takes. He'd say, "Oh, I didn't like this, I didn't like that," and be too critical....All the rest of us, we just kind of went along for the ride, because it was really Peter and the doctors [owners of Up-town Records] that were producing it, and so Peter pretty much had the musical side covered, as far as what he wanted....

When you have two "horns" like that, the bass player is not go-ing to get a hell of a lot of solo space on the record, especially if it's going to be mastered by Rudy Van Gelder. You'll probably barely have forty minutes on the whole record. He likes to cut a master to forty minutes. In fact, he actually likes it to come in between 36 and 38. If you look at all the Blue Note records that he's mastered—you have to remember that the Blue Note records, yes, they were rec-orded by Rudy Van Gelder, but a lot of the first pressings of all the ones, even through [Herbie Hancock's] *The Prisoner* and beyond that, were actually mastered by him. In other words, he cut the mas-tering plate as well as did the original recording. The way you can tell is, if you look on your Blue Notes, on the inner vinyl, right next to the label, they'll say "Van Gelder" stamped on the black. That means it's an actual Van Gelder mastered record. Some of the Im-pulses are like that as well. I'm talking original now. They were far superior than subsequent pressings.

Regarding Pepper Adams and Peter Leitch, John Hicks told the au-thor in 1988, "Those guys are real students of Monk. They played good together. They had a real empathy for that kind of music, that phrasing and stuff. They were really together." During rehearsals for the date, said Hicks, "they'd have a little question about the phrasing or something on one of the tunes that he and Peter were playing the heads together on. [Pepper] would have some little remark, usually about how he was deal-ing with it, but it could've been Peter that was fucking up, but he wouldn't say that. He'd let him know that something wasn't right, and he'd just say, 'It was probably my fault.'"

JAMES L. DEAN
841119
19 November 1984, private recording of rehearsal at Allan Namery's house, Lodi NJ: John Marshall tp; Frank Foster ss, ts; James L. Dean cl, as, ts; Pepper Adams bs*; Noreen Grey p; Earl Sauls b; Glenn Davis dm.

a   Dance of the Infidels[1]
b   Mood in Question[2]
c   **Generations***

d   Titter Pipes[3]

[1]Dean and rhythm section.
[2]Dean and Grey duet.
[3]Foster, Dean, and rhythm section.

See 850125.

AL COHN-PEPPER ADAMS-KENNY BURRELL
841228
28-29 December 1984, private recordings, Blackstone Hotel, Chicago:
Al Cohn ts; Pepper Adams bs; Stu Katz p; Kenny Burrell g; Dan Shapera
b; Wilbur Campbell dm.

See Author's Note above 580000A entry.

AL COHN-PEPPER ADAMS -KENNY BURRELL
841230
30 December 1984, private recording, Blackstone Hotel, Chicago: Same
as 28 December 1984:

a   **Wee**
b   **How Deep Is the Ocean**
c   My One and Only Love[1]
d   **Valse Celtique**[2]
e   Don't Get Around Much Anymore[3]
f   **Yardbird Suite**
g   **Secret Love**
h   **Blue Monk**
i   Chelsea Bridge[4]
j   Take the "A" Train[5]
k   Do Nothing 'Til You Hear from Me[6]
m   **It Don't Mean a Thing (If It Ain't Got that Swing)**
n   **All the Things You Are**
o   **'Round Midnight**
p   **Woody'n You**
q   **unknown blues**

[1]Burrell and rhythm section.
[2]Adams and rhythm section.

[3]Cohn and rhythm section.
[4]Adams, Burrell and rhythm section.
[5]Burrell and rhythm section.
[6]Cohn and rhythm section.

See Author's Note above 580000A entry.

AL COHN-PEPPER ADAMS-KENNY BURRELL
841231
31 December 1984, private recording, Blackstone Hotel, Chicago: Same
as 28 December 1984:

See Author's Note above 580000A entry.

HOD O'BRIEN–OPALESSENCE
850102
2 January 1985, Van Gelder Studio, Englewood Cliffs NJ: Tom Harrell
tp, flh; Pepper Adams bs; Hod O'Brien p; Ray Drummond b; Kenny
Washington dm; Stephanie Nakasian voc.*

a	**Opalessence**	Criss Cross (Neth) LP: CRISS-1012
b	**Touchstone**	
c	**Bits and Pieces**	
d	**Joy Road**	
e	**Joy Road**	Criss Cross (Neth) CD: CRISS-1012
f	**A Handful of Dust**[*]	Criss Cross (Neth) LP: CRISS-1012
g	**The Blues Walk**	
h	**Detour Ahead**	Criss Cross (Neth) CD: CRISS-1012

All tracks on Criss Cross (Neth) CD: CRISS-1012.
According to Ray Drummond, in an interview with the author in
1989,

We had a rehearsal over at Hod's place and that went smoothly....I
remember that [Pepper] wasn't getting around quite like he was....It
was a little more difficult, and he was just saying, "I'm feeling not
so good as I did when I just saw you [on 17 November 1984]....He
was beginning to not have the kind of stamina, the strength, that he
had had as the old Pepper I knew. His playing was *never* affected! It
was *never* affected! He always played the same, regardless of how

he felt…but I'm just talking about getting out of the car. Walking up the steps, he'd have to gather his breath for a minute.

In his liner notes to the LP, Hod O'Brien wrote, "Pepper has been a major influence of mine since the very early days when I started hanging out on the New York scene in the mid-'50s. I remember first hearing him at sessions that used to be held at a private loft on East 28th Street in New York owned by Ken Karpe."

PEPPER ADAMS
850112
12 January 1985, audience recording, Far and Away, Cliffside Park NJ: Pepper Adams bs*; Noreen Grey p; Earl Sauls b; Al Harewood dm.

a   **After You've Gone***
b   **Witchcraft***
c   Times Have Changed
d   **Dear Old Stockholm***
e   **How Am I to Know***
f   **Played Twice***
g   I'm Confessin'
h   **All God's Chillun Got Rhythm***
i   **unknown title***

See 801101.

JAMES L. DEAN
850125
25 January 1985, Van Gelder Studio, Englewood Cliffs NJ: Same as 19 November 1984, except Vinnie Cutro tp* replaces Marshall; Frank Foster√ ss, ts; Pepper Adams bs†:

a	**Generations***†√	Muse LP: MR-5313
b	**Generations***†√	Muse unissued
c	**Dance of the Infidels**†√	Muse LP: MR-5313
d	**Stablemates**†√	
e	**Titter Pipes**†	
f	**Titter Pipes**†	Muse unissued
g	Mood in Question[1]	Muse LP: MR-5313

h   Milestones√
i   Inventory√
j   Inventory√   Muse unissued
k   Rendevous for Clarinet and Piano[2]

[1]Duet for Dean and Grey.
[2]Dean and rhythm section.

-a, -c, -d, -e on Camden-BMG (Neth) CD: 74321-610882.

In an interview with the author in 1989, Frank Foster said about his former student, Jim Dean:

> He produced the session himself. He got the studio, he got the rhythm section and the rest of the musicians, and rented this little studio over in Jersey [for the rehearsal,] and did this thing, and then got Joe Fields to buy the master. My total understanding was that it was his album, and he was trying to get himself established as a player, and use Pepper and me as guest artists to kind of give him a boost....I don't know how Pepper was feeling, but he was outplaying everybody!...Pepper played brilliantly on every cut!

In an interview with the author in 1989, James L. Dean said that this date

> was not released right. It was a bad deal, and, actually, I didn't know it was going to be issued that way. The problem is I got into hot water with Frank Foster. The problem with that session was it was released as a Pepper Adams-Frank Foster date and it wasn't, and Joe Fields at Muse assured me that it wasn't going to be issued that way. I did have a problem with Frank, because he didn't believe me. He thought that it was done behind his back. He thought that I had something to do with it, that I conspired against him, you might say, to release the album, and that's not true at all. I had no idea it was going to be released that way. I was shocked! I couldn't believe my eyes! The problem is I couldn't take any legal action against anybody, because I didn't have the money to do it. At that point in time, it was my first album....What I did was I sent [Foster] a newspaper clipping that I took out in the musician's newspaper, clarifying that he was the special guest star. I went public with it, but, believe me, it was fruitless. Unfortunately, that album didn't get as far as it should have gotten, because Frank Foster was calling

up all these people that he knew and says, "Don't review that record." Maybe it was best that it didn't get reviewed, because I think
it would have added more fuel to the flame. It was my initiation into
the world of jazz record producing! I couldn't take on Joe. All he
simply said, when I called him up, was, "If I released it under your
name, nothing would have happened." Actually, I didn't know what
the hell to do, really. I was so disillusioned and disgusted with it.

PEPPER ADAMS
850131a
31 January 1985, audience recording, Bull's Head, London: Pepper Adams bs; Tony Lee p; Spike Heatley b; Bobby Orr dm.

a **Lover Come Back to Me**
b **'Round Midnight**
c **My Shining Hour**
d **Solar**
e **Time on My Hands**
f **You Took Advantage of Me**

PEPPER ADAMS
850131b
31 January 1985, audience recording, Bull's Head, London: Same as 31
January 1985, except Terry Jenkins dm for Orr:

a **How Deep Is the Ocean**
b **The Days of Wine and Roses**
c **Chelsea Bridge**
d **Milestones**
e **A Child Is Born**

PEPPER ADAMS
850202
2 February 1985, audience recording, Bull's Head, London: Same as 31
January 1985, except add Peter King as*:

a **I Love You**[*]
b **Star Eyes**[*]
c **I'll Remember April**[*]
d **Scrapple from the Apple/Audobon**[*]

e   **How Long Has This Been Going On**
f   **Yardbird Suite**[*]
g   **Wrap Your Troubles in Dreams**[*]

PEPPER ADAMS
850203
3 February 1985, audience recording, Bull's Head, London: Same as 31
January 1985, except Terry Jenkins dm for Orr:

a   **Conjuration**
b   **Quiet Lady**
c   **It's You or No One**
d   **Three Little Words**
e   **Day Dream**
f   **The Days of Wine and Roses**
g   **Played Twice**
h   **'Tis**
i   **Between the Devil and the Deep Blue Sea**
j   **Chelsea Bridge**
k   **Valse Celtique**
m   **Milestones**
n   **A Child Is Born**
o   **My Shining Hour**
p   **Lady Luck**
q   **'Tis**

PEPPER ADAMS
850205
5 February 1985, audience recording, Bull's Head, London: Same as 31
January 1985, except Terry Jenkins dm for Orr:

a   **Solar**
b   **Isn't It Romantic**
c   **That's All**
d   **Polka Dots and Moonbeams**
e   **Lady Luck**
f   **'Tis**
g   **Gone with the Wind**
h   **A Child Is Born**

i   **Softly As in a Morning Sunrise**
j   **Wrap Your Troubles in Dreams**
k   **'Tis**

PEPPER ADAMS
850210
10 February 1985, audience recording, Bull's Head, London: Same as 31 January 1985, except Terry Jenkins dm for Orr:

a   **Falling in Love with Love**
b   **I Let a Song Go Out of My Heart**
c   **Solar**
d   **'Tis**
e   **The Days of Wine and Roses**
f   **A Child Is Born**

PEPPER ADAMS
850216
16 February 1985, audience recording, Bull's Head, London: Same as 31 Janary 1985, add Tommy Whittle ts*:

a   **Between the Devil and the Deep Blue Sea***
b   **How Deep Is the Ocean***
c   **Dearly Beloved***
d   **I Let A Song Go Out of My Heart***
e   **'Tis***
f   **It's You or No One***
g   **Port of Rico***
h   **You Don't Know What Love Is**
i   **'Tis***

PEPPER ADAMS
850218
18 February 1985, audience recording, Bull's Head, London: Same as 31 January 1985, add Peter King as*:

a   **Scrapple from the Apple/Audobon***
b   **How Deep Is the Ocean***
c   **My Shining Hour***

d   **Barbados**[*]
e   **Witchcraft**[*]
f   **I've Got It Bad (And that Ain't Good)**
g   **'Tis**[*]

PEPPER ADAMS
850219
19 February 1985, audience recording, Bull's Head, London: Pepper Adams bs; Bill LeSage p; Terry Smith g*; Dave Green b; Bill Eyden dm.

a   **Min and Maj Blues**[*]
b   **Quiet Lady**[*]
c   **Pent-Up House**[*]
d   **'Tis**[*]
e   **Ephemera**[*]
f   **Valse Celtique**[*]
g   **I Carry Your Heart**
h   **Milestones**[*]
i   **'Tis**[*]

PEPPER ADAMS
850221
21 February 1985, audience recording, Ship Hotel, Weybridge, England: Pepper Adams bs; Tony Lee p; Spike Heatley b; Tony Crombie dm.

a   **Lady Luck**
b   **That's All**
c   **I Let A Song Go Out of My Heart**
d   **'Tis**

Recorded by the Weybridge Jazz Club.

PEPPER ADAMS
850223
23 February 1985, BBC-2 radio broadcast, Bull's Head, London: Tony Coe cl*, ts; Pepper Adams bs; Tony Lee p; Spike Heatley b; Terry Jenkins dm.

a   **My Secret Love**

b **I Let a Song Go Out of My Heart**
c **A Child Is Born**[1]
d **Scrapple from the Apple/Audobon**
e **'Tis**
f **Lady Luck**
g **In a Sentimental Mood**
h **Three Little Words**
i Body and Soul[2]
j **'Tis**
k **Hellure***

[1]Adams and rhythm section.
[2]Coe and rhythm section.

PEPPER ADAMS
850319
19 March 1985, RF radio broadcast, Le Petit Opportun, Paris: Pepper Adams bs; Georges Arvanitas p; Jacky Samson b; Charles Saudrais dm.

a **Dobbin'**
b **Doctor Deep**
c **Diabolique II**
d **I Carry Your Heart**
e **Three and One**
f **'Tis**
g **Played Twice**
h **Bossallegro**
i **Quiet Lady**
j **Min and Maj Blues**
k **In Love with Night**
m **'Tis**

Adams was booked for a week-long engagement, but could only play the first four nights due to illness. His lung cancer was discovered in Boden, Sweden a week earlier.

PEPPER ADAMS
850412
12 April 1985, audience recording, Far and Away, Cliffside Park NJ: Pepper Adams bs*; Noreen Grey p; Earl Sauls b; Al Harewood dm.

a   **Consummation**[*]
b   Summer Night
c   **How Am I to Know**[*]

See 801101.

PEPPER ADAMS
850413
13 April 1985, audience recording, Far and Away, Cliffside Park NJ:
Same as 12 April 1985:

a   **Between the Devil and the Deep Blue Sea**
b   **That's All**
c   In a Sentimental Mood[*]
d   **After You've Gone**
e   **How Long Has This Been Going On**
f   Earl's Vamp[*]
g   **In Love with Night**
h   **'Tis**
i   **Wrap Your Troubles in Dreams**
j   **Get Happy**

[*]Rhythm section only.

See 801101.

PEPPER ADAMS
850501
1 May 1985, CBC radio broadcast, Yardbird Suite, Edmonton, Canada:
Herbie Spanier tp; P.J. Perry as; Pepper Adams bs; Ken Chaney p; Dave
Field b; Jerry Fuller dm.

This was produced by the Edmonton Jazz Society, who maintains a
library of their broadcasts.

ERIC FRIEDENBURG
850503
3 May 1985, CBC radio broadcast, Yardbird Suite, Edmonton, Canada:
Eric Friedenburg ts, fl; other musicians; GUEST: Pepper Adams bs.

This was produced by the Edmonton Jazz Society, who maintains a library of their broadcasts.

PEPPER ADAMS
850504a
4 May 1985, CBC radio broadcast, Yardbird Suite, Edmonton, Canada:
Bob Tildesley tp; Jim Pinchin ts; Pepper Adams bs; Tommy Banks p; Dave Field b; George Ursan dm.

This was produced by the Edmonton Jazz Society, who maintains a library of their broadcasts.

PEPPER ADAMS
850504b
c. 4 May 1985, CBC radio broadcast, Yardbird Suite, Edmonton, Canada: Gary Guthman tp; Jim Pinchin ts; Pepper Adams bs; Tommy Banks p; Dave Field b, e-b*; George Ursan dm; Judi Singh voc.†

a **Valse Celtique**
b **Scratch**
c **A Touching Refrain**[*]
d **Claudette's Way**
e Alice In Wonderland[1]†
f **Binary**

[1]Duet for piano and vocals.

This event was sponsored by the Edmonton Jazz Society and broadcast live for the program *Edmonton on Stage*.

JAZZ CITY JAM SESSION
850505
5 May 1985, CBC radio broadcast, Yardbird Suite, Edmonton, Canada:
Pepper Adams bs; Tommy Banks p; other musicians.

This was produced by the Edmonton Jazz Society, who maintains a library of their broadcasts.

HIGHLIGHTS IN JAZZ
850517
17 May 1985, private recording, New York University's Loeb Student Center, New York: Jon Faddis, Lew Soloff tp; John Mosca, Benny Powell tb; Dick Oatts, Paquito D'Rivera as; Frank Foster ts; Pepper Adams bs; Roland Hanna p; Toots Thielemans harmonica; Bob Cunningham b; Kenny Washington, Mel Lewis dm; Ray Barretto cga.

a   unknown title[1]
b   Body and Soul[2]
c   unknown Swedish folk song[3]
d   A Night in Tunisia[4]
e   Sacred Love[5]
f   In a Sentimental Mood[6]
g   Anthropology[7]
h   **Mean What You Say**[8]
i   **Dylan's Delight**[9]
j   Star Eyes[10]
k   **A Night in Tunisia**[11]

[1]Powell, Thielemans, Hanna, Cunningham, Barretto.
[2]Thielmans, Hanna, Cunningham, Washington.
[3]Hanna, Cunningham, Washington.
[4]Faddis, Soloff, Foster, Hanna, Cunningham, Washington.
[5]Unaccompanied bass solo.
[6]Foster, Hanna, Cunningham, Washington.
[7]Faddis, Soloff, Hanna, Cunningham, Washington.
[8]Mosca, Oatts, Adams, Hanna, Cuningham, Lewis.
[9]Adams, Hanna, Cunningham, Lewis.
[10]Mosca, Oatts, Hanna, Cunningham, Lewis.
[11]Washington out.

This was a tribute to Mel Lewis. *See* 781215.

PEPPER ADAMS–THE ADAMS EFFECT
850625
25-26 June 1985, Van Gelder Studio, Englewood Cliffs NJ: Frank Foster
ts; Pepper Adams bs; Tommy Flanagan p; Ron Carter b; Billy Hart dm.

a	**Binary**	Uptown LP: UP-2731
b	**Binary**	Uptown unissued
c	**Valse Celtique**	Uptown LP: UP-2731
d	**Valse Celtique**	Uptown unissued
e	**Dylan's Delight**	Uptown LP: UP-2731
f	**Dylan's Delight**	Uptown unissued
g	**How I Spent the Night**	Uptown LP: UP-2731
h	**How I Spent the Night**	Uptown unissued
i	**How I Spent the Night**	
j	**Claudette's Way**	Uptown LP: UP-2731
	Adams and rhythm section:	
k	**Now in Our Lives**	
m	**Now in Our Lives**	Uptown CD: UPCD-2731
n	**Now in Our Lives**	Uptown unissued
o	**Now in Our Lives**	

It's not known what tunes were released from either date.
All tracks on Uptown CD: UPCD-2731.
This is Adams' twentieth and final date as a leader.
About Pepper Adams, Tommy Flanagan told the author in a 1988
interview: "He was very strong on that date. Just judging from the way
he played—so strong—you could just say, 'This cat's gonna lick this
thing.' They were mostly his originals....He felt really good about having Frank Foster there. They had been tight for *years!"*
Uptown owner and physician Mark Feldman told the author in 1988,

Somehow it worked out where we were trying to get all Detroit
people, and we actually talked to Elvin Jones' wife and the money
wasn't right there, so we talked about a bunch of other drummers,
and I think Billy Hart was one of the first people we mentioned, and
that was one of the first people that was most agreeable to [Pep-
per]....Pepper was very well set in his ways, and there was a certain
caliber of musicianship that he wanted, especially on a recording....
I remember discussing material with Pepper. Pepper had a way of
letting you know right away. I mean, when he said, "No," it was just

a "No," and then there was silence, and you knew there was no point in discussing it....[This] session was worked out where it was in between therapy, and during a period of time when the risk of side effects would be much, much less. It was very good timing, and that worked out very well.

According to Billy Hart, in an interview with the author in 1988,

I was in awe, because I had been so moved by him from the start. But he's like Kenny Burrell, or Thad, or Johnny Griffin: He immediately tests your professionalism. Once you're on the bandstand with him, there's a lot of stuff you have to know. In other words, you don't want to disturb his creativity. That means, all of a sudden, there's pressure on you to know a whole repertoire of pieces immediately, because you don't know what he might play in his solo or what he might quote....But then, this time, he had a very high level of professional *mechanics* around him. You look over and see Ron Carter. But then there was Frank Foster too, and people don't realize what an *excellent* musician Frank Foster—I mean, those cats don't make mistakes, on any level! They read everything the first time perfectly, with the right inflections, their solos are going to be incredible the first time. If there's going to be another take with those cats, it's because *I* did something wrong! It brings out the humility in most, I would think.

According to Uptown owner and oncologist Bob Sunenblick, in an interview with the author in 1988, Pepper

was on the fourth cycle of chemotherapy. He was pushing his complete response, and he really wasn't having a lot of nausea from the chemotherapy, because I remember talking to him about it. I scheduled the recording for eight, nine, ten days after he received his cycle of chemotherapy, and he was in good shape when he came in there. He didn't look very well, but he was in very, very good shape. If you shut your eyes, it was the old Pepper. He was very strong. It turned out excellent.

There was no way to know what he was going to play. He didn't tell anybody what he was going to play until he showed up. I remember asking the guy I was doing the records with, Feldman, and he didn't know what he was going to play either.

Sunenblick had compiled a list of some thirty tunes that he suggested to Adams for this recording:

> I had asked him to play In a Sentimental Mood. I think I asked him to play Sophisticated Lady or some kind of Duke Ellington tune. He was very fond of Duke Ellington's music, and he was fond of Rex Stewart's music also. My Funny Valentine was another, [but Adams told him], "It was a dumb tune with a dumb refrain, and he didn't want to do it. I said, "Well, gee, you were known with that." I said I thought it would be fantastic if we could get a version of you playing this tune, and he didn't want to do it. I said, "I liked your version very much that you played with Stan Kenton," and he was surprised that I ever heard it. The only tune I could talk him into playing was How I Spent the Night. That was a tune on the first Frank Foster record [Foster] ever made, on a ten-inch Blue Note that was a beautiful tune that had a Tadd Dameron feel to it, and, actually, wasn't totally successful on that record. Apparently, Pepper had heard it, because he agreed with me, because Benny Powell didn't seem to pull it off very well on that record. Pepper felt that this tune deserved to be done again. That's almost his exact words. Frank Foster actually had to go back and transcribe it. I don't think he had the music.
>
> Pepper didn't like rehearsals. Pepper felt that he didn't need them. So that was it. We went to the recording session. It was one of the strangest recording sessions, in the sense that I didn't know what they were going to play. I was surprised, because I wasn't totally enamored with Pepper Adams' original compositions, but they sounded good with Frank Foster on them. They sounded fantastic! It was not a very difficult recording. There were a lot of takes on each. Pepper sounded very strong throughout. I remember, on the date, Billy Hart playing the drums real loud and Rudy going berserk. He sent me and [Uptown co-owner Mark] Feldman out into the studio, and he said, "Do you hear something?" and neither one of us knew what he was talking about.
>
> Rudy makes reference to this on his own [NPR radio] interview with Ben Sidran: How that, when he was doing the two track dates with Blue Note, the drummers—this is before the era of multi-track—would always know that they were too loud, and they would try to blend in with the other players. But Billy Hart is a drummer of the era of multitrack, and he felt this could be fixed up in the mix. Well, there is no mix! So, I had to talk to Billy Hart several times,

that he had to play softer. He's a very, very nice guy, but he is a loud drummer, and, I think if you ask him to do something like that, that's not the way he plays. Rudy, I remember, took the window and isolated him from everyone else. That's why it came out good. On some of the original, unissued tracks, Billy Hart's drums are too loud.

Pepper chose every single person. These are the people he wanted. I think Pepper knew it was his last record under his own name. He didn't want any pictures of him. I remember that. When we were going to do the cover photo, he would only pose with a group photo. They did it [in Rudy's backyard.] Afterwards, I wanted to get some photos of him in New York City, which I like to use as backdrops for all the albums. I couldn't get him to pose for any photos.

Regarding Rudy Van Gelder, Billy Hart told the author in 1988:

He's got a drum booth. The last time I recorded [at Rudy's] outside a booth is before he had a drum booth. It was with McCoy Tyner. When you go hear the playback of any mix, Rudy has the drums up real loud, but that's his sound. But when it comes out on the record, it's this classic sound that no engineer has been able to equal. He's definitely got the "head" of an innovator, and the aloofness of one. When you're dealing with him, it's just like dealing with Miles or Art Blakey. I mean, he was part of those cats, and he acts like that.

NOREEN GREY-EARL SAULS
850630
30 June 1985, audience recording, St. Peter's Church, New York: Pepper Adams bs; Noreen Grey p; Earl Sauls b; Keith Copeland dm.

a   **Falling in Love with Love**
b   **Reflectory**
c   **That's All**
d   **Now in Our Lives**

According to Keith Copeland, in an interview with the author in 1988, this was a Sunday Jazz Vespers concert:

We rehearsed and did a lot of Pepper's tunes. I loved it! It was great, because I got a chance to play a lot of Pepper's tunes. His tunes were not easy. He did things with forms: He changed forms around. Not that they were really unorthodox, but they were just different. There was no A-A-B-A forms with Pepper's music. Most of that stuff was different. It had all kinds of extensions in it, and different harmonic places than you thought it would go. It sounded like they were tunes that only he could play really well. He seemed to have written them specifically for baritone, and for his voice to make his horn sound the way he wanted it to sound.

MICHAEL WEISS
851004
4 October 1985, audience recording, Angry Squire, New York: Richie Vitale tp*; Pepper Adams, Gary Smulyan bs†; Michael Weiss p; Dennis Irwin b; Kenny Washington dm.

a **If You Could See Me Now**[1]
b All God's Chillun Got Rhythm[2]
c Riverbed[3]
d **Three Little Words**
e **Milestones**
f **Lover Come Back to Me***†
g **Theme**

[1]Adams and rhythm section.
[2]Rhythm section only.
[3]Rhythm section only.

Michael Weiss told the author in a 1988 interview,

I always wanted to have an opportunity to play with [Pepper Adams] at some point or another. I was sort of beginning to form some kind of a relationship with this club, the Angry Squire. In 1985 I played there with a trio, and I played there with the same trio plus Junior Cook, who I had been working with for a while. I didn't have much exposure to New York, and I was looking for as many opportunities as I could to be able to surround myself with great players as a learning experience, to develop as a player, and, also, for professional reasons, to establish myself in the city. This was another opportunity to perhaps hire a headliner as a special guest soloist, and a chance to work with Pepper.

I think I got ahold of Pepper through Al Harewood, who I had worked with for quite a while at that time, and Al was very tight with Pepper. He used to drive him to the airport and stuff. Pepper was into doing the gig. He wasn't interested in rehearsing. I was hoping to have an opportunity to play a lot of his music. I knew he had a book, and I wanted to have a crack at playing his tunes. It was, basically, very loose, whatever we wanted to do, but he wasn't too interested in pulling his things out. He eventually did pull out a few things, and we played them. There was a waltz we did that was pretty complicated—Valse Celtique. The harmony was very complicated....We might have done one other one. We just played common knowledge repertoire: standards and bebop tunes. We played old Milestones, though. I remember doing that. The Milestones that John Lewis wrote that Bird and Miles recorded. We played Lover Come Back to Me. That's the tune that Smulyan sat in on. I remember Ronnie Cuber just sort of bogarted his way onto the bandstand, and a couple of other people wanted to sit in. There were some singers and stuff. This wasn't a steady gig, and I didn't feel at the time that I wanted to turn my gig into a jam session. That isn't what I went through the trouble to arrange. I had a contractual misunderstanding with the club, or they had a misunderstanding with me, and that was the last time I worked there, as a result. They didn't treat the musicians right, and they packed it. We did wonderful business, and that was unfortunate. It wasn't a name jazz club, a headline jazz club, so there wasn't that kind of money going in and out. It was minimal. I don't remember what I got, actually, but it was enough to make it worth his while.

I thought [Pepper] played really good. We didn't really talk that much, and I remember we drove to the gig together with Al Harewood, and [Pepper] was kind of cranky. I didn't really know him. That particular weekend, at least from my own personal experience, he wasn't terribly approachable. You could say something, and he sort of took it a different way than you meant, but he sure played his ass off. He played as hard, with the same kind of energy and forcefulness, as he always does.

According to Tim Horner, in an interview with the author in 1990,

That was supposed to be my gig with Jeremy [Kahn] and Ed Howard. They had actually hired us, and I called Pepper, asking him if he wanted to do it. Next thing I know, I was calling Pepper about doing a rehearsal and he said, "Rehearse for what? I've got this gig with Michael Weiss." It was really strange! I went back and talked with the club owner, and the club owner confessed that he took it on because Michael wanted less money. Then Michael turned around and hired Pepper; kept Pepper on the gig, because Pepper already knew about it.

"The last time I saw Pepper Adams, he was playing at the Angry Squire," Don Friedman told the author in an interview in 1988:

I went to see him because I knew that he was very sick, and I wanted to see him. So I went down there and it was very interesting to me, because I had known Pepper all these years, but we were never what you would call good friends or close friends. I didn't know him that well, and for many years I didn't even see him. We didn't have so much to do with each other, but we always knew each other, and I think he liked me as a person, and I always liked him and respected him. It was interesting, because, that night that I went down there to see him, he and I got into this very heavy conversation about him and his disease and his sickness and all this stuff, and he opened to me. It was unbelievable, because I always perceived him before as kind of a conservative person in his personality. He wouldn't tell you all about himself just like *that*. He was very unemotional, and saved everything for his music, I guess, and I'm sure he had very close friends, who he shared his inner feelings with, but I wasn't *that* close to him before. For some reason, that particular night, he just opened up to me, and he told me all this stuff about all these things that happened to him, and his sickness, and his medication that he was taking—that he had trouble walking after it—and he told me about the chemotherapy. Then he told me, besides having the lung cancer, he had a brain tumor. All these things. It was unbelievable! And to see him: He was this gaunt—he looked dead already, really, but he still stood up there and played, and he played with power and strength! It was unbelievable! It was unreal! I don't think everybody there realized who they were listening to, how great a cat he was, but he *was* getting a great response from the audience. Ronnie Cuber sat in that night and they played battle of the baritones. [Pepper] chewed him up and spit him out, man! There was no contest, really. Ronnie is a good player, but he's not in a league with Pepper. And it was great to hear them, because it was so clear, so obvious.

According to Adams' friend Doris Moreau, in an interview with the author in 1987, "Mel Lewis was there. He sat in on drums. He wasn't part of the [band], but he sat in because he was there in the audience. I asked [Pepper] to play Cindy's Tune, and he said, "I can't, because I can't reach the register.""

According to Mel Lewis, in an interview with the author in 1988, Pepper was losing his place in the tunes. "That's the first time I ever noticed him doing that," Lewis said. "He sort of laughed, and he'd always find it, but that was unusual for him to do. He'd just forget where he was."

PETER LEITCH
851012

12 October 1985, audience recording, Universal Jazz Coalition, New York: Pepper Adams bs; Mulgrew Miller p; Peter Leitch g; Ray Drummond b; Kenny Washington dm.

a **Played Twice**
b **Bouncing with Bud**
c **How Deep Is the Ocean**
d My One and Only Love[1]
e **Exhilaration**
f **Speak No Evil**
g **Slugs, in the Far East**
h **Trinkle Tinkle**
i Solar[2]
j **Rhythm-a-Ning**

[1]Leitch and rhythm section.
[2]Piano trio feature.

According to Peter Leitch, in an interview with the author in 1987,

Pepper was ill at the time and, in fact, I think it was one of the last appearances he did in New York....He was not fond of the compositions of Wayne Shorter. He didn't like the way Wayne used harmony in his compositions. He liked him as a person very much. I believe at one point he lived in the same building as Wayne. At this concert we played [Shorter's] Speak No Evil. He was reluctant, but I got him to play it, and, of course, he sounded wonderful on it.... Pepper had one quote about Wayne Shorter. Towards the end, Pepper would really just say what he felt. He didn't seem to care. He said, "Wayne Shorter uses harmony like a bored housewife uses detergent." He told me that backstage at the concert. For some reason [he also told me] about the first time he played with Miles in Detroit: He said to Miles, "What are we going to play?" Miles said, "Let's play Milestones." Pepper said, "I don't know that tune." It's really complex harmonically. I guess Pepper was quite young at this point anyway, and Miles said to Pepper, "Well, it's just Perdido with some altered changes."

According to vibraphonist Warren Chiasson, in an interview with the author in 1988,

I was lucky to have caught Pepper just before he passed. He did a thing over at Cobi Norita's with Peter Leitch, the guitar player, and the piano player was Mulgrew Miller, so it was a *really* great performance, and Pepper had to go for rests in between tunes. Well, actually, he played the tunes, but, I mean...he would sit off to the side and try to get his strength up for the next tune...kind of get recharged again, but he certainly played very, very well.

PEPPER ADAMS
851015
c. 15 October 1985, RAI TV broadcast, Salon delle Feste, San Remo Jazz Festival, San Remo, Italy: Pepper Adams bs*; Ricardo Zegna p; Dodo Goya b; Ronnie Burrage dm.

a **Conjuration***
b **Dobbin'***
c **unknown waltz**
d **unknown blues**
e **Doctor Deep***

According to historian Francesco Martinelli, Zegna was a last minute replacement for Franco D'Andrea, and drummer Gianni Cazzola also played with Adams on part of this tour. Zegna, Goya, and Paolo Pellegatti backed Adams at a gig on 14 October 1985 in Valenza, Italy.

PEPPER ADAMS
851021
c. 21 October 1985, audience recording, Widder-Bar, Zurich: Pepper Adams bs; Vince Benedetti p; Jimmy Woode b; Svend-Erik Nørregaard dm.

It's unclear if the audio exists.

PEPPER ADAMS
851029
29 October 1985, audience recording, Pellerina Bar, Turin, Italy: Same as c. 15 October 1985, Paolo Pellegatti dm replaces Burrage:

a **Falling in Love with Love**
b **All the Things You Are**
c There Is No Greater Love[1]
d **I Can't Get Started**
e **'Tis**
f **Bye Bye Blackbird**
g **Bossallegro**
h **Just Friends**
i **'Tis**
j unknown title

[1]Rhythm section only.

PEPPER ADAMS
851030
30 October 1985, audience recording, Mandracchio Club, Trieste, Italy: Pepper Adams bs; Marcello Tonolo p; Marc Abrams b; John Betsch dm.

a **Dewey Square**
b **Ephemera**
c I Could Write a Book[1]
d **Body and Soul**
e **'Tis**
f **Time After Time**

g **Bossallegro**
h **Snowball**
i **Conjuration**

¹Rhythm section only.

JOHN SPIDER MARTIN
851108
8 November 1985, audience recording, Dade County Community College, Miami: Jimmy Owens tp, flh; John Spider Martin ts; Pepper Adams bs; Chris Taylor p; unknown b; unknown dm.

It's unclear if the audio exists.

PEPPER ADAMS
851114
14 November 1985, audience recording, Regina Public Library, Regina, Canada: Pepper Adams bs; Jon Ballantyne p; Ken Coffey b; Andy Cree dm.

a **It's You or No One**
b **Three and One**
c **'Tis**

PEPPER ADAMS
851115
15 or 16 November 1985, audience recording, Basement Jazz Club, Saskatoon, Canada: Same as 14 November 1985:

a **It's You or No One**
b **Three and One**
c **'Tis**

PEPPER ADAMS
851120
20-23 November 1985, CBC radio broadcasts, Yardbird Suite, Edmonton, Canada: Pepper Adams bs; Tommy Banks p; Bob Miller b; Tom Foster dm.

These were produced by the Edmonton Jazz Society, who maintains a library of their broadcasts.

PEPPER ADAMS
860115
15 January 1986, audience recording, Artists' Quarter, Minneapolis: Pepper Adams bs; Dean Magraw g; Paul Madsen b; Phil Hey dm.

a **Three Little Words**
b **Quiet Lady**
c C.O.D. [1]
d **The Days of Wine and Roses**
e **Pent-Up House**
f **'Tis**
g **Hellure**
h **Bossallegro**

[1]Rhythm section only.

Also performed that night was Chelsea Bridge, Lovers of Their Time, My Funny Valentine, and Softly As in a Morning Sunrise.

According to Phil Hey, in an interview done with the author in 1990, Pepper Adams

> was very ill when he came here. In fact, one of the more telling moments: At the end of the four nights [18 January 1986], we were both on the far side of the bar. The way the Artists' Quarter was set up, the bar was actually in a different room, and, at the end of the night, there was a customer in between us and we had both ordered a Guinness Stout. The customer moved away, right as we both got our beers, and I turned and looked at Pepper Adams, who was smoking a cigarette and sipping his beer. He must have known what I was thinking and he raised his glass to me and he said, "It can't hurt now!" He knew he was on his way out.
>
> He had some bad moments emotionally on the gig. He got kind of upset with the guitarist and the bass player a couple of times over nothing. But when the guitarist, Dean Magraw, and I picked him up to go to the airport the next day, he was in a great mood! Real funny and upbeat. He told us some funny stories about coming up in De-

troit. I remember laughing a lot at the stories. A couple of them involved Elvin Jones....

What stands out for me about Pepper Adams was how much energy he put into his playing, and then just kind of collapse at the end of his solos. He'd sit there with his head down. I mean, he really looked awful, and a lot of people commented on that to me at the Artists' Quarter. You know how people are: They pick up more on the visual than they do on the audio, and I remember a lot of people saying that they really didn't think he was playing, but he was playing great!

According to Dean Magraw, in an interview done in 1990 with the author,

At that time, they had no piano at the Artists' Quarter, and [Pepper Adams] was asked to choose between electric piano and guitarist, and I was the guy that got the nod. I'm not sure who made the connection first. It might have been through Phil. We worked together a little bit, but not much, and we all worked with different groups and knew each other from playing with different groups.

We knew that [Pepper] was really sick. In fact, we were amazed he came out....I remember enjoying his originals. He said, "We'll play some standards and we'll pass around a little bit, and then you'll do a trio tune." Not really all that much instructionally. He just asked us some of the standards that we might know, and then said we'll look at some out of the book. I would say he was very physically frail, but he was *very* focused in on getting up on the stand and playing his butt off. That was his main focus, pretty much his only one.

Oh, I thought he played *incredibly* well! *Oh*, my God! When we were on the stand, we were all thinking it, and then, when we heard the tapes, we thought it again. There was one incident when he got pissed off because he thought that we had lost our places—me and Paul. He came back and said a couple of things one night. I went back and listened to the tape, and, actually, we did not lose our place. I think it was Alone Together. Then there was another place where he kind of went ahead in the form and Paul and I hung back. I mean, usually in the tunes, all the forms were right and everything was fine. He did get a little irritated one time, and I know people that are on some of those cancer medicines can have mood swings. Oh, on one piece he got like two beats ahead or something, and, on

Alone Together, there was a discrepancy as to where the bridge was.

We don't want to mess up playing with Pepper Adams. We want to give him the best possible support we can give him, so he can get natural and do his utmost. There he was, really sick and frail. Especially, we don't want to cause any musical trouble for him....If he messed up, he messed up almost not at all! I mean, if there was a little discrepancy on when to go to the bridge, or he was hearing some different voicings, or whatever the situation was, it was tiny. I didn't have any problems.

He was just playing like a son-of-a-bitch! Chorus after chorus of it....I never could remember, anyway, a moment in time when it felt like he was struggling to find something. He might have been struggling with the fingering, or he might have been struggling with his breath, but not with his ideas. He was constantly flowing. You got the sense that if he lived to 150, he would have kept growing and growing and growing.

PEPPER ADAMS
860116
16 January 1986, audience recording, Artists' Quarter, Minneapolis:
Same as 15 January 1985:

a **Time on My Hands**
b **Bossallegro**
c C.O.D.[1]
d **Stella by Starlight**
e **How Long Has This Been Going On**
f **'Tis**
g **My Secret Love**
h **Day Dream**
i **Played Twice**
j **'Tis**

[1]Rhythm section only.

See 860115 notes.

PEPPER ADAMS
860117
17 January 1986, ̄audience recording, Artists' Quarter, Minneapolis:
Same as 15 January 1985:

a   **Alone Together**

See 860115 notes.

PEPPER ADAMS
860118
18 January 1986, audience recording, Artists' Quarter, Minneapolis:
Same as 15 January 1985:

a   **Three and One**
b   **Lovers of Their Time**
c   **'Tis**
d   **The Days of Wine and Roses**
e   **Pent-Up House**
f   **I Can't Get Started**
g   **'Tis**

See 860115 notes.

JOSHUA BREAKSTONE–ECHOES
860219
19 February 1986, Eras Studio, New York: Pepper Adams bs; Kenny
Barron p; Joshua Breakstone g; Dennis Irwin b; Keith Copeland dm.

a	**Oblivion**	Contemporary LP: C-14025
b	**Oblivion**	Contemporary unissued
c	**Oblivion**	
d	**It's Easy to Remember**	Contemporary LP: C-14025
e	**It's Easy to Remember**	Contemporary unissued
f	**My Heart Stood Still**	Contemporary LP: C-14025
g	**My Heart Stood Still**	Contemporary unissued
h	**My Heart Stood Still**	
i	**Even Steven**	Contemporary LP: C-14025
j	**Even Steven**	Contemporary unissued

k	Even Steven	
m	To Monk with Love	Contemporary LP: C-14025
n	To Monk with Love	Contemporary unissued
o	Bird Song	Contemporary LP: C-14025
p	Bird Song	Contemporary unissued
q	Bird Song	
r	Bird Song	
s	Quasimodo	
t	Quasimodo	
u	Down at Roger's Place	
v	Down at Roger's Place	

All issued titles on Victor (J) CD: VDJ-1125.

According to Kenny Barron, in an interview with the author in 1988, Pepper

> didn't really look bad. He was in good spirits and he really played exceptionally well. It kind of amazed me, because here's a guy going through chemotherapy; not only that, a whole bunch of personal problems at the same time—his wife leaving him, and stuff like that. Again, with his physical condition, being able to play the way he did was really amazing....Any time you do a lot of takes, it gets to be hard and you start competing with yourself. Actually, that wasn't really *that* hard. I've been on dates where I've done twenty-some takes of a tune. That's hard, because, after a while, you don't feel like it any more. But, for a jazz date, I guess that was considered difficult. Most of the jazz dates I've been on, two takes is usually it. [Pepper] seemed to be all right.

In an interview with the author in 1988, Joshua Breakstone said,

> For me, playing with Pepper was a really great experience. I had done two records, and it came time to do a third, and the producers wanted to do something that was a little bit of a departure from what I had done on the previous two, which was quartets. They wanted me to bring in another instrument or try something different. We settled on the idea of getting a saxophonist and Pepper was the first person I really thought of. I like the combination of guitar and baritone sax quite a bit, and...I thought the baritone would be the best thing. And, of course, where Pepper comes from and where I come

from is kind of the same kind of place. There are some all right baritone players, but Pepper is something else!

I grew up around [New York] and, for me, the Vanguard was
the only club in town that they used to let me into when I was four-
teen, fifteen years old. They weren't supposed to. I went to this private school in New Jersey. We used to get out of school at 5
o'clock, we'd get on the bus to New York, we'd get down to the
Vanguard at 6:30, right when they'd be opening the doors. They'd
be cleaning up from the night before, and we would sit there from
6:30 until when the music started at 10:00. We'd be there sometimes big band night (Monday nights), sometimes during the week
to hear whoever was in there. We'd always have the best table,
though! But I remember, when I was a kid, growing up with the big
band. Pepper was always *the* cat in the big band that always freaked
us out—for me anyway. The image that I used to have of Pepper in
that big band at that time was, he played so hard and so long, I
thought he was going to blow the saxophone up. I thought that the
instrument was going to come apart, the keys were going to fly off
the thing! Honest to God, that's how he played at that time! Yeah,
that is exactly how I thought; that he was going to blow the keys
right off the saxophone! He used to sit right behind the pole. You'd
just see the bell of the saxophone sticking out.

So, I called Pepper for the date. We had only met on a few oc-
casions. Pepper was a sweetheart and he was very complimentary to
people. He knew how to handle people very well, I think. I didn't
know him very well but I called him for the date. I didn't know that
he knew who I was, but he said that he did....I knew he had been
sick and I didn't know if he would even be able to make it....He
said he'd love to make it, but it depended on his therapy treatments.
We talked for a while about what we wanted to do on the record.
The quartet was working, so it was just a matter of adding somebody to the quartet. He liked the sound of it a lot. We discussed the
tunes, the basic approach. He said, yeah, he'd like to do it. He asked
for quite a bit more money than we were ready to pay. In fact, he
got more money than me for this record. But I knew he needed the
bread and I didn't want to argue at all. Pepper asked for a grand,
and that's a little bit more than the budget was calling for. I went to
the producers, and they didn't like it, but I said, "Man, just do it."
So we set the date. It was the first few days of January—January 5th
or 6th, or something—and he got sick again. He couldn't make it. I
don't know if he was in the hospital, or if it was just a matter of

chemotherapy which rendered him very weak after those treatments. So we tried for January and now it didn't work out. Then we set the date for February, and he must have been in the hospital maybe about two weeks before the date, or something like that. I know he had been traveling. I know he was up in Canada, but he came back and said, "O.K., we're going to try and do it." We had to have a rehearsal, so I called him about the rehearsal, because I wanted to really not overwork him on this stuff. I understood the predicament. I said, "Listen: I'll come out there and we'll rehearse." He goes, "Oh, no, no, no!" He was too ridiculous: "No, no, no, no, no, no! You're the leader. I'll come to you to rehearse." I'm all the way out in Jersey. He seemed to have this protocol that I'm the leader and that he should have to come over here, and I couldn't argue him down, man! He insisted! So we got together. He came over here. It's not that far, but I didn't want to make him have to do it. It didn't matter to me where we rehearsed.

This was just a little rehearsal, him and me. I had the music.... We had some stuff to go over, definitely. We were messing around and putting some harmonies onto some things. I remember he said, "You mind if I smoke?" and I said, "Hey man, I think you're old enough to decide for yourself what you want to do. I don't want to tell you what to do," so he was smoking. He was just being polite. My inclination was to say, "Hey, motherfucker, forget it! You can't smoke around me! You're dying and no way! I don't wanna let you kill yourself!" but what are you going to do? We talked about this and that. He was checking out the classical records. We were talking about Bartok for a while. We were talking about sports....What Pepper did say was that he considered doing Oblivion on his first record date, and that he had been thinking of doing that his whole life. Virtually every record date that he had, he had considered recording Oblivion, and he had never gotten to record it, which I thought was pretty interesting....

He didn't look too terrible. I had seen him a few times around then, so I knew how he looked. He didn't look great, but he didn't look awful. He looked sort of status quo. Then we had another rehearsal about two days before the date. We had that over at Don Sickler's studio and went over some stuff. It was a real short rehearsal. I remember there was snow on the ground and Pepper came up, walking through the snow. Like I said, the quartet, the four of us, were working. We had done a week at the West End, I think, probably the week right before the record date, and had a few other things here around town. The rhythm section was great!

So the time came to go into the studio. We got there on time and everything, and set up, and the first take that we did—we just had our axes out—was Oblivion, the take that's heard on the record....We went right from that to the next tune to the next tune. He was sitting on a stool the whole time. Pepper wasn't standing, playing at that time, and he looked terrible at the date. He looked *real* tired, really kind of whipped, but he was playing great! He was playing better than he did at either of the rehearsals. Stronger. I almost have a sense, on the record, that this is somebody that knew that he didn't have much time, and he was just going to play with everything he could.

There were a few little incidents at the date. I remember he was getting a little cranky. He was getting a little tired, and it wasn't an easy situation for him. The four of us had been together. We could tell the beginning and the endings of our solos. We didn't have to look at each other. I could tell when Kenny's going to end his solo like a chorus before. I could hear him, the way he tends to let down on his things, but Pepper hadn't been there. I usually just run the recording sessions like, let's get together, we'll play, and they can record it. So Pepper was into this thing. I remember he said something. It was very funny, but it wasn't funny at the moment, because I got ticked, but he had a very good point. He said something like, "Listen: You may not be wearing a tuxedo, but, remember, you're still the leader. Cue everybody in and out of their solos." Something like that. So, from that point on, when it got to the end of my solo, I was jumping up and down, practically, looking at him making motions, doing everything. It was cool. So then we were playing and playing, and, finally, he was getting tired. He got up and he said, "Man, I don't have any lip left. How about just giving us five minutes?" I said, "Any time you want five minutes—you want ten minutes, you want fifteen minutes—just take it. Just get up and do it. I don't mean to be a tyrant over the thing." That was it. The date went very smoothly and that was it.

According to Keith Copeland, in an interview with the author in 1988,

On the date, Pepper was sitting right in front of me! I'm facing Pepper. Pepper's sitting on a stool facing me, and Kenny's over farther, on the other side of the room. We're doing a whole album in five hours, and Josh is doing take after take after take because he wants to be able to pick. They were doing a lot of takes because they're all direct-to-two-track digital. Pepper is sitting there on the stool, looking at me, chain smoking cigarettes! This man is sitting on the stool, just as calm [as can be], playing his *ass* off, chain smoking cigarettes, and I'm thinking, "Well, damn! I know he's really sick, man. I know this cat is gonna split soon. I know it. He knows it. It would seem to me, in my mind, that, if he wants to play good on the date, or anything else he's going to leave as a legacy, or possibly extend his life a little bit longer, he wouldn't do something that might possibly shorten that." The cat is playing his ass off! I'm playing, and he's playing so much shit when he plays, that I'm literally holding on for dear life! I'm giving up every ounce of creativity and energy I can to keep up with Pepper. The cat to keep up with on the date wasn't Kenny, it was Pepper! Pepper was killing everybody! He was like saying, "Well, you know, I know I'm not going to have too many more record dates, so I'm going to play some shit that I always *dreamed* about playing that I never got a chance to play!" I got that feeling, man. I never heard him play no shit like he played on Josh's date. He had gone beyond what Pepper would normally play. He was playing polyrhythms, and seven groups—artificial groups: Seven against four, and seven against one, shit like that; Stuff that Trane used to do—and all kinds of shit in his runs, and it was swinging more than I ever heard him. He was doing *that!* Unbelievable! Just doing that with such energy and force. I don't like to close my eyes on the date, because you gotta keep your eyes open in case there's a cue to do something, but, I was playing with such intensity, it was hard to keep my eyes open. We were doing something and I could feel my eyes were gonna close, but, the whole time Pepper was playing, he was looking dead at me, dead-panned, just dead at me, sitting up there on the stool with his legs crossed sometimes, and just looking at me. It was like he knew what I was thinking, because every time I would see him smoke a cigarette, I'd think, "Man, how can he do that?" He can see me looking concerned. He just kept doing it and he just kept playing his ass off! I guess I felt that he thought I was questioning why he was doing that. This was like mental telepathy. He would do it more and play even more to let me know, "Man, if you're upset about that and you're concerned, don't worry about *me*. Worry about *you* keeping up with this shit! That's what you need to worry about." Man, that was like the heaviest lesson I ever had in my life! Being on that date, and seeing how Pepper played.

A couple of times he got a little irritable, because Josh wanted to keep doing takes, one after another, over and over, and physically, after three hours—I mean, we weren't taking any breaks to listen back to nothing! Once they got the level in the studio, we kept going. I think we did that whole date and maybe stopped one time for a break. At the end I could see that was starting to wear on Pepper just a little bit. He just needed a little bit of time, but, finally, after a while, he would say something for a second. You could tell he was maybe getting a little irritable, but then he would cool out. But the main thing was the cat was just like steel; like he was looking death in the eye and spitting in death's eye. I got the feeling he thought, "I've been doing this shit all my life. I've been smoking cigarettes, and I know I'm gonna split and that's it, and I'm not worried about it, and I'm going to go out the way I've been doing it all my life. Why change now?"

DENNY CHRISTIANSON
860224

24 February 1986, Studio Victor, Montreal: Denny Christianson flh; Roger Walls, Laflèche Doré, Ron DiLauro, Jocelyn Lapointe tp, flh; Patrice DuFour, Muhammad Abdul Al-Khabyyr, André Verreault tb; Bob Ellis btb; Joe Christie Jr. as, ss, bs, fl, pic; Pat Vetter as, cl, bs, fl; Richard Beaudet ts, cl, bs, fl; Jean Lebrun ts, ss, bs, fl, pic; Jean Frechette bs, bcl; Kenny Alexander p; Richard Ring g; Vic Angelillo b, e-b; Pierre Pilon dm; Paul Picard perc; GUEST: Pepper Adams bs.

a	**Arlequin**	Justin Time (Can) CD: JUST-19
b	**Autumn Leaves**	
c	**Captain Perfect**	
d	**Osage Autumn**	

-d on Enja (Ger) CD: CD-9079-2.
All tracks on Justin Time (Can) CD: CD-19-2.
See 860225.
Denny Christianson told the author in 1987,

I found that I really had to adjust my timing to play heads with [Pepper]. It was very hard to play a head in time, because he liked to back-phrase. He liked to pull the time. In fact, on a couple of the recordings we made, it got to the point where he was back-phrasing so much, I told the rhythm section, "Don't pay any attention to what we're doing on the head. Just keep the time straight." *Very* pulled back! If you listened to it and went with it, you'd start to drag, but that wasn't what he wanted to do. He wanted you to play time and he wanted to pull *his* time back. It's part of his style....Arlequin: that's an original by me. He wasn't terribly fond of it, because it was straight eighths. He hated straight eighths. He made no bones about it: "Goddamn tight-assed straight-eighth rhythm!" He liked straightahead swing....

The real date was 24 and 25 February. The 24th: The first three hours were piss-off. We didn't really get any good cuts and we were getting the sound down and all of that, and then, *bang!* We took a break and had pizza and beer, and then we started rolling. We had three or four nice takes and everybody was happy.

We came back the next night and started again, and, within half an hour, we were getting good takes. By the end of three hours, we had a whole album in the can. [Pepper] was feeling good, and I said, "Do you want to keep going?" and he said, "Yeah! Let's do some more!" So, I said, "I got a lovely arrangement of Funny Valentine." I knew that tune had been recorded to death. "I don't know how you feel about that. If you don't want to do it, we'll pass on it." I said, "How do you feel about doing Funny Valentine?" and he said, "That's a lovely tune. I'd be delighted to do it." It surprised me a little bit. Somebody in retrospect said that it was he and his wife's "tune." I didn't know that. What happened was we went in and I ran it once so he could tell where it went, because it's got a couple of written parts that don't fit the melody. And then: "Everybody ready?" "Yeah." We went back. One cut and magic! When the tape stopped, you had a chill up and down your spine, because you knew that was it!...

I chose stuff that was compatible for him: From his background, that he would feel comfortable in. I would have never chosen this particular stuff; if it hadn't been for Pepper, I wouldn't have put this stuff on record. I wouldn't have recorded it. Alf Clausen tunes, for example, which are very much in the style of the Thad Jones-Mel Lewis [band]: I wouldn't ordinarily want people to hear my band and say, "Well, that sounds like what Thad was doing." I don't want to sound like what Thad was doing fifteen years ago, but I had these charts. I love the charts, but, as far as making a musical statement, I said, "All right, that's something Pepper would like," and he did! He played them and he said, "Let's do these. So we did that....I wanted Pepper to record [Sophisticated Lady], but he didn't like the arrangement. He made it very clear what he liked and didn't like, and I respected that. I didn't force him into things that I wanted to do. There was altered changes in the arrangement. "How could anybody fuck with Duke Ellington's original changes?" he said. "It's beyond me!" He said, "It's gorgeous changes, and somebody's gotta go fuck with them!" That, plus there's sections that go into bossa nova. It goes from the straight [eighths] Sophisticated Lady, Ellington-style, into a bossa nova, kind of double-time....We did this on the radio show [*see* 841024a], but he let me know that he preferred not to do it on the album.

DENNY CHRISTIANSON–SUITE MINGUS
860225

25 February 1986, Studio Victor, Montreal: Same as 24 February 1986, add Daniel Doyon* tp:

a Mingus—Three Hats*:   Justin Time (Can) LP: JUST-15
    Theme
    Slop
    Theme
    Fables of Faubus
    Theme
    IX Love
b **Lookin' for the Back Door**
c **My Funny Valentine**
d **Trollin' for Thadpoles**
e **A Pair of Threes**
f **A Pair of Threes**   Justin Time (Can) unissued
g **A Pair of Threes**

-c on Enja (Ger) CD: CD-9079-2.
All issued tracks on Justin Time (Can) CD: JUST-CD-15-2.
See 860224.
In a 1989 interview with the author, saxophonist Don Palmer said,

I think that thing that he has on record there is wonderful, especially in context. The pictures on the album show Pepper looking very deep into his cancer, I think, because he had no hair. I remember Denny telling me [about] Pepper struggling up the steps to the recording studio with his baritone. He didn't want anyone to carry it. He wanted to do it himself, but he had to take two or three steps and then stop and huff and puff. And then you hear the recording and it sounds as big and as full as I ever remember Pepper sounding!

In an undated radio interview done with Denny Christianson, possibly for the CBC, after Pepper Adams' death, Christianson said the following about the Mingus project:

The first time I brought Pepper up to do a show with us in Montreal, we did pretty much standard material, some of the things which you're going to hear on the album. *Mingus* we didn't have time to rehearse, but, when we decided to do an album together, I asked Pepper if he wouldn't mind if I made that the focal point of the album. He said, "Sure. Why not? I used to work with Mingus anyway, so it seems very appropriate." What Pepper brought to it was an *immense* talent and experience, not only as a musician, but as a human being. He was a *rare* person....I would say I've only been fortunate enough to meet a few in my lifetime that touched me both as a musician and as a human being. When we had the chance to do this album, I looked at it as a rare opportunity, for myself and for the band, that we were given the opportunity to make music with somebody that I consider a giant of his time.

In an interview done with the author in 1987, Denny Christianson said,

I don't think anybody ever focused totally a big band album around [Pepper Adams] that showcases him. I went into record stores looking around and said, "Shit! Nobody's done this! It's amazing!" Every number is focused on him....There's one tune on the second side of *Suite Mingus*. The tune is called A Pair of Threes, and I had to do three cuts, because the time kept pulling back, pulling back. Now, this is the slowest of the cuts. I don't like it from the standpoint of energy, but the solos are phenomenal, especially his....He liked the changes, and he just went blazing into the solo. It was just an excellent cut. He didn't have the energy that he had maybe a few years before, but he made up for it on this album. He was like an Old Master, picking his spots—when to burn and when to lay back—but his musical ideas were still there....We're running the rehearsal once, the day before we're recording this. We're going through the last section, and he says, "Are you sure these changes are right?" I said, "Well, geez, I think so. I mean, we've been playing them a long time. They're Mingus' changes, from what I can tell. That's Curt Berg's interpretation." He says, "Well, I shouldn't be surprised. I used to play with Mingus for an hour at a time and not understand anything!..." Bear in mind that I took Curt's original thing and I made cuts in five places and trimmed it down to fifteen minutes. I cut out some repetitious sections. It's Curt's themes and Mingus' tunes. It was my idea to put arco and baritone together in a few spots....

When we recorded Mingus, he was still playing on a partially collapsed left lung and he was in a hell of a lot of pain. I just looked at him. I said, "We can do this any way you want. If you get in the middle of a cut and you're feeling pain or discomfort, just drop out and we'll go back and dub your part in later. "No, I don't think it will come to that." I said, "O.K. Any way you want it. Just so you know that I'm aware of it, and I can handle it any way you want to handle it." That's one thing: I did and still always will have an enormous respect for him, and I wanted this to be comfortable for him. I wanted it to be a warm experience, and as easy as possible. He was playing in a lot of pain. He had lost a lot of weight. I know. He told me. I asked him, because he didn't say anything. It was like, "I'll take care of it. Don't worry." I said, "Are you in pain?" "Yeah, it hurts a lot." There's one point in Mingus: In his solo he starts his solo in the middle of Fables of Faubus and he plays a couple of measures. He stops—coughs—he had to clear his chest before he could go on. Yeah, you can hear the cough in the background; just barely. I left it, because that's the way it was.

BENEFIT FOR PEPPER ADAMS
860306

6 March 1986, audience recording, 880 Club, Hartford CT: Lee Katzman tp; Sonny Costanzo, Steve Davis tb; Jackie McLean, Joey Roccisano as; Bill Barron ts; Pepper Adams bs; Don DePalma, Mark Templeton p*; Nat Reeves b; Mike Duquette, Larry DiNatale dm†.

a   **Have You Met Miss Jones**[1]
b   **Body and Soul**[2]
c   **Billie's Bounce**[3]

d   **All the Things You Are**[4]
e   **Stella by Starlight**[5]
f   **Groovin' High**[*][†][6]
g   **'Tis**[*] [†][7]

[1]Katzman, McLean, Adams, DePalma, Reeves, Duquette.
[2]Katzman, McLean, Adams, DePalma, Reeves, Duquette.
[3]Katzman, Costanza, Davis, McLean, Adams, DePalma, Reeves, Duquette.
[4]Entire band, Templeton and DiNatale out.
[5]Entire band, Templeton and DiNatale out.
[6]Entire band, Reeves and Duquette out.
[7]Entire band, Reeves and Duquette out.

Recorded by the Artist's Collective. All proceeds from this benefit were given to Adams to help him pay his medical bills. An award from the Artist's Collective, an organization headed by Jackie and Dollie McLean, was presented to Adams. Part of this concert was broadcast on television stations in Hartford and, according to saxophonist Yusef Lateef, in Amherst, Massachusetts. The broadcast included an interview with Adams.

According to Bill Barron, in an interview with the author in 1988, Pepper

> was in good blowing shape. He sat down a bit. I think, after he finished playing, he kind of rested a bit, but you couldn't tell that anything was wrong, because he was playing as forcefully as ever. I guess when he picked up the horn, his strength came back, but you could tell he needed to rest. I was very happy I was able to be there for that thing. He called me on the phone and asked would I be happy to do it.

PARADISE VALLEY JAZZ PARTY
860315
15 March 1986, audience recording, Camelback Inn Hotel, Scottsdale AZ: Joe Newman tp*; Urbie Green tb√; Buddy Tate ts∆; Pepper Adams bs; Buddy Weed†, Ray Bryant p◊; Richard Davis b; Jeff Hamilton dm.

a   **Struttin' with Some Barbecue**[*][†]
b   **On the Sunny Side of the Street**
c   **Time on My Hands**√∆◊

d **Lovers of Their Time**√∆◊[1]
e **Undecided**√∆◊

[1]Adams and rhythm section.

Hosted by Don and Sue Miller. According to Don Miller, roughly thirty sets are typically played in their seventeen hour, two-day event.

In an interview with the author in 1988, Richard Davis said, "Man, it was hard for me looking at him! He always looked like a robust guy. That's when I knew he was *really* sick."

Saxophonist Lew Tabackin told the author in a 1988 interview,

I remember being with him not too long before he died. There was a festival in Scottsdale: Paradise Valley. I tried to spend as much time with him as I could, because he was really in bad shape. For some reason, musicians didn't seem to be too empathic. We hung out. I tried to get him to eat, but he was having difficulties eating because he couldn't taste anything. The scary thing was, man, when he got on the bandstand, I couldn't believe it! He could play with so much intensity, and then he'd finish playing, and then he'd be just wasted, just the way he was before. It was just amazing the way he could summon up so much energy. It was a spiritual thing; it transcended the physical. It was very inspirational. I've seen it in other musicians too. A lot of times, when you're feeling badly—you're sick or you're weak—somehow you summon up enough energy to maintain a level. Sometimes, you even play better, but, I think when you know your time is limited, it must create another dimension. The old cliché, "Everytime you play, you play like it's the last time you're gonna play," kind of starts to hit home. That was the last time I saw him. Pepper wasn't even sitting on a chair. He was standing up, and [a baritone] is a heavy thing!

In an interview with the author in 1988, trumpeter Clark Terry said,

I'll never forget. Pep was on one of the sets that I had. You know, they have a tendency to make up sets—all these guys who quarterback these parties—and they usually make the trumpet players the leaders. Dick Gibson started that. He said he did so because the trumpet is the loudest instrument, so most of them follow the same policy. The Millers got their ideas from the Gibsons. So, I had a set, and, on this particular set, all I'm thinking of was Pepper. I just wanted to throw a little challenge to Pep. Even though he was sick, he didn't want any pity. He was just that type of person. He wanted to do his *damnest* until the last breath. We were playing a very swift thing, so I said, "Hey, Pep, you wanna take one *naked?*" He shook his head, "Yeah." So we gave him a stop-time chorus, and he went through that with flying colors, man! When it finished, he got a standing ovation. All the cats were so thrilled! I remember saying to him, after the set, "Pep, that was *fantastic!*" You know how we always talk to one another. I said, "Man, you played your ass off!" and he seemed very, very pleased. I think he was pleased with himself, because he knew that he put forth his best effort and it came out good!…He was a *bad* motherfucker!

ORANGE COUNTY COLLEGE BIG BAND
860320
20 March 1986, private recording, Orange Coast College, OCC Jazz Festival, Costa Mesa CA: Orange County College Big Band; Charles Rutherford cond; GUESTS: Pepper Adams, Nick Brignola bs; Claude Williamson p.

a   **Song for Pepper**

This tune, written by saxophonist Bruce Johnstone, was commissioned in Adams' honor, especially for his appreance at the Festival.

PEPPER ADAMS
860323a
23 March 1986, private recording, Orange Coast College, OCC Jazz Festival, Costa Mesa CA: Pepper Adams, Nick Brignola bs; Claude Williamson p; Art Davis b; Carl Burnett dm.

a   **All the Things You Are**
b   **Isn't It Romantic**
c   **After You've Gone**

Curtis Fuller and Jack Sheldon were originally slated to be part of a sextet that was to record for Fantasy on this date.

According to festival producer Fred Norsworthy, in an interview with the author in 1987, Dick Bock videotaped the entire two hour concert, and there was enough taped material for two recordings, which Fantasy ultimately rejected. "There was a ballad that [Pepper] did," said Norsworthy. "He dedicated it—I forget the name of it now, but it would be on the tape. For the first time, when I heard it, it sounded like he knew that he was dying. It was like his final statement. I could hear, the way he played it. I just sat there crying. I mean, I just sat there weeping."

According to Claude Williamson, in an interview with the author in 1988, "If you didn't know Pepper, you'd never know that he was dying. He just stood up there and played as if everything was O.K. I knew, pretty much when he left, that I wasn't going to see him again. A very sad time."

SHORTY ROGERS
860323b
23 March 1986, private videotaping, Orange Coast College, OCC Jazz Festival, Costa Mesa CA: Jack Sheldon tp, Bud Shank as, Pepper Adams, Nick Brignola bs; Claude Williamson p; Art Davis b; Carl Burnett dm; Shorty Rogers cond.

According to festival producer Fred Norsworthy, in an interview with the author in 1987, Dick Bock videotaped the performance. On this second half of the two-set concert, said Norsworthy, "Shorty Rogers couldn't play at the time, because he [was still recuperating from an] operation, so the band was the same group [as 860323a], and then they augmented with Bud Shank and Jack Sheldon, and Shorty brought in the arrangements and conducted it."

According to Claude Williamson, in an interview with the author in 1988,

Dick Bock was going to record the whole group...but, after he heard the group rehearsing, he decided not to record it. It didn't really come together as a unit. Pepper and Nick Brignola were blowing everyone off the bandstand, and the rhythm section really wasn't making it....That was a problem, and the other two players were just so outclassed, Dick just decided to back off. I think it was a wise move, although I think Dick missed the boat by not setting up a separate session with Pepper and recording him.

RADIO TELEFIS EIREANN ORCHESTRA
860404
4 April 1986, RTE radio broadcast, Main Auditorium, National Concert

Hall, Dublin: Benny McNeil, Davy Martin, Eoin Daly, Mike Nolan tp; Dave Weakly, Johnny Tate, Harry Knowles, Jack Bayle tb; David Carmody, Fergal O'Ceallachain, Brian Jack frh; Peter Healy, David Agnew oboe; Sam Ellis, Carole Block bassoon; Elizabeth Gaffney, Ann Kinsella fl; John Finucane, Jean Lechmar cl; Mike McMullen, Rory McGuinness, Len McCarthy, John Curran, John O'Connor reeds; Jim Doherty p; Des Moore g; Dave Gausden b, e-b; John Wadham dm; John Fennessy, Richard O'Donnell perc; Ellen Demos, Bob Whelan voc; Helen Davis harp; string section; GUESTS: Bobby Shew tp, flh; Sonny Fortune as; Pepper Adams bs; Lex Jasper p.

a   In a Mellow Tone[1]
b   In a Sentimental Mood[2]
c   **Cotton Tail**[3]
d   I Got It Bad (And that Ain't Good)[4]
e   Come Sunday
f   **Caravan**[5]
g   Everything But You
h   Lush Life[6]
i   Take the "A" Train[7]
j   **Day Dream**[8]
k   Take the Coltrane

[1]Fortune and orchestra.
[2]Shew and orchestra.
[3]Adams and rhythm section.
[4]Jasper and orchestra.
[5]Shew, Fortune, Adams, and orchestra.
[6]Jasper and orchestra.
[7]Fortune and rhythm section.
[8]Adams and orchestra.

PEPPER ADAMS
860509
9 May 1986, audience recording, Far and Away, Cliffside Park NJ: Jerry Dodgion as*; Pepper Adams bs; Noreen Grey p; Earl Sauls b; Ron Marabuto dm.

a   **Wrap Your Troubles in Dreams**
b   **Lover**

c   Beautiful Friendship[1]
d   **You Don't Know What Love Is**
e   **Out of Nowhere***
f   **Three and One***
g   This Is Always[2]

[1]Rhythm section only.
[2]Rhythm section only.

According to Red Rodney, in a 1988 interview with the author, "Just before [Pepper] died, he was playing Far and Away in Cliffside Park and I went over to see him. He looked so bad. It was pathetic, but he played beautifully! Sometimes he missed the first bar, picking up the horn and getting his breath even. He'd miss the first bar, maybe, but, after that, he'd play beautifully."

In an interview with the author in 1995, Earl Sauls said Adams was occasionally sitting on a stool when he played.

See 801101.

PEPPER ADAMS
860510
10 May 1986, audience recording, Far and Away, Cliffside Park NJ: Same as 9 May 1986, omit Dodgion:

a   **If I Love Again**
b   **How Deep Is the Ocean**
c   Bittersuite[1]
d   **Urban Dreams**
e   **It's You or No One**
f   **After You've Gone**
g   **'Tis**

[1]Rhythm section only.

See 860509, 801101.

LAIRD JACKSON
860531
31 May 1986, private recording, New York: Joe Shepley, Marky Markowitz, Jerry Gonzales tp; Jerry Dodgion, George Young as; Frank Wess,

Frank Foster ts; Pepper Adams bs†; Bob Dorough p; Al Schackman g,
vib, harmonica; John Beal b; Richie Pratt dm; Leopoldo Fleming bongos*; Laird Jackson voc.

a　**I Got Rhythm**†
b　Goodbye Pork Pie Hat†
c　**Caravan***†
d　When Was the Last Time[1]
e　**Naima**†[2]
f　Ceora*†
　　Jackson and rhythm section:
g　Brother, Can You Spare a Dime
h　That's All I Want from You
i　On Top of Old Mount Tipsy
j　My One and Only Love

[1]Jackson, Young, and rhythm section.
[2]Jackson, Adams, Young, and rhythm section.

PEPPER ADAMS
860620
*c. 20 June 1986, audience recording, Penn Harris Ballroom, Harrisburg
PA:* Valery Ponomarev tp; Pepper Adams bs; Reuben Brown p; Rufus
Reid b; Billy Hart dm.
　　Recorded by the Central Pennsylvania Friends of Jazz.
　　According to saxophonist George Coleman, in an interview with the
author in 1989,

> That was the last time I saw him. This particular night he had said,
> "Man, I would sure like to stay for your performance," because he
> had worked overtime. He was just charged up! But he said, "Man, I
> get kind of weak." But he was all charged up. He played around two
> hours, I think. He really played, and he sounded great. He gave me
> his apologies and said, "I'm gonna get some rest."

According to Billy Hart, in an interview with the author in 1988,

> Pepper came all the way from Canarsie to Englewood, [New Jer-
> sey], picked me up, and drove all the way to Harrisburg. He would

not let me drive, whatever that new car was that he had. He was amazing! When he drove me to Harrisburg, man, that's a long, fucking ride! I started asking him all these questions, like you would ask your heroes. One of the things I asked him: I said, "Man, should you be smoking those cigarettes?" because I heard he was really sick, and he was smoking Camel unfiltereds, and his attitude was, "Don't fuck with me." I mean, very clearly, with enough edge. He didn't use any profanity, but it wasn't polite. He knew where he was with me and I'm sure he knew where he was with most people when it came to that point: "Don't fuck with me. I'll do what I want to do! Your concern isn't necessary." I said, "Do you need me to help you drive?" and he said, "No, I got it," in a way like, "Don't ask me again." As I say, I was so moved by the tenderness in his music, I just assumed he was like that. It didn't have to be *sweet*, say, sweet for the ballads. It was smooth. [His] rhythm changes was smooth, like Sonny Stitt or Stan Getz, even though his tone was hard like Coltrane. It was smooth and clear. In other words, whatever it was, you didn't want to interfere with it. If you couldn't enhance it, you certainly didn't want to interfere with it. He was that kind of cat. The rest of the time I would ask him things about who he played with, the time he played with Donald Byrd, and he would give me memories of things. We talked about a lot of things. He didn't want to accept any help. I'd ask little things like, could I help him with his saxophone case or something. So it led me to believe that he was going to make it. He was moving a little slow, but I really thought he was going to make it. But then, on the other hand, I could see something inspiring for me. He went out playing. He played his ass off! He drove me all the way back home!

PEPPER ADAMS
860702
2 July 1986, CBC radio broadcast, The Spectrum, Montreal Jazz Festival, Montreal: Pepper Adams bs; Kenny Alexander p; Vic Angelillo b; Cisco Normand dm.

a **Conjuration**
b **Quiet Lady**
c **Dobbin'**
d **Ephemera**
e **Bossallegro**
f **Chalumeau**

g   'Tis

According to Denny Christianson, in an interview with the author in
1987, Adams chose Christianson's rhythm section for this concert because they had played together for a CBC radio gig in late 1984 (*see*
841023b).

This was Pepper Adams' last public performance. Cisco Normand, in
an interview with the author in 1990, said that there was a standing ovation for Adams even before he began the opening number.

According to saxophonist Charles Papasoff, in an interview in 1987,

I spent the day with Pepper. I went to get him at the hotel and we
went down to the [Spectrum] together. The first thing that they did
was the soundcheck. When the soundcheck was over, Pepper called
me up and said, "What do you think, Charles?" I said, "I think that
the sound man should come and listen to you play without the microphone for, like, twelve bars." He said, "Well, go get him," and I
went to get him, and the guy said, "What do you want?" The guy
does rock sound. Usually, at the Spectrum it's mainly a rock club.
Even if he might have done jazz bands, it doesn't mean that he ever
heard up-close a baritone saxophone, because it's a seldom used instrument. "Hey, listen to the sound, man!" and he came up, listened
to Pepper's sound. The guy was a good sound man. There's no
doubt about it. He went back, made some adjustments, and at the
concert—I don't know about the recording—the sound in the hall
was incredible! Pepper was relaxed, just sitting down and playing
really mellow, and it sounded gigantic! It sounded really big! It was
really great!

According to Denny Christianson, in an interview with the author in
1987, Pepper

came up to do this last thing at the Jazz Festival. One of the nicest
things I'll ever have happen to me is when I walked in the trailer,
when he was waiting backstage to go on. I walked in and he looked
at me, and his eyes lit up with a warm smile, like he was really happy, almost a relief, that I made it before he went on. I never expected that. It was just a wonderful feeling to know that he felt as
warm about me as I did about him. We didn't want to break the
moment. We hung together for about twenty minutes, just to be with

each other. People around him were saying, "Oh, he looks great!" but, my God, he couldn't even get up and down the steps, without somebody holding each arm, and his eyes were real red all around his eyes, and they were bloodshot and sunken in his head. As soon as I looked at him, I knew he was in bad shape. I knew from February how much a toll it had taken. By the time I had seen him in July—and people had said, "Oh, he looks better"—and I looked at him, I said, "Bullshit! He looks *much* worse." When I saw him in July, when I said goodbye, I knew that was the last time I was going to see him.

AUTHOR'S NOTE
Pepper Adams died at home in Brooklyn, New York on 10 September 1986, the day after Elvin Jones' birthday, three weeks after Dizzy Gillespie had called him to say that Elvin's brother, Thad Jones, had died in Copenhagen, two months after his final performance at the Montreal Jazz Festival, and one month shy of his 56th birthday.

Appendix 1
Dates as Leader

During his forty year recording career, Pepper Adams was a prolific sideman and session player, with a discography exceeding 700 entries. Fortunately, Adams also recorded twenty dates as a leader. Below is a list only of those recordings led or co-led by Pepper Adams, for which he had artistic control. Many dates attributed to him, such as posthumously released live dates, for example, are not included. Moreover, all but two of the Donald Byrd-Pepper Adams Quintet recordings are not listed, even though the band was a co-led, working unit, because the contract with Blue Note was in Byrd's name. I've listed only the original title, original label, and recording date, since full details are available in the book.

Pepper Adams Quintet (Mode): 12 July 1957
Critics' Choice (Pacific Jazz): 13-14 August 1957
The Cool Sound of Pepper Adams (Savoy): 19 November 1957
The Pepper-Knepper Quintet (Metrojazz): 25 March 1958
10 to 4 at the Five Spot (Riverside): 15 April 1958
Unreleased (Stinson?): December 1959
Motor City Scene (Bethlehem): mid-November 1960
Out of This World (Warwick): January 1961
Pepper Adams Plays the Music of Charlie Mingus (Workshop): 9 and 12 September 1963
Unreleased (Workshop): 3 December 1963
Mean What You Say (Milestone): 26 April, 4 and 9 May 1966
Encounter (Prestige):11-12 December 1968
Ephemera (Spotlite): 9-10 September 1973
Julian (Enja): 13 August 1975
Twelfth and Pingree (Enja): 13 August 1975
Reflectory (Muse): 14 June 1978

The Master (Muse): 11 March 1980
Urban Dreams (Palo Alto): 30 September 1981
Live at Fat Tuesday's (Uptown): 19-20 August 1983
The Adams Effect (Uptown): 25-26 June 1985

Appendix 2
Broadcasts and Recordings That No Longer Survive

PEPPER ADAMS
550000
c. 1955, TV broadcast, Detroit: Curtis Fuller tb; Pepper Adams bs; Tommy Flanagan or Hugh Lawson p; Ernie Farrow b; Hindal Butts dm.

According to Curtis Fuller, in a conversation with the author in 1989, the group performed two or three tunes on "Soupy's On," an evening show hosted by comedian Soupy Sales.

PEPPER ADAMS
560000
c. 1956, TV broadcast, Detroit: Curtis Fuller tb; Pepper Adams bs; Ray McKinney p; Ernie Farrow b; Hindal Butts dm.

See 550000 above.

PEPPER ADAMS
570901
c. 1 September 1957, TV broadcast, Detroit: Curtis Fuller tb; Pepper Adams bs; Tommy Flanagan p; Ernie Farrow b; Frank Gant dm.

See 550000 and 560000 above. Adams' friend, Bob Cornfoot, told the author in 1987 that the group did this date soon after 570823.

PEPPER ADAMS
790716
August 1982, private recording, Studio le Garrec, Ploneour-Lanvern, France: Pepper Adams bs; Louis Stewart g; Patrice Galas org; Papamutt dm.

a   **Binary**
b   **Day Dream**
c   **Let's Cool One**
d   **unknown Adams composition**
e   **Irish Ballad**
f   **French popular tune**

Adams was in Brittany, performing with Stewart. For this date Papamutt also functioned as the engineer. Sometime after the session, when Papamutt listened to the recording, he unilaterally decided that the sound was "too raw" and destroyed the master. A few months later, when Stewart asked Papamutt about the recording and learned about his decision to destroy the tape, Stewart was furious. "You're an idiot!" Stewart scolded him. "That's like an art dealer throwing away a Van Gogh because he doesn't like the colors he used."

Bibliography

Works cited in the text are listed below. For a more thorough bibliography of Pepper Adams, see pepperadams.com.

Adderley, Cannonball. Liner notes to Joe Zawinul's *Money in the Pocket.*

Amram, David. *Vibrations: The Adventures and Musical Times of David Amram.* New York: Macmillan, 1968.

_____. Liner notes to Amram's *Triple Concerto.*

Balliett, Whitney. "Mingus Regained," *The New Yorker,* 21 August 1989.

Bloom, Mike. "Pepper Adams," *Klacto,* January 1982, pp. 4-6.

Bruyninckx, Walter. *Sixty Years of Recorded Jazz.* Mechelen, Belgium: Self-published, 1981.

Carner, Gary. *The Life and Musical Times of Pepper Adams.* MA thesis, City College of New York, 1985.

_____. "Pepper Adams," *Cadence,* January 1986, pp. 13-16.

_____. "Pepper Adams" *Cadence,* February 1986, pp. 5-12.

_____. "Pepper Adams," *Cadence,* March 1986, pp. 1-17.

_____. "Pepper Adams," *Cadence,* April 1986, pp. 5-10.

_____. "Pepper Adams' Rue Serpente," *Jazzforschung 22.*1990, pp. 119-138.

Cerulli, Dom. Liner notes to Manny Albam's *Jazz New York.*

Christie, Agatha. *And Then There Were None.* New York: St. Martin's, 2001.

Danson, Peter. "Pepper Adams." *Coda,* 1 August 1983, pp. 4-9.

Delauney, Charles. Review of Dizzy Gillespie concert, *Jazz Hot,* August 1978.

Dostoyevsky, Fyodor. *Crime and Punishment.* New York: Random House, 1956.

_____. *The Brothers Karamazov.* New York: Norton, 1976.

Emerson, Keith. *Pictures of an Exhibitionist.* London: John Blake, 2003.

Gardner, Marc. Liner notes to Pepper Adams' *Ephemera.*

Gleason, Ralph J. Liner notes to Quincy Jones' *Go West, Man!*

Johnson, Bo. Liner notes to Thad Jones-Mel Lewis Orchestra's *Live at Jazz Jantar.*

Keepnews, Orrin. Liner notes to Thelonious Monk's *Blues Five Spot.*

Kirchner, Bill. Liner notes to *Joe Henderson Big Band.*

_____. Liner notes to *The Complete Solid State Thad Jones-Mel Lewis Orchestra.*

Lohmann, Jan. Pepper Adams concert review, *Orkester Journalen,* December 1972.

Martin, Douglas. "David Young Dies at 71," *New York Times,* 3 June 2001.

Monk, T.S. Liner notes to *Thelonious Monk at Town Hall.*

Myers, Marc. "Urbie Green: Persuasive Trombone," Jazz Wax Blog, 21 September 2011.

_____. "Interview with Rhoda Scott," Jazz Wax Blog, 14 October 2011.

Newsom, Jim. "Big Bad Bari Man," jimnewsom.com/PFW05-GlennWilson.html.

O'Brien, Hod. Liner notes to Hod O'Brien's *Opalessence.*

Palmer, Robert. Liner notes to Thelonious Monk's *In Person.*

Pirie, Christopher Anthony and Siegfried Mueller. *Artistry in Kenton: The Bio-Discography of Stan Kenton and His Music, Volume 1.* Vienna: Mueller, 1969.

Porter, Bob. Liner notes to Gene Ammons' *The Big Sound.*

Priestley, Brian. Liner notes to *Charles Mingus: The Complete Town Hall Concert.*

Ronzello, Robert. "Sittin' in with Pepper Adams," *Saxophone Journal,* May 1982, pp. 35-37.

Ruppli, Michael and Ed Novitsky. *MGM Records Discography,* Westport: Greenwood Press, 1998.

Santoro, Gene. "Town Hall Train Wreck," *Village Voice* [supplement], 7 June 2000, pp 1-5.

Sidran, Ben. *Talking Jazz: An Oral History—43 Jazz Conversations.* New York: Da Capo, 1995, pp. 209-220.

Smith; Arnold Jay. "The Essences of Spice." *Down Beat.* 3 November 1977, pp. 18-19, 40.

Stanton, Jeffrey. "Experimental Multi-Screen Cinema," westland.net/expo67/map-docs/cinema.htm, 1997.

Stephenson, Sam. "Interview with David X. Young," *Double Take,* Fall 1999.

Tomkins, Les. Interview with Bill Perkins, jazzprofessional.com /interviews/bill_perkins.htm, 1987

Tucich, Rudy. New Music Society program notes to World Stage concert, 28 March 1956.

White, Keith. *Autobiography.* Montreal: Self-published, 1987, pp. 103-115.

Wild, David. *The Recordings of John Coltrane.* Ann Arbor: Wildmusic, 1979.

Wilson, John S. "Twenty-Piece Band at Birdland," *New York Times,* 22 April 1961.

Zipkin, Michael. Liner notes to Norman Bishop Williams' *One for Bird.*

Filmography

Below are films, TV broadcasts, and private films cited in the text.

Films and Documentaries
The Arrangement, Elia Kazan (USA, 125 minutes), 1969
Bowling for Columbine, Michael Moore (USA, 119 minutes), 2002
A Dandy in Aspic, Anthony Mann (USA, 107 minutes), 1968
Dizzy Gillespie's Dream Band, Stanley Dorfman (USA, 89 minutes), 1982
Don Byas Come Home, Nick van den Boezem (Netherlands, 55 minutes), 1970
Everything You Always Wanted to Know About Sex but Were Afraid to Ask, Woody Allen (USA, 88 minutes), 1972
For Love of Ivy, Daniel Mann (USA, 101 minutes), 1968
Hawaii, George Roy Hill (USA, 189 minutes), 1966
Jerry Seinfeld: Comedian, Christian Charles (USA, 81 minutes), 2002
Mingus, Thomas Reichman (USA, 59 minutes), 1966
Nous Irons Tous au Paradis, Yves Robert (France, 110 minutes), 1977
Passing It On, David Chan and Ken Freundlich (USA, 23 minutes), 1985
People, People, People, John and Faith Hubley (USA, 4 minutes), 1975
To Be Alive, Francis Thompson and Alexander Hammid (USA, 18 minutes), 1964
US, Francis Thompson and Alexander Hammid (USA, unknown duraton), 1969
We Are Young, Francis Thompson and Alexander Hammid (USA, 30 minutes), 1967
The Wiz, Sidney Lumet (USA, 135 minutes), 1978

TV Broadcasts
Bob Dorough on "Schoolhouse Rock," ABC TV (New York), 20 June 1973
David Amram and Friends on "Soundstage," WTTW TV (Chicago), 29-30 January 1978

David Amram at the Horn and Hardart Automat, Westinghouse TV (New York), 4 May 1973

Donald Byrd-Pepper Adams Quintet on the "Jim Gerard Show," unknown TV network (Indianapolis), c. March 1961

Eddie Phyfe Big Band, NBC TV (Washington, D.C), c. 1971

Lionel Hampton at La Grande Parade du Jazz, RF TV broadcast (Les Jardins des Arènes de Cimiez, Nice), 13 and 16 July 1978

Lionel Hampton at the Northsea Jazz Festival, AVRO TV (Prins Willem Alexander Zaal at the Concertgebouw, The Hague), 14 July 1978

Lionel Hampton in Chicago, WNEW TV (possibly Plugged Nickel, Chicago), c. 7 July 1964

New York Jazz Repertory Company at La Grande Parade du Jazz, FR3 TV (Les Jardins des Arènes de Cimiez, Nice), 17 July 1978

New York Jazz Repertory Company at La Grande Parade du Jazz, RF TV (Les Jardins des Arènes de Cimiez, Nice), 12 July 1978

Pepper Adams, RAI TV (Pérgine, Italy), 10 July 1980

Pepper Adams, RAI TV (Trento, Italy), 6 July 1981

Pepper Adams-Al Jarreau on "The Grammy Awards," NBC TV (Shrine Auditorium, Los Angeles), 24 February 1982

Pepper Adams at the Barcelona Jazz Festival, TV-3 (Palau de la Música, Barcelona), 1 December 1983

Pepper Adams at Captain's Cabin, TV North broadcast (Edmonton, Canada), 26 November 1973

Pepper Adams at the Domicile, unknown TV network (Munich), 13 August 1975

Pepper Adams at Maison de la Radio, RF TV (Paris), 17 March 1982

Pepper Adams at the San Remo Jazz Festival, RAI TV (Salon delle Feste, San Remo, Italy), c. 15 October 1985

Pepper Adams on "AM Weekend," KGO TV (San Francisco), 30 April 1978

Pepper Adams on "AM Weekend," KGO TV (San Francisco), 12 November 1978

Pepper Adams Benefit, unknown TV network (880 Club, Hartford CT), 6 March 1986

Pepper Adams on "Music from The Flags," Granada TV (Liverpool), 10 August 1981

Pepper Adams-Kai Winding Sextet at Jazz Middelheim, BRT TV (Antwerp), c. 17 August 1978

Shorty Rogers on the "Stars of Jazz," KABC TV (Los Angeles), 4 February 1957

Sixty Minutes with Spoon, CBC TV (Toronto), c. Summer 1963

Sture Nordin in Stockholm, SR TV (Mariahissen, Stockholm), mid-August 1978

Swing Into Spring, CBS TV (New York), 10 April 1959

Thad Jones-Mel Lewis Orchestra, BBC-1 TV (London), 15 September 1973

Thad Jones-Mel Lewis Orchestra, CTVSC TV (Los Angeles), 26 September 1975

Thad Jones-Mel Lewis Orchestra at De Doelen Concert Hall, NRU-NOS TV (Rotterdam), 9 September 1969

Thad Jones-Mel Lewis Orchestra at the Domicile, ZDF TV (Munich), 8 July 1976

Thad Jones-Mel Lewis Orchestra at Graabroedre Torv, DR TV (Los Angeles), 2 September 1975

Thad Jones-Mel Lewis Orchestra at Jazz Middelheim, BRT TV (Antwerp), 18 August 1973

Thad Jones-Mel Lewis Orchestra at La Grande Parade du Jazz, RF TV (Les Jardin des Arènes de Cimiez, Nice), 13 and 15 July 1977

Thad Jones-Mel Lewis Orchestra at the International NOS Jazz Festival, NOS TV (Singer Concertzaal; Laren, Netherlands), 25 August 1973

Thad Jones-Mel Lewis Orchestra at the Kongsberg Jazz Festival, NRK TV (Kongsberg, Norway), 30 June 1974

Thad Jones-Mel Lewis Orchestra at Maison de l'ORTF, ORTF TV (Paris), 8 September 1969

Thad Jones-Mel Lewis Orchestra at Montreux, RTSR TV (Congress Hall, Montreux, Switzerland), 5 July 1974

Thad Jones-Mel Lewis Orchestra at Ronnie Scott's, BBC TV (London), c. 25 March 1972

Thad Jones-Mel Lewis Orchestra at the Theater Het Spant, AVRO TV (Bussum, Netherland), 29 June 1974

Thad Jones-Mel Lewis Orchestra in Cologne, WDR TV (Sartory-Festsaal, Colgone), 7 September 1969

Thad Jones-Mel Lewis Orchestra in Søborg, TV-Byen (Søborg, Denmark), 3 September 1969

Thad Jones-Mel Lewis Orchestra in Stuttgart, SDT TV (Saal's Stuttgarter Liederhalle, Stuttgart), 5 September 1969

Thad Jones-Mel Lewis Orchestra in Waldshut, SDR TV (Waldshut, Germany), 16 September 1976

Thad Jones-Mel Lewis Orchestra in Tokyo, unknown TV network (Tokyo), 26 February 1974

Thad Jones-Mel Lewis Orchestra on "Jazz Casual," KQED TV (San Francisco), 22 April 1968

Thad Jones-Mel Lewis Orchestra on "Jazz Vivo," TVE TV broadcast (Sitges, Spain), 24 July 1976

Thad Jones-Mel Lewis Orchestra on "Live from The Top," PBS TV (Rochester NY), 8-9 November 1974

Thad Jones-Mel Lewis Orchestra on the "Mike Douglas Show," KYW TV (Philadelphia), 26 January 1967

Private Films and Videotapes

Bill Berry Big Band at the OCC Jazz Festival, unknown director (USA; Orange Coast College, Costa Mesa CA), c. 25 March 1983

Lionel Hampton at the Casino, Otto Flueckiger (Divonne-les-Bains, France; 25 minutes), 24 July 1964

Pepper Adams at Musée des Beaux-Arts, Keith White (Montreal, Canada; 60 minutes), 5 November 1978

Shorty Rogers at the OCC Jazz Festival, unknown director (USA; Orange Coast College, Costa Mesa CA), 23 March 1986

Thad Jones-Mel Lewis Orchestra in Copenhagen, unknown director (Denmark), c. early August 1977

Thad Jones-Mel Lewis Orchestra in Hibaya Park, Billy Harper (Japan, 60 minutes), 5-6 March 1974

Thad Jones-Mel Lewis Orchestra in Russia, Billy Harper (Russia), 1972

Industrial Film

Unknown title and director (USA; soundtrack by George Gruntz), 1969

Index

About the Author

Gary Carner, an independent jazz researcher, is the author of *Jazz Performers* and *The Miles Davis Companion*. From 1984 until Adams' death in 1986, Carner collaborated with Pepper Adams on his memoirs. Carner's Adams research, collected at pepperadams.com, spans four decades. Carner has produced all 43 of Adams' compositions for Motema Music, and he's commissioned arrangements of Adams' tunes for jazz orchestra and chamber ensembles. *Pepper Adams' Joy Road,* the first book ever published about Pepper Adams, is a companion to the author's forthcoming, full-length Adams biography.